EUGENE A. FORSEY, OC, FRSC, author of numerous books and articles on economics, labour, government, and public affairs, was director of research for the CCL 1942–1956 and for the CLC 1956–1966, retiring from the CLC in 1969 as director, special project. He served as a member of the Senate of Canada from 1970 to 1979.

We are apt to think of labour unions as a feature of a relatively advanced industrial society. It therefore often comes as a surprise to many to learn how long ago in Canadian history they actually appeared. Unions already existed in the predominantly rural British North America of the early nineteenth century. There were towns and cities with construction workers, foundry workers, tailors, shoemakers, and printers; there were employers and employees – and their interests were not the same.

From this beginning Dr Forsey traces the evolution of trade unions in the early years and presents an important archival foundation for the study of Canadian labour. He presents profiles of all unions of the period – craft, industrial, local, regional, national, and international – as well as of the Knights of Labor and the local and national central organizations. He provides a complete account of unions and organizations in every province including their formation and function, time and place of operation, what they did or attempted to do (including their political activity), and their particular philosophies.

This volume will be of interest and value to those concerned with labour and union history, and those with a general interest in the history of Canada.

EUGENE FORSEY

Trade Unions in Canada
1812–1902

UNIVERSITY OF TORONTO PRESS
Toronto Buffalo London

© University of Toronto Press 1982
Toronto Buffalo London
Printed in Canada

ISBN 0-8020-5485-4 (casebound)
0-8020-6388-8 (paperbound)

Canadian Cataloguing in Publication Data

Forsey, Eugene A., 1904–
Trade unions in Canada 1812–1902
Bibliography: p.
Includes index.
ISBN 0-8020-5485-4 (bound). – ISBN 0-8020-6388-8 (pbk.)
1. Trade-unions – Canada – History – 19th century.
2. Industrial relations – Canada – History – 19th
century. I. Title.
HD6524.F67   331.88′0971   C81-094650-5

Contents

vi Contents

vii Contents

Preface

This book was commissioned by the Canadian Labour Congress as its Centennial project. There were many problems facing its research.

First, a general labour historian ought to have been able to draw on a series of specialized studies on particular unions, unions in particular places or regions, unions in particular periods, particular aspects of unionism, and particular episodes. But anything of the sort was precious scarce, and, where it did exist, often left much to be desired.

Second, especially for the nineteenth century, secondary sources, such as government reports, were spotty and often contradictory, while general histories contained only occasional, incidental, and not always correct, mention of the labour movement.

Worst of all, of course, was the absence of primary records, such as union minutes, for most organizations in most places, for most of the early period. Even union newspapers had often disappeared, or survived only in bits and pieces. Fire, flood, and fecklessness had all taken their toll.

Since most Canadian unions in 1963 were, and had long been, branches of international unions, with headquarters in the United States (or in a few cases, Britain), one might have expected that histories of such unions would fill some of the gaps. For the most part, they did not. Understandably enough, especially till almost the end of the nineteenth century, the international unions were not too much concerned with Canada; so their histories usually said little about it.

Hence, most of the work, even the academic work, which had been done on the history of Canadian unions simply could not be relied on. To do a proper job, everything had to be checked and rechecked, sifted and resifted. In most cases, I had to start from scratch, and much of the scratching had to be done in the files of daily newspapers, which provide a plethora of material, sometimes inexplicably contradictory, on some things, and tantalizing little, or nothing at all, on others which may have been just as important.

This book is an attempt to fill in the factual gaps in our knowledge of early unionism. It presents few opinions or arguments, and attempts few analyses; I have an ingrained distrust, inherited from a long line of English ancestors, of generalizations based on inadequate knowledge. But there is now an impressive number of brilliant young professional Canadian labour historians, hard at work on the special studies which will, in due course, I hope, provide the substantial material which, in my judgment, is necessary for valid generalizations, conclusions, and analyses. All I would venture to claim for this book is that I think it will give people interested in the subject, and people working on it, a lot more information, a lot more accurate, a lot better arranged and documented, and a lot more clearly written than they ever had at their disposal before I set to work. I think it will materially help those who want to go farther to know where they are likely to find the most profitable areas for investigation and what sort of material may be available. All the rest I cheerfully leave to my youngers and betters.

This book has been published with the help of a grant from the Social Science Federation of Canada, using funds provided by the Social Sciences and Humanities Research Council of Canada, and a grant from the Publications Fund of University of Toronto Press. For this assistance, my profound thanks.

E.F.
Ottawa 1980

Acknowledgments

My thanks are due first and foremost to the Canadian Labour Congress, which, by a heavy investment, from 1963 to 1969, cast its bread upon the waters and is only now receiving it back. I have also to thank the Canada Council for generous help in financing graduate students; Professor Irving Abella and the Labour History Committee of the Canadian Historical Association, without whose exertions this book would never have got into print; the Public Archives of Canada (where Eldon Frost, Nancy Stunden, and Danny Moore were as tireless as they were invaluable); the Nova Scotia and British Columbia Archives, the New Brunswick Museum, the University of British Columbia Library, and the Toronto Reference Library; the McGill-Queen's University Press (for making available to me the criticisms of four scholars who read the first and second drafts of the work); and, very notably, the University of Toronto Press (especially R.I.K. Davidson), for their professional expertise and almost infinite patience. I owe a heavy debt to a variety of individuals: to the (then) graduate students who collected most of the material (Brian Atkinson, Lloyd Atkinson, George S. Bain, Elizabeth Blouin, Anthony Butler, W.J.C. Cherwinski, Huguette Demers, Michael Holmes, Jacques Martin, Michael O'Farrell, Richard Rice, David Spring, and Lorne Thompson); to Professor Greg Kealey for much invaluable information on the Knights of Labor; to Professor Rolf Hattenhauer for most of the information on Newfoundland unions; to Mary Jordan for material on Winnipeg; to my indefatigable, and unfailingly patient and cheerful, secretaries, Dawn Dobson (who personally gathered much essential information) and Betty Eligh (who typed the whole of the original work); and to Gus Richardson, whose diligent and perspicacious editing has much improved even my own revised text. My indebtedness to various other people and institutions will be evident from the footnotes. I crave the forgiveness of anyone whose help I ought to have acknowledged but have not. My wife, of course, has been a constant and much enduring support.

E.F.

Abbreviations

AASRE	Amalgamated Association of Street Railway Employees
ABC	American Brotherhood of Carpenters (after 1887, UBCJ)
AFL	American Federation of Labor
ARU	American Railway Union
ASCJ	Amalgamated Society of Carpenters and Joiners
ASE	Amalgamated Society of Engineers
ATLA	Allied Trades and Labor Association (Ottawa)
ATU	Amalgamated Trades Union (Halifax and Dartmouth)
BLE	Brotherhood of Locomotive Engineers
BLF	Brotherhood of Locomotive Firemen
CASE	Canadian Association of Stationary Engineers
CCMTM	Conseil central des métiers et du travail de Montréal
CFMTM	Conseil fédéré des métiers et du travail de Montréal
CIU	Coopers International Union
CLC	Canadian Labour Congress
CLU	Canadian Labor Union
CLU (Hamilton)	Central Labor Union
CMIU	Cigar Makers International Union
CMTC	Congrès des métiers et du travail du Canada
CNMTC	Congrès national des métiers et du travail du Canada
DA	District Assembly of the KOL
FLU	Federal Labor Union (either AFL or TLCC)
GMA	General Mining Association
HTLC	Hamilton Trades and Labor Council
IAM	International Association of Machinists
IBEW	International Brotherhood of Electrical Workers
IMIU	Iron Molders International Union

ITU	International Typographical Union
IWA	International Workingmen's Association
JTUA	Journeymen Tailors Union of America
KOL	Knights of Labor
LA	Local Assembly of the KOL
LBA	Labourers Benevolent Association
MMLPA	Miners and Mine Laborers Protective Association
NAME	National Association of Marine Engineers
NATSE	National Alliance of Theatrical Stage Employees of the United States
NTLCC	National Trades and Labour Congress of Canada
NUM	National Union of Molders
ORC	Order of Railroad Conductors
PWA	Provincial Workingmen's Association (later, Provincial Workmen's Association)
SLP	Socialist Labor Party
TLC	Trades and Labor Council
TLCC	Trades and Labor Congress of Canada
TTA	Toronto Trades Assembly
TTLC	Toronto Trades and Labor Council
TTU	Toronto Typographical Union
UBCJ	United Brotherhood of Carpenters and Joiners
UBRE	United Brotherhood of Railway Employees
VTLC	Vancouver Trades and Labor Council
WFM	Western Federation of Miners

TRADE UNIONS IN CANADA 1812–1902

I
Introduction

We are apt to think of labour unions as a feature of a relatively advanced industrial society. So it comes as something of a shock to most people to find out how far back in Canadian history they actually go. That there could have been anything of the kind in the primitive, frontier, predominantly rural British North America of the early nineteenth century seems almost incredible. But there was, as early as the War of 1812; nor, on reflection, is it so surprising after all. There were towns and cities. They had to have construction workers. They had to have tools, and stoves, therefore foundries and foundry workers. They had to have boots and shoes and clothes, therefore tailors and shoemakers. They had to have printers. And even in that simple society there were employers and employed, and their interests were not identical. The employed soon found that out, by experience; found out also the employer's strength and their own weakness in individual bargaining on terms and conditions of employment, and so started organizing to prevent their employers from taking advantage of them.

This the employers were only too ready to do. The first half of the nineteenth century was the heyday of laissez-faire, and quite as much in America as in Britain. 'Each, seeking only his own interest, [was] led as by an Invisible Hand to promote the interest of society': so ran orthodox economic theory, and nothing could have been more to the taste of the enterprising capitalists, big and little, who set out to develop the remaining British North American colonies. Ruthless competition was right, its results were good, for everyone, and it was inevitable. Any attempt to thwart it was not only reprehensible; it was senseless, since it was bound to fail.

Then as development proceeded there grew up some really big industries, notably the timber trade, and with it shipbuilding and shipping, with large labour forces, where the harshness of laissez-faire could not be softened by the close contact between employer and employed on the small construction job or in the small factory.

Moreover, much of the working force, even in Quebec (in Montreal and Quebec City), was made up of British or American immigrants, who had already tasted the joys of laissez-faire in their own countries, and who brought with them, increasingly as time went on, experience of unions in those countries.

Another factor which helped to buld up Canadian unions was the mobility of labour across the border between British North America and the United States. There were none of the later legal obstacles to this movement, and both employers and employed found it to their advantage. The employers were able to drive a thriving reciprocal trade in strikebreakers. The employees, finding work slack on one side of the line, went to the other: the records of transfer cards given and accepted by locals of such unions as the Typographers and the Molders read like a lesson in North American geography.

What were the early unions? Mutual benefit societies? Often they were, in part, as in Britain and the United States. But, from the beginning, they were essentially concerned with negotiating, or (where they were strong enough) imposing, terms and conditions of employment: wages, hours, safety precautions, exclusion of non-unionists. Very soon, finding that the method of collective bargaining (as the Webbs were later to call it), even when supplemented by the method of mutual insurance, was inadequate, or too slow, to give them what they wanted and felt they had a right to, they started using also the method of legal enactment.[1] This meant demanding a wider franchise and reforms in the electoral machinery in order to give union members the power to influence political decisions; otherwise, they would ask in vain for legal protection of the unions' existence and funds, and laws to prevent the exploitation of at least women and children, the swindling of men, the killing or maiming of workers by industrial accidents or negligence, and the destitution of the dependants of those so killed or injured. Generally, the method of legal enactment took the form of putting pressure on the existing parties; but from the 1870s on, increasingly, there was an insistent demand for independent political action through working-class representatives (even if 'Lib-Lab' or 'Cons-Lab') or a working-class party; and in spite of repeated rebuffs and disillusionments the idea would not die. It was to become one of the things that distinguished Canadian from American trade unionism, even when the Canadian unions concerned were locals of international unions with their headquarters and the bulk of their membership in the United States.

Why did certain unions spring up first in certain places? Why did they grow, or dwindle, or die, in this, that, or the other place? Why were most early unions organizations of skilled crafts? Why did certain unions disappear? Why did local unions gradually give way to international in most occupations and industries?

At least partial answers to some of these questions are easy, even obvious. For example, unions of longshoremen sprang up in large ports, unions of miners in mining camps, unions of the building trades or the clothing trades in large towns.

Some unions dwindled or disappeared because technological progress knocked them out: the Saddlers, the Leather Workers on Horse Goods, the Horseshoers, the Cigar Makers, the Shipwrights, the Sailmakers, the Riggers, the Piano and Organ Workers, the Carriage Workers. Others were created by technological progress: Electricians, Telephone Workers, Automobile Workers, Rubber Workers, Oil Workers. Unions rose here because new resources were discovered, died there because the resources were exhausted or more profitable ones had been discovered elsewhere. Changes in tariffs, our own or other people's, made and broke industries, and unions with them. Transcontinental and trans-border railways made the great railway unions. Skilled craft unions usually came before unions of the unskilled because the skilled workers were usually scarcer and therefore in a better bargaining position. International unions generally supplanted local, regional, or national unions because of the mobility of labour across the border (down to the late 1890s) and because the international unions usually had more money, more experience, more organizers, and more skilled negotiators and so could do a more effective job of representing the workers concerned.

More detailed answers are unlikely to be forthcoming till there is a much more extensive literature on Canadian economic and social history than we now possess, as well as special studies of particular places, regions, industries, and unions. The sheer task of finding out which unions were where, when, and for how long is gargantuan, and far from accomplished, even for the period with which this volume deals.

What does emerge, unmistakably, and most surprisingly, from the knowledge we have is the persistence of problems, of attitudes towards them, of methods of dealing with them, of arguments about them. There have been so many changes, especially in the last 40 years, notably in labour-relations legislation (which hardly existed before 1940), that one might have expected to find the accounts of unions and their activities in the last century of almost purely antiquarian interest: 'old, forgotten, far off things, and battles long ago'; what the victories and defeats were all about, obscure or undiscoverable. On the contrary, what one finds is, over and over again, startlingly contemporary. It is only necessary to change a few names, dates, and absolute figures, and the tale might have come from yesterday's newspaper. The unions were so often fighting for the same things they are fighting for now, wielding the same weapons, using the same arguments; employers were so often resisting exactly the same things, wielding the same weapons, using the same arguments. Governments were so often acting, or not acting, for precisely the same reasons, or lack of reasons, as now. Of course there are also vast differences. But the similarities are more numerous, more striking, and more important. There was no golden age when unions were unnecessary because employers, and economic conjunctures, were so benevolent; when such unions as there were were too 'moderate' or 'responsible' ever, ever to strike; when union demands were generally recognized as 'reasonable' and 'justified'; when employers were always rational and 'gentlemanly' in their dealings with their employees. The world of the nineteenth century, and the early twentieth, was in these respects basically the same as the world of today.

The history of trade unionism in Canada may be said to fall into five broad periods, which, of course, cannot be neatly divided by particular dates: the edges are necessarily blurred.

For example, the first period, down to 1859, may be described as that of purely local craft unions of skilled workers. But one has to add at once that the first international union, the Amalgamated Society of Engineers (British), set up its first Canadian branch, in Montreal, as early as 1853, and that there were a few unions of unskilled workers, such as the Ship Labourers (Longshoremen) of Saint John, founded in 1849, and Quebec, founded in 1857. None the less, nearly all the unions down to 1859 were purely local, without any formal ties even with others in the same city or town: and nearly all of them were made up of skilled craftsmen or tradesmen, such as printers, carpenters, cabinet-makers, masons, stonecutters, painters, blacksmiths, shoemakers, sailmakers, shipwrights, caulkers, bakers, and tailors.

The second period, from 1859 to 1880, is marked by the entry of a series of international unions (both British and American), and by the setting up of the first local central organizations and the first national central organization.

The third, from 1881 to 1902, is characterized by the entry of many more international unions (all American); by widespread organization of the unskilled; by the effective spread of the movement clear across the country, from coast to coast; by the reorganization of the old local central bodies and the creation of many new ones; by the establishment of a permanent national central body; and by the existence of a single inclusive movement which took in every possible kind of genuine labour organization: local, provincial, national, international, Canadian, British, American, skilled, unskilled, of one occupation or many.

The fourth, from 1902 to 1956, is the period of consolidation of the major national central body, of its exclusion of all unions 'dual' to (rivals of) the American Federation of Labor affiliates, and of the splits and attempts to create rival centres and rival movements, based on various principles.

The fifth, from 1956 on, is the period of reunion, or attempted reunion.

PART ONE

The early period of unionism

2

The period of local unionism 1812–59

The first unions in British North America were almost certainly in New Brunswick and Nova Scotia. Before the end of the War of 1812, Saint John had a building boom which shot rents up by 40 per cent in one year. With the increased demand for labour, 'the wages of Mechanics of every description were enormously increased, and their unwarrantable combinations being adhered to for lessening the number of hours which were to be considered as a day's work, it became impossible to procure workmen for the various purposes for which they were wanted; and the Public were in these respects at the mercy of the few mechanics that the city afforded.' However, a number of mechanics, particularly masons and housewrights, had arrived in the city from Massachusetts just before war was declared. Against this competition, the unions promptly memorialized the mayor to enforce the law that only freemen of Saint John could employ their trade within the city. The mayor could scarcely refuse, but he was most reluctant to deprive the master builders of their cheap labour. The difficulty was that only British subjects could be made freemen. He got around this by directing the Yankees to get themselves sworn as British subjects. The commissioner for administering the oath was strongly anti-union; so, though he doubted the legality of the performance, he duly swore about 40 of the immigrants. The mayor then admitted them freemen, and the employers were able to hire them with at least a show of legality.[1]

Saint John may well have been the chief centre of union activity from the late 1830s to the late 1850s. As early as 26 September 1835, the sawyers of Saint John and Portland must have been organized, for in a newspaper of that date they informed their employers that they were determined to take no less than 6s. 6d. per day to 1 November, and 5s. per day from then to 1 April; or so much per hundred feet of various woods.[2] There is a peremptoriness in this which suggests that the sawyers must have been in a position to stand no nonsense. On 20 March 1841 we find another notice in the same terms.

The Sawyers Association may well have had a continuous existence till 23 May 1849, when a meeting of the Saint John City and Country Sawyers Society took place 'for the purposes of organizing themselves into a legal Society, to make rules and regulations for their future guidance – as to their wage and the number of hours per day for working – and so that a perfect understanding may be had between themselves and their employers.' The meeting also decided to set up a charitable fund to relieve poor and disabled members, with each member contributing 1s. 6d. per month. Sixty-two men signed up, and the society set a new scale of prices for various woods.[3] In the same month the ship carpenters, or shipwrights, met to 'form themselves into a legal Society,' along the same lines as the sawyers. About 150 signed up. They established a mutual benefit fund and set the same hours as the Labourers Benevolent Association,[4] a longshoremen's organization formed in the same year.

At about the time of the first Sawyers' advertisement, the United and Friendly House Carpenters and Joiners Society was formed. It was still going strong in March 1838.[5] On 25 March 1837, a Painters Society held its regular quarterly meeting. A few weeks later we find notices of the Tailors Society and the Journeymen Cabinet-Makers. The Tailors Society was still in existence more than a year later.[6]

By 1840 we have ample evidence of the existence of a considerable number of unions in Saint John. It comes chiefly from accounts of two trades processions: one, 27 May to lay the corner-stone of the Mechanics Institute, and the other, 22 July, to welcome the new governor-general, Charles Poulett Thompson. What makes these doubly interesting is that the second is explicitly described as 'another Trades Union Procession'[7] and that the societies concerned show every sign of being well established and indeed enjoying substantial public respect.

In the first parade, 'owing to the shortness of the notice, several of the Trades who intended to join, were unable to make the necessary preparation.' None the less, 1200 men from 10 trades marched: Blacksmiths, Founders, Hammermen, Horologers, Carpenters, Tailors, Painters, Bakers, Cordwainers, and Cabinet-Makers. They paraded in style. The Blacksmiths ... carried banners inscribed with such slogans as 'Industry and Benevolence unite us in Friendship,' 'By Hammer in Hand, all Arts do stand,' and 'Arts, Trades and Manufactures.' The 'Sons of Vulcan' were accompanied by a car, 'drawn by black horses, with a representation of two smiths at their anvil, the loud and unceasing strokes of whose hammers (which appeared to be worked by machinery) were greeted with frequent cheers.' The Carpenters, who were very numerous, wore red scarves, and carried long white wands. They bore two banners, one with the five architectural orders, and one with their arms, on which were inscribed the words 'Great Britain, Ireland and the

Colonies – Union is Strength.' The Tailors were preceded by the Golden Fleece, and each man wore a blue scarf. Their banner was inscribed '*Concordia parvae crescunt.*' They were accompanied by a car 'drawn by splendidly caparisoned horses, representing the Garden of Eden. In the centre stood a large tree, hung with abundance of beautiful fruit: the old serpent was twined around the trunk, and the figures of Adam and Eve, as large as life, stood under the branches.' The Bakers each wore a straw hat and blue ribbon, and a white apron and gloves. They carried a large horn of plenty and the banner of their trade, with the motto 'For Good of All.' The cordwainers, another numerous body, were dressed in white pantaloons and white gloves, with aprons of chamois leather, bound with blue ribbons and rosettes. Their banner bore their arms and the motto 'Frères Cordonniers.'[8]

For the second procession there was more time to prepare, the trades having held a meeting five days before the event. There were about 1500 men in the trades' procession which followed the governor-general from the landing place to the court house, comprising Carpenters, Riggers, Cordwainers, Tailors, Blacksmiths, Hammermen, Founders, Coopers, Shipwrights, and Bakers. The Bakers had been assigned the duty of keeping the door of the court house, and of receiving the governor-general, while the Coachmen, Cartmen, and Draymen of the city formed a mounted guard of honour. As one newspaper remarked, the trades' 'display of banners, badges, emblems, models and devices far exceeded all expectation, and made a most imposing spectacle, one which, we doubt, could scarcely be equalled in all British North America.'[9]

A third procession took place 13 years later, this time for the turning of the first sod of the European and North American Railway. It included the mayor and corporation of Saint John, the mayor and corporation of Fredericton, the police magistrates of Saint John and Portland, the magistrates of the city and county of Saint John, the high sheriff of the city and county of Saint John, and the president and directors of the railway. Most of the unions came near the head of the procession, and many were accompanied by floats.

The House Carpenters and Joiners led the trades with a carpenters' workshop, with men 'busy in the various occupations of the craft, and a sash machine ... at full work.' Next came the Ship Carpenters, or Shipwrights, whose union had just been reorganized.[10] Described as one of the largest and finest bodies in the Procession, they came from sixteen different shipyards, and were 'dressed in appropriate uniforms, and ... bore emblems of their trade. ... Models of vessels in various stages of construction were drawn upon waggons, suitably decorated.' Then came the blacksmiths and founders in four divisions: Blacksmiths, Founders, Edge-Tool Makers, and Farriers, each with banner and motto. They mustered about 200. After them, but belonging to the same body, came the men from the foundries, over 300. They were followed by about 40 or 50 painters, with a marshal and a banner bearing their arms – a shield supported by St Luke, their patron saint, and a leopard – and their motto, *Amor, honor et obedientia.*

The Masons and Stonecutters mustered about 150, and their float represented a brickyard hard at work: 'the stone cutters plied the chisel and mallet busily, and on one car were borne barrels of cement, plaster, &c. – Their banner showed an arch, with a railway train passing over it.' The Saint John Bakers Friendly Association turned out 80 or 90 strong, bearing a banner with 'sheaves of corn and men in working dress – motto "For the good of all." They bore gilt peels, dokers, &c.'

Next came the Printers. 'The Printing Press was drawn by four greys. Supporting the canopy were the figures of Faust, Gutenberg, Caxton, and Franklin. The car bore the inscription "Knowledge is Power." Attending on the Press was in a devil in proper shape, horn, hoof and all.' Copies of a song composed by a Mr Redfern were thrown off as the procession moved along. The song had 13 stanzas in praise of science, the railway, and, above all, of course, of the printing press. The final stanza is a fair sample:

Splendid fount of lore and light;
Bulwark of a people's right;
Gibbet for the base transgressor
Scourge of tyrant and oppressor;
Friend of science, art and knowledge;
Aid of author, school and college;
Source of human happiness –
Hail transcendent, peerless PRESS!

The Cordwainers, about 250, were accompanied by King and Queen Crispin. The Tailors numbered 139: 'Adam and Eve stood their part well.' They were followed by 'a Golden Lamb and the trades Banner. Two Camels, with the motto "*Concordia parvae Crescunt.*"' The Riggers and Sailmakers 'mustered 100 strong, dressed in frock coat and white trousers, Banner, Ship, with Riggers at work. Motto – "Go on and Prosper."' The Cabinet-Makers, about 90 or 100, had a work bench, with workmen in full operation, and a carriage with furniture. They were in full dress, and each carried a mahogany staff. Towards the tail-end of the procession came the Millmen, 1100, dressed in white shirts, black trousers, black belts, and glazed hats.[11]

This makes 13 unions, and this without the Labourers Benevolent Association. Why it was not in the parade is a mystery. In the first 16 years of its existence, its fortunes ebbed and flowed,[12] and in 1853 it may have been at a low point in its history.

Fourteen unions at this early date, in a place the size of Saint John, may seem fantastic. But in the 1850s, Saint John (with the adjacent town of Portland) was bigger than Toronto, twice the size of Hamilton, and more than half as big as Montreal.[13] It was the centre of flourishing shipping, shipbuilding, and lumber industries.[14] Some idea of its prosperity may be gained from the fact that, even as late as 1875, 15 local employers, within a matter of minutes, put up what was for those days the fabulous sum of $58,500 towards a $100,000 strikebreaking fund, and the next day's newspaper account added, casually, 'the balance of the $100,000 will be doubtless made up to-day, without much effort.' Three days later, it had in fact reached $106,000 with 62 merchants contributing.[15]

The Bakers Association was still in existence in 1858, as were a fair number of other unions, including the Ship Labourers, Shipwrights, Riggers, and Caulkers.[16] and very probably the Printers, Millmen, Carpenters, Painters, Cordwainers, and Tailors.[17]

The *Miramichi Gleaner* of 26 May 1840 printed a notice of a Carpenters and Joiners Society meeting.[18] It seems clear that in Chatham, as in Saint John, unions appeared early. It also seems clear that in New Brunswick as a whole unions were not secret societies, and they appear to have run into none of the legal prohibitions they encountered in most other parts of British North America.

In Halifax, in 1815, the Benevolent Society of Journeymen Tailors was meeting regularly. It must have been only one of a number of vigorous unions, for in 1816 the legislature passed a ferociously anti-union act, whose preamble complained that 'great numbers of ... Journeymen and Workmen, in the Town of Halifax, and other parts of the Province, have, by unlawful Meetings and Combinations, endeavoured to regulate the rate of wages, and to effectuate illegal purposes.' The Act proceeded to annul all contracts, covenants, and agreements in which such bodies sought to obtain an advance of wages, lessen or change their usual hours of work, decrease the quantity of work, prevent or hinder any person from employing anyone he chose, and control or affect anyone in carrying on his trade or business. Journeymen or others entering into such contracts, or combining for such objects, or enticing men not to take employment, or to leave their employment, or hindering or trying to hinder employers from hiring men or refusing to work with other employees, could be sent to jail for not more than three months, or to a house of correction for not more than two. Further, the Act was not to be construed as preventing any such disreputable characters from being indicted, prosecuted, or punished under the common law for combination or conspiracy.[19]

It seems plain that the Nova Scotian unions must have been doing almost everything that a modern union does in pursuit of collective bargaining, and with some success. There was a Carpenters' and Joiners' Union in Yarmouth, from 25 March 1834 till at least 2 July 1851.[20] There was also a Printers' Union somewhere in the province, probably Halifax, in 1837: a fraternal delegate from Nova Scotia was seated with full powers at the convention of the (American) National Typographical Association, predecessor of the Naitonal (now International) Typographical Union.[21]

A Mechanics' Society or Union, open to all tradesmen, was founded in Newfoundland on 3 March 1827 and was still in existence after the turn of the century. Initially, it may have been a purely benevolent association; in 1896 it transformed itself into a local federation of unions.[22]

There may have been a Sealers' Union as early as 1845.[23] Certainly there had been successful strikes by sealers, 27 February 1838 and 18 March 1842, both over berth money. On 17 April 1845, the employers precipitated fresh trouble by announcing a reduction in the berth money for common or ordinary hands, for after- and bow-gunners. Three thousand men met at Brigus and sent delegates to St John's. There they called on Captain Henry Supple (who had figured prominently in the 1842 strike) to come to Brigus and lead the men. He agreed, and when he arrived at Chapel's Cove he 'was given a reception seldom or never tendered to any man before – nor in all probability has it since been equalled. He was drawn on a sleigh, while over his head waved a silk banner, trimmed with green satin, in the centre being a red satin St George's Cross. The Temperance Band of Hr. [Harbour] Main accompanied the men, who left for Brigus, the "seat of war."' At a big meeting there, the employers agreed to give berths at 'Ios. per man, persons shipped for gunners to bring a good gun with a spare lock and use the same,' and to provide free outfits. When some of the employers welshed on the agreement, there was a successful lawsuit to enforce it, in which Supple, in lively exchanges with the employers' counsel, Sir Bryan Robinson, seems invariably to have come off the better.[24]

The Shipwrights Union was organized in 1851 and was still in existence in 1897. The Seal-Skinners Union, organized in 1855, was still in existence in 1936. Its early records were destroyed in the 1892 fire. It did no collective bargaining and never signed any formal agreements.[25]

QUEBEC

Quebec City had a Printers' Union in 1827, though it does not seem to have lasted long.[26] In 1836, however, the printers organized again, in the Société typographique canadienne de Québec. The objects of this union were 'to raise the position, maintain and protect the interests of the craft; to establish and maintain a just and equitable rate of wages, and to regulate all matters concerning the welfare of the members; to influence the apprenticeship system towards a higher degree of intelligence, capacity and ability, in the interest of both employers and employed; to try to replace strikes, and the rebuffs and pecuniary losses which they cause, by arbitration and conciliation in the settlement of all disputes over wages and working conditions; to make suitable provision for members' funerals; to work by all honourable means for the interests and welfare of employer and employed; and to encourage all legitimate measures which might raise the position of the craft.'[27]

This body, which included both French-speaking and English-speaking members, apparently was active for some years. In 1839, it addressed a petition with 66 signatures to the master printers, asking for an increase in rates. (What are now called demands were in those days embodied in petitions or memorials, and wages were called prices or rates.) It was couched in very respectful terms, but the content is thoroughly modern. The cost of living had gone up; other trades, with shorter apprenticeship (such as carpenters and joiners) got more pay; and the current wages were not high enough to allow the workers to make ends meet. The union disclaimed, however, any intention of engaging in 'what in English is called a "strike,"' assuring the employers that it relied wholly on their goodwill and on the justice of its request.

This Quebec union, which corresponded with the York Typographical Society, seems to have faded out in 1844. It was reorganized in 1852 but lasted only a few months. In 1855 it was reorganized again, and from then till 1872, when it became locals 159 and 160 of the International Typographical Union, there is a pretty complete list of presidents, arguing for reasonably continuous activity.[28]

In 1840 the Quebec ship carpenters formed the Société amicale et bienveillante des charpentiers de vaisseaux de Québec. Both a mutual benefit society and a trade union, it must have owed something to middle-class leadership, for its first secretary was a notary. Its stated aim seems to have been to defend the interests of the ship carpenters against the master shipbuilders and against the competition of unskilled labour. In the very year of the Société's foundation, there was a strike over wages, which seems to have failed. The union suffered severely from the economic crises of the late 1840s, but in 1850 it was strong enough to seek incorporation, and throughout that decade it seems to have flourished.[29]

There must have been a Painters Union in Quebec in 1841, for in October of that year, seven journeymen painters were found guilty of conspiracy.[30]

Quebec had a Seamen's Union before 1847. Its enemies called it 'the Crimps,' alleging that it procured seamen by decoying or impressing them. In fact, on the same testimony, it seems to have established something like a closed shop, and what the employers called 'an exorbitant rate of wages.' It must have existed for some time and enjoyed considerable success, for in 1847 the Legislature passed an Act which forbade shipowners or shipmasters to hire anyone who did not have an official register ticket. The Act did not crush the Crimps, for in 1852 the employers were still complaining of the closed shop and the 'exorbitant wages.'[31]

The Quebec Cordwainers Society, at the end of 1853, had won a strike for a wage increase, and was demanding a closed shop.[32] In 1857 the Quebec longshoremen (at that time almost all Irish) formed the Ship Labourers Benevolent Association, a powerful and durable union which, by the turn of the century, had five branches, and which lasted till at least the 1940s.[33] In 1858 a group of newly arrived British sailmakers formed a union at Quebec.[34]

Montreal had unions of shoemakers and tailors in 1830, and both seem to have lasted till at least 1834. There is some indication of a shoemakers' union in the spring of 1854, and a large contingent of shoemakers took part in the celebrations at the opening of the Grand Trunk Railway in November 1856.[35]

By 1833, there was a Printers Society, which seems to have lasted till 1844; a new one was formed in February 1854.[36] In February 1833 the carpenters organized as the Mechanics Mutual Protection Society. They asked and got a 10-hour day. But a year later the master carpenters counter-attacked, demanding restoration of the 11-hour day. The union replied by publishing a book of wage rates, calling for an increase of 16s. a year and providing for strike pay. The employers remained adamant, and a strike took place. In 1856 a Carpenters Union took part in the Grand Trunk celebrations, and in 1858 there was a Canadian Society of Carpenters and Joiners, Inc.

In 1858 there was a Journeymen Tailors Protective Society.[37] There seem to have been unions of Bakers and of City Firemen in 1834; the former appear also to have had a union in the spring of 1854. There may also then have been a Carters' Union. A Painters' Union took part in the Grand Trunk celebrations of 1856.[38]

The Montreal Stonecutters, organized in 1844, later became a local of the Journeymen Stonecutters of North America and lasted till 1938. They struck in May 1854.[39]

In 1853 Montreal got the first Canadian branch of the Amalgamated Society of Engineers (ASE), a British Union. This branch had an initial membership of 21; by 1857 it had reached 55; in 1859 it was 42. Its first year's income was £23, expenditure £5. It provided sick benefits and, from 1854 on, funeral benefits.[40]

ONTARIO AND THE WEST

Hamilton had unions of shoemakers and foundry workers between 1827 and 1842. By 1833, it had a Typographical Society. This must have succumbed, for by 5 August 1846 there was a new one 'recently organized.' This was still in existence on 6 March 1849, when, at the Toronto union's anniversary banquet, a representative, Mr Nicholson, responded to the toast, 'The Hamilton Typographical Society,' and, in his turn, proposed 'The Toronto Typographical Society.' This second Hamilton union also must have faded out, for on 26 July 1852, the Hamilton printers organized a fresh society 'in connection with their brethren from Toronto.' Perhaps with an eye to the law of conspiracy (the pre-1791 English common law on this subject had never been amended by the Legislature of Upper Canada or of Canada), the society emphasized that it was 'united to support, not combined to injure.' Its main objects were to work for the mutual benefit of the employer and employee, to maintain a regular rate of charges, to assist journeymen in obtaining employment and fair wages, 'and in every other manner to uphold the dignity of the craft.' The society said it intended to connect itself with the union recently established in the United States.[41]

The Hamilton society seems to have had a short life. We find a new one in 1854. This also proclaimed itself 'united to support, not combined to injure.' At the time of its third anniversary dinner it apparently enjoyed good relations with its employers, for one master printer rose and said how pleased he was to see the society in such a flourishing condition. He approved of the principle of association 'when such association aimed at the elevation of the social conditions of the employee and the protection of the employer.' The Toronto Typographical Union had a deputation at the dinner, and a letter was read from the London Society of Compositors (significant, this, of the close ties between Canadian workers and those of the Old Country). All printers in the city were either members of the organization or had taken steps to join. This union was still in existence in 1860.[42]

Two new unions were formed in Hamilton in 1853. By mid-June a Shoemakers Trade Union Society was functioning. A year later it was on strike: nine shoemakers were charged with combining not to work for a particular firm. Circulars of the Journeymen Shoemakers of the United States and Canada, formed in Baltimore in 1855, indicate a local in Hamilton in April and June 1858. The House Carpenters organized about mid-March 1853. They promptly demanded a one-third increase in wages and struck when it was refused. Some employers gave in; some of the strikers formed companies and took on work themselves.[43]

The next Hamilton union was probably the Journeymen Tailors Protective Society, formed on 13 February 1854, to oppose the introduction of sewing machines in Lawson and Bros' establishment. The tailors had already struck twice and won wage increases; the machine was probably part of a counter-attack. In the picturesque phrases of the *Hamilton Spectator*, 'A terrible row has been going on in the city for the last eight or ten days among the sons of the goose and the needle ... The fiend that has come amongst them is ... none other than the steam engine with his sewing machines and other implements of evil, threatening extermination to the whole craft. It is no wonder, therefore, that they have come out and separated themselves from the evil and have left the monster alone in his glory with his gussets and seams and shirts.' The employer advertised for 50 tailors who were 'not afraid of machines,' and William Ferguson, president of the society, on another page of the same issue, had a notice informing outsiders of the strike. Fifty American tailors duly arrived, but the Hamilton tailors forced them to go home.[44]

With the end of the Crimean War came an influx of skilled workers from Britain, notably into the railway shops, and this was probably what led to the formation of the Hamilton branch of the ASE in 1857. The branch began with 14 members and lasted till 1920. In 1858 the membership rose to 30, but in 1859 it was down to 23. Its income in the 1850s ranged from £19 to £51, its expenditure from £4 to £75, and it had a sick benefit scheme.[45]

The first Toronto union was probably the United Amicable Trade and Benefit Society of Journeymen Bricklayers, Plasterers, and Masons, which, in 1831, demanded a 10-hour day: 6 am to 6 pm, with two hours off for meals. In December 1833 this body resolved that its members would work only for masters of the respective trades and only with other members of the society. Wages it left entirely to each employer. The carpenters appear also to have had a union in 1833, and in December the 'Journeymen Carpenters, Bricklayers, and Masons of York' petitioned for a law to compel proprietors to hold back from contractors enough money to pay wages. This must have been a joint effort by the two unions.[46]

The second Toronto union was the York Typographical Society. Twenty-four printers had been in the habit of meeting on Sunday afternoons in an old orchard near the present Allan Gardens (the furtiveness which this suggests was not accidental). They decided to form a union 'owing to the many innovations which [had] been made upon the long established wages of the professors of the art of printing, and those of a kind highly detrimental to their interests.' On 12 October 1832 Joseph H. Lawrence called a meeting in the York Hotel, which, with W.A.C. Myers in the chair, decided to set up the York Typographical Society. Daniel Bancroft was elected president, and the dues were set at 1s. 3d. a month.

The constitution seems not to have been adopted till April 1833, when it was signed by 25 members of the craft (both journeymen and foremen). It stipulated that no member was to work for less than £1 15s. a week, that wages must be paid weekly, that any work over the usual 10 hours a day must be paid overtime at 10d. an hour, that apprenticeship should be not less than 4 years (changed to 5 in 1835), and that no member should work in any office where there were more than 2 apprentices unless it was the last year of the eldest apprentice's time. Any member who did not get paid weekly should leave his job, and the society should pay him 10s. a week for 3 weeks and, if he left town because of unemployment, a lump sum of £1. If any journeyman refused to comply with the society's rules the members working in the office concerned should notify the employer and refuse to work until the objector either complied or left the office.

On 15 October 1833, the society held an anniversary dinner. Twelve members appear to have been present, with two apprentices and ten guests. Five of these were newspaper owners: Robert Stanton, King's Printer, the *Gazette*; William Lyon Mackenzie, the *Colonial Advocate*; George Gurnett, the *Courier*; Mr Collins, the *Freeman*; and Mr King, the *Correspondent*. One was a deputy from the Hamilton union.

There were eleven or twelve formal toasts, followed by nine volunteer toasts that were responded to with impromptu speeches. Toasts were drunk to the king, the queen and the royal family, the king's ministers, Sir John and Lady Colborne, and the 'diamond forms of Upper Canada.' These were followed by toasts of the York Typographical Society (proposed by Mackenzie), the proprietors, the press, printers around the world, and York.

The proprietors' and master printers' references to the society were most cordial. This may have owed something to the conviviality of the occasion, but it seems to have been mainly the result of the statement of aims in the constitution: 'the mutual interest of employers and employed.' Mackenzie praised the society's 'consistent and moderate policy – nothing that savoured of exclusive privileges – but on the contrary arrangements that would secure respectability to journeymen without interfering with the interests and prerogatives of the employers.' Stanton believed such societes, 'when conducted upon proper principles and with due regard to morality to their members ... were calculated to benefit society generally.' Gurnett said he was glad the society existed, and Bull said he 'belonged to a similar Society in Montreal.'

The Society set up a committee in December to revise the constitution, and on 25 March 1834 what now became the Toronto Typographical Society came into being. In October the society set up a committee to draft a petition to the Legislature for the better regulation of apprentices (a recurrent problem both for this union and for its successor).[47]

Like all the early unions, the society was wretchedly poor, and in the fall of 1836 was nearly bankrupted by the payment of £3 2s. 6d. to a sick member. None the less, it decided to strike all the Toronto papers. The cost of living was rising, and tales of higher wages in such centres as New York whetted the appetite of the Toronto printers. According to one of the employers, William O'Grady, they were already getting 35s. a week and 10d. an hour for extra work. William Lyon Mackenzie said he was paying $7 to $7.50 a week, and the union wanted $8, with a 10-hour day. O'Grady said the society was demanding New York rates for piece-work. Apparently there was also a demand to limit apprentices to two per office. Stanton, of the *Gazette*, granted this; Dalton, of the *Patriot*, kept five, Mackenzie apparently four.

The master printers were furious at the demand for higher wages and refused it. The union then struck on 22 October. The strike must have been pretty effective at first, for O'Grady apologized to his readers for the delay in getting the paper to them, and Mackenzie informed the legislature that if the strike continued he could do no more work for it. But the apprentices and foremen seem to have rallied to their employers' side, for both O'Grady and Mackenzie were soon operating normally enough to publish their opinion of the union's demands. O'Grady was relatively mild. He contented himself with pointing out that the Toronto master printers got less than those in New York and that rent and food were much cheaper in Toronto than in New York.

Not so Mackenzie. The tribune of the people, the champion of the mechanics, the great revolutionary, let fly with everything he had. The demand for higher wages would be ruinous unless he had several months' notice so that he could negotiate a new contract with the Assembly. (To this the union replied that he had taken the contract at too low a figure.) He had discharged the six journeymen he was employing and told the foreman he must leave the union or be discharged also. The foreman complied. 'But for him and my apprentices,' said Mackenzie, 'this paper would have been the size of a seven by nine pane of glass.'

Mackenzie could see no excuse at all for the strike. The printers had steady employment and worked in a warm comfortable room. There had been no employers' combination to cut wages. The journeymen printers would do well to 'employ their evenings studying the true principles of economy which govern the rule of wages.' Combinations such as the printers' were 'useful when not carried too far. But when they begin to foment divisions and animosities in society, when they array classes against each other who could otherwise be united by a common interest, when they attempt to deprive the youths of a city ... of the privilege of choosing the trade they would desire to pursue, when they attempt to establish a monopoly in the rate of labour instead of leaving it to be regulated by supply and demand, they become injurious to society.' Mackenzie ended with an admission that 'Labour sometimes needs protection' – witness the horrors of child labour in English factories – but added, defiantly, 'it is not so here.'

By the end of the month, the union had lost, but the men got their jobs back. Astonishingly, the union survived its defeat, lasting till it was virtually abandoned in the aftermath of the rebellion.

Two features of this union's activities are noteworthy. The first is that members were severely disciplined for withdrawing from any office in an improper manner, or discharged for misconduct. A second offence carried a fine of £1; a third meant expulsion. The second is that the society, from the very beginning, was in touch with printers' unions elsewhere. On 2 May 1833, one Baird, of the Cork Typographical Society, deposited his membership card from that body and was not only accepted but, on his plea that he could find no work in York, given 17s. 6d. to help him go to the United States. During 1836, the society corresponded with similar bodies in Montreal, Quebec, Washington, Boston, Philadelphia, New York, and Albany.[48]

In 1844 the present Toronto Typographical Union (TTU) was formed. The organization meeting was held early in February at the Mansion House, where the union continued to meet till the end of 1849. Daniel Bancroft presided and was elected president of the new union. Three other veterans of the first union were also elected to the executive: John Jones, vice-president; R.W. Clindinning, secretary; and James Lumsden, member of the standing committee.

This union, like its predecessor, was a response to action, or expected action, by employers. According to the first annual report, a section of the employers, early in 1844, conceived the idea of forming a coalition to reduce wages. 'What was urged for departing from the settled wage of the Trade has, perhaps, never fully transpired; but it is believed, that the pre-eminence of the existing rate of wages of this, over the other provincial towns, was the main point of attack.' Threatened with reverting to the wage rates of Kingston and other places, the journeymen printers decided to call a general meeting. Though there was no visible result from the masters' meeting, the men went ahead with their plans. Although the old society had fallen into decay, its scale of wages had, in the main, been upheld. Its constitution also had been preserved and was now taken over by the new union, with some slight alterations and minor additions based on the rules of the societies of Quebec and Montreal. 'In the wording of the various articles, everything calculated to give offence to the employers was studiously avoided.'

At a subsequent meeting, 33 were present, including several foremen. The constitution and by-laws were adopted, and in the scale of prices in the press department, 'some sweeping concessions were made.' The constitution and by-laws, with the scale, were then printed, partly to furnish the masters with a copy. Plainly, these were no revolutionaries, and their moderation is underlined when the annual report, with modest pride, notes that during the year several new members had joined without coercion.

The new union did not have an altogether easy life. The same report dwelt at some length on the growing problems associated with the apprenticeship system: 'The mania for taking boys seems stronger than ever.' This was bad enough. But it was by no means all. The union faced, alone, a small group of tough employers and the competition of immigrant printers brought in by the employers.

The toughest of the employers seem to have been the Browns, father and son, and they lost no time in coming to grips with the union. In May 1845 the members were informed that John Carter, their secretary, and Clindinning, now president, had both been dismissed by George Brown for their union membership. To replace Clindinning, Brown had secured the services of one Clancy, a member of the union's standing committee, who in return for permanent employment had agreed to work at $6 a week, which was below the union rate.

According to Clindinning, Brown had told him that he was determined not to employ any union members. Clindinning had replied that he could not stay much longer at the present rate of wages. He complained that he had to work till midnight, one or even two in the morning, for $7 a week, and that hours off in lieu of overtime were not compensation. He had been 14 years in Toronto and had never even once been offered $6 a week. Brown said he had no objection to paying Clindinning $7 if he would leave the union, but he would not be 'dictated to by the Society as to what wages I must give men belonging to it. I will not be compelled to pay every hand $7 a week.' He added that there were only two offices in the city willing to support the union – the *Colonist* and Rowsell's. The rest were opposed.

Clancy, so far from being repentant, actually asked the president to call another special meeting, at which he was prepared to undertake that if every member 'would give him a week's work, by withdrawing alternately for that purpose, he would not accept $6.' The union's response to this proposition was to strike Clancy off the roll, and to provide 14s. a week to Carter while he remained unemployed (and the same to Clindinning if he was dismissed), raising the money by a levy of 1s. 3d. per week per member. By June both Carter and Clindinning had resigned from the union to go into business on their own account. Brown's office had been unanimously ruled unfair, on the ground, among others, that it was the one office in the city paying wages below the union scale. This, of course, put it out of bounds to union members and so it remained for two years.

On 2 July the union decided to carry its case to the public. It composed and printed 250 copies of a 'Plain Statement of Facts' on the dispute. This document makes it plain that Brown's had been the hand behind the abortive coalition of master printers to reduce wages, which led to the society's formation. The established scale of prices had remained untouched and unobjected to until Brown's arrival two years before. Although unsuccessful in his attempt to get the other employers to regulate or reduce wage rates, he had persisted in his efforts to remould the industrial relations of the Toronto printing trade nearer to his heart's desire. 'After nearly filling his office with boys (some two or three of whom were Apprentices who had absconded from offices at a distance, and four who had left different offices in this city) about two months ago he discharged two of his journeymen, *professedly* because they were members of the Typographical Society, but really because they refused to work for *less* than the regular and established rate of wages.' The statement observed that this rate had been considered fair and just by 'all the *respectable* Proprietors,' and it contrasted their papers with the *Banner*, 'that "*liberal*" and "*responsible*" establishment.' It is quite evident that none of the union's members would have posed for the figure at the foot of Brown's statue on

Parliament Hill: a working man, tools in hand, gazing adoringly up at the champion of his rights.

The firing off of this blast must have taken some courage. It was done in the teeth of the recorded protest of the union's own vice-president, Hill. He objected on three grounds: first, that the 'malicious representations' against the union were not worthy of notice in such a manner; second, that the statement 'would call down upon them the vengeance of the public press, with which they have not adequate means to cope'; and third, that 'the public ... are averse to any kind of combinations among workmen, how mild soever their form, or righteous their intentions,' an illuminating commentary not only on the attitude of the newspapers and the state of public opinion at the time but also on the militancy of most of the members.

The same meeting which decided to issue the statement expelled a member (Mallon) for working in the *Banner* office. On what happened next, the minutes are silent, for eight pages have been torn out. When the record begins again (probably in April 1846), the first item is the statement that there has been no meeting for six months, and that henceforth the meetings are to take place quarterly instead of monthly. (If this was intended to encourage members to turn up oftener, it was not very successful: the very next page, for 6 May 1846, notes that a meeting on that date could not be held for lack of a quorum.) The last echo of the Carter-Clindinning dismissals came on 5 August 1846, when the ineffable Clancy asked to be readmitted to the union, and was turned down.

Apart from a recurrence, in November 1846, of the perennial difficulty over apprenticeship, the next trouble came in March 1847. The union was evidently still none too strong; otherwise, it would scarcely have accepted the Master Printers' proposal that a committee of five from that body should meet with a committee of five individuals chosen by the journeymen printers generally, without any reference to the union, to consider the subject of wages. The union jibbed at the date, but agreed to the rest; the journeymen, union and non-union, met, and a joint meeting of employers and employees followed. The employers opened by saying they wanted to elevate the condition of the men. Their means to this high end were a wage cut. Predictably, the conference collapsed.

The union meeting of 1 February 1848 received the melancholy news that the funds were sinking very fast and that many members were in arrears. This was one reason why the standing committee proposed that the provisions of a provident society be added to the constitution. The benefits were to be for disease or accident or incapacity, 10s. a week for 3 months, after which the committee would decide whether to continue, reduce, or stop the benefit; for unemployement, 10s. a week for 3 weeks; for leaving the city, a lump sum of 10s. to £1; for funeral expenses, £2 10s. In addition, any member dismissed for standing by his union principles would receive 12s. 6d. a week (less any casual earnings of more than 2s. a day) until he secured permanent employment. Except for this last benefit, no one would be entitled to more than £5 in any 1 year. To qualify for benefit, a member had to be six months registered, and if he was over two months in arrears, he could get nothing till three months after he had paid up in full. No member would get anything if he had been discharged for misconduct or if his 'disease' had arisen from 'drunkenness or debauchery.' No member receiving relief from the sick fund was to remain abroad after sunset. All this was adopted.

The results were at first discouraging. On 1 June 1848 the attendance was so poor that one member gave notice of motion to dissolve the society. The notice was not pressed, but it stood on the books for the next few meetings. By September, however, things were apparently looking up, for the meeting received notice of motion to carry out the benefit provisions of the constitution. In October, the quarterly financial statement showed expenditure of £3 5s.7½d., receipts of £10 4s. 5d., and a balance of £6 18s. 9½d. By November the members were feeling so exhilarated that they were lamenting the absence, hitherto, of any festivities to mark the union's progress. They proposed to fill the gap with a professional dinner on the anniversary of the society's founding.

After elaborate preparations, the dinner was duly held, and was a roaring success. It lasted from nine in the evening till three the next morning, with fourteen formal toasts and eleven impromptu. In spite of a deficit of £2 5s., the members were so pleased that they ordered the *British Colonists*'s report to be inserted in the minutes, where it duly appears, in the back of the book, upside down!

The after-dinner speeches began with one by the society's president. He noted that the union now included nearly all the practical printers in the city. Then came the toasts, drunk with musical honours. To 'The Day We Celebrate,' the treasurer replied at great length in a speech replete with puns on technical terms of the printing craft. He expatiated on the benefits organization had brought, notably in the printers' moral condition. Before the union's advent, printers often 'could not be recognized by any other badge than the rags of drunkenness'; but now there were 'very few ... who could not be called sober men, and an increasing majority who felt more delight in "the cup that cheers, but not inebriates," than they formerly did in the glass that was "filled with the nectar that Jupiter sips."' The evening wound up with a toast to the printers' households (there had already been one to 'Wives, sweethearts and children') and a second toast to the press.

The annual report presented in January 1850 showed a further improvement in every respect. At the beginning of 1849 there had been 34 members; there were now 44. There was a surplus of £18. The union had given the retiring president a pair of gloves, paid three weeks' sick benefit and a funeral allowance, and shouldered half the cost of helping 10 members leave the city. All this had been accomplished on a subscription of 1s. 3d. per month, despite the fact that fines had not been collected.

The report exhorted the members to look carefully at the character of every applicant for membership before proposing him and, by way of tightening up, recommended that in future new members should be admitted by ballot. The executive recommended another anniversary dinner (which was approved) and also a demonstration, for the particular purpose of showing the numerous new offices, especially the Queen's Printer, how strong the union was. It also recommended a new constitution and lamented the indiscriminate employment of apprentices.

There were elaborate preparations for the 1850 dinners and a long and rather stormy discussion on whether to invite Lord and Lady Elgin (which led to the resignation of the president). On 2 March 1850 the dinner committee reported. The affair had cost £23, and the sale of tickets had brought in £21 15s. There had been fewer guests than the union had hoped, but all but one of those invited had promised future support. Those invited included, wonder of wonders, the Browns! Ryerson, who was not able to attend, donated $4, and the society responded with a resolution of thanks and deepest sympathies in the 'melancholy bereavement which prevented his coming.' But in spite of the absences, the committee was thoroughly pleased with the whole affair: 'The twig, planted some few years ago, has become a fair and stately tree; and your Committee ... predict, that when the blasts of winter shall have gathered to Mother Earth the leaves which at present adorn its branches, a future spring shall call it forth in more than pristine vigour – its roots deeper – and its waving boughs more greenly fresh, more wildly free.'

By 9 March, however, the tree had begun to wilt. Only about half the membership turned up for a special meeting to adopt the new constitution. The next meeting was scarcely better attended. A special meeting, 11 January 1851, to consider another festival, was so sparsely attended that the members decided in favour of a dinner for the whole trade, union and non-union. By 1 November, however, they had decided on a union anniversary dinner.[49]

In both 1853 and 1854 Toronto had city-wide printers' strikes. Both times, the men wanted wage increases. Both times, the *Globe* took a strong line. In 1853 it brought in strikebreakers from 'other places'; in both years, it 'kept ... going ... partly by hiring boys and young women ('Brown's harem,' said the printers).' Brown professed to have no objection to unions as such; but they could function only as benevolent societies. The 1853 strike cannot have amounted to much, for the union's own historian, in 1905, calls the 1854 trouble the 'first strike of note' in many years. But the 1853 walkout resulted in an increase in overtime from 3d. an hour to 4d., even, apparently, at the *Globe*.

Almost a year later, the union presented new demands: an increase from 1s. 3d. per thousand ems to 1s. 6d. and an increase from 4d. for overtime. According to the *Globe*, it gave the employers one week to comply. The union had seized a strategic opportunity, for even the *Globe* admitted that the demand for printers in Toronto was greater than the supply and that the usual effect of such a state was a rise in wages. This was, of course, merely the normal operation of the sacred law of supply and demand, to which the employers could not, and in fact (according to the *Globe*) did not, object. What they did object to were the way the claim for higher wages was presented and the inordinately high increase asked for overtime. The men should have come to them prepared to discuss the matter freely. Instead, they 'had used their Society organization to issue arbitrary commands, accompanied by threats in case of non-compliance.' As for the overtime increase, it 'could not be assented to by any employer without serious injury to his business.' The proposed increase for overtime would be nearly five times the wage increase: 'The wise heads have resolved that there should be no night work ... It has been the custom to pay a higher price for night work, which no newspaper proprietor objects to ... [But the Typographical Society] are for prohibition ... and they say that if 6d. an hour of extra wages will not do it, they will lay on a shilling and if the proprietors will not consent, they will take away the men and prevent the daily newspapers being published at all.' The result of abolishing night work, the *Globe* contended, would be that people would have to take Buffalo, Rochester, or New York newspapers to obtain the latest news.

The master printers made the printers an offer of $9 a week, or 1s. 5d. per thousand ems, and 1s. 7d. per thousand ems for night work. They also proposed to divide their men into two groups, to take the night work on alternate nights. But, adds the *Globe* indignantly, 'There was not even a meeting of the Society called to consider the offer, although the regular meeting did not take place until a week after the striking time. They passed it over with supreme contempt, and issuing their mandates yesterday [7 June], withdrew every man ... they could influence from the various printing offices.' All the newspapers had been put to 'inconvenience and annoyance' by 'unreasonable proceedings of the workmen.' The tone of outraged majesty is unmistakable.

Four days after this blast, Brown returned to the subject: 'We still continue to engage as many young men and boys as come forward, to whom we impart as rapidly as possible the art of type setting. We have also resolved, as well, ... to employ females in type setting. They have been so engaged for some years in the States. A female who knows how to read and write, can earn in a printing office twice as much as she would receive in any other employment. We have made arrangements to provide room especially for the female department of the printing offices and everything will be done to render their situation comfortable.'

Brown was not content with editorial thunders and hiring strikebreakers. He had the strike leaders arrested for conspiracy and succeeded in getting them fined a penny each. But he seems not to have succeeded in breaking the strike, except at his own office, for the union's historian says that after a long struggle, the society got increases at every office but one. It is not hard to guess which one.[50]

The extant minute books of the Typographical Union begin again in January 1859 with the annual report for 1858, which seems to have been an uneventful year. But 1859 was to be very different.[51]

It opened with a letter from Toronto to New York, Local 6 of the National Typographical Union, asking whether it accepted Toronto transfer cards (an acceptable union card was, of course, indispensable for work in any unionized shop). New York replied that Toronto cards were accepted, and had been for a long time. Other American unions gave 'assurances ... of their desire to reciprocate every kindness.' Between 1859 and 1866, when it joined the NTU, the Toronto union corresponded with several American typographical unions: New York, Buffalo, Louisville, San Francisco, Boston, Mobile, Charleston, Milwaukee, Chicago, Indianapolis, Albany, Cleveland, New Orleans, Peoria, Detroit, Sacramento, and Memphis.

Hard times in Toronto made themselves felt in May 1859, when the *Colonist*, which had been rather favourable to the union, announced it wanted to reduce wages from 33⅓ cents per thousand ems to 28 cents, as paid at the *Globe*. The society reacted, first, by closing the *Globe* newspaper office (not the job office, which paid union rates) to all union members; second, by instructing members in the *Colonist* office to demand continuance of the established rate until the *Leader* also asked for a reduction. The *Leader* promptly did, and the hands of both offices met to consider the situation. The *Colonist* management said that, if it did not get the reduction, it would either have to close down or cut the paper to a size where few, if any, journeymen would be needed. The union decided that because of the depressed state of the economy and of trade generally in Toronto, a slight reduction was reasonable, and it proposed a new rate of 30 cents per thousand ems, with 5 cents extra after midnight.

With this proposal it waited on the two papers. The *Leader* accepted the 30 cents, but balked at the extra 5, saying that it was already trying to get rid of work after midnight. The *Colonist* said it would pay 33⅓ cents for the moment. The matter was amicably settled, apparently on the basis of the 30 cents alone; the removal of the seat of government from Toronto (which had much reduced the union's membership) had also much reduced the need for night work.

The annual report for 1859 had paid its compliments to both Brown and his employees: 'Nothing of a more liberal nature [the union was fond of these sarcastic plays on the word 'Liberal'] could be expected from an employer who has ever been noted for his endeavours to curtail the wages of those employed in his establishment by whose midnight toil he has benefitted, and it was but retributive punishment to men who have unnecessarily isolated themselves from their brethren in the city and who refused to cast in their lot to assist those of their unfortunate brethren who might be suffering from sickness or be in distress.' The 1860 report noted again the depressed conditions and took another shot at Brown and the *Globe*'s non-union workers (union members had by this time been squeezed out of the job office as well as the newspaper).

In 1845, the Toronto tailors organized their first union, 'for mutual protection and the standard rate.' They got the rate, one York shilling per hour, but by 1849 the union was gone.[52] In January 1852 a second union, the Journeymen Tailors Operative Society, was organized, to prevent the use of the new Singer machine. The union got Walker and Hutchieson to take out the machine and to send back to New York a girl who had been brought in to work on it. On 26 January the members paraded, about 200 strong, with the city band and banners, from the Mechanics Institute to a dinner, at which the union presented the firm with a silver crouching lion, the emblem of their establishment. Employers and workers sat down to a dinner of cabbage, goose, and toasts. The occasion, though festive, must have been sober, for we are told that 'the greatest number drank the crystal fluid.'

The proceedings were denounced by the *Globe*, and the beautiful harmony did not last. Within a few months a machine had been installed in Yorkville, and in 1854 Hutchieson broke away from his fellow employers, refusing to accept the union rates all the rest had agreed to pay. His employees promptly struck, and he replaced them by women. The union members all contributed one York shilling per week to support the strike, and the union had a horse and buggy follow Hutchieson's rig all over the city, warning people that he was not on the fair list. Hutchieson took legal proceedings against the union, and on 7 November 1854, the tailors were found guilty of conspiracy.

This may have temporarily knocked out the union, for a third union, the Tailors Protective Society, was formed in 1855. This proved more durable. In 1865 it changed its name to the Toronto Operative Tailors Society; in August 1886 it became the Golden Fleece Assembly (LA 8527) of the Knights of Labor; in July 1891 it left the Knights to become Local 132 of the Journeymen Tailors of America. As such it was still flourishing at the end of 1902.

The Carpenters Union (whether the old one or a new one) was flourishing in April 1853, when it demanded an extra 25 cents across the board, to bring those who had previously been getting $1 a day up to 6s. 3d., and those who had previously been getting $1.25 up to 7s. 6d. The *Globe* made the kind of comment that might have been expected: 'No one denies that a rise in wages must sometimes be necessary according to the fluctuation of the labour market; the objection chiefly made by the masters in this case is not that the journeymen have made an altogether unreasonable request, but that they chose an improper time for making it. They say they made contracts for the season at rates proportioned to the former wages, and that it is not fair in the journeymen to insist on them being raised until those contracts are filled. If the strike had taken place in January there would have been little trouble about the matter for all the contracts were entered into just before the opening of the spring.' If only the men had been decent enough to strike when there was little or no work, everything would have been lovely.

The employers refused the demands, and the union struck on 1 May. It sent out notices all across the province, warning carpenters and joiners elsewhere that the strike was on. On 13 May the employers made an offer. Apparently only about half, and those not the largest, agreed to the union's terms. A year later, therefore, it struck again, for a uniform rate of 10s. for carpenters and 8s. 9d. for joiners. This union was still in existence in May 1857 but gone by June.[53]

The Toronto Stonecutters was organized in March 1853, and there was a Bricklayers and Masons Union in existence in April, when it decided to ask for a wage increase. In July a number of the Bricklayers and Masons struck for an increase in the daily rate; in August the union threatened to strike the next week if the increase was not forthcoming.[54]

A Private Coachmen's Society was organized in February 1854; and there may have been a Teamsters' Union, since in May teamsters were reported on strike. Some time during the year a Painters Society was organized, by one Jeremy Sears, among others. It cannot have lasted long, as he is reported to have organized, with a Mr Fairclough, a second such body, at some later date.[55]

Much more important was the Cordwainers Union, which was active in June 1854. According to the *Globe*, some elderly shoemakers had broken ranks, and the union had ordered them out of the city for a specified period of time. They went 'on tramp,' but came back before their time was up, and were beaten.[56]

This union apparently survived and appears to have become a local of the Journeymen Shoemakers of the United States and Canada, to which it certainly belonged in April and June 1858. It may well have been while it was in the international union that it struck Dack, Scandritt, and Gemmell's in 1857. Evidence in the resulting conspiracy case showed that the union had about 80 members. It had sent the employers a printed schedule of wage rates, embodying increases. Dack refused the demands, but Gemmell paid the higher rates for two months. He then told his men he was going back to the old rates, whereupon some quit work at once and the rest followed. Gemmell said he had been told not to employ outside shoemakers, and the union seems to have set a watch on the three firms which were trying to maintain operations. One employee of Dack's, who had kept working, accused the union of having lured him into the street, where he had been stoned and shot at. It had also, he said, demanded from him monies which it claimed to be due to the union, and threatened to force him out of Dack's shop if he did not pay. He paid and attended a meeting at which, he said, the union decided to set the watch. As a result of this man's complaint, 10 of the union's members were charged with conspiring to raise wages and to force the complainant not to work, assault, riot and assault, assembling for the purpose of creating a riot, and unlawful conspiracy to awe workmen. The men were successfully defended by Dr Connor, QC.

The Toronto moulders organized in 1857. By June 1857, the Carpenters' Union was gone. By 1859, there was a new Carpenters' and Joiners' and Bricklayers' Association. The Toronto branch of the ASE was formed in 1858, with 11 members. By 1859 it had 15, an income of £38, expenditures of £19. It paid sick benefits of 10s. in its first year; in its second it paid out £2 15s. in sick benefits and £9 8s. 2d. in donations to distressed members.[57]

London had a Printers' Union (said to have been a local of the NTU) in 1855. On 11 February 1856 it struck the *London Free Press* for increased wages. The men had been getting 25 cents per thousand ems, which was said to give an ordinary man about $9 a week and an expert printer about $12. The union wanted 28 cents, or $10 a week. Josiah Blackburn, the editor, was highly indignant: printers in Toronto and Hamilton, he said, generally made only about $9; if they made more, it was simply because they worked many more hours. The London rates were 'as high as it is possible for us to pay in order to leave a margin of profit.' He was resolved to resist, especially as the increase asked for was 'quite irrespective of the capabilities of the man, so that the worst "botch" that ever slurred a sheet of paper with printers' ink, is expected to be paid as much as his more practiced fellow-workman.'

Blackburn soon showed that he meant business. To the people of that day, the employment of women in industry was 'shocking and revolutionary'; yet Blackburn boldly advertised: 'FEMALE HELP WANTED: ... Young persons of industrious habits, could earn, after a month's practice, from Four to Six dollars a week ... Good wages to begin with.'[58] One wonders what Blackburn's idea of low wages must have been!

There seems to have been a London moulders' union, organized perhaps as early as 1856 or 1857.[59]

The shipwrights and caulkers of Kingston were organized between 1848 and 1850, and there is evidence of a Carpenters' Union asking for Toronto wages in May 1853.[60] Oshawa may have had a Shoemakers' Union in March 1854, when the shoemakers there struck for higher wages. So may St Catharines, whose shoemakers' strike was reported amicably settled when the employers accepted the men's demands, in May 1854. Brantford certainly had its branch of the ASE, founded in 1858 with 15 members. It was closed in 1863, reopened in 1868, and closed again, finally, in 1874. Guelph seems to have had a Tailors' Union from 1858 till at least 1887.[61]

On 17 January 1859 the bakers of Victoria, British Columbia, formed a society, to get a wage increase and the abolition of Sunday work.[62]

From this sketchy and scattered information, several things seem clear. First, by 1859, there must have been at least 30 to 36 unions, in almost every settled part of the country. Second, except for the four ASE branches, all seem to have been purely local, and very few seem to have had any relations with other unions. Third, there seems to have been a fairly high mortality. Fourth, certain crafts predominated, notably printers, engineers, waterfront workers, a few construction trades, moulders and foundrymen, shoemakers, and tailors. Fifth, the only organizations of the unskilled were the two longshoremen's unions.

3

The entry of the international unions 1859–80

The first American international union to enter Canada was probably the Journeymen Shoemakers of the United States and Canada, whose circulars of April and June 1858 indicate that it had locals in Hamilton and Toronto. The Hamilton local cannot have lasted long, as the Hamilton shoemakers formed the Sons of St Crispin in 1860. The Toronto local also probably disappeared in short order.[1]

The next international shoemakers' union was the Knights of St Crispin (KOSC), for a time the most powerful international union on the continent. Formed in 1867, this union lost no time in coming to Canada. Montreal Lodge 122 was apparently chartered in 1867 or 1868. By April 1869 Toronto 159, Saint John 171, Quebec 174, and Guelph 202 had been added. Hamilton 212 was probably chartered later in 1869, along with Georgetown (Ontario) 214, Stratford 234, London 242, Three Rivers 246, and Windsor (Ontario) 250. By April 1870 Montreal Central 201 (English-speaking), St Hyacinthe 271, Prescott 284, Halifax 306, and Toronto 315 had been added, and by 1 December 1870 Chatham (Ontario) 326, St Catharines 340, Petrolia 341, Brampton 347, Strathroy 349, and Barrie 353. Toronto 356 was in existence by February 1871. Later in that year, or early in 1872, a second New Brunswick lodge was chartered. By February 1873 there were lodges also in Galt and Orillia. In short, at one time or another, the order had 26 Canadian lodges, in 22 places.[2]

In Ontario, the KOSC had found the ground well prepared. Sons of St Crispin or Disciples of St Crispin had existed in Hamilton from 1860 to 1867, and a Fraternity of Shoemakers in London in 1865. By 21 August 1867 the Hamilton and London unions had both become Journeymen Shoemakers, and the London union had summoned all shoemakers' organizations in Ontario to meet in Toronto, 18 September, to form a provincial union. The convention duly met, with delegates from Toronto, Hamilton, London, St Catharines, Brantford, Stratford, Guelph, and Georgetown, and set up the Boot and Shoemakers' Union of the Province of Ontario.[3] It is possible that the provincial union went into the Crispins *en masse* in 1869; it is certainly highly probable that its local unions soon became, or gave place to, Crispins' lodges. It is possible also that the Saint John lodge was simply the old Cordwainers gone international.

Almost immediately after their formation, three of the Canadian lodges, Saint John, Montreal, and Quebec, were embroiled in strikes.

The Saint John strike cost $200. It probably failed, for in February 1869 15 Saint John Crispins established a co-operative shoe factory. The Crispins, like the Moulders, were ardent supporters of the co-operative principle, which they considered 'a proper and sufficient remedy for many of the evils of the present iniquitous system of wages that concedes to the labor only so much of his own production as shall make comfortable living a bare possibility, and places education and social position beyond his reach.' The Saint John co-operative was only one of several the Order started, though probably the only one in Canada. By July 1869 the co-operative had 150 members, had hired a building and put in machinery, and was planning a greater expansion. Shares were $50 each, purchasable by any Crispin anywhere. Their sale is reported to have realized $20,000, and the factory then set in motion is described as the best shoe factory ever started in Saint John.[4]

Montreal had three strikes. The first, reported to the grand lodge meeting of April 1869, must have been costly, for the meeting authorized the executive to pay bills up to $1200. The second broke out 31 August 1869, involved some 1000 workers, and lasted over two months. The workers were getting $5 to $8 per week. They wanted increases of 20 to 25 per cent to meet the increase in the cost of living over the previous four or five years. The employers pleaded inability to pay. Some of them seem to have granted the increases early in the strike, but many of the strikers seem to have trickled back on the employers' terms and over 150 left for the United States. American unions contributed $2200 in strike aid. The third strike, a small affair beginning 20 October 1869, is said to have been inspird by a grand lodge delegate who urged the workers to demand a wage increase. It failed, costing the Grand Lodge $299.[5]

The Quebec strike broke out 8 September 1869 and lasted nine weeks. It involved almost all the factories in Quebec City, and cost the Grand Lodge $3472.78. What was worse, it failed. The grand scribe reported to the 1870 meeting: 'Our lodge in Quebec is in a very low condition indeed, the men are persecuted for being members ... and they have even asked me to give them an honourable discharge ... At the time of their grievance they were in bad shape, but Brother McLaughlin went to their assistance and succeeded in doing them a great deal of good.'[6]

Montreal Lodge 122 had two delegates at the 1869 grand lodge meeting: Alexander Vincent and H. Brennan. Vincent was probably French-speaking, Brennan English-speaking. Apparently there had already been difficulties between the two groups, for the meeting was told that in Canada 'those who do not understand each other, on account of the language, may be divided into two separate lodges.' At the 1870 meeting we find Brennan representing one lodge and Louis Blanchet a second.

Saint John Lodge 171 had a delegate at the 1869 meeting, C.H. Birkinshaw. So did Toronto 159: Thomas Clark. Clark, Vincent, and W.O. Smith from New Brunswick were appointed to a committee to discuss with other unions a system of lecturing. This meeting also made provision for translating the rituals and constitutions of the Knights and their lodges into various languages, French among them.[7]

At the 1870 meeting Canada was well represented: Toronto by William J. Cameron; Montreal 122 by Louis Blanchet; Montreal 201 by Hugh Brennan; Saint John 171 by Thomas Beatty; Halifax 306 by Thomas Lambert; Quebec 174 by A. Chabot; Hamilton 212 by J. Pryke; and London 242 by W. Phillips. Cameron and Lambert were promptly appointed to offices denoted only by the letters 'I.S.' and 'O.S.,' and Brennan to the committee on credentials. Pryke was later elected to the committee to revise the constitution, Phillips to the committee on ritual, Blanchet to the committee on appeals, Beatty to the committee on a 'Communication from Messrs Pratts,' Chabot and Cameron to a committee to prepare a digest of the Order, and Cameron to a committee on unwritten work. Cameron was elected first grand trustee. An Ontario grand lodge had been organized, which survived till at least 1873. Fourteen out of sixteen lodges listed had paid into the international treasury sums varying from $1.80 (Halifax) to $69 (Montreal 122), a total of $262.03. Only two (Montreal 122 and Toronto 159) paid in more than $50 and only six (these two and Hamilton 212, London 242, Saint John 171, and Toronto 315) more than $10.

There were reports of grievances at Quebec, Montreal, Saint John, London, Georgetown, and Prescott. Of the London and Saint John strikes we know only that they cost, respectively, $12.50 and $422; of the Prescott strike only that it was recognized by the New York state lodge, and that no figures of the cost were available. On the others, we have fuller information.

The Georgetown strike, recognized by the Michigan state lodge, lasted five weeks, and cost $745 in strike pay for 13 married men, 6 single, and 28 children. Of this amount, the local lodge had received from the international or other local lodges $121.65.

The Saint John lodge, which had almost ceased to exist, had been visited by Mr McLaughlin, who had revived it 'to a healthy and active condition.' This suggests both that the strike had failed and that the co-operative had collapsed.

There had evidently been some kind of trouble in Montreal also, perhaps two kinds. The convention received a letter from H.S. Myers, claiming a grievance. It also listened to speeches by Brennan and Blanchet explaining the troubles. From the fact that after Brennan had finished, Blanchet next took the floor, and gave his view of the matter, one may surmise an internal rumpus between English-speaking and French-speaking members.

In the late fall of 1870, when the Toronto Crispins were approaching a strength of 600, their 1869 contract came up for renewal.[8] They asked for some increases. Most of the employers agreed to sign, but one demanded the union accept his simple word instead. The union refused, and, after a short strike, he gave in. But late in December, or early in January 1871, he broke the agreement by cutting some men's wages, and the union struck again. Twenty-seven members broke their union oath, went back to work, and were expelled. The employer, Childs and Hamilton, and a second firm, Henry Cobley and Co, thereupon closed their shops to union members. The strike went on into the spring, with the employers using Canadian immigration agents in England in attempts to recruit 400 shoemakers for Toronto, Hamilton, and London.

Early in April, another firm, Damer and King, refused to discharge a number of boys whom it had hired without union permission. It also refused to recognize a union of the women workers which the Crispins had helped organize. The last straw was the employer's insistence that the workers enter and leave the shop by a 'back lane so full of dirt and slush that we could not help but wet our feet.'

On 4 April 1871, four or five hundred shoemakers, with the band of the 10th Royals at their head, and carrying British and American flags, paraded to the Great Western station, to see off to the United States some 50 members who had been locked out. They were addressed by H.L. Beebe, president of Lodge 315. The *Leader*, seizing on the fact that the American flag had been carried in the procession, attacked the Crispins as a 'seditious and Yankee controlled threat to all things Canadian.' Next day, shoemakers were alleged to have assaulted a man at a Yonge Street workshop, and two men were arrested. Then, in the night of 6–7 April, somebody broke into Childs and Hamilton's factory and destroyed machines, work in progress, shoemakers' kits, and a foreman's outwork records. The destruction was confined to areas where strikebreakers had worked.

Naturally, the employers and the press blamed the Crispins. Equally naturally, the union repudiated any connection with the outrage, and, indeed, offered a reward for the discovery of the perpetrators (an offer withdrawn when evidence appeared which suggested the thing had been instigated by the employer himself, to damage the union's reputation).

The strikes continued through the summer, but failed.

By 1872, Thomas Lambert, of Nova Scotia, was first grand trustee. Two new Canadian lodges had been chartered, one in New Brunswick and one in Ontario and the Chatham lodge had sent in $16.30. But this was the only cheerful news from north of the border. There were no Canadian delegates, but a series of gloomy letters from Thomas Haisley, Toronto, provincial grand trustee of the Ontario grand lodge; G. Fewings, London, provincial grand sir knight; and Michael Denham, Toronto, provincial grand scribe. All were apparently in relation to their 'late' troubles and perhaps hinted that the Ontario Crispins would be better off on their own. The letters were referred to the committee on ways and means, which recommended that the Canadian Crispins be retained in the international and that, 'owing to the bad state of our Order in the Canadas financially (owing to debts contracted by them to sustain grievances), the delinquent Lodges throughout the Provinces be instructed to remit all taxes due this Grand Lodge to the Province Grand Lodge, and that said Province Grand Lodge send all said taxes to sub-Lodges that are financially low. Also that all debts contracted prior to 1871 be repudiated.' The recommendations were referred to the committee on the constitution, which appears not to have acted on them.[9]

The Halifax Crispins struck 16 January, at the boot and shoe factory of William Taylor and Co. The previous day, one of the workmen had been discharged by the foreman, but immediately rehired by one of the sub-foremen employed on piece-work. When the foreman discovered this he ordered the man to leave the factory, telling him that he could not work there in any capacity. The man, a Crispin, had the sympathy of most of the employees, who were also members. They unsuccessfully tried to induce the foreman to take him on again. On the 16th, they sent a deputation to the owners to demand that he be employed again. The owners refused, and the men and boys in the establishment, about 70 in all, struck. According to the report, 'a number of these were not members of the St Crispin's society, and ... were willing to continue work but were induced, if not intimidated, into joining the strike.' A few men went back next day, but most stayed out, and were still out a week later. By 14 February, however, the factory was again in full operation, all the men having resumed work except the one whose discharge occasioned the strike.[10] Though the strike failed, the union survived for at least two years.

Somehow or other, the Ontario lodges must have weathered the storm of 1872. The provincial grand lodge met in February 1873 with representatives from all three Toronto lodges and from Hamilton, Galt, London, Guelph, Stratford, Barrie, Brampton, Chatham, Orillia, Montreal, Quebec, Three Rivers, and St Hyacinthe. St Catharines also must have been in existence. It was there in March, and by June it had the provincial grand scribe. Georgetown and Prescott did not belong to the Ontario grand lodge. In March 1873 the Orillia lodge struck when one employer tried to go back on the bill of wages which had been agreed on. One employee was discharged, the rest went out. Though two went back, and four strikers were arrested for conspiracy (and acquitted), the strike succeeded.[11]

The Ontario grand lodge broke away from the international union in 1873. Toronto Lodge 159 became Lodge 1, and new lodges were organized in 1873 and

1874 in Peterborough (Lodge 12), Brantford (Lodge 13), Belleville (Lodge 14), Thorold (Lodge 15), Ingersoll (Lodge 16), and Preston (Lodge 17). This grand lodge met for the last time in 1876.[12]

The international order virtually collapsed in the United States in 1874. It was revived in 1875, in 'really a distinct movement,' which lasted till 1878. The Ontaio grand lodge, in 1875, sought affiliation with the new, or revived, international.[13]

METALWORKERS

During this period, the first international union to enter Canada, the British ASE, added appreciably to its strength. At the end of 1859 it had 4 branches (Montreal, Hamilton, Toronto, and Brantford) with a total membership of 91. In 1861 it added Kingston (closed 1865, reopened 1872). In 1863 Brantford was closed, but it was reopened in 1866 and lasted till 1874. In 1874 branches were opened in London and Stratford, both of which lasted till 1920. In 1876 and 1877 there was a branch in St Catharines. By 1880 the ASE had 6 Canadian branches with 231 members. Montreal had grown from 45 to 75, Hamilton from 23 to 33, Toronto from 15 to 53. In 1880 Kingston mustered 14, London 30, and Stratford 26.[14]

Our second American international union was the National Union of Iron Molders (NUM), organized 5 July 1859. This probably took in five existing local unions; at any rate, before 1859 was out it had five Canadian locals: Montreal 21, Hamilton 26, Toronto 28, Brantford 29, and London 37. All except London were represented at the 1861 convention. In 1863 Montreal had to be reorganized, but by the end of the year it was in working order again. During that year, the international president made a tour of Canada, visiting the five locals, and apparently trying to organize new ones in Chatham, Woodstock (Ontario), Oshawa, Belleville, and Kingston.[15]

The only immediate result seems to have been a Woodstock branch of the Brantford local, with its own vice-president and recording and financial secretaries, which lasted at least till April 1864. But before the decade was out, the Molders had organized no less than 13 other locals, stretching from Halifax to St Catharines. It was the second international union to enter the Maritime provinces, with the organization of St John 176 in April 1867 and Halifax 181 in May of that year. It had already, in 1866, organized its sixth Canadian local, Oshawa 136. In February 1868 it added Woodstock 189 and Woodbridge 191 (both in Ontario), and in October, Brockville 197. Meanwhile, Halifax had been suspended in December 1867 and Saint John in September 1868. The close of that year, therefore, saw nine Molders' locals in existence in Canada, eight of them in Ontario. Brantford was suspended in June 1869; Hamilton and Oshawa in April 1870; Woodstock in August 1870; Woodbridge in March 1871; and Brockville in May 1871. This reduced the total to three, but in October 1871 Hamilton was reorganized.[16]

At this point, the Molders' president, William Saffin, made a revealing report in the union's journal: 'Unions Nos. 21, 28 and 37 have for some time past been the only organizations we have had in Canada.' In Montreal, there were at least 100 moulders, of whom only about one-tenth belonged to what had been once a flourishing union. The Toronto local, in contrast, was one of the strongest in the whole organization, with nearly all the local moulders belonging. John H. Dance, of Toronto, third vice-president of the international had been reorganizing Hamilton, where there were about 150 moulders and good prospects that they would all join. The Brantford local was gone: 'How or why it ever went down is a mystery ... If an earthquake had swallowed up the city, the Union could not have been more completely wiped out.' Oshawa had 'died we believe from a dose of too much "wheels" or helpers. One good UNION MAN agreeing to do the work of two molders with the assistance of a helper ... and the other Union men agreeing to it by breaking up the Union.' Woodstock, Woodbridge, and Brockville had all been 'spasmodic efforts ... About all they accomplished was to fill up a number. In each of these places there is urgent need for [moulders] Unions, as well as in Kingston, Quebec, and other places throughout the two Provinces.'

Saffin followed up the report by visiting Hamilton, 18 January 1872, and holding a big meeting. He attended a grand ball held by the local next day and reported that the local expected a membership of 100 by March. He paid high tribute to Dance's work. The Hamilton local reported that it had more members and money than ever before. Saffin went on to Brantford, where he reorganized the local with an initial 28 members; then to London, which he reported 'in bad condition ... The stove shop which employs nineteen men is out of the pale of the Union, and will remain so no doubt, until a merciful Providence sees fit to remove the present foreman to a more genial clime.'[17]

In May 1872 the moulders of Chatham were making efforts to reorganize, but nothing seems to have come of this. Oshawa was reorganized in February 1873, and in June Cobourg took over Woodstock's old number, 189, bringing the number of Canadian locals back to seven.[18]

The Molders came through the depression of the 1870s remarkably well. From three locals in May 1871, they rose steadily to eleven in March 1874, never fell below eight (September 1877 to September 1879, and February to April, 1880), and by August 1880 had ten.

Peterborough 191, organized in October 1873, survived for 80 years. St Catharines 201, chartered at the same time, was suspended in February 1880. Brockville was reorganized in March 1874, and a Kingston local, 236, chartered. This lasted only till September 1876. In August 1877 Brantford was suspended again, and in the next month Cobourg. In September 1879, however, Smith's Falls 239 was chartered, and in April 1880, Quebec 176. In July 1880 Smith's Falls was suspended, but in August Cobourg was back and Three Rivers 195 was chartered.

It was not that the depression of the 1870s did not hit the Molders. It did, and hard, from 1873 on. While only a little over a third of the locals had reported trade as dull or bad in the 1860s, the number rose to two-thirds in 1874, and to over four-fifths in 1876. It is surely proof of the Molders' extraordinary vitality and organizing ability that they set up three new locals in 1873 and two more the next year, and that they lost only one local in 1876, the worst year of the depression.

What effect the depression had on the number of members only a most minute examination of the incomplete monthly reports of initiations, and transfer cards received and granted, would show; and even then the results might be far from satisfactory.[19]

One thing is certain: the Molders' Canadian locals did not lose their militancy. There had been eight strikes and one lockout in the 1860s; in the 1870s there were fifteen strikes and six lockouts.[20]

Of the early strikes we know very little. The Great Lockout of 1866–67, according to the union, was the work of an employers' combination formed at Albany, New York, 14 March 1866. The employers agreed that 'the obnoxious notice' (probably requiring union men to quit the union on pain of discharge) was to be posted in all plants, in the hope that the men would walk out, thus making the stoppage a strike rather than a lockout, and so shifting the odium to the union. The 1867 convention report says the lockout extended to all parts of the country, including London, Local 37; it says also that the employers' organization 'tumbled to pieces almost at once.' If so, what the employers would doubtless have considered a saving remnant survived in London and fought on, lustily. For on 10 April London reported, 'We are locked out'; on 10 May the same; and on 10 June, 'The lockout continues.' On 10 July Elliot's shop had 'given in to the Union, and agreed not to interfere with the union laws,' but 'The lockout still continues in Anderson's and McLary's,' which were still holding out on 10 December, with at least one still out in August 1867. The 1867 international convention (2–9 January) was told that London had lost one shop, but that otherwise the struggle had been a success for the union. But the cost, to September 1866, was $796; and the local which in December 1865 had 36 members had, by March 1867, shrunk to 5.[21]

The strikes and lockouts of the 1870s are usually better documented.

The first, Toronto (14 December 1870 to 15 April 1871), was against Gurney's, a perennial foe. Gurney's brought in strikebreakers: 'The hordes of Buffalo have swooped down upon them, and now it is a war of extermination.' All the powers of the law were invoked, the local reported: some men had been heavily fined and thrown into prison. Money was coming in for the strikers, but they appealed for more (February 1871). By 20 April Dance was able to report that the strike had been 'ended ... by all the men who were on strike getting work elsewhere'; in other words, Gurney's had won. But, Dance added, the union had not been crushed; no Molders' strike had been better supported (it cost the international $1276.17), and the local was 'in as good, if not better condition than she has been for years past.' By September Dance was reporting 'Trade splendid, Union ditto'; and the international convention of July 1872 was informed that while Local 28 had been 'not wholly successful,' it had 'administered a slashing defeat to Gurney & Co., had subsequently got a general wage increase in all the other shops, won over a non-union shop which had held out for years and increased its membership by fifty per cent.'

The next stoppage was in Hamilton, 10 May 1872. It arose out of the Nine Hour Movement, which involved the Molders 'through no desire of their own, but from a general determination of their employers to kill the union in that city by a general lock-out of its members.' One shop kept it up till 24 May; the others caved in after a few days. The local vaingloriously reported that it had 'completely "busted" the bosses' lockout in two weeks, and on condition that they would say no more about it the bosses conceded an advance in wages.'

In February 1874 Oshawa asked the international for authority to demand restoration of a wage cut, got the authority, struck, and won a complete victory. This strike cost the international $206.

An epic struggle broke out in Hamilton in August 1874. The *Molders' Journal*, in a special article said: 'The Canada employers in our trade seem to be the only employers in America who ape the customs of the British employer, by endeavoring to compel a compliance with their wishes by resorting to what is known as a "lock-out".' In December 1873 the Hamilton employers had cut wages by 10 per cent, promising to restore the old rate 'as soon as trade brisked up. ... Nine months have elapsed ... but not a word from the employers about the ten per cent. Trade was rushing. Two of the firms, employing sixty-nine molders, were so busy as to be unable to fill their orders or contracts.' The union demanded that the 10 per cent be restored. The employers refused. The union offered to submit the dispute to arbitration. The employers refused. When the union, in a letter of 26 August to Burrow, Stewart & Milne, asked that firm for the increase, the reply was that seven employers had resolved that, owing to the 'depressed state of trade' and 'low prices,' they could not grant the increase, though they would be 'happy to do so in more favorable circumstances'; and that if the union struck Burrow, Stewart & Milne, all seven shops would lock out their employees. The union promptly struck the one shop, and the employers closed the lot. The union declared that the whole thing was instigated by Gurney's, a scab shop with a large accumulation of unsold inferior products that it hoped to dispose of by getting its competitors shut down. (The two largest shops were union shops, the next two, though scab, were half manned by union members.)

At first the lockout did not altogether live up to the employers' hopes. The Hamilton local's September report said that some of the men there were back at work at the increased rates demanded, and later reports make it clear that W.J. Copp, one of the employers, had caved in. The same report added, ominously, that the shops there were half idle; that it seemed to be the local employers' policy not to employ union men, at least not local members; and that union men from other places were coming in and taking jobs in locked-out shops, in some cases even signing a document denying they were union members. Copp's apparently made up its mind to restore the old wage rates as soon as it could, and get rid of the union; and other employers dug their heels in harder.

For they had intended the Hamilton lockout to be the first, and decisive, step in a national policy of maintaining prices and cutting wages. 'By accident,' in September 1874, the *Molders' Journal* got hold of a printed circular of the Canadian Iron Founders Association meeting of 19 November 1873 that caused it to revise drastically its former belief that the stoppage was simply Gurney's bright idea for unloading his unsaleable stocks. The whole association had decided in November 1873, on motion of W.J. Copp, that there should be no change in prices till February 1874, but that wages should be cut 10 per cent on 1 December 1873. Copp had carried out the decision, though he had told his men that he was against the cut and had fought it at the meeting. When he was forced to restore it, he seems to have set to work at once to get back to square one. At any rate, the association's meeting of 11 November 1874 heard the glad tiding that both Copp and McKillop (Toronto) would, after 21 November, be taking back the increase wherever they had granted it, and that from 1 January 1875 their shops would be non-union. Stimulated doubtless by this militancy, the association resolved that it would maintain prices till the next meeting and would set up committees for three districts of Ontario (Kingston and below, Hamilton and below, and all west of Hamilton) 'to get the co-operation of foundry men in those districts in endeavoring to gain control of their own shops after January 1st next.'

Copp Bros duly sent a letter 17 November to about a dozen of their moulders, announcing that henceforth the shop would operate on non-union principles, 'to avoid, if possible, a repetition of the experience of last September, which has caused us so heavy a loss, and has also created an estrangement between employer and employed which is not desireable.' By way of ending the estrangement, it announced that it was discharging the recipients of the letter, but would take them back if they left the union. Moulders in Hamilton generally were apparently invited to sign a contract which bound them to work for a given employer during his pleasure only, but bound the employer only to pay current wages for such time as suited him. John Campbell, the local's president, called this 'an agreement worthy of the veriest tyrant,' adding that 'the men who would sign it, would degrade themselves below the standing of a Chinese coolie or African slave.'

None the less, plenty of them evidently did sign, for the international convention of 1876 was informed that the 1874 lockout in Hamilton had cost the international $1968.64 and had nearly destroyed the local, 'as some of its most honored and trusted members proved traitors.' Copp's was lost, as we learn from two searing comments in the *Molders' Journal* for 10 March and 10 April 1876. The first said: 'James W. Kerr and Fred. Walters, the two lowest scabs in Canada, are such arrant hypocrites that they are holding a prayer-meeting in the shops in Hamilton every Saturday afternoon. We wonder if they ever preach on "perjury".' The second corrected 'shops' to 'Copp's' shop, and added that in that establishment the wages were 'ninety cents in cash, ten cents in prayers.'

The Novelty Works, at Brockville, locked out its moulders in December 1874 with the ultimatum, 'Leave the Union or leave the shop.' The union won in this shop, after a long struggle, though at a cost of $836.82. Cossill Bros, in the same town, approached by Gurney to lock out its employees, answered that they could attend to their own business.

The *Molders' Journal* of 10 January 1875 reported that no demands had been made on the Canadian locals, with the exception of the two shops already noticed. But the ink was scarcely dry on this heartening word before two other employers tried their hand at carrying out the iron founders' policy.

Hart and McKillop, in Toronto, locked out their employees in January, in what the president of the Canadian Labor Union later called a 'vile conspiracy' to 'destroy the Iron Moulders' Union of Toronto.' The attempt failed. Part of the story was reported by John Nolan, corresponding representative of Local 28, Toronto, in excruciating doggerel:

McKillop to Buffalo went, to get scabs was his intent. Nine scabs from Buffalo came, with McKillop in the train; but a telegram ahead of them came from Martin: 'Nolan, watch the train.' The boys posted right and left, and did the business you may bet. At seven o'clock the train arrived, and McKillop he was overjoyed. The party left the depot very soon, and were rapidly driven to the King's saloon. We had a man, his name was Smitt, who acted his part in German wit; McKillop did not know what he said, and he soon with the scabs a bargain made. The foreman went out to see, if he could get the scabs boarding free; the landlord insisted on cash pay, and to borrow the money the foreman went away. He had hardly made his first tack, before the scabs were in two hacks, and being driven to Western Row, to take the train back to Buffalo. O was it not a ... shame, for Union men to spoil such a scabby game. The end. John Nolan.

This sounds like an early and a happy ending, but as late as January 1876 the local was reporting only that it had been 'fairly successful.' Evidently final victory was slow in coming, and it cost the international $831.71 (though this included a strike on a single job in Armstrong's in October 1875).

On 12 January 1875 two other old antagonists of the union in Hamilton locked out their employees: Gurney's, and Burrows and Stewart. In the first case the men failed to get the two-thirds vote of all locals which was necessary for international recognition and financial support of any strike or lockout. In the other case recognition was forthcoming, and the international paid out $1512 before the long and bitter contest was declared officially ended on 5 March 1875.

Altogether, Canadian strikes and lockouts between August 1874 and May 1875 cost the international $5156.17, nearly a third of its total expenditure on strikes and lockouts on the whole continent for the two years from July 1874 to July 1876. Hamilton, with $3480.64, got more than any other of the 28 places listed.

In April 1878 Oshawa was evidently in the midst of a strike or lockout at Carmichael's for on 18 April there was a grand parade, 'when the "scabs," etc., brought to the town by Carmichael, were marched to the depot, surrounded by all the molders of the locality, headed by a band of music, and put upon the train, with orders to go, and sin no more. Oshawa men were determined, but no violence was allowed.'

Two stoppages began on 19 March 1879. In Brockville four men were locked out by Smart & Shepherd, because they stood by their union principles. This lockout lasted ten weeks and cost the international $280. The 1882 convention was told that the union won, but the *Molders' Journal* for 31 July 1879 had reported the strike badly supported. The Montreal strike involved nine men in William Glendenning's stove department who refused to take a 25 per cent wage cut. This strike lasted two weeks and ended in victory. A much bigger strike broke out in Montreal on 2 April. Twenty-five men in H.R. Ives & Co struck against a wage cut of 15 to 25 per cent. In May 1864 the *Journal* had described 'Ives and Allen' as 'the greatest rascals on this Continent. They have made their boasts of how they broke up the Union when it was first formed. So steer clear of them as you would a pestilence.' The strike was sanctioned, and the international imposed a strike tax of six cents on every member of every local. The stoppage lasted 12 weeks; the union won.

After these distressful events, it is pleasant to find Brockville Local 197, in December 1879, holding a ball and supper. The ballroom 'presented a neat and tasteful appearance, having been appropriately decorated for the occasion. The attendance was large, and dancing was kept up with unflagging zeal and energy.' For supper, the revellers adjourned to the St Lawrence Hall, where 'mine host Robinso– well maintained his established reputation. The dining room was gay with decorations, while the tables groaned under the following bill of fare.' After raw oysters, and a choice of 2 kinds of soup, the diners had their choice of no less than 20 kinds of cold meat, 3 kinds of fish, vegetable salad, Boston baked beans, and 18 relishes. They could then select what they fancied from among 16 confections. The repast could be topped off with 'raisins, filberts, soft shell almonds, English walnuts, pecans, Brazil's, snow apples, dates, crackers and cheese, green tea, coffee and black tea.'

The ball must have come early in the month, for the Brockville monthly report said the moulders in Smarts were out on strike for 15 per cent, promised to them when times became good. The January 1880 report says the strike had ended with the local winning a 10 per cent increase, but on 20 April a fresh strike broke out, with the men demanding a 10 per cent increase (presumably at some other shop or shops). This lasted only a few days, and succeeded.

The Canadian locals during these years played a not inconsiderable part in the international. From 1861 on they were usually well represented at international conventions. Most of their delegates served on important committees. As early as 1864 Canadians were elected recording secretary and assistant recording secretary, and in 1865 a Canadian was elected second vice-president. From 1868 on there was always a Canadian as one of the secondary vice-presidents: R.G. Breeze, Oshawa, 1868–70; John Dance, Toronto, 1870–74; John Nolan, Toronto, 1874–78; and R.G. Eansor, Oshawa, 1878–82.

The prominence of the Canadian locals is further illustrated by the part they played in the international's attempts to get itself incorporated by the United States Congress. By January 1873 the bill had been introduced, with John Dance as one of the proposed incorporators. The name was to be the Iron Molders International Union for two reasons. One was that the moulders of Canada were thoroughly organized, and the other, that it would be 'impossible to have an appropriate design for a seal without presenting the two nations.' The word 'international' had apparently been used to tag the Molders as communist, linked to the International Workingmen's Association of Europe. The 1872 convention had passed resolutions denying any such connection, but the belief persisted. The president triumphantly produced the union seal in the incorporation bill as alone 'sufficient refutation of the charge of "Communism." For the seal in the center bears an impression of the United States shield ... and an impression of the royal crown ... with clasped hands. Now if we know anything of Communism, the sight of a crown is to a Communist like water to a mad dog. And, as we propose to keep the crown on our seal, until Canada ceases to be a colony of Great Britain, we rather think the Communists will give us the cold shoulder.' After several years' persistent effort, however, the project was dropped in 1879.[22]

The shadow of defaulters falls across the Canadian locals in these years: Malone, of Hamilton, 'a scabby old defaulter, who stole our funds' in 1871; John C. McAvoy, Montreal delegate to the 1861 international convention; and Hugh McKee, of Hamilton.

McAvoy in April 1874 was held up to union execration in the *Molders' Journal* for 'having robbed Union No 23, of Chicago, by a system of fraud seldom equaled, never excelled.' In January 1876 he was pilloried again: 'McAvoy ... is leading the life of a worthless dog in Ottawa, Ontario. There are too many Union men in Canada for him; he is shunned by all classes; and we are expecting to hear of him committing suicide at any time.' But in July 1880 we find McAvoy bobbing up serenely in his old local, in Montreal, as one of the six members of the committee for the 'Grand Picnic!'

In December 1879 the *Molders' Journal* reported that Hugh McKee, financial secretary of Local 26, Hamilton, had defrauded the local of $33.50 between September and November 1879. He had been paid a salary of $26 a year, and his actions, according to his local, 'ought to place him lower than any scab in the country or on the continent.'

The same number of the *Molders' Journal*, however, records something more agreeable: a testimonial to John Nolan from the Toronto local, on his departure to set up a stove business. Nolan got an address and a gold watch, and the reporter wound up his account with a gay, 'if you will take the word of an old man speaking from his coffin, Nolan's stoves will keep the life in you.'

Some other leading figures of the union who graduated to the employing class got curses rather than blessings. The most notable was Norman Van Alstyne, international president in 1861, who, by September 1867, had set up his own shop in Montreal and earned from the local the description 'our most bitter enemy.' On a smaller scale, a union foreman in a Brockville shop, in March 1876, was denounced for having 'done all he can against the Union, by discouraging men from joining, hiring scabs, etc.'

The Canadian Molders in these years were, of course, mainly concerned with bread-and-butter unionism, but not entirely. In September 1867 Saint John reported that it had leased ground for a co-operative foundry, which was being built. In March 1868 a letter in the *Molders' Journal* from Toronto declared that strikes were 'played out,' and that unions should go all out for the co-operative movement. Where Saint John and Toronto led, the international soon followed. At its Toronto convention in July 1868 it changed its name to the Iron Molders International Co-operative and Protective Union, with appropriate amendments to the constitution, and provision for serious promotion of co-operatives. We hear no more of the Saint John co-operative foundry. However, in September 1873 Fred Walters wrote from Hamilton that co-operative foundries were 'the sovereign balm for all our wounds; the morning star, hailing the coming day of labor's redemption.' But he added that any such enterprises had to be very carefully planned.

Other signs that some Canadian members were thinking in larger terms than mere wages and hours appear in two long letters on economics from W. Arnold of Toronto in the *Molders' Journal* for August and September 1879 and in a paraphrase, December 1879, of an article in the Brantford *Equalizer*: 'The manufacturers, through the influence of capital, have taken their foreign competitors by the throat, and now they are seizing the workmen in the same manner. Every right-thinking man will acknowledge that the hour has come when the mechanics of Canada should better themselves, and by combination present a bold front, demanding justice. To permit the lion's share of the profits to pass into the hands of capitalists, while the mechanics drag out a miserable existence, is to tolerate a condition of affairs which is inimical to the best interests of the country.' None the less, the Molders in Canada do not seem to have engaged in, or supported, any direct political activity during the 1870s. This is hardly surprising, for, even apart from the depression of the 1870s, the atmosphere was not propitious. True, Walters, in the letter already quoted, was able to record a considerable improvement from 1859 to 1873, and, not without reason, to chalk it up to the union's credit: 'twelve years ago, the ideal mechanic was being black and greasy, smoking a dirty, black pipe, with a strong smell of whisky about him – one who knew but very little about anything but working, sleeping and drinking. All is now changed. Workingmen occupy positions of honor and trust. We even have mechanics in our legislative halls, and they vie in intelligence and ability with the college-bred whose hands have never been soiled by labor.'

RAILWAY WORKERS

The Brotherhood of Locomotive Engineers (BLE) established its first Canadian division, no. 70, at Toronto, 5 December 1865; its second, no. 68, at London, six days later. These were followed by seven others: 89 (Point St Charles, Montreal), 7 March 1867; 118 (Brockville), August 1870; 133 (Hamilton), September 1871; 188 (Stratford), 1875; 189 (Belleville), 23 December 1875; 132 (St Thomas), 11 April 1876; and 142 (Richmond, PQ), 1 April 1877.[23]

By the fall of 1876, the BLE had signed up about 90 per cent of the Canadian engineers and was ready for the major struggle in which it soon found itself. The Grand Trunk Railway (GTR) had compounded the effects of the depression by a ruinous rate war. In March 1875 it tried to recoup its losses by cutting wages. The BLE forced it to restore the cuts and to adopt a seniority rule. But the company wriggled out by reclassifying the men, and simply disregarded the seniority rule in favour of non-unionists. Early in December 1876 it reduced wages and discharged 66 of 375 engineers, and 71 of 365 firemen. Most of the discharged engineers were BLE members; some 50 were told to quit the union or quit the service. The grievance committee, augmented by the grand chief engineer of the BLE, tried to negotiate, but was met with evasions and blatant anti-strike preparations. On 29 December the BLE gave the company two hours to negotiate; it refused, and the strike was on.[24]

It lasted four days, tied up the line pretty thoroughly, and was marked by considerable (though relatively minor) violence, which brought out the troops. However, as the *Molders' Journal* noted with satisfaction, the troops 'came, but they did not either fire upon or bayonet the strikers. They were workingmen themselves.' The GTR tried to hire strikebreakers, but when it got them they too often joined the strikers. By 2 January the company was prepared to reinstate all the discharged men except those who had been guilty of violence, and ready to negotiate a complete agreement. The men went back next day, and on 5 January the company met the grand chief engineer and the committee and reached a final settlement.

It was a famous victory. In 1875 there had been three grades of engineers and two of firemen. Then the company had added an extra grade for each, and downgraded many of the senior men. Now there were to be just two grades for each, to be paid at the 1875 rates. In addition: no engineer or fireman was to be discharged without a fair and impartial trial; all shunting engineers were to get $1.75 a day for the first year, and after that, it there was no serious report against them, $2 on shunting, and first-class rates on mainline, service; all second-class engineers were to go to first class at the end of one year's service; all who had been entitled to promotion on 1 December 1876 were to have their promotions date from that day; all general disputes, not decided by the mechanical superintendent, were to be arbitrated by a committee of engineers before the general manager, whose decision would be final; all discharged employees were to be reinstated; the conduct of all who had struck in accordance with general orders was to be overlooked; warrants against strikers were to be withdrawn, except where men had been guilty of personal violence; all road engineers shunting at terminal stations were to get 20 cents an hour.

The Brotherhood of Locomotive Firemen established its first Canadian lodge, no. 65, at Brockville, 11 March 1877. This lasted only till September 1879, but the three others formed during this period were more durable; 66, Belleville, March 1877; 67, Toronto, March 1877; and 38, Stratford, January 1880.[25]

The Order of Railway Conductors formed its first Canadian division, St Thomas 13, in 1880.[26]

THE INTERNATIONAL TYPOGRAPHICAL UNION

The National (after 1869 International) Typographical Union (ITU) certainly entered Canada in 1865, with the chartering of Saint John 85, on 16 December. There may, however, have been earlier affiliates, notably the London union of 1855. The second certain affiliate in Canada was the Toronto union, which, on 23 May 1866, became Local 91. Next came Montreal 97, 12 March 1867; then Ottawa 102, 17 June 1867. Hamilton 129, 4 September 1869, was followed by Halifax 130, then London 133, 22 November 1869. Montreal Jacques-Cartier, Local 145 (French-speaking), was formed on 21 November 1870; St Catharines 416 (not its original number), 22 December 1870; Quebec City 159 (French-speaking), 10 September 1872; Quebec City 160 (English-speaking), 31 October 1872.[27]

Some of these locals lapsed before 1880: St Catharines on 2 September 1875, and Saint John late in 1877. In 1878 Montreal Jacques-Cartier 145 merged with the English-speaking local because of troubles over language. Halifax 130 made its last report to the international office in 1877 and therefore ceased to be in good standing in 1879, but it apparently continued as a purely local union, for we have reports of elections of officers in July 1881 and January 1882.[28]

This left, in 1880, seven Canadian locals in six places.

On Saint John 85 we have little information except lists of officers. In 1866 it reported that it had initiated 98 members, had 16 in good standing and a total of 90. One of Local 85's officers, William H. Coates (recording and corresponding secretary in 1869, 1871, and 1872, and member of the international executive committee, 1871 and 1872), was later to play a prominent part in the Saint John Trades and Labor Council and the TLCC.[29]

On the Toronto local, 91, we have the minute books for the whole period, a mine of information not only on the Toronto local itself but also on ITU locals elsewhere and other unions in Toronto.[30]

Except for the great strike of 1872, Local 91 itself seems to have led a somewhat more tranquil life than before it joined the international. Membership, which at the end of 1865 had been down to 31, by 1869 was up to 162, and the local and its members were prosperous enough to give help to a number of other unions involved in strikes or lockouts: the Toronto Cigar Makers in January 1867; the Montreal Typos in April 1869; the Toronto Crispins in February 1871; the Ottawa Typos in August 1873; the Toronto Tailors in November 1873; the Toronto Stonecutters in July 1875 (a lawsuit, this); and the London Typos in June 1880.

At the end of 1866 the local asked for a wage increase from the existing $9 a week to $10, and got it without a strike. In April 1867, however, the incorrigible George Brown counter-attacked by cutting piece-work rates to 28 cents per thousand ems. The union considered striking, but decided against it and the issue fizzled out by 8 May when the *Globe* had no hands at all on piece-work. In 1868 there was a rumpus about members being paid in American silver, which the merchants refused to take except at 10 per cent discount. The trouble was particularly acute at the *Leader*; eventually it paid in gold. In November 1869 the local memorialized the employers for a reduction from 60 hours per week to 58. The petition was not granted, but the union appointed a new committee on the subject, which Brown refused to meet; and the matter slumbered until the great 'Nine Hours' strike of 1872. The chief effect on the local itself seems to have been to cause it to toy with the idea of making itself a secret society.

The depression brought a wage reduction to 30 cents per thousand ems in the newspaper offices, which the union reluctantly accepted, 4 November 1876. The bolder spirits insisted on a special meeting to reconsider the decision, but after a spectacular row the president ruled the reconsideration motion out of order, and his ruling was sustained. A similar reduction in rates in the book-printing offices followed. As usual, Brown was tougher than his fellow employers, and on 31 March 1877 he gave notice that on 2 April he would cut wages in his job-room to 28 cents. By a vote of 33 to 32, the local decided to leave the men in the shop with work permits, but some apparently declined to stay, for on 7 April we find the local granting to men who left the *Globe* $6 a week for married men, $4 for single, for 4 weeks.

In August 1877 there was further trouble. The *Mail* was reported 'taking away from the men the ads. and having the same composited by boys.' A motion to strike the *Mail* was carried but declared lost because it had not got the necessary two-thirds' majority. The president still had 'several motions to put to the meeting but owing to the uproarious conduct of members he could not & having lost control thereof he adjourned it until next regular meeting.' At this a motion allowing the *Mail* hands to accept the manager's terms carried 37 to 13, apparently without untoward incident. But later, after a short address by D.J. O'Donoghue on matters pertaining to the craft, disorder broke out again. 'Mr Addison moved That any person coming here intoxicated be ejected ... Moved & sec. in amendment That men coming to this meeting in a state of intoxication the President request them to withdraw and in not complying with the request forceable means be used ... Carried.' A little later, two members were fined for misconduct towards the chair. After some intervening proceedings, Addison 'spoke of the blackguard conduct which had prevailed in the meeting for some time back. The remarks received the approbation of the majority in the room; but exception being taken by one or two members the President declared them out of order.'

By February 1878 Brown was at his old tricks. The foreman in his job-room had warned members working there that in future $11 per week would only be paid them for 60 hours. Militancy seems to have been at low ebb, for it was moved and seconded to accept the ultimatum, but an amendment to have the executive report at the next meeting carried. So did a motion to maintain the existing wage rate. Meanwhile, the two men had refused Brown's terms and walked out; and the union granted them $4 a week for one month.

The executive did not report at the next meeting, perhaps because by that time there was fresh trouble elsewhere: Bell & Hawkins had increased their hours to 57 per week. The union was in favour of upholding the scale of prices and decided to close the shop to members till it went back to 54 hours. It was not until 30 November that the *Globe* matter was disposed of by refusing members permission to work in the job-room for 28 cents per thousand ems or $11 per 60 hours. On 9 May 1880, however, death put an end to Brown's long struggle with the union. The executive committee, whether by way of rejoicing or as a mark of Christian forgiveness, decided that the local should attend the funeral 'as a Union, which was concurred in and the Union attended accordingly.'

By 2 October a new paper, the *World*, had started. It had assured the local that it wanted to operate as a union office, but had asked to be allowed to pay 25 cents per thousand ems, the same rate as in the *Telegram*, till it had established itself. The local granted it permission to do so.

At the last meeting of the year we hear the first rumble of a long struggle to come: a motion to strike John Ross Robertson, publisher of the *Telegram*, off the list of honorary members; but it was left in abeyance.

The local's minutes have a number of miscellaneous items of interest during these years: a dinner early in 1867; an anniversary 'Soirée, Literary entertainment, and Supper, and dance' in February 1868 ('the table to be kept open to the dancers the entire evening,' but the press to be excluded); and a picnic of all the unions of Toronto, under the auspices of 'the Trades' Union,' at Mimico, 24 August 1867. A second such picnic in 1868 was recorded as a 'failure, the Bricklayers' Committee having appropriated their receipts from the sales of tickets.' There is a long account of proceedings of the executive committee against one Crozier, the financial secretary, who had defaulted to the tune of $115, skipped town, and been expelled. He was subsequently run to earth in Buffalo, where he offered to pay up (with a guarantee by a Mr Lee), provided he was given time and reinstated as a member, a proposition which was turned down. Not the least interesting item is a recommendation by the executive in its annual report for 1868: 'with the advancing prosperity, there should be a corresponding activity on the part of the Union, intellectually and socially, for the establishment of a reading-room, and the formation of a library, where the members of the craft can have access in leisure hours, for the enjoyment of study and mental recreation, and where may be ever within their reach increasing facilities for the acquisition of whatever in the Art it may be of advantage to know. In unity there is strength, and knowledge is the lever which, while it opens the door to the Temple of Truth, levels with the earth the structures of error.'

The Ottawa Typos had existed as a purely local union as early as 15 April 1867.[31] By 8 May they were corresponding with the Toronto Typos. In December 1869 they were engaged in a strike, on 12 January 1870 they are described as having sustained their scale of prices (25 cents per thousand ems, and $8 a week for day hands, as against 30 cents and $10 in Montreal and Toronto, though the *Citizen* is said to have raised its rate to 26 cents in November 1869). By 9 February the local was on strike again, and the Toronto brethren sent it $75. The *Citizen* is reported to have raised its rate to 27 cents. In January 1872 the master printers generally agreed to raise the rates to 27 cents and $9, and in January 1873 the union got a new agreement, with $33\frac{1}{3}$ cents on morning papers, 30 cents on evening, 40 cents for Sunday work, and $10 per week of 58 hours for day hands, with 25 cents an hour overtime. The

Ottawa *Times* commented that this was an increase of 75 per cent on the pay that printers received five years ago, but, perhaps fearful that the whole improvement might be chalked up to the union's credit, added: 'which is another illustration of the fact that the price of labor is increasing in all branches.'

By March 1873, however, D.J. O'Donoghue, president of the local, was charging that the *Citizen* had got a parliamentary printing contract at a price which was unfair to honest printers and had been trying to reduce wages, an effort which the union had successfully resisted. Apparently the *Citizen* kept at it and got support from other offices, for on 2 August the Toronto local had word of an Ottawa master printers' lockout. It granted the Ottawa local $100, if needed. It was, for on 4 August the Ottawa local struck the two evening papers, the government printing bureau, and Mr Woodburn's job-office. Two of the *Citizen*'s printers, Felton and Armstrong, were promptly arrested on a charge of leaving their employment without due notice, convicted, and each fined $1 with $1 in costs. By 16 August the Toronto local had sent Ottawa a total of $200, leaving its treasury empty, and a week later was imposing a levy of $1 on all its members in regular employment and 50 cents on casuals, for two quarters. The strike failed because of the importation of strike-breakers from England.

The Ottawa local survived none the less. There are references to it in the Toronto local's minutes throughout 1875, at the beginning of 1876, in July 1878, and throughout 1879 and 1880. It was represented on the national or international executive committee from 1868 to 1874 and it sent a delegate to the international convention in 1875.

Of the Hamilton local we know little. It was represented on the national or international executive committee from 1870 to 1874 and it figures twice, inconspicuously, in the Toronto local's minutes. It struck for an increase in May 1872 and on 25 May was reported jubilant because the employers could not get the strike-breakers they had telegraphed for and it was believed they would have to cave in.[32]

London, Local 133, had as one of its first objectives the payment of its members in cash instead of in orders on shops which advertised in the employers' newspapers. A single employee might come home on pay-day with as many as 50 of these orders. If he did not want to buy at the particular shops he had orders on, he could try to collect the cash from those shops. Sometimes he got it at once, sometimes a week or two later, sometimes not at all. As wages were miserably low, this was a serious matter. The union seems to have dealt with it successfully and without too much trouble.

Working conditions in London printing were bad. Lighting and ventilation were poor, hours were long, and tuberculosis was rife. None the less, the local at first got very little public sympathy, since it was believed to be anarchistic. But it seems soon to have dispelled this impression and to have become one of London's strongest unions.[33]

The Montreal Typos had some stormy passages. On 20 April 1869 Local 97 struck all the papers except the *Star* and the *Nouveau Monde*, which had already granted the wage increase the union was demanding. On 23 April the Toronto local sent Montreal $150 (imposing a levy of 50 cents a week to get the money). Some of the employers advertised for girls of 14 or 15 to learn the trade. On 29 May the local reported the battle 'progressing favourably: eleven offices have conceded the scale, and three still hold out.' None the less, in January 1870 the local admitted that the strike had not been as successful as hoped, and it seems clear that many of the men went back on the employers' terms, while a considerable number emigrated to the United States. The local struck again in June 1878, for about a week, against a 20 per cent wage cut at the *Herald* and the *Gazette*, and lost. There was a further stoppage in July 1878.[34]

The Montreal Typos were plagued by problems of bilingualism and biculturalism. In November 1870 they organized a separate, French-language local, 145. There was to be no change in the scale of prices without the consent of both locals, and members of each were to be allowed to work in shops of the other. This union version of associate states was presumably expected to produce a situation where everybody would live happily ever after. It failed disastrously. There was constant friction, and one international convention after another had to devote considerable time to trying to sort things out and establish some kind of peaceful coexistence. The 1876 convention had to listen to charges by Local 97 against Local 145. A committee recommended that a referee visit Montreal, investigate the situation, and settle it. The referee, who bore the perhaps unfortunate name of O'Rourke, spent several weeks in Montreal and produced a 'drastic document,' ordering Local 145 to disband and its members to join the English-speaking local. This produced strong protests from Local 145, and international president McVicar was obliged to tell the French Canadians to pay no attention, as disbanding a local was beyond O'Rourke's powers. The matter then came to the 1877 convention, which sustained McVicar, but ordered the surrender of the charter of Local 145, on conditions which are said to have been acceptable to its members: that both languages should be used for the constitution, by-laws, motions, reports, and documents; that there should be an English-speaking president, and French-speaking vice-president, recording secretary, and secretary-treasurer one year, and the reverse the next; and that the board of directors should be half English-speaking and half French-speaking. The amalgamated local was to be No 176.[35]

In 1873 the international convention met in Montreal. The Canadian locals were well represented and cut something of a figure. Toronto sent E.F. Clarke (later MP); Montreal 97, Thomas Atty and Charles Curran; Montreal 145, Peter Crossby and Pierre Griffard; Ottawa, Georges Cloutier and Henry Webb; London, a delegate whose name is indistinct; and Quebec 159, Siméon Marcotte. Crossby chaired the committee on female labour, a committee on which Marcotte and Cloutier also sat; Clarke was on the committee which recommended the creation of union districts; and Local 97 played host at the shooting of the Lachine rapids.[36]

Meanwhile, Local 145 had been running into heavy weather with the Roman Catholic bishop of Montreal, the redoubtable Mgr Bourget. On 26 June 1873 it had received a letter from the bishop's palace informing it that 'Your Society is interdicted, because it engages in things unjust and condemned; for example, to make strikes and to prevent honest and quiet workmen, who do not belong to the Society, engaging in an office in which your members work, or to oblige those who do not belong to your Society to join, under penalty of being refused work.' To this fundamental challenge, the local returned a soft answer. Crossby, the president, submitted the local's constitution to the bishop, humbly asking him to suggest amendments. The bishop replied by striking out all references to the international, travelling cards, and the number of the local. Crossby begged him to reconsider, and the bishop obliged with a revised series of demands. First, the local must formally disavow any connection with the International of Europe (as much a bogey to employers and the church then as its successor was to be half a century later, and as useful a stick to beat the unions with) or any other organization intended to undermine the social and religious order. Second, it must prohibit strikes. Third, it must undertake 'not to apply unjust means or those opposed to individual freedom, to lessen the number of printers.' The local meekly accepted these orders. It probably dared do nothing else, since the bishop had already applied sanctions by refusing burial in consecrated ground to one of its members, Samuel Chabot, who had drowned. In the circumstances of the time, it was more than enough to make the union knuckle under, at least formally; there is no sign that in fact it did anything to lose its standing with the international. Its meekness did, however, earn a scathing denunciation from the Chicago *Workingman's Advocate*, under the heading, 'Cowardice vs. Principle.'[37]

For Quebec Local 159, we have little more than an incomplete list of presidents (1872, and 1876–78), a full list of officers in November 1872, and the fact that in 1873 it was represented on the international's executive committee by Siméon Marcotte. For Local 160 we have only the fact that it was represented on that committee by Edward Murphy.[38]

THE CIGAR MAKERS INTERNATIONAL UNION

The Cigar Makers National Union (CMIU) formed in New York in 1864, may have entered Canada as early as 1865, though it was not till 1867 that, because of the desire of Canadian local unions to affiliate, it changed its name to 'International.'[39] The Canadian local unions were probably the Toronto and Hamilton branches of the

Journeymen Cigar Makers of Upper Canada, formed at Toronto in November 1865, and a Montreal union started in the same year by Hungarian workmen from the United States. There had been a Brantford local of the Upper Canada union, but it must have collapsed, for a new, purely local body was formed there 20 May 1866. This was reorganized on 18 May 1869 as Local 59 of the CMIU. The Hamilton cigar makers, local, provincial, or international, held their third annual ball and picnic on 26 July 1868.[40] Toronto, Local 27, had a delegate at the international convention of 1867. Toronto 27, Hamilton 55, Montreal 58, Brantford 59, and St Catharines 64 were all represented at the 1869 convention.[41]

The St Catharines local lasted only till May 1870. Its members were then being paid in American silver, a depreciated currency, which brought their rates down by 7 to 15 per cent; they struck for payment in current funds. The local was then suspended, and the members left town to seek work elsewhere. The Toronto local was suspended in September 1874 for violating the constitution by frequently failing to pay its assessments to help strikes by other locals. It was reinstated in November. The Montreal local was suspended for the same reason in February 1875, but it had a good excuse for its apparent misbehaviour: its secretary had been collecting the money for the assessments and pocketing it, destroying the reports to the international office. The local found him out in January 1875 and fined him, *in absentia*, $100. It also circulated a description of him: he was about 21, had 'a sneakish look,' and was 'very talkative – his principal conversation being about sporting events. Beware of him!' The international office, apprised of all this, reinstated the Montreal local in March, but in September was again compelled to suspend it, for unstated reasons. The Hamilton local was still in existence in October 1876, but seems to have fallen by the wayside some time between then and 1879, when it was reorganized. Toronto, Montreal, and Brantford seem to have survived the depression of the 1870s, and before the decade was out Local 19, London, had been added to their number, making a total of five locals in 1880.[42]

The Toronto Cigar Makers, in January 1867, asked the Typos for a loan, to help them resist a wage reduction. The Typos obliged with $15. The resistance must have been successful, and promptly, for in February the loan was repaid. On 30 June 1871, however, some members had to strike again to maintain the bill of prices on certain cigars.[43] At the beginning of December the strike was still on, though the prospects were favourable: the employers were paying the union rates, and the only remaining difficulty was that a few strikebreakers were still employed, while 12 union men were still out. At the beginning of the stoppage, the employers had brought in non-union men from Chicago, to replace the strikers. Ten came. The union paid the fares of the first four home again and let the other six join the local without paying an initiation fee. Later, it was 'much troubled with unfair men from Chicago and Pennsylvania,' whom it was evidently unable to get rid of. Twenty-seven other locals sent in funds, to the tune of $87 weekly, but, even so, in September the local reported an urgent need of money.

Even while the strike was on, the local had reported that, though it no longer had 'the position it occupied in years gone by,' its prospects were 'brighter now than they have been for some time.' By the end of the year, it was able to announce that 15 or 20 cigar makers could find steady employment at C.P. Reeds, on Front Street. In March 1872 its per capita arrears to the international were only 55 cents, and it played, as we shall see, a prominent part in the Toronto Trades Assembly.

Early in 1873 the Toronto local had another and far bigger strike which it candidly confessed a failure. This cost $1851.82, of which $18 represented payments to non-union men to leave town; $86, repayment of a loan from the Molders; $36, repayment of another loan; and most of the rest strike pay to 30 men out of work for from 1 to 15 weeks. Fifty-four other locals sent in $1679 ($27 from Hamilton, $5 from Montreal, and the balance from the United States), leaving the Toronto local with a debt of $172.82.

The failure of this strike must have hit the union hard, but by February 1874 the *Ontario Workman* was able to report that its prospects were encouraging and that its membership was increasing. Apart from occasional items such as its contribution of $18.45 to a strike in Albany in May 1875 and its participation in the Toronto Trades Assembly, this is about the last we hear of it during the 1870s. It seems probable, however, that it was responsible for the organization, in January 1879, of the Toronto Co-operative Cigar Association, in which the Toronto Typos took 20 shares (with a down payment of 50 per cent), and to which they appointed a representative. This association was probably, as so often then and later, an attempt to provide work for strikers.

The first few mentions of the Hamilton Cigar Makers nearly all strike a festive note: the annual balls and picnics in 1866, 1867, and 1868 and the organizing of a quadrille class in December 1868.[44] Reasonably regular monthly reports begin in October 1869. On 16 May 1871 the local struck to enforce its regulations on apprentices (the employers had evidently been up to their customary tricks of trying to dilute or supplant skilled men by excessive use of apprentices). Twelve men were involved. By 17 June, with the help of 31 other locals, the union had won a complete victory.[45]

The Hamilton Cigar Makers do not seem to have taken part in the Nine Hours demonstration of May 1872. By May 1873 they were reporting 'no jobs and no money'; but in July they were contributing $10 towards the fund to support cigar makers in Kingston, New York, on trial for conspiracy (Toronto contributed $4, Montreal $5). In February 1874 they sent $40.20 to a strike in Cincinnati (being one of the locals which collected most for this purpose); in May they sent $30 to Boston; and in September $7.50 to Syracuse. In April 1875 they suspended 11 members and in May contributed $17.50 to a strike in Albany. The local was reorganized in 1879.

For Montreal Local 58 we have, again, pretty regular monthly reports from October 1869 to July 1875.[46] Its first conspicuous appearance comes early in August 1870, when it reported 'no work, no money in the treasury,' and listed 4 rats, and, again, in September 'no work, no money' and 12 rats. A month-long strike involved 21 men, some of whom remained out of work and drew strike pay for as long as 6 weeks. The French-Canadian membership of the local must then have been small, for only 6 of the strikers had French names. (Of 16 rats, half had French names.) The strike cost $440, of which the international contributed $420. The result we do not know, but the union must have come out of the trouble in reasonable shape, for by 15 April 1871 it reported an immediate need for 15 good cigar makers. By August, however, it was the familiar 'no work and no money in our treasury.' In September the local sent $2 to help strikers in Buffalo. In May 1873 Montreal, though not assessed for the purpose by the international office, sent $9 to help strikers in St Louis, which argues a degree of prosperity; in July it paid $5 to the Kingston 'Conspiracy Fund' and in August a special assessment of $4 for St Louis; and in September it sent $5 to help strikers in Cleveland. In February 1874 Local 58 was imposing fines of $5 on members for 'rolling bunches' and warning wandering cigar makers that there were no jobs in Montreal. By August 1874 the only union shop was on strike, against a wage cut, and in September, to halt a decrease in membership, the local withdrew all charges against members and cancelled all loans they owed. None the less, it sent $7.40 to help strikers in Elyria. In June 1875 it was in arrears to the international.

The local struck J.N. Fortier's factory, 1 October 1879, for a wage increase, and the police intervened. Of this strike nothing further seems to be known.

Brantford makes only routine appearances until 28 June 1871, when a portion of its membership struck to enforce the apprenticeship regulations law. Several members were arrested for conspiracy. The international office approved the strike and ordered aid, but the trouble ended before it was needed. Unfortunately, it broke out again, 9 July. There were further arrests for conspiracy. The local appealed for $100 aid immediately, and the international office at once asked 20 other locals to respond.[47]

The strike figures show that CMIU locals were generally small. The few other figures we have confirm this. In June 1874 Toronto had 30 members, Hamilton 26, Montreal 14, and Brantford 6. Brantford had come up from 4 members the year before, and in February 1875 it reported 7 applications, which, if it had kept its old members, would have brought it to 13. In the circumstances, the fact that Toronto, Montreal, Hamilton, and Brantford seem to have survived the decade is remarkable; the more so since by the fall of 1875 a great many of the American locals had succumbed to the depression.[48]

WOODWORKING AND BUILDING TRADES

A Halifax branch of the National Association of Plasterers of England and Scotland was organized in 1867. It seems to have been short-lived.[49]

The Coopers International Union was founded in 1870. London already had a local union in May 1870. So had Halifax in July. The London union probably joined the international almost at once, and certainly by July 1873. Toronto Local 3 took the lead in organizing the Trades Assembly in February 1871. By October the international had 14 locals in Canada and had already accomplished something evidently considered noteworthy: 'the rule of twenty hours a day has been broken down.' By September 1873 Bowmanville 17, Seaforth 8, and St Catharines 13 were represented at the Canadian Labor Union (CLU) convention. In August and September, Thorold 14, and locals 9, 10, and 16, locations unknown, were corresponding with the Toronto Trades Assembly. In May 1873 and again in January 1876 there was a local at Oshawa, which the *Workingman's Advocate* then described as 'one of the best unions in the Dominion.'[50]

The Thorold local, 'extinct' in July 1875, was reorganized in January 1876. The St Catharines Coopers had delegates at the CLU convention of 1875. The Toronto local played a prominent part in the Trades Assembly and may have survived the 1870s, since a 'Coopers Society' turns up in the Toronto Trades and Labour Council minutes for 21 July 1882.[51]

The only coopers' local of which we have any further information is London. The local body there had sprung from an unsuccessful strike for higher wages in November 1869. Coopering was becoming an active trade in London at the time, because of the boom in the oil refining industry. In July 1873 the local struck for higher wages, flatly refusing the slight increase the employers offered. Many of the strikers left the city and got work at nearby places; the rest stuck it out, leaving the city almost bereft of coopers and entailing great loss to the merchants from the almost total stagnation in the trade. The boss coopers' difficulty was at least partly a matter of the oil refiners refusing to pay more for the barrels. Finally, when they saw no barrels would be forthcoming till they did pay more, the refiners gave in, the boss coopers offered a further wage increase, and the men returned to work.[52]

There may have been members of the British Amalgamated Society of Carpenters and Joiners (ASCJ) in Hamilton as early as May 1864, when a Carpenters Union struck for higher wages. But the first branch was officially established only in March 1871, in London. This lasted till 1923, the year before the ASCJ's Canadian branches merged with the United Brotherhood of Carpenters and Joiners of America. It was followed, in 1872, by a Hamilton branch, which lasted till 1924; in 1873 by a Toronto branch, which also lasted till 1924; in 1873 or at the beginning of 1874 by a St Catharines branch (closed in 1881, reopened in 1906, closed in 1924); and, in 1877, a Kingston branch, closed in 1886. By 1880, therefore, this union had 5 Canadian branches, with 108 members. London had grown from 18 members to 22, Hamilton from 19 to 20, Toronto from 38 to 40, and Kingston from 16 to 22. St Catharines had dropped from 15 to 4. Total income had grown from $110 for the one branch of 1871 to $1260 for the four which reported in 1880; expenditure from $76 to $1244.[53]

Toronto, at the beginning of 1872, had a purely local Bricklayers and Masons Union; Ottawa had organized one in April 1872, and London one in July.[54] All three seem to have wanted to join the National Bricklayers Union of the United States, and Toronto, at the end of 1871 or the beginning of 1872, actually applied for a charter. The other two waited to see what would happen before trying their own luck.

The difficulty was that the NBU was constitutionally restricted to the United States. Its officers, however, decided to take a chance on persuading the convention to authorize a charter *ex post facto* and to change the union's name to International. On 5 April 1872 they granted the Toronto union (which had just emerged from a strike for the nine-hour day, with a shorter Saturday and a wage increase) a provisional charter. Alas! when the convention met, early in 1873, the committee on the president's address refused to concur in chartering Toronto and reported against changing the name to International. Annulment of the Toronto charter was carried 37 to 29.[55]

This stuffy and inhospitable attitude earned the censure of the *Workingman's Advocate*, which had already devoted some attention to the question of international unionism. On 15 July 1871, under the heading, 'A Word with our Canadian Friends,' it had said:

There is no phase of the labor movement in which we have of late taken a greater interest than the desire evinced by our Canadian brethren to join the organized army of labor and make common cause with their co-workers across the line. We rejoice the more ... because in the past this element has generally been regarded with distrust, and the word Canadian looked on as synonymous with scab. We can recall struggle after struggle in our border cities, in which if left to their own resources, employers would have been compelled to comply with the reasonable demands of honest labor, but who, relying upon Canada as their legitimate recruiting ground, and the will of her workmen to accept their terms, have been enabled thereby to triumph. The fruits of such servility may be seen in the quarries of Vermont and the factories of Maine, where colonies of French Canadians have fairly swamped the native element, *because* they would work for what they could get, and as a consequence wages in these sections are lower than in any part of the country.

We are however speaking of the *past*. We have brighter anticipations for the future ...

There does not and there never has existed a valid reason why the mechanics of Canada and the United States should not co-operate in their efforts to sustain each other against the aggressions of capital. So far as tested by the International Union of Cigar Makers, Printers and Coopers – the Canadian organizations have maintained a reputation of which they have every reason to feel proud ... In a recent difficulty the membership of the Cigar Makers' Union of Montreal found it to their advantage to know that they would be sustained by the moral and pecuniary support of every honorable fellow craftsmen enrolled in the 150 Unions of the International, while in the memorable strike at Cincinnati, Brantford, and Montreal gave us cheerfully as Dayton and Columbus.

It is also well known that during the existence of the Shipcarpenters' and Caulkers' Union, its members in Quebec were regarded in point of independence and reliability, the equal of any corresponding number of men in the country.

With its preoccupation with the dangers of cheap, unorganized Canadian immigrant labour (it seems to have been totally unaware that the traffic in strikebreakers was a two-way affair), the *Advocate* was naturally both incensed and disgusted by the Bricklayers' action, which it considered a serious setback for American labour itself. On 25 January 1873 it argued:

It is not at all likely that any definite action will now be taken on the application of the Canadian Unions before the Baltimore session in 1874, and it is more than probable that since their proposals for amalgamation have been virtually rejected, our brethren across the line may reconsider their action, and refuse to renew such propositions.

It is all very well to assert ... that the fewer entangling foreign alliances we have the better ... Canadian unionists are supposed to have some pride as well as American unionists, while their interests are identical with our own – and why should they be denied admission and representation to our counsels, while expressing a willingness to accept all the obligations and responsibilities required – is a question which they will be very apt to ask, and which will be somewhat difficult to answer.

The *Advocate* was confident that the presidents of the Molders, the Typos, and the Cigar Makers would say their organizations had materially benefitted by the connection, and would not dissolve it if they could.

The *Advocate*'s concern with international unionism as self-defence for American unions, the Toronto Bricklayers' anxious desire to go international, and the NBU's refusal to touch them with a barge-pole all provide an instructive contrast to the orthodox middle-class Canadian conviction that the entry of international unions into Canada was pure trade-union imperialism, or pure greed for power and money by American union bosses. Only a couple of months before the American Brick-layers had so decisively insisted on staying out of Canada, no less a person than Goldwin Smith, in a lecture to the Mechanics' Institute of Montreal and the Literary Society of Sherbrooke, had said:

Let me add, with regard to Canada specially, that we have industrial interests of our own to guard. An American agitator comes over the lines, makes an eloquent and highly moral appeal to all the worst and meanest passions of human nature, gets up a quarrel and a strike, denounces all attempts at mediation, takes scores of Canadian workmen from good employ-ment and high pay, packs them off with railway passes into the States, smashes a Canadian industry, and goes back highly satisfied, no doubt, with his work, both as a philanthropist and as an American. But Canada is not the richer or the happier for what has been done. Let us settle our family concerns among ourselves: nobody else understands them half so well, or has half so much interest in settling them right.[56]

No NBU charter seems to have been granted in Canada till 1876, when Toronto Local 1 was established, and even this solitary local seems not to have lasted long.[57]

A Journeymen Stonecutters Association of the Welland Canal struck for a wage increase in August 1874. The Journeymen Stonecutters of Thorold struck, 15 November 1875, against a wage reduction, demanding an eight-hour day at 30 cents an hour. The strike lasted till 15 February 1876 and ended in a compromise, after the employers had tried to bring in strikebreakers from Montreal.

Both these organizations may well have been branches of the international union. Certainly, by February 1877 there were branches, in both Thorold and Pelee Island, of 'the Society of the General Union in the United States.' The Pelee Island branch struck against a foreman's refusal to pay the men $14 to pay their inter-national dues, and the Thorold branch endorsed the strike. The Thorold *Post* says the real cause of the strike was 'a system of tyranny which the Emperor of Russia would scarcely dare inflict.'

In January 1878 the Thorold union formed a co-operative 'to compete with some of the many sub-contractors now doing and seeking to do so much of the work, and with so little satisfaction to the government or the workmen.' By November the co-operative was successfully working the Beaver Dams quarry, as well as succeed-ing in its work at Stonebridge. In February the Thorold union struck again. Strike-breakers were brought in from Buffalo, the union staged a march, revolvers were drawn, the mayor summoned the Ontario police, and two men were convicted of assault on non-unionists. On 15 February the mayor met union officials to discuss the situation. The Thorold union may have collapsed late in 1879 or early in 1880, for in May 1880 we find a Thorold Stonebreakers Union No 1.[58]

The Machinists and Blacksmiths International Union had two branches in Canada in the 1870s. Its Local 1, Toronto, was in existence as early as 4 August 1871 and seems to have lasted till at least July 1883. Its Local 2, Hamilton, was in existence by 17 January 1872 and still there in September 1873. There is mention of a union of Hamilton machinists 9 April 1879, perhaps the same organization.[59]

The Sailors (or Lake Seamen's) International Union, formed in 1877, extended, in 1880–81, from Port Dalhousie to Port Colborne. It had locals in St Catharines (1880–83), Toronto (1881–83), and Kingston (1879–84).[60]

The Flint Glass Workers Local 13, Hamilton, must have been in existence in 1879, for it held its third annual ball on 18 April 1881.[61]

In 1879 there was a St John's (Quebec) local of an international union of china workers, for it struck, in January, against a 15 per cent wage reduction. The strike was said to have been inspired by the American headquarters.[62]

At the beginning of 1859 there had been just one international union in Canada, the ASE. By the end of 1880, there were probably 12: the ASE, Molders, BLE, Typos, Cigar Makers, Amalgamated Carpenters, Machinists and Blacksmiths, BLF, Sailors, Stonecutters, Flint Glass Workers, and ORC. They had probably 52 locals: 43 in Ontario, 9 in Quebec. Hamilton had 8, Toronto 7, London 6, Montreal 5; Kingston and Stratford 3 each; St Catharines, Belleville, Brockville, Ottawa, St Thomas, and Quebec City 2 each; Oshawa, Peterborough, Brantford, Thorold, Pelee Island, Cobourg, Three Rivers, and Richmond (Quebec) 1 each. One organization, with 6 branches, was British; the rest were American. At least 4 other international unions had been in Canada during the period 1859–80: the Crispins, Coopers, Bricklayers, and Ship Carpenters. The probability is that the internationals reached their pre-1880 peak in 1873, with 81 locals: the Crispins had 26, Coopers 17, Typos 11, Molders 7, ASE and BLE 5 each, Amalgamated Carpenters and Cigar Makers 4 each, Machinists and Blacksmiths 2.

4

Local and regional unionism 1860–80

The entry and spread of the first dozen or so American unions was one of the distinguishing marks of the period 1860–80. But purely local unions continued to spring up and even to flourish. Indeed, in the Maritime provinces most of the unions throughout this period were purely local or regional.

In Halifax two were started in December 1863: the House-Joiners Union Society of Halifax and the Shipwrights and Caulkers Association of Halifax and Dartmouth. Both were incorporated in 1864 and both lasted well beyond 1880. The house-joiners struck late in May 1864 for a wage increase from their existing 5s. to 6s. to a straight 8s. a day. By 3 June about 150 carpenters were out, and the building trades were at a standstill. Next day, most of the employers had granted the demand. Within a fortnight, they had revoked part of the increase and agreed only to a uniform rate for first-class journeymen; this despite the opinion of one newspaper that wages had practically stood still since 1815 while prices had more than doubled. In April 1872 we find the house-joiners considering whether to ask for the nine-hour day or a wage increase. They decided in favour of a 10 per cent increase, from 1 May, but indicated they had no intention of striking to get it.[1]

The shipwrights and caulkers had their first battle with the naval dockyard, which refused to hire union members. The union won. It seems also to have struck for higher wages at the same time as the house-joiners. It tried to stop the hiring of out-of-town journeymen and refused to work with non-unionists. The employers invoked an 1864 act forbidding the use of coercion by an employee against an employer or a fellow-employee, but the government sent the petition to a legislative committee, which dismissed it. In June 1870 the union struck again, for an increase of 25 cents a day, and brought the yard to a standstill for a time. Nine days later, 'a number of the inferior hands' had 'ratted,' but 'the practical hands' were standing firm, though some had left the province.[2]

The Stone Cutters and Masons Association of Halifax and Nova Scotia was formed in 1865 and incorporated in 1866. A group of masons formed their own union in 1868 and promptly struck in May against the employment of non-unionists. There may have been some kind of local organization of locomotive engineers in the 1860s.[3]

A Journeymen Bakers Society was formed in March 1868 and lasted till 1879. Almost at once, it struck for a 12-hour day and $8 a week ($9 for foremen). The master bakers agreed to cut the 16-hour day by one hour, but refused to budge an inch beyond that. They argued that compliance with the union's demands 'would entail ... a largely increased expenditure for oven accommodation, and materially enhance the price of bread,' and they would not allow any association to enforce on them any scale of wages. If the men struck, the masters would refuse to employ any union members. The union's leading opponent was Moir and Co, which tried to break the strike by employing women and boys, and people from the Deaf and Dumb Institute. The strikers, with the help of other unions, established a co-operative bakery, and after three weeks most of them were re-hired at the wage demanded and with a shorter working day.[4]

By the beginning of 1869 a Painters and Glaziers Association was well established. On 1 February it demanded $2 a day (instead of $1.50 in summer and $1.20 in winter). The employers refused. The resulting strike led to a court case. A striker and a renegade unionist came to blows. The union member was convicted and fined $20 (though the act stipulated a year in jail). The strike produced a heated controversy in the *Evening Express and Commercial Record*, which on 9 April denounced all such combinations as 'wicked and injurious to the extreme ... The law of supply and demand will always regulate the value of labour; and ... combination ... can never succeed in forcing and keeping up wages beyond their natural levels. This is an arm of political economy which workmen are sometimes apt to forget.' There was a Painters' Association in 1882.[5]

The Coopers Union, formed in July 1870, lasted throughout this period. The Sailmakers Union Club, established in 1871, struck that same year. On 12 August 1873 its 25 members went to McNab's Island for their annual dinner. In March 1874, the union struck for a 25 cent wage increase (from $1.50 a day to $1.75). The employers refused and advertised for strikebreakers.[6]

The truckmen organized their society in March 1872, and a Truckmen's Union existed in March 1884. A Halifax Plasterers Union was organized in February 1873. It probably did not last out the 1870s, since in March 1883 we find a Plasterers Union being formed. A Labourers Society of longshoremen was organized 19 June

1873. This also may not have survived the 1870s, since there was certainly a fresh organization formed in the spring of 1882. A sailors' organization struck early in 1873 and stayed out for at least three weeks.[7]

We get several glimpses of union activity in Halifax in 1872 in the accounts of an abortive project, by a joint committee of the different trades societies, to build a mechanics' hall. We are given ample details of possible locations, probable cost, financial arrangements, and even the (rather unfortunate) name of the owner of one property considered for purchase: G.W. Dupe. But there is not one word to indicate which unions were involved, except that the several meetings to discuss the subject were held in the Crispins' lodge room.[8] By the end of 1873, there were a dozen unions in Halifax, two of them (Crispins and Typos) international.

The dominion election of January 1874 produced a curious episode which sheds a little more light on which unions existed and were active at that time and provides the second example of common action among them. An unsigned advertisement appeared in the papers, calling a meeting of the 'Trades Unions of this city and Dartmouth ... for the purpose of nominating a "Workingman's Candidate."'

The *Evening Express* was outraged that a workingman should be 'proposed for the county ... There is no need in this country for such class representation ... not a single good reason why the ... commercial interests of the city should be represented by a workingman ... We protest against ... the beginnings of that dangerous species of combination among workmen which gives so much distress to the authorities and inflicts so much ultimate evil on the workingman himself.'

Some of the unions were equally indignant, though for different reasons. Fifteen hundred men turned up for the meeting, 26 January, but no one appeared to take the chair or assume any responsibility. Finally, Robert F. Murphy mounted the platform and read a formal protest, signed by the presidents of the Typos, Sailmakers, Coopers, Crispins, and the Shipwrights and Caulkers. They said they had not been consulted and would oppose the project. A master plasterer did eventually run as a workingman's candidate, but he was only a camouflaged Conservative.[9]

Halifax was not, however, the only centre of organization in Nova Scotia in these years. One of the most significant developments in the labour movement in the whole country began in Pictou County, in the coal mining industry.

THE PROVINCIAL WORKMEN'S ASSOCIATION

The Nova Scotia coal industry already had a long history of labour trouble. The failure of the McKay firm, in Pictou County, just after the War of 1812, produced a demand from their workmen for full payment of arrears of wages. There appear to have been a successful strike of miners at the Albion mines, also in Pictou County, in 1840; another, also successful (the miners seem to have asked only that the proposed wage cut should be only half as big as the owners wanted), from 19 November 1841 to 9 February 1842; and a third, also in Pictou, in 1846. The Albion Mines Union Association was incorporated in 1864. How long it had existed does not appear.[10]

In 1864 there was a bitter strike at Sydney Mines, which the government met by two drastic measures. It sent in troops, an expedient which was to become almost standard practice in the miners' strikes. It also passed, double quick, an act which 'slammed the door against effective action on the part of workmen to achieve their goals or settle disputes.' Early in 1868 there was a strike at the Glace Bay Coal Co's mine; later in the same year two more, both at the Blockhouse mine at Morien, Cape Breton, one lasting a month, the other two months. In May 1873 the employees of the Intercolonial Coal Co, Pictou County, struck for six days; in April 1875 there was a strike at Reserve, Cape Breton; and in 1876 the men at Sydney Mines struck unsuccessfully against a wage cut.[11]

None of these rows, spectacular and prolonged as several of them were, seems to have produced any permanent organization. But early in 1879 the Spring Hill Mining Co reduced wages at a time when its profits were commonly believed to be at an all-time high. A few months later it repeated the performance, and this time the miners decided to resist. According to one account, they took to the woods around the town to discuss their many grievances. 'They had no say in mine inspection. They ... were not allowed to appear before a coroner's jury following an accident. [There was a] total lack of sickness, accident, or death benefits ... of opportunity to rise in the service on the basis of merit or knowledge ... of protection against dismissal without cause. They had no way of settling disputes except to strike, no way of hoping for justice through legislation because only one miner in nine had a right to vote; no way of forming legal unions.' So a few days later, when the second wage-reduction notice was posted, feeling ran high against it and in favour of a protective association. By late summer a formal organization was beginning to take shape, and on 29 August a large meeting of miners launched the Miners Association. Tom Leadbetter, a labourer, was elected president, and Robert Drummond, an overman and part-time newspaper reporter, was elected secretary. A constitutional committee was set up and three days later the local lodge was chartered.

According to another account, Drummond, who wrote for the Halifax papers, found out that the company's chief customer had not asked for a reduction in the price of coal and thereupon took the side of the men. He spoke and wrote in support of their case and joined with Leadbetter and Robert Maddin (afterwards provincial inspector of mines) in organizing the union. (Drummond himself, incidentally, ended up a member of the Legislative Council.) There was a five weeks' strike, which forced the company to restore both wage cuts, and it was this resounding victory which led to the association.[12]

The committee elected at the 29 August meeting immediately formed itself into a provisional grand council, and on 1 September submitted a constitution to a second meeting of the Springhill mine workers. This formed itself into Pioneer Lodge, No 1, of the Provincial Miners Association, with a membership of 126. On 11 September it added 96 more.

The grand secretary had been instructed to proceed at once to Pictou County to form lodges there. He did. Cameron Lodge, No 2, Westville, was organized within a fortnight, not without difficulty. The only available hall was denied the men; so they met in Mr Cameron's building. The secretary had an oil barrel for a table, and the miners 'had to dispose of themselves in every imaginable position.' Fifty men signed up there and then, and a few evenings later 50 more: by 25 September the new lodge, named after the kindly owner of the building, had 160 members.

Meanwhile, Drummond had gone to Stellarton, where the going was even stickier. At his first meeting, only one man turned up. At the next, 40 or 50 appeared, but only half of them responded to his appeal to join. At the third meeting, 89 were ready to join; and at the fourth, 19 September, Fidelity Lodge, No 3, was organized with 146 members.

On 14 October the Drummond Colliery in Westville reduced wages without notice. The grand council met and after prayer by the grand chaplain (who appears to have been an ordinary member of Cameron Lodge) apparently decided to try to negotiate. Its efforts failed, and on 1 December it sanctioned a strike which lasted two days, with what result neither the Council's minutes nor its official organ, the *Trades Journal*, gives any indication.

Before the strike, however, another lodge had been organized, McBean, No 4, at Thorburn (Pictou County); and on 17 October delegates from the four lodges met at Truro and formally set up the Provincial Miners Association, with a membership of 646.[13]

The year 1880 opened with the dismissal of the grand master, Robert Wilson, by the Spring Hill Mining Company. The association was too weak to get him reinstated, and he was forced 'to seek a home elsewhere.'

About the same time, Cameron Lodge struck again, as a result of the earlier strike against the unwarranted reduction in wages. There were 60 places available in the Drummond mine. The men wanted to draw for them and, as further places became available, have them filled by the regular employees, with no outsiders brought in till all the local men were employed. The company had other views. It advertised for 150 men and actually brought in 19 from Cape Breton, who, however, promptly sided with the strikers. The strike was won, apparently in March or early April.

A second Westville lodge, Gladstone No 5, was formed in May 1880. The *Trades Journal* commented on the broadmindedness of its members in choosing that name, since the majority of them were Canadian Conservatives.

Soon after this, there was a successful strike at the Acadia mine, which won a substantial wage increase not only there but at the Albion and Thorburn mines (all in Pictou County). The association had now won recognition throughout Pictou County.

Neptune Lodge, No 6, South Pictou, was organized before 23 June 1880. At the end of September 884 men from the 6 lodges marched in an anniversary parade in Stellarton. The *Trades Journal* adds that many members did not fall in because they lacked regalias.

The association, still officially an industrial union of miners and other workers about collieries, was already thinking of broadening out. In April 1880 the grand secretary visited the Acadia Iron Works. He reported that the time was inopportune for forming a lodge there, but that the union still hoped to take in workers from other industries. Accordingly, when representatives from the first five lodges met in grand council at Truro, 15 October, they changed the association's name to the Provincial Workingmen's Association (PWA). Later it became the Provincial Workmen's Association of Nova Scotia and New Brunswick.

Just before the meeting of the grand council, Pioneer Lodge had shown its strength by getting an obnoxious worker at Springhill discharged; and McBean Lodge was asking for a union shop. Immediately after the grand council meeting, the PWA organized a seventh lodge, Visatergo, composed of trimmers on the wharves at Granton, Pictou County.[14]

Like many other early labour organizations, and for solid reasons of employer and government hostility, the PWA partook of the nature of a secret society, with religious overtones and an elaborate ritual. Lodge meetings were normally opened with prayer, led by the membership-appointed chaplain. The chairman was addressed as master workman. Latecomers had to give a secret knock and a password.[15]

The Saint John Shipwrights Union, reorganized in 1853, had almost disappeared by the next year, because most of its members fled the city to escape an outbreak of cholera. By 1856, however, most of them had returned, and the union was again reorganized. By 1866 it must have run into financial difficulties, for it got itself incorporated, 'for the purpose of pecuniary affairs and no other.' The Shipwrights struck, 28 August 1871, for a full day's pay for work on Saturday (when they stopped work at 5:00). They were out one day and won. The union struck again, briefly and successfully, in April 1874. In May 1875, during the great Longshoremen's strike, there was some question of the Shipwrights going out in sympathy, but they apparently decided not to. The Great Fire of 1877 threw them into a state of disorganization, but in 1880 they reorganized.[16]

The next Saint John local union was the Caulkers Association of the City and County of Saint John, organized in January 1864. It promptly demanded a nine-hour day, which the employers promptly refused. A bitter strike followed, lasting many months. Many of the caulkers left Saint John to seek employment in the United States. But the union held firm. By mid-1864 the employers had given in, and the nine-hour day was established. Two years later the same union got the eight-hour day. All members working for one hour in the morning or evening before or after the hours stated, or during the dinner hour, were to receive one-quarter-day's pay, or be fined two dollars for each and every violation. The system of fines gave the individual member a strong incentive not to let his employer break the overtime rule, and there is no reason to believe that this strong union was at all lax about enforcing the fines.

This union was incorporated in 1866 again for its pecuniary affairs only. Like the Shipwrights also, it declined to go out in sympathy with the Longshoremen in 1875.[17]

From at least 1866 till at least 1872 there was an Indiantown Raftsmen's Association, with some 150 members, including many of the employers.[18]

Whatever riggers' organization took part in the 1840 and 1853 processions must have disappeared by 1868, when we find a Riggers Union being organized. Unlike the Shipwrights and the Caulkers, it struck in sympathy with the Longshoremen in 1875. It was still active in 1880 and indeed seems to have lasted till 1902.[19]

In 1868 there was a Coopers Society, which may have existed as far back as 1840. There was a Plumbers Union in 1870.[20]

There was a Bricklayers and Masons Society (or Masons and Plasterers) from 1870 to 1874. On 5 November 1874 all the bricklayers and masons employed by one Causey struck because he continued to employ a union member who had fallen badly behind in his dues. The man offered a compromise, but the society refused and asked for his dismissal. Causey refused, and the strike followed. There may have been a Boilermakers Union in June 1872, when men of that trade struck for a wage increase, demanding $2 a day for rivetters and fitters-up, $1.66 for clippers and caulkers, and $1.20 for apprentices.[21]

A Millmen's Union struck for higher wages in May 1873 at the Adams mill. The employer immediately shut down and said he would stay shut. This is probably the same union which, in April 1874, engaged in a major battle with the lumber-mill owners. Its official name was, apparently, the Millmen's Association, or Millmen's Protective Union; the employers, perhaps with malice aforethought, called it 'the Club.' Its drive to organize the unorganized roused the owners to fury, which the union's assurance that it had no intention of asking for a wage increase before January 1875 did nothing to diminish.[22]

The employers struck the first blow. On 21 April 1874 Miller and Woodman discharged the half of their working force which belonged to the union. The other half, believing this to be very arbitrary conduct, left their employ. Next day the union marched 250 to 300 strong, to S.T. King's mill, where the members tried unsuccessfully to get King's men to join. King told them they were an illegal gathering and must not interfere with his workmen. If he was compelled to shut down his mill, he would support every man who would not join the association. The crowd tried vainly to get King's men to take membership cards and after some grumbling dispersed.

Next day the mill owners and lumber shippers set up their Lumber Exchange, which denounced the union as threatening one of the largest interests of this port and 'likely to prove subversive of orderly and legitimate business'; declared it was the duty of all mill owners to refuse employment to men combined against them; and asked the police magistrates 'to detail a sufficient force to disperse the large gatherings of men and boys visiting the various places of business in and about the city, as disorderly and dangerous to the best interests of the community.' The resolutions were signed by no less than 15 firms.

The union disclaimed any intention of striking for higher wages or interfering with non-unionists. It did not look for any wage increases until the beginning of 1875. The *Telegraph* insisted there had been 'large bodies of millmen, marching to mills and endeavouring to induce those employed therein to join the organization.' The editor warned his readers of the 'probable effect on the trade and prosperity of the port, of the triumph of the employees over the employers of labor. Already we have an illustration at hand of the consequences which follow labor combinations in the working of the laborer's society, which has already established a sort of despotic authority over the shippers of lumber from this port. If the manufacturers of lumber get into the hands of a similar organization, St John may bid goodbye to its present prosperity and prepare for a period of financial difficulty if not of financial ruin. We do not say this in the interest of any one class ... but ... the entire community, which depends largely on the prosperity of the lumber trade ... Manufacturers dare not make contracts ... Shippers, ship-owners are all kept in a state of doubt ... With such dangers ahead, it is evident that the present conflict is one in which nine-tenths of the community are interested, and in which they must take sides.'

The Lumber Exchange met again on 27 April. It adopted a constitution, elected officers, and members signed a pledge not to employ any members of the union. Most of the exchange's members undertook to subscribe money 'for the purpose of employing a special force to give protection to our workmen and also for the further purpose of furnishing extraordinary facilities to those having contracts to fill.' This is notable for its hint that the magistrates had been insufficiently accommodating in providing police, and that the employers were quite prepared to supply the deficiency.

Next evening, the union held a large meeting and amended the union constitution to make it clear that there had never been any intention of asking for a wage increase, even after the end of the year, or of a strike on 1 January 1875. By 2 May the *Telegraph* would have liked to believe that the trouble was over, but on 6 May it was obliged to report that the difficulty had been revived the day before.

One of the mill owners had been reluctant to join the exchange and had kept on his union men. Finally he joined and told the men they must give up their union tickets, though he would not ask them to sign 'the document' undertaking not to become or remain a union member. They refused and struck. This meant six mills shut down. Both sides declared stridently that they would not give way; the employers talked of bringing in strikebreakers from Maine; and their organ, the *Telegraph*, observed complacently: 'It will not be long till numbers of them [the millmen] will be without any means of supporting their families. The owners have capital to back them on their side – the employees nothing. Within a very few weeks they must yield or starve.' The strike seems to have petered out by 24 June, with the union dropping its demand and the employers their document. The sequel was a meeting of the exchange, 10 December, which elected six arbitrators to settle future disputes. All were members of the exchange.

Contrary to the expectations of the *Telegraph*, the union survived, for on 5 April 1875 we find a notice of a meeting for the election of officers, with the remark that the initiation fee has been reduced to 25 cents. Moreover, it was still capable of kicking. In May 1875 Dunn's announced that henceforth its mills were to operate an extra hour every Saturday. The men simply walked out, at 5:00, and the owners retaliated by closing the mills.

A Carpenters Union was invited to strike in sympathy with the longshoremen in 1875.[23]

THE LABOURERS BENEVOLENT ASSOCIATION

In Saint John, the longshoremen's Labourers Benevolent Association (LBA) had, by 1865, reached a state where some of its members with more advanced ideas felt it needed to be reorganized. Accordingly, on 12 June they called a meeting and re-enrolled no less than 1500 members. They settled on a standard wage rate and drew up by-laws. The LBA took on a new lease on life and, during the 1870s, made labour history in Saint John.

The first major dispute of that decade seems to have been to some extent between two organizations, both concerned with longshoring: the LBA and the Boss Scowmen's and Stevedores Association, organized in March 1870. According to the LBA, the Boss Scowmen decided to set a rate of $2 per standard for delivering cargo and storing it aboard a vessel. This would have meant an increase of 29 per cent in costs to the shipowners. The Boss Scowmen tried to get the longshoremen to go along with this. The merchants, shipowners, and shipbrokers took fright, and some 30 of them wrote to the LBA urging it to refuse. The merchants complained that the Boss Scowmen not only wanted to raise rates but also to take from the owners, masters, and consignees of vessels the right to select a stevedore, who would be responsible to them for the manner in which he did his work. The merchants said they recognized in the LBA 'a union which has been productive of benefits to its members, and the means of bringing a better class of labor into the market, in this way proving a benefit to the trade of the Port. But, should this Society, by any arrangement with the Stevedores' and Boss Scowmen's union, or otherwise enable or assist them to carry out the high handed measures contemplated by that body, we do not hesitate to say that our confidence in the management, which has heretofore kept the Society by itself and aloof from those who would use it for their own selfish purposes, will be very much impaired.'

Whether because of this appeal or otherwise, the LBA by a small majority, repulsed the advances of the Boss Scowmen. The leaders of the Boss Scowmen, James and Robert Mahoney, and one of their colleagues, William Dunlavey, then tried to get along by engaging 'outsiders' (non-members of the LBA or members not in good standing; otherwise known as 'rebels'). The longshoremen took the stand that no ship in the harbour should be loaded or unloaded by outsiders. The Mahoneys and Dunlavey claimed that they had been given to understand in March by the LBA that the prices for scowing deals would be $2 per day, and that for piling, 9s., but that it had subsequently raised the price for piling to $2. Dunlavey had made a contract based on the lower prices, and so was forced to engage outside men at lower rates. By the beginning of June 1870 the Mahoneys and Dunlavey had contracts for handling a series of ships and were using outsiders or rebels and trouble erupted.

On 13 June a large number of LBA members, unauthorized by the union, drove the rebels off one ship, chased the Mahoneys into a shop, and were with difficulty prevented from dragging them out. Three longshoremen were arrested, and warrants issued for ten others. Another gang drove rebels off another vessel, whose captain came near firing on them a small gun loaded with spikes and other missiles. Fifty men boarded a third ship and ordered the men there to leave or be thrown overboard. They left.

Even the anti-union *Telegraph*, however, admitted that one of the LBA officers had helped prevent the attack on the Mahoneys and that the treasurer and secretary had assured the paper that the officers had tried to dissuade the men from carrying out threats against Mahoneys' and Dunlaveys' men. Moreover, when the rebels resumed work under police protection, and the longshoremen massed again, the secretary went to the wharf and got them to disperse. The men who had been arrested were admonished by the magistrate, and bound over for six months. The rebels celebrated their triumph by a 'free concert on the programme of which "Shoo Fly" occupied prominence.'[24]

So the wildcat effort to enforce a union shop in the harbour failed for the moment. But on 2 August the *Freeman* was reporting that the LBA had resolved to suspend immediately all work in the harbour until the rebels were discharged. This produced results in short order. On 6 August the *Freeman* reported that the rebels had submitted to the authority of the LBA and had been readmitted to membership. Work resumed on all the vessels.

The LBA could count on the support of others. In October 1870 a new ship was being masted and ballasted. Mahoney, employing outsiders, had charge of loading the vessel. The Riggers Association members working on the masting consequently struck work. Their employer got outsiders and was proceeding with the work, when a large number of longshoremen and riggers congregated about the vessel. The police were sent for, but since there was no actual molestation they did not interfere. However, during the afternoon the outsiders stopped working.

The *Telegraph* promptly denounced a system where shipowners, shippers, or their agents had nothing to say about who should do the work or how much they should be paid: the union settled that. If the employer hired a non-unionist, the union struck. This was 'tyranny ... a deadly assault upon professional independence – a most flagrant outrage upon men's most cherished rights.' But if the strike failed, there was the 'brute force' the city had seen during the year; and there was 'another form of intimidation.' When a union member died, all the others had to go to the funeral, and 'the long procession, walking two and two' showed the public how big the union was. These displays were probably not meant to intimidate, but they did; and 'the Society derives quite as much benefit ... from their lengthened processions as they have ever obtained from attacks on 'outsiders.''' 'One might enquire the loss to the laborers themselves, as to the city generally, from lost time spent in these processions ... and whether the new order has produced any better workmen, either among the scowmen, the ordinary laborer who handles deals or saws wood, or among masons and plasterers?' (Evidently unions of these two crafts were then in existence, and also practised this distinctively Canadian 'method.')[25]

By the summer of 1873 Saint John unions generally must have succeeded in winning something like a closed shop in the organized occupations. For the *Telegraph* complains on 10 June that 'Labor, as now understood in the city ... is obtainable only through societies who sit in judgment over employers, and dictate what they shall pay ... the employer being obliged to accept and pay for the work of men of whom he has no knowledge ... If the employer is not satisfied with a man's way of earning his high rate of wages, he cannot discharge him; that power being alone in the hands of the society to which the man belongs. The employer, of course, may refuse the services of a man belonging to the society, but should he do so without the consent of the society's representatives, all the other laborers leave his work.' This was a sad change from the days when 'laborers were at liberty to work for any person who would employ them at wages agreed upon between the employer and employed, the rate of pay being in accordance with the value of the work done and such as was sufficient to keep the laborer independent alike of the capitalist and his fellow-laborer.'

The *Telegraph* was, however, particularly incensed by the behaviour of the LBA, especially as that union had, it alleged, made a deal with the Tug Boat 'combination' not to bring any vessel into port unless the captain promised to use only LBA members for discharging and loading, while the LBA undertook not to work on scows or woodboats towed through the Reversing Falls by non-members of the Tug Boat Association. The result, the *Telegraph* claimed, was to raise costs in Saint John harbour to uneconomic levels, which drove business away from the port.[25]

A day or so later, the president of the Saint John Board of Trade said that unless something was done the trade of the port would be damaged to the extent of $600,000. One remedy was for the shipper to arrange to deliver the deals directly to the ship. Work costing $22 or thereabouts in Saint John, it was said, could be done for $16 at Miramichi, Richibucto, Bay Verte, and other places.[26]

By the fall of 1874 a situation prevailed which, according to the sympathetic *Morning Freeman*, threatened the very existence of the union. Unemployment was rife: of the 1400 to 1600 members of the LBA, only 250 were at work. None the less, the union insisted that its members should not take less than $3 a day and forbade them to work with non-union men at any wage. With winter coming on, some of the unemployed longshoremen were tempted to break the rules. Naturally, the employers took advantage of the fact. Equally naturally, the union expelled members who violated its rules. By 10 November the rebels were evidently numerous, for it was then reported by the hostile *Daily News* that on the discharging of six of the vessels then in port none but rebels were employed. The union apparently tried unsuccessfully to take away the unloading of one ship, the *Alps*, from one particularly tough and enterprising master stevedore, Alexander McDermott, who was employing rebels. The trouble apparently went on smouldering throughout the winter.[27]

It produced a lively exchange of editorials between the *Daily News*, supporting the employers, and the *Morning Freeman*, generally supporting the union. (There may have been an ethnic element in this: the *Freeman* was the organ of the Irish, and the union was overwhelmingly Irish.) The *News*'s accusation that the union kept the men idle 'to satisfy a secretary who receives a salary ... or a treasurer who is making a fortune by having the use of the society's funds without interest' shows that the LBA had at least one full-time paid officer and a substantial amount of money. It evidently spent the winter preparing for a showdown. On 9 March 1875 it resolved not only to maintain its rate of $3 a day, but to apply it to steamships as well as sailing vessels (the rate for steamships had formerly been 40 cents an hour).

A number of the rebels had been allowed back into the union, and it was believed others would soon follow, so that when the spring work began the LBA would be in as strong a position as ever it was.[28]

Two weeks later the union resolved to support the scowmen and stevedores in any rate of wages agreed on and laid down fresh restrictive rules. It was clearly feeling more and more confident, not to say ready for a fight, and on 30 March the lid blew off. Six rebels working on a steamer for Scammell Bros were assaulted because they were taking $2 a day for work for which union members had been getting $4. That same evening, a union meeting defeated a motion to accept lower wages. One of the men assaulted took proceedings under an act of 1869 which imposed a penalty of not less than two years' imprisonment, with or without hard labour, on anyone who, in pursuance of an unlawful combination or conspiracy to raise the rate of wages, unlawfully assaulted any person or used violence or threat of violence against such person. No arrests seem to have taken place, but the mere possibility may have induced a chastened mood, for on 6 April the union reduced its standard wage to $2 and a few days later the members were reported to be offering no resistance to rebels.

The calm was short-lived. On 24 April Mr Scammell, a prominent employer of longshoremen, was struck by an unknown assailant; the blow was almost fatal. The Scammell firm immediately offered a reward of $500 for the arrest of the assailant. The union promptly called a special meeting to deny responsibility for or countenance of the assault. It said that when the Scammells refused to employ union men, the members had hoped that the rebels would be unable to do properly the work coming to the port, but that when they saw this was a mistaken idea they lowered their wages to the same rate as the rebels. The union unanimously offered its regrets and a $200 reward for arrest of the assailant. The merchants of the city also offered a reward and the lieutenant-governor published a proclamation offering $500 to anyone providing information leading to a conviction.

Within a few days, fresh trouble broke out. On 28 April the scowmen working for Edward Elliot refused to bring deals alongside the steamship *Vanguard*, since it was being loaded by rebels. The union secretary tried unsuccessfully to arrange a settlement. The scowmen struck, and an LBA meeting that evening resolved that the whole union should strike and refuse to go back unless it had the discharging and loading of all vessels coming to the port.

The strike left nine ships idle and five being worked by rebels. The mayor swore in special constables, but the LBA decided not to hold a procession, as it thought most of the rebels would give up ship work as soon as the lumber mills opened, and then the merchants would have to come to terms.[29]

The merchants, however, felt otherwise. In the previous fall, the Board of Trade and the Lumber Exchange had appointed a joint committee to produce a report dealing with the labour question. A joint meeting of the board and the exchange took place, 30 April, to hear the report.

It was a long and elaborate document. It complained of 'many and excessive charges unusual to this trade in other ports ... largely reducing our profits, and making it exceedingly difficult to compete,' and pinned the blame squarely on the unions, and in particular the LBA and the tugboat combination. It admitted that most of the longshoremen earned barely enough to support their families, but blamed this on the high daily rate which produced 'an unnatural over supply of labourers ... the result of which is loss of time equivalent or more than equivalent to the increase in wages. The law of supply and demand ... is imperative, and must be recognized, as well as the perfect freedom of choice, on the part of him who sells, and him who buys.' The report wound up denouncing the union as 'an engine of tyranny ... oppressive to its own members and ... other laborers, who do not choose to become members, as well as dangerous and destructive to business,' and recommending the employers to discountenance all combinations and encourage 'free labor.'

After some discussion, the report was adopted without amendment. There was, however, a general feeling that resolutions were not enough: there must be action. Mr Alexander Gibson, of Nashwaak, 'was called upon to give his opinion, which he did in a modest yet practical manner.' 'Practical' was the right word: he said what was needed was to get labourers from outside the LBA. This required money, no less than $100,000. He would put up $25,000 if others would put up the rest. This was received with applause. An executive committee of five was appointed and a subscription list, which promptly produced $58,500 from Gibson and 15 others, was opened. By 5 May the fund had reached $108,500. It is interesting to note that one of the merchants, in moving the appointment of the executive committee, noted that it was 'the principle which had proved so successful in the case of the millmen a year or two ago.'

Clearly the merchants had no objection to combinations of the right kind, and their own promptly proceeded to act with the utmost energy. It advertised, repeatedly, for 300 men to scow deals and load ships at $2 a day for a guaranteed period of three months and asked the papers in St Andrews, St Stephen, Moncton, Woodstock, Fredericton, Halifax, and Yarmouth to copy the advertisement. The results seem to have been rather meagre: by 5 May only 52 men had signed up, and the merchants had decided not to import labourers, 'in view of the large number of idle men about town.'

The merchants' energy and determination, and their willingness to say it with money, and big money, must have impressed the LBA. Almost immediately after the employers' meeting, the union appointed a committee to meet the merchants' committee. A conference duly took place, but no arrangement could be made. Rebuffed, the longshoremen met afterwards and resolved to continue their strike.

Both sides then settled down to a grim struggle. The civic authorities, fearing violence, took strong measures. The chief of police kept all the night men on the force on duty, old batons were brought out and scoured and revolvers carefully cleaned and loaded. The mayor swore in special constables; but this very nearly backfired. The regular constables, who got $1.25 a day, objected to the special constables getting $1.50. The strike ended before this could produce anything more than grumbling (though the special constables were not relieved from duty till a week later). But the grumbling of the regular men must have increased the nervousness of the authorities, for on 6 May the *News* reported that about 30 men of the 62nd Battalion Volunteers had been called out for duty, apparently by the mayor. Actually, there was no violence at all: the LBA's members made no attempt to interfere with the rebels or the imported strikebreakers, and even the fiercely anti-union *News*, at the end of the strike, offered grudging congratulations to the LBA on its members' good behaviour.

The men's self-restraint is the more remarkable because the association was in no position to hold out for any great length of time. It had about $6000 and each of its 700 members was entitled to draw $4 a week while on strike. As early as 4 May the LBA was trying to get the other unions, notably the Carpenters and Caulkers, to strike in sympathy. At its meeting on that day, representatives of the Carpenters and the Caulkers were present. Both undertook to consider the question promptly. Both unions felt 'that if the Labourers' Association were destroyed the others must follow, and therefore joint action is advisable.'

The prospect of a partial general strike worried even the *Freeman* and stirred the *News* to send a reporter to prominent members of the Shipwrights, the Riggers, and the Caulkers to get their views.

The replies were not altogether reassuring. The Shipwrights so far had not promised to go out, but if they saw the merchants trying to crush the LBA, they were 'not prepared to say that they would not do their best to defeat such an object.' Their president had advised the LBA to call off the strike. The Caulkers Union seemed to favour striking. The *News* observed that if its 80 members did strike, it would be next to impossible for the merchants to fill their places. If other unions struck in sympathy with the LBA, the Caulkers were prepared to join. The Riggers were in sympathy with the longshoremen, but not likely to be among the first to encourage a strike of other unions.

The Riggers actually came out, 7 May. The Caulkers, the same day, announced that they would not. There is no further word of any action by the Shipwrights or the Carpenters, and no mention of any other unions (except, of course, the Millmen, who had struck on their own account). It looks as if the LBA appealed for help only to the waterfront unions, for it is pretty certain that the Crispins and the Typographical Union were in existence at the time, and it seems probable that the Bakers, Tailors, Painters, and Cabinet-Makers were also.

As early as May some LBA members were scowing deals to some of the lumber yards. Both the *News* and the *Freeman* reported that some had left to take work in the Miramichi mills or at the North Shore. On 11 May the LBA decided to work on vessels on which there were no rebels, and next day both the longshoremen and the Riggers went back, the former hoping to work out all the rebels in a few weeks.

Throughout the strike the newspapers had bombarded each other vigorously, the *News* and the *Telegraph* supporting the employers, the *Freeman* and the *Globe* the men. The *News* called the strike a 'most puerile and tyrannical attempt at trampling down and stamping out the rights of others,' and appealed to the 'large number of thoughtful, reasonable and sober-minded' men in the union to 'withdraw from an organization that has fallen under such evil guidance.' The *Telegraph* specialized in rhetorical questions, such as, 'Is it not a fact that it is a disagreeable, if not even a hazardous duty for any man to speak out plainly in regard to these Labor Combinations?' and 'Is it not a fact that many of these "fourteen hundred members" have votes or can influence votes?'

On the first question the obvious comment is that the merchants and their papers seem to have performed their hazardous duty not only with singular heroism but without any sign of finding it disagreeable. To the second, the *Freeman* replied: 'Not half, not a quarter as many as those who feel aggrieved by the actions of the labourers have and can influence.' This last, indeed, was one of the *Freeman*'s favourite points. At the merchants' meeting on 30 April H.A. Austin, MPP; William Elder, MPP and editor and owner of the *Telegraph* and the *Presbyterian Herald*; and A.L. Palmer, MP, had all taken a prominent part and a strong line. The *Freeman* said it was 'curious to note how eager the politicians who attended the meeting were to have the Society crushed,' and wondered if they would have been so outspoken if the 1400 LBA members all had votes. For the most part, however, the *Freeman* confined itself to answering the economic arguments put forward at the merchants' meeting ('sheer nonsense') and to commenting on the clumsy work of the rebels and their imported allies and doubting whether they could really break the strike.

The strike had failed. A week after the longshoremen went back, they even passed a resolution to work on any vessel, provided only that no others, except those rebels who had been guaranteed work for three months, were engaged. But their meekness did not evoke any conciliatory response. On the contrary, on 29 May the *Freeman* lamented that the executive committee of the association of merchants and shippers had resolved to employ no labourers who belonged to the LBA. It had also recommended that a clause be inserted in every charter binding the master of every ship coming to the port not to employ any labourers belonging to the LBA. The *Freeman* feared that 'in the present state of the labour market perhaps the effort to crush the Society out of existence may be temporarily successful.'

This gloomy prognostication was not fulfilled, but trouble soon began to smoulder again in the form of the breakfast question. On 20 August some labourers presented themselves at 6 am. The employer insisted they start at 7, without the usual hour for breakfast (8 to 9). The men struck until after dinner. The union was now once more full of ginger, and on 23 August resolved to stick to 6 am, with an hour for breakfast. The employers had evidently also been imposing a further wage cut, for it resolved to demand the former rate of $2 per day.

Next day the men employed upon five or six vessels presented themselves at 6 am. Their offer was again declined, and the men refused to work on any other conditions. As a consequence, the ships had to rely on men outside the union. On 26 August the *Telegraph* reported 'comparatively little inconvenience has been felt from the new labor difficulty.' A meeting of the merchants' committee had resolved 'to sustain the efforts of those who seek to retain the privilege of naming the hours of labor for those they employ, so long as that privilege is used in reason.'[30]

The employers must have won their point, for in April 1876 there was a fresh strike for $2 per day. Clearly, the employers had been able to make the second 1875 wage cut stick.[31]

In the light of what we do know of the LBA's troubles in these years, it is a marvel the union survived at all. Survive it did, however, and by January 1880 it was apparently back in good fighting trim, for it struck the ship *Crown Prince* because an old enemy had members of an opposition society working on several vessels. The opposition society was doubtless the Longshore Labourers, apparently organized in December 1879.[32]

There were one or two other local unions elsewhere in New Brunswick. In Chatham in October 1872, with 30 to 40 vessels loading lumber and the mills going night and day, the workmen had formed a society which demanded $2 a day. Whether the workmen were millmen or longshoremen is uncertain. But by the early summer of 1874 a Labourers' Association of longshoremen, with nearly 700 members, was strong enough to enforce a closed shop. In April 1875 the employers tried to break out of this, and the men struck. The strike lasted till July, but the men appear to have lost.[33]

Trade unionism even made its appearance in Prince Edward Island during this period. In June 1869 the Summerside ship carpenters struck to get their wages in cash. They may have had a union. The Charlottetown Journeymen Shoemakers, in May 1874, certainly had, and on 11 May they threatened to strike for a nearly 40 per cent increase in wages. The Halifax *Evening Express* says that 'it was generally admitted that this class of workmen are underpaid' and that there was 'a good prospect that the employers, who appear ready to meet all reasonable demands, and their work people will soon come to an amicable understanding.'[34]

In Newfoundland, a retail clerks' union, the United Assistants Association, felt it necessary to disband in 1868 because it was being blamed for violence. Within 10 years, it had been reorganized, but seems to have lasted only a few months. the Mechanics Society and the Shipwrights and the Seal-Skinners of course continued.[35]

QUEBEC

In Quebec City during the 1860s and 1870s, the Ship Labourers were both active and powerful. The years 1860–73 were the last prosperous phase of the export trade in square timber. The merchants were well off, and the longshoremen were indispensable. In 1862 the union was incorporated, and on 9 June of that year, it formed Local 5. In 1865, faced with an influx of French Canadians into what had been an Irish preserve, it formed a French-Canadian Local No 3. There were eventually five branches, and in its heyday the society had 2000 members and, as it showed in 1866, effective control of the longshoring labour force.

The Ship Labourers Benevolent Society provided benefits, both sick and burial, and at one time paid the then not inconsiderable sum of $6 a week for 13 weeks to any member injured on ship. This, with the fact that the two key officers got small salaries, suggests the possession of substantial funds, even though the dues were at first only 25 cents a month for the 6 months that the port operated.

But though the society, like many unions then and since, was in part a mutual insurance organization, it was none the less a true union. Early in the summer of 1866 it published a list of minimum wage rates for various categories of work. The employers ignored the list, and in the first days of July the society struck. At first the shipmasters and the merchants stood together. The shipmasters began by moving their vessels across the river to Lévis, which was only partly organized. The society replied by calling a complete stoppage on both shores enforcing it in Lévis by strong-arm methods, even invading the navy yard. Bluejackets, marines, and ordinary strikebreakers were called in. But the society was too strong to be knocked out, and the shipmasters, anxious to get their profitable cargoes loaded and away, failed to maintain employer solidarity. On 23 July they met the union leaders and accepted their terms. The merchants felt betrayed. They denounced what they considered the perversion of a benevolent society to collective bargaining. They warned the men that 'labour was simply a commodity, like everything else, and was regulated by the same laws.' But huffing and puffing was all they could do. They were beaten, and they knew it. On 24 July they caved in.

The strike must have established the society as one of the powers of Quebec and given it a considerable standing in the community, for its annual 23 July parades seem to have become an institution. The members assembled at the Mariners' Chapel, in Lower Town; then paraded, four deep, up Palace or Mountain hills and circulated through Upper Town and back to the coves by way of the Plains of Abraham, a distance of eight miles. Members who did not walk were fined; so were those who stopped at pubs en route, or who joined the parade part-way along in a 'refreshed' condition. The parade displayed the great banner of the society, showing a ship being loaded, with the inscription, 'We support our infirm; We bury our dead.' The members wore their best clothes, with cockades and cascades of rosettes of various colours, and the townsfolk replied in kind.

As French Canadians began to infiltrate longshoring and the society itself (the early officers, as in Saint John, bore such emphatically Irish names as Burke, Grogan, Corcoran, Mullins, and McFall), disputes broke out over the demands of the French-speaking members for a share in political influence and available work. The latter dispute was eventually settled by dividing the work equally between the two groups. Meanwhile, some French-Canadian longshoremen had formed the rival Union canadienne des débardeurs. The two unions came to blows in 1878, and in August 1879 there was a pitched battle, during which the ship labourers barricaded themselves in their headquarters and defended it with cannon. The contemporary *Illustrated News* had several cuts picturing the clash, with the members of the Union canadienne, 'some in top hats ... defending their banner from the more functionally attired Irish.'[36]

The Quebec Ship Carpenters were still strong and active in 1867 when they struck, 2300 strong, 24 September, for a 35 cent increase to $1.25 a day. The employers offered $1. The strike was a stormy affair. The employers brought in strikebreakers, whom the police protected. Troops were called out and in a large demonstration on 28 October a man was killed. Two days later 19 leaders were arrested, then released on bail of $1400. Well on into December the strikers paraded daily in the streets. Then what were apparently non-union delegates chosen by the carpenters asked the board of trade to arbitrate. The board proposed small increases, which the employers and the carpenters accepted, the latter demanding the rehiring of all the strikers. The shipyards reopened on 24 December.[37]

Thus the newspaper accounts. But a letter in the Chicago *Workingman's Advocate*, 8 February 1868, signed 'L.C.L., W.P. Union No. 35,' says the Ship Carpenters and Caulkers had refused the board's terms and reported that the situation was still the same as it had been four months before. The board had demanded that the men sign the infamous 'document.' Most of the members had refused, and all who had signed 'are as true to the union as ever.' All the union's officers had been arrested for being officers of an illegal combination.

The Quebec Bargemen formed in 1870 a union which struck in 1871 for overtime after eight hours. The employers brought in strikebreakers and invoked the aid of the police, who protected the strikebreakers and arrested three strikers. The union is said to have lasted six years and to have been broken up by the employers' use of the 'document.'[38]

Montreal is said to have had a Union of Wharf Porters, organized in 1865. By the spring of 1867 there was a Carpenters and Joiners Union, which had struck and got a 25 per cent wage increase. The Printers also got a 25 per cent increase, and the Cabinet Makers struck and got 12½ to 15 per cent. There were also Bakers and Masons unions at the time, and of course the Stonecutters, the ASE, the Molders, the Locomotive Engineers, and the Cigar Makers. A large number of other unions either existed already or were organized in the spring of 1867. On 6 April Médéric Lanctôt founded the Grand Association of Canadian Workingmen. This took in unions of carpenters, printers, cabinet makers, bakers, masons, and what may have been new unions of bricklayers, ship carpenters, labourers, painters, plasterers, cable makers, jewellers, tinsmiths, coopers, teamsters, brushmakers, shoemakers, saddlers, curriers, tailors, tobacco workers, and carters.[39]

The Grand Association, which is said to have had 8000 members, is interesting for more reasons than one. Lanctôt clearly intended it to become at least province-wide; he is said to have hoped to include farmers as well as urban workers; he set to work at once to organize what he called co-operatives, and the Montreal *Gazette* of 8 June 1867 reported that 'The Association is also beginning to manifest political proclivities, and there is a muttering that it ought to be represented' (apparently in the dominion Parliament). Lanctôt was already a member of the city council. It is notable that the head of the association was a French Canadian and that French-Canadian names predominate in newspaper reports of its activities.[40]

The Bakers struck late in May under the auspices of the Association. They were getting $5 to $6 a week and wanted $8 and day work. The master bakers were said to have been getting men to work at night for lower wages and then discharging their ordinary employees. By the end of May some of the employers had granted the demands but 20 bakers were still out. On 12 June the strike was still in progress. The Masons struck 10 June to get two rates, according to qualifications. The Carpenters had already struck, successfully, in February and March, for a 25 per cent wage increase, on rates varying from $1.20 to $1.50 a day.[41]

The association's first co-operative store, started in May, provided groceries at a 25 per cent saving on ordinary prices. Members' dues were 10 cents a month. A dry-goods store was to be established immediately, and drugs and medicine were to be made available on the same principle at Quévillon and Desjardins drug store. A house had been rented for another store in St-Jean-Baptiste village. Carters and labourers were to be admitted to benefits from the stores, and ordinary householders were to pay an annual fee of $5. The grocers were said to be indignant.

By 12 June Lanctôt was writing to the *Gazette* that there had been strikes every year for 30 years past and reporting progress in his co-operatives. A bakery turning out 700 loaves per day was to be in operation the next day. Dry goods were available at Quévillon's and at Larivée's. There would be a store in St Lawrence Main the next day. Hardware would soon be available at Saucère Bros. The entry fee for all these was to be sixpence.[42]

The association's most spectacular manifestation was a torchlight procession on 10 June 1867. The Locomotive Engineers and the ASE apparently did not take part, but at least 22 other unions did: Typos, Tailors, Tobacconists (Cigar Makers?), Brushmakers, Plumbers, Bricklayers, Saddlers, Carriage Makers, Molders, Curriers and Tanners (perhaps two separate unions), Coopers, Blacksmiths, Nail Cutters and Finishers (one account lumps these with the Blacksmiths), Stonecutters, Masons, Painters, Ship Carpenters and Caulkers, Tinsmiths, Cabinet-makers, Carpenters and Joiners, Shoemakers, and (according to one account) Bookbinders and Carters. The Carpenters and Joiners took part in the St-Jean-Baptiste parade of 1868 and appear again in 1872.[43]

The Stonecutters had a strike in 1869 and two in 1877, both on the Lachine Canal. The first, 1 March on section 4, was for a 40 cent increase to $1.60 a day. They were out two days and won. The second, 31 March on section 6, was for an increase to the rate paid the previous fall. It seems to have petered out.[44]

The Ouvriers de bord struck in June 1877 against a rumoured wage cut from 15 to 12 cents an hour. The Allan company took on strikebreakers at 25 cents an hour, with the usual police protection. The strikers attacked the police with stones and tried unsuccessfully to block the hiring of other longshoremen at the harbour. Allan then offered $1.50 a day to strikebreakers, and longshoremen from other companies joined the strike. The men offered to go back if wages were not cut and if the companies would pay the longshoremen for the time lost while on strike. The companies refused. The men went back after eight days at rates of 15 to 20 cents an hour. About 1000 workers were involved. The same union struck in August 1880 for an increase from 12 to 15 cents an hour, which they said had been promised them. They were replaced by strikebreakers under police protection.[45]

In June 1880 the Montreal Bricklayers struck, 150 strong, for a wage increase of 50 cents, to $2 a day. Five days later most of the employers (who included the Grand Trunk Railway) had granted the increase. St John's, Quebec, had a strike of unionized glass blowers in November 1879. The 30 men involved were replaced by strikebreakers.[46]

ONTARIO

In Kingston, a Sailors Union struck in October 1872.[47]

Thanks to being chosen as the capital, Ottawa produced a union movement early in the 1860s. The erection of the Parliament Buildings brought in skilled stonecutters who, by 19 May 1864, had formed a union. Men who had taken part in an earlier strike were on trial when the union struck, ón or about 19 May, demanding discharge of a non-striker, no further hiring of apprentices, and an hour for dinner.[48]

The *Labour Gazette* says that Ottawa blacksmiths and bricklayers and stone masons formed unions in 1867. The Bricklayers and Masons Union must have been short-lived: the *Ontario Workman* reported a Bricklayers and Masons Union formed 6 April 1872. This union got down to business at once, and to some effect, for a labourers' meeting 24 April was told that its purpose was 'not to bring about a strike but merely to raise laborers' wages in proportion to increases newly made for brick-layers and masons and other tradesmen.' This meeting resolved that the minimum pay of a labourer in Canada should be no less than 7s. 6d. per day and appointed a committee to wait on the contractors. But another meeting a few days later was told that the committee had not seen the contractors. When someone suggested forming a union, the chairman objected, saying that it would lead to strikes. The upshot was the formation of the Laborers Mutual Aid Society, which apparently confined itself to providing benefits.[49]

The next Ottawa local union was the Plasterers, formed in mid-May 1872. This, with the Typos, the Bricklayers and Masons, the Stonecutters, and the Carpenters (who had organized by this time), took part in a joint union presentation to Sir John A. Macdonald, 5 September 1872, a testimonial of thanks for his Trade Unions Act. The Stonecutters, Typos, Bricklayers and Masons, and the Carpenters paraded in that order, and the presentation committee handed Sir John a gold-headed ebony cane. Both Macdonald and Tilley spoke in reply.

Early in November the Journeymen Saddle and Harness Makers Union number-ing about 50, struck for a wage increase. On 12 December it was still out.[50] By 19 December 1872, there were two stonecutters' unions, Limestone and Sandstone. In January 1873 a seventh purely local union, the Tailors, made its appearance. At the first Canadian Labor Union (CLU) convention in September, the two stonecutters' unions, the Bricklayers, and the Tailors were all represented.[51]

By the end of March 1874 an eighth local union, the Carters, is reported as burying one of its members. A Stonecutters Union was still on hand in the spring of 1876; so, probably, were the Bricklayers and Masons.[52]

Ottawa made labour history in 1874 by electing the first independent labour member of any legislature in the country, Daniel J. O'Donoghue. O'Donoghue had twice been president of his own union, the Typos. He was a member of the first executive of the Ottawa Trades Council and in July 1873 had become its president. He was a member of the Typos' international executive and first vice-president of the CLU. When Hon R.W. Scott vacated the Ottawa provincial seat to enter the dominion cabinet in November 1873, Ottawa workingmen felt the moment had come to send one of their own to Toronto to represent one of the chief union centres of the province.

On 11 January 1874 a mass meeting of workingmen, after some squabbling, unanimously nominated O'Donoghue. On 20 January he issued his election manifesto to the 'Independent Electors of the City of Ottawa.' He presented himself 'as the workingman's candidate on Independent principles.' He appears to have been an early practitioner of the art of consensus, for his platform appealed to a wide swath of electors and contained little that was radical, even by the standards of the time: extension of the franchise 'to a certain amount of income,' lowering of the assessment qualifications of voters (presumably in municipal elections), the amendment of the Mechanics' Lien Law, and the cancelling of the contract granting convict labor to any private company. He promised to support 'all measures tending to a judicious emigration of the classes most required for the development of the resources of the country' and also 'all public works of utility ... While being economical of the finances of the country, I will ... [always] advocate the development of the immense resources of the Province.' He wound up by asserting his confidence that the workingman's candidate would be elected by a large majority. In fact he did get a large majority over his only opponent, the Liberal candidate, who was very ill during the campaign. O'Donoghue's opponents claimed he had had Conservative support, but the vice-president of the Trades Council and Donald Robertson of the Stonecutters issued a statement that the new member was a genuine independent, not bought by anyone.

On 4 November 1874 O'Donoghue was renominated for the general election. He said the premier had indirectly promised to amend the Lien Law; he himself favoured giving the vote to anyone with an income of $400 a year. He claimed he had voted with the government in all but one or two cases because he thought it deserved his vote. He was re-elected, apparently with Liberal support. Only about half the voters turned out.

Like many another workingman's MLA or MP after him, O'Donoghue seems to have slid gradually into the Liberal party. In the dominion election of 1878, though he was careful to say he would make no references to the candidates for the Ottawa seats, he spoke against protection and in favour of a tariff for revenue only.[53]

The Toronto Crispins continued as a purely local union till 1886, when they entered the Knights of Labor as LA 6250. In 1868 there was also a Shoemakers Union, with two branches, 'peg men' and 'sewing.' The former had five officers and two trustees, the latter four officers. In 1877 a group of factory operatives formed the Wholesale Boot and Shoemakers' Union, which seems to have lasted till at least 1887.[54]

The Toronto Cigar Makers in June 1864 were meeting once a month, and the Tinsmiths once a week. The Tinsmiths were asking their fellows in Canada, if 'favorable to the formation of an international union, to correspond, if east of Toronto, with J.D.B. Clark, corresponding secretary, Toronto, and with James Clark, corresponding secretary of grand union, Hamilton, if west of Toronto.'[55]

The Toronto Bricklayers Union, formed in 1866, was going strong in 1868. There was an Apprentices Union (probably printing) in February 1867, and an Apprentices Union (the same or another) which struck early in March 1872. There was a Bookbinders Union in April 1869, when it joined the typos in petitioning against removal of the 15 per cent duty on imported books, and it seems to have been still in existence in January 1870. But the Toronto Trades Assembly minutes indicate that by the fall of 1871 it was gone, to be succeeded by a new one early in 1872. It was this new union which, later in that year, served as a channel for a gift of £20 from the Bookbinders Consolidated Union of Great Britain to the Toronto Typographical Union, to help defend the arrested members of the Typos' strike committee.[56]

By 1868 the Friendly Society of Carpenters and Joiners of Toronto was holding regular meetings. It must have been a body of some size, for it had six officers, three trustees, and a committee of seven. It was still in existence in January 1882. By 1868 there was also a Bakers Union meeting regularly. It was almost certainly the same which was present at the organization of the Trades Assembly and which lasted till 1875 at least.[57]

The Toronto Stonecutters Association seems to have been founded in 1870 and survived well into the twentieth century. It figured in a celebrated prosecution in the summer of 1875 when, according to the *Molders Journal*, there was an effort to send members of this union to prison for conspiracy, because they induced an employer to discharge a scab. The Stonecutters asked, and got, $50 from the Toronto Typos towards the expenses of their defence and some $97 from other unions, as well as the help of the Toronto Trades Assembly; but the accused were convicted and sent to prison.[58]

The Tailors Union had a strike in October and November 1873. The Painters, organized in 1872, were still present in February 1878.[59] A Plasterers Union, formed in June 1872, was still on hand in the spring of 1876. There was a short-lived Dry Goods Clerks Early Closing Association in the summer of 1871. There were smaller organizations in Saint John and Ottawa, but the Toronto Association seems to have been the only one to get recognition as a union.[60]

There was a Cabinet-Makers Union in 1871 and a fresh one organized in 1872. The Toronto Trades Assembly organized a Coachmakers Union in 1871 and a Varnishers and Polishers Union. There was a Brass Founders Union in April 1872. A Harness and Trunk Makers Union was formed in May, a Tinsmiths Union in or before July, a Hackmen's Union in or before January 1873 (still in existence in March 1878), a Labourers Union in or before May (dead by June 1877), a Longshoremen's Union in or before September 1873, and a Millers Union in November 1873.[61]

Some musicians formed the Toronto Musical Union on 20 February 1874 with 22 members and Mr Hewitt (presumably of the coopers) in the chair. The third meeting, in March, changed the name to Association and adopted a constitution. Members were to be between 14 and 50 years of age and of good health. The association's objects were to be the 'moral and intellectual elevation of its members, Relief in sickness and distress, To bury the Dead, and promote the general Welfare of its members.' The next meeting adopted a scale of prices. The association lasted till 7 May 1877 when it was dissolved and its funds divided among its members.[62]

Hamilton was a great centre of local unionism during the 1860s and 1870s.

In 1860 the shoemakers organized as the Sons of St Crispin, a body which, under that name or as the Disciples of St Crispin, seems to have lasted till 1867, when it became Branch 4 of the Boot and Shoemakers Union of Ontario. This branch was still in existence on 6 May 1868. It may have become Lodge 212 of the Knights of St Crispin.[63]

The Hamilton Journeymen Bakers Association was organized 23 July 1862. The bakers were working as many as 18 hours a day. This night system, with its slavish hours of labour, seemed oppressive, ridiculous, and pointless. By modern standards the day system they wanted, a 12-hour day (4 am to 4 pm) sounds modest indeed, and so the association thought. It claimed that the day system had already been tried in several shops and proved to be an inconvenience neither to the master bakers nor to the public; it also claimed that the majority of the master bakers agreed, but felt it could be brought into effect only if all the employers accepted it. Hence the necessity for the journeymen to unite for the common interests and benefits of masters and men. However, many of the master bakers insisted that the public demanded fresh bread, delivered early in the morning. They refused to budge on this ground and threatened their employees with dismissal if they persisted in their attempts to abolish the night system.

The press, for once, seems to have sided with the union. The Molders unanimously resolved to boycott those master bakers who refused to accept the day system and urged the whole working class to join in the boycott. None the less, the association's efforts were on the whole unsuccessful. It threatened, if the master bakers held out, to organize a co-operative bakery. In 1869 its members were still agitating for the day system, with a reduction of hours from 16 to 12.[64]

In June 1864 the Hamilton Tinsmiths were meeting regularly once a week; the union was still there in 1868. In February 1872 however, we find the Journeymen Tinners meeting to organize a union, which they did a week later. In May 1882 there was a meeting of tinsmiths and sheet-iron workers to form a third union.[65]

In May 1864 there was a Carpenters and Joiners Society, which seems to have considered itself a branch of the British Amalgamated Society of Carpenters and

Joiners. The Hamilton Society asked and got the leave of the Trades Assembly to strike.[66]

In 1866 and 1867 we find a Brushmakers Union which took part in the demonstration of May 1872. In 1866 Hamilton had a Seamen's Union.[67] A Tailors Union (whether the one founded in 1854 or a new one) reappears on the scene in 1867. A new one was formed in 1870. In 1872 it was working for a uniform scale of prices in all shops; in 1873 it is said to have represented fully half the tailors in the city. It continued as a purely local body till 1892, when it became Local 149 of the Journeymen Tailors of America.[68]

On 13 July 1867 the butchers organized themselves into a benevolent society. There is some indication of a Bricklayers' and Masons' Union organized in 1868, though we can find no reliable signs of its existence before 1881. The Hamilton Coopers struck in June 1869 for an increase of five cents per oil barrel and on 3 August were reported as about to hold their annual picnic. The union was still in existence in January 1872. Whether this was a purely local body is not clear.[69]

The Hamilton boilermakers were organized in March 1872 and the cabinetmakers in May. The latter month also saw an unsuccessful attempt at organization on the part of the labourers. We also find the first mention of five other unions in 1872: the Marble and Stonecutters Association, the Hatters, the Stonemasons, the Boltmakers, and the Harnessmakers.[70]

The Hamilton plumbers may have been organized in 1873; they held their first annual supper 16 December 1874. The Carriage-Makers held a ball on 26 December 1875. There was a Hackmen's Union by March 1878. The Marble and Stonecutters Association must have fallen by the wayside, for in March or April 1880 a new union, the Hamilton Stonecutters Association, was formed.[71]

London had a purely local Bricklayers Association in 1863, before the Bricklayers International Union was founded at Baltimore. This local union lasted 15 years. In 1876 it adopted a sick benefit plan to create more interest in the organization and in 1877 it changed its name to the Bricklayers Benefit Society. But the benefit plan was its undoing: the membership was too small to support it. In 1878 expenditures exceeded revenues by 55 cents, and on 6 August of that year the union was dissolved.

London had a purely local Carpenters Union by 10 April 1865. For about a year, regular monthly meetings followed. There was a Fraternity of Shoemakers in July 1865, and it was the London shoemakers who started the provincial union in 1867. The tailors organized a Protective Association on 2 October 1865. They told the employers wages were too low in comparison with the advancing markets and demanded an increase, which was granted.

The oil boom about this time had made coopering an important trade in London. In November 1869 the coopers struck unsuccessfully for higher wages. Their failure apparently convinced them they needed a union. In April 1870 they set about forming one and launched it in May.

In London also 1872 was a big year for organization. The cabinet-makers seem to have had a union by February, the painters by May, and the bricklayers' labourers by July. The bricklayers' labourers had struck, just before they formed their union, for an increase of 12½ cents a day, basing their demand on a recent increase in the bricklayers' wages. They formed the union to put pressure on the contractors. This union probably survived for at least a year, for on 21 June 1873 the bricklayers' labourers were again on strike, for an increase to $1.50 a day.

By September 1874 there was a union of carriage-makers. In March 1878 the hackmen, dissatisfied with the police commissioner's new rules for their job, decided to form an organization and to affiliate with the hackmen's unions in Hamilton and Toronto. There was a Railway Brakemen's Union in 1878. On 29 January 1880, the Plumbers and Gasfitters Society held its annual supper.

London witnessed an attempt at labour politics during these years when, in May 1872, a tanner, a cooper, and a shoemaker, with the editor of the *Western Workman*, founded the Workingmen's Progressive Political Party. There is no indication that this Ontario version of the Three Tailors of Tooley Street accomplished anything, nor is there any sign that it had any official union support.[72]

Brantford had a Carpenters Union in June 1864. The printers' social in December 1871 might indicate an organization; the machinists, in the same month, held their first annual ball. As we have seen there was a Shoemakers Union in 1867; and the Carriage Makers had a picnic, with a number of speeches, in July 1873.[73]

There was the short-lived provincial organization of cigar makers, the Journeymen Cigar Makers of Upper Canada, which held a convention in Toronto.

The Niagara peninsula was a centre of early local unionism. St Catharines had a Welland Ship Canal Ship Carpenters and Caulkers Union in June and July 1861, formed a few months before, with all the hands employed on the canal as members. In 1867 its Journeymen Shoemakers became part of the provincial union. In January 1868 the St Catharines *Weekly Journal* reported that the grammar school teachers of Ontario intended organizing an association: 'We suppose they will succeed as associations are quite popular just now.' Whether anything came of this amazingly early attempt to organize professional workers we do not know; it is not even clear that it originated in St Catharines. In May 1871 the St Catharines teamsters gave notice of an agreement to increase rates for their services, which may indicate an organization. There may have been unions of carpenters in April 1872 and of ship carpenters and joiners along the canal in June. The carpenters were certainly demanding a wage increase (to $2 per day) and threatening to strike if they did not get it. The ship carpenters and joiners were also threatening to strike, but against a proposed wage reduction.

The tailors certainly had a union as early as March 1873 which lasted till at least the fall of 1877. In 1873 the journeymen house painters of St Catharines formed a union in connection with the National Union and demanded an immediate wage increase, threatening to strike if they did not get it. The presidents of various unions in town were present and addressed the organization meeting. There were then at least four, perhaps six unions: Crispins, Coopers, Typos, Tailors, and possibly the Cigar Makers and the ASE. The Painters Union was still in existence in 1874, with a membership of about 30 and in 1875. In 1875 the president of the Trades Assembly, William Carroll, of the Tailors, told the Canadian Labor Union that St Catharines did not require further organization as the various trades were already organized. By 1876 there was also a Tinmen's Union, and the ASE had certainly established itself in St Catharines.[74]

Port Colborne had a sailors' strike for higher wages in April 1872, which may indicate a sailors' Union. In November 1878 about 80 Beamsville stonecutters struck for a wage increase. In February 1879 both the Beamsville and Queenston Heights stonecutters struck. In Beamsville, the issue was the discharging of union members; in Queenston Heights, the refusal of unionists to work with non-unionists. The strikes ended in May, with the men returning to work at the same wages as before. Perth had a Journeymen Shoemakers Union in April 1872.[75]

BRITISH COLUMBIA

Victoria had two purely local unions. The first was the Shipwrights and Caulkers Association, formed in 1862 or 1863. The second was the Victoria Typographical Union, organized in 1863.[76]

The third British Columbia union was the Miners Mutual Protective Society, of Wellington, near Nanaimo. Its formation seems to have been preceded by several strikes in the Vancouver Island coal fields. A big strike at the collieries of Dunsmuir, Diggle and Co, early in 1877, failed, but the union persisted till at least January 1884. It was founded 26 February 1877 and was intended to cover the whole mining district. It resolved to have its general committee collect money to defray the expenses the miners had already incurred to send Dunsmuir's strikebreakers out of the country; to have the same committee draw up a code of rules and regulations, to be endorsed by the men at the different collieries, and then printed, with a copy to each member; and to organize locals forthwith. But on 15 August 1883 we find a regular quarterly meeting to consider forming branch unions at Nanaimo and East Wellington. The probability is that the prolonged and unsuccessful strike of August to November 1883 broke this union.[77]

5

Local central organizations before 1880

Until the 1860s local unions seem to have felt little need to co-ordinate their activities with other unions in their area. There is some evidence of attempts to form central organizations in Montreal in March 1834 and in Quebec City in April. But the first local central which lasted for any appreciable length of time seems to have been the Hamilton Trades Union or Trades Assembly set up before 21 December 1863.[1] None of its records seems to have survived. It must have had considerable support and been endowed with large powers, for when the Carpenters and Joiners Society was contemplating a strike at the end of May 1864 it said it could hardly act unless it got leave from the assembly, since otherwise it would not be entitled to support from other unions. The leave was granted, and the assembly also set a rate for the maintenance of the strikers.

In November 1864 the assembly started a co-operative society. In July 1872 it presented Sir John A. Macdonald with an address and a small token of its gratitude 'for the readiness with which he removed from the statute books those restrictions which prevented workingmen from unlawfully combining to maintain trade privileges.' On 1 October 1873 it held a celebration in honour of Joseph Arch, leader of the British National Agricultural Labourers' Union. On 26 February 1875 the assembly passed a resolution endorsing the action of E. Irving, MP for Hamilton, in bringing forward the repeal of the Criminal Law Amendment Act, in the House of Commons, and pledged itself to use all legitimate means to secure the bill's passage.[2]

With this, the curtain falls. It seems probable that the early strength must have dwindled by 1871, for in the voluminous records of the Toronto Trades Assembly of 1871–78, with their numerous references to Hamilton, there does not seem to be a single mention of the Hamilton assembly. The same applies to the *Ontario Workman*, the official Toronto labour paper, in 1872–73.

There appears to have been a central organization in Toronto in 1867. On 10 August 'a deputation from the Trades' Union' visited the Typos to request their co-operation in a proposed picnic for all the unions in Toronto. The Typos agreed to take part and appointed a committee. The picnic was reported a great success. The following year the picnic was run by 'the Committee of Trades Unions.'[3] But it was not until 1871 that the Toronto Trades Assembly was organized.

This body has left complete minute books for almost the whole of its existence, with, for most years, much more than merely formal entries.[4] This is particularly fortunate, for the Toronto assembly was not just a local body like those in Hamilton, Ottawa, and St Catharines. It was responsible for starting the first national central organization, the Canadian Labor Union (CLU). Till that body was established, the TTA served almost as a national centre itself, and throughout the existence of the CLU, the TTA was its backbone.

In February 1871 the Toronto local of the Coopers International Union appointed a committee, John Hewitt, E.S. Gooch and James Judge, to confer with the various unions of the city, 'for the purpose of agitating the question of forming a Central Body, to be known as the Toronto Trades Assembly' (no mention of the unskilled). This committee visited each of the other unions, asking them to appoint similar committees.

The result was a meeting, 3 March 1871, of representatives of the Coopers, Crispins, Typographical Union, Cigar Makers, Iron Molders, and the Bakers to see what could be done. Lodge 159 of the Crispins sent five delegates, Lodges 315 and 356 three each, and each of the other five unions three each. Hewitt was elected chairman, and J.S. Williams, of the Typographical Union, recording secretary.

The Crispins' delegates were generally favourable to the idea of an assembly, but had no definite instructions from their lodges. The Bakers also were generally favourable, but wanted further information. Other delegates said much the same. No one was prepared to act decisively, but a motion was carried that the meeting thought an assembly desirable and that the delegates pledged themselves to further its formation.

They evidently took their pledge seriously, for on 12 April the assembly was actually formed. This time delegates were present not only from the original six organizations but also from the Tailors. The Crispins, Cigar Makers, Molders, and Coopers were all ready to go ahead. The Bakers' delegates thought they would co-operate. The Tailors had no instructions and were not prepared to take action. The Typographical Union wanted to know the basis of the proposed assembly before committing itself. None the less, the meeting formally established the Assembly and set up a committee on a constitution and another to draft rules and regulations. On this latter committee all seven unions were represented. In spite of the non-committal position of his union, J.S. Williams continued as recording secretary.

On 5 May the assembly met again, with delegates from the Coopers, the Molders, and Lodges 159 and 356 of the Crispins present as full members. It was decided that other delegates, 'properly accredited but not possessing full credentials' (a delicate and rather mysterious distinction) should be considered full members till the next meeting. Since the previous meeting, the Cabinet-Makers Union and the Amalgamated Carpenters had been seen, and the president of the former and a delegate from the latter were present and duly introduced and invited to remain.

The meeting then proceeded to elect officers. Hewitt was elected president; John Dance (Molders) vice-president; Williams, recording secretary; H.L. Beebe (Crispins 159), corresponding secretary; McLaughlin (Cigar Makers), sergeant-at-arms; Stewart (Bakers), financial secretary; and James Dean (Crispins 159), treasurer. The laws and regulations drawn up by the constitutional committee were then adopted. The executive was authorized to buy stationery and notice was given that the Homestead Act would be discussed at the next meeting. From then on, regular meetings were held every two weeks, with occasional special meetings. At the third meeting, 19 May, the Bakers, the Typographical Union, and a third lodge of Crispins were represented, bringing the number of member organizations to six, with eight local unions in all.

One of the first things the assembly did was to set up an organizing committee. This had two tasks: to get all the other existing unions into the assembly, and to organize new ones. It lost no time getting to work on both. On 2 June it reported that it had visited the Engineers (ASE), the Carpenters (ASCJ), and the Cabinet-Makers to bring them into membership, and also groups of bookbinders, boilermakers, carriage-makers, painters, builders, and hackmen. The following week it reported that the bookbinders, watchmakers, and boilermakers were arranging to be associated; that the hackmen and the hatters were moving in that direction; and that the men in the rolling mills wanted a union. On 16 June it reported that the brushmakers had been seen. On 7 July the Dry-Goods Clerks Early Closing Association was admitted to membership. On 15 September the Blacksmiths came in. On 3 November the organizing committee reported having organized unions of coachmakers, and varnishers and polishers (a little belatedly, this last, since delegates of the Varnishers and Polishers Union had just been seated), and added that the bookbinders were likely soon to have a union. On 22 November the ASE joined, and on 13 December at a summoned meeting, the last of the year, the committee reported that the upholsterers and the cabinet-makers were likely to establish a union. (The Cabinet-Makers Union of May had evidently fallen by the wayside). By the end of the year, therefore, and after only about 8 months' work, the number of unions in the assembly had grown from the original 4 to 9, and the total number of unions in Toronto had increased to at least 14.

On 1 March 1872 the TTA admitted representatives of the Bricklayers and Masons Union, with voice and vote, though their credentials had not yet arrived. On 5 April the Bookbinders Union was admitted, and the organizing committee reported that it had visited the tinsmiths and found them ready to organize, with over 30 members. On 9 May the *Ontario Workman* reported the formation of the Journeymen Harness and Trunk Makers Union; the next evening the assembly's organizing committee said that the tinsmiths were to meet in the TTA hall and that the cabinet-makers, carvers, and chairmakers would organize the next day. On 17 May the committee reported that the chairmakers, cabinet-makers, and carvers had been organized. The painters reported on 21 May that they wanted a delegation from the assembly to organize a meeting and on 7 June that they had in fact formed a union and were earnestly at work in the short-time movement. The plasterers had also organized. On 21 June the list of members of the assembly's committee for the presentation to Lady Macdonald showed representatives from the three Crispins' lodges, the Molders, the Coopers, the Cigar Makers, the Typos, the Bakers, the Coachmakers, the ASE, the Varnishers and Polishers, the Machinists and Blacksmiths, the Bricklayers and Masons, and the Bookbinders: 12 organizations with 14 locals. On the same date the Painters were asking for an explanation of the benefits of joining the assembly, and the committee was instructed to visit them for this purpose. (A week later, they promised to join.) There was a complaint from the Lathers and Plasterers (who seem not to have been members of the assembly). On 19 July the Stonecutters were admitted, the Painters on 6 September. On 18 October the ASE said it wanted to withdraw. A committee went to see the society, and, on 1 November, complained of the manner in which it had been received. By 10 December, however, the ASE delegates were again present. On 1 November the Plasterers said it was impossible to keep their union together and asked for a bill for the amount they owed. At the next meeting the Crispins reported that Lodge 356 had been absorbed by Lodge 159.

By the end of 1872, therefore, the assembly had 14 organizations with 15 locals, and the number of unions in the city was at least 21. Of these, 7 were American internationals, 1 was British, and 13 appear to have been purely local. All represented only skilled workers.

The Tailors Union joined the TTA on 17 October 1873 in the midst of a strike. On 21 November the organizing committee reported having helped organize the millers. So at the end of 1873, the assembly had 15 member organizations. The total number of unions in Toronto was at least 25, of which 16 were purely local, 1 was British, and 6 were American internationals.

The Plasterers Union either did not disappear, as it had gloomily expected, or else was resuscitated some time before November 1874, for on 6 November the assembly's organizing committee reported that it had visited the organization and thought it would join, which it did at the next meeting, bringing the total of member organizations to 16, the highest figure it ever reached. By the end of 1874 Toronto may have had a total of 27 unions, as the assembly's 6 November meeting was told that the 'Musical Union' and the Expressmen both wanted to use its hall.

The 1875 minutes do not record the formation of any new unions and at the end of the year show only nine member organizations: the Typographical Union, the two Crispins' lodges, the Bricklayers and Masons, Painters, Tailors, Stonecutters, Bakers, Plasterers, and Molders. It is notable that the Coopers and the Cigar Makers, both founding organizations, do not appear, nor do the Machinists and Blacksmiths, the ASE, Varnishers and Polishers, Bookbinders, and Coachmakers. However, the financial secretary's report of 19 January 1876 shows that the Coopers, the Cigar Makers, the Machinists and Blacksmiths, and the ASE were all still in existence.

On 16 February 1876 the Plasterers withdrew, and on 1 March the Molders. The organizing committee visited the Plasterers and the Amalgamated Carpenters in the early spring. It came away with hopes of getting the former to come back, but with a flea in its ear from the Carpenters, whose mass meeting told it its services were not required. It is not till 6 December that we find a note that the committee is to meet the Carpenters, the ASE, the Molders, and the Cigar Makers to get them to join or rejoin.

The Cigar Makers did in fact come back, 21 March 1877; uncredentialled delegates from the ASCJ were seated at the meeting of 20 June; and the Molders and the ASCJ agreed to co-operate in the assembly's picnic. On 20 June, also, uncredentialled delegates from the Friendly Society of Carpenters were seated. The Laborers Union of May 1873 had evidently collapsed, for on 6 June J.S. Williams reported that the labourers had called upon him for information on how to form an association. He had, of course, given the information but he was not sanguine of results, and apparently there were none. On 4 July Lodge 159 of the Crispins suddenly popped up again, with three delegates, but on 5 December, with a total of only seven delegates present, the assembly was so discouraged that there was actually a motion (later withdrawn) to convene a meeting of the unions of the city to consider whether it was desirable to keep the assembly in being.

In 1878 the assembly held the last three meetings recorded in its minute book; but even at the last, 20 February, it had spirit enough to arrange for a joint deputation with the CLU's parliamentary committee to demand from D.J. O'Donoghue, Labour MLA for Ottawa, an explanation of some conduct of his with which both organizations were dissatisfied. At this meeting the expiring assembly had proof that its fame had spread: the corresponding secretary reported that 18 unions in Chicago, which were organizing a trades assembly, had written the Toronto assembly asking for information, which he had duly supplied.

The Typos' minutes suggest that the assembly must have been 'an unconscionable time a-dying.' On 2 March 1878 De Vere Hunt moved that the union withdraw, but the motion was lost. On 5 April 1879 Heffernan gave notice of motion to the same effect. The motion seems never to have been moved, but on 3 May 1879 the union asked J.S. Williams to report on the assembly at the next meeting. On 1 November the union had a letter from the secretary of the assembly asking the union to appoint two more delegates, and stating that the TTA was giving up its hall. The union, appointed two members 'to act in conjunction with delegates to Trades Ass.' At an executive committee meeting on 29 November the delegates stated that there had been no quorum at the meeting. There are scattered references to the assembly thereafter, but on 16 April 1881 the union's committee decided that the time had come 'to form a "Labor League," to protect the interests of Unionism in our city, composed of delegates from all sister Unions; and that we take the initiatory step by corresponding with all sister Unions.' Even after that, however, on 11 June, Williams was making a lengthy report on the trades assembly and receiving a vote of thanks for his work as a delegate to it. At the meeting called 23 July to organize a labour league (which was promptly named the Trades and Labor Council), Carter stated 'that the old Trades Assembly was not quite dead, but that they were willing to turn over to a properly organized body the property and money in their charge.' The council's trustees were empowered to take charge of the property of the assembly on 3 September, but the negotiations with the assembly's trustees were not completed till 6 January 1882.[5]

The Toronto Trades Assembly, during its seven years' effective existence, might almost be said to have taken the world for its parish, and counted nothing human alien to it. It took a leading part in the nine-hour movement. It agitated for better legislation on a variety of subjects. Through lectures and a TTA library, it undertook workers' education. It listed union and non-union shops and organized boycotts. It carried on correspondence with labour organizations in other parts of Canada, in Britain, and in the United States. It took the lead in organizing the Canadian Labor Union. It started a labour paper, organized demonstrations, picnics, concerts, and moonlight excursions. It encouraged co-operatives. It made representations to governments on immigration and on prison labour. It discussed apprenticeship and the incorporation of unions. It published a history of its own activities (unfortunately lost).

THE NINE-HOUR MOVEMENT

As early as 1 October 1871 notice was given in the TTA that at the next meeting the question of the eight-hour day would be discussed. The next mention of the subject is 3 November, when the notice was extended till January. All that emerged from the meeting of 19 January 1872 was a resolution in favour of a 55-hour week. This was hardly surprising. In Britain, from which many of the early Toronto unionists had come and in whose union movement they maintained a lively interest, the nine-hour day was only in process of being won.[6] To attempt to go farther and faster than the world's leading unions must have seemed, to most, completely impracticable.

The individual unions evidently favoured a nine-hour movement, for on 2 February the assembly undertook to call a mass meeting of the workingmen of Toronto to introduce the idea. The radicals moved amendments in favour of a 51-hour week and of shortening hours, but these were defeated. Meanwhile, in Hamilton, James Ryan had already founded a Nine-Hour League, and on 1 March the TTA received a letter from him, asking its co-operation on 'the reform question.' This produced a motion to form labour reform leagues in each ward of the city, 'to be composed of working men to discuss matters pertaining to them as working men and using their united efforts for advancing the interests of Labour.' This, however, did not meet with approval. Instead, the assembly adopted an amendment to have the different trades direct their efforts to get the nine-hour system adopted with the assembly's aid.[7]

A meeting held five days later received a letter from Richard F. Trevellick, president of the National Labor Union of the United States, suggesting that he might address a meeting on labour and its rights and the Nine-Hour Movement, a suggestion which the assembly adopted. The 12 March meeting heard three letters from Ryan asking for money to help him visit business centres 'to canvass the working men in relation to the nine hour movement' and to provide strike pay for the Hamilton workers who might have to strike for the nine-hour day. The assembly said its funds were too low. It went on to discuss a date for launching the nine-hour movement in Toronto. The Typos favoured immediate action, and J.S. Williams, now president of the assembly, proposed that their union be permitted 'to demand it, or enforce it, at such time as they saw fit' with the 'hearty support' of the assembly. It was also proposed that the 'subordinate' (affiliated) unions should be allowed to form nine-hour leagues, no doubt for the purpose of bringing in workers who did not belong to any union, as had been done in Britain.

Actually, Williams was asking the assembly to accept a *fait accompli*. For on 29 February the Typographical Union had notified the printers of King Street that it wanted a new scale of prices and a nine-hour day. On 7 March it made provision for strike pay at $5 per week for married men and $3 for single, to be raised by a levy of $1 per week. The strike committee was given power to stop strike pay to any man 'who conducts himself in any way unbecoming a member ... by intoxication on the streets or elsewhere'; and a committee was appointed to consider setting up a co-operative printing establishment. The master printers flatly rejected most of the demands, including the nine-hour day, and on 13 March their reply was read to a union meeting. The union thereupon set 25 March as a deadline: if its demands were not granted by then, it would strike.

On 15 March the Trevellick meeting took place, with the American leader addressing a large and enthusiastic working-class audience. He claimed that workmen had a natural right to the nine-hour day, for education and improvement. On 19 March the master printers issued their counter-ultimatum: they would pay $10 for a 60-hour week, not 54, as the union demanded. From this they would not budge, and they made arrangements to pool their resources if a strike took place.

On 21 March the assembly heard that the TTU had set 25 March for the nine-hour day to begin. The assembly, 'recognising ... that the avowed object of the employers is to crush the grand principles of unionism,' appealed 'to all tradesmen in the Dominion of Canada to give all moral and financial support that may be required to frustrate the weak and foolish efforts made by the master printers (with the honorable exception of Mr James Beaty, MP of the Leader) to annihilate the existence of Unions.'⁸

Clearly, both employers and workers regarded the Typographical Union and its demands as the spearhead for a general nine-hours campaign; clearly also, the assembly felt the struggle was more than a local one. In effect, the Toronto centre constituted itself a national centre, proclaimed the Toronto printers' strike a national strike, and called for nation-wide support.

Foolish the master printers' efforts ultimately proved. Weak they were not. George Brown, the head of their alliance, responded to the union's challenge with the greatest energy and conviction, and the union mustered all its resources. The assembly voted to send Andrew Scott (ASE) to Oshawa for a mass meeting there on 28 March. It also passed a vote of thanks to Beaty. Beaty, alone of all the newspaper proprietors in the city, conceded the printers' demands. He also wrote editorials in defence of the printers, published long and favourable news accounts of their activities, and printed their advertisements and the angry letters of the strikers and their wives.

On 12 April another special meeting of the assembly decided to organize a workingmen's demonstration on the 15th and was assured that the Coachmakers, Coopers, Molders, Bookbinders, and Brass Founders would take an active part; every member of the assembly was to wear a red ribbon. The assembly accepted offers from the Young Irishmen's, the Queen's Own, and the Christian Brothers' bands to provide music, and for good measure decided to invite the 10th Royal Band. It offered $5 to each band.

The demonstration was impressive. Ten thousand people took part. Soon after noon the crowd began to gather. The procession was headed by the band of the 10th Royals, followed by the British ensign. Then came the Molders, the Bricklayers and Masons, then workingmen of no organization. Next, the band of the Christian

Brothers Academy led the Cigar Makers, the Machinists and Blacksmiths, R. Hay & Co's employees, and the Bakers. Then came the Queen's Own band, followed by the Varnishers and Polishers, the Knights of St Crispin, and the ASE. The Young Irishmen's band, followed by the Union Jack and Stars and Stripes entwined, preceded the Typographical Union, the Bookbinders, and the Trades Assembly. The procession moved from the Trades Assembly Hall, on King Street, via Brock, Queen, King, George, Yonge, and College Streets to Queen's Park. There were thousands of spectators, and 'the windows of the houses were also filled with ladies, who cheered the procession as it passed ... The processionists on passing THE LEADER Office cheered lustily, but on passing THE GLOBE Office a contemptuous silence was observed, with the exception of a few who could not refrain from giving vent to a groan.' There was a heavy snowstorm as the demonstrators neared the park, but this appears to have had no dampening effect. The *Ontario Workman* said there had never been a larger meeting in the history of Toronto; so large, in fact, that it had to be divided into two, with the speakers addressing the crowd from both sides of the platform. On the platform were a Dr Hall, E.K. Dodds, D. Riddell, Beaty, Hewitt of the Coopers, Grant of the Stonecutters, and Scott of the ASE.

The speeches ranged over a considerable field. Shorter hours figured prominently, but the orators also discussed monopolies, the monetary system, apprenticeship, organization, general education, the co-operative movement, and arbitration in industrial disputes (a term then often used to cover negotiation, mediation, and conciliation, as well as arbitration proper). No doubt because Brown was a leading Liberal and Beaty a leading Conservative, there was emphasis on the fact that this was a completely non-partisan workingmen's demonstration.

At its 21 March meeting, the TTA had decided to memorialize the employers for the nine-hour system, and a committee had been set up to draft the document. While this hung fire, the iron trades had formed a nine-hour league and members of the Machinists and Blacksmiths at the Fensom works had been dismissed for agitating the short-time movement. The bookbinders had struck on the same day as the printers, and there was talk of a general strike for the nine-hour day to take place in June. The employers held a mass meeting of their own to discuss this, and on 8 April issued a 'manifesto of defiance.' Tempers were rising, and the master printers decided to act. Warrants were sworn out, and on 15 April 14 leading strikers, members of the TTU's Vigilance Committee, were arrested on charges of conspiracy.

The Trades Assembly had said the master printers were seeking to annihilate unions. Here was proof. For if the strikers were convicted not one union in Ontario, perhaps not one union in Canada, could survive. They would all be totally illegal.

The unions seem to have been thunderstruck. This is astonishing, but apparently everyone had forgotten Brown's 1854 prosecution of the printers or else had assumed that Confederation had changed all that. But the fact was that in Ontario the old blunderbuss of the English common law was still in working order, and Brown and his fellow-employers had only to pull the trigger.

The arrests produced a fresh mass meeting. Four thousand people gathered in the city hall square and listened to speeches by A.W. Lauder, MLA; E.P. Roden, of the *Leader*; and Grant of the Stonecutters. The Chicago *Workingmen's Advocate* of 27 April 1872 says 12 unions took part: the Typos, Molders, Crispins, Cigar Makers, Coopers, Machinists and Blacksmiths, Bricklayers and Masons, the ASE, Bookbinders, Coachmakers, Bakers, and the Varnishers and Polishers. Next day, the court proceedings began, and the magistrate surprised even the employers by brusquely announcing that they need not bother to prove overt acts of intimidation or molestation: they had proved that there was a union, and that it had struck. That was enough. Unions were illegal combinations; nothing could make their actions lawful.

On 19 April the TTA's regular meeting devoted almost its whole attention to the arrests and related matters. Hewitt spoke of the 24 men under indictment and successfully moved that a fresh mass meeting be held on 24 April 'to call forth the repeal of these laws and for the appointing of the Magistrates in the hands of the people.' The corresponding secretary was then instructed to get in touch with all the nine-hour leagues. There were already such leagues in Hamilton, Montreal, Dundas, and St Catharines. At this meeting, there was a letter from the St Catharines league asking the assembly to send a delegate to a mass meeting it was planning to hold, which was agreed to. There was also a letter from the indefatigable Ryan, enclosing a memorial intended for presentation to the workingmen of Great Britain. The assembly also decided to write to 'the Trades authorities in London England for a Copy of the Trades Union Bill and requesting details regarding the Arguments which the unions purposed making thereon.' The meeting took up the question of the assembly's own memorial to the employers. The drafting committee reported that nothing had yet been done and successfully recommended adoption of the same form as those being used by the iron trades. If there had ever been any idea of joint presentation of a single memorial to all the employers, it was dropped: as with the iron trades, each shop and trade was to present the document for itself.

By this time, Sir John A. Macdonald had taken a hand in the proceedings. Brown had hit the unions with the English common law. A chance to hit Brown with a Canadian version of Gladstone's trade union legislation of 1871 was not to be neglected. Macdonald gave notice of his intention to do so, and the TTA lost no time in supporting him. At the 19 April meeting the assembly acknowledged with gratitude the action taken by Macdonald. The secretary was instructed to present the acknowledgment and to ask whether Macdonald intended to adopt the British act.

The case of the 14 strikers was adjourned 18 April, briefly resumed 6 May, and adjourned again till 18 May. The magistrate ruled that the men should stand trial at the next assizes, adding that the law might well be changed by then. It was, and the accused were never tried. Meanwhile they were out on bail.

The 24 April meeting was duly held. The *Ontario Workman* reported 4000 people present. J.S. Williams, Richard Nye, George H. Wiggins (Molders; vice-president of the assembly), Gibson (Molders), Scott, and Matthew Ryan (a Montreal lawyer) all spoke.

James Ryan was now proposing a council to be held in Hamilton, 3 May 'for the purpose of defining the position of the Hamilton League and to ascertain if possible what financial support the Hamilton men would receive if they came out on Strike.' He wrote to invite the TTA to send representatives. A special meeting, 2 May, agreed to send three delegates. There was a good deal of discussion about what they could say and do once they got to the council, especially about financial support.

'Mr McGennott did not see what we could offer as the Assembly had no power to levie an assessment on any Union. Mr Stephens did not see as we could instruct them to act until the matter was laid before each local organization. Mr Doughtie explained the object of this convention, it was expected that the Employers would be present and the position could be better defined. Delegates were to be present from Dundas, Sarnia, Ottawa, Oshawa, Montreal, Ingorsall [sic] & St. Catherines, and suggested that the delegates be instructed to say that this Assembly would use it full influence to obtain financial support, but could not promise more at present ... Mr Hewitt spoke of the Labor convention as being the first ever held in Canada and suggested that there be a grand Convention of Labor held in Toronto after the New Year in conjunction with the Ontario Parliament and further suggested that there would be a comit. appointed to strike bye-laws to be presented at the Toronto Convention Labor Convention.'

The delegates must have made all speed home from Hamilton, for they reported to the TTA on the evening of 3 May. The council had consisted of 12 delegates from Hamilton, 3 from Toronto, and 1 each from Montreal, Brantford, and Dundas. There had been letters and telegrams of support from London, St Catharines, Oshawa, Ingersoll, Guelph, Sarnia, and other places. The council had proceeded to form the Canadian Labor Protective and Mutual Improvement Association, whose object was 'to form similar local organizations throughout the Dominion for the purpose of uniting all classes of workmen for mutual benefit.' Its officers were John Pryke (Hamilton), president; William Moore (Montreal) and D. Buchanan (Brantford), vice-presidents; John Hewitt (Toronto), corresponding secretary; James Ryan (Hamilton), recording secretary; and John Ballantine (Dundas), treasurer. As its official organs, the new association adopted the *Ontario Workman* (Toronto) and the *Northern Journal* (Montreal). It hoped to form leagues in every city ward, each with its own meeting places, library, and reading room, 'and having all the requirements suitable for the intellectual and social improvement of the working class after their hours of labor.'

Meanwhile, the printers had been winning some victories. The *Leader*, of course, had not been struck; neither had the newly founded Conservative *Mail*, nor one other small plant. By 2 May the *Workman* was reporting that the printers had gone back on favourable terms at the *Irish Canadian*; McLeish and Co; the *Canadian Freeman*; Rowsell and Hutchinson; Copp, Clarke and Co; the *Express*; the Church Herald Printing Co; and Bell and Co. At the 17 May assembly meeting, McMillan, the Typos' president, spoke of the victory already gained, but warned that all branches of industry must keep up the agitation for shorter hours, or what had been won would prove fruitless. He said everyone was watching Toronto and strongly supported a motion for a fresh demonstration on 1 June.

This gave rise to a lively discussion. The real question was, what did a 'demonstration' mean? If the employers resisted, would it mean a general strike? Gibson thought the assembly should not vote till the various unions had been consulted. Someone asked how far the memorials for a nine-hour day had been presented to the employers. Levesley (Machinists and Blacksmiths) replied that he thought that in the iron trades they had been fairly thoroughly distributed and in most cases replies had been received. Allen (Crispins) said his union could not be ready for a demonstration before 1 July, which suggests he thought it might well involve a general strike. Carrie and Lucas (Bricklayers) said their union would probably move for nine hours and wanted to know when other trades proposed to do the same 'if a strike was to be resorted to.' Willard (Molders) said his union was not in favour of any demonstration and thought the question should be left to each union. Allen thought none of the unions was in a position to take part in a general strike. Others thought that 'if it was to be unanimous their unions would probably act.' Gibson argued that if the men were firmly united the struggle would be short and decisive. He did not believe the employers' association amounted to much and felt there would be little to fear from that quarter. Not surprisingly, an amendment to lay the whole thing over till the next meeting carried. The assembly did, however, decide to send a delegate to a mass meeting of the Guelph nine-hour league on 28 May.

POLITICAL ACTIVITIES

On 7 May Macdonald introduced his Trade Unions Bill and his Criminal Law Amendment Bill into Parliament. There had already been mutterings in the *Ontario Workman* that if they merely followed Gladstone's acts they would not be enough. The TTA lost no time in appointing a committee to study the two bills. On 21 May this committee reported that it favoured striking out a section of the Criminal Law Amendment Bill which prevented individual members of trade unions from being forced to pay assessments or dues. However, given the lack of time, it felt that 'it would be well [to] accept ... the Bill as it now stands.' Most of the assembly members present agreed that the bill was deficient but also that it should nevertheless be passed. In the end they decided to 'take no steps of recognition at the present but allow the bill to pass.'

Macdonald's two bills went through without amendment and with very little debate and received royal assent 14 June. Meanwhile, the printers' strike had been officially ended. On 1 June the Typographical Union voted by more than two to one to reopen the closed offices and stop strike levies. Even in the plants where they had not won an outright victory, the men had gained wage increases for day printers and a shorter day on Saturdays. (The 14 arrested men were still out on bail, and the warrants against the 10 others had not been executed; in November, the charges were dropped.)[9]

The demonstration contemplated for 1 June had not come off, and with the end of the printers' and bookbinders' strikes, it looked as if a good deal of the steam had gone out of the nine-hour movement. Some members of the TTA certainly thought so, for at the 21 June meeting, Hewitt moved 'that this assembly recommend that all organizations cease any active measures for the present in the short time movement to enable the various unions to organize more efficiently.' The motion was defeated. None the less, the movement in Toronto had, for the time being, stopped moving. But its political repercussions were only beginning. Five days after Macdonald's bills had become law, Hewitt, now corresponding secretary of the TTA, wrote the prime minister that the unions would like to make a presentation to Lady Macdonald 'as a slight token of our appreciation of your timely efforts in the interests of the operatives of this Dominion.' Macdonald agreed with alacrity, and the presentation duly took place with great éclat; producing, incidentally, an internal rumpus whose echoes were still reverberating in March 1873.

Meanwhile, the dominion general election of 1872 had taken place, and a considerable number of prominent members of the TTA had plunged into it on the Conservative side. Hewitt and Scott spoke at a workingmen's meeting in Hamilton which endorsed the Conservative candidates, Chisholm and Henry Buckingham Witton, the latter himself a workingman. In Toronto, Wilkes, a Liberal candidate, was rash enough to call a workingmen's meeting, which promptly elected as chairman John McCormack, TTA president, and, after listening to speeches by Scott and Williams, pronounced in favour of Shanly, the Conservative candidate. Later, in Hamilton, Hewitt spoke from the same platform as Sir John himself, and Williams again supported the government. Witton was elected, and the *Ontario Workman* proudly proclaimed him the first workingman ever elected to a Canadian Parliament.[10]

The TTA does not seem to have shared this opinion, for on 6 February 1874 it congratulated the Ottawa Trades Council on being 'the pioneers in establishing the [right] of labor to direct representation in this Province by bringing out Mr Daniel O'Donohue our fellow trades unionist and placing him on the floor of the legislature of this Province were we hope he will be ever redy to rase his voice in the interest of labor.'

None the less, the assembly showed no desire to follow the Ottawa example. For the rest of its existence it stuck to less spectacular forms of political activity. It had earlier asked its member unions to present to it a list of members entitled to vote in parliamentary and municipal elections, but only one did. The assembly had other and more important political fish to fry. It wanted provincial legislation on mechanics' liens and on employer-employee relations, and it wanted the dominion Parliament to repeal the Criminal Law Amendment Act of 1872.

This act had never been acceptable to the unions, and even before Macdonald left office they had tried to get it repealed. On 21 March 1873 the TTA authorized a petition for repeal and urged other organizations to do the same. On 10 April a special meeting discussed a reply from the Ottawa Trades Council which said that it had itself appointed a committee to draft and circulate a petition and was ready to co-operate. The assembly then proceeded to appoint a committee to draft a petition. On 16 May there was word from the Oshawa Coopers' Union that it had sent petitions to be presented by Mr Witton, MP, and a letter from the Ottawa Trades Council giving a detailed account of an interview between its committee and the prime minister. The assembly then set up a parliamentary committee to 'have under their charge all matters relating to legislation on Trades Union Bill, etc.'

Apparently the unions got nowhere with Macdonald, but they lost no time in going after the new government of Alexander Mackenzie. On 6 March 1874 the assembly wrote the Ottawa Trades Council that nothing less than total repeal of the offending act would be satisfactory. On 31 March the corresponding secretary was instructed to write the various unions and ask them to pass repeal resolutions. On 17 April a delegate called attention to the fact that Mackenzie, in answer to a question by Aemilius Irving, MP (who had replaced Witton), had told the House that the government would not act until the British commission on this matter had reported. This, of course, would not do at all, and the assembly immediately embarked on a prolonged series of efforts to get action. It wrote MPs, notably Thomas Moss and Aemilius Irving, the latter of whom introduced an amending bill of his own. This in its turn produced a government amending bill, which was passed 8 April 1875.

The new act, however, satisfied neither Irving, who wanted more considerable changes, nor the TTA, which wanted straight repeal of the 1872 act. During the parliamentary recess Irving arranged to meet the assembly to discuss his own bill, and the assembly appointed a committee 'to Carefully Look over the Original Criminal Law Amendment Act & Mr Irwins Amendt to post themselves to Discuss the Matter with Irwin.' The committee reported that it could not see any difference and it wanted to urge Irving to press for the total repeal of the act. Irving, after meeting with the TTA, agreed to support total repeal.

A by-election in West Toronto gave the TTA a chance to redouble its efforts. On 20 October 1875 it appointed a committee to attend public meetings and question the candidates on the laws affecting trade unions. On 3 November Mr Oakley (Stonecutters), one of the committee, reported that he had attended one meeting, where the Liberal candidate, Mr Turner, had promised to support repeal. The corresponding secretary was instructed to write Edward Blake, the minister of justice, asking him to state his views at a meeting he was to address the next evening. He did, and must have indicated his intention to introduce an amending bill, for on 1 March 1876 Williams read the bill introduced by Blake, and after considerable discussion the TTA approved it, adding its thanks to Blake for the prompt action he had taken.

A week later, the TTA held a special meeting to make arrangements for a mass meeting on Blake's bill. A committee was formed to frame resolutions on the bill. It produced three: 'That this meeting approve of the Bill relating to violence, threats, and molestation, introduced by Mr. Blake, and, that the best thanks of this meeting are due to Mr. Blake for the prompt action he has taken ... Whereas, a Bill is before the Dominion Parliament to so amend the Bill ... at its second reading there were certain obnoxious suggestions made which would totally nullify the objects of the said Bill, be it therefore resolved that this meeting views with alarm the said suggestions, and would respectfully urge upon the Government to pass the Bill as introduced. That the thanks of this meeting are due to Mr. Blake, and that copies of these resolutions be transmitted to him.'

The resolutions were passed, and on 15 March Williams reported that he had sent copies to Blake, Irving, O'Donoghue, and William Magness, of St Catharines, grand scribe of the Knights of St. Crispin and president of the Canadian Labor Union. Blake had assured Williams that every consideration would be given the subject, and the bill had passed.[11]

The TTA next turned its attention to the Breach of Contract Bill. On 7 March 1877 Williams read a letter from Blake in which he promised to have the bill further amended. On 21 March another letter from Blake produced a resolution that the Breach of Contract Bill, ... will not be generally satisfactory until railway and other companies are liable to prosecution for breach of contract, when such breach will have the tendency of stopping trains, the supply of gas, &c. &c, so as to place them upon the same footing as employees in regard to breaches of contract.' On 17 April Williams read the bill to the assembly, which then passed a resolution that, 'while regretting that the Minister of Justice could not see his way clear to place railway and municipal companies in the same position as the workmen or other person committing breaches of contract, [this assembly] wishes to express its thanks to the Minister ... and the members ... who assisted in carrying the bill ... such bill ... being a great boon to the working classes of Canada, as it tends to place employer and employee on a footing of equality before the law in reference to such breaches.'

The TTA seems to have begun its activities in provincial affairs on 17 January 1873, when it instructed the corresponding secretary to write Adam Crooks, provincial treasurer, for copies of the government's bills 'on the subject of a Lien Law and "to adjust disputes between Masters and workmen."' It also set up a committee which made elaborate arrangements for a mass meeting to discuss the lien law, the Master and Servants' Act, convict labour, the ballot and extension of the franchise, and amendments to the Municipal Assessment Act. To this meeting, the Ottawa Trades Council appointed two delegates, Canada Labor Unity (Hamilton) and the Hamilton Molders one each. Crooks' lien bill was not satisfactory, and on 20 November 1874 the assembly considered a private member's bill on the same subject, introduced by O'Donoghue. The committee appointed to deal with the Criminal Law Amendment Act was entrusted with the task of watching the progress of this bill also, and on 4 December it was empowered to petition the legislature in favour of O'Donoghue's bill. The bill passed.[12]

On 20 October 1875 Mr Oakley drew the TTA's attention to the case of a Hamilton glassblower who had suffered under the Master and Servants Act and suggested that the assembly should make some effort to have the act amended. The president replied that the Canadian Labor Union had the matter in hand and would no doubt attend to it.

On 17 November the assembly appointed a parliamentary committee. On 1 December it reported that it had met with O'Donoghue and that he had agreed to express the assembly's views in the House on the immigration policy of the government.

In 1877 James Bethune, MLA, introduced a cumulative voting bill, to give property owners extra votes in municipal elections: the larger the assessment, the greater the number of votes. This naturally stirred the assembly's anger, and on 17 January it appointed a committee to act with a committee of the national central body, the Canadian Labor Union, to oppose the bill. A joint mass meeting 'proved a decided success.' The bill was withdrawn. In 1878 Bethune tried again; the TTA and the CLU held another mass meeting, and the bill was again withdrawn.

On 20 February 1877 Williams read a letter from O'Donoghue on the Labour Lien Act. The letter was evidently unsatisfactory, for the TTA's last recorded act, apart from authorizing payment of the rent, was to provide for a deputation, with the CLU parliamentary committee, 'to see Mr. O'Donoghue, and ask an explanation and then wait on the Government in regard to the Lien Act. Also, Secty to inform Mr O'Donoghue that the com shall wait on him friday night.'

The TTA seems to have intervened in municipal politics only twice. On 16 June 1875 it received a committee of citizens who wanted it to appoint a representative to attend a mass meeting 'with relation to Building up the Queens park also showing plan of the Intended Building Lots.' The assembly thanked the deputation and appointed a committee to attend the meeting. In the second case, the TTA's action produced an internal rumpus.

On 17 November 1875, the TTA instructed the corresponding secretary to write supporting the city council's motion to exempt no property from taxation. On 1 December Nolan (Molders) asked for information about this letter and proceeded to condemn the assembly's action on the ground that it 'would interfere with their relations to Trades Unions.' A warm discussion followed, and Carter moved, seconded by Strachan (Crispins), that the assembly's action be referred to the various unions for their consideration, but the motion was lost. On 15 December he moved it again; this time it carried.

By 5 January 1876 Strachan had become president of the assembly and Carter recording secretary, and things began to hum. Strachan reported that his union thought the assembly's letter ought to have been submitted to the individual unions before action was taken. Stevenson (Molders) said his union had condemned the assembly's action. Hunt (Painters) read a resolution from his union saying the action had violated the assembly's constitution. However, McCormack (Bricklayers) said his union endorsed the assembly's action.

On 19 January Jury (Tailors) reported that his union thought it would be better not to discuss the subject, but Nolan said that unless the assembly's letter was retracted, the Molders would withdraw their delegates. Williams reported that the Typos endorsed the assembly's action. Carter moved that that action be declared unconstitutional. The constitution said the TTA was to examine and discuss 'such laws as may be considered contraventions of the rights of workingmen, & present them before the various organizations with a view of devising ways and means to abolish or amend them. Mr Carter thought that the Trades Assembly would have plenty to do to legislate for unions & union men without legislating for the outside public. He contended that the question was one they had no right to deal with, he thought that if the Constitutional aspect of the question had been put before the unions, very different reports would have been sent back.' Hunt seconded the motion. Williams disagreed and moved an amendment, seconded by Jury, but it was ruled out of order. Jury moved another amendment, which met the same fate. After a good deal of further argument, Carter's motion was lost.

On 16 February Carter resigned his office as financial secretary (to which he had been transferred on 19 January) because of the taxation question, and his resignation was accepted. On 1 March the Molders withdrew, as they had threatened to do. But on 1 July Carter was re-elected financial secretary; the row had apparently fizzled out.

OTHER ACTIVITIES

The TTA's efforts at workers' education began very early indeed. In 1871 it sponsored two lectures by presidents of international unions: Martin A. Foran, of the Coopers, and John Fehrenbatch, of the Machinists and Blacksmiths. In December 1874 it organized one by Goldwin Smith which produced a deficit. In 1875 a Mr Galbraith tried unsuccessfully to interest it in a disquisition to financial reform. In 1876 it tried to get J.W. Bengough, the cartoonist, to lecture, but he came too dear.

The first effective mention of a library seems to be on 16 February 1876, when MacMillan reported that 'Messrs Belford Bros. had made a present of some 15 books to the Trades Assembly Library.' The corresponding secretary was instructed to thank the Belford brothers and a committee was appointed to procure a bookshelf. It turned out this would cost about $20. The mere mention of such a sum produced a motion 'that each delegate ... bring the matter of a library before their respective unions, and ask for a grant to enable this Assembly to erect a book-shelf.' This carried. At the next meeting, the Typos responded with $5 and the Painters with $2; on 3 May the Stonecutters added $2; and on 20 June the Bricklayers and the Crispins put in $5 each. There must have been some further contributions, for on 20 September the library committee reported receipts of $22 and expenditures of $20.50.

The books, apparently about 30-odd, were a varied collection. They included: *Distinguished Men, Christian Miscellany, Canadian Independence, Condensed Novels*, four volumes of the dominion *Hansard, Nicholas Nickleby, Protection of Home Industry, Vicar of Lansdowne, Richelieu*, and *The Last of the Barons*.

The TTA ordered the library to be open during the day for the use of unemployed members of unions. The bookshelf and at least some of the contents seem to have survived the assembly, and been turned over to its successor, the Toronto Trades and Labor Council, in 1881.

The listing of union and non-union shops also began early, but petered out within a few months. On 2 June 1871, Crispins' Lodge 159 submitted a list of wholesale boot and shoe manufacturers with the union shop. It promised a list of retail shops at the next meeting. The Molders reported: '*Union Shops* – Armstrong and McKillop. *Non Union Shops* – Gurney's and Beard's.' Other organizations gave oral reports, and the business was then laid over till the next meeting. At that meeting the Bakers, Cigar Makers, and Iron Molders all presented written repors, whose terms are not recorded, and several other members gave oral reports.

On 15 September Wiggins (Molders) asked whether anything had been done with regard to advertising the union and non-union shops of the city. After considerable discussion the matter was laid over till November, a committee being appointed to find out how the various unions felt. The matter came up on 1 October, when the Blacksmiths said they were not in favour of publishing lists, but would abide by any decision of the assembly. The Molders favoured publication. The Coopers 'thought it would not be necessary for them to move in the matter, as they had no shop to report.' This was discouraging, and the assembly seems then to have dropped the idea.

The TTA's activity in industrial disputes took varied forms. One of the most persistent was its effort to act as an arbitrator between unions and employers. On 4 August 1871 Wiggins moved to set up a committee to settle disputes in struck shops, but an amendment to consult the individual unions carried. On 15 September Hewitt resurrected Wiggins's motion, but after considerable discussion, the matter was allowed to drop. At the next meeting, however, Dean said the matter had been brought up before his union, and it favoured setting up such a committee and having it try 'to settle existing difficulties, but a report must be given to the Unions concerned before final action.' Beebe thought the existing difficulties 'were of such a delicate character, that it would be better perhaps that the Assembly should not interfere in this case.' After considerable discussion, he moved that the president appoint a committee of three to consult with the employers who were 'at variance' with their employees, after it had consulted with the executives of the unions concerned. Dance, the president, left the chair and spoke in favour of the assembly trying to arbitrate 'in the matter concerned,' and, after further discussion, the motion carried.

On 20 October Williams reported that the committee had met with Childs & Hamilton; Damer, King and Co, and E. & C. Gurney. It had had a cordial reception. On 3 November the same committee reported having visited the Crispins and having explained to them 'the result of interviews with various firms, and obtained from them a bill of grievances with certain propositions, which they were to submit to the Messrs Damer, King & Co.' At the same meeting, two delegates of the Machinists and Blacksmiths Union 'made explanations as to difficulty that had occurred in connection with their Union, at the works of Messrs Dickey, Niel, & Co.' After some debate, Hewitt successfully moved that a committee be appointed to confer with the company. On 22 November the committee reported that 'under the circumstances of nearly all the men having gone to work, it was not deemed advisable to see the firm at that time.'

By 19 January 1872 the Coach Makers were reporting a grievance in one of their shops. They were willing to have the assembly arbitrate. The president then appointed a committee to confer with the employers by the end of the month, if the trouble had not been settled sooner.

On 12 March Rose (ASE) told the assembly that a united meeting of the ASE and the Machinists and Blacksmiths had resolved that Mr Fensom, who had discharged a union man (allegedly for agitating the short-time movement), must reinstate him at once or the unions would close the shop. The meeting had also decided to ask the assembly to appoint a committee to meet Fensom and try to settle the matter amicably. The effort failed.

On 20 December 1872 the assembly merely records the Cigar Makers' strike and its sympathy with the strikers. By 17 October 1873, however, it had apparently decided to have another go. The Tailors were on strike, and it wrote to the merchant tailors tendering its good offices. The employers indicated they had no wish to compromise, and the assembly decided to appoint a committee to act with the Tailors' Union to get up Saturday night entertainments to raise money for the strikers; and to give the Tailors free use of the assembly's hall for a mass meeting, to be attended by a delegation from the assembly. On 7 November, however, Jury (Tailors) reported not only that the position of both parties was unaltered, but also that the proposed Saturday night entertainments had not been received favourably by the Tailors.

S. Stephenson (Molders), financial secretary, reported on a Molders' strike on 20 January 1875. The assembly not only passed a motion of sympathy, but also resolved to call a mass meeting if the Molders approved. On 3 February Nolan reported that the strike remained unsettled and 'Mr McMillian formed a com to cooperate with the Moulders Com Messers Carter and A. McCormick.' But the approval sought was not forthcoming: 'the Moulders held out hopes of regaining the Shops now locked out and wished to be careful not to widen the Breach that now existed.'

On 7 April 1875 it was the Bricklayers' turn. The master bricklayers had passed a resolution showing they intended cutting wages, and the union proposed to hold a mass meeting. The assembly appointed a deputation of three. Two weeks later it received the news that a satisfactory arrangement had been reached.

In May the Stonecutters were having trouble with their employers, and in June the dispute was still on. In the minutes of 16 June the matter occupies considerable space. The TTA recorded 'Its strong Disapprobation at the recent Decision of the police Magistrate as being in our opinion Both unlawful and unjust and at the same time to accord to the convicted stone cutters our sincere sympathy in this their Hour of Trial and pledges Itself to use its Legitimate Efforts to obtain their release from prison & the punishment of the man who Has so unjustly incarcerated them.' Copies of the resolution were sent to the press. The Stonecutters were allowed the use of the assembly's hall for a mass meeting under the assembly's auspices, and a committee of four was appointed to attend. On 7 July the Stonecutters reported the end of their trouble. Their legal expenses had amounted to $450, towards which they had received $147 from other unions.

By 6 June 1877 the Bricklayers were involved in another dispute and the TTA was voting sympathy and assistance. On 20 June it was told that the Bricklayers Union probably 'would not oppose the Assembly should it think proper to bring about a meeting between the disputants.' After a good deal of discussion, the assembly decided to appoint a committee to try to bring about an amicable settlement. This committee was empowered to call a public meeting to give the parties a chance to explain their positions. On 4 July, however, the strike was still on.

The TTA seems to have made at least one attempt to get together rival unions – the Bakers and the Confectioners – on 19 January 1872. A standing committee reported that it had 'conferred with Confectioners, but as there was some difference with Bakers nothing definite were derived at, but expected to hear from them shortly.'

Relations with unions in other countries took up a surprising amount of time. The first American organization to get in touch with the TTA was the Cincinatti Trades Assembly, which sent a letter, with a copy of its by-laws and a circular it had issued agitating the formation of a State Trades Assembly. This was received 3 November 1871. If it was intended as an invitation to Toronto to join up, it failed, for the communication was simply placed on file. Cincinnati wrote again, with similar results, in December and on 2 February and 19 April 1872.

Meanwhile, on 22 November 1871 the TTA had received the first of a series of letters from W.J. Jessup, president of the New York Trades Assembly, and later secretary of the New York State Workingmen's Assembly. On 17 January 1873 he informed the TTA that the New York assembly would be meeting that month and requested correspondence if Toronto so desired. A committee was appointed to draft a reply. By 10 April the indefatigable Jessup had written again, and this letter also had been placed on file.

On 7 June 1872 Winnett (Cigar Makers) had made a speech on the need for 'a more thorough and compact organization between local unions in the matter of support in time of need' and advocated 'taxation' for this purpose ('taxation' meaning assessments by the assembly). 'This brought up considerable discussion on the relation the sub unions owed to their International depts.' Gibson (Molders) disagreed with Winnett, and was supported by Tutton (Machinists and Blacksmiths); they said the assembly had no authority to tax unions for this purpose. Hewitt intimated that the problem would be solved if more unions joined the assembly. Scott supported Winnett 'and urged such organization irrespective of International Dept.'

On 15 November 1872 there was a letter from Cleveland concerning the National Labor Union (NLU), and the assembly appointed a committee to draft a series of resolutions in sympathy with the NLU's convention. On 20 December there was a letter from 'Mr Saffin, in connection with the National Labor Congress.' There seems to have been no suggestion that the Toronto assembly should be represented.

On 21 February 1873 the corresponding secretary was instructed to write Jessup regarding the refusal of the International Union of Bricklayers to recognize the branch in Toronto. (This was the branch provisionally chartered on 5 April 1872.) As there was certainly a Bricklayers Union in the assembly throughout 1874 and 1875, and no international local was chartered till 1876, we may surmise that the letter to Jessup produced no effect.

Relations with the British labour movement seem to have begun on 15 November 1872, when 'Mr Whelmsly Representative of the labor interest, of England' addressed the assembly at some length on the condition of the working classes of England. Whelmsly was the first of a number of British union VIPs. The next was the celebrated Joseph Arch, of the National Agricultural Labourers Union. On 19 September 1873 McMillan (Typos) asked if the corresponding secretary had received any communication about Arch. The answer was no. McMillan said he thought someone 'was a little remiss in not finding out about the whereabouts of J. Arch.' This soft impeachment produced, at the next meeting, the appointment of a committee 'to find the means of entertaining Mr Arch.' On 7 November Hewitt handed in a 'partial report of the committee ... for a Banquet in Honor of Mr Joseph Arch.' On 6 November 1874 Williams presented a bill for 'the address to J. Arch,' and 'the Treasurer was requested to foot the bill.'

Meanwhile, on 18 September 1874 the TTA had had a letter from Henry Taylor, secretary of the Agricultural Labourers. On 29 September Williams reported that Taylor had gone to Muskoka and had not returned; 'Mr Taylor seemed anxious to meet prominent Unionists to ascertain personally the feeling of Unions in matters interesting to him' (chiefly immigration). On 2 October there was a letter from Taylor acknowledging an invitation to meet the assembly. Taylor, however, proved rather elusive, and the TTA fought shy of getting involved in any public meeting held for Taylor by a Mr Laidlaw, though it was willing to send a deputation. Finally, on 4 December, Taylor turned up and addressed the assembly.

On 5 May 1875, the assembly ordered the secretary to get 50 copies of the British Criminal Law Amendment Act from George Potter, of the London, England, *Bee-Hive*, which, from 1861 to 1872, was the chief English working-class newspaper. On 19 May 1875 the assembly provided Carter with credentials for a trip to England, and on 18 August he gave an account of his visit, together with an account of the position of trade unions, 'the state of the labor question, and recent legislation relating thereto. He also kindly presented members with copies of the "Beehive" ... containing copies of bills affecting trades unions, carried through the British Parliament.'

On 15 September Williams, reporting for the special committee on immigration, recommended that a statement of the condition of trade in Canada be sent to labour papers in England. A discussion concerning the wage rates in different trades throughout Canada followed, and a letter containing the resulting statement was sent. A letter acknowledging receipt of the statement arrived on 20 October from George Howell, secretary of the parliamentary committee of the Trades Union Congress. The next month a letter in reply arrived from Henry Broadhurst, another secretary of the TUC's parliamentary committee. The letter was evidently perfunctory, and the assembly, stung to the quick, assumed a pose of outraged dignity. Carter 'thought the Assembly had been treated disrespectfully by the Labor Congress Union Committee of England in the matter of the correspondence ... inasmuch as our communication was not so much as read in the congress. Mr Williams said the "Bee-Hive" in its report of the doings of the Congress had not one word in reference to the matter contained in our circular. Moved & Seconded that the corresponding Secretary drauft a letter to be sent to the "Bee-Hive" in reference to this matter. Carried.'

There was another letter from Broadhurst on 15 December. This also must have been disrespectful, for Carter promptly moved that the corresponding secretary write to the TUC concerning the treatment the TTA's circular had received, and also that he send copies of the circular to the *Despatch, Lloyd's Newspaper*, and *Reynold's Newspaper* (all English papers). Nevertheless, the corresponding secretary's annual report took pains to emphasize that though 'the correspondence did not receive the courtesy and attention that might have been expected; yet it is hoped that the correspondence will not stop here, but that future communications between the representative bodies of workingmen in the two countries will be more frequent and fraternal. The letters that were sent to several of the English papers for publication will ... have their due weight and influence with English workingmen in informing them on the prospects of emigration to our Dominion.' Perhaps Broadhurst learned his lesson, for on 17 May 1876 the assembly received from him a copy of the 1875 report of the TUC and a copy of the '"Compensation to Workmen" Bill, and the "Reform of the Jury Laws,"' and there are no huffy comments.

The assembly's pretensions to some sort of 'international personality' had perhaps had their origin long before this. On 1 December 1871, after receiving a letter from the IWA, the assembly instructed its secretary to continue the correspondence. However, this brief flurry occurred before there was a central labour organization in Canada, and it apparently was not repeated.

The creation of a central labour organization, to do for Canada what the TTA did for Toronto, had been proposed as early as May 1872, but it was not until the following May that a motion, moved by Hewitt and seconded by Williams, was made to organize a labour congress. Correspondence evidently began at once, for on 6 June there were replies from the London Coopers' Union, the provincial grand lodge of the KOSC, and from 'Mr Pryke, CLU Hamilton.' There were favourable replies as well on 15 August from locals 16 and 9 of the Coopers, and the Hamilton Typos. The TTA then decided, 22 August, to circularize various unions to encourage them to attend the proposed congress. It also elected three delegates to the congress and provided them with $2 per day in expenses.

By 5 September favourable letters had come in from CIU locals 10 and 17; KOSC lodges in Barrie, Orillia, and Toronto (No 315); the Toronto and Jacques Cartier (Montreal) typographical unions; the Toronto Painters Union; and the ASE. On 19 September no less than 15 letters came in, 2 from individuals (Daniel O'Donoghue and Donald Robertson, of Ottawa) and 13 from unions: CIU locals 8 (Seaforth), 14 (Thorold), and 17 (Bowmanville); KOSC Lodge 159; Local 1 of the Machinists and Blacksmiths; the Hamilton local of the ASE; the Hamilton Tailors Protective Society; the Coburg Iron Molders; the Toronto Tailors; the Toronto Longshoremen's Union; and the Toronto local of the Amalgamated Carpenters. The TTA decided that the Toronto delegates should form a reception committee to meet those arriving from outside the city, and was informed that Hewitt had permission to take them all to the Normal School's museum. The congress began on 23 September.

On 3 July 1874 the TTA got a circular from the Canadian Labor Union about a second convention. On 17 July the assembly decided to send a delegate. Williams was elected by acclamation and voted $25 expenses. Carter successfully moved that the unions not sending delegates be asked to contribute to defray part of this sum. Jury observed that the CLU executive had not listed the questions to be discussed, and successfully moved that 'our delegate be instructed to move such a resolution as will rectify this omission in the future.' The Assembly also opposed having to pay CLU dues, resolving that trades assemblies were not subject to the per capita tax of three cents stipulated by the CLU constitution. On 22 August, following the CLU convention, Williams delivered his report of the proceedings to the assembly.

On 2 June 1875 the TTA resolved that Hunt and Jury be deputed to visit the local unions to urge them to send delegates to the forthcoming CLU convention. The assembly continued to press the Toronto unions and on 21 July appointed Williams as its own delegate. Domestic affairs prevented him from attending the convention, which was being held in St Catharines, but he took upon himself the responsibility of delegating his authority to one Vennell, of Lodge 1 of the KOSC. On 1 September Vennell submitted a report of 19 closely written foolscap pages to the assembly, but it was not read until 6 October.

On 17 May 1876 the TTA resolved to form with the executive of the CLU a committee, to be chaired by the Assembly's president, to make arrangements for the forthcoming CLU convention. The assembly elected three delegates on 19 July, and on 16 August Carter, one of the delegates, made his report.

On 20 June 1877 Williams read a circular from the CLU which reported that its next meeting would be in Toronto. The assembly appointed three delegates on 18

July, and on 19 September Williams, one of the delegates, was voted $2.50 a day in expenses. This was the last convention of the CLU, and the TTA itself virtually came to an end five months later.

The TTA's efforts to start a labour paper, and keep it going, seem to have begun on 1 March 1872, when Hewitt presented a resolution for the purpose and intent of publishing a Co-operative weekly Journal in the interests and under the control of the working men of Toronto,' through a joint-stock company. It was to be a genuine co-operative, the Toronto Co-operative Printing Association. The resolution passed unanimously, after several strong speeches in its favour. Until the new paper could get going the assembly adopted the Hamilton *Standard* as the organ of the working men of Toronto, and instructed the corresponding secretary to write the editor about opening a Toronto agency. On 6 March the editor replied, and the assembly appointed a committee of five to consider the best means of establishing an agency. But on 18 April the first number of the *Ontario Workman* made its appearance.

Like most labour papers, it was not long in getting into difficulties. On 5 September it announced a change of management. The co-operative's shareholders placed it in the hands of Williams, its superintendent, and Sleeth and McMillan, two practical printers. They bailed themselves out of their financial difficulties by getting a loan, on chattel mortgage, from Sir John A. Macdonald. Needless to say, they did not reveal this at the time, and the loan was without strings. Macdonald said he expected to give them enough government patronage to work off the amount ($500), but he didn't. When the mortgage came due he renewed it, remarking to his agent that he did not suppose he would ever get the money, 'but I may as well keep it over them as security for good behaviour.' However, he seems not to have put any pressure on Williams (who was a Conservative anyway), and the paper seems to have preserved a reasonable degree of independence. It ceased publication in February 1875.

On 7 April 1875 the TTA received a letter from the CLU referring to a new labour paper, but laid the matter over for two weeks. In fact, it did not come up again till 5 May, when the assembly decided to issue a circular urging the republication of the *Ontario Workman*. On 18 August it appointed a special committee to visit 'the various trades unions urging the claims of that journal for their support.' The committee pegged away, and on 15 September it handed in a report, with subscription sheets signed by members of various unions. On 6 October it reported further that every union had been visited with the exception of KOSC Lodge 6. By 21 February 1877 the *Workman* was presenting books to the assembly's library. On 17 October Williams presented 'the Record and Workman Newspaper and made some explanatory remarks also presenting copies to the members present,' and Carter successfully moved that the assembly's card ... 'be inserted in the Social and Workman for twelve mths.'[13]

The discussion and arrangement of picnics, excursions, concerts, and other forms of entertainment took up a great deal of the TTA's time, for they were not only a pleasure but a matter of business: they brought in money, or at least the assembly always hoped they would.

The picnic of 14 August 1871 involved elaborate preparations stretching over almost two months. There were two special trains to take people to the picnic and a band. Activities at the picnic included separate races for men, women, boys, and girls; quoits; and weight throwing. An interim report on 15 September shows receipts of $257.45 and expenditures of $241.96. Arrangements for a second picnic for Dominion Day, 1872, ran into snags. Railway fares had gone up 25 per cent, and some grounds owners refused to rent their land to the assembly at any price. This time, the net proceeds were about $50.

The approach of the first CLU convention produced a suggestion for a picnic in the Crystal Palace on the second day of the congress, but there was an immediate amendment to appoint a committee to see if the Horticultural Gardens could be had for a promenade concert, and another to have a concert and hop with a torchlight procession. After seven delegates had spoken, all three motions were lost.

In 1874 the TTA considered both a picnic and a moonlight excursion, but neither came off. In 1876 the picnic pops up again. This time the assembly took to the water, going to Humber by the steamer *Water Town* and including in the festivities a swimming race. As in the other cases, prizes were solicited, presumably from merchants.

The 1876 financial results may have been disappointing, for the 1877 motion for a picnic struck a new note: each union was to get five cents for each ticket sold by its members. This worked: net proceeds were $142.45, after a $35.05 discount to unions.

Concerts and other entertainments also figured prominently among the TTA's activities, again largely as a means of raising money. An 1872 concert produced enough money to pay at least some of the assembly's debt to the Molders and the Crispins for furniture in the hall. In 1873 there was a concert to celebrate the first anniversary of the assembly's founding. In September 1874 it was decided to celebrate the opening of the assembly's new hall with readings, recitations, and singing. Tickets were to be 25 cents. The committee had some trouble getting female singers and a pianist, but the affair came off and seems to have shown a small profit.

A second anniversary concert, in the spring of 1875, netted $10.75. For the anniversary of the hall opening, 27 December 1875, the assembly held a 'concert & Hop with refreshments to consist of Tea, Coffee and unintoxicating drinks.' The celebration of the 1877 anniversary of the assembly's founding took the form of a concert.

The TTA's attempt at running a co-operative newspaper has already been noted. But this was not the sole manifestation of its interest in the co-operative movement. For example, on 15 May 1874 Levesley gave notice that at the next meeting he would 'bring forward the question of a workingmans cooperative building society.' The next April Stevenson (Molders) 'gave notice respecting a limited Co-operative Society.' In October 1877 one Davis, secretary of the Toronto Co-operative Society, made a few remarks before the assembly on the current state of the society. On 19 December the assembly was thanked by the society for the loan of its hall.

As might be expected for a period of growing depression of trade, the question of immigration cropped up several times. As early as 16 May 1873 Scott (ASE) suggested issuing a manifesto on the subject. Then there was the business of the Laidlaw-Taylor meeting late in 1874, and the statement of the condition of trade sent to England in the fall of 1875. On 1 December 1875 O'Donoghue spoke to the assembly 'mostly on the subject of immigration, and said he would do all in his power to stop unnecessary immigration.'

Prison labour got a good deal of attention at first. On 4 October 1872 the TTA appointed a committee to interview the provincial attorney-general on 'the proposed introduction of convict labor into the central Prison.' Levesley saw Crooks, the minister, and at the next meeting the committee reported the results.

Crooks' first line was the familiar one that his government was only carrying out measures started by the previous one, the abandonment of which would entail heavy losses. Second, he had assured the mechanics of Ontario that the employment of convict labor would not conflict with their rights, as prisoners would be employed only as 'laborers, mere hewers of wood, drawers of water.' He gave details of the contract with the Canada Car Co, which was buying the convicts' labour for 7½ years (with option of renewal) at 55 to 65 cents a day.

The TTA was not satisfied with Crooks' arguments, and the committee was instructed to see him again. Levesley reported on the second meeting on 15 November. In his opinion it was time the mechanics of Ontario protested the contract between the Ontario government and the Canada Car Co. After a lively debate the assembly decided to call a mass meeting, but the plan fizzled out.

On 16 January 1878, the assembly's secretary was instructed to draw up resolutions protesting prisoners' employment by the city. The TTA, together with the parliamentary committee of the CLU, was to meet the city council to protest.

Apprenticeship seems to have come up only once, on 3 November 1871, when Clarke (KOSC Lodge 159) and Hewitt successfully moved that the TTA establish a standing committee to act 'in connection with all organizations to examine all apprentices (on application for membership) to ascertain whether they are qualified to enter such Union as a Journeyman.'

The incorporation of unions came up in March 1874, when Williams read the new incorporation act to the assembly in order to provoke discussion on the possibility of unions incorporating under its provisions. A deputation was sent to confer with Oliver Mowat, the provincial premier, to ascertain the government's attitude, and on 31 March Williams delivered its report. Maddeningly, that is all we are told. The minutes have lighter touches which deserve to be recorded. On 10 May 1872, for example, 'Mr Gibson spoke ... about the proper cleansing of the halls,' and the assembly promptly empowered the hall committee 'to procure a sufficient number of spittoons.' On 21 May the committee reported having bought 24; but alas! on 20 January 1875, 'Mr Carter complained of the very dirty Manner in which the Halls were kept by Members of the various unions through Tabacco Spitting.' An entry for 20 January 1875 says: 'Bill Submitted by Mr. Leversley for Gas Fitting and Work done to Hall Amt $32.75 Moved & Sec that the Bill be paid if found Carried.' The 'if found' has an earlier parallel: a resolution, 19 June 1874: 'That the Treasurer pay the rent as soon as he gets it.' The assembly was never very flush, though its expenses were not, by modern standards, high. For example, at this same meeting, it was decided that the hall cleaner should be paid $5 per month. This, or a later, cleaner was not at all satisfied; for on 19 September 1877, 'Mr McMillan made a report as to caretaker striking for higher pay – hold the job for one month longer.'

The problem of absenteeism also existed even in these early days. On 4 October 1872 the TTA resolved that absent officers be fined 25 cents, and that absent members be fined 10 cents. This seems to have had some effect, at least for a while. But the corresponding secretary's 1875 report says sadly: 'The attendance of delegates has been medium, but has certainly not been all that could be desired. During the year 24 meetings have been held. The presiding officer was present at 22 meetings, the VP was absent 15 times, present only 9 times. The Cor. Sec. was present 24 times. The Rec. Sec. was 9 times present, absent, 15 times. The Fin. Sec. was present 19 times, absent 5 times. The Trea. was present 22 times, and absent on 2 occasions. The Sergt. at Arms was present 7 times, absent 17 times.' Only 1 delegate had a perfect record, and only 2 had over 20 attendances; 3 had never turned up at all. 'The full representation, was 30 delegates, whilst the average attendance was about 14 delegates.'

The Ottawa Trades Council was formed 19 December 1872. Our information on it is scanty. The Bricklayers and Masons, the Limestone Cutters, the Sandstone Cutters, the Plasterers, and the Typographical Union were all represented on its executive. The Typos were represented by D.J. O'Donoghue, their newly elected president, who was to figure so long and so prominently in Canadian union history, first in Ottawa, then in Toronto. The council was soon corresponding with the Toronto Trades Assembly. It engaged in various joint activities with the TTA in 1873 and

1874. It had six delegates at the Canadian Labor Union convention in Ottawa in 1874. We get occasional glimpses of it in the Ottawa newspapers: electing new officers, July 1873, February 1874, and January 1876; listening to a speech by John Hewitt in December 1873; sending a deputation to the minister of justice in March 1874 to get his views on the repeal of the Criminal Law Amendment Act; announcing a musical entertainment to raise funds in June 1874. There seems to be no trace of it after 1876, and the official records have apparently disappeared.[14]

Of the St Catharines Trades Assembly all we can say is that it sent a delegate to the 1875 CLU convention, held in St Catharines itself.[15]

6

The first national central organization

The Canadian Labor Union, the first national central body, was, as we have seen, the child of the Toronto Trades Assembly. Its first convention call must have gone out to a considerable mailing list.[1] In 1874 the secretary of the new national body corresponded with upwards of 70 unions and union locals, and there must in fact have been many more, probably at least 125, when the 1873 convention met, 23 September. Only 31 sent delegates.[2]

Those that did were: from Toronto, the ASE (one), the Friendly Carpenters (two), Typos 91 (three), Crispins 159 (three) and 315 (one), Bricklayers and Masons (two), Iron Molders 28 (two), Coopers 3 (one), Machinists and Blacksmiths 1 (one), the Longshoremen (three), the Operative Tailors (two), the Bakers (one), the Painters (one), and the TTA (three); from Hamilton, the ASE (two), Typos 129 (one), Crispins 212 (one), Iron Molders 26 (one), and Machinists and Blacksmiths 2 (one); from Ottawa, one each from Typos 102, the Bricklayers and Masons, the Tailors, the Free Stone Cutters, and the Limestone Cutters; from St Catharines, one each from the Crispins (who sent their grand scribe), Coopers 13, and the Tailors; from London, one each from the ASCJ and Crispins 242; from Bowmanville, one from Coopers 17; from Cobourg, one from Iron Molders 189; from Seaforth, one from Coopers 8; a grand total of 45 delegates. Almost two-thirds were from international unions; four from the British (three ASE, one ASCJ), twenty-two from the American (seven Crispins, five Typos, four Molders, four Coopers – plus one of the TTA delegates – two Machinists and Blacksmiths). From purely local unions there were one Bakers' (Toronto), four Tailors' (two Toronto, one Ottawa, one St Catharines), two Carpenters' (Toronto), three Longshoremen's (Toronto), one Painters' (Toronto) (plus one of the TTA delegates), three Bricklayers' and Masons', one Free Stone Cutters', one Limestone Cutters' (all Ottawa). All the delegates were from Ontario. Montreal Typos 145 (Jacques-Cartier) and Quebec

Typos 160 had wanted to send delegates, but could not, the latter, like the Barrie Crispins, saying that it could not afford the expense.

The 1873 Toronto convention was the largest and most representative the CLU ever had. The basis of representation was one delegate for every 50 or fraction of 50 members. The figures would indicate a membership of over 100 for the Toronto Typos 91, Toronto Crispins 159, and Toronto Longshoremen, and a membership of over 50 for the Toronto Carpenters, Toronto Bricklayers and Masons, Toronto Iron Moulders 28, Toronto Tailors, and Hamilton ASE. It was chaired, pro tem, by J.W. Carter, of both the Toronto Painters and the TTA. John Hewitt, of both the Toronto Coopers and the TTA, was elected secretary, pro tem.

Carter opened the convention 23 September 1873, with a keynote speech: rather grandiose, far-reaching, and ambitious, yet moderate:

You meet today to inaugurate one of the grandest events in connection with the labor movement that has ever taken place in the Dominion of Canada. Its significance may be gathered from the fact that from all centres of industry in the provinces of Ontario and Quebec the working classes have determined to centralize their energies to promote the adoption of those laws and regulations which must be established for the good and protection of the laborer.

You do not meet to create an agitation for supremacy or power, nor to create hostilities between capital and labor; but you do meet for the purpose of disseminating the true principles of unionism; to foster a spirit of common brotherhood throughout the Dominion; to seek the protection of those laws which shall make no distinction of man as man.

I urge upon you the necessity of being wise and moderate in your deliberations and enactments, and let those who are watching your movements at this, the first Canadian Labor Congress, be compelled to admit that we are honest, earnest and prudent workers.

The convention's first act was to set up committees: constitution and rules, ways and means, prison labour, imported and cheap labour, arbitration, hours of labour, printing, organization, legislation and labour bureau. Of the 44 delegates apart from the chairman, 8 were appointed to 2 committees each, 32 to 1 each, and only 4 to none at all.

The committee on the constitution and rules brought in its report next day. The preamble of the constitution set forth that 'the workingmen of the Dominion of Canada, in common with the intelligent producers of the world,' felt the necessity of co-operation to secure 'just compensation for their toil, and such limitation of the hours of labor as may tend to promote their physical and intellectual well-being.' It also declared that most of labour's troubles came from 'want of proper organization.'

The first four articles were adopted with only one amendment. They gave the organization its name. They stated its objects: the passing of beneficial, and the repeal of oppressive, laws; the use of 'all means consistent with honor and integrity ... [to so] correct the abuses under which the working classes are laboring, as to insure to them their just rights and privileges;' promoting union organization. All trade unions and protective labour organizations were to be eligible for membership. Each organization was to be entitled to 1 delegate for the first 100 members of fraction thereof; 2 for 100 to 200 members; 3 for over 200 members. The officers were to be a president, three vice-presidents, a secretary, a treasurer, and a warden, with the three vice-presidents acting as a board of trustees. Carter was elected president; O'Donoghue, first vice-president; William Magness (grand scribe of the KOSC), second vice-president; J.I. Hodgins (Machinists and Blacksmiths, Hamilton), third vice-president; John Hewitt, secretary; and J.C. McMillan, (TTA) treasurer. No warden seems to have been elected.

Revenue was to come from a $5 fee for charters to subordinate unions, per capita dues of twenty cents a year from each such union, and per capita dues of three cents per year from other unions represented at the annual congress. From the beginning the CLU proposed to charter unions, distinguished between these unions and other (affiliated) unions, and set per capita dues at figures which, by the standards of those days, were very high indeed.

Article VI ordered the president, when officially notified of a strike or lockout involving a union that had offered to arbitrate, to circularize all unions for money to sustain the affected workers. This provision is remarkable. First, it displays a high degree of solidarity, startling in a country with so few and such widely scattered unions. Second, it vests great power in the president, once a union has asked for help. Third, it makes the help conditional on the union's having tried to settle the dispute by arbitration. However, in those days arbitration and conciliation were not always clearly distinguished, and local trades assemblies or trades councils often proposed themselves as 'arbitrators'.

Article VII provided that any union composed of at least 13 workingmen 'who are not under expulsion, rejection or suspension in any existing labor organization and have no existing chartered organization in their respective trades or calling' and who acknowledged the jurisdiction of the CLU could get a CLU charter. They did not have to belong to a single trade or calling, though if there were enough belonging to any one trade, the CLU president would have to instruct them to seek a charter from their own trade organization, if there was one. Obviously, the CLU had set its face firmly against dual unionism. It would not charter unions made up of people who had been thrown out of other unions for disloyalty, strikebreaking, or other improper conduct, nor would it issue charters for unions in any trade where there was already an organization in the field. Perhaps the most noteworthy feature of this article, however, is the provision for unions of more than one trade or calling. This may have been borrowed from the mixed local assemblies of the Knights of Labor (KOL) which later enabled that body to organize so many small places in Canada with such spectacular success.[3] At the same time, the CLU provided safeguards against the rivalry between trade organizations and mixed locals which caused so many difficulties during the heyday and decline of the KOL.

Any subordinate (affiliated) union with a grievance was to try by every honourable means to settle the difficulty peacefully. If it failed, it was to report the case at once to the CLU president, who was to take immediate steps to secure the pecuniary aid provided for in the constitution. The subordinate unions were to be under district or county committees (probably another borrowing from the Knights of Labor). Subordinate unions were to be at liberty to set up mutual benefit plans, but all of them had to guarantee each member a respectable funeral ('in case of death,' adds the constitution, cautiously).

Article VIII provided that the constitution could be amended only at a regular annual congress, and only by two-thirds' vote of the members present.

Meanwhile, the convention had been grappling with particular issues. Perhaps because of the experience of the Toronto printers' strike, the first subject tackled was political action. William Joyce (Toronto Typos) moved, seconded by James Levesley (Toronto Machinists and Blacksmiths),

that it is essential to the recognition and establishment of the just and equitable rights of the workingmen of this country that they should have their own representatives in the Dominion Parliament, and with this idea in view, it is the opinion of this Congress that a workingmen's platform should be put before the industrial classes of the country, and that the President do appoint a committee to draw up such a platform.

Joyce said union organization, though essential, was not enough.

'Were the working masses as united as either of the great political parties ... then success would be certain. Lock-outs, strikes, etc., with their concurrent evils, would happily be a thing of the past; for they should send their representatives to the National Parliament there to demand and get justice! ... [Workingmen] have their unions, 'tis true; but they are scattered, weak and disconnected. This Congress was a stride in the right direction. They must drill their army to fight manfully at the great battle-ground – the polls – and teach the enemy that election funds are of no avail against men determined not to sell their birthright for dollars. It had been whispered in his ear: "Look out for anything like Communism or the attempt to make a political machine out of this Congress." Well, he thought this Canada of ours could get along without the Commune as can any other free country where the masses are not goaded into desperation by the despotic acts of their rulers. If they would continue to send men to Parliament whose only objects were the exaltation of their Party and the furtherance of their schemes of self-aggrandizement, the workingmen have only themselves to blame. As for politics he went heart and soul for the workingmen's ticket, knowing neither Reformer nor Conservative, and would vote only for that man who pledges himself to support any measure brought forward for the amelioration of the toiling masses, and would watch that he fulfil his pledge.'

O'Donoghue supported the motion, dwelling 'at some length upon the importance of having a workingmen's platform independent of Party politics. Until this was established the interests of the industrial classes would invariably be neglected. As it was, they often found men willing to make numberless promises to workingmen, in order to secure a seat in Parliament, which were as readily forgotten as soon as their election was made certain.' The resolution was referred to the committee on legislation and seems to have died there.

But if the delegates were disinclined to go in for political action in general, they were by no means backward about demanding particular political actions from both dominion and provincial governments. The committee on imported and cheap labour condemned 'the practice of importing labor into this country, that is to say, making a contract in a foreign country for less wages than are actually paid here; and ... the practice of the Government in paying a premium to persons so engaged' and called on MPs and MLAs to remedy such evils.

This promptly brought out what was to be for many years a perennial division in the labour movement on the subject of immigration. One group thought of the immigrant, especially the assisted immigrant, as a competitor likely to underbid the Canadian worker. The other thought of him as an impoverished, unfortunate, perhaps oppressed, even persecuted, human being who deserved a chance in a new, free, rich, developing country.

The committee's report was squarely on the side of the former. But it was not forthright enough for Hewitt, who moved that it be referred back to add a 'strong condemnation of the system pursued by the Local and Dominion Governments of voting large sums of money for the purpose of bringing out immigrants to this country. In his opinion, the system of immigration was one of legalized robbery. Immigration was legitimate only when not carried on with other people's money. Every person in the country was taxed forty cents to bring labor from the old country to compete with those here.'

Thomas McDuff (Toronto Bricklayers and Masons) thought this 'most selfish. There were many worthy persons in the old country who could not afford to pay their passage out.' A. McCormick took a middle line: 'More of the money voted for immigration purposes went into the pockets of the immigration agents and shippers, and hence the great amount of wrong information given to the workingmen of the old country [this was to be a recurrent theme for many years]. One immigration agent stated in a public speech that railway laborers received in Canada fourteen shillings a day ... Pamphlets were also published in England at the present time quoting prices of wood, and provisions that obtained here ten years ago.'

Hewitt, unchastened, replied that 'every immigrant should work out his own salvation without Government assistance. He objected strongly to paying a tax of forty cents to bring out labor to compete with him.' McDuff moved that the report be adopted unamended. It was.

The committee on prison labour was also concerned with unfair competition. It said it had not had time to go into the question fully, so would present only 'a few of the most glaring evils of this iniquitous ... contract system.' First, the inspector of prisons had 'not taken into consideration the best means of ameliorating the condition of the criminal without conflicting with the best interests of the various branches of industry.' Apparently, he tried simply to make the prisoner self-supporting while in prison, not thinking 'of the great cost of bringing to justice and convicting law-breakers. By this course he has left a wide field for capitalist and speculator to step in and realize a handsome margin. We further think the present system of punishing crime to be entirely wrong, as in a great measure placing a premium on crime, which system unscrupulous men are not slow in taking advantage of for the aggrandizement of their own pockets and to the detriment of the honest laborer.' It attacked the contract between the Ontario government and the Canada Car Co for convict labour. It considered it unjust to give any company power to employ prison labour, since it would enable it to undersell all competitors. The committee recommended 'that the community at large strongly discountenance the contract system'; a surprisingly mild resolution, which seems to have been adopted without discussion.

The committee on legislation and labour bureaux may have felt that the report on prison labour was rather mealy-mouthed, for one of its recommendations (all of which were adopted) was 'that the whole united power and influence of the labor of this country be brought to bear on our lawmakers to bring about the abrogation of the contract system in our Dominion and Provincial prisons.' It also made five other recommendations.

First, it called for the repeal of the Criminal Law Amendment Act.

Second, it demanded that the dominion and local legislatures enact a more stringent apprenticeship law. This reflects the predominantly skilled-worker composition of the congress, and a progressive concern with what would now be called vocational and technical training. It reflects also a cagey desire to make certain that no plea of want of jurisdiction should prevent the enactment of the desired legislation. To be sure, the passage of the Trade Unions Act seemed to indicate that labour matters belonged to the dominion; and Lord Watson had not yet, in the words of his admirer and follower, Lord Haldane, 'established and expounded the real Constitution of

Canada,' as against what the Fathers of Confederation and most Canadian judges supposed it to be.[4] But there were already murmurs about 'property and civil rights,' and Mowat, 'the little rebel,' was already firmly seated in power at Toronto, and determined to magnify his office.

Third, the committee recommended steps to secure a law to prevent the employment of children under 10 years of age in factories, mills, and other manufacturing establishments where machinery was used. Fourth, it demanded 'a just and equitable lien law.' Finally, the committee recommended asking the dominion government to create a bureau of labour and statistics.

The committee on hours of labour recommended that hours should be reduced from 10 to 9 per day, with Sunday, and Saturday afternoon, off in order to promote 'advancement in the moral and material condition of the working classes.' It added a 'decided objection to overtime as being calculated to defeat the benefits accruing from short hours.' A motion for the eight-hour day was defeated, but evidently got considerable support, for the main motion was carried by only two votes.

The committee on organization stressed the necessity of organizing the large number of workers still unorganized. It recommended the issuance of printed circulars, 'setting forth the advantages to be derived from union ... to the committeemen of each county, to be distributed ... in localities where no organizations at present exist.' It also recommended asking the organized, and those willing to organize, 'to communicate with this Canadian Labor Union, with a view to solidification and concentration of power, by sending their delegates to represent them in this body.' Where there were not enough of one calling to form a union of any one trade, the committee recommended forming 'a protective body ... of those working at all trades ... to be called an Amalgamated Labor Union, or some other appropriate name,' though membership should not be open to those already in a trade union or numerous enough to form one. As for unions not yet represented in the congress, the committee recommended sending them a copy of the constitution with a recommendation to join.

The convention ended with a banquet for nearly 200 in the TTA hall. After the usual loyal toasts, drunk with tremendous enthusiasm, the chairman proposed '"the volunteers" coupling it with the name of Mr McCormick. Mr McCormick in responding, after alluding in touching terms to his devotion to the "cause," urged upon those present the necessity of adhering with fidelity to the Union. Merchants and others combined to regulate the prices of their goods, and why should not the workingmen regulate the rate of remuneration for their [labour]?' The chairman then proposed 'the visiting delegates,' which was acknowledged by delegates from Hamilton, London, Ottawa, Seaforth, St Catharines, Bowmanville, and Cobourg.

The chairman then proposed 'the press.' He hoped that the future would see the press more favourable to the claims of labour than at present. Williams responded on behalf of the *Ontario Workman*, and could not 'forbear cautioning [the Union] not to put too many irons in the fire at one time, but to heat one well first. The press was the great medium by means of which their views were circulated throughout the country, and the agitation, necessary to secure their rights, promoted. He urged upon the Union the necessity of enlisting the influence of the press on its behalf.'

Next came 'The officers of all trade unions in Canada,' followed by the 'Canadian Labor Union,' to which Hewitt replied. He attributed 'the present reduced condition of the working classes to their isolation,' and said the CLU 'now sought to establish labor organizations in every town and village in the Dominion.' He took a whack at the hostility of the Toronto Grit sheet (the *Globe*) which had not published any report of the meeting of the congress. After referring to a 'contemptible and criminal' letter on the labour question in the Seaforth *Expositor*, he urged 'the workingmen to be temperate and just in whatever course of action they pursued.'

The next toast was 'The organization of labor in the United States.' The convention had had a letter from the Industrial Congress of that country, with 'copies of proceedings and constitutions ... correcting several false impressions that seemed to prevail in the Dominion concerning the Industrial Congress ... [It had] denied any exclusiveness ... towards members of foreign unions. The mistaken impression arose from a report of the proceedings ... erroneously giving a resolution in its unamended form.' This letter may have been the reason for the toast. In any event, Levesley replied to the toast in a speech which seems to have made no reference at all either to the United States or to its unions. He dwelt at some length 'upon the advantages of trades unions. Those branches of labor, the members of which were the most thoroughly organized, did the minimum of work and obtained the maximum of pay. One good result of union was shown in the prevention of the overcrowding of certain trades by the admission of too great a number of apprentices.'

The second CLU convention, in August 1874, enjoyed the distinction of meeting in the dominion Parliament Buildings, but mustered only 14 delegates, again all from Ontario. Ottawa had the largest delegation: six (trades council). Toronto had three (one from the trades assembly, one Painter, one Tailor). St Catharines had two (Crispins and Molders). Kingston had two (ASE and Molders). Hamilton sent a solitary delegate (ASE). This time, the international unions had just over a third of the delegates (two ASE, two Typos, one Molder), the building trades had one delegate, the metal trades four. Ottawa was probably too far away from most of the Ontario centres for them to afford to send delegates.

This convention on its first day did nothing but listen to a speech by O'Donoghue and appoint a credentials committee. Next morning it appointed committees on organization, the constitution, ways and means, officers' reports, laws affecting trade unions, hours of labour, and printing. It then discussed the possibility of appointing a chief organizer when finances permitted.

After lunch Carter made his presidential address. The past year, he said, had been 'peaceful and comparatively prosperous ... but with one exception, and that the tailors of Toronto, the relations between capital and labor have been very little disturbed.' The labours of the congress had not been in vain and 'the signs of the times indicated a growing disposition to mutually arrange an amicable settlement of all disputes on the labor question.' Seven societies had identified themselves with the CLU. The present financial position, though not 'flourishing,' was satisfactory. He recommended some system of communication with England on the question of immigration, by which employment might be supplied for emigrating mechanics. He was sorry so few unions throughout the province had sent delegates and hoped the deliberations and decisions 'would be remarked for their wisdom and moderation.' He hoped also that the congress would discuss the Criminal Law Amendment Act, the Masters and Servants Act, and the application of the laws of conspiracy. He wound up by suggesting that the committee on officers' reports would 'recommend the approval of a suggestion in the Secretary's Report concerning the Reciprocity Treaty.'

The secretary's report spoke of the depressed state of trade. It noted that the Crispins and the Molders had each added 10 or 12 Canadian branches during the year. It also came out strongly against the proposed Reciprocity Treaty: 'It is high time that this Dominion was laying aside its swaddling clothes and becoming self-sustaining, and we can only become so by a fair and liberal protection. Let our struggling industries become once established; let us manufacture our own iron, wool, etc., and the day may come when we can open our ports, and defy the world. But in the meantime I think we do not ask too much when we claim the right to get a foothold upon our own soil without being pushed down by foreigners.'

The committee on officers' reports took the president's hint on this matter and approved the secretary's remarks on the treaty. But the convention jibbed. Carroll (St Catharines, Tailors) moved reference back, with instructions to strike out this part of the report, and his motion carried. He explained that he agreed with the secretary, but thought that the proper channel for such suggestions was the president.

The convention amended the constitution to provide that every union should have 1 delegate for the first 50 members or fraction of 50; 2 for over 50 to 100; and 3 for more than 100 with no union entitled to more than 3. It also reduced the fee for charters from $5 to $2. A committee endorsed the principle of a legal nine-hour day. The congress 'dissected' the report of the committee on immigration and observed that 'the present system of Immigration was ... a fraud and a delusion alike to the immigrant and the Canadian artisan. The bonus system was particularly condemned.'

Sixteen delegates attended the August 1875 convention of the CLU in St Catharines. A delegation of eight arrived from Toronto: one each from the TTA, Typos 91,

Crispins, Stonecutters, Operative Tailors, and Plasterers, and two from the Friendly Carpenters. Six delegates came from St Catharines itself: one each from the trades assembly, Crispins, and Painters, and two each from the Coopers and the Tailors. An ASE delegate arrived from Hamilton and a Molders delegate came from Oshawa.

Carter was in England, so his presidential address was read by the secretary, William Joyce. It began by lamenting that 'The cause of unionism had not for years received a severe check, or been subjected to severer struggles, than during the past twelve months, both in the United States and in England. In Canada no very disastrous events had come upon them, though the year was not without its difficulties ... The mean and contemptible objects sought by some ... Canadian employers had been frustrated by this wise and conciliatory spirit of leading workingmen. He referred to the vile conspiracy concocted by Messrs Hart and McKillop to destroy the Iron Moulders Union of Toronto and the abortive attempts made against the Stonecutters of Toronto.'

The address then congratulated O'Donoghue for the success of his efforts to get amendments to the Mechanics' Lien Act and credited Irving and Moss, MPs, for their attempts to get the Criminal Law Amendment Act repealed. It complained that the government's bill left the unions 'as much open to abuse as they were before.' The address concluded by urging the unions to insist on repeal of the act, and with the hope that the convention would vote for direct representation in both houses of Parliament.

The convention established six committees: organization, constitution, ways and means, officers' reports, laws affecting trade unions, and auditing. The acting president set up four other committees on printing, hours of labour, immigration, and prison labour.

Two of the convention's committees reported very briefly. The committee on organization recommended, though with some doubts, virtually 'the mixture as before,' and urged the re-establishment of a labour paper. The committee on the constitution said it needed considerable amendment, and proposed that the incoming executive undertake revision and mail a draft to the unions with the circulars calling the next convention.

The committee on the laws affecting trade unions dealt with four acts: the Dominion Criminal Law Amendment Act, the Ontario Masters and Servants Act, the Trade Unions Act, and the Lien Act. On the first, it thanked Moss and Irving for getting a definition of the application of the law of conspiracy and urged them to persevere till all the obnoxious clauses were repealed. On the second, 'a piece of class legislation of the most despicable character,' it wanted amendments to make breach of contract by either party a civil offence, to prevent the application of the law of conspiracy to breach of contract, and to bring the law into line with the English acts of 1875. On the third, it wanted power for unions to buy and hold property; on the fourth, amendments to give priority of claim 'to labor ... on any enterprise or building,' and to provide that previous payment to contractors should not relieve the owner of liability.

The presidential committee on the hours of labour suggested their reduction but, considering the state of the economy, recommended 'that no hasty action be taken.' The committee on prison labour recommended that the CLU use 'all its influence to induce the government to utilize prison labor in such a way that it would not come into direct competition with free labor and private enterprise.'

The report on prison labour produced some strong remarks. Prickett said 'it was entirely unjust to mechanics ... to have convicts competing with them under disadvantageous circumstances. It amounted to a system of pampering the worst classes in the country ... Prisoners should be used on road work instead of gaining free instruction in trades which they plied in competition with those who had paid to learn ... There were many harbours and breakwaters as well as roads in the new districts to be built. Criminals could be used on these.' Jury felt 'that if certain classes were to be merely hewers of wood and drawers of water then the convicts should be these.' Magness pointed out 'that it was a very complicated matter ... If the goods made by convicts were sold at the going prices no harm would be done to the legitimate labor.'

The report of the committee on organization produced an interesting discussion. Gilbert McFedries said the mass of working people were very poorly informed about the CLU, whose funds were low. William Magness said the county committee plan had not worked, and the union should devote itself more to 'the securing of just privileges to working men than to undertaking organization.' He also wanted a new labour paper. Alfred Jury thought it had been a mistake to hold the second convention in Ottawa, 'which was entirely outside the centre of trade and industry in Canada.' He hoped for a new plan of organization. In the centres of trade, there were already assemblies which did some of the job, the rest could best be left to the organized trades. The CLU 'should partake more of the nature of a general parliament of the Trade Unions.' George Vennell thought the CLU 'could do a great deal to nurse and instruct young societies,' notably by public meetings. 'The great want felt by the various unions was to get speakers to address the meetings.' William Carroll said that in Ottawa organization was dead, and that in St Catharines the various trades were already organized. He did not think much of Vennell's public meetings and thought the existing plan of organization should be pursued. McFedries insisted on the importance of the press in arousing interest and called for continual agitation. E.F. Clarke thought the great obstacle was the 'ignorance and apathy among workingmen ... as to the laws which tended to operate against them. The mass of workingmen did not see clearly ... why they should organize, and if they did, petty jealousies often interfered ... This strongly showed the necessity for a newspaper organ ... It was almost impossible to get ... a meeting of the unorganized workingmen of Toronto no matter who was to address them. What they wanted was a newspaper to reach the masses and to stir them up to the need for looking after their own interests.' He thought the suspension of the *Ontario Workman* was due mainly to 'the manner in which it was conducted ... A workingmen's newspaper should steer clear of politics except where the views expressed had the clear endorsation of the working men.' Carroll, Vennell, and S. Brooking all thought the *Workman* had devoted too much space to 'matters foreign to the immediate interests of the workingmen.'

The committee on immigration strongly disapproved of the government's method of attracting immigrants to Canada. It invoked orthodox economic theory, declaring that it was 'a gross violation of economic law to import large numbers of skilled workers into the country when the market ... was already overstocked.' It also objected to having to pay heavy duties on consumer goods while 'their labor had to be sold in the open market against that of others who had been bonused out of government funds.' Under such conditions a free labour market could not endure. It regretted that the government had not adopted the CLU policy of closing all immigration offices. It wound up by suggesting that the federal government could obtain needed farm labourers by contact with the agricultural labourers' unions in England. Clarke, moving adoption, denounced the unsuitability of most of the immigration agents, who were mainly political appointees. McFedries agreed, adding that 'what was wanted was able-bodied agricultural workers [who] should be assisted in the clearing of land and be given seed grain at low prices. This would develop the back-bone of the country and allow the industrial part to grow on sound foundations.' Magness said that 'one of the most serious abuses ... was the importation of pauper children ... Many of these unfortunate children were going to ruin as fast as possible.'

Two important resolutions dealt with a labour newspaper and the extension of the franchise. The first pledged the CLU 'to use every legitimate means in its power to support any paper that may be established to reflect the views of the masses of our workingmen on matters affecting their welfare by agitating for the repeal of those laws which now bear heavily and unfairly on trade unionists as a class.' Jury proposed (and later withdrew) an amendment requesting the proprietors of the *Ontario Workman* 'to re-publish that organ on purely non-political and non-sectarian principles.' He had differed entirely from both the political and religious views it had advanced and argued that its failure had resulted from its not getting 'enough support in money and literary contributions from the workingmen. They could not expect a newspaper that would faithfully represent their views on all subjects. It would be necessary at times for such a newspaper to discuss political matters affecting the workingman such as manhood suffrage on which the movement might be divided.' The CLU, having twice endorsed the *Workman* as its official organ, was 'morally bound to support it.' Vennell thought they ought not to pledge themselves to any particular scheme. Clarke thought the *Workman* had failed largely because of the introduction of political and religious matter into its columns and urged the delegates to defeat the amendment because it might bar some other paper. The original resolution carried.

The resolution on extension of the franchise proposed giving the vote (municipal and parliamentary) to every man with freehold property worth over $100. Vennell favoured manhood suffrage but felt 'the people had to be educated up to that point.' Many workingmen now could not vote. Jury wanted an amendment to provide for manhood suffrage. McFedries favoured a wider franchise but not manhood suffrage. Clarke favoured manhood suffrage but suggested leaving the matter to the next convention, which was done.

The convention elected as its officers Magness (president), Jury (first vice-president), Clarke (second vice-president), Vennell (third vice-president), Joyce (secretary), and McFedries (treasurer), with J.S. Williams as a member of the executive committee.

The August 1876 convention, held in Toronto, had 22 delegates, all from Ontario. The largest delegation, which numbered 18, came from Toronto itself: 3 each from the TTA and the Typos; 2 each from the Crispins, Tailors, and Painters; and 1 each from the Friendly Carpenters, ASE, Molders, Stonecutters, Bricklayers, and Bakers. A delegation of 3 came from St Catharines: 1 each from the ASE, Tailors, and Tinmen. A solitary ASE delegate came from Kingston.

The first act of this convention was to adopt a resolution for manhood suffrage. The delegates were evidently more radical than their predecessors: not one is recorded as speaking against the motion. Vennell, Stephenson, Carter, McFedries, A. Oakley, and Jury all spoke strongly for it. Jury took pains to emphasize its essential respectability by quoting Edward Blake, in the famous Aurora speech ('the franchise, as it at present exists, is logically indefensible'), and by disclaiming any inclination to universal suffrage ('politics should be left to the men while women attended to their domestic duties'). The motion carried unanimously.

The convention then listened to an address by Jury, in his capacity as vice-president (Magness was not present). He noted with pleasure the new provisions of the Criminal Law Amendment Act, reducing the maximum penalty for conspiracy to $100 or three months. He called for changes in the Master and Servant Act and hoped the convention would 'act on behalf of the domestic portion of the community as it did for itself.' He denounced assisted immigration and 'the apathy shown by working people in matters of political economy.' J.S. Williams, acting secretary (Joyce had resigned), presented a report which repeated some of what had already been said and noted that Ontario provincial expenditure on immigration had been cut in half. He blamed the small attendance at the convention on the depressed conditions of trade. The committee on the constitution recommended changing the name of the CLU to the Trades Union Congress, but the convention decided instead to make it the Canada Labor Union Congress.

The committee on prison labour reported in effect no progress and urged perseverance. Oakley introduced a new note: 'Many persons became convicts through adverse circumstances and ... everything possible should be done to enable these men to become better citizens. While the government should not make these men a burden upon the community, they should attempt to reform them and make them honest. Prison labor should not be brought into direct competition with free labor, and the products of prison labor should not be sold at less than the products of free labor ... This matter should be taken into serious consideration by the government, with a view, if possible, of doing away with prison labor.' Only the second part of this somewhat contradictory pronouncement appealed to Jury, who thought 'prison labor should be kept at the lowest level. Prisoners should not be taught trades which they could use on release to compete with honest workingmen. This tended to degrade the community ... All prison labor from an economic standpoint was wrong.'

The convention passed resolutions approving the amendments to the Criminal Law Amendment Act, calling for the establishment of trades assemblies or councils in all centres of industry and urging all unions to join such assemblies or councils where they existed, calling for direct labour representation in Parliament and recommending that the executive committee 'embrace every opportunity to bring labor candidates forward where there is a large industrial constituency,' calling for the establishment of a government labour bureau with 'a collection of information bearing upon the Labor question ... similar to the collections ... in the Departments of Commerce, Agriculture, etc.,' urging the unions to give 'the subject of co-operation their earnest and thoughtful consideration, believing as they do that co-operation in its brightest sense is ultimately destined to work great and beneficial results,' and calling for further amendments to the Mechanics' Lien Act.

This last resolution produced some discussion. Oakley pointed out a difficulty: some contractors took several jobs and workingmen were employed on all of them, and it was hard to know which property should be attached by a lien. Carter said the trouble workmen were having was much worse when they 'let their wages lie for two or three weeks,' instead of being paid by the day. Insistence on weekly payment would help.

A resolution on apprenticeship occasioned much discussion. James C. McMillan moved that there should be an apprenticeship law flexible enough to meet the needs of different unions, that it should provide for indenture, that the employers' prevailing policy in 'employing turn-over apprentices without making proper inquiry as to their indentures should be discountenanced,' and that the law should provide for a board of examiners, with an equal number of employers and employees, to examine all apprentices for fitness before they were allowed to become journeymen. Carter supported the resolution, though he thought it would be hard to get the legislation. Employers had got into the habit of hiring boys for two or three years and then granting them journeyman status. Oakley said the existing situation was bad for all tradesmen and even worse for the boys. They were 'picked up indiscriminately, often stay only a short time ... never learn a trade, and end up unable to get anything but inferior jobs.' J.L. Lumsden said the congress held in Philadelphia had gone on record that no one should be allowed to work as a journeyman till he was 21. No trade suffered more from the employment of boys than printing. Stephenson 'spoke of the injustice felt in the carpentering trade through the employment of boys. They were like flies in the summertime: the first time you saw them, they were full-sized and ready for action.' Carroll said he knew of carpenters in his town, St Catharines, who were unable to get three days' work a week because of the employment of boys. 'From the employers' point of view if a boy could drive a nail he was a carpenter. However, what he complained of most was the employment of girls in the tailoring trade.' His union had passed a resolution that no tailor be allowed to employ girls. J. McMillan (St Catharines ASE) supported the resolution. The Northern Railway shops, where an apprenticeship system was in force, produced some of the best mechanics in the country.

A committee on the Masters and Servants Act recommended amendments to place workpeople on the same footing as their employers and suggested getting a copy of the Employers' and Workpeople Bill introduced into the British House by Mr Cross. In the discussion, it was pointed out that test cases were very expensive: the Toronto Stonecutters' case had cost that union about $500. 'This was a financial strain no union could bear.' Further discussion produced a reference back and an amended report practically identical with that of 1875.

The convention also listened to a speech by Carter and a paper by one of the McMillans on trades societies. Carter said trade unionists were more provident, and better mechanics, than others. Through combination men bettered their position and obtained 'a fair day's pay for a fair day's work.' He also mentioned sickness and death benefits, and shorter hours. McMillan said the need for trade societies was increasing with the increasing immigration of mechanics.

The committee on immigration reported that it saw no reason to change the CLU policy of opposition to indiscriminate immigration especially of skilled workers. Large numbers of workingmen 'were already unable to support their families. Many had been forced to accept the aid of benevolent individuals and organizations.' Vennell condemned 'the colonization mode of immigration in which immigrants of different nationalities were being located by themselves in the Northwest.' Williams thought the CLU should thank the government for cutting down expenditure on immigration and thought the policy now being followed provided little ground for complaint. Jury thought all immigration activities should be carried on by government agencies and not by interested people in Britain. The report was adopted.

The convention elected Jury president, Carroll vice-president, Williams secretary, and Carter treasurer, with A. Young, Vennell, Oakley, T. Mellon, James C. McMillan (TTA), and A. Gibb (TTA) as members of the general parliamentary committee.

The August 1877 convention, the last, was again held in Toronto and apparently had 20 delegates, though the reports name only 17, and for 7 the organizations which sent them are not named. Of the delegates from Toronto, 3 came from the TTA, 2 from the Tailors, and 1 each from the Typos, ASCJ, Friendly Carpenters, and KOSC Lodge 6. An ASE delegate came from St Catharines, and there was a delegate from an unidentified tailors' union.

The convention elected T. Mellon (Toronto Crispins) president, and R. Roddy (Toronto Typos) recording secretary. Mellon then addressed the convention. He spoke of the severe trials workingmen had faced since the last convention because of the depression in Canada, Britain, the United States, and most of Europe. Wages had been greatly reduced, and the unions' strength severely taxed in trying to prevent such reductions. But the biggest cuts had been in places where there was no organization. The convention would discuss remedies for the depression. The Masters and Servants Act, the Mechanics' Lien Act, and shorter hours were also worth discussing, and he had hopes that arbitration as a way of settling disputes between capital and labour would soon be universally adopted. Direct representation in Parliament was important. He also touched on the importance of co-operation, on better means of dividing profits, on convict labour, and on the need for a government bureau of labour. The convention elected James C. McMillan secretary, and Alfred Jury treasurer, and then listened to the secretary's report.

Next day Jury moved 'That the present depression ... is caused from overproduction and over-importation of goods and labor, and the way to mitigate future panics is so to regulate our tariff as to meet the exigencies of the revenue.' Williams promptly moved an amendment for a protective tariff. Jury opposed this, voicing the usual arguments against a protective tariff and begging his listeners 'not to be led astray by the deluding cries of the Conservatives ... During the term of office of Sir John MacDonald the country needed protection just as much as it does now, but the Conservatives took care not to impose a protective tariff knowing that the country would be ruined.' Williams replied that 'the closed market of the United States and the open market of Canada were unfair to the latter. Both should be on an equal footing.' W. Ternent said he had asked one of the leading men in Hay and Company (chair makers) his opinion of the cause of the depression. The reply was they wanted the 'same policy as prevailed across the line. If the conditions were equal, they would be able to compete with the Americans in all lines.' Moffatt said free trade was good for England but not for Canada. 'Wages in the United States were higher than ... in Canada. The self-interest of the workingmen demanded protection.' Gibson said the wages of railway men in the United States were not higher. Roddy said printers' wages were. J. Rose thought wages were about equal in the two countries. Jury, closing the debate, said Williams's amendment 'would mean that our tariff would be made by the Americans ... We should make our own tariff. The people of Canada should be allowed to buy in whatever market they liked. The manufacturing industry of Canada – mite that it was – could not be built up by protection. The reduction in wages in the United States had occurred mostly in those trades artificially built up by protection.' None the less, the amendment carried by two.

Ternent presented a paper on immigration. He wanted a minister of immigration. 'Neither school masters, ministers nor publicans should be, as had been, appointed immigration agents. The great majority of immigrants had improved their position. This was especially true of the farming community. Only the proper kind of immigrants should be encouraged to come here. Those immigrants unfit for the country should be encouraged to go home.' Stephenson objected to immigration agents and said it was 'sheer nonsense to bring out people at present.' A delegate named Bentley said 'the men wanted were men ready to take up the land waiting for them. Mechanics were not wanted. Immigration had overstocked the various trades with apprentices.' Rose thought the bonus system had: 'People should be left to themselves to come out and not be encouraged by the government.' Williams said all agents should be withdrawn during the present depression. Jury thought the law of supply and demand should regulate immigration. Ternent said he had been informed that the government was 'almost forbidding mechanics to come out.' The secretary then successfully moved that the dominion and local governments cease all expenditures for immigration, 'and that in future we will discountenance any such grants.' The customary resolution on the Lien Act followed.

Next day the convention tackled hours of labour. The secretary moved that hours should be reduced from 10 to 9 per day, which would be followed 'by the advancement intellectually and morally of the working classes.' McMillan added that it would 'result in the employment of a number who were out of work.' Bentley dealt with the allegation that workmen would not know how to use the extra time: 'It would at least give a man the opportunity of giving himself and his family an airing in the country.' Ternent spoke of the half-holiday system in Edinburgh, which had 'brought out latent talents in the workingman.' Thomas suggested most workingmen were against a reduction of hours. Gibson felt that close co-operation among the workingmen, as in Britain, would soon bring the nine-hour day. He would like to call for eight hours. He believed 'in the four "eights" – eight hours work, eight hours play, eight hours sleep, and eight shillings a day.' Moffatt favoured shorter hours 'to give the workingman time to improve his mind.' McMillan closed the debate with a strong condemnation of piece-work and overtime, and the motion then carried.

Williams moved a resolution in favour of boards of arbitration and conciliation wherever possible. He cited the progress arbitration had made in Britain and America. He believed feeling in Canada was steadily growing in favour of arbitration and against strikes. He quoted the London *Echo* and noted that arbitration had been accepted in the shoemaking industry in the United States, averting 149 strikes. He emphasized that arbitration 'had to be arranged by mutual agreement between the parties.' In the abortive bricklayers' strike in Toronto, the attempt at conciliation had come in the heat of the struggle. To be successful, arrangements for 'arbitration and conciliation had to be made when both parties were calm and cool.' McMillan wanted a bureau of labour statistics, to provide accurate information on such matters. He could not see why the government should not establish a board of arbitration also. Williams considered this 'impracticable because of the diversity of interests to be represented.' His motion carried, unanimously.

Jury next moved: 'That, whereas it is impossible to secure thorough representation on the floor of the House of Parliament of the working classes until we are represented by men of our own class, therefore be it resolved that this Congress pledge itself to use all legitimate means in its power to secure the election of workmen to Parliament and to support any workingman's candidate nominated by the Parliamentary Committee or the local labor organization in the locality in which they reside.' Jury said the presence of a dozen workmen in Parliament 'would have a most beneficial effect. This was not class division; this was trying to break down class differences. There was class legislation now. They wanted to create universal representation by the inclusion of the only class that was not represented now. The Licensed Victuallers were represented in Parliament, and surely the workingman was quite as important to the community as these gentlemen. The temperance party was represented, and the lawyers were in Parliament in great force; but the laboring classes had only one man, and they had only half of him.' Ternent did not take so sanguine a view: 'Mr O'Donoghue was no longer a representative of the labor party, and he held that until they could get a laboring man who would faithfully attend to the interests of his class, there was no good in sending a man to Parliament.' McMillan 'held that because one man might not have satisfied the electors there was no reason to suppose they could not get a man that would do so.' The discussion seems to have ended without a decision.

Moffatt moved a resolution on co-operatives in production and distribution, asserting that 'until we put this principle into practice we can never hope to place ourselves in that position in society to which our usefulness and industry entitles us.'

Williams called co-operation 'the panacea for all of the evils of the workingman.' Gibson insisted on the necessity of efficient and trustworthy management of the co-operatives. He had invested $40 in a co-operative society and lost every cent of it. But he knew these societies operated well in Scotland and Ireland. Jury thought more good would come of co-operation in production than in distribution. He believed 'strikes might be obviated through co-operative establishments. It would also allow them to get rid of the "middlemen" who preyed upon the working class like vultures.' The ASE 'might set up a co-operative factory. It would be well ... for the bricklayers and others in the building trades to start co-operatives.' The motion carried, unanimously.

Next came the perennial subject of convict labour. Bentley moved: 'convict labor should be so utilized as not to come unduly into competition with free labor, and such convict labor should not be let to any company or individual, but should be used by the Government for the benefit of the whole country.' Rose said it should be employed in manufacturing what was required by the government. 'The prisoners were kept at the cost of the country and it was right that some use should be made of them.' Jury voiced his usual sentiments. Stephenson said he had heard 'of several owners of machine shops complaining of their business being ruined by prison labor ... Prison labor might be employed in making the banks of the Don river a beautiful place. It would improve the city very much, and in the part which needed it most.' Mellon said convict labour interfered with free labour in boots and shoes, stonecutting, and the machinists' business. He favoured using prison labour in clearing land for settlers. The motion carried, unanimously.

The convention next passed a resolution in favour of a bureau of labour statistics; elected a parliamentary committee of nine comprising Jury, Carter, Gibson, Williams, Stephenson, Mellon, J.C. McMillan, Thomas, and Rose; passed a number of votes of thanks; and adjourned. 'E'en the ranks of Tuscany,' in the shape of the Toronto *Globe*, felt obliged to cheer to the extent of saying that it could not be denied that the delegates 'present their views in a manner calculated to excite respect even where they may not command acceptance.'

The CLU was still in existence in February 1878, when the TTA minutes mention its parliamentary committee; but that is the last we hear of it.[5]

It is noteworthy that the Locomotive Engineers and the Locomotive Firemen seem to have taken no part whatever in the central organizations, thus establishing a pattern for the railway running trades which, with rare exceptions, was to hold good till 1956.

7

The Knights of Labor 1875–1902

With the adoption of the National Policy and the building of the Canadian Pacific Railway, Canadian Industry began to revive and grow, and Canadian unions with it. The 1880s saw the organization of a host of purely local unions, most of them short-lived, and the entry of 17 new international unions.[1]

But the most spectacular feature of the decade was the growth of the Noble and Holy Order of the Knights of Labor (KOL). This organization had been formed in the United States in 1869. It was a secret society, complete with ritual and offices with such imposing names as general master workman (president), grand worthy foreman (vice-president), venerable sage (past president), grand scribe (secretary), and unknown knight.[2]

This caught on. So did the fact that the Knights were prepared to organize everybody, skilled and unskilled, men and women, black and white, in cities, towns, and villages. Their distaste for strikes had a special appeal in a period of acute economic depression. Their advocacy of co-operatives and of political action touched a vein of idealism. They became for a time the leading labour organization in the United States and Canada and spread to Great Britain, Ireland, Belgium, Australia, New Zealand, and Hawaii.[3]

They entered Canada in 1875, at Hamilton, with Local Assembly (LA) 119. By 1880, however, this was moribund,[4] and the real history of the Knights in Canada begins, again in Hamilton, probably in the fall of 1881, certainly not later than April 1882. The first LA was LA 1852 (painters), organized in the basement of the unfinished Canada Life Assurance building. July 1882 saw the first Canadian 'mixed' assembly (taking in various occupations), LA 2056 (St Catharines). This was followed, in August, by two more Hamilton assemblies, LA 2132 (shoemakers) and LA 2156 (bakers), and by the first two Canadian assemblies of the Knights' National Trade District 46 (United Telegraphers of North America): LA 2163 (Toronto) and LA 2191 (Montreal).[5]

The Telegraphers' assemblies spread rapidly. Till late in 1883 they made up a large part of the Knights' strength Canada. The Montreal assembly was followed by Hamilton, London, Barrie, Brampton, Guelph, Stratford, Ottawa, Brockville, Kingston, Peterborough, Belleville, Port Hope, St Catharines, Haysville, Brantford, St Thomas, Saint John, Quebec, Rivière-du-Loup (en bas), Campbellton, Moncton, Simcoe, Sherbrooke, Halifax, North Sydney, New Glasgow, Winnipeg, and Truro. Sherbrooke lapsed in May 1883, as did Simcoe in June. The other 28 were still on hand for one of the most spectacular events in Canadian labour history: the Telegraphers' strike of 1883.

This was our first nation-wide strike and the only genuinely international strike we have ever had. It was a strike for equal wage increases in Canada and the United States and for equal pay for men and women. It was declared and carried on not by factory workers, nor by skilled artisans with a tradition of organization and class solidarity, but by white-collar workers. Four of the six members of the board which ran the strike were Canadian-born.

On 16 July 1883 the executive board of the Telegraphers presented to the telegraph companies in both countries, and to two American telephone companies, a memorandum of demands. The Canadian demands were identical with the American, except that the Canadians already had Sunday overtime (40 cents an hour) and the Americans wanted it.

The demands were substantial: first, a reduction of hours from nine to eight for day work and from eight to seven for night; second, a 15 per cent salary increase for everyone, with 20 per cent for those getting from $45 to $65 a month, and a flat increase of $35 a month for those getting under $45, with a 25 per cent commission for all operators on commission work. The New York *Herald* estimated that for an American day operator earning $75 a month, this would mean an hourly increase of about 27 per cent. In Canada, it would have been higher, as the union put the average commercial operator's salary at $37.49. The highest-paid operator in Toronto was getting only $70, and some operators working 'good wires' were getting as little as $20. Rates for comparable white-collar workers were: bookkeepers with four or five years' experience, $90 to $150; retail dry-goods salesmen with four years' experience, $40 to $80; commercial travellers, $80 to $150; court stenographers, $140 to $200 plus several weeks of vacation.

The companies, except Canada Mutual, flatly refused to recognize the 'Brotherhood,' and just before noon on 19 July the code message, 'General Grant is dead,' went out over the wires. From New York to San Francisco, from New Orleans to Winnipeg, and from Winnipeg to North Sydney, 'the operators rose from their keys as one man,' except at Canada Mutual, which, however, was struck the next day.

The Brotherhood's Canadian membership at the beginning of the strike must have been about 1200. The Canadian assemblies went into the struggle with certain

advantages. Their members belonged to a highly skilled occupation whose operations were essential to the business of the time. Their organization covered the
country, since some LAS took in not only the place they were named for but nearby
smaller places as well. They were backed by a big and apparently powerful international organization, with some 18,000 to 19,000 members, affiliated to an even
larger body. The Canadian members were enthusiastic, loyal and disciplined, and
strongly supported by other labour organizations. They also enjoyed a surprising
amount of public sympathy, especially at first. The Brotherhood was up against a
phalanx of powerful and iron-willed employers, notably, in Canada, Western Union
and Great North-Western.

The strike seems to have taken the companies by surprise. The demands had
been presented only 48 hours before the walkout, and without any statement of
intention to strike if they were not met. The Brotherhood said it feared any such
statement would have been construed as intimidation and that, accordingly, it had
given the companies only 24 hours' notice after their refusal to negotiate. It probably
felt the employers would use any period of notice only to perfect plans for carrying
on with a skeleton staff and bringing in strikebreakers.

The strike seems to have been almost total, and most of the Canadian strikers
seem to have stayed out till it was officially called off on 18 August. Just how
thoroughly it tied up the telegraph system is not altogether clear. The Brotherhood
and the companies of course gave different versions. The Brotherhood's seems the
more accurate. But in a good many places the companies were able to provide
enough service, of a sort, to prevent the strike from being, as the strikers had
expected, a short march to triumph over employers rendered helpless.

One reason the union had been so confident was that the air was full of highly
circumstantial stories of the organization of a new, pro-union company to compete
with existing lines. Nothing came of this. Another was the strong financial support of
other labour organizations. The parent Knights of Labor announced at the outset of
the strike that it had placed $100,000 to the Brotherhood's credit and would provide
ten times that amount at a moment's notice, if need were. This offer turned out to be
illusory: the Brotherhood had expected $500 from each of the order's 1500 LAS; it
got an average of $3 per assembly, enough to pay the strikers only $1 a week. But
the Toronto Trades and Labor Council; the Toronto Bricklayers, Shoemakers,
Tailors, and Machinists and Blacksmiths; and the Oshawa Knights came forward
manfully to the tune of some $2000.

The companies seem to have been thoroughly unpopular, and the strikers
enjoyed considerable public sympathy. The Toronto *Mail* was markedly pro-union
throughout the stoppage, the Montreal *Gazette* only less so. Newspaper after newspaper called for public ownership.

But Jay Gould and his colleagues were too much for the Brotherhood. The strike was called off 18 August, the union advising its members to try to get their jobs back. By October the Telegraphers had left the Knights.[6]

The collapse of the strike might have been expected to stop the KOL's progress in Canada, or at least slow it down. In fact, it seems to have had little effect. In 1882, apart from the Telegraphers, 14 LAS had been organized (7 in Hamilton, 2 in Toronto). In 1883, before the strike, another 16 were organized (5 in Hamilton and 1 each in Burlington, Toronto, and Montreal). In the last 4 months of the year, another 10 were added, and in 1884, 20 more, including 3 in British Columbia and 1 in Winnipeg. In 1885 the pace quickened: 36 new LAS (9 in Toronto, 5 in Montreal, 4 in St Thomas, 2 each in Brantford and Stratford, and 1 in Quebec City). In 1884 Hamilton had been the centre of the KOL in Canada, with 13 LAS to Toronto's 8. In 1885 Toronto had overtaken its rival, with 17 LAS to Hamilton's 11. Montreal by then had 7, and Quebec City, Winnipeg, Victoria, Nanaimo, and Wellington 1 each, and another 43 were scattered around Ontario. St Thomas had 5, Brantford 4, London and Belleville 3 each, and Stratford and Oshawa 2 each.

The year 1886 produced a tremendous surge of organization: some 133 new LAS. Toronto got 3, Montreal 23, Hamilton 10; London, St Catharines, Windsor, and Thorold 3 each; St Thomas, Stratford, Berlin, Chatham, Cornwall, and Gananoque 2 each; 35 other places in Ontario 1 each. Winnipeg got 2, Vancouver 2, Kamloops and New Westminster 1 each. The Quebec towns of Sherbrooke, St John's, Richmond, and Upper Bedford also got 1 each.

Some of the earlier LAS had lapsed. But, at some time or other in 1886, there were pretty certainly 203 Canadian assemblies. Of these, 159 were in Ontario (46 in Toronto, 20 in Hamilton; 6 each in London and St Thomas; 4 each in Stratford and Windsor; 3 each in Guelph and Thorold; and 2 each in Ottawa, Brantford, Belleville, Chatham, Port Hope, Oshawa, Woodstock, Berlin, Gananoque, and Cornwall). Vancouver had 2, and there were 4 others in British Columbia. Winnipeg had 3. Montreal had 30, Quebec City 1, and there were 4 others in Quebec.[7]

The 23 new LAS organized in Montreal in 1886 are particularly notable because the KOL had been having trouble with the Roman Catholic church in Quebec. Long before, the Knights had run into heavy weather with the church in the United States. But by 1882 they had managed to set themselves right with the American hierarchy and clergy, with only isolated exceptions. In Quebec, at first, at least in Montreal, the clergy rather encouraged French-Canadian workers to join. But in September 1884 the Quebec hierarchy moved the Vatican to charge the bishops to deter their people from belonging. Archbishop Taschereau, of Quebec City, complied in a circular letter 2 February 1885. This was followed by a letter from all the bishops, read in the churches 20 June 1886. This specifically declared the Knights 'forbidden ... under pain of grievous sin,' because they were a secret society, because they required an unswerved obedience to occult chiefs,' and because their 'cosmopolitan character ... necessarily exposes many of their members to execute the orders of a Council residing in a foreign country, which Council at a given time may not only have interests at variance with those of the government to which the members owe allegiance, but may even be at war with God.' The faithful were admonished to leave the KOL at once and to file with their parish priests declarations that they had done so.

Archbishop Taschereau's letter may have had some effect in 1885, though all five Montreal LAS organized during that year came after the letter was issued. Ten of those organized in 1886 appeared before the bishops' letter, the other thirteen after it. The ecclesiastical thunders may have had something to do with the disappearance of four Montreal LAS and the two at Richmond and Upper Bedford. But it is remarkable that all the other assemblies in the province seem to have survived. The chief effect was apparently a marked decline in membership.

The 1886 pastoral letter caused a considerable commotion in Quebec and out of it. It was not altogether well received even by members of the church in the province. The *True Witness and Catholic Chronicle* attacked it at once in strong terms. It pointed out that the order enjoyed the approval of many of the American bishops. It was no more secret than temperance, benevolent, and other societies which no one thought of condemning. Every important communication or instruction from the general master workman or the general executive board was given to the newspapers. The 'occult chiefs' were among the best-known men on the continent. A semi-official Vatican organ had published an article favourable to the Knights. The *True Witness* suggested there were grounds for an appeal to Rome.

General Master Workman Terence V. Powderly was alarmed, not only by the immediate decline in the Knights' strength in Quebec but also by the possibility that the effect might spread to other parts of Canada, and even to the United States. He interviewed the bishop of Montreal, without much effect. He issued a statement explaining that the situation in Quebec was something special: 'There are so many anarchists in Canada they have reason to be suspicious. The French are much harder to manage than our people. We have some anarchists in the United States but not of the dangerous class. The French are of a very different temperament. We can take our people and pack them in a solid mass from one end of Market Street to the other and there will be no harm. But take an equal number of Frenchmen and the result will be serious.' Powderly also had an interview with Cardinal Gibbons, of Baltimore, on 28 October 1886. This bore fruit.

Gibbons and other American bishops were sympathetic to the KOL and most reluctant to see the church made to look anti-labour. Gibbons's interview with Powderly satisfied him that the KOL was unobjectionable from the church's point of view, and by the end of March 1887, with the help of Cardinal Manning, he succeeded in getting the Holy Office to say so. Archbishop (now Cardinal) Taschereau jibbed as much and as long as he could. On 12 April 1887 he suspended, until further notice, his sentence against the KOL, but only on severe conditions, which included exacting from every Knight a promise to leave the order the moment the Holy See banned it. Knights who accepted the conditions were again admitted to the sacraments, which had been denied them for some time, and most of them hastened to put themselves right with the church. Press reports said that priests took down the names and addresses of penitent Knights, just in case the Vatican should later renew the ban. But this was a vain hope. On 26 July 1887 the pope decided there were no grounds for interfering with the KOL, and the condemnation in Quebec accordingly came to an end.[8]

The Quebec Knights promptly took on a new lease of life. In 1887 Montreal got 3 new assemblies, giving it a total of 29. Quebec City and Lévis got 12, giving them a total of 13. Buckingham got 1. This, with the 2 in Sherbrooke and St John's East, brought the provincial total to 45. Moreover, both Montreal and Quebec continued to have substantial numbers of assemblies long after the order had begun to go down hill elsewhere, as Table 1 shows.[9]

All told, at one time or another, the KOL must have organized some 400 LAs in Canada, in every province, except Prince Edward Island, and in what is now Alberta. None was set up in Newfoundland or in what is now Saskatchewan. The LAS were attached either to one of the district assemblies (DAs) listed in Table 2, or to a national trade district or simply to the general assembly.[10]

How many members did the KOL have in Canada? At the outbreak of the telegraphers' strike a Toronto brotherhood speaker claimed there were 2000 to 3000 Knights in the city, apart from telegraphers; a few days later the Hamilton telegraphers put the membership in that city at 2000. But the proceedings of the 1883 general assembly show only 289 members in 3 Toronto LAS and 880 in 6 Hamilton LAS.[11] Table 3, based on the general assembly's figures, indicates the spectacular growth of the KOL in Canada in the 1880s.[12] But the lack of information about total Canadian membership after 1888, and the dwindling Canadian representation at general assemblies, suggest a marked decline in numbers after the fall of 1888. Nevertheless, in 1894 DA 20 denied an Associated Press report that 10,000 Knights in Quebec, Montreal, and parts of Ontario were proposing to leave the order.[13]

The average size of LAS varied considerably from 1882 to 1887. It started at 31; jumped to 134 in 1883; fell to 90 in 1884, and to 68 in 1885; rose to 137 in 1886; and fell to 72 in 1887. However, these averages conceal wide variations in the membership of individual LAS, which in the years 1883–85 could be as low as 10 or as high as 439. Also, membership in a particular LA was often highly volatile. In DA 61 (Hamilton) in the years 1883–85 the membership of LA 2225 rose from 20 to 439 and then fell back to 61; of LA 2132 from 25 to 141 and then back to 47; of LA 2586

TABLE 1
KOL LAS 1887–1902

	1887	1888	1889	1890	1891	1892	1893
BRITISH COLUMBIA	5	5	3	4	3	4	4
Calgary (NWT)	1	1					
MANITOBA	5–6	2	1	1			
NOVA SCOTIA			1	2			
QUEBEC	45	46	36	32	31	32	35
Montreal	29	29	21	17	15	18	22
Quebec City-Lévis	13	14	13	13	14	12	12
Other Quebec	3	3	2	2	2	2	1
ONTARIO	148	121	86	68	57	54	52
Toronto	50	37	37	37	36	37	36
Hamilton	14	10	10	3	3	2	
Ottawa	3	3	3	9	7	6	8
St Thomas	4	1	1	1			
Windsor	4	4	2	2			
Kingston	3	4	1	1	1		
Belleville	3	3					
Gananoque	4	2					
Thorold	2	2	1				
St Catharines	2	5	4	2	2	2	2
London	6	6	2	2	1		
Berlin	5	5					
Other Ontario	48	39	25	11	7	7	6
Total Canada	204–5	175	127	107	91	90	91

SOURCES: See note 9.

from 27 to 134 and then back to 72; and of LA 3040 from 44 to 145 and then back to 41. The membership of LA 2311 (Brockville) rose from 50 to 258 and then fell back to 11, while that of LA 2355 (Oshawa) went from 151 to 278 to 16.[14]

What did the Knights do in Canada? What, rather, did they not do? They seem to have got into every conceivable form of working-class activity: organization, collective bargaining, strikes, lobbying, independent political action, the co-operative movement, labour journalism, and the promotion of local and national central labour oganizations.

Theoretically, they believed in organizing all workers, skilled and unskilled, men and women, into one single body, to work for the abolition of the wage system and the establishment of a new society. Theoretically, they were not much interested in organizing particular crafts or occupations. In practice, however, at least in Canada,

1894	1895	1896	1897	1898	1899	1900	1901	1902
3	2	2	1	0				
				5	5	5	5	0
32	30	25	14	14	16	21	16	15
21	21	16	5	5	7	11	9	9
9	9	9	9	8	9	8	6	6
2				1		2	1	
20	14	10	4	4	6	6	11	11
13	6	5	3	3	5	5	6	6
							1	
3	4	1	1	1	1	1	3	3
							1	2
4	4	4						
55	46	37	19	23	27	32	32	26

they put a great deal of water in their wine. They organized not only the mixed assemblies that might have been expected (probably something like one-third of the total), but also craft or occupational assemblies of at least 75 occupations, from coal miners to musicians, and including railway employees, sailors, longshoremen, teamsters, carters, cabmen, street-railway employees, harbour carpenters, ship carpenters, coal-miners, ironworkers, moulders, steelworkers, agricultural-implements workers, brassworkers, machinists, boilermakers, blacksmiths, horseshoers, tinsmiths, steamfitters, stove mounters, carriage makers, woodworkers, saw-mill hands, pavers, stonecutters, granite cutters, marble workers, carpenters, painters, plasterers, electricians, cabinet-makers, box-makers, varnishers and polishers, upholsterers, shoemakers, tailors, hatters, garment workers, fur fleshers and shavers, cotton workers, spinners and weavers, sewing girls, leather workers, saddlers, harness makers, trunk makers, tarpaulin makers, coopers, wheelmakers, butchers, bakers, cigar makers, tobacco workers, barbers, reed-organ builders,

TABLE 2
KOL DAS 1883–1908

DA number	Place	Years of existence
61	Hamilton	1883–90
114 (sub-DA 1)*	Montreal	1886–90
114 (sub-DA 2)†	Montreal	1886–90
125	Toronto	1886–93
138	St Thomas	1886–90
174	Windsor	1887–89
203	Nanaimo and Vancouver	1887–89
204	Winnipeg	1887–90
207	St Catharines	1887–93
235	Belleville and Gananoque (Ont)	1888–90
236	Uxbridge and Peterborough (Ont)	1888–90
241	Berlin	1888–89
18*	Montreal	1890–1907
19†	Montreal	1890–95
20	Quebec City	1890–1907
6	Ottawa	1892–95
35	Glace Bay (NS)	1898–1901
180	Toronto	1900–1908

* English-speaking
† French-speaking
SOURCES: See note 10.

TABLE 3
KOL membership in Canada 1882–88

1882	560
1883	2,283
1884	3,134
1885	2,906
1886	14,132
1887	12,553
1888	10,151

SOURCE: See note 12.

musicians, clerks, salesmen, letter carriers, glassblowers, bottle blowers, nail-makers, jewellers, silver-platers, watch-case makers, wallpaper printers, book-binders, and (though apparently only a single assembly) labourers.

Gerald Grob writes that though the mixed assembly 'might agitate for reform or participate in politics, [it] could never become the collective bargaining representative of its members [and] could never be more than a study or debating group.'[15] For Canada, this is an overstatement. It seems perfectly clear, for example, that the mixed assembly at Smith's Falls succeeded in getting recognition, and in bargaining collectively, at the Frost and Wood Agricultural Foundry, where the Molders had failed. The mixed assembly 3484, in Montreal, in August 1887 speaks of having had 'a little strike.' It seems to have been a mixed assembly which struck at Gananoque in 1887. It was probably the mixed LA 2311 (Brockville) which was locked out for some months before July 1884 and which succeeded in getting a rather reluctant general executive board to send $1000 and to try to find jobs elsewhere for the men who were out. (The landlords and grocers 'were beginning to push these men to the wall for back debts, and the magnificent hold obtained by the Order in that section of Canada was necessarily jeopardized by the prospect of defeat and forced withdrawal of large numbers from the Order.'[16]

Certainly, there were plenty of strikes by Knights' craft or occupational Assemblies in Canada. The Hamilton Stove Mounters' Assembly (probably LA 2225) struck in January 1883 against Gurney, Copp Bros, and James Stewart & Co, who, as usual, were trying to reduce wages, this time by 10 per cent. On 22 March the strike was still on, and the Toronto *Wage-Worker* commented: 'The ruffianly scoundrels of manufacturers must insist on the reduction. Shylock like they must have their pound of flesh. Yet some of these wretches disgrace the Church by their presence. We are led to believe, that these avaricious wretches, and others like them, may continue to rob their employees until they are about to depart this life, and if they, before they die, sincerely repent of their sins they will be rewarded in heaven. On the other hand, their victims who may have been driven to crime are to be rewarded with eternal punishment. Is it any wonder that the working classes are being gradually estranged from the Church?' The report also notes that during the election in June 1882 'workingmen were told that the N.P. [National Policy] would raise wages,' but that the stove manufacturers' behaviour shows that 'the N.P. does not increase wages unless it suits the employers' fancy to do so. Also that the bosses will not scruple to lie for an excuse to cut wages. The remedy for the working classes – ORGANIZE.' The strike failed.[17]

The Toronto Knights had 16 strikes from 1883 to 1892.[18] LA 3499 struck Dale's Bakery from October to December 1883. LA 2622 struck the Massey works, the largest Toronto employer, in 1886. The men wanted the wage list printed and fortnightly, not monthly, payment of wages. Massey refused, discharged one of the men's committee, and said he would discharge any employee who joined a labour organization. He then proceeded to discharge five. The assembly demanded they be rehired. Massey refused, and the men struck, 400 strong. The Molders struck in sympathy. The strike lasted one week and the men won. The company said there had been a misunderstanding and promoted the Knights' district master workman to foreman.

The most spectacular of the seven 1886 strikes was against the street railway company. In the fall of 1885, when the men were unorganized, three were dismissed for belonging to the Knights, and all the rest were forced to sign an undertaking that they would not join a union, on pain of dismissal. The men sought the aid of the Knights, and on 8 November 31 men formed LA 4534. The company promptly fired the whole lot, and the Knights' Toronto leaders advised them to dissolve their assembly, which they did, some joining mixed LA 2305. Representatives of the men went to see Hon Frank Smith, head of the company, to ask what the Knights had done, individually or as an order, 'to the injury of the company.' Smith did not reply, except by saying that he would not employ any member of a labour organization.

On or about 7 March 1886 the men held a meeting, which signed up 32 new members and a dozen or so who had secretly belonged to other assemblies. Within 2 or 3 days, 132 of the 350 employees had joined. On 10 March the whole 350 found themselves locked out. On 13 March 240 of them applied for membership in LA 2305.

By hiring non-union men, the company succeeded in getting about half its cars in operation by noon of 10 March. Each car carried three policemen, applied for beforehand. But the company was highly unpopular: from the first, public sympathy was strongly on the side of the men. 'Cars were turned sideways on the tracks, horses were unhitched, and friendly coal drivers blocked the way with their carts, or proceeded at a snail's pace just ahead of the streetcar. By four o'clock no cars were running ... as a result of such action by Knights of Labor sympathizers.' Within two days the mayor wrote Smith a stiff letter, saying the city would hold the company responsible for any injury done to any policeman while he was protecting company property, and for any damage done to city or private property. The city would also insist on the company fulfilling its charter obligation to operate cars at intervals of not more than 30 minutes for 14 hours a day. 'You have,' said Mayor Howland, 'by your act produced this trouble, having in the face of the knowledge of the result (as your application for police protection in advance of your own act proves) deliberately locked out a large body of your men, not on account of any claim for higher wages or shorter hours, but simply for exercising a legal liberty in joining a lawful body or society.'

The company, however, was adamant. Smith said it had suffered hardships from union action in the past and was determined not to hire union members; its men had signed an agreement not to join a union, and they would be rehired as soon as they promised to honour their pledge. Meanwhile, he kept trying to hire strikebreakers, without much success; 'Few men,' writes D.R. Kennedy, 'were willing to take the cars out in the face of [the] strong public opposition. Amid jeers and catcalls, filth and missiles were hurled at the cars as they passed down the streets empty except for their police escort ... [Coal drivers and loafers] manhandled the cars so that they were unable to proceed. The company applied for further police protection, but the police were no match for the quick-witted crowds which attacked each car.'

All this was a spontaneous manifestation by sympathizers of the locked-out men, who themselves made no attempt to interfere with the service. 'They were kept off the streets by their executives and urged to abstain from rowdyism and drinking while out of work.'

The city authorities were not pleased with the company, but they were certainly not pro-union. They provided extra police. With this help, the company made a determined effort to get the cars out and keep them running. It was not a great success. Large and hostile crowds surrounded the cars, showering bricks and mud upon them. One car, with 12 policemen aboard, was obstructed by coal carts and express and railway lorries. The police tried to urge the lorry horses forward, whereupon the crowd unhitched the horses and sent them off to their stable at a gallop. Another car, also with 12 police aboard, was luckier. Its way was blocked by coal carts, but they were forced to move. Opposite the *Globe* office, the police rushed the crowd, using their batons with 'telling effect.' Mounted police used their batons so freely that 'many innocent citizens protested that they were charged and beaten while walking on the sidewalks ... On Front Street near Jarvis where a large crowd had gathered ... an old man who had been hit on the head with a baton ran about shouting "murder, murder," while an explosion on the tracks was mistaken for a pistol shot. The crowd was thrown into a panic by the sudden appearance of the Twelfth Battalion, which, as it turned out, was on its way to a funeral. The mob was cleared away with some difficulty and the cars were taken back to the company's yards.' Some people were arrested, convicted, and severely punished.

The mayor then issued a proclamation ordering everyone to give free passage to the cars and forbidding obstruction of the right of way and congregating on the public highways. Two committees of aldermen were appointed, one to see the company, one the men. The men agreed to return to work if those who had been discharged were taken back, and to make no further demands. Smith appeared to agree that he would take everyone back unconditionally; but he later insisted that the men had come back on the old condition, a pledge that they would not join a union. They had been out only five days.

The resumption of work proved to be only an uneasy truce. 'For a week or two,' says O'Donoghue, 'all went well.' Then the superintendent started discharging men on various pretexts. 'Later on he told them plainly that they were being discharged because they were Knights of Labor, and that he intended to weed them all out.' New employees were required to sign the 'ironclad document' which Alderman Walker thought Smith had promised to drop. The men then drafted a list of grievances, including requests for shorter hours and higher wages, and appointed a committee to wait on Smith. One member presented himself and handed Smith the list of grievances, which that worthy refused to take. The same aldermen who had helped settle the lockout were asked to intervene again. One refused. Another agreed to try, 'but he was so received that under no circumstances, he said, would he ever go to see Mr Smith again.' The men then brought the matter before the Trades and Labor Council, which instructed its president, R.J. Whitton (a Knight), to appoint a committee of three to interview Smith and 'take such action as they deem necessary.'

The committee reported, 7 May that it had called several times at Smith's office, but he was in Ottawa. It had tried, in vain, to see other company officials, and one prominent shareholder. It had left a letter to which it had received no reply. It was going again next day, when Smith was expected home.

Nothing came of this; in fact on 8 May the men struck. Soon after noon, not over 40 of the 350 employees were at work. After dark, no cars at all were running. On 9 May there was a meeting of the KOL, Mayor Howland issued a proclamation, the police said they were determined to protect life and property, and Smith declared, with disingenuously literal accuracy, that no committee had called on him before the strike. He also said the company had given an increase after the lockout, bringing wages up to $8.50 to $10 a week. He denied breaking the agreement of 15 March. He simply would not have a 'secret union' running the company's business. Franklin, the company's superintendent, put in his twopennyworth by announcing that he could man 700 cars.

The *Globe*, wonderful to relate, took the men's side in several strongly pro-union editorials, one of which urged the company to recognize the Knights and make a two-year agreement with them. It also took pains to emphasize, repeatedly, the peaceable and orderly behaviour of the strikers.

On 10 May there were no crowds, and no signs of disturbance, and only about 20 cars running. Next day the strikers started a line of buses of their own. They charged nothing: passengers could contribute to the strikers' funds if they chose. They did choose, and the free buses were well patronized. By 14 May there were about 30 on the streets, and the strikers were getting about three days' work a week driving them. The men had procured 30 covered buses, with horses, from the Hamilton streetcar company, which was only too pleased to disoblige Smith: some little time before it had needed extra equipment, had tried to borrow it from Smith, and had been brusquely refused. Even with this accession of strength, the men were advertising for another 50 teams.

Meanwhile the company and its strikebreakers were having a slim time of it. On 11 May two or three drivers had been pelted with stones, and one of them seriously injured, by what the *Globe* was careful to call 'irresponsible parties not known to the strikers.' Two people were arrested for obstructing a car. On 15 May the *Globe* published figures showing that next to nobody was travelling on the company's cars. Franklin complained bitterly that the strikers had left 630 horses with only 2 foremen to look after them, the men whose job it was having been intimidated by the Knights (which the Knights of course denied).

On 25 May about a dozen new buses for the free line arrived from Oshawa and were greeted by a procession, which packed them to the doors as they wound through the principal streets while the company's cars rattled by empty. The company's drivers were greeted with cries of 'rats' and 'scabs,' and one or two car windows were smashed; but the police remained admirably cool and no serious trouble occurred. Two days later another consignment of buses, from Kingston, was met by another procession. This time there was some disorder, though not by the Knights. Six car windows were broken, and there was 'a doubtful injury of one lady's cheek.' But at least 500 American newspapers carried lurid accounts of 'mob rule,' of 'over thirty street cars wrecked,' and of 'many persons hurt' in a commotion lasting more than three hours. The *Globe* was highly indignant. It blamed the whole thing on the *Mail*. As a result of that paper's nefarious behaviour, 'organized labor of this law-abiding city has been held up to the outside world as the fit ally of the Chicago anarchists.'

Meanwhile, on 19 May there had been a mass meeting of the strikers and their sympathizers. The mayor was present and congratulated the men on their peaceableness and urged dominion legislation to deal with the trouble. The meeting passed, with only one dissenting vote, resolutions in support of the strike and, unanimously, a resolution favouring formation of a strikers' bus company.

This seems to have caught on at once. On 4 June the municipal committee of the Trades and Labor Council reported that it was 'pleased to notice that the late Street Railway employees have been able to start a line of Buses in competition with that monopoly.' Alfred Jury told the council that the 'free Bus system ... [had] been such a paying success, that [the strikers] were induced to start a line ... on the Co-operative principle ... Some hundreds of shares had been taken up,' at $5 each, with an entrance fee of 25 cents. Jury asked each delegate to lay the plan before his own union, to encourage members to take shares in the co-operative. He argued that 'if this was allowed to be a failure it would retard greatly the standing of Unionism in the City, by showing ... [its] weakness to compete against capital.' On 18 June the committee told the council that it was pleased to find that 'the K of L buses continue to be patronised and ... [called] on all union men to take stock in the Bus Co.'

But the co-operative was running into difficulties with its own employees. It had hired teamsters from Oshawa and elsewhere and now wanted them to accept $2.50 per day and board for their teams rather than $3.50 or $4. They refused, but went on running the buses on their own, patronized by a public unaware of the dispute. At the same time, differences arose between the strikers and the Knights' leaders. These latter, full of co-operative zeal, put money into the bus company instead of strike pay: in the first month, strike pay amounted to only $20 per striker. Even so, the co-operative was losing money. The Knights did not want to go into debt. DA 125 took over the management, and on 24 June a general meeting of the Co-operative Bus Association decided to dissolve the company and return to the shareholders whatever they had paid in, less their share of expenses.

The Knights had spent a good deal on the strike. They had been well supported by the rest of the labour movement in Toronto, and indeed beyond, and by private citizens. The Plasterers Union gave $500 (exactly the amount the Knights had to spend to buy buses). The Carters and Teamsters gave 200 buses and 200 horses. The Trades and Labor Council set up a committee on 4 June to work with a general committee, evidently of citizens, to raise funds to help the strikers. At the same meeting, the council resolved to accept, for 14 June, the offer of a Mr Turner to place 'the Boats of his Co at the disposal of the strikers for one day to assist them in obtaining their rights against the unjust demands of the Car Co.' The resulting jaunt to Toronto islands on Turner's boats produced $800 to $1000. The Oshawa Trades and Labor Council called on the Toronto council to join in ostracizing Smith if he stumped the country in the election, as he would, and in sending a copy of the resolution to Sir John A. Macdonald. (Smith had not only steadfastly refused to negotiate, or to submit the dispute to conciliation or arbitration, but had, from his place in the Senate, denounced the working men of Toronto as thieves.) The Toronto council concurred, adding a rider that demanded Smith's removal from the cabinet.

The strike seems to have fizzled out in July. The Knights and the unions had done their best, and many citizens had rallied nobly to their support. But 'Vain faith, and courage vain!' vain the contributions of Mr Turner's boats, vain even the support of the *Globe*! The strike failed.

Before the streetcar strike was over, the Toronto Plumbers and Steamfitters, LA 5493, were threatening to go out. They wanted a minimum of 25 cents an hour for journeymen, a working day of 9 hours in summer (with Saturday afternoon off) and 8 hours in winter, none but union journeymen to be hired in future, and all non-union men already employed (except for those doing first-class work) to be discharged unless they joined up. The assembly's 42 members included, the *Globe* said, 'all the better class of workmen in the city.' The deadline for the demands, which were presented at the end of May, was mid-June. Eight firms agreed to the 25 cent minimum wage and a 9-hour day with 10 hours' pay, a Saturday half-holiday, time-and-a-quarter for Saturday work after 1 pm, time-and-a-quarter for work after 6 pm, and double time for Sundays. The assembly apparently dropped the demand for a union shop, but it struck the firms which refused to accept the compromise.

By the end of June the master carpenters were refusing to sign an agreement, jibbing at a demand for a minimum wage. Three organizations were involved: the ASCJ (two branches); the American Brotherhood of Carpenters, Local 27; and the KOL, LA 8235. The masters and the unions eventually compromised on a 9-hour day (8½ in winter), with no other change.

But the unions were not satisfied, and on 22 January 1887 they presented a new series of demands: an increase of 2½ cents, to give a uniform minimum of 25 cents an hour (abolishing the masters' right to limit the minimum to those they considered qualified workmen); a 54-hour week (5 hours on Saturday); time-and-a-half for work after 5 pm Monday to Friday and after noon on Saturday; double time on Sundays; pay for time spent walking about the shop to collect their wages; and an hour's pay for any carpenter discharged, so that he could grind his tools and put them in order. The masters reluctantly agreed to meet the men's representatives, but absolutely refused to discuss anything. The 1886 terms were good enough for them. They even refused to accept arbitration.

The original deadline had been 1 May but the men took no action till 4 May, perhaps partly because the DA refused to sanction a strike. By this time, the Bricklayers were asking for an increase of 2½ cents to 35 cents an hour; the Stone Masons for one of 2½ cents to 30 cents. The masters in all three trades declined to take any action. So, on 9 May, over the opposition of the Knights (who felt that themselves could represent all these trades), the Carpenters, Bricklayers, Stone Masons, Plumbers, Painters, and Stone Masons' Labourers, formed a Building Trades Federation.

In the carpenters' dispute, the employers still would not budge, so on 10 June the ASCJ, the ABC, and the KOL decided to strike the next day. Between 600 and 700 union carpenters, and another 400 or 500 non-union, went out. On 13 June 27 employers agreed to the new rates, and their 400 employees went back. On 30 June, however, in an effort to bring the strike to an end, the unions called these men out again, and building operations were completely paralysed. For a time a general strike of all the building trades seemed possible, but the federation was against this and urged the carpenters to work for the employers who had accepted the demands. By about mid-August the master carpenters were getting all the non-union labour they needed. By 19 August the Knights had decided to let their men go back; two days later the other two organizations officially declared the strike over. The men went back on substantially the old terms without an agreement, though they seem to have got a one cent increase in wages.

The three organizations had, till almost the end, stood firmly united. Other unions had supported them, the Bricklayers alone contributing $1000. Once again there was a benefit concert on the Island, which brought in about $1500. But all this was not enough to offset a wage loss of $48,000.

LA 3181 (varnishers and polishers) and LA 3684 (woodworkers) struck the Heintzman Piano Co, Toronto, in the spring of 1887. The company had discharged three old polishers. DA 125 asked to have them reinstated. The company refused. The DA proposed arbitration by the board of trade. The company twice refused and discharged the master workman of LA 3181. The LA demanded his reinstatement, and LA 3684 supported it. The company again refused arbitration and the men struck. On 28 March the DA endorsed the actions of the two LAs, and David R. Gibson, the Knights' Canadian supply agent, went to see the company. He got a courteous reception, but the company's proposals were not acceptable. After seven weeks the company accepted arbitration by a board of which the district master workman was to be a member.

A Toronto LA, organized in 1886, secured from a boxmaker employer a 20 to 30 per cent wage increase in 1887. But by January 1888 it had struck unsuccessfully against the employment of a non-union man.

Hamilton Bakers LA 2156 struck in April 1886. They were working 13 to 14 hours a day, for wages ranging from $1.25 a day to $5 a week. They demanded the day system of hours, a nine-hour day, a three-year apprenticeship system, and restriction of apprentices to one per shop. By the end of the month five master bakers had fallen into line, and the assembly threatened to boycott the rest. The recalcitrant master bakers, loud in their denunciations of the assembly for presenting its bill of grievances at all, apparently stood firm, for on 14 May the strike was still in progress.[19]

LA 6582 (spinners and weavers) in Cornwall struck twice in 1887 against the Stormont Cotton Mills and the Canada Cotton Co. According to one account, the first strike at Canada Cotton was against a 28 to 33 per cent cut in weavers' wages. It was settled by arbitration, though the company refused to sign an agreement. The men alleged that the company then broke the agreement, and a second strike followed, lasting a month. The summer strike at Stormont Cotton resulted from a demand by 18 Knights, dyers of raw cotton and cotton yarn, for a reduction in hours from 10 to 9. The manager locked them out, refusing conciliation. In both cases, the discharge of employees because they were Knights seems to have been a factor, though the companies denied this, or blamed it on a single overseer.

The Cornwall weavers struck again, in 1889, for five weeks, and secured a compromise agreement. This was almost certainly a Knights' strike. LA 6582 may have been gone by this time; but LA 6583 (mixed) was certainly still there, and LA 358 was organized in 1889.[20]

The organization of the Amherst (Nova Scotia) local assembly, in April 1890, provoked an explosion from the local employers. They had told the Royal Commission on the Relations of Capital and Labour in 1888 that they had no organization among their employees, though they felt obliged to add that one man belonged to the Coal Cutters Union.[21] This idyllic state of affairs had evidently continued, for the Halifax *Morning Herald*, commenting on the appearance of the Knights, observed on 1 May that Amherst had been 'heretofore without experience in the ... conflict between capital and labor,' but seemed 'now to be beginning the war in good shape.' 'A number of dissatisfied hands claiming they had grievances owing to the way in which the Amherst boot and shoe management was conducting their outside business ... [had begun] the formation of a knights of labor society, and some fifty of the hands [had] become connected with the organization.'

But, though only the boot and shoe workers were involved, the employers rallied in an impressive display of class solidarity. On 25 April 19 employers addressed a printed letter to their employees. The firms had heard of a movement to establish an assembly. They were aggrieved that those involved in the matter had not 'deemed [it] advisable to take the employers nor all the workmen into their confidence.' Heretofore there had been 'mutual confidence and good feeling between employers and employed.' The future prospects of the 'now flourishing town' depended on 'the continued success of its factories and workshops ... Anything tending to come between those who are furnishing the capital and giving employment and those who are employed, but who are quite as much interested in the success of the town, many of whom own property in it, would undoubtedly break up that harmony and good feeling and replace it by distrust and enmity and strike a death blow at our now prosperous industries; we think therefore that a movement of this kind should be carefully considered ... before it is allowed to get a foothold here.'

This consideration they then proceeded to give:

Let us examine ... the objects aimed at by the Knights of Labor: It is claimed that its main object is to enable workmen to protect themselves, and regulate the prices and hours of labor, etc. In reply we would ask, do not the laws of 'supply and demand' regulate wages as well as other commodities in defiance of any society? If wages are too low in any factory or town is the workman not free to go to any other place where he can get more? He is more independent than the employer who cannot move his factory at will; but if the workman by means of labor organizations succeeds in forcing the price of his labor higher than the market will warrant, does it not lead either to the closing down of the workshops or the manufacturers combining in trusts, as they have done in the United States, to protect themselves against the unreasonable demands of trades unions?

Second. It is claimed that by having a general fund the workmen will get relief in case they are thrown out of employment. How would this work for Amherst? Supposing the workmen of Amherst had contributed to the Knights of Labor during the last ten years, who would have got the greater benefit, the mechanics of Amherst or the loafers and strikers in the United States?

Third. In your experience, when you have had a difference with your employer, has it been better to settle the matter with him yourself, or would it have been better to try to force him to your way of thinking by means of a strike dictated by the Knights of Labor?

Fourth. So far, have you seen in Amherst any number of industrious capable men out of employment, or not receiving wages in proportion to their ability? Do you know of any town where they pay better wages than Amherst, or where the mechanics as a rule are more prosperous? If so why not go there? The Royal Commission report shows that the wage earners of Amherst are as well paid and better satisfied than in most other towns in Canada.

Fifth. Why have Amherst and other small towns been more successful as a rule in manufacturing than Halifax, St John, and other towns where they have trades unions? and why as a rule are the mechanics better off and more contented?

In conclusion we would refer to the fact that nearly all the managers of the principal manufactories of Amherst have been wage earners, and can assure their fellow mechanics that they did not get their present position by means of trades unions, and we feel sure that all level-headed workmen who are capable of doing a good day's work and earning a good day's pay will not feel that they need a union to get their rights, and that they are not willing to sacrifice their independence to any society which proposes to regulate their affairs, nor to contribute to keep up loafers or strikers in the United States or elsewhere; and they will decide with the undersigned fellow citizens that Amherst does not want a branch of the 'Knights of Labor' or any other organization which will interfere with the satisfactory relations which now exist between workmen and employers. We feel sure that the majority of workmen are totally indifferent or opposed to the organization referred to, but in order that there may be no doubt in the minds of those few who are agitating for it, we the undersigned manufacturers think it prudent to state that we will not employ any person whom we know to be a member of the 'Knights of Labor' or any other Society which proposes to come between us and our workmen.

This sublime effusion is a classic; its only novel feature is its explanation of the rise of trusts in the United States.

But the employer most concerned did not 'divorce the feeling from her mate, the deed.' On 1 May a number of the Knights were discharged from the shoe factory, and on 2 May all of them, about 50, were discharged when they refused to leave the KOL.

The sequel was reported in the *Morning Herald* of May 26:

The labor trouble seems to have been reduced to whether 20 or 30 hands of shoe factory who are off, shall have the American order of knights of labor, or whether the 150 hands who remain at work shall have a lodge of the Provincial Workmen's Association. What seems therefore to have been an injustice from the presentation of one side only, resolves itself into a matter of easy adjustment. With the excellent order of Provincial Workmen's Association – a provincial [body] incorporated by our legislature – we cannot see why these persons will not accept it in preference to the American societies. The Provincial Workmen's Association will soon be a fixture at Amherst and 'tis hardly to be supposed that the vast majority of this firm's hands, backed by Manager Pride, who has, we learn, offered material assistance to the PWA lodge, will be induced to favor the knight's order. 'Tis admitted by both parties that some misunderstanding existed on both sides regarding these societies, but we have it on good authority that the employers of labor in Amherst will give their general support to the provincial order, and would induce their hands to join it in preference to the American order. With so little difference we look for an early settlement.

This was too optimistic. In July the men were still on strike. Also, the PWA, perhaps not too happy about the material assistance of Pride and the general support of the other employers, did not charter its Concord Lodge, No 24, till January 1891.[22]

In 1898, however, the Knights tackled another part of Nova Scotia, the Cape Breton coal fields, where the PWA had been established for something like two decades. The Knights had secured the support of a former prominent member of the PWA, the legendary A.B. McGillivray, then and long after magistrate at Glace Bay.[23] At the 1898 general assembly McGillivray appeared as the delegate of DA 35, which was described as made up largely of miners. In 1899 he was present again. This time he moved a resolution to have the general master workman and the grand secretary interview Mr Whitney, head of Dominion Coal Co, who was checking off 'Miners Union' dues and refusing to do the same for the Knights. The resolution carried, but seems to have had no effect. At a special general assembly in June 1900 McGillivray again represented DA 35 and was elected general worthy foreman (the second-highest office in the order). At the regular general assembly in November 1900 he was present, but seems to have taken no part in the proceedings. In 1901 he was not present, but the general assembly was told that the district had not been very successful in 'keeping its LAs in good condition ... owing entirely to the opposition of the Dominion Coal Company: This deprives us of the presence of our esteemed Brother, A.B. McGillivray.' With this, the curtain descends on DA 35.[24]

One of the most spectacular strikes in which the Knights were involved was in the Ottawa and Hull lumber-mills in 1891 and 1892. Twenty-four hundred men struck nine firms.[25] In 1890 the mill hands had been getting $7 to $9.50 per week of almost 60 hours. In the late spring of 1891, the employers announced a wage cut of 50 cents a week, with a 10-hour day. The wage cut materialized; the 10-hour day did not. The men asked the KOL for organizational and strike assistance. The Knights replied that their rules required six months' notice of a strike, and that, as cutting would end in six months, there was no use trying to force negotiations that season.

On 12 September eight or nine men at Perley and Pattee's asked to have the old wage rate restored. The employer refused. The men struck, 14 September, and the foreman closed the mill, laying off 350 men. Mr Pattee said the cut was the general policy of the employers. The men thereupon marched to the other mills and invited their workers to join the strike: 800 from Booth's, 300 from Buell, Orr and Hurdman's, and 500 from Bronson and Weston's did so, as did the workers on the docks and in the shipping yards adjacent to the mills. They demanded the restoration of the old wage rate and a 10-hour day. Mason's, in Mechanicsville (Ottawa), was willing to accept the men's demands; the other employers were not.

Three thousand strikers met at Booth's mill and decided to appeal to the KOL and the Ottawa Trades and Labor Council for help. Next day, the strikers tried to get the women, girls, and boys employed at Eddy's, and the labourers working a 13-hour day on the construction of Eddy's new paper mill, to join them. Eddy and his managers tried to keep the strikers from entering the premises, and fights broke out. Eddy was jostled, kicked, and struck with a stone. The Hull police made a few arrests and operations ceased. At Mason's, where work had resumed, the strikers forced teamsters to stop work, and in the scuffle Mason's son struck a striker with a stick and was beaten up by the rest.

Next day, at a rally at the Chaudière, attended by a large number of police, Napoléon Fauteux, the strikers' leader; J.W. Patterson, president of the Ottawa Trades and Labor Council; and ex-alderman Farrell, of the ITU, exhorted the strikers to stand firm and assured them of labour solidarity and support. That evening, the employers induced three magistrates to requisition the militia. Fauteux, Patterson, Farrell, and A.B. Ingram, MP and a prominent Knight, tried to get the government to refuse, but under the Militia Act it had no power to do so. Four militia companies were called out, issued with ten rounds of ball ammunition, and marched to Hull in time for the beginning of work next morning. Taunting and jeering strikers lined the streets, but there was no confrontation, and non-striking carpenters at Eddy's resumed work. Fauteux and Patterson, with six strikers, visited Eddy; assured him that only a few of those involved in the earlier violence were strikers, led by an outsider; and offered, if Eddy would send the militia home, to provide reliable men to protect his property and non-striking employees. Eddy demurred, and when the militia colonel himself urged that the soldiers be sent home, the magistrates jibbed. Next day 4000 strikers and sympathizers paraded around Parliament Hill, without incident, and squads of strikers replaced the militia around the mills.

The mill owners now issued a statement, saying that granting the strikers' demands would add 20 per cent to the cost of lumber, at a time when the industry was already in difficulty, with many mills closed and the rest on half-time, as a result of poor markets in Britain, political trouble in South America, and inferior timber which had to be brought from farther away. They claimed also that the men should have given 30 days' notice of striking. Patterson replied at a mass meeting that giving the notice would merely have given the employers time to bring in strikebreakers. He added that, though the strike had been spontaneous and unorganized, the KOL 'as an organized body would take up the matter and see them through it.' The meeting ended with the strikers cheering Fauteux and the queen.

The Hull merchants called a meeting for 20 September. A crowd of at least 5000 jammed the Main Street square. The warden of Ottawa County presided. Alfred Rochon, MLA and former mayor of Hull; C.H. Mackintosh, Conservative MP for Ottawa; Mayor Birkett of Ottawa; and several Hull aldermen (two-thirds of the Hull council supported the strike) all spoke in support of the strikers' demands. Patterson said the depression, used as an excuse for the wage cut, was over, and prices were even better than in 1890. The chairman said a large number of Ottawa and Hull merchants had declared their support for the strikers, and a meeting in the Ottawa City Hall had set up a citizens' committee consisting of himself, Birkett, Rochon, Mackintosh, Patterson, a Hull priest, and three Protestant ministers, to seek a settlement. Rev Dr Ryckman, a Methodist, said the Old Testament called the oppression of the hireling in his wages a sin; the workman should be paid enough to enable him to educate his children and to prevent his wife from having to work. (The 1889 report of the Ontario Bureau of Industries had indicated that the mill yardman's wages would leave him $10.13 short of meeting his annual cost of living.) Father Whelan advised the strikers to go back to work and trust the good faith of the mill owners; the strike was a last resort, and he did not think it was yet necessary in this case.

The citizens' committee got nowhere with the employers and reluctantly advised the men to return to work. They refused. By 21 September LA 2966 (Chaudière) and LA 2676 (La Canadienne) had each contributed $75 to the strikers' funds (the Knights as a whole eventually contributed $1500); the printers at the government printing bureau gave another $30; the Ottawa Hackmen's Union gave $100. Two stores were set up to distribute contributions of food, and tea, flour, bread, and pork were contributed by local merchants and private citizens. DA 125 pledged money, and there were rumours of a further promise of $15,000 from Toronto sympathizers. The Trades and Labor Council sent letters to labour organizations in other cities seeking aid, and delegates left for various points in Canada and the United States on the same errand. The men were confident that the KOL would prevent strikebreakers from being brought in. Montreal workmen promised not to handle 'hot' lumber.

On 24 September a mill foreman circulated a message urging the men to return to work, promising a favourable settlement. The leaders agreed, and next morning a large number gathered at the mills, only to discover that the favourable settlement was an offer of an extra quarter-hour for lunch. The men refused.

In the second week of the strike, Sheppard and Morse accepted the strikers' demands, and on 29 September *Le Spectateur* announced that three firms, including Mason's, had agreed to the ten-hour day. A few strikers (higher-paid saw-filers at Bronson's) tried to return to work but were restrained by other strikers, who threatened to tar and feather them if they broke ranks again. The strike leaders began to encourage the men to look for other work in Hull or elsewhere, and by 30 September over 600 were reported to have left the area.

The remaining strikers stood firm. The Knights predicted that 700 would join LA 2676 and another 1500 LA 2966. Ottawa's LA 5222 voted $125 for the strike fund, and the clerks' assembly $100. Two hundred families received relief daily. Dr Ryckman preached a second pro-labour sermon; Dr Armstrong, a Presbyterian, said diplomatically that wages must be ruled by supply and demand but that the worker must have a living wage. Father Ladislas denounced the employers who still stood out for treating their men like slaves.

By the end of the third week, Buell, Orr and Hurdman, and the smaller mills and yards, had caved in. Booth, Perley and Pattee, and Bronson and Weston stood fast. They were said to be offering board and $1.50 a day to strikebreakers from outside the area. The strikers tried to stop the strikebreakers, but by 30 September enough had got in to permit shipping to begin. Trouble broke out; the Ottawa police arrived and drove the men back; and Fauteux restored order. Two men who were arrested were later fined.

Twenty-five men resumed work at Bronson's, but next day 600 strikers marched into the yards, and the strikebreakers and office staff working there fled. At Bronson's, the police were too few to be able to act. At the other mills, enough were on hand to prevent the strikers from acting. The mill owners and the police conferred every day on 'protective' measures, and on 3 October the Ottawa police commissioners swore in 20 special constables.

The relief stores closed 7 October and by 12 October the strike was virtually over, though the strikers did not officially acknowledge this till 19 October. So many men had left the district that only 1100 remained at the Chaudière. The mill owners had won on the 10-hour day issue, but economics forced them to restore the wage cut.

The resumption of work at Bronson's did not last long. On 14 October, the men took the opportunity to find out their terms of employment. When they found they were to get the 1890 wages and one hour for lunch, 200 of them struck again. They got no support from their fellow workers, public sympathy was exhausted, the Ottawa police turned up in force, and at the end of the week the men gave in. They had lost about $150,000 in wages. The sheer economic strength of the employers, backed by the Ottawa police, was too much for them. Lack of a strong organization was another factor. The local Knights were active and zealous, but the order as a whole far from it. Powderly, the general master workman, was in Toronto at the time, but did not even visit Ottawa. Worse, though he expressed his sympathy with the strikers, he said they did not belong to the order and therefore he could not bring their case before his executive board.

None the less, the workers' spirit was not crushed, nor their faith in the KOL destroyed. On the contrary, in March 1892 they organized DA 6, with over 2000 mill hands and general workmen as members, and J.W. Patterson as district master workman. A labour paper, the *Free Lance*, was established, labour became active in local politics, and in the years immediately following 1891 the Chaudière mill owners were obliged to recognize the Knights and settle disputes by negotiation.

Sometimes it was a DA which handled a strike. In 1884 Knights in the Gardner Sewing Machine Co in Hamilton struck. 'In order to save the organization in other and larger factories in [the] city,' DA 61 felt it necessary 'to call the balance of our members in the Gardner factory out until an arrangement had been effected'; and it got the general executive board to send in $600 to help. In 1887 the general strike assistance fund was abolished, and the LAS and DAS had to finance their own strikes and lockouts. (This was the same year in which the order collected, from all its LAS on the continent, $70,000 for the relief of the families of 177 coal miners killed in an explosion at Nanaimo.)[26]

The Knights' lobbying activities were both direct and indirect. All five members of the special parliamentary committee appointed by the Trades and Labor Congress in 1887 were Knights. This committee devolved most of its duties concerning the dominion Parliament on the Canadian legislative committee of the KOL established by the general assembly (at the request of DA 61) in October 1887. The two committees met together on 3 March 1888 and agreed that all TLCC affiliates sending petitions to Parliament were to notify Alfred Jury, of the KOL committee, in Ottawa, 'of the dispatch of such petitions and the name of the member to whom they were sent.' It was also decided that Jury could call on the assistance of members of the TLCC committee if need arose. A.W. Wright, of LA 7814 (Toronto), helped Jury in his work while in Ottawa for a brief period.

In 1889 the TLCC president, J.T. Carey, of LA 7025 (St Catharines), reporting on his 'efforts on behalf of Labor legislation while present during the parliamentary session last winter,' paid special tribute to the help he had received from the St Catharines, Hamilton, Toronto, and Montreal district assemblies of the KOL. The executive reported that on 10 January 1889 it had met the members of the KOL's Canadian legislative committee and that the two had agreed to seek legislation along the lines laid down by the 1888 Congress convention. The Knights' committee did the bulk of the work. Carey's report to the congress covers less than two pages; that of Elliott (chairman of the KOL legislative committee) to the general assembly nineteen. Carey's confines itself to seven subjects, and says almost nothing about any but two; Elliott's deals with twenty. What is more, it is clear that the Knights' committee went into several of these subjects with some care. The Knights' committee reported, with obvious satisfaction, that it had had an interview with Sir John A. Macdonald and that he had given it a cordial invitation to call on him at any time.

The Knights' committee still existed in 1890, but it submitted to the general assembly a much briefer report. The congress had, by now, clearly asserted its primacy in representations to the dominion government and Parliament, and its executive's report to the 1890 convention does not even mention the KOL committee. But the congress president and vice-president, and four other members of the executive of nine, were Knights, and it was President Carey who, again, represented the congress during the parliamentary session, after the committee's initial meeting with four ministers.[27]

Between lobbying and independent political action, it is not always easy to draw a precise line. A number of active and prominent Knights became members of the Ontario and Quebec legislatures and of the dominion Parliament: notably A.B. Ingram (St Thomas, MLA and MP), William Garson (St Catharines, MLA), Joseph Béland (Montreal, MLA), and A.T. Lépine (Montreal, MP). But only Lépine seems to have been advanced as a genuine *labour* candidate independent of any party affiliation, and even he was elected with Conservative support.[28]

The Knights nominated Edward Williams, a locomotive engineer, as labour candidate for the Ontario legislature in Hamilton in 1883, but he polled only 1222 votes to the 2077 and 1922 cast for the other candidates. Kennedy says the Knights ran candidates in all three divisions of Montreal in the provincial election of 1886; certainly there were three labour candidates. All were defeated. In the dominion election of 1887, the Knights joined the Montreal Central Trades and Labor Council in supporting H.J. Cloran, 'National Liberal and Labour' candidate, also defeated.[29]

This series of defeats was broken in the dominion by-election of 1888 in Montreal East. The Conservative member had died. The Liberals nominated A.E. Poirier, the Knights Alphonse-Télesphore Lépine, printer, journalist, recording secretary of LA 3484, first corresponding secretary of the Central Trades and Labor Council, and publisher of a labour paper, *Le Trait d'Union* (a bilingual pun?). The Conservatives supported Lépine, who declared himself in favour of the Conservative policy of tariff protection. He also advocated: a bureau of statistics; land for colonists (meaning, probably, unemployed workers); equal legal protection for capital and labour; public health measures; recognition of unions; cash payment of wages, guaranteed by a lien on the workman's product; abolition of contract labour on public works; compulsory arbitration; regulation of work in prisons and factories; an income tax; issue of money by the state; prohibition of alien labour; nationalization of public services; expansion of the co-operative movement; and the eight-hour day.

Lépine was elected by a majority of nearly 700. He was introduced to the House by two prominent Conservatives, Sir Hector Langevin, minister of public works, and J.J. Curran, and chosen to second the address in reply to the speech from the throne. In 1891 he ran as a straight Conservative and was re-elected; he was defeated in 1896. He seems to have shown a certain independence on labour questions while he was in the House.[30]

The Knights seem also to have backed J.W. Patterson, president of the Ottawa Trades and Labor Council, when he ran for the House of Commons in 1891. He was defeated, though not by a large majority.[31]

The Knights also took part, indirectly, in the 1886 British Columbia provincial election. The Vancouver Island assemblies formed the Workingmen's Party, which nominated John M. Duval, editor of the *Industrial News*, a labour paper, and A.J. Smith for Victoria; and James Lewis and S.H. Myers for Nanaimo. The party's platform included a nine-hour day, legislation to protect miners, amendment of the Lien Law, provision of public lands for settlers, exclusion of Chinese immigrants, and taxation of land speculators 'out of existence.' This savoury mixture, however, did not prove tempting enough to get any of the candidates elected.[32]

The Winnipeg Knights in 1886 appointed a parliamentary committee to confer with the prohibitionist Dominion Alliance on a joint candidate for the provincial elections; but the project fell through, as the Knights insisted on a labour candidate, who was defeated.[33]

By way of redressing the balance, the Vancouver Knights, in the same year, made an alliance with the local vintners' association for the municipal election. The joint program included restriction of Chinese immigration, establishment of public libraries, municipal and financial reforms, and, amazingly, limitation of liquor licences. As the Knights had always excluded from membership anyone who made his living from the manufacture or sale of intoxicating drink (other exclusions were lawyers, bankers, stockbrokers, and professional gamblers), this alliance is as astonishing as the last of its objects. Presumably the Knights wanted the restriction of licences to promote temperance, and the vintners to lessen competition.[34]

Individual Knights also took part in municipal politics. In Quebec City in 1892 James Dussault was elected alderman, and George Parent councillor. In Hull in 1894 the mayor and 9 of the 12 aldermen were Knights.[35]

The Knights strongly favoured the co-operative movement and showed it by deeds as well as words. There was a KOL grocery co-operative in Hamilton in 1885, and a printing co-operative in Toronto in 1887. LA 3305 (London) tried twice, in 1886, to get the general assembly's authority to start a co-operative paper, but the GA refused, apparently doubtful of its success. The Chatham Knights had a co-operative biscuit and confectionery works in 1886–87. The Nanaimo Knights, in September 1887, reported that a highly successful co-operative store had been started there three years before, and that it now had 225 members, capital of $17,500, and sales of over $5000 a month. In December 1887 DA 203 reported that it was agitating the establishment of a co-operative paper and already had a number of shareholders. Montreal, in 1887, had a co-operative shoe company for which DA 125 sought the general assembly's aid in 1888. In April 1888 LA 6632 (Sherbrooke) reported that about a year before it had started a small co-operative grocery store which had been a great success. In 1887 the Norwich (Ontario) Knights formed a joint-stock company which bought the local knitting factory. It was capitalized at $3000 and the shares were $5 each. It was not 'a conspicuous success ... and the knitting machines were sold to the people of Norwich.' In 1888 DA 114 asked the general assembly's approval to offer stock in a tobacco co-operative.[36]

The KOL was also much involved in labour journalism. In Toronto the *Wage-Worker* became a KOL paper just before its end in 1883. A.W. Wright, a prominent Knight, took over the Hamilton *Palladium of Labor* and published it in Toronto between the years 1885 and 1887. O'Donoghue's *Labor Record*, published between 1886 and 1887, merged with the *Canadian Labor Reformer* in 1887. The merged paper was the organ of both the Toronto Trades and Labor Council and DA 125. After a lapse of a few months, it reappeared in the fall of 1889. Another paper, the *Labor Advocate*, published in Toronto between 1890 and 1891, was endorsed by both the council and the assembly. Other KOL papers were the *Canada Labor Courier* (St Thomas, 1886?–87), the *Industrial News* (Winnipeg, 1886–87), the *North-West Call* (Calgary, 1887–88), the *Canadian Workman* (Montreal, 1888), *Le Trait d'Union* (Montreal, 1888), and the *Industrial News* (Victoria, 1885–86).[37]

The Knights were responsible for the organization of the Montreal Central Trades and Labor Council in 1886; their Winnipeg district assembly is said to have provided the basis for the Trades and Labor Council there in 1886–87;[38] and, after some difficulties in getting admitted, in 1884, they took a very prominent part in the Toronto Trades and Labor Council. They were active in other councils also, and for some years dominated the TLCC.

The Canadian Knights took a considerable part in the affairs of the organization as a whole.[39] Canadian delegates (three) appeared first at the general assembly of 1883. One, W.J. Vale (Hamilton), was nominated for general worthy foreman (and got 17 votes out of 105) and elected to the co-operative board. The 1884 general assembly again had three Canadian delegates. George Collis (Hamilton) was nominated for general worthy foreman, but got only a handful of votes. Collis and J.F. Redmond (Montreal) were both appointed to the committee on state assemblies, which reported on the Canadian desire to have a Canadian general assembly. The committee recommended that wherever there were 10 or more assemblies in a foreign country, they should be permitted to form a general assembly of their own, and that the American and foreign general assemblies should exchange representatives (1 each), who would have voice and vote on the secret work of the order. The delegates rejected this but, perhaps by way of consolation prize, voted to hold the next general assembly in Hamilton.

Despite this, and the much larger number of Canadian LAs by then, there were only five Canadian delegates in 1885. D.J. O'Donoghue, representing ten Toronto LAs, and one Oshawa and one Guelph LA, was appointed to the general committee on legislation. D.R. Gibson, from DA 61, was nominated for the co-operative Board, and defeated, but elected Canada supply agent. Gibson also figured at a special general assembly in May and June 1886 as grand internal esquire. The special assembly was called to deal with a proposed treaty, between the Knights and the national and international unions, which did not come off.

At the regular 1886 General Assembly, in Richmond, Virginia, there were four delegates each from DAS 114 and 138, and two each from DAS 61 and 125. There were a number of LA delegates as well. J.T. Carey, of St Catharines, represented two each in St Catharines and Thorold and one each in Toronto, Welland, Port Dalhousie, and Port Colborne. James R. Brown, of Oshawa, represented three in Oshawa and one each in Uxbridge, Lindsay, and Port Perry. Edward Doyle, of Guelph, represented two in Guelph and one in Hespeler. Thomas E. Kilroy, of Windsor, represented three in Windsor and one each in Amherstburg and Essex Centre. And Richard H. Leahey, of Quebec City, represented LA 4003.

This array of Canadian delegates is imposing not only for its number, but also for the number of places represented, the variety of occupations of the delegates, and, most of all, the prominence of several of the delegates. Urbain Lafontaine and J.T. Carey were both to be presidents of the TLCC, and D.R. Gibson (who was to become an international vice-president in the Bricklayers Union) was to be vice-chairman. Brown and Leahey had just been elected to the executive of the congress.

In 1887 there were only six Canadian delegates: from DAS 61, 114, 125, 174, 204, and 207. The sharp decline in the number probably reflects economic difficulties, notably strikes, for the proceedings contain no less than 20 requests from Canadian LAs for relief from assessments.

On 30 September 1887 the Canadian Knights had held a convention in Toronto, which had passed a resolution in favour of a joint committee from itself and the general assembly on the relations between the American and Canadian Knights. It wanted a dominion assembly, subordinate to the general assembly, but with a large degree of autonomy. The dominion assembly would have control over district and local assemblies within its territory, collect all moneys, levy all assessments, and distribute all supplies in Canada. It would pay to the general assembly a proportion of the per capita tax it received from the Canadian assemblies and would get supplies from the general assembly at a price which would leave the dominion assembly a fair profit. Cards issued by American and Canadian assemblies were to be mutually recognized. DA 61 presented this proposal, and one for a Canadian legislative committee, to the general assembly in Minneapolis a few weeks later. The request for the legislative committee was granted; the other scheme was referred to the general executive board, which sat on it.

At the 1888 general assembly there were six Canadian delegates from DAS 61, 114, 125, 174, 235, and 236. A.W. Wright (DA 125) was elected to the general executive board. O.D. Benoît (DA 114) was nominated for the general co-operative board. The 1888 general executive board report had a good deal on requests from various Canadian LAS to get out of, or into, this or that district assembly or national trade assembly. St Catharines LA 2056 did not want to be part of DA 61 and was duly assigned to the new DA 207. Five Berlin LAS wanted to get out of DA 61, but Hamilton LA 2481 protested against any division, and the general executive board ruled that the consent of DA 61 was necessary. None the less, the new Berlin DA was established. LA 6583 wanted to get out of DA 235 and into DA 114. Quebec City LA 10,061 wanted to get out of DA 114 and into a new, Quebec City, DA. Lévis LA 10,123 wanted to get out of DA 114, which in turn protested against attaching Quebec City LA 10,987 to national trade assembly 216 (shoemakers). DA 114 wanted to be made a provincial assembly. The general executive board was willing, if the Montreal LAS would agree. (Seven of them had, in 1886, asked to be put into a separate French-language DA, and the general assembly had been willing, but DA 114 had jibbed.)

At the 1889 general assembly, there were four Canadian delegates, from DAS 125, 207, 235, and 236; in 1890, two, from DAS 125 and 207. In 1891, 1892, and 1893, Wright, who throughout had been a member of the general executive board, represented DA 125, and he took a prominent part in the row which, in 1893, unseated Powderly as general master workman, and in the rumpuses which followed. In 1893 he had two fellow delegates.

From 1894 till 1899 inclusive, only the Quebec DAS were represented at the general assemblies, except for the appearance of DA 35 (Glace Bay) in 1898 and 1899. DAS 18 and 19 were represented in 1894 and 1895, DAS 18 and 20 in the years 1896–98, and DA 18 in 1899. In 1900, DAS 18 and 35 sent a delegate each. The LAS in DA 20 were on strike, so could send no one. The new DA 180 (Toronto) sent Isaac H. Sanderson, who was elected to the general executive board, succeeding Sarsfield Fitzpatrick of DA 18, who had served since 1897. In 1901 DA 180 alone had a delegate, Sanderson, who was re-elected to the general executive board. In 1902 Fitzpatrick re-appeared from DA 18, along with Sanderson from DA 180, who was elected general worthy foreman.

PART TWO

The international unions 1880–1902

8

The revolutionary, railway, and building trades unions

In the first half of the 1880s, the Knights of Labor unquestionably held the centre of the stage. The international craft unions, indeed, more than doubled the number of their locals between 1880 and 1885. Two unions (the Machinists and Blacksmiths, and the Sailors) seem to have disappeared altogether. A third, the American Flint Glass Workers, maintained itself in Hamilton till at least the fall of 1897; Montreal Local 24 appears in 1891 and was still there in 1902; Montreal Local 54 marched in the 1899 Labour Day parade; and a Wallaceburg local formed 17 October 1898 was still in existence in February 1902.[1]

But though two internationals disappeared, a host of new ones came in; the unions already established by 1880 added many new locals; the movement spread from Ontario and Quebec into all the other provinces, and from the larger cities into many smaller cities and towns; and the unions, old and new, moved into new industries. Even at the end of the period, however, organization was heavily concentrated in a few areas in Ontario, railway union locals (running trades and others) made up almost 30 per cent of the total, building trades locals almost another 20 per cent, and metal trades almost a further 12 per cent. Between 1880 and 1890 the growth was rapid; from 1890 to 1897, relatively small. The American Federation of Labor's organizing drive, from 1898 to 1902, more than tripled the 1897 total of locals and took unionism into secondary and service industries and into the ranks of the unskilled (notably the Railway Trackmen and the Longshoremen). Revolutionary unions also made their appearance (see Appendix).

THE REVOLUTIONARY UNIONS

The revolutionary unions were, first and foremost, the Western Federation of Miners (WFM); then the two industrial railway unions, the American Railway Union (ARU) and the United Brotherhood of Railway Employees (UBRE); third the Western Labor Union (WLU), No 155 (Phoenix), organized 5 May 1901.[2]

The WFM had been started in the United States in 1893 as a craft union, but soon developed into an industrial union covering both metal and coal mines. Its members were generally rough frontiersmen, migrants who recognized no international boundaries. Hard conditions and tough, powerful employers made the miners receptive to radical, even revolutionary, ideas; though the WFM joined the conservative American Federation of Labor (AFL) in 1896, it disaffiliated in 1898, and stayed disaffiliated till 1911.[3]

It entered Canada rather quietly. Between 1886 and 1892 various deposits of gold, silver, copper, lead, and zinc were discovered and worked in the Kootenays of British Columbia. The Kootenay mines attracted a mixed labour force: veterans of the Cariboo gold rush, American immigrants, and Welsh, Cornish, and other British miners. They also attracted American, British, and Canadian capital. The British miners brought with them the traditions and habits of British trade unionism, and on 16 July 1895 the first Canadian WFM local, No 38, was established in Rossland. For a time, however, the miners seem to have devoted their energies to a mild form of political action. They wanted a law enforcing an 8-hour day for a 10-hour wage. In the provincial election of 1898 they supported and elected candidates who favoured such a law and who proceeded to pass it. This outraged the employers, who organized to nullify it by posting bonds of $2500 that they would either pay the existing rate of $3.50 a day for the established 10-hour day or $3 for an 8-hour day. They also refused to recognize the union.

The miners' reaction to the bond must have disappointed and startled the employers. Within a year 13 new WFM locals were established. Local 81 (Sandon) was organized 5 December 1898, and the following locals in 1899: 85 (Ymir), 76 (Fernie), 95 (Silverton), 96 (Nelson), 79 (Whitewater), 8 (Phoenix), 22 (Greenwood), 43 (Camp McKinney), 97 (New Denver), 62 (Slocan City), 71 (Moyie), and 59 (Lethbridge). Moreover, in spite of the fierce opposition of powerful employers, all these locals except perhaps Lethbridge seem to have been still in existence in 1902. In 1900 the WFM added Kaslo 69 and Kimberley 100; in 1901 Kamloops 112, Texada 113, and Lardeau 119; and in 1902 Morrissey 120 (coal), Grand Forks 180, Nanaimo 177 (coal), almost certainly Fairview 134, and Michel (coal).

The spurt of organization in 1899 had a by-product which must have seemed ominous to the employers. In the 1898 election the miners had supported candidates of any group or party, provided they pledged themselves to an eight-hour day law. In 1900 the miners nominated a labour candidate of their own, a working miner and a prominent member of the WFM, Chris Foley. He was defeated, but his nomination marked a new stage in the development of independent labour political action in British Columbia.

One result of the miners' political action had been the prohibition of the employment of Chinese or Japanese in the mines. This anti-Orientalism, to modern eyes most unedifying, and out of tune with the humanitarian ideals the labour movement had always professed, was common to the whole North American labour movement of the time and had been for some years. It had ugly tinges of racial prejudice, but also a solid, and more respectable, economic base. Oriental immigrants, accustomed to an abysmally low standard of living, naturally were delighted to work for wages which they thought almost paradisiacally high, but which North American workers thought infernally low. Naturally, the employers took advantage of this, and of the Oriental workers' ignorance of English, which prevented them from even understanding, let alone trying to enforce, expensive safety regulations. The white miners, equally naturally, were afraid of having their standard of living undercut by 'coolie labour,' and their lives shortened by the almost inevitable, and involuntary, Oriental disregard of safety precautions. So they were pleased with a law that said 'No Chinese or Japanese underground in mines,' and correspondingly disillusioned when the dominion government disallowed the act. This may have been one thing which led them to swing away from political action towards industrial. (This alternation between political and industrial action, as each in turn fails to produce the results hoped for, is, of course, a recurrent theme in labour history on both sides of the Atlantic.) Another factor was unquestionably the growing truculence of the employers, whose determination to nullify the eight-hour day law produced a series of shut-downs.

In September 1899 the Slocan mines were on strike. The employers sent a man east in an unsuccessful attempt to find strikebreakers at $3 a day. The management of the Payne mine sent five men from Montreal, who arrived in Sandon armed with Winchester rifles. However, on hearing from the local union officers what the situation was, they refused to work. The company shut the mine down. A few days later, the Silver Lead Mines Association was advertising for 2500 men at $3 a day. This also must have failed, for within a week the association was announcing that it would close all its members' mines 'until the present labor difficulties are adjusted.' That same week all the men at Whitewater walked out because of a row with the acting superintendent. In February 1900 the Slocan lockout was still on, and the Vancouver Trades and Labor Council was watching trains and boats and employment agencies there to ensure that no union men went to Slocan under a misapprehension. About 10 days later, the mine owners offered to pay $3.25 a day (which was what the strikebreakers were getting), but refused to recognize the union. The closing of the War Eagle and Centre Star mines at Rossland, and the Hall Mines at Nelson, alarmed union men, since they feared that if they did not go to work at once they would lose their only chance. By 17 February the Sandon union had declared the strike off, and the men were working at $3.25. Rossland, however, was 'prepared to fight to the bitter end' for the eight-hour day. In two years, the local had grown from 180 members to 1800. It said the War Eagle and Centre Star mines were closed not because of the owners' resistance to the eight-hour law but because they were not safely timbered. In March there were strong complaints of violation of the Alien Labour Act. By April 5 the Rossland Board of Trade was announcing that the troubles there had been 'brought to a satisfactory conclusion' and that the settlement might be regarded as permanent.

This turned out to be wishful thinking. According to Frank Woodside, secretary of the Rossland local in 1901, there had been reasonable harmony between employers and workers there for the five years before 1899. But in October 1899 the British American Corp with seven mines, and the Gooderham syndicate, with two, both came under new management. In February 1900 the Gooderham mines, and then one of British American, were closed 'for repairs to machinery.' They stayed closed for two months. Then British American announced it was prepared to reopen its mine on the contract system. The union was at first unanimously opposed, but finally, under pressure from the dominion and provincial governments, voted in favour. The company proceeded to install spotters in the workforce and to blacklist union members. The president of the local succeeded in getting rid of the spotters, but factional disputes in the union, and the failure of members to attend meetings, weakened it. The company took advantage of this to forbid the secretary to solicit members on company property, which he had been accustomed to do, usually when they were going on or off shift. It also began bringing in new men from the United States. This was a violation of the Alien Labour Act, and the union managed to get it stopped. But things were clearly hotting up.

Common labour in Rossland at this time was getting 50 cents a day less than in other camps, and the local decided it was time to wipe out this differential, bringing the Rossland rate up to $3. The union also demanded that the companies stop discriminating against its members. It knew that there was an accumulation of ore at the smelter in Northport, just over the border, and that this was therefore an unpropitious time to strike. Nevertheless, the men's patience was wearing thin, and the smelter itself had just been organized. So on 8 April 1901 the Rossland local took a strike ballot. The vote in favour of a strike was 12 short of the necessary three-quarters' majority required by the WFM constitution, and for the moment the union could take no action.

Both sides, however, were girding for battle. The employers tried to get the Slocan mine employers to agree to shut down if Rossland did, so that contributions from the Slocan union men would not come in to help Rossland strikers. The Slocan employers, however, were unreceptive. The 1899 strike had been severe and had put back mining in the Slocan a couple of years.

The union was relying to some extent on a co-operative started some months earlier. The local businessmen, during the earlier strike, had refused the miners credit. The men had then organized a co-operative, which was prepared to extend credit to the amount of two-thirds of each man's holdings. As most of the miners owned their own homes, they felt reasonably confident of their ability to hold out for some time, especially as the companies had made heavy investments in machinery and had paid few or no dividends.

The atmosphere was clouded by trouble over Italian immigrant miners, on whose loyalty the companies were believed to be relying, and whom the local merchants found poor customers. The union suspected that special constables sworn in the year before, and still on hand, were Pinkertons. Some of these had wormed their way into the union and acted as spies. The union alleged that contrary to the agreement arrived at in 1900 the walking delegate had been prevented from approving the employment of non-union members, because he was personally obnoxious to the management. There was also the question of the contract system, which some of the men feared would be used to cut wages, especially as the management said that contract rates negotiated with the union were impracticable.

What precipitated the long and bitter struggle which raged throughout the summer and fall was the situation at Northport, where Rossland ores were smelted. The local there had been organized in March. About the middle of May the smelter was closed down 'for repairs' (the turn-of-the-century equivalent of the Mohawk Valley formula a generation later), and the manager called in the men with the grim statement, 'Bring your withdrawal cards [from the union], or don't come.' One came, and Northport was officially on strike from 24 May. This, coming on top of its own experiences (which included the companies' refusal even to acknowledge the union's demands), convinced the Rossland local that the employers were out to break the union. If the Rossland miners went on working while the Northport smelter was closed, ore would simply pile up still further there, and when the smelter reopened the companies would say they now had enough ore to supply the smelter for some time and would close the mines accordingly.

The immediate dispute was with Le Roi Co, which owned the Northport smelter and two mines at Rossland. On 3 July 1901 the local decided that a strike vote should be taken next day. At this time there were between 700 and 900 members in good standing. According to the WFM constitution, no strike vote could be taken unless a meeting of the local so decided; and there had then to be 24 hours' notice of the taking of the vote, by secret ballot. The constitution also required that no strike should take place, even after a secret ballot had given a three-quarters' majority in favour, without the approval of the international executive board. The board had to have 15 days' notice of any changes in 'working time or wages advocated by the [local] union, unless an employer or employers attacked the rights of any members of a [local] union or its established principles without allowing the local sufficient time to notify the Executive Board.' Apparently the local officers thought this last gave them a right to act immediately and to disregard the 24 hours' notice rule. The vote was taken, beginning a bare 12 hours after the local's meeting. The members voted in favour of a strike and went out on 11 July at the Le Roi, War Eagle, Centre Star, and some smaller mines. Next day, the Gooderham miners also went out, bringing the total on strike to about 1000. All the struck mines were completely shut down.

Six of the smaller mines accepted the union's demands. The other companies insisted they were unable to grant the increase. They also were unwilling to recognize the union, although they claimed they did not insist on their employees leaving the union. Centre Star and War Eagle were kept closed, but Le Roi brought in strikebreakers, in violation of the Alien Labour Act, and, despite a successful prosecution, continued to do so. Centre Star and War Eagle chose legal means to break the union: they sued it, and won $12,500 damages; they also got injunctions against it.[4]

By the time Mackenzie King, the dominion deputy minister of labour, arrived on the scene on 9 November 1901 the two Le Roi mines were both working with, the management claimed, some 500 to 600 men employed, and the strike had virtually collapsed. King, greatly daring, asked the companies for a statement of their position. He got it, in writing, from an altitude of perpetual frost. The Le Roi company said its mines were in full operation, its employees were satisfied with their hours and wages, and were 'working peacefully.' It felt it was 'useless to discuss a past condition of affairs which no longer concern us.' War Eagle said there was an abundant supply of labour, and it could operate its mines whenever it chose, and wound up with the same lofty phrases as Le Roi. King thereupon submitted the letters to the local union executive and asked it to call a meeting of the local, 'at which I might read these communications and make a statement to the members of the situation.' The executive refused. King, indefatigable in his pursuit of peace, then saw one of the officers of the District (WFM District 6, established in December 1899) and tried to get him to consent to a meeting of the local. He got the same answer.

In justification of their position, the officers urged that to declare this strike at an end, without having received some definite acknowledgement from the mining companies, as to what they were prepared to do in the matter of considering the increase demanded in the wages of the muckers, would be to leave in a precarious position the interests of muckers in other mines in British Columbia, and that, consequently, if necessary, the strike would have to be perpetuated indefinitely. The exact position of affairs in Rossland will accordingly be seen from the statements of the companies, and the officers of the union. So far as any formal declaration of the strike being at an end is concerned, it has not been made, nor is it likely that it ever will be made. On the other hand, the situation as it affects the companies is probably best expressed in their own words.

Here ended King's report. His distinctive literary style, and his characteristic attitude towards unions, had already taken shape.[5]

Meanwhile in February the Van Anda miners had organized a local and struck against the employment of Japanese miners and engineers, and the employers' refusal to 'guarantee white men wages.' This strike, however, was declared off early in April, as the management issued assurances that the Japanese were out of the mines, which were now to be operated by the bondholders, not the old company.[6]

As the deputy minister foresaw, the Rossland strike never was officially called off. Industrial action having failed, the WFM swung back towards politics. It succeeded in getting a provincial act outlawing injunctions and suits for damages in certain kinds of labour disputes. But this was not enough. In March 1902 District 6 summoned central labour bodies, and single tax, socialist, and other reform bodies in the province to a convention in Kamloops on 14 April. The Progressive party which resulted never got off the ground. By the end of this year it was dead. The WFM international convention declared for socialism in June; the socialists took over District 6; and Eugene Debs, the American socialist leader, denounced the new party. Apathy did the rest.[7]

The WFM's coal locals had an interesting history. Fernie soon won recognition and a wage increase. The formation of other coal locals and an urge to expand into Vancouver Island led the WFM on 7 December 1901 to set up District 7, to cover coal miners on the Island and in the Crow's Nest Pass and Lethbridge. The new district was not, however, formally constituted till 25 November 1902. Meanwhile the Michel local, with 160 members, had struck on 3 November to protest the discharge of the local president who, the company claimed, was interfering with the operation of the mine. The strike lasted till 17 November and the union lost.

District 7's life was short and violent. It succeeded in taking over the TLCC's Miners and Mine Labourers Protective Association at Nanaimo in December 1902, but the Island coal companies refused to deal with the WFM. Strikes and lockouts followed; WFM coal locals deserted, early in 1903, to the United Mine Workers of America; and District 7, for all practical purposes, came to an end in November 1903, though its charter was not formally revoked till 1904.[8]

The WFM of course survived, and remained a potent factor in British Columbia, and to some extent elsewhere in Canada, for many years. The other two unorthodox international unions were hardly more than 'apparitions sent to be a moment's ornament.'

Debs' American Railway Union (ARU) had a local, No 243, in the Winnipeg Trades and Labor Council at, or soon after, its formation in 1894. At the council's 5 February meeting, William Small of the ARU was chairman. During the Northern Pacific strike that summer the Winnipeg ARU was described as solid, and on 1 July, during the Pullman strike, the men at the Winnipeg shops, with the firemen, struck. The Winnipeg ARU survived the collapse of the strikes. It marched in the 1894–96 Labour Day parades, and Small (still, or again, chairman of the Trades and Labor Council) was one of the leading figures in the founding of the Winnipeg Labor party in October 1896. But on 19 June 1897 Local 243 reported to the council that it was withdrawing, as its membership had 'considerably dwindled.'

An ARU local was admitted to the Vancouver Trades and Labor Council on 16 January 1896, but by 16 July 1897 it had been obliged to surrender its charter. In Toronto on 11 July 1896 the recording secretary of the Trades and Labor Council reported that 'meetings were being held in the interests of the American Railroad Union – Mr. Goodwin the Organizer would hold a public meeting on the 18th to which the Council was invited.' W. Spence, of the ARU, cast in his lot with the Industrial Brotherhood in London in 1897, so there had evidently been a local there.[9]

The other radical union was the United Brotherhood of Railway Employees (UBRE). A purely local union of this name had been established in Winnipeg on 15 September 1898, made up mostly of CPR clerks, freight handlers, carmen, shop employees, and bridge and building men. After about a year 'the men from the shop departments formed class craft unions, and the brotherhood was left to only men of the freight department.' Early in 1902 it decided to go international and on 25 April became Division 70 of the UBRE. Vancouver Division 81 was chartered 24 June and admitted to the Vancouver Trades and Labor Council on 4 December. Three other divisions were organized in Revelstoke, Nelson, and Calgary some time in the fall.[10]

Meanwhile, during the summer, the Winnipeg division had been having a battle with the CPR and the Canadian Northern Railway. The CPR had dismissed some UBRE members, and the international president, George Estes, had come to Winnipeg to see what he could do about it. He held several meetings which, according to the TLCC,

were highly successful in bringing into the ranks of their union, not only many in the service of the CPR, but also the largest proportion of those employed on the CNR. Among the latter were engineers, firemen, conductors, brakemen, switchmen, freighthandlers, clerks and other classes, most of whom had never previously belonged to any trade union, and worked for a corporation which exerted an influence that hitherto had defied all attempts to organize their employees.

In the meantime, the employees of the CNR machine shop after several attempts to deal collectively with the management, had gone on strike, and through their committee agreed to act in co-operation with the local representatives of the UBRE. Organization meetings, under the auspices of the UBRE, were being held with the result that the original organization of less than 100 members had been increased to approximately 1,000.

The movement had the hearty sympathy and co-operation of all local Trade Unionists. In due course schedules for the various classes of employees were prepared, and presented. ... The CNR management refused to recognize any committee representing the men or any trade union. In subsequent attempts to open negotiations the president of this corporation openly declared his determination to defeat the trade unions at its headquarters, which he flatteringly called Winnipeg. The UBRE called out their members and their order was loyally obeyed. [The *Labour Gazette*'s version is that on 30 June some 220 freight handlers and others struck, partly in sympathy with the machinists.] A general meeting was held, and Mr A.G. Broatch, a highly respected member of the ... Machinists, was elected chairman of the strike committee. Mr. Broatch was one of the machine shop employees who had previously gone out. This attitude of the company ... concerned not only the men who were on strike, but every member of trade unions in Canada. Mr Mackenzie, the president of the Canadian Northern Railroad, is the same gentleman who, as president of the Toronto Street Railway, refused to recognize trade unionism in the latter city. He is a magnate who controls undertakings employing large numbers of workmen all over the Dominion, and, therefore, every thoughtful trade unionist will readily see the far-reaching effects the result of the present strike will have.

The men on strike have used every effort to induce the company to meet them. The deputy minister of labor, the city council, the local government, have all intervened, only to receive the same response as the representatives of the men – that recognition of trade unions would not be granted.

The cessation of work of several hundreds of members of the UBRE seriously crippled the business of the company. The passenger service was continued under difficulties, as the engineers, firemen and trainmen and some of the switchmen, did not join the UBRE and those who joined did not cease work. Some few train hands were members of the brotherhoods, but as employees of the CNR, they derived no benefit whatever from their membership.

Largely as a result of the critical position they were in, and encouraged by the friendly attitude of the committee in charge of the strike they severally held meetings and actually negotiated with the general strike committee for the presentation of schedules along with those of the UBRE, and the distinct understanding was arrived at, that no agreement would be made until all schedules presented were dealt with and signed. No better evidence could be adduced to attest the sympathy of the engineers, firemen, and other train hands with the men on strike. The schedules were drafted by the officers of the UBRE, and were taken back to them to be amended in accordance with the wishes of the trainmen in question. Action, however, was delayed until representatives from the respective headquarters of the brotherhoods arrived in the city, when meetings were held, and afterwards the international officers immediately were received by the management of the Canadian Northern Railway, with the result that public announcement was made that these international officers had signed schedules with the company for their respective brotherhoods. The various classes of men belonging to the UBRE were ignored, and also the obligations entered into by the firemen and others.

The company that boasted its determination to defeat trade unionism were beaten, and knew that their only salvation was to accept the schedules of the trainmen. The latter knew that it was impossible to procure the schedules but for the position created by the rank and file of the UBRE. It is thus clear that the trainmen – conductors, engineers, firemen – entered into a common understanding to defeat the men who had legitimately combined and struck for laudable ends, and had done this at the instigation of the grand officers of the leading Railway Brotherhoods.

The men belonging to the UBRE represent the majority of the railroad trade union workers in Winnipeg. Their joining the UBRE had the countenance of the Trade Council and the enthusiastic approval of all local trade unionists. Their accession to union ranks seemed the climax of years of faithful effort to organize them. It cannot then surprise this Congress that locally the action of the brotherhoods in question is regarded as traitorous in the extreme, and that we cannot expect less from the central body of Canada than an endorsement of the action of the Winnipeg Trade Council in declaring the CNR unfair, and that every member of the brotherhoods in question working under their 'stolen' schedules are entitled, in every sense of the word to be called 'unfair.' The action of the brotherhoods in thus disregarding the broad principles of co-operative action between unions as well as individuals is sincerely deplored and will constitute the blackest page in the history of trade unionism in Manitoba.[11]

The *Labour Gazette*'s version of these events suggests the hand of Mr Bowdler: 'an arrangement ... of the various schedules presented by several of the orders, viz.: the Brotherhoods of Firemen, Conductors and Telegraphists, avoided difficulties with those organizations.' This, and 'the return of the freight clerks, left the struggle mainly with the members of the United Brotherhood of Railway Employees.'

The TLCC's account of the strike is necessarily summary. Certain details are worth filling in. For one thing, the earlier part of the strike was marked by several of what the *Labour Gazette* was careful to call 'alleged' acts of violence, for which the UBRE consistently disclaimed responsibility. At Port Arthur, some 40 Italians hired by the agent of a steamer loading freight were ordered, says the *Labour Gazette*, 'to quit work and did so' (the UBRE must have had some organization, or at any rate influence, well east of Winnipeg).

Support for the strike by Winnipeg unions generally was shown in unmistakable fashion. On 16 July 800 workers from various unions paraded in sympathy with the strikers and listened to speeches supporting the strike. Later the Trades and Labor Council asked the provincial government to try to get a settlement (the company president told the acting premier he refused to recognize the strikers). On 28 July the council registered an emphatic protest against the CNR's attitude, which had been made perfectly clear on 17 July when 'a committee representing a number of the recent employees of the company discussed their grievances with the vice-president.' He told them the company had already filled a number of vacancies left by the strikers and would have to keep faith with these new employees. It was prepared, however, to reinstate 'as many as possible of the men who are still out,' but they would have to make individual application to the heads of the various departments. Wages would be as on the CPR. Departmental schedules were to be discussed with a committee appointed by a majority from each department (those already employed, and those reinstated). The proposition was presented to Division 70, which rejected it without discussion, as an insult.

The September *Labour Gazette*'s sole comment on the strike is that the 'company claims to be no longer embarrassed.' The October issue has nothing. Amazingly, however, the strike was not completely lost. By December the *Labour Gazette* was reporting: 'It is understood that the United Brotherhood of Railroad Employees is negotiating with the Canadian Northern Railroad, with good prospects for a settlement.' In February 1903 it reported that a settlement satisfactory to both sides had been arrived at. The question of union recognition had been waived, but in 'several lines of work an increase of pay over competing lines of railway was secured.'[12]

This, apparently, was enough to keep Division 70 alive and strong enough to survive the much bigger and longer, but disastrous, 1903 strike on the CPR. For on Labour Day of that year it contributed a long article to the Trades and Labor Council's souvenir programme. The article laid heavy emphasis on the UBRE's respectability: 'It is the policy of this brotherhood to act conservatively and judiciously ... and to espouse no cause or movement which it does not deem absolutely right and just, or which it may not, with propriety, maintain before all the world. To avoid the exercise of arbitrary and tyrannical methods ... recognizing ... that unionism, improperly conducted, may become as great a tyranny as that of capital unjustly administered; to avoid and discourage strikes by exercising moderation in its dealing with employers; by conducting negotiations in a business-like and conservative manner; by observing the rights and privileges of employers, and by strictly adhering to its written laws in handling matters for adjustment.' It seems scarcely possible that this is the same organization that a royal commission had just damned with bell, book, and candle. True, the commission would probably have seen the cloven hoof peeping out in the statements that another part of the UBRE's policy was 'To refrain from declaring itself for, or pledging its support to any capitalist political party'; that 'Labor politics' were the answer to repressive legislation: 'We are going to cut loose from the old parties and make a fight to obtain control of the political power now held by a small minority of capitalists. We are nominating men from our own ranks and will attempt to secure seats in the halls of legislation. We understand that there is a class struggle, and that the Lord helps those who help themselves,' and that in British Columbia 'the labor and Socialist parties are especially active, and it is within the probabilities that five or more labor representatives will be elected to the ... legislature on October 31st.' The commissioners would certainly have smelt sulphur in the further statement that the UBRE was at one with the American Labor Union 'in its alliance with the International Socialist Party.' Clearly, some Winnipeg workers had already learned to roar as gently as any sucking dove. The mixture of ordinary union aims and tactics with revolutionary fervour would reappear.

But the clinching proof of the moral turpitude of the UBRE the commission would have found in the Winnipeg division's statement that the UBRE card was interchangeable with and accepted by any branch or section 'of that mighty and growing force in the labor world, the American Labor Union and its sister body, the Western Federation of Miners.' For the commission was to declare: 'There is ... a class of so-called union developing rapidly in Western America which is not really a trade union at all, but a secret political organization ... The primary object ... is to confiscate all franchises and natural resources without compensation ... To this class belong the American Labor Union, the Western Federation of Miners and the United Brotherhood of Railway Employees.' The two latter, the commission added, are 'affiliated with the former ... All these bodies have declared for socialism.'[13]

THE RAILWAY TRADES UNIONS

Down to the end of 1902, the UBRE played only a very minor part in the labour movement. But another new railway labour organization, the Brotherhood of Railway Trackmen (later, the Maintenance-of-Way Employees), was already playing a very large one. This union had been formed in 1887 but seems not to have entered Canada till 1899. Meanwhile, however, the Canadian trackmen had been organizing on their own. At some unknown date, some unknown person had formed a Canadian 'Order of Section Foremen,' but it did not last long. In 1892, however, the Canadian trackmen formed the United Brotherhood of Railroad Trackmen (UBRT), with headquarters in Ottawa. In 1893 this took in a Nova Scotia organization. In the same year, it received the adhesion of most of the members of a small defunct organization of the same name in Battle Creek, Michigan. It remained, for all practical purposes, a Canadian national union; but perhaps the presence of the Battle Creek division was enough to sully its immaculateness from the point of view of Canadian employers, who, from time to time, indulge in at least modified raptures over purely Canadian unions. At any rate, one such employer, the CPR, declined to recognize the UBRT till 1901; before that, members had to attend meetings in secret and 'often risked discharge for taking [the Brotherhood organizer, A.B. Lowe] from place to place on their hand cars.'

None the less, the Canadian Brotherhood produced results. It needed to. In 1892, in at least one Ontario town, the CPR was paying $1 to $1.15 per ten-hour day with no overtime; with board at $15 a month, this left only about $11 for other expenses. A little later, a married man was getting $32.50 a month, with free fuel and a house. When a committee went to Montreal to ask for a wage increase, the management made a poor mouth about the company's financial position: it could not afford a wage increase. It was prepared, however, to make one concession: the foremen could have the hay along the right-of-way (worth about $5 a ton), if they cut it on their own time.

In 1897, on the CPR's eastern division, the Brotherhood got an increase of 10 cents a day across the board, 'and at the same time 20 cents per day for foremen and 10 cents for men on the Ontario and Quebec Division and a cut of $5 per month for foremen and 10 cents per day per man, restored on the Western Division from Fort William to Laggan ... The same year the Canada Atlantic boys quit work for four days and gained a 10 cent increase. Next year the Ontario & Quebec and Eastern Division to Fort William received a 5 cent increase (in some parts for foremen) and the Atlantic Division foremen in New Brunswick were increased in pay to $1.70 per day on main line and $1.60 on branch lines, the previous rate being $1.45. The following year the Canada Atlantic men were increased to $1.75 and $1.15 per day, and the Intercolonial Railway men to $1.65 and $1.20 per day.'

John T. Wilson, head of the American union, had, from 1897 on, tried to bring the two unions together. He attended the Canadian union's convention in both 1897 and 1898, but, though he had A.B. Lowe on his side, Canadian national feeling was too strong for him. The American union set up an amalgamation committee in 1898, and the Canadian in 1899. But the Canadian committee dragged its feet, and in 1899 and the early months of 1900 an estimated 1500 to 2000 Canadian trackmen joined the international union. Within a short time the amalgamation had taken place.

The international union was not long in making its weight felt. On 18 April 1901 a committee of CPR maintenance-of-way workers met the general manager to ask for a wage increase, time-and-a-half after 10 hours and for Sundays, a grievance procedure, seniority rights, no discrimination against union members, and other concessions. The general manager said the committee should have gone first to the local officials. All he would agree to do was investigate, and call the committee back by the end of May. Meanwhile, employing a technique which has become familiar, he increased the wages of some of the trackmen and issued a statement of company rules containing some of the basic provisions the committee had asked for. The union also heard reports that the company had been spreading false rumours about the conduct of committee men in Montreal and had been sounding out individual employees about their attitude to a strike. There were also indications that the company was rushing work on the tracks to be ready for a trackmen's strike at the end of May.

None the less, the union president wrote the general manager, giving him, in detail, the 'objectives and purposes of the Brotherhood and its wish to act in good faith in entering into any agreement.' He received no reply. When the committee came back at the end of May it got no results, and on 17 June 1901 the maintenance-of-way men on about 4000 miles of CPR track walked out. The union claimed the strike was about 95 per cent effective (it said about 5000 men went out and about 20 per cent went back in a few days). The company pooh-poohed this.

The strike lasted till 30 August. By 1 July the CPR was importing strikebreakers, in violation of the Alien Labour Act. On 31 July President Wilson and the secretary of the men's committee were arrested on a charge of criminal libel against a defector from the union, but they were released on bond, and the action was dropped after the strike was settled. The employers' friends, notably the Montreal *Herald*, reproached the Brotherhood for having struck the CPR, which paid the highest wages of any Canadian line: was this 'British fair play?' Wilson replied that the CPR employees had organized and paid dues: '[was] it fair for the public to condemn them when they ... make united efforts to bring about improved conditions for themselves and their families, because the same class of men on other roads have not got the brains or the courage to do likewise?' In August the general chairmen of other unions on the CPR tried to bring about a settlement, but the best they could offer was what Wilson called 'an unconditional and disgraceful surrender'; it was not till the Trainmen's board of adjustment arrived in Montreal that acceptable terms were worked out. The CPR confirmed the concessions it had granted before the strike and undertook to negotiate an agreement at the end of six months.

When the parties met in March 1902, however, the company contended that the union was authorized to represent only the permanent first and second men in the maintenance-of-way gangs and proposed arbitration on this point. The union stood firm, the company gave way, and the two reached agreement on working rules. Wage increases were left to a board of arbitration, made up of one nominee of the company, one of the union, and a judge. On 8 May 1902 the board awarded an increase of 20 per cent over the 1897 rates, and by June the final agreement was signed, and a copy handed to every union member on the CPR. The Grand Trunk promptly granted the same increase.[14]

Just about the time the strike was being settled, the Trackmen seem to have secured the accession of the Canadian members of the International Brotherhood of Railroad Bridgemen. An AFL organizer named Stamper had started Bridgemen's locals in the west in 1899, and by January 1900 he was reporting that the union was 'extending to Halifax.' (He also reported a Western Trackmen's Union, with headquarters in Winnipeg, and covering 'the Canadian Railroad Co's system' from Fort William to Vancouver). In March 1900 he reported locals in Nelson and Revelstoke; in May in Crow's Nest and as far east as Rat Portage (Kenora); in July at Fort William (with a successful convention of the craft at Moose Jaw). By March

1901 he had left the Bridgemen, since he felt they should join the Trackmen. In February 1902 he was reporting, from Moose Jaw, Trackmen's lodges at Winnipeg, Belmont, Portage-la-Prairie, and Minnedosa, on both the CPR and the Canadian Northern. In June 1902 he reported lodges at Kashabowie, Fort Frances, and Winnipeg.[15]

The Rossland strike and the Trackmen's strike were spectaculars. They were big. They showed that the unskilled were on the march. But they were not sudden explosions at the end of two decades of unruffled calm. Sir George Parkin, in 1895, had said that labour problems were unknown in Canada (partly because the 'Canadian winter exercises upon the tramp a silent but well-nigh irresistible persuasion to shift to a warmer latitude');[16] but this is only an astonishing illustration of the fact that in Canada, as in Disraeli's England, there were 'two nations.' We have already seen that from 1860 to 1880, even the most respectable craft unions had plenty of trouble, grievances, difficulties, or, in plain terms, strikes and lockouts. They continued to have plenty from 1881 to 1902; so many, in fact, that it is quite impossible to give more than an outline of most of them, with some detail on the more important ones. Strikes and lockouts were not, of course, the international unions' only, or even main, activity during the two decades. They were, in fact, a mere by-product of their main activity, collective bargaining, and, as often as not (or oftener than not), 'employer trouble,' rather than labour trouble.

The Brotherhood of Locomotive Engineers (BLE) caused a considerable commotion in both labour and government circles in 1882. It started organizing the engineers on the Intercolonial. The Department of Railways and Canals, which ran the railway, promptly ordered the new members to leave the union or face dismissal. Twenty members who stood firm were discharged, and the anti-union Halifax *Chronicle* smugly observed that the trouble seemed to be over.

It spoke too soon. The BLE had powerful friends in the Conservative party, and promptly got to work on them. It also invoked the aid of the Toronto Trades and Labor Council. The council was divided, pretty clearly on political lines. The Liberals plainly welcomed an opportunity to censure the Conservative government, the Conservatives pleaded for delay and more information, and there appears to have been some grumbling about the BLE's tendency to look down their noses at the rest of the union movement.

By a narrow margin, the Conservatives won, and by the time the council came to consider the matter again, the BLE had won its battle. Deputations to Sir John A. Macdonald and Sir Charles Tupper, the minister of railways and canals, had produced a spectacular victory. All the dismissed men were reinstated, with full pay for the time they had been out, and the BLE was, in effect, granted recognition.[17]

The BLE had another battle in 1883. By December of that year, the still unfinished CPR was in serious financial trouble. It decided on a wage cut. It announced that engineers' pay would be cut by $6 a month and that all engineers must sign a statement formally accepting the cut. The BLE countered by asking for an increase of 25 to 50 cents a day (to a rate of $4). The Firemen asked for 40 cents, to bring them to $2.25. The railway refused. The Engineers struck on 11 December from Thunder Bay to Calgary, and the Firemen went out in sympathy. Inadequate lodging at divisional points, and expensive meals, were added grievances of long standing. By using supervisory staff the CPR maintained some service from the beginning of the strike. On 18 December it brought in strikebreakers from Chicago, and some violence followed. Next day the BLE acting president signed the document accepting the wage cut, and the strike was over.[18]

THE BUILDING TRADES UNIONS

The Amalgamated Society of Carpenters and Joiners (ASCJ) struck in Toronto in April 1882: a joint walk-out with the American (later United) Brotherhood of Carpenters and a local union, but with T. Moor of the ASCJ as chairman of the strike committee:

For some years [the Toronto carpenters had been] in a disorganized state ... In 1878 the current wage was $1.25 per day, with $1.50 for first-class men. In the spring of 1880 ... after a three-months' agitation they succeeded in getting an additional 25 cents per day, which was in some cases taken off again in the fall ... In 1881 the employers were notified ... that an advance of 25 cents per day for first-class men would be asked for on May 1st, and after some negotiations the request was granted ... thus placing the day's wage at $2.00 ... One of the results ... was the better organization of all operatives, and at the beginning of 1882 the carpenters ... decided to demand, on the 3d of April, an additional 50 cents per day. It was not the minimum wage of $2.50 per day, as some employers endeavoured to make out, but ... the maximum ... Some of the bosses ... gave their men an increase of 5 cents per hour, but others positively refused, agreeing, however, to compromise by allowing ... 25 cents per day.

The strike was lost, and the Master Carpenters' Association blacklisted the strikers.[19]

The ASCJ took part in the general strike of carpenters in Toronto in 1887, and in London in the same year, when a few of the employers conceded an increase but the majority did not.[20] It was also involved in the great Hamilton building trades lockout of 1888. The master builders, alarmed by efforts to form a building trades council, organized the Builders' Exchange on 12 March. The exchange promptly demanded that the Building Labourers work a ten-hour day. They refused, and were discharged. The Bricklayers and Masons refused to work on non-union materials. The exchange retaliated by refusing to employ any union men whatsoever after 28 March. It locked out the carpenters, bricklayers, painters, plumbers, tinsmiths, plasterers, lathers, and the stonecutters. The unions now refused to recognize the exchange, which collapsed in May. Some of the unions got increases, some went back under their own contracts. This is John Flett's account long after the event.

The Ontario Bureau of Industries said the affair began with a dispute between one member of the Builders' Exchange and the members of the BLU. The exchange supported its member firm and notified all members of the building trades that they must leave their unions or be discharged. Nearly every worker refused, and the whole lot were then locked out for almost four weeks. The unions offered to arbitrate, but the employers refused. Then the architects 'stepped in, and the exchange, knowing the value of their friendship, at last consented.' A meeting took place, but the employers refused to consider any proposition unless the workers renounced their respective unions, which the men refused to do. After the conference had failed, the strike continued for about a month. Finally, the parties agreed on terms (unspecified) for the rest of the season.[21]

The ASCJ also had a strike in Montreal in June and July 1894, and in Winnipeg in 1899. The Winnipeg branch won a reduction of hours from 60 to 56 per week, and wage increases, from 25 to 27½ cents an hour. A second Winnipeg strike in October 1901 failed.

In 1881 the ASCJ had 4 Canadian branches and 132 members. In 1883 it organized Winnipeg; in 1888, Montreal; in 1889, Vancouver. By 1890 there were 10 branches and 299 members; in 1895 8, and 176. Two new Toronto branches in 1902 brought the membership from 359 to 899 in a single year. The bulk of the membership was in Ontario. Toronto preponderated heavily till 1890 and represented the largest single group of members right down to the end of 1902. Throughout the period, the Canadian branches were part of the union's American district council, and from 1888 on the union was affiliated to the AFL. Till 1900, the ASCJ and the United Brotherhood of Carpenters got on well together and accepted each other's membership cards. In 1900, this came to an end, as a result of rows in the United States.

Down to 1880, the Canadian branches had shown a small surplus: a total of $16. From 1881 to 1902 there was a total deficit of $4509. Montreal, Vancouver, Victoria, New Westminster, Kingston, and Guelph had surpluses, but Toronto, Hamilton, and London had deficits (Hamilton's was $5458).

The ASCJ paid sick, funeral, 'trade privilege,' unemployment, and, from 1895 on, superannuation benefits. From 1881 to 1902 unemployment benefits per member for the whole Canadian membership ranged from 47 cents in 1881 to $14.31 in 1894. The pattern varied considerably from place to place. Montreal got off lightly. Its highest average benefit was $4.57, and in 10 of the 14 years in which it reported the average was below $2. London, in its bad years (1885, 1888, 1895, and 1896) averaged from $11.94 to $16.48; Hamilton (1889, and 1894–97) from $11.99 to $18.14; Toronto (1892–97) from $9.08 to $19. Vancouver and Victoria had only one bad year, 1894, when Vancouver averaged $11.91 and Victoria $16.37. Winnipeg in 1894 and 1897 averaged $11.99 and $9.98; in 1895 and 1901, between $8 and $9; in 1886, 1891, and 1893, between $7 and $8.[22]

The Hamilton Bricklayers and Masons,[23] organized as a purely local body on 9 February 1881, became on 7 July Local No 1 of Ontario of the international union. In January 1882 it notified the employers that wages for the ensuing season would be $2.75 a day from March to June and $3 from then on. Either the employers agreed or the union backed down, for there was no strike in 1882. In 1883, however, there was. It lasted two weeks, involved an assessment of 10 cents a week, cost the international $1676.23, and was successful. In 1883 also, D.R. Gibson (prominent in both the Bricklayers and the Knights of Labor) was elected international vice-president.

By 1885 the Hamilton local was one of the most flourishing unions in the city and well enough off to have its own room, which it kept open the whole winter for the use of its members. In April 1885 the local showed its loyal and martial spirit by exempting from dues and assessments all members called for active duty in suppressing the Northwest Rebellion; it also resolved to give their families all the help it could. The Bricklayers were out two weeks in the 1888 Hamilton building trades lockout. The international imposed an assessment of 5 cents a week and paid $1912 in strike pay.

Local 5, London, was chartered in October 1882. It struck in 1884 and got a satisfactory settlement in such short order that no assessment was necessary. On 2 May 1887 it struck again for higher wages. The international gave it permission to stay out two years, if necessary, but the members were determined to settle the question forthwith: if the employers were adamant they would pool their money and take up contracts themselves.

The contractors professed nonchalance: contracts and bricks were scarce. Perhaps in the hope that the international would hear of it, they charged the local with going on strike simply to get the strike benefit of $5 per week. This unlikely yarn the local president of course at once denied. He added that he could get plenty of bricks 10 miles out of town, and that new contracts were in the offing.

The union set up pickets on construction sites and patrols to watch incoming trains. The local press reported that within a week all the members who were not doing picket duty had left the city to take work in other places in western Ontario, where good bricklayers were in demand. One employer had given in and was paying the higher rates. He had at once got all the available union labour and appeared to be doing well out of it. The international's report says that this strike also was settled satisfactorily without having recourse to any assessment; it does not even say how long it lasted.

Toronto Local 2 had a big strike in 1890 lasting seven weeks. The international imposed an assessment of 18 cents and paid $11,523 in strike pay; the union won. Toronto had another strike in 1899, for a wage increase from 32 cents an hour to 40 cents. The employers offered 26, the union refused and struck on 1 May. In March 1902 the Toronto Bricklayers, then getting 35 cents an hour for an 8-hour day, demanded 45 cents effective 1 May. They refused an offer of 41, and struck, 350 strong, on 1 May. They were out 1 day and got 42 cents.

Brantford Local 6,[24] formed in the early spring of 1886, struck in August and won. By 1890, however, it was defunct. Nothing came of a movement to revive it, and a new local appeared only on 4 March 1898. It was chartered on 23 March 1899 as Local 9.

The new local at once distinguished itself by instructing its delegate to the international convention to vote against the eight-hour day. It was also against the international affiliating itself to the AFL, though it left its delegate free to use his own judgment about affiliation to the National Building Trades Council. It favoured affiliation to the TLCC. On 7 October 1901, after a heated discussion, it decided to demand a wage increase to 33⅓ cents an hour, with a 60-hour week and a Saturday half-holiday, 1 May to September. So say the local's minutes; the *Labour Gazette* says a 9-hour day with 5 hours on Saturday.

Ottawa Local 7,[25] formed 22 July 1889, struck in the spring of 1890 for a nine-hour day, as required by the rules of the international. By 2 May the independent contractors had given in, but the Contractors Association was still holding out. In June 1893, when the Building Labourers were on strike, the Bricklayers refused to handle non-union materials; but the matter seems to have been promptly settled by the Building Labourers scaling down their demand from $1.50 to $1.40 per day, and the contractors accepting this.

In May 1899 the local struck against Bourque and Poulin, contractors on the main drain, complaining that this firm was unfair both to the workers and 'honest contractors,' paying its men only half-pay for 10 hours' work. The local added that Bourque and Poulin were aided in their suppression of the union 'by religious and other institutions which should know better.'

In 1900, when the Building Labourers were again striking for an increase, the Bricklayers wanted to refuse to handle non-union material, but the masons (part of the same union) seem to have objected that any interference in the BLU strike was contrary to the international constitution. This argument seems to have prevailed.

The Halifax Bricklayers[26] got the 9-hour day and 30 cents an hour, as required by the rules of the international, immediately after they joined that body in 1899. On 7 April 1901 they asked for 36 cents, to take effect 1 May. They noted that the Sydney rate was already 50 cents and that in the Halifax climate they could expect to be employed only about 25 weeks a year. The increase was granted.

The Vancouver Bricklayers,[27] organized 1 February 1890, were suspended 5 July 1893 for non-payment of dues. Disbanded on 29 April 1895, they reorganized in the fall of 1898. The local signalized its reappearance by a masquerade ball, towards the end of March 1899. Within a week or so it was showing its sterner side.

In December 1898 the 90 or so members had decided to ask for an increase from 45 cents an hour for a 9-hour day to 50 cents. About 1 January 1899 they notified the employers, setting a deadline of 1 April. The employers seem to have paid no attention till 6 April when they formed an association of their own and decided to refuse the demand. Protracted negotiations followed. The employers' position was weakened by the fact that they had an unusually large number of contracts to fulfill. While still 'vowing they would ne'er consent,' they did, in fact, start paying the 50 cents from 1 April, under protest, adding that they would formally accept the new rate only if the working bricklayers would 'agree in turn to refrain from accepting small contracts, which they have been in the habit of doing all along.' The union seems finally to have won its increase and the employers to have gained some amendments to the union's by-laws.

Meanwhile, the New Westminster local, which had made the same demand, had been refused, and about 40 members had struck against the firm of Coughlin and Hay. The strike seems to have been won before the middle of April.

On 21 December 1899 the Bricklayers were once more in festive mood: they held a ball. But by 2 April 1900 they were on strike (along with the Painters). The employers had accepted the Carpenters' demands but balked at the others' (the Bricklayers wanted an eight-hour day with the old nine hours' pay). At first it looked as if the strike would be won in a couple of days. But the employers wanted to put off the eight-hour day for three months. The union said they had already had three months' notice, that one contractor building a church on a contract based on the old rates had been offered exemption for that job (the union paying the extra 50 cents a day itself) but that the Builders' Exchange had refused him permission to sign on this basis, and that employers outside the exchange were already paying the $4.50 for 8 hours. The Stonecutters and their apprentices struck in sympathy 10 April, declining to work on any job where non-union bricklayers or masons were employed. The Quarrymen and Drillers did likewise. The Bricklayers then met to decide whether to refuse to work on any job where non-union stonecutters or quarrymen were employed, and presumably agreed to do so. By 27 April the Brick-layers were still holding out and claimed they could sustain the strike indefinitely, while the contractors could not.

Their confidence must have been ill-founded, for by 21 August the men were at work, getting only 50 cents an hour for a 9-hour day. In New Westminster, how-ever, they were getting 56¼ cents for 8 hours, and the international headquarters was insisting that the 8-hour day must be enforced.

The American (after 1887 'United') Brotherhood of Carpenters organized close to 90 locals in the two decades 1882–1902. But the mortality was very high. Of the 45 locals in existence at the end of 1902, only 7 had been organized before 1898. Nearly all the others dated from 1900–02.

The January 1882 *Carpenter* has an interesting account of the formation of the first Canadian local, Hamilton 18. 'Over 130 had placed their names on our list, but when it came to paying the initiation fee our number was reduced to thirteen, but has since increased to twenty-seven active members. A great many more say they are going to join, and by our union joining the Brotherhood we will bring them in ... Our agitation for a union has caused a number of carpenters to join the Amalgamated Carpenters, which is working in harmony with us.' The two apparently held a joint ball on 23 December 1881.

A joint meeting on 17 January 1882 decided to ask for an increase of 2½ cents an hour (from 17½) from 1 April. The going rate was $1.75 to $2 a day. 'Bricklayers here have got $2.75 per day ever since latter part of last Summer. They have a strong union. The carpenters ... are at the tail end of all the trades.'

The next month's *Carpenter* said: 'The "bosses" grumble at our demand ... They saw we have hurt the trade and kept back the work. The Bricklayers ask $2.75 from March and $3 from June. Plasterers are getting $2 and want $2.25 from April 3. They have formed a union recently. There is very little noise made about all this, until the "Chips" made their demand, then the newspapers take it up and interview the bosses and create unnecessary alarm, predict trouble, and in trying to toady to the bosses, damage the interests of both bosses and men.' We hear no more of the Hamilton unions' efforts that spring.[28]

In the 1882 Toronto Carpenters' strike the American Brotherhood and the purely local union (probably the Friendly Society of Carpenters) apparently came out before the ASCJ and went back sooner, for the *Carpenter* says:

Our strike is closed by the bosses offering some concessions. We were out four weeks. Over 600 men came out on April 3, and our numbers swelled daily until at one time we had over 1000 on strike. All we asked was 50 cents advance per day ... The Typographical Union ... granted us $250 and the Bricklayers liberally assisted us. So did other trades. Four hundred dollars were raised by a concert. We paid single men $3 per week and married men $5. Two prominent citizens waited upon the bosses to adjust the difficulty, but were insulted. Then five church parsons tried it with like treatment. At last the Mayor called a citizens' meeting, April 19, to hear both sides ... Then the bosses offered a compromise of 25 cents a day ... [to] be the standard wages for twelve months ... Any notice of alteration of wages ... [to] be given by either party annually in January to come into operation ... [in] May ... any dispute ... to be submitted to arbitration. Furthermore we are to have one hour's time or one hour's money to grind our tools on being discharged. During the strike we sent away numbers of men; our railway bills amounted to over $700, and yet we had special rates with one of the companies. We consider we have won in many respects. The bosses have had enough this time not to try it for another year.

The Bricklayers' contribution to the strike fund had been $200, 'while the Stone Cutters and the Seamen emptied their treasuries.' The amount spent to help men leave the city totalled $879.45.[29]

By August 1885 the local was growing rapidly. It had secured the 55-hour week with a Saturday half-holiday; it was helping its members when they were ill, paying a disability benefit of $250 and death benefit of $250 on the death of a member and $50 on the death of a member's wife.

The 1884 international convention had no Canadian delegates. The main Canadian news was the report of the strike of Victoria Local 48, formed 25 July 1883. It had 125 members, earning from $3 to $3.50 per day. It struck 1 March 1884 for a nine-hour day and was out two months. The strike 'at first was successful on many jobs, but the influx of immigration poured in so that the men were not able to secure their demand and finally compromised with eight hours as a day's work on Saturdays. In their struggle they received financial aid voluntarily from San Francisco, Seattle and Portland.' The Victoria *Colonist* says that of eighteen contractors eight were in favour of granting the nine-hour day, two against, and eight undecided. The members must have felt the strike had failed for the local was disbanded within the year.[30]

The 1884 convention heard also that Guelph Local 46, chartered 5 May 1883, had 'expected to make a move to establish a rate of $2.00 per day, but owing to the Chicago strike then being on hand, they decided to postpone their movement.' The decision must have been fatal, for this local also was disbanded in 1884. St Catharines, however, had won a reduction in hours.

The 1886 convention had delegates from Hamilton, Toronto, St Catharines, and Belleville. Five new locals had been chartered. Hamilton had got a 55-hour week with a Saturday half-holiday; Belleville had shorter hours on Saturdays. Toronto, St Catharines, and St Thomas had inaugurated the 9-hour system; but the international had refused to let Toronto strike for the 9-hour day, as the constitution did not 'make ample financial provision' for strikes. So Toronto had gone ahead on its own and won.

The 1888 convention had delegates from Hamilton, Toronto, and St Catharines. Eleven new Canadian locals had been chartered in two years; one had been disbanded. The chief Canadian events had been the great 1887 Toronto strike and the 1888 Hamilton building trades lockout. Local unions had sent $481.95 to Toronto; the international $2326.75. For Hamilton the local unions had sent $1144.46 and the international $658.74.

By 1890 seven new locals had been organized, three disbanded, and one consolidated with another local. Toronto, Ottawa, Saint John, Vancouver, Victoria, New Westminster, Windsor, St Catharines, Peterborough, and Belleville were now all 'nine-hour cities.'

The 1892 convention also had a good deal of Canadian news. The protective fund had spent $300 in Halifax, which now joined the nine-hour cities, along with London, Winnipeg, and Nanaimo. Peterborough, however, had fallen out (its local had disappeared in 1891). Toronto was down to 50 hours. The international now had organizers in Toronto, Winnipeg, and Halifax. Six new locals had been chartered; ten were gone.

In 1894 the international office reported a district council in Montreal, but a net drop of seven locals. Calgary joined the nine-hour list, Peterborough returned to it, and Toronto, Halifax, and Nanaimo are absent.

The protective fund had spent $5310 in Montreal, where, on 1 May 1894, the United Brotherhood and the ASCJ had struck 1900 strong, for a wage increase to 20 cents an hour, a 9-hour day, and 30 cents an hour overtime. The unions provided $6 a week strike pay. By 7 May 50 of the 175 contractors had given in, but 600 men were still out. The Cigar Makers, Stonecutters, and Painters all contributed money towards the total union aid of some $10,000. By 5 June 80 contractors had accepted the union's terms, and the strike came to an end.

In 1896 the international set up a general executive board of five, with one representative each from New England (including New Brunswick and Nova Scotia) and the middle states (including Ontario and Quebec) and two from the western states (including Manitoba and British Columbia). Toronto and Halifax were back in the list of nine-hour cities; Hamilton, Winnipeg, and Ottawa were absent. There were no new Canadian locals; two had lapsed or been suspended.

In 1898 only one new local had been chartered; two had disappeared. Winnipeg and Ottawa were back in the list of nine-hour cities.

By 1900 eleven new Canadian locals had been chartered; three were gone. The list of nine-hour cities disappears; Toronto appears in an eight-hour list. The most noteworthy feature of the Canadian statistics is a net gain of three locals in British Columbia.[31]

By the end of 1902 the UBCJ was broadly based: twenty-five locals in Ontario, seven in Quebec, five in British Columbia, three each in Nova Scotia and what is now Alberta, two each in Manitoba and New Brunswick, and one in Prince Edward Island.

When Vancouver Local 617 was organized on 19 May 1890 the city had two other carpenters' unions: the ASCJ, and a purely local body. It was, apparently, the purely local union which decided to join the United Brotherhood; though there must also have been some connection with the ASCJ, for a week after the formal establishment of Local 617, the local had a statement from the 'Financial sectery of the old Union showing how this Union 617 stood with the Amalgamated Society of Carpenters & Joiners of this city financially, up to the time of the dissolution of the old Local Union, and the formation of this branch of the Brotherhood.' The meeting of 19 June 1890, which decided to join the UBCJ, had first heard, and approved, the minutes of the previous meeting.[32]

The first formal meeting of Local 617, on 21 August 1890, with 56 members,[33] 'adjourned at 9:45 after which we had the pleasur to listening to a little Harmony from some of the Bretheren.' A week later, there was the report from the financial secretary, and a decision to exchange membership lists with the ASCJ. On 4 September the local was informed that it owed the ASCJ $10.40, and it decided to invite the president of that body to attend its Labour Day social. On 2 October there was a request for information on starting a local in Nanaimo, and 'Bro Smith proposed a Rev Gentlemen Mr. [be] an Honorary member of this Union but it seemed the opinion of the members that he was not a fit person to join our order.' The local decided to ask the ASCJ to join in getting a meeting room.

The minutes of the first few meetings are full of appeals for financial help from all and sundry for a variety of purposes (holding a ball, building a hall, helping sufferers from a cyclone). By 23 November, when Frankford Local 422 was asking Vancouver to buy tickets in aid of their relief fund, the members' patience gave out, and the secretary was instructed to write the international secretary, complaining of 'the frequency of these begging communications' and asking that they be discouraged. At the same time, the local paid a bill for $2.50 for two cases of soda water, and on 4 December followed this up by paying $3.50 for 'One Keg of Beer used at the opening of this Hall.' But, though drinking, whether of soda water or beer, was apparently approved, smoking was not: a motion to allow smoking at the meeting, 'for the comfort of the Bretheren,' was lost.

Bilingualism cropped up in Local 617 in 1891. On 8 May there was a payment of 25 cents duty on French versions of the international's constitution, presumably for the use of the fairly numerous French-speaking members: Duclos, Chapdelaine, 'Le Franger,' Blondin, Boudette, 'Tardiff,' 'Larivée,' and Gagnon are among the names. Some of these appear again in 1893.

By 12 November 1891 there had been so many claims for sick benefit that the local conducted a careful investigation and decided that either benefits must stop or dues be raised. The question was, for the time being, left in the air: 'there Being no further business to transact The worthy President Bro Franklin was asked for one of his favourite songs which he rendered in his usual style.' On 19 November payment of sick benefit out of general funds was stopped, and on 3 December an assessment of 25 cents a month was imposed to continue benefits to those already on the list; this lasted till 7 January 1892.

In March 1892 a joint special meeting with the ASCJ agreed to demand an eight-hour day from 1 January 1893, with nine hours' pay from 1 May. On 26 May a motion for a general strike of carpenters was amended to provide that the local should wait to see if the contractors' action endangered the *nine*-hour day, and only if it did not, to co-operate with the ASCJ in asking for eight. By the time 1893 came, the local was allowing members to work with non-unionists, and even earlier, the ASCJ had been letting its members take any job that paid $3 for 9 hours.

In the fall of 1892 the local was coping with a perennial problem of all unions at all times: apathy, chronic failure to turn up at meetings. The remedy adopted was to raise dues to 75 cents a month and rebate 25 cents for attendance at the first meeting after the increase, allowing, of course, for illness, absence from the city, or other legitimate excuse for default.

On 5 April 1894 the local agreed to act with the ASCJ in organizing the Royal City Factory sawmill hands, and by 10 May it heard that the Union of Factory and Sawmill Machine Men had been duly organized.

On 14 April 1892 it recorded its opposition to a militia corps as 'a menace of a help to us.' On 2 March 1893 it voted against free trade and in favour of a single tax in municipalities. On 11 April 1895 it was instructing its delegates to the Trades and Labor Council to protest 'against the high tax on cigar stores that is to be brought up in the City Council.'

On 24 March 1892 the local resolved to have only soft drinks at its social, as several temperance men said they could not attend if beer were served. When the fall social was actually held, the minutes record, somewhat ambiguously: 'Entertainment Committee reported social Dec 24th. High old time, all went home sober.' On 18 September 1893 we get a tantalizing glimpse of another kind of entertainment, doubtless at the Labour Day celebrations: 'The tug-of-war committee was not present to infuse new life into the apparently played out committee.' On 19 October the local appointed a new committee.

The revival of trade in the late 1890s galvanized the two Vancouver carpenters' unions into new activity. On 12 January 1899 they agreed to hold a public meeting of carpenters. On 9 February Local 617 voted unanimously for an eight-hour day. On 9 March a delegation from the ASCJ urged joint action for shorter hours. The ASCJ itself had passed a resolution in favour of a 9-hour day, 5-day week, with 5 hours on Saturday, at 36 cents an hour and time-and-a-half for overtime. Local 617 accepted an invitation to send delegates to an ASCJ meeting.

A 5 April meeting was told there were about 300 carpenters working in Vancouver. On 26 April the *Province* put the number at 400 or 500. About 150 had turned up at a 25 April meeting whose purpose was to see if the two unions could unite 'and become affiliated with either the Amalgamated Union of Carpenters or the Brotherhood of Carpenters.'

On 3 May there was a second mass meeting of about the same size 'to consider what steps should be taken to ensure improvement in the condition of members of the carpenter trade.' Those present received the depressing news that only about 100 of the city's carpenters belonged to either union, 'and being hopelessly in the minority could not accomplish anything.' Local 617 reported that 28 contractors were in favour of an 8-hour day with 9 hours' pay, and everybody present agreed that this ought to be the goal. The difficulty was not only the numerical weakness of the unions but the fact that more than half the carpenters were comparatively unskilled, and if a strong union were formed, the employers would 'naturally show a preference for those who were skilled mechanics, to the detriment of members who were not so skilled.'

The two unions seem finally to have agreed to ask for a minimum rate of 33⅓ cents (an increase of 3⅓ cents), a 9-hour day for 5 days a week, and a half-holiday on Saturday. On 30 March the men met to hear the employers' replies. The employers (who had demands from other unions on their hands also) were ready to grant the demands, and no strike took place.

By the fall of 1902 discussions were under way on new demands. On 26 November the new rules were finally hammered out: from 1 April 1903 to 31 March 1904 a 44-hour week at 40 cents an hour, with time-and-a-half for overtime and double time on Sundays; no piece-work; payment every 2 weeks; and holidays on New Year's, Thanksgiving, the 24th of May, Dominion Day, Labour Day, and Christmas.

A few miscellaneous items from the Local 617 minutes are worth recording. On 21 December 1893, 'Bro Walker reported ... that new carpets could be got at prices ranging from 25 to 75 cents per yard but as it was the feeling of the meeting that the Union could not afford a new carpet it was resolved that a mat be got to cover the hole in the present carpet. Bro Gagen was appointed to see after the mat.' On 27 December 1894, 'A communication was read from the Co-operative Protective Union. On motion it was consigned to the waste basket.' (This was probably the 'Socalled Local Union' of carpenters which turns up again on 11 December 1902.)

On 3 November 1898 the members favouring holding a provincial congress of unions, 'providing it would not cost too much.' In April or May 1899, 'Bro Doidge advocated having an Intelligence Office.' This sounds like an anticipation of later union research departments. It was probably merely the 'central place for unemployed carpenters to register' which the local, on 1 June, tried to get the ASCJ to join in providing. Whether or not, it was disposed of with beautiful simplicity: 'Bro Dixon said that he would see to it.'

On 2 November 1899 two delegates reported themselves pleased with the lecture by Eugene V. Debs and regretted there had not been more union men at the meeting, which had showed a deficit. A fortnight later, the union met for the first time in its new hall, a former Methodist Church at the corner of Homer and Dunsmuir streets. On 25 April 1901 the local suggested that each union member contribute 50 cents to the expenses of Labour Day or that each union contribute 50 cents per member, instead of collecting contributions from merchants. (The Labour Day celebration of 1899 had netted $700.)

The Ottawa locals of the UBCJ had an off-again-on-again-out-again-in-again-gone-again-Finnegan existence, appearing and disappearing with bewildering rapidity. The last of them during this period, Local 674, struck 3 June 1901 for a minimum rate of 25 cents an hour, a 9-hour day, and a union shop. A week later, the members formed a 'last Nail Club: each member has placed a nail in the lapel of his coat. It will stay there until they win.' Three days after that, the employers offered a compromise: an open shop, a minimum rate of 15 cents, and 3 rates above this, of 20, 22, and 25 cents an hour. The union of course rejected this unanimously. It then offered to appoint a committee with full power to settle the dispute, but the employers rejected that. On 2 July the city council passed a motion in favour of having this and other strikes settled by a court of arbitration consisting of Mackenzie King, deputy minister of labour, and one nominee each of the unions and the employers. Next day, a public meeting endorsed this in principle, but asked the unions to submit their cases to King alone for adjustment, and only if that was unacceptable to all parties to proceed to the court. The unions promptly agreed to accept King as sole arbitrator, or, if the employers balked at that, to appoint as the unions' representative on the court John Coates, president of the Ottawa Board of Trade (who had initiated the whole effort for settlement). The employers, who had earlier said that they would not accept arbitration and had rebuffed Coates's efforts, still refused to budge. The carpenters then voted to fight to a finish. They claimed that over 50 carpenters had left the city by 5 July. The strike was never officially ended, but the local finally decided to let its members go back to work anyhow, which they did 15 July.[34]

The Halifax local struck, 159 strong, on 1 June 1901 for a 7 cent increase. The dispute went to arbitration, and the men got 4 cents, with a provision that all future disputes were to be arbitrated without stoppage of work, and that notice of changes must be given by 1 March of each year.[35]

In May 1901 the Windsor local adopted the policy of a 9-hour day, time-and-a-half for overtime, and a 20 cent minimum wage. Twelve of the thirteen contractors accepted the demands, but one refused. The Carpenters thereupon struck that one firm 1 August and the Bricklayers struck in sympathy, along with two labourers on a job where the carpentry work had been given to a less recalcitrant contractor. On 12 August the employer caved in, on condition that the union get rid of all 'incompetent artisans.' In May 1902 the union demanded union recognition and a 10 per cent wage increase for 30 carpenters and machine hands in 3 planing mills. This time, one employer agreed, and two balked. The union struck the two mills 19 May and five days later won.[36]

The Winnipeg Carpenters tried in the summer of 1898 for 30 cents an hour, but failed. At the beginning of 1899 they gave notice that they wanted 30 cents, effective 1 May. Eleven employers agreed, nineteen did not; whereupon the men struck the whole lot. By 12 May the initial 200 or so strikers had grown to about 300. They struck again, 400 strong, on 8 August 1901 for a 9-hour day and 40 cents an hour. They went back 28 September on the understanding that in January 1902 they would give notice of another demand for higher wages in the summer. In June 1902 1 contractor, with 16 employees, refused to observe the 9-hour day. The men struck 24 June and won 26 June.[37]

The Toronto Carpenters, 400 of them in 25 establishments, struck 1 May 1902 for a 5 cent wage increase (to 30 cents) and an 8-hour day. By 10 May the outside men had gained practically all they asked; mill hands got the increase, but in some cases still had to work a 9-hour day.

Victoria Carpenters got the 8-hour day on 1 May 1902, with the same hourly rate of 33⅓ cents an hour. On 15 May, however, 7 carpenters working on the new Government House demanded 37½ cents and, after a 2-day strike, got it; a number of other contractors then granted the 37½ cents.[38]

The UBCJ had had a Calgary local in 1892, but it had not survived the year. It was only at the beginning of 1902 that the Brotherhood effectively entered Alberta, with the chartering of Frank Local 1012. The organizing meeting took place on a bitterly cold February evening in the town's main saloon. The charter was issued 26 February. Most of the members were recently arrived Americans; every carpenter in town joined.

The Frank local promptly elected Robert Robinson organizer for the province. He lost no time getting to work. On 16 March he arrived in Calgary; two days later, in the Co-Operative Hall, he organized Calgary Local 1055. In a stirring speech he compared carpenters' wages in Nelson, with a minimum of $3.50 for 8 hours, with Calgary's maximum of $2.75 for 10 hours. Twenty-nine members signed up and the local was chartered on 2 April. Late in October Robinson arrived in Edmonton, where he organized Local 1235 (chartered 11 November).

Calgary 1055 struck 13 establishments, with 90 employees, on 4 July 1902. The ruling wage rates had been $1.50, $1.75, and $2.75 for a 10-hour day; the union demanded a minimum of $2.75 for 9 hours. On 21 July it got nearly all it asked for.[39]

On 17 November 1902 40 St Catharines carpenters struck because their employer brought in men from Thorold who were not Brotherhood members, but belonged to an AFL FLU. The strike lasted till 22 November when the Thorold Carpenters agreed to affiliate wih the St Catharines Brotherhood local and work under its system of working cards.[40]

The Painters, Decorators and Paperhangers Union may have chartered its first Canadian local in Hamilton on 15 March 1887. A Painters and Decorators Union certainly took part in organizing the Trades and Labor Council on 12 November 1888, and Hamilton Local 27 of the Painters and Decorators Union had a delegate at the 1892 TLCC convention. This local had faded out by 30 August 1895, when the Hamilton Trades and Labor Council had a letter from the Carpenters on organizing a Painters Union. Attempts, next month, to reorganize the painters failed, and Hamilton seems to have had no local of the international again till 26 June 1900.[41] By the end of 1902 the Painters had 29 locals: 20 in Ontario, 3 in British Columbia, 2 in Nova Scotia, 1 each in Quebec, New Brunswick, Manitoba, and what is now Saskatchewan.

The Painters figure in a fair number of industrial disputes during these years. They were, of course, involved in the great 1888 Hamilton building trades lockout. They struck in Toronto between 7 and 23 May 1888 for higher wages and shorter hours. They had trouble in Toronto December 1891 with a Mr Hovenden, who had 'taken the contract for the work at the new Parliament Buildings at a very low figure' and was trying to cut wages accordingly. They also struck in Ottawa in December 1892 against a Mr Shepherd because he refused to pay the regular proportion of a day's wages for the short winter day of seven hours.[42]

In January 1890 the Montreal Painters, Local 74, demanded $2 a day from 1 April. Only five employers complied, and the union struck. One painter wrote La Presse that at the existing rates he was $82.04 in debt at the end of a year's work; with the increase he would come out $28.94 ahead.[43]

After winning a wage increase in Ottawa in May 1900 without a strike, the Painters got into a stoppage there in March 1902. The local had about 115 members. In February it asked for a wage increase, effective 15 April, to $2 a day for painters and $2.25 for paperhangers, sign writers, and grainers. Four employers locked out their men, some 34 strong, on 11 March, refusing to recognize the union. By 25 March one had given in, some of the strikers had found work with other contractors at union wages, the union had opened its own shop at 180 Bank Street, and the Plumbers had voted $30 to support the Painters. The union paid the strikers $6 a week each, and the international's fourth vice-president, Charles March, of Toronto, had arrived to do his bit. On 15 April, as the employers generally showed no signs of granting the increase, the union struck, except against some employers who had given in the day before. By 21 April most of the employers had granted the increase, with a preference for union members, though not all the strikers were able to get their old jobs back. On 26 May one shop was out again, because the employer was employing a man who had left the union during the April strike and now refused to rejoin.[44]

The Kingston local, in March 1901, wanted a 9-hour day and a 15 cent wage increase. The 3 employers concerned, with 35 employees, refused, and the union struck 1 March. It went back on 16 March when the employers granted the demands and agreed to a union preference shop, with the proviso for a special wage rate for men incapable of earning $1.75 per day.

On 16 July 1901 the Toronto local struck James Casey's shop with 12 men because one of them was getting only 22½ cents an hour instead of the union rate of 25. By the end of the month 9 of the strikers had got other jobs, though some who had got other jobs earlier were discharged by their new employers the moment these gentry discovered they were strikers from Casey's shop. This strike seems to have petered out.

Toronto had a lockout from 31 March to 15 April 1902, because 40 employers refused the union's demands for an 8-hour day at 30 cents an hour, instead of 9 hours at 25 cents. The employers offered 27½ cents for 8 hours, but the union refused and held out till the employers finally conceded everything.[45]

The Vancouver Painters in January 1900 demanded a 9-hour day, a minimum wage of 33⅓ cents an hour, 1 extra hour at standard wages to finish any job, time-and-a-half for all work after 6 PM, a grievance procedure, and a union shop (non-members being given one week to join up). All this was to go into effect 2 April for 1 year, with 30 days' notice of any changes. The employers rejected the demands, and the union struck 2 April. By 5 April, after several meetings with the employers, many of the painters (the union had about 75 members) went back to work 'on the assurance ... that their views would be met and the papers signed,' and all the rest were expected to go back next day on the same terms. This seems to have been the end of the trouble, except for one shop, where the strike was still on as late as 16 June. On 19 April 1901 the local struck again, for a one-year continuance of the existing rates, and a union shop. Two days later the strike was won.[46]

The Journeymen Stonecutters of North America seem to have entered Canada in 1888 at Winnipeg. By 4 January 1889 the Toronto union had affiliated, Montreal certainly did so before October 1901. By the end of 1902 there were two branches in British Columbia, one in Manitoba, at least nine in Ontario, and probably one in Nova Scotia.[47]

By 3 August 1888 the International Association of Journeymen Plumbers, Steamfitters, and Gas Fitters had a Toronto local, which seems to have lasted till the advent of Local 46 of the present United Association on 1 September 1890.[48] Fifteen more followed, and by the end of 1902 there seem to have been sixteen locals: ten in Ontario, three in British Columbia, two in Quebec and one Manitoba.

The Winnipeg Plumbers by 20 May 1898 had got a union shop agreement for all the firms in the city, and before the year was out had established a rate of 30 cents an hour. They then asked for 40 cents and adoption of the union's rule of 1 apprentice in each shop. The employers ignored the notice and the union struck 1 May 1899.[49]

Montreal had a strike on 1 May 1902 of 145 men in 60 firms, because the contractors refused to sign an agreement for a 9-hour day with a minimum wage of 25 cents an hour. By 1 June most of the employers had given in.[50]

The Toronto Plumbers, 250 strong, came out on 17 June 1902, demanding an increase of 10 cents an hour (to 37½ cents); on 8 July they got 2½ cents, with a further 2½ to come on 1 January 1903.[51]

The Ottawa Plumbers struck 25 August 1900 for a minimum rate of 25½ cents (a 2½ cent increase) and various changes in working conditions. They went back 4 September with a 25 cent minimum and an undertaking to negotiate the shop conditions.

In August 1902 the Ottawa local asked for $1.50 a day for a journeyman in his first 6 months and after that the standard rate, with a minimum of 25½ cents an hour (a 3 cent increase). It also demanded that the masters should not send out any helpers or apprentices to do plumbing or steamfitting, and that there should be one apprentice for every five plumbers in each shop. The employers were willing to pay 25 cents for competent men, but refused to allow the union to enforce its shop regulations. Early in September, however, they offered to negotiate the shop regulations and most of the strikers went back.[52]

The Vancouver Plumbers, on 4 May 1900, complained to the Trades and Labor Council that 'the shop of T. Marshall persisted in employing "scab" labor ... A committee of one from each of the building trades was appointed to take the matter in hand ... The plumbing by-law had been a dead letter for the past year, and ... there were plumbers working in the city without the certificate required by law.' The measures were effective and by 15 June Marshall's was a union shop, 'and acted more fully up to the union by-laws, than any other in the city.'[53]

The history of locals of the Builders' Laborers International Union in Canada is somewhat obscure. There was certainly a local in Toronto on 4 May 1888, but it seems to have suffered an early death. There is evidence of a Local 4 in Ottawa, formed in 1892; a London Local 8, formed 21 October 1895; a Hamilton Local 1 and a fresh Toronto local by October 1901; a Local 2 in St John's, Quebec, on 4 October 1902; and a Montreal local in November 1902. The Ottawa local apparently left the international in 1898 but had got a new charter in December 1900.[54]

The first Ottawa local had a strike in June 1893. Most of the contractors met the union's demands promptly; a few were prevented from coming to terms by the Contractors and Builders Association. When two of the employers put non-union labourers to work on their contracts the Bricklayers refused to handle the materials. The contractors then offered the Builders' Laborers a $1.50 minimum (or maximum; the reports are confusing) for a 9-hour day; the union asked for the offer in writing; and the Building Trades Federation threatened to strike unless the contractors gave the Laborers what they were asking. The contractors' negotiating ommittee refused a union offer to take a $1.40 minimum for a 9-hour day, but a full meeting of the builders involved accepted it.

In May 1900 the Ottawa union (with 225 members), now apparently thinking about getting back into the international, decided to demand an increase of 3⅓ cents an hour (to 20 cents) for 9 hours, effective 15 July. The Laborers 'felt they should share in the profits' of rebuilding the large part of the city destroyed in the fire of 1900. They pointed out that the Toronto building labourers were getting 23 cents and Hamilton 19.

The employers refused, so the union struck early in June. When the Masons jibbed at the Bricklayers' refusal to handle bricks brought them by non-union labourers, the Bricklayers went back to work and the Laborers' strike collapsed on 15 June. The men accepted a rate of 15 cents per day, less than the employers had at one stage offered them. The defeat clinched the men's determination to get their international charter back.[55]

In April 1901 the Toronto Builders' Laborers, 'one of the strongest and most important bodies' in the city, was asking for an increase from 22 cents an hour, and got 2 cents. A year later it wanted an extra 3 cents, with time-and-a-half for overtime. The employers offered 25, with no overtime. The union balked.

In May 1901 the Hamilton local struck for 3 cents (to 21 cents an hour). It was out 2 days and got 20.[56]

The Plasterers' Toronto local, No 48, was chartered 30 March 1889. Seven others followed, and Montreal, whose union had rejoined the international in 1896, and left it in 1897, seems to have been reorganized some time in 1902.

Montreal had a strike between 14 and 17 May 1902 for a 9-hour day and a 3 cent increase (to 28 cents an hour), which it won.[57]

Ottawa had a 2-day strike in June 1901, involving 36 men in 11 firms. The union wanted 30 cents an hour for 7 months of the year, 28 cents during the winter, and a Saturday half-holiday with 4 hours' reduction in pay. It got them all.

The Toronto Plasterers in January 1902 asked for an increase of 4 cents (to 40 cents an hour). They got, without striking, 38 cents, effective 1 May.[58]

9

The International Typographical Union, the Cigar Makers International Union, and the Amalgamated Association of Street Railway Employees

THE INTERNATIONAL TYPOGRAPHICAL UNION

In Toronto in April 1881 Local 91 of the ITU succeeded in getting 27 cents per thousand ems on the evening papers. In March 1882 it decided to ask for further increases, on both morning and evening papers, and on book and job work. This brought varying responses from the employers, mainly unfavourable or procrastinating, and a strike vote failed to get the necessary two-thirds majority. The *Telegram* had refused even to meet the union, and in May the local called out the men there. Two came out, one stayed in. The union then set up a committee to see the advertisers and persuade them to boycott the paper. Some merchants cancelled their advertisements at once; others promised not to renew their contracts; and the campaign is said to have cost the paper 6000 subscribers.

The 1882 efforts to get increases had failed, so in March 1883 the local renewed its demands, with some variations. It pointed out that over the past few years, the various skilled trades had had wage increases of 10 to 25 per cent, but the Toronto printers had had none. This time, it got favourable replies from most of the employers, and struck the rest. It paid strike pay of $7 a week for married men and $4 for single, raised by a levy on the members at work.

Early in April, a Trades and Labor Council committee waited on John Ross Robertson, owner of the *Telegram*, apparently without result. A second interview, by this committee and one from the Typos, was equally fruitless.[1]

By July 1884 the union was once again locked in combat with the *Globe*, and this time also with the *Mail*. Both papers had cut wages. A Trades and Labor Council deputation visited the two managements. The *Globe*'s acting manager pleaded inability to pay, but was willing to go to arbitration (the manager refused to back him). The *Mail*'s manager truculently asserted 'his right to do as he liked.' The council gave up for the moment. But when the *Mail* posted a notice requiring all employees to promise not to join any union or the Knights of Labor, under penalty of immediate dismissal, and dismissed John Armstrong (former international president of the ITU), the delegates were furious. They set up a committee to draft a boycotting circular, which called on 'the labouring classes ... the business community ... [and] the people,' to withdraw their patronage from the *Mail*.

The *Mail* was in ill odour; but the *Telegram*, an old foe, was, for the moment at least, emerging into respectability. It had opened its offices to union men, and the council on 21 November responded by allowing the *Telegram* reporter once more to attend its meetings.

On 16 July 1888 the *World* locked out its printers, violating (so the union alleged) the agreement it had made a year before. The Trades and Labor Council condemned this action and pledged itself to use every legitimate means to defeat the paper.

By December 1890 Local 91 had before it an elaborate draft scale of demands for book and job work, weekly newspapers, and magazines. It was still asking only for a 54-hour week, though now at a rate of $13.50. The job scale was adopted 28 March 1891 when the weekly rate asked was cut to $12. The reduction was presumably the result of a review of rates and hours elsewhere, which showed a weekly rate of $10 to $11 in Montreal; $11 in Hamilton; $9 to $10 in London; $8 to $11 in Quebec City; $10 in Halifax; and $9 in Kingston. Only London reported a 50-hour week; the others reported a 10-hour day.

On 30 September 1890 the local had reports from 59 chapel fathers, covering 79 employers and 489 employees. Of the non-unionists working in shops where union members were also employed, there were 39 men, 4 women, 172 boy apprentices, and 32 girls. By the end of March 1891 the chapel fathers reported a total of 520 union men. Of the non-unionists, there were 49 men, 39 women, 62 extra men, and 200 apprentices (nearly all males).

At the end of 1890 the *Telegram* and the *Truth*, and the Mortons' and Hill and Weir's shops had been closed to union men. Otherwise, Local 91 was free of disputes, and a 'kindly feeling' existed between it and the employers.[2]

In August 1891 things began to hot up.[3] The Central Press Agency discharged its union printers and refused to hire any new ones. Of course it was promptly struck, in spite of a state of trade described as 'but fair.' This strike succeeded: by 19 September the CPA had discharged its non-union men and hired union members in their places. Meanwhile, the union had sent a circular to the Employing Printers' Association, with a new scale of job wages; the association had replied with an ultimatum; the local had approved the scale and sent it to international headquarters. By November the ITU's president, W.B. Prescott (who had left the presidency of Local 91 only in July), had replied that the international was in no position to support a strike, and the local would have to accept the employers' scale: $11 for 54 hours.

At the end of September 1892 the *Telegram* had been boycotted; on 20 October there was a lockout at the *News*, over the scale for machine operators, and the business committee recommended a two per cent assessment to fight the paper. By 19 November the *Telegram* had been unionized; by 7 December the local had accepted a compromise agreement with the *News*. By 7 January 1893 every daily paper in the city had been unionized. The *News* lockout had cost $1295.14, of which the international had provided $890. But the local now had two other stoppages on its hands.

On 16 December 1892 the Stereo Co, which had become an open shop, was struck, or had locked out its union employees. This stoppage lasted til 22 January 1893, when the company agreed to become a union shop by June, and was granted permission to retain, till then, in a separate room, three non-union men. On 6 May however, the Stereo committee reported that the company had broken faith again: that on 8 April the three union men employed had got dismissal notices. The company then organized a company union; by this time trade was too slack for the local to take any action.

The original Stereo stoppage had cost only $56.35; but meanwhile there had been large expenditures for the other and much bigger stoppage at the *Presbyterian*. That paper was employing women apprentices on machines, and just before Christmas, its management had declared it an open shop. The union struck on 10 January 1893. Twenty-two union men, two non-unionists, and six boys came out. The union on 14 January imposed a two per cent assessment to finance the strike, to be increased to five per cent if the international union did not help. The management brought in strikebreakers in large numbers. The union replied by picketing, by writing to the advertisers in both the United States and Canada to withdraw their advertisements, and by getting subscribers to cancel their subscriptions. In spite of terribly cold weather in the first three weeks of the strike, the pickets were on duty from 6:30 to 6:30. Thirty strikebreakers were taken out or stopped from going in, some being sent out of town. By 16 February four union men and three boys were still out of work, the rest of the strikers having got jobs in other offices. By 4 March the local had spent $760 in strike pay; by 18 March its finances were in precarious shape. By 6 May the strike was plainly lost, though the *Presbyterian* was closed to union members. What was worse, the Employing Printers' Association, of which the *Presbyterian* was a member, refused to negotiate on the book and job scale until the *Presbyterian* dispute was settled. The local's annual report in May 1893 had described 1892 as the year of the biggest crisis since 1872. 1893 was not, apparently, much better.

In May 1894 a committee on unemployment reported that the whole of Canada had suffered from a depression in trade over the past year; that there had been much suffering among printers; and that the widespread use of typesetting machines had made printers' unemployment worse. It recommended an assessment of 50 cents a month for 2 months on all working members to help their unemployed brethren. The local amended this to 80 cents for members earning $10 to $11, 90 cents for those earning $12 to $14; and $1 for those earning $15 or over. At the same time the *Presbyterian* office was opened to union members, to give employment; though with the consoling reflection that this was the only principal office not controlled by the union. Membership had by this time declined to only 271, not much more than half what it had been 3 years before.

In 1895 the local turned down a Montreal proposal for a district union (which Hamilton favoured). It told the Trades and Labor Council in February that if the Pressmen came in, Local 91 would go out (which it did in July, though it came back in October, after the ITU had arrived at an agreement with the Pressmen and the Machinists). In May there was an agreement that offices which wanted to work less than 54 hours a week should pay 21 cents an hour, with overtime after noon on Saturdays. At the end of July the local struck the Toronto Type Foundry; by 24 August the foundry had agreed to become a union shop within four months. By the end of the year the local had 289 male members and 1 'union female.'

By July 1896 the Allied Printing Trades Council (established in February 1894) was favouring a weekly rate of $11 for a 49-hour week.

By 6 March 1897 the local was receiving a report that the Pressmen, and the Allied Trades, had failed to unionize the *Telegram* pressmen, though all other offices were observing the union by-laws and paying union wages. Local 91 was against striking the *Telegram*: there was too much unemployment. By November things must have been looking up, for the wage scale committee reported in favour of a rate of $11 for a 48-hour week with 35 cents an hour overtime, 50 cents after 11 pm and on Saturday and Sunday, and 5 nights' night work at 35 cents an hour.

In March 1898 Local 91 left the Allied Printing Trades Council. By May it was down to a membership of 289 but by June had recovered to 334. All the morning papers were reported to be ready to adopt a new union scale with a few minor amendments; the two evening papers had objections to the bonus scale but the union negotiators felt they would come round. By September the local was back on the Allied Printing Trades Council.

By 1899 trade was good. In January membership stood at 324. In February there were more than 500 members working (though not all paid up). At the 4 March meeting, the question of a union label for the *Star* 'was well stirred about,' with a 'nice warm time,' and settled only by the president's casting vote.

In April 1899 the local tackled the machine question, adopting an elaborate scale. Trade had recoverd, and the union was prepared to strike on 16 July, by which time it was also demanding overtime on eight holidays. Nothing happened, however, except that the weekly papers and the book and job printers, in July, offered a weekly wage of $12 with overtime at time-and-a-quarter, which the union accepted. In November it adopted a scale for machine tenders, but this also seems to have come to nought. It was not till June 1900 that the newspapers accepted a new machine scale: morning papers, $2.50 per night of 7 hours, with work over 23,000 ems at 8 cents per thousand, and 50 cents an hour overtime; evening papers, $2.35 per day of 8 hours, with work over 29,000 ems at 8 cents per thousand, and 40 cents an hour overtime. In the same month a union committee made recommendations to deal with the perennial problem of apprentices: one apprentice to the first three journeymen, one to the second three, one to each additional six, and no more than six in any one office.[4]

In November 1900 the local asked for an increase of $3 to bring the weekly wage to $15 for 54 hours. The employers wanted a four- or five-year agreement covering 'every branch of the trade in order to prevent continually recurring disagreements and demands from separate branches of the trade.' In January 1901 joint negotiations between the Employing Printers' Association and the Typos, Pressmen, and Bookbinders resulted in an agreement, to run till 1 June 1904. Proofreaders, compositors, and journeymen printers were to get $13 for a 54-hour week from 1 June 1901 until 1 June 1902, then $13.25. Overtime was set at time-and-a-third. A detailed set of rates was established for day and night work, overtime, kinds of type used, and special work (such as foreign languages, and that involving figures, tables, and columns). Scales were also set for machine operators in book and job shops: $17.50 per 48-hour week for night work, $15.20 per 51-hour week for day work, and time-and-a-half overtime.[5]

This, however, did not prevent the Typos from asking on 28 April 1902 for a uniform scale for all printers in newspaper offices: $21 a week for night work, $18 for day. In May they got $18 for night machine operators and some other classes on morning papers, with a 7½ hour night shift, and $16 on evening papers for an 8-hour day.

Meanwhile, on 16 April the local had called out two union printers employed by Eaton's, which refused to run its composing room on-union rules. Five pressmen also came out, and several bindery girls who refused to do the men's work were discharged. Not till 27 November could the union inform the Trades and Labor Council that the strike had been won for the compositors; the Pressmen and the Stereotypers, on 11 December, reported that for them Eaton's was still 'unfair.'[6]

The Saint John local of the ITU, No 85, was revived in 1881 as a result of a circular signed by upwards of 85 journeymen, but only 59 were present at its first meeting on 26 February.[7] Printers in most offices were then getting $9 a week, or 25 cents per thousand ems, and they had long believed that this was insufficient. On 11 June the local set up a committee to report a scale of wages. Its report on 10 September, which was in favour of the existing scale, was not accepted by the members.

After a long and heated debate the local decided to ask for a new scale: for compositors on evening papers, 30 cents per thousand ems; for pressmen on evening papers, 25 cents an hour and $10 a week; and for compositors working by the week, $9 for a 10-hour day with 25 cents an hour overtime and double time for Sundays.

A committee headed by the president, W.H. Eaton, was appointed to lay the scale before the employers and demand an answer by 17 September. Unfortunately, Eaton was also foreman of the *Daily Sun* office. Torn between the two positions, he resigned the presidency, and the rest of the committee were so demoralized that they did not even interview the employers. The emergency meeting of 17 September accordingly 'adjourned without transacting any business.'

The employers said they could not pay higher wages: they had not yet recovered from the Great Fire of 1877. None the less, the union members in the *Sun* office managed to get an increase to 28 cents per thousand ems. But the increase was granted under protest, and within a few days the *Sun* discharged the father of the union chapel, George E. Day. The employer and Eaton insisted that the discharge was 'solely owing to a personal misunderstanding' between Day and Eaton. The members thought otherwise, and when the employer refused to reinstate Day and discharge Eaton, they struck on 24 September with disastrous results. They had no authority, and hence no support, from the union, and the employer had no difficulty finding enough substitutes to carry on. Of the eleven men who struck, four went back a week or so later, and the rest left town. The chief result of the whole affair was that Day laid charges with the local against Eaton and three other members accused of ratting; they were exonerated, however, probably because the strike was unofficial.

The local opened the year 1882 with 61 members and $96.23 in the treasury. By July attendance was so poor that there was a notice of motion to disband; this was lost 12 August without opposition. By November things had clearly improved, for in the *Sun* newspaper office there were ten union members, one non-union printer, and one apprentice; in the job office one unionist, two non-unionists, and five apprentices; and in the press room one unionist and one non-unionist. In the *Telegraph* composing room there were sixteen union members and two apprentices, and in the press room one apprentice and one journeyman.

From April 1882 till December 1883 Local 85 devoted much of its energy to a campaign to get school books printed in New Brunswick.[8] Despite poor attendance and financial difficulties, the union must have been getting stronger. In May 1883 it was able to send $20 to help the Pressmen's strike. Wages, by July, had reached 28 cents per thousand ems, or $7 to $9 a week; in November the union decided to ask for 28 cents and a straight $10. By the end of the year the *Telegraph* was a union office; the *Sun*'s news office was unionized, but not its job room. J. and A. McMillan's was a union shop. The *News*, however, was non-union throughout; so were

Barnes & Co, George W. Day's, George A. Knodell's, and the *Visitor*. 'In some of these offices, there are as many non Union as Union men employed.'[9] In January 1884 Knodell's became a union shop.

In January 1885 the Brotherhood of Carpenters asked the local's help in forming a Carpenters' local in the city. The Typos went so far as to pass the letter on to some carpenters. At the same meeting, it considered a long circular from Ottawa Local 102, on forming a Canadian National Typographical Union. The circular was referred to a committee of five 'to write for information for the purpose of presenting some plan of action.' There must have been considerable dissatisfaction among Canadian Typos at this time. The Saint John committee reported progress on 14 February and 9 May. On 9 May the local heard a letter from Ottawa Local 102 describing the progress being made towards the formation of the national Union. On 15 June there was a letter from the Montreal Jacques-Cartier local on the subject, and one from Toronto asking whether Local 85 favoured the project. The members voted in favour of the idea, but nothing seems to have come of it. In Saint John attention was perhaps diverted by the disappearance of the treasurer, who skipped town with $192.66, and by the urgency of the apprentice question.

A year later the local was engaged in negotiations over a new wage scale. The employers were 'not unopposed' to an increase, but wanted to put it off till 1 January to finish their contracts and raise their prices. The union wanted it to start 12 October. On 11 October a special meeting was told that the *Sun*, the *Globe*, the *Telegraph*, Barnes' and McMillans' had all agreed, and special thanks were tendered to the firm of Day and Reed 'for the manner in which they had stood up for unionism.'

By November 1886 plates, which virtually eliminated compositors' work on the matter involved, were coming into widespread use, though not yet in Saint John. The local appointed a committee to look into the question. By December, when it reported, ready-made plate news was being used on one local paper and seemed likely to be introduced on others. The local decided to prohibit its use, but to allow members working in offices where it was already in use to continue working there until 1 January 1887.

The paper which had been using plate collapsed before battle could be joined there, but by August 1887 a new weekly, the *Gazette*, was reported to be up to the same game. The local notified its union printers that they were violating union regulations. The *Gazette* pleaded poverty, but its men struck, then went back.

This, however, was only the beginning of an acrimonious dispute. The *Gazette* was being printed in the *Sun* office. Two men quit, and the *Sun* chapel said that if the *Sun* went on printing the *Gazette*, its members would strike. It did, and they did. The local approved, and appointed a committee to confer with the employers. A *Globe* man had worked in the *Sun* office one night, so there was a threat to strike there. The owner of the *Globe* refused to deal with the union at all; the owner of the *Sun* could not be seen. About three weeks later, on 8 October the *Globe* men decided to go back on any honourable terms, and the *Sun* men were ordered back because of the arrival of non-union men. On 12 November one Berry, a reporter and member of the local, who had worked despite the strike (which he claimed was illegal) was expelled, and G.W. Day's office was declared 'rat.' The same meeting was informed that the *Globe* was willing to pay 30 cents instead of 28 on books.[10]

By June 1890 almost every office was on a nine-hour day, with a Saturday half-holiday. In August the local decided that it was inadvisable to organize a national union, as suggested by the Montreal Jacques-Cartier local.

At the beginning of 1891 the local appointed a committee on a new wage scale. This reported in favour of 28 cents per thousand ems and a 9-hour day, which was accepted by the employers.

There was a notable strike at the *Progress* in 1892. In October that paper had taken on two women compositors. On 5 November the union wrote to the owner, E.S. Carter, pointing out that his had heretofore been a union office, and that it was against the union's constitution for members to work with non-members. The local asked for a meeting for 8 November, a request which seems to have been ignored. The printers then struck.

Carter, after the strike broke out, declared that the *Progress* had not been a union office since February, when he had decided that it 'would not be guided by the Union or its rules ... owing to the lack of protection extended to the paper at that time by the union.' He claimed that the foremen and the men had been told so, and that on 7 November the compositors were asked whether they 'proposed to stand by or not through the impending difficulty.' Plainly, Carter had already decided to fight, and within hours his foreman was informed that the union had called out all its members.

According to Carter's account, nine employees failed to turn up next morning. Pickets were set up to warn women compositors against working at the paper, to persuade the employees still working to join the strike, and, at the railway station, to prevent printers from coming in. The union also notified jobless compositors elsewhere in the province not to come to Saint John. The *Progress* reported also that the press foreman had joined the strikers after the first day: 'He had not sufficient moral courage to withstand ... their overtures'; it added that the work proceeded faster after he had left.

Carter warned the union that he would not dismiss the women compositors. He claimed he had raised his wage rate to 27 cents per thousand ems when other city establishments were paying only 25 and insisted that the *Globe*, *Gazette*, *Sun*, and George W. Day all had non-members working with union members, and that five of the *Progress* strikers themselves had come from offices where girls were working.

(Three of these were from places where there was no ITU local.) He further accused some union member of insulting language to the female compositors, and the union's walking delegate of having thoroughly frightened a new *Progress* employee as she arrived at the station.

The paper also congratulated the union's members on being able to stay out of jail, thanks to the *Progress*' having 'felt disposed to treat them leniently.' It said the *Telegraph* was the only union office in the city and wound up by declaring roundly that the *Progress* 'will be run according to the idea of the proprietor, and free from the dictation of its employees or their mistaken advisers. If the way in which it is run does not suit the latter, so much the worse for them.'

The international rallied with financial support; pickets continued to watch all incoming trains; the local started a paper, the *Workman*, which was to last till May 1894; the Shipwrights, Carpenters' Local 397, and other Saint John unions gave their support; and the Halifax Typos promised that no 'rodents' would be furnished from that city. But all this was in vain, for in October 1893 a committee was interviewing Carter on opening the *Progress* to union men, and he was replying that though he was willing to hire union members he would not discharge his rats or unionize the office. Till November 1895 the paper remained closed to union members.

By November 1893 still another paper, the *Record*, was being printed at the *Progress* office, and the local's executive was conferring with other unions on a boycott of this journal. The *Record* was still closed to unionists on 11 May 1895.[11]

In February 1894 the local unanimously agreed to ask each member to give 10 cents a week for 4 weeks to keep the *Workman* afloat; but it sank, and only 1 copy survives, that of 26 November 1892. It contains a sharp reproof to the Chatham *World*, which had commented on the *Progress* strike, and an exhortation to 'look closer home for labor problems'; a comparison of unions with the legal profession ('If any body of tradesmen or laborers conducted such a "Union" as the Lawyers of St John, they would immediately be branded as rebels'); a series of letters attacking a Saint John reporter, one McDade, for his reporting of the Ship Labourers' strike of 1875; and a long letter from R.W. Bradbury, of the Infantry School in Fredericton, who had been hired to work on the *Progress*. He had arranged a special leave, and was actually on his way to Saint John when he was 'made aware of the facts ... and then fully made up my mind not to go to work.'

In the summer of 1895 the Saint John Trades and Labor Council asked the city council for a grant towards a Labour Day parade, and Local 85 was soon deep in plans for its part in the occasion. On 24 August it was decided that the members should march in a black suit, white tie, white gloves, and silk hat, wearing union badges and buttonhole bouquets, and carrying canes. At the head of the Typos' section of the parade there was to be a banner, followed by a printer's devil in black tights, tin helmet with horns on the sides, cloven hoofs and a tail, and under his arm a large roll of paper labelled 'copy.' There were also to be bannerettes with the inscriptions 'Patronize Union Offices and Keep Taxpayers at Home,' 'Boom No 85 for next year,' 'In Union there is Strength,' and 'Live and Let Live.' There was to be no float: too expensive. The minutes of the next meeting have a full statement of the costs: 'Tights, $1.00; One shirt, $1.00; Dying, .40; Moustache and goatee, .25; Mask, tin hat and horns, .45; Horse, $2.50; Cloven hoof, .35; 12 bannerettes, $5.92; 62nd. Fusiliers' Band, $30.00; 5 doz. roses, $3.00; 60 badges, $9.30.' Against this the union had collected $5.55 for the bannerettes and roses.

In 1895 also Local 85 drafted a scale for Merganthaler Linotype machines and took steps to set up a new labour paper, the *Weekly Toiler.*

In November 1901 the local heard a paper from the Saint John Fabian League (organized in April with its object 'the municipal ownership of gas plants, street railways, etc.'). The local appointed a committee to attend a league meeting on 12 November. On 14 December the chairman reported: the league was doing good work; the meeting had been a respectable one, and had good objects. He felt all union men should attend. At this same meeting of the local the league (of which H.E. Codner, a prominent member of the local, was secretary) circulated a petition to the legislature to enact a workmen's compensation act on the lines of the British act. It got 53 signatures, which must have covered nearly the whole membership. Among the signatories were those of President Emms and W.H. Coates, vice-president of the TLC.[12]

The Halifax Typographical Union, which had ceased to be in good standing with the international in 1879, probably continued as a purely local body. Certainly it was in existence in July 1881, January 1882, and January 1883. Early in 1883 it wrote to the international union asking how it could get back into good standing, and on 5 March its charter, as Local 130, was reissued. The extant minute book begins on 6 January 1883 but the rest of the year runs to only 10 pages, with little of any consequence except a note of a bill for rent from the Amalgamated Trades Union (ATU) the first Halifax central organization.[13]

In February 1884 the local was invited to join the ATU. It heard a report that the *Chronicle* press room was working at rates less than union wages and appointed a committee to prepare a scale for April. In May the local joined the ATU; in June it boycotted the *Herald.* The *Herald* had evidently been requiring employees to sign an ironclad contract. In October the manager, Mr Stewart, was assuring the local that 'the paper had been abolished and that any man could obtain work there without signing such.' After some discussion the local appointed a committee to see Stewart 'and explain the matter more fully.'

On the same date the delegates to the ATU reported that it had a deficit of $75 and wanted Local 130 to contribute its share. The local resolved to take no action until officially notified and urged its delegates to scrutinize the ATU's accounts 'rigidly.' The deficit was for the ATU picnic, and on 1 November the local paid its share of $15. Moreover, the per capita dues to the ATU, which were evidently in arrears, were ordered to be paid at once.

On 6 December the committee to explain matters to Stewart reported that his assurances had been a trifle premature: 'The paper was certain to be done away with but had not yet passed the Board of Directors.'

By May 1885 the ironclad contract had been abolished in the *Herald* office. A committee was promptly appointed to interview the men there and get them to join. On 6 March 1886, however, the local heard that the *Herald* was not open to union printers. It promptly boycotted the paper, assessing every member 25 cents a week for the purpose; it also appointed a committee to interview the management. This reported two weeks later, 'a very satisfactory arrangement by the "Herald" management in reference to opening the said office to Union men.' A committee was to wait on the men in the composing and job rooms to see how many wanted to join. On 23 April 23 new members came in. Encouraged by this, the local sent a committee to wait on the hands at the *Recorder*; they were reported nearly all ready to join.

In February 1887 the local appointed a chapel father for the *Recorder*, who took his place with his counterparts for the *Citizen*, *Chronicle*, *Herald*, and *Wesleyan*, indicating a pretty considerable organization of printers in the city.

In April the members were faced with the question of whether to take part in the celebration of the Queen's jubilee. Rather surprisingly in loyal Halifax, there was considerable discussion; more surprisingly still, it was moved and seconded that the local should take no part in the street procession of trade unions. An amendment to confer with the ATU was moved and seconded. The 'ayes seemed in majority,' but the meeting 'adjourned in disorder,' apparently without any decision. Perhaps this is why the next meeting authorized purchase of a copy of Cushing's *Manual*.

In June 1887 the situation in the book and job-offices came up for discussion. It was resolved that the weekly rate of $9 was 'insufficient to sustain life in a comfortable manner' for journeymen book and job printers and those working with them. Continuance of such a rate 'must result disastrously to both branches of the trade (newspaper & job) as well as to the bosses.' Men leaving book and job-work to go to the newspapers were 'tending to lower the standard of fine book and job work.' A committee was accordingly appointed to draw up a circular to the employers, to request respectfully $10 a week at the earliest possible moment. Because of the slackness of work, however, the committee refrained from approaching the employers.

The chief items of interest in 1888 concern the Labour Day parade, then a purely local affair, late in July. The local agreed to take part. Its representatives were to carry a banner, modestly inscribed, 'The press, the light of the world,' and the members were to wear dark clothes, a hard felt hat, and white gloves in the procession. The last item evidently struck the members as swank: an amendment to omit the gloves carried.

In 1889 the parade took up far more time and energy. It was agreed that the members should have banners and sashes, that the apprentices should be invited to join, and that the marshal should be mounted. Then the fun began. There were evidently two parties: aristocrats, intent on maintaining the dignity of the profession, and militant proletarians, who wanted no part in such highfalutin' nonsense. The proletarians opened by moving 'that we don't want beavers on parade.' The aristocrats countered: 'Amended that we do wear beavers. On a standing vote being taken, it was declared a tie. The president then cast his deciding vote in favour of hard black hats. Notice of reconsideration at next meeting was given. At this juncture Mr. Mayo was fined for using improper language.' Things quieted down long enough for the meeting to decide on hiring a barouche for elderly members to ride in. Then it was 'Moved and carried that we have a uniformed devil in the parade. Notice of reconsideration at next meeting was given. Moved and carried that we do not carry a walking stick. An amendment was made to the foregoing that we do. Notice of reconsideration at our next meeting was given.' By the next meeting tempers had cooled a little: the reference to Mayo was ordered stricken out and his fine remitted, and 'Mr Stokes was allowed to withdraw his notice of reconsideration in regard to beavers. Moved and carried that we parade without the devil. Moved and carried that the walking stick question be struck out.'

In 1890 the parade question again caused a dust-up, especially over the rival claims of black hard hats and high silk hats. But in 1891 the discussion was apparently entirely amiable. It was agreed to wear dark clothes, beaver hats, light neckties, white gloves, bouquets, and badges; to spend $25 for refreshments; to have a barouche; to have a banner and a mounted marshal; and to invite the employers and proprietors to attend in barouches.

In 1892 the discussion was again non-controversial but took up a good deal more space in the minutes. It was agreed, in May, to have sashes, a saddle cloth for the marshal's horse, and 125 badges. In June, however, the saddle cloth was dropped from the plans: too expensive. In July it was reported that the sashes would cost $3.50 and the badges $107.55. The president said the local would not lose by selling the badges for 87 cents each. It was agreed to have barouches; the marshal was to procure a horse; and the employers were to be invited. A week later, the local decided on the uniform: silk hats, dark clothes, white gloves, bouquets and badges. It also instructed the committee 'to procure 10 gallons of ale, 10 doz. bottles of temperate drinks, with some biscuit and cheese.' The paraders were to assemble at seven in the morning; the union would ask the employers for a holiday, with suspension of the newspapers; and invitations would go out to sister unions (presumably to enjoy the refreshments). After the parade, it was reported that the refreshments had cost $9.73, and that the union had received $19.80 as its share of the profits, including a $6 loan to the Labour Day general committee.

In 1893 the Typos paraded in the same uniform as the year before. In 1895 the Labour Day celebration again figures prominently. The marshal was to be on foot, but, by way of compensation, was to carry a sword. The dress was to be the same as in 1894; an amendment in favour of white vests, silk hats, and dark clothes was defeated.

In 1901 the Typos were to head the procession with a carriage, and they made preparations accordingly. There were to be vests and canes, and a photograph of the printers. The local was to nominate a man for grand marshal of the whole parade (which it did), and its own marshal was to be mounted. Expenses were not to exceed $5. Four apprentices were to help carry the banner, and were to get $2. The net proceeds were $26.39.

Meanwhile, of course, the local had been doing plenty of serious business. On 2 March 1889, there was a lengthy and stormy discussion on 'Mr. McNab making his hands work Saturday afternoon for 45 cents, when it should be called a half day proper, or strictly speaking, extra time. This matter was brought up by Mr. Wm. Melvin, who took half an hour to explain where 5 minutes would have sufficed, had he plainly stated his case and not kept jumping to his feet with interruptions to other speakers who attempted to help him out in his argument.' McNab's men were to be notified of the union rates, and if they did not govern themselves accordingly, they were to be expelled.

Not surprisingly, the secretary's free comment on Melvin's oratorical style, or lack of it, produced, at the next meeting, 'some little discussion in reference to the wording of one portion of minutes'; but it withstood the criticism. Two months later, the main item was a proposal to pay the secretary $15 a year, out of which he would have to pay postage. This was lost, and the final decision seems to have been to pay him $6, let him off his dues, and pay the postage on union letters. In September, financial matters came up again. This time, it was a question of arrears of dues: 'William Anderson was read out by the financial sec. as being in debt sufficiently to the union to warrant his expulsion, which was accordingly done. Mr. Ryan was also in the same fix, but stated to the union that he was in the soup, & requested a little time, which was granted.'

In October there was notice of motion to ask for a $10 weekly wage for men paid by the day. This was carried on 2 November, to go into effect on 11 November. On 9 November it was reported that two employers were against it. The local decided that all men not getting $10 per week should strike. Single men were to get $3 a week strike pay, and married men $6, but nothing if under the influence of liquor. All were to report to the secretary daily, and working members were to be assessed for the money. The men were still on strike on 7 December.

In June 1890 the secretary got an increase: $12 a year, but to pay his own postage. The same meeting appointed a committee to draw up a circular prohibiting the employment of union and non-union men in the same office after 1 August. Someone promptly moved reconsideration at the next meeting. In August we find a fresh decision for a circular to the same effect, to come into force after 1 October. The circular was adopted with a resolution to enforce it by 6 October. But on 4 October the matter was laid over for a month, partly, perhaps, because the members were now thinking of trying for a nine-hour day.

On 1 November a committee was appointed to confer with the employers on establishing a 9-hour day and 54-hour week, at the present wages, to come into effect in December. On 26 November a proviso that the union would temporarily allow a 55-hour week, with a Saturday half-holiday was added. The employers agreed, and the union must have prospered in the months that followed, for on 2 May 1891 it made a presentation to the treasurer. He tried to express his thanks, but his 'surprise ... was so complete ... that he was entirely unprepared for the attack, & requested to be excused from further remarks.'

On 1 August the local unanimously voted against an international office request to adopt a general demand for a nine-hour day, with eight on Saturday. The secretary was instructed to tell international headquarters that Halifax already had a 9-hour day and 54-hour week 'and did not care to provoke a strike in this city for 1 hour extra per week.'

In January 1892 the local proposed a new scale of prices. Morning papers were to pay 35 cents per thousand ems, and evening 30 cents. The employers accepted the terms, with slight changes, and they came into effect 1 February. In April the local had a letter from the two Quebec locals asking for its views on forming a Canadian typographical union. Halifax was against it. In August the *Herald* announced it would reduce its rate to 30 cents on 22 August. A special meeting appointed a committee to meet the manager, Mr Burgoyne. It had no luck. What was worse, the *Chronicle* intimated it proposed to do the same. The local asked to have the ITU district organizer, James Patterson, of Ottawa, come to Halifax. He did, and suggested a compromise of 33⅓ cents, which was accepted.

In January 1894 Halifax was disturbed by the apprenticeship question, and the local appointed a committee to meet the employers. It was not a good moment for negotiations. Unemployment was rampant. The union was paying relief at $4.50 for married men and $3 for single. Moreover, it was having trouble with a non-member, one Kelly, at the *Herald*. He was apparently a member of the Printers' Protective Fraternity, a company union which existed in both Canada and the United States, and which had caused major trouble in Ottawa and Montreal in the spring of 1892. The minutes do not record what happened to the apprenticeship discussions.

By January 1896 all the printing establishments in Halifax were so thoroughly unionized that the local was expressing doubt of the benefit of having the union label. In March 1897, however, it adopted the ITU label on all work. A month later it endorsed the 1893 wage scale, but decided that all apprentices on machines must be union men, at $11 a week for day work and $14 for night; that the apprentices were to be employed only for 2 months; that no men were to operate machines for more than 5 days or nights a week; that the men teaching on the machines must be union members; that the executive was to 'set a figure of competency on machines'; that there was to be no piece-work and no bonus on machines; and that all men in machinery offices were to be considered the same as operators.

The *Herald* refused the proposed machine scale and said it would do as it pleased. When the *Herald* refused to negotiate the local telegraphed for the ITU district organizer, George W. Dower. He arrived a few days later and persuaded the *Herald* to consider a scale which the management accepted but refused to sign. While the result was hardly all that the local could have wished, it was scarcely in a position to fight. On 1 September it listed 30 members out of work; on 6 November it was providing loans to help members elsewhere.

In February 1898, though there were still 15 members out of work, the local asked for several changes in rates and conditions. A 55-hour week was to be permitted if Saturday was a half-holiday; guaranteed time was to be 6½ hours on night work. Sunday overtime for compositors was not to apply to their regular hours' work for Monday morning papers. Matter over three columns was to be paid double price. Piece-workers were to have a five-day week. Waiting time on machines was to be 33⅓ cents an hour at night. The employers apparently accepted the changes.

All through that spring the local was preoccupied with unemployment and relief. On 6 March it held a draw for unemployed members which netted $115.50. It was paying, to members with six months' standing, means-tested benefits of $2.50 a week for single men and $4 for married, provided they had not lost their jobs through their own fault and were not found using liquor. It was also providing foremen with lists of unemployed printers. On 19 March it was co-operating in a petition of unemployed members to the city council. On 2 April the petition had been cordially received and the number of unemployed members stood at 11. On 7 May word came that relief would have to stop for the time being.

In June the local set to work on a scale for stereotypers; on 16 July it held a special meeting to draft an emergency scale to go into effect a week later. On 22 July it was told that a union stereotyper had been discharged, and that this was taken as a discharge of all the *Herald* and *Mail* union men. The job-room men had been asked to set the paper, had refused, and had been discharged. The members resolved to fight 'to the bitter end.' On 6 August three members were expelled for ratting, three others were reported to be working, and ten were out of work. The local imposed a 10 per cent assessment on working members for August to support the strike.

The strike in the news room lasted till December; in the job-room it was still on in January 1899. The employer brought in alien labour. The union invoked the Alien Labour Act and on 3 September reported that the law would be enforced next week and that it hoped soon to have the alien strikebreakers quit. It also started publishing a union paper, the *Weekly News*, which, initially, was pronounced a success.

On 3 December the strike committee reported. It had had several conferences with Stewart of the *Herald* and the *Mail*. The strike was evidently none too successful, for Stewart had told the committee that some men would be taken back immediately and 'some provision made for those remaining out until such time as they were reinstated in the Herald office; also that in the future preference would be given to union men, as he, Mr. Stewart, believed in union offices.' Conferences with Mr Dennis, Stewart's principal, had, however, been unsatisfactory. None the less, the committee recommended accepting Stewart's terms. Strike benefit from the international had ceased; if the union balked at Stewart's terms the *Herald* would probably be closed to union men for all time, while if it accepted it would eventually gain the office. The local voted for acceptance. The total assessment for the strike had been $268.83.

On 26 December there was an emergency meeting to hear a proposition from Stewart and Dennis: they would take back three men at once, another on the first vacancy, and two others on extra work as before the strike. This was accepted. The job-room was still on strike, but its manager was said to be open to conferences. The union decided to be on the safe side and give the executive power to levy a further assessment.

The truce seems to have been a rather uneasy one, for on 7 January 1899 the local resolved that any member found 'making a companion of the rats in the Herald office [should] be charged with a misdemeanour.' By 1 April the union had written to Stewart listing violations of the agreement. The letter added that after 9 May the union would allow no union man to work in the *Herald* or *Mail* offices till they were unionized; nor would any union man patronize the *Herald* or the *Mail* 'or any of its supporters, politically or otherwise.' The union was sure Stewart never intended to have a union office. It set up a committee for a campaign against the two papers.[14]

The *Weekly News*, established to give work to the strikers, blossomed into something more considerable. In December 1898 it was moved that the local borrow not more than $500 to stock an office to print the paper. An amendment, to investigate buying a printing plant, carried. On 17 December a committee reported that an office could be started for $400. It was empowered to borrow this amount 'for the purpose of purchasing a plant for the publication of the *Weekly News*.' By 4 February 1899 the *News* was going behind. A month later the local voted to continue it for a further month. By 1 April its liabilities were $87.60 and its assets $65.80, and the local was levying an assessment to wipe out the debt. This was discouraging; but a later strike, in 1902, produced another paper, the *Toiler*, still in existence at the beginning of 1903.

On 13 May 1899 an emergency meeting heard the report of a rather inconclusive interview with Dennis, who said that he had never been notified and that he had not broken the agreement. The committee thought another interview might produce something definite; meanwhile, the local assessed all members $1 to carry on the strike and appealed to sister unions for aid. On 20 May a planned campaign against the papers was postponed till the committee could have a further interview with Dennis, since it thought he would agree to hire only union men in future. He flatly refused.

On 19 June the local was informed that Dennis, in a final interview, had refused to discharge any of the non-union men already working for him, but had offered to give union men a preference in future and to take back two of the strikers at once and a third if the union brought him back. The local voted against accepting the offer, and the strike went on. On 5 August a considerable amount of money was coming in from other unions. By 4 November the strike was settled: the three strikers were to get the first three vacancies; 'a show' was to be 'given, in future, for capable union men'; the union men were to be allowed to learn the machines. This settlement applied only to the newspaper office; the job-office was still on strike, and a settlement there was reported only on 6 January 1900.

In August 1900 it was the turn of the *Chronicle* and the *Echo*, the *Herald*'s and *Mail*'s Liberal rivals. The local presented a new scale: $2.50 per night for night work, with 40 cents an hour overtime; $13 a week for day work, with 35 cents an hour overtime. In October a monoline machine scale followed: 9 to 11 cents per thousand ems, with 35 cents an hour overtime. The management offered 8 to 11 cents. The union also wanted 30 cents an hour waiting time; management offered 25 cents during the day and 30 cents at night. This was rejected in January 1901, and the union started drafting new proposals.

These appeared in March. They provided, for one, that an apprentice was to be allowed to learn how to operate the machines only during the last six months of his apprenticeship, and only if he applied for union membership. The proposed rates for monoline machines were to be 9 cents per thousand ems day work, and 11 cents night work; for typesetting machines, 8 and 9 cents respectively. The day shift was to be 8 hours, the night shift 7. There was also a detailed set of rates for special work. Overtime was to be 30 cents an hour, and the agreement might be terminated by either side on 30 or 60 days' notice.

This must have produced some agreement, for the next news we get of the *Echo* comes in October 1901, when it was reported that there were non-union men working on that paper, and that the union men had refused to work with them. A committee was appointed to see the manager. It did not get much satisfaction, but the foreman discharged the non-unionists.

This was followed by a new scale for book and job work: $12 a week, with an agreement terminable by the union on 90 days' notice. This, in its turn, was followed by the formation of a book and job printers employers' association.

In April 1902 Dennis announced that he did not intend to have a union office at the *Herald*. The union's reply was to co-operate with the Pressmen in preparing a new scale. This was sent to the ITU's president, in mid-June; he returned it, with minor amendments (notably a 54-, not 55-, hour week in book and job-offices) a week or so later. The unions gave notice to the employers that they wanted the new arrangements to come into force 1 August.

A committee presented the new scale early in July, in the absence of Dennis. It was well received, and the committee expected an answer by 15 July. By that date Local 130 had a letter from the *Herald*. It quoted the letter of agreement of 21 October 1899, in which the paper undertook to employ the best men it could find in Halifax, which the union had accepted. It wanted to know whether the new scale meant the repudiation of this agreement, and whether, if the scale was refused, there would be a strike. The union replied that it was not proposing violation of any existing agreement, but the adoption of a new one after 'frank and friendly discussion,' in which the employers could state any objections they had. It withdrew the August deadline, and said a strike was not anticipated.

Next evening, there was a lockout at the *Chronicle*. A non-union man had been found working there; he refused to join. Dunn, the manager, insisted on keeping him, and the union members refused to work with him. The local asked the ITU to send an organizer and arranged for a committee to see Dunn on 17 July. On that date, the local appointed a strike leader. The union set up pickets, and watched all incoming trains for strikebreakers. It also interviewed the parents or guardians of four boys working in the office, to see whether they would take them out. On 20 July the ITU's organizer, McMahon, arrived. He interviewed Dunn, but had nothing favourable to report. He had also had a meeting with Dennis and was to get an answer from him later. During the next three days he had meetings with one of the directors, who gave him no satisfaction, and with the secretary of the Retail Merchants' Association, which was sending a committee of its own to see Dunn. Meanwhile, there had been a belligerent letter from Dennis; the boys had gone out and been provided with two weeks' strike pay; and the Typothetae (the employers) had refused to increase wages.

By 4 October all four newspapers were struck, and the local was considering holding a public meeting on the subject. It decided, instead, to appoint a committee to visit the other unions in the city. This produced results. The Carpenters sent in

$20, the Painters $10, the Stonecutters $30, the Coopers $15, the Retail Clerks $5, and the Bricklayers $10. The Machinists promised to do all they could. The contributions were needed, for the international could send no more money, and the local was paying $5 to each man locked out. The strike was still on as late as 7 March 1903. By that time there were 143 members. The strike had evidently not seriously affected the local's numbers, since only six members are listed as dropped, eight as expelled, two as having left the city, and one as suspended (for non-payment of dues).

Kingston Local 204 began with a meeting, 18 February 1886, of seven *Whig* printers to discuss forming a union. On 5 March a larger meeting drafted and discussed a constitution and by-laws, and decided to be a local of the ITU. There were 11 charter members.[15]

Not till 19 May 1887 did the local get round to drawing up a scale, and to appointing committees to wait on the *Whig* and the *News*. There was difficulty with the *News*, and, while awaiting a decision from the international, the local tried to have the trouble with the *News'* compositors arbitrated. This apparently failed; for early in July a deputation informed the publishers that the local was going to strike, and a member was sent to the Knights of Labor to ask for their sympathy.

On 11 July the local adopted a scale, decreed that any office refusing to accept it would be considered unfair, and gave the employers till nine o'clock to agree. They must have done so, for in November we find a committee waiting on management to explain certain features of the agreement on both papers and to deal with alleged violations.

On 28 March 1892 Local 204 sent its 'hearty sympathy' to the Canadian National Typographical Union, though it does not seem to have proceeded further in the matter. On 6 October 1893 it proposed to other unions throughout Canada action to give work to the unemployed and backed this with a resolution 'that for every member not holding a steady sit, this union pledges to give those out of work at least two days' work a week.' The local must by this time have been in pretty low water, for the same meeting had a notice of motion to surrender the charter. But by 3 November the notice was withdrawn.

In May 1896 the local drew up a new scale: 22½ cents per thousand ems for hand compositors working on evening papers for a 7½-hour day; $9 a week for job-offices and time hands for a 59-hour week; 25 cents an hour for overtime; and $9 a week for machine hands for a 54-hour week. In June 1898 the local received a telegram from the Tailors' Union, suggesting that the two unions hold a joint celebration of Labour Day: an indication of how little Kingston was then unionized.

In August 1898 the local appointed a committee to wait on the job-offices to try to get shorter hours. By September there were sixteen members in good standing, with four liable for suspension, and it was reported that ex-members setting up offices and cutting prices made the nine-hour system 'well nigh impossible.' In December the shorter-hours committee was empowered to draft a proposal, to be signed by the papers and the job offices, to go into effect 1 January 1899. In March 1899 the local adopted the 9½-hour day and agreed to notify the book and job-offices. By May there were several trades unions in the city, and it was felt that it was 'time for joint action to celebrate Labour Day.'

In February 1900 there was notice of motion to adopt a machine operators' scale of $9 per week for the first 100,000 ems, with a bonus for all work over that figure to be arranged by the different staffs; by April all the employers but one had signed. By 14 January 1903 a new scale of $12 a week for day hands, $14 for foremen and machine hands, and $12 for 'Act' men and job hands had been adopted.

Seventeen Vancouver printers met early in May 1887 and formed a purely local union which, however, was to apply at once for an ITU charter.[16] This seems to have been Vancouver's first union. It antedated the arrival of the CPR. Almost at once, the union was involved in a strike at the *News*, where the unionists went out for a few days while non-unionists got out the paper. Three members raised $150 to carry on the strike. 'Pete Mayer [the sergeant-at-arms] was given $40 for picket duty and told to stay at the Bridge Hotel, next to the False Creek bridge at Westminster Avenue (now Main Street), the only highway where "rat" printers could enter the city from the south. The strike was settled on the same day the first CPR overland passenger train arrived in Vancouver.'

Most of the local's pioneers left for the United States in May and early June. The ITU charter was issued 20 June but never reached Vancouver, having possibly got misdirected to Vancouver, Washington. On 22 January 1888 nine printers met in the White Swan Hotel to start a new union. Only two of the original seventeen seem to have been present, though another five turn up in the records within a few months. The new charter was issued 7 February 1888, with eleven charter members (five had been members of the earlier local).

The new union at once adopted a constitution, by-laws, and a scale of prices. 'The nine-hour day was firmly established at $21 a week for time work, with piece work on newspapers at 50 cents per 1000 ems for night work and 45 cents for day work.' Plainly, Vancouver was already a high wage area. Before the year was out, the local was trying to form a trades and labour council, though the only other unions in the city at the time seem to have been the purely local Stevedores' Union (formed in the spring); Locomotive Firemen, Lodge 276 (formed 24 March); and Railroad Trainmen, Lodge 144 (formed 26 June); and perhaps the purely local Longshoremen's Union (formed 17 November). The attempt failed.

In 1889 the local had 35 members. On 16 September there was a strike at the *World* 'over the observance of a "style" board. The editor-in-chief had assisted the chapel to make up a set of rules for the use of "editors, reporters, compositors and proofreaders." ... Any changes of style from "copy" were ringed, i.e., the office would make the alterations in type, or pay extra to the piece-worker to do so. In the argument, the foreman discharged a compositor, hence the walk-out, which lasted two days, over who should make the correction from lower case "i" to capital "I" in the word "independence."' The managing editor had for some time been making exceptions to the style board as he saw fit, till the exceptions were almost as many as the rules; and 'independence,' not inappropriately, was the last straw. The union won, after only two days, and the strike went down in history as 'the "cap I" strike and became the josh of the town. Nat. Goodwin, the actor, then performing at the Vancouver Theatre, made fun of the whole affair. The managing editor was at the show.'

In 1890, the Vancouver local circularized all the ITU locals in Canada, urging them to make a united demand for a legal eight-hour day; and two Vancouver Typos were the first western delegates to attend a TLCC convention (one representing the local, the other the Vancouver Trades and Labor Council).

In 1891 the Vancouver local came out for equal pay for equal work by men and women, the formation of 'labour lecture bureaux ... for discussion of economic questions,' and a nine-hour day (eight hours on Saturday).

On 5 September 1892 the local presented a new scale of prices to the newspaper publishers. Negotiations began on 9 September but failed. A strike broke out on the *World* and *Telegram* on 21 October, and though it lasted only two days, the local issued a paper of its own to support the strikers. The *New World*, announced as an evening daily, had, for its one issue, 'the largest circulation of any daily paper in Vancouver' (not quite so empty a boast as it sounds, for, though the *World* and *Telegram* were shut down, the *News-Advertiser* continued to operate, under protest). The *New World* was sold out within an hour, and had to print a fresh run. The newsboys got it free and sold it for five cents.[17]

The new scale provided for 50 cents per thousand ems on night work, 45 cents on day work; 6½ to 7 hours' continuous composition; waiting time at 1200 ems per hour; time work $3.75 for 9 hours, night, and $3.50 for 9 hours, day; night foremen $26 per 6-day week; day foremen $24 per week.

In February 1893 the local had to contend with the arrival of machines. It was assured that only union men would be used on them, and it promptly drew up a provisional scale: an 8-hour day; $10 a week for the first week's operation by learners; $15 a week for the next 5 weeks; and $21 a week for the next 6 weeks; after that, reconsideration of the rates. The *News-Advertiser* and the *World* accepted this, and in July accepted the reconsidered rates: $21.50 a week, day work; $22.50, night work. George F. Leaper, a member of the local, started a co-operative labour paper, the *People's Journal*, which lasted three months. In September a committee of three was appointed to help organize country towns as part of the Vancouver local. The membership now stood at 55.

In January 1894 the machine scale committee reported in favour of new rates, but, because of the depression, negotiations were held in abeyance. During this year, because of the hard times and 'large numbers of idle and hungry men,' wages were reduced in all trades in Vancouver except printing; work for printers, however, 'was curtailed fifty per cent, hand work being replaced by machinery.'[18] By the end of 1895 'Vancouver was slowly emerging from the dark days of the depression ... though most of the unions were financially broke; consequently general inactivity prevailed in labor organizations.' Earlier in the year a member of the Typos' local had declared that it was 'useless for parents to send their children to the printing trade. The calling is dead to what it was even ten or fifteen years ago ... Something should be done to stop any more apprentices learning the trade for at least ten years.' Membership was down to 22.

In 1897 the city of Vancouver was asked to put the union label on all city printing. The local's secretary wrote the Typographical Association in Sydney, Australia, to see whether Australian Typos accepted Orientals as members (a Chinese printer on a CPR liner had wanted to join the Vancouver local). There seems to have been no reply, nor does the official history record whether the Chinese printer got in.

In 1898 'the eight-hour day was made complete in all Vancouver composing rooms.' A joint Vancouver-Victoria scale committee 'opposed [the] proposed bonus system on machine composition of 10 cents per 1000 ems for all type set over 30,000 ems per day of eight hours. It was held that pace-making was not in the best interests of the general membership. This did not prevent a superior workman receiving a stated wage higher than the union minimum scale.'

In 1899 the local bought 35 shares (one for each member) to buy the Homer Street Methodist Church for a proposed labour temple; a fine of $5 was imposed on any member not attending the Labour Day parade; trade had improved; and the union had two chapels in both the *Province* and the *News-Advertiser* and one each in the *World*, *Town Topics*, Evans and Hastings, Thomson Brothers, Trythall & Son, and Timms Publishing Co.[19]

In 1900 the local came out strong for independent labour political action and was unanimously in favour of setting up a labour paper, the *Independent*. One of the local's most prominent members, George Bartley, resigned as delegate to the Trades and Labor Council (a position he had held since its inception) to become editor. The local invested $200 in shares of the new Labour Hall, and members were asked to buy shares as well. The local resolved that overtime should be paid price-and-a-half and that union proofreaders should be employed on city papers at the printers' scale. To the list of union offices were now added the *Independent*, the Record Publishing Co, J.A. Fulton, Webber & Philipps, and Stoney & Barclay.

In 1901 Timms broke away, got the city printing contract, and of course lost the union label. The local's members were asked to refrain from patronizing Chinese laundries. It was deemed 'inadvisable for proprietors holding active membership in the Union to be also active members of the proposed Typothetae Association [employers].' The local also went on record in favour of compulsory arbitration. To compensate for the loss of Timms, there were new chapels in the *Ledger*, *Trade*, *Budget*, and Trythall & Son.

In 1902 the local sent a delegate to the provincial political convention at Kamloops, but he recommended that the union have nothing to do with the Progressive party. The local decided to have nothing to do with any party. It also endorsed the proposal to do away with Sunday work throughout Canada; adopted a new scale of $21, $21.50, and $22.50 per week; and added to its chapels *Citizen and Country* (a labour paper), the *Canadian Socialist*, BC Printing and Engraving, and 'Keystone.'

From 1889 to 1902 the local had also been active in the Trades and Labor Council and, from 1898, the Allied Printing Trades Council. In 1894 it supported the Trades and Labor Council's effort to establish a co-operative store.[20]

The Montreal consolidated local, after four years' experience, had found it impossible to continue. Half the members were French-speaking but, though few of them were bilingual, all the proceedings were conducted in English. By 1882 not only was the local riven by disputes but half the printers in Montreal were unorganized. The French-speaking members accordingly asked to have the old Jacques-Cartier Local 145 restored, and on 14 July 1882 it was, the English-speaking printers continuing as Local 176. Within the year this local had an unsuccessful strike at the *Star* to secure the dismissal of five non-unionists.[21]

Evidence before the Royal Commission on Capital and Labor casts a lurid light on the Montreal Typos' problems during the 1880s. The *Gazette* was a union shop. The *Star* professed itself indifferent about unionism and employed both unionists and non-unionists, at (so it said) higher than union rates. The *Witness* was blatantly anti-union. The foreman of its composing room said it was 'because I find this union business a drag, and it enables the drones to live upon honest men.' The *Witness* had closed its office to the union after the labour troubles of the 1870s and had taken on girls. The foreman boasted: 'We have some of those girls to-day, and we have never had any strikes since, and I don't think we ever will, so long as we have girls to fall back on. They know that we are independent of them.' The *Witness* paid less than union rates.

The union's worst headache was the job-printing establishments. The most serious cheap-labour threat came from the Reformatory, which operated a printing shop with convict labour, and from the friars of Coteau St-Louis, who, the union claimed, operated one of the largest shops in the Montreal district. The smaller establishments did mainly lawyers' factums, and the competition of the convicts and the friars had cut the price of these by a third in the previous 10 years, with, of course, a corresponding effect on wages.[22]

On 30 May 1890, the Typos struck the *Herald*. They wanted piece-work and double rates for the nightly correction of the financial column. The management refused, and hired strikebreakers. Those who came from Toronto the union persuaded to go back, 'by numerous acts of intimidation' (said the newspapers). The union president and 4 strikers were arrested for conspiracy, and 13 other strikers for desertion, under the Masters and Servants Act. American strikebreakers replaced the Toronto variety, and by 26 July the strike was over: lost.[23]

In February 1893 Local 145 appointed a committee (including Urbain Lafontaine) to organize a national typographical union. Before the month was out, the committee had issued an appeal to all printers, pressmen, bookbinders, and stereotypers to join the new organization. A few days later, the national union was 'in process of being organized'; before the middle of March, *La Presse* was announcing the first meeting of the 'national Association of Printers of Montreal.'[24] But Local 145 seems in the end to have remained loyal to the international union, and the national union to have died aborning.

Local 176 got a wage increase in the leading offices in October 1899. In January 1901 both locals demanded increases, and some of the largest employers agreed at once. By March Local 145 had signed agreements with nearly all the French-language employers. By April apparently all the French offices had fallen in line.

A year later, five English offices had agreed to grant a 9-hour day, with $11 a week for hand work and $15 for machine work, while the rest were negotiating. There was an inconclusive strike of 15 printers in 1 shop in May and June 1901, because the employer refused to grant a wage increase.[25]

In 1882 a member of the Ottawa local, one Teague, contributed one of the three practicable plans for reorganization of the international union. In the fall of 1883 the Ottawa local struck the *Free Press*. The strike was evidently unsuccessful, for in April 1886 we find the local condemning the *Free Press* and the *Journal* for not recognizing the union and not paying union wages, and for hiring women and boys. It also regretted that the city had given municipal advertising to the delinquent papers. At this time, the local had agreements with the *Citizen* and *Le Canada*.

By the spring of 1892 even the *Citizen* agreement must have collapsed, for on 20 April the Toronto local had a letter from J.W. Patterson, of Ottawa, in which he speaks of the prospect of getting that paper back into the fold. He also describes some incidents of the fight which the union was waging in both Ottawa and Montreal against the Printers' Protective Fraternity: 'We performed a *coup-d'état* last Sunday and kidnapped five of them, among them their Vice-President, took them to the country, struck terror to their hearts and shipped them to parts unknown.' He added that there was a good prospect of organizing the Montreal *Herald*, as well as the Ottawa *Citizen*. By 4 June he was able to report that the Ottawa local had 'cleaned' the *Citizen* of all the PPF men but one, that that organization was beyond recovery in Ottawa, and that the Montreal local was 'in a fair way to gain the "Herald."'[26]

In September 1900 the Ottawa local had a dispute with the Government Printing Bureau important enough to produce a delegation to Sir Wilfrid Laurier. The delegation consisted of the international's president, the presidents of the Toronto and Montreal locals, and Patrick Draper and S. Anders of the Ottawa local. The men wanted an increase of wages from $12 a week to $15.[27]

In May 1901 the Ottawa local had been asking for $13.50 a week for compositors (an increase of $2.50) and a corresponding increase in overtime rates, and $15 for linotype operators (also a $2.50 increase). The publishers offered $12 for the compositors and agreed to the other demands, but wanted the option of piece work on linotype at 7 cents per thousand ems day, 8 cents night. The union balked at this option, but eventually the parties compromised. The agreement also provided for a nine-hour day.[28]

On 25 January 1901 reporters from the Ottawa papers had met and decided to organize under the ITU. In February this News-Writers' Union was expected to be in working shape by March, with a membership of about 15.[29]

The Winnipeg local, No 191, soon after its formation, succeeded in raising the scale on morning papers from 40 cents to 45, and the weekly rate from $16 to $18. All the newspapers granted this unconditionally, but some of the job offices very unwillingly, 'threaten[ing] that they [would] replace those at present employed by cheaper hands if the [could] get them.'

This was in May 1882. Five months later, the local ran into trouble. Some days before 18 October 1882, the *Free Press* compositors, on arriving at work, found a notice of dismissal effective in two weeks. They sent a deputation to Luxton, one of the proprietors, to find out why. He replied that he had a staff engaged at 40 cents per thousand ems and that he 'had secured new men because he was sure those then working for him would not accept the reduction.' He intimated, however, that any of them who would accept it could stay. The union decided that the new hands were a mere flight of fancy, just Luxton's way of demanding a reduction. They decided to insist on the existing scale. Luxton meanwhile telegraphed for one new hand, but when he arrived he refused to work except at the union rate. Luxton was obliged to give in.

But only for the moment. By the last week in October both the *Free Press* and the *Times* tried to impose a wage cut, and the union struck. On 2 November the *Trades*

Union Advocate carried this information, with the added news that on 31 October the strikers' places had been 'filled by gutter-snipes and scurvy scabs procured in Chicago.' In the 9 November issue comes this choice morsel:

Albert Horton, lately one of the proprietors of the *World* of this city, and an honorary member of the Toronto Typographical Union, but who was recently pitchforked into the editorial chair of the Winnipeg *Free Press*, on the occasion of the printers' strike in that city, cast aside all the moiety of manhood in his composition, and proved that he was a miserable, sneaking, pandering cur. Sacred history tells us that Zimri slew his master, but justice overtook him, and in a fit of remorse he burned himself to death. Some centuries later Judas betrayed his master, and so strongly did his conscience rebuke him that he hanged himself. Some centuries later Albert Horton betrayed his fellow-workmen, but he will neither burn nor hang himself, for the simple reason that he has not the least vestige of a conscience left, it having been silenced long ago. A dose of *delirium tremens*, with its hobgoblins and demons is preferable to companionship with a creature like Albert Horton, editor of the Winnipeg *Free Press*.

The Toronto Typos contributed $50 to this strike, and on 2 December received three Winnipeg refugees by transfer card.[30]

Looking back, in 1903, the Winnipeg local was able to say that it had 'steadily increased in numbers and influence till the advent of typesetting machines.' This had caused a revolution in the trade, in Winnipeg as elsewhere, and within a few months of the installation of machines, the local's membership was reduced from 110 to less than 70. 'However, after the first shock had passed, things began to look brighter, a general increase of work in all branches followed, particularly in newspaper composition, and it was not long till the membership began to assume its old time proportions.' On 1 May 1902 the membership totalled 95; a year later it stood at 112.

This last may well have resulted partly from the agreement the union won for job shops and for 'ad' men on newspapers on 1 February 1902 without a strike. This cut the work week from 54 to 53 hours for day work, with a minimum wage of $17, and established a 48-hour week for night work, with a minimum of $19; overtime, in both cases, at time-and-a-half. For machine work the work week was to be 48 hours day and 45 night. On the Mergenthaler machine, the day work minimum was to be $19 a week; night work, $21; time-and-a-half overtime in both cases. On the Rogers machine, day work was to be paid 14 cents per thousand ems; night work, 16.[31]

The two Quebec City locals were merged on 7 April 1893 into a new local, No 302. By 1900 the combined local had only 35 members. By January 1901, however, it had won an agreement with the publishers which set a wage of $9 per 54-hour week for day work, with overtime at 25 cents an hour, and an $11.25 50-hour week, night work; 27 cents per thousand ems day work, 32 cents night work. Day hands got 50 cents an hour for Sunday work (with no piece-work allowed, except on morning papers), and $12 per 48-hour week for work on evening papers. Learners on machines were to get $11.25 on morning papers and $19 on evening and apprenticeship was to last 8 weeks.[32]

The Brandon Typos had a short life. Organized 2 July 1898, chartered 13 July, they were faced from the outset with the employers' adamant refusal to recognize the union. When the local presented its demands orally, the employers asked to have them in writing. When the union complied, all but two men were dismissed within two or three days. Both the local and the international representative (who had been called in) were ready to make what the Winnipeg *Voice* called 'humiliating concessions' from the initial demand for $12 a week. But they were not accepted, and the local died 29 May 1899.[33]

The London local struck in November 1899 for the first wage increase it had asked for in 25 years. The employers were not able to get competent men and lost Christmas business; the local union was so flush with funds that it was able to pay strike benefit without drawing on the international. It got a satisfactory agreement in the early summer of 1900.[34]

THE CIGAR MAKERS INTERNATIONAL UNION

Of the Cigar Makers during the years 1881–1902 few records seem to survive. We are thrown back on incidental references by other unions, trades and labour councils, the TLC, or the newspapers. This is a pity, for cigar-making was in these years a very considerable and widespread industry, and the Cigar Makers International Union played a notable part in the Canadian as well as the international labour movement.

The mere number and distribution of the locals are impressive. By the end of 1902, there were at least twenty: nine in Ontario (Toronto, Hamilton, Brantford, St Catharines, London, St Thomas, Berlin, Stratford, and Kingston), four in Quebec (Montreal, Quebec, Sherbrooke, and St Hyacinthe), five in British Columbia (Vancouver, Victoria, New Westminster, Nelson, and Kamloops), one in New Brunswick (Saint John), and one in Manitoba (Winnipeg). There is also some evidence of locals in Nanaimo and Sault Ste Marie; and there had been others in Tilsonburg, Paris, Guelph, Galt, and Ancaster.

The CMIU had a troubled history during these decades. In September 1880 the international office had issued an order that there were to be no strikes for increased wages till the spring of 1881. The moment the ban was off, the strikes must have started, for the 1883 convention reports that 'During the last two years the expenditures were enormous, involving a large portion of our income.' To support various strikes, the CMIU had sent $822.05 to London, No 19; $913.30 to Hamilton, No 55; $3380.55 to Montreal, No 58; $92 to Brantford, No 59; $22.80 to Tilsonburg, No 64; and $114.68 to St Catharines, No 140: a total of $5345.38. The next convention, in 1885, recorded 3 strikes for Toronto, No 27, and 1 each for Hamilton, No 55, Montreal, No 58, and Tilsonburg, No 64, costing a total of $8270.78.

The next 2 years were quieter. In 1887 the strike expenditure in Canada since 1885 was shown as $269.45 for London 19, only $7.30 for Toronto 27, a modest $84.85 for Hamilton 55, a slightly higher $91.95 for Montreal 58, and only $69.30 for Brantford 59 (1 strike each). But the 1889 convention was informed of 3 strikes in Toronto (cost, $6023.10), 2 in Brantford (cost, $374.75), and 1 for the new Montreal Local 226 (cost, $36). Again, the next 2 years showed a marked slackening off: 1 strike each for Toronto 27, London 278, and St Thomas 195.

At this same convention, 1891, William V. Todd, of Toronto, the CMIU's third vice-president, reported on the situation in Canada. There were 3048 cigar makers in the country, of whom about 500 were in the union's 8 locals (2 in Montreal, 1 each in Toronto, Hamilton, London, Brantford, St Catharines, and 1 other, unidentified). Quebec had 2117 of the total, Ontario 788, New Brunswick 69, British Columbia 53, and Manitoba 21. Todd said Canada's adoption of the national policy had cut off the supply of cheap European cigars, and 'brought into requisition ... the cheap labor abounding in the eastern provinces ... with the result of forcing into competition the cheap labor districts of Western Canada [by which Todd probably meant western Ontario], thus placing the membership of the International Union in Canada in a position best described as ... between the devil and the deep sea.' Curiously enough, Todd did not mention Oriental labour, though the 1883 convention proceedings had had a special note on 'the Anti-Chinese Law being pushed in the Canadian Provinces,' and a committee had recommended giving the CMIU's president 'discretionary powers ... to act in conjunction with other labor organizations,' and appropriating 'a sufficient sum of money to defray such expense.'

Most of the eight Canadian locals, Todd said, were

in extremely weak condition, and all of [them] resemble beleaguered camps engaged in a continual struggle to keep out the foe. The only weapon we have to fight with is the union label, and it is only effective in places that are fairly well organized, outside these places the demand is general for the very cheapest grade of goods, rendering it well nigh impossible for union label goods to obtain a foothold ... Our brothers in Canada ... operating under very low bills of prices, have not hesitated to freely expend money in agitating on behalf of the label. I have heard of voluntary assessments made for the purpose of organizing and for advertising the union label by our brothers in Montreal, which, considering the low prices that are being paid for work in that locality, had been veritable sacrifices in the cause of unionism ...

Union 27 in Toronto is well organized; all the shops strictly union; the goods manufactured bearing the union label and the city a trade union center. Yet, after a prolonged fight, it has been unable to raise the bill [wage rates]. I am persuaded the only remedy ... in this and similar cases, is a well directed sustained effort to organize the non-union element.

In London, Ontario, the center of the cheap labor district of Ontario, wherein the great majority of those employed are of the female persuasion, the employment of a female organizer would, I am sure, be attended with the best results.

Todd also noted that the government had substantially reduced the excise duty on cigars made from Canadian leaf, and the manufacturing licence fee; that one manufacturer who had the label had accordingly started using Canadian leaf; and that 'the label [had] suffered in consequence – for cigars made from Canadian leaf are the vilest of the vile.'[35]

It is possible to piece together a good deal more about the activities of the various locals. In Hamilton, in May 1881, Local 55 demanded and got an increase of $1 per thousand on hand work, with proportionate increases on fancy brands. Next month, the local held an extremely successful first annual picnic, with more than 1500 people present. In April 1883 came the strike which cost the international so much money. It arose over the employment of too many apprentices in the shops. The employers, not surprisingly, threatened to go to Montreal and elsewhere for men to replace the strikers, but, very surprisingly, said they would then set up their shops along strict union lines. They alleged that the Hamilton local's practice in regard to apprentices was unique. The union stuck to its position and talked of setting up a producers' co-operative. By August the local had more than a hundred members.

Some time between the 1883 strike and the beginning of 1885, the officers must have been involved in some shady doings, for on 15 February 1885 the members were told that they now had an efficient staff of trustworthy officers, and could rest assured that there would be no repetition of the 'crooked transactions' from which they had suffered so much in the past.[36] The efficient and trustworthy staff was needed, for the union was soon involved in July 1886 in a prolonged strike or lockout by all the manufacturers in the city. By 1 May 1886 all the union shops in the city had secured an eight-hour day. Some of the cigar manufacturers had formed an association, which now proposed to cut wages by 15 per cent. As the men's average wages were less than $6 a week, they balked. The employers then locked the men out, and the men boycotted all the members of the association. Arbitration was invoked, but was unsuccessful, and the employers brought in strikebreakers from other places. 'The united efforts of organized labor,' however, produced a break in the ranks of the manufacturers, 'after which a gradual weakening of the combination [of employers] was perceptible until the early fall, when the majority of the shops were employing union labor again.' One by one, in fact, all but two of the employers agreed to keep the old prices.

The two die-hard employers, Reid & Co, and Simon, not only brought in strikebreakers, but tried to organize them into the Knights of Labor. There had been a Knights of Labor cigar makers' assembly in April 1884, but it was now apparently defunct, for the two employers tried to get their strikebreakers admitted to LA 2225, which in March 1884 had described itself as a machinists' and blacksmiths' assembly. LA 2225 refused to accept the applicants, and the employers were apparently on the point of settling with the International Cigarmakers' Union, when a new element entered the picture.

Three officers of District Assembly 61, D.R. Gibson, W.J. Vale, and George Collis, told the strikebreakers they should organize a new assembly and have the KOL label placed on their product. This was done. Local 55 of the CMIU of course, promptly censured Gibson, Vale, and Collis for interfering with its activities and accused them of having an agreement with Reid and Simon. Adolph Strasser, international president of the CMIU, appeared on the scene, calling a meeting of all workingmen to expose the activities of men who, he alleged, were working with the Home Club – 'a secret organization whose grand object was to get control of the Knights of Labor for selfish purposes.' The Strasser meeting unanimously censured the Knights, and called for support of the CMIU label.

When DA 61 refused to revoke the charter issued to the cigar makers assembly, the Central Labor Union threatened to boycott all and any cigars which did not bear the CMIU's blue label. When DA 61 still did not come to heel, the resolution in favour of the boycott was put and carried.[37]

London Local 19 had its share of troubles. On 11 February 1882, it struck Kelly and Sons. Fourteen men walked out, demanding the dismissal of three non-union employees. Two days later, two of the non-union men did not return to work; the third did, and the union men stayed out. The *Daily Advertiser*'s comment sheds an interesting light on contemporary ideas in London. Apparently, all previous strikes had been for higher wages or some other improvement in working conditions, for the editor said a strike for a closed shop was 'somewhat of a peculiar character.' In September, the employers locked out most of the members to forestall a demand for equalization of wage rates in the various shops. The employers immediately tried to get new workers, but their efforts were quietly and effectively frustrated by the union. The strikers lay in wait at the Grand Trunk Railway station, met all cigar makers arriving in town, and tried to induce them not to accept any job. The *Advertiser* says reproachfully that in the case of non-union men among the arrivals, 'it was claimed that measures resorted to had not always been such as could be approved.'

On 19 October two employers turned up to do counter-picketing. The constable on duty, acting on instructions from the superintendent, told the men to move on; but they claimed they were there to buy tickets to East London and had a right to stay till the ticket office opened. By December, the employers had succeeded in bringing in a certain number of cigar makers from Pennsylvania. Organized labour in London denounced the employers' action and pledged its support to the strikers; and the employers were still short-handed.

On 9 December S.M. Hodgins, the local's president, wrote this account of the whole affair:

About three months ago we came out, seventy in number, to equalize a bill of prices in this city, as some shops were paying more than others; and we were actually compelled to take such action by some of the bosses who were paying the least ... Instead of waiting upon us like men, many locked their shops against us on Saturday. Furthermore, they signed a bond of $500 not to employ any man who dared ask his just rights for the term of five years. Many also pledged themselves not to buy leaf from any agent who would dare to sell to or employ any one of those men they had locked out. Again, they vowed that they would starve No. 19 clear out of existence. But what is left are still living in our city. We have six on strike-list and two working for Mr. Hasselgrove and the old Union shop. Mr. John Clark stood out against all the bosses; so did the Union shop, Mr. Russ Woodward, L. Arbucal, and of course they can buy all the tobacco they can pay for.

We have succeeded in shipping off all but seven or eight of the new arrivals. Of course the old rotten mechanics will die here. We have eight or nine in the city that we would back against the United States. Harry McKenna was out West for a few months, and had some $14 on his card. On his return he had the hardihood to tell Mr Kennedy, one of the bosses in this city, that the Union did not amount to anything. Moreover, he has never refunded the money the Union lent him to help him over the road. Thomas Kenny ... was acting Treasurer of Union 19. He got drunk one night, losing the money belonging to the Union, which was in his possession. We were about to shut down upon him, when he pleaded his case so well that the men had mercy on him and granted him time to pay up. This he never did IN FULL. No! he waited until we were in trouble with the manufacturers, then he ... not only went back to work the next day, but made himself solid with the boss by helping him to down the very men who had befriended him in his trouble ... John Garlic stayed out one week, then found out he could not live on $4 per week; but he can peddle plaster images when he cannot get a chance to make himself solid with the bosses. Then we have the conglomerate of corruption ... Thomas Fitzgibbons. He was one of the very worst kickers of the whole lot previous to the lockout; yet he was one of the very first to turn around and help the bosses, by misrepresenting matters so as to get an excuse for going back. It is well that we have the means of showing up these fellows to the craft in their true colours. We wish that this may meet the eyes of those sixty or seventy true men who left town on the strike.[38]

London had another strike on 24 August 1886, at Olmstead's. The union, which seems to have had no members in the factory, wanted an increase of $1 per thousand cigars. Olmstead refused. The local wanted the Trades and Labor Council to send a delegation to Olmstead, but the council, noting the absence of union members in the shop, considered such a move pointless, and merely filed the request.

This was about the end of Local 19. By 12 January 1888 the CMIU witness before the Royal Commission on Capital and Labor supposed there were not then three union cigar makers in the city: those who had been there were working in Stratford. After the 1882 strike, the London employers, by a bonded, three-year agreement, had blacklisted union men.[39]

A second London local, No 278, established in February 1891 with 25 members, had a strike on its hands almost at once. Eighteen men went out on 7 April and stayed out till 30 May. They lost. But by September 1900 this union was the largest in London, with about 170 members. It had a series of strikes in 1901.

On 2 January 18 men went out for a wage increase. They got it on 29 January. On 11 January another 18 men went out against a wage reduction. At the end of February women and children had taken the places of the men, but in August the company reverted to a union shop. On 23 April five union men were discharged and replaced. The lockout lasted for the rest of April and most of May, and the union lost. On 31 July seven men were locked out for refusing to make a superior class of cigars without extra pay. This stoppage lasted till 12 August, and the union won. In 1902 also this local had trouble: it refused to grant the union label to one of the employers, who, on 27 January, locked out his nine employees. By 12 February most of them had found work elsewhere, and the rest had come back, on the employer's terms.[40]

The Brantford local, No 59, seems to have covered also Woodstock, and, except when they had their own locals, Guelph, Galt, and Paris as well. Like some other locals, it had to cope with a rival Knights of Labor assembly which included cigar makers. In 1886 the workers were split between the two; but by August 1887 Local 59 must have carried the day, for its strike of that month was supported by all the other labour organizations in the city, which pledged their members to use only the CMIU 'Blue Label' cigars.

From 17 April to 26 May 1888 Local 59 was engaged in a further strike. It lost.[41]

A Toronto strike in the summer of 1888 apparently involved all the cigar factories in the city, and the union, by 20 July, had offered to accept arbitration by a board of three union nominees, three employers, and a referee chosen by these six.

The 1896 convention report, strangely, says nothing about three Toronto strikes in the early months of that year. Trouble at the Spanish-Canadian factory in January continued till March, when the union won. A second strike, at Eichorn and Carpenter's in February, over child labour, was still in progress in May, and there was fresh trouble at Maddox. By 22 July 1897 the Spanish-Canadian factory had locked out its employees because they refused to let it 'infringe on the apprentice laws of the union.' On 12 August the Trades and Labor Council resolved to circularize all the other councils on the subject; on 26 August the trouble was still unsettled.

On 27 April 1899 Local 27 had presented to the employers a list of demands (including a rate of 40 cents) to which they had acceded by 11 May, after a strike.[42]

The Saint John local, organized on 12 April and chartered 28 April 1894, seems to have got off to an excellent start. It 'placed the matter before the ... manufacturers ... who favored the move the men had made.' One of them had by 7 June adopted the union label. The Trades and Labor Council unanimously resolved that 'Whereas the Bell Cigar Co ... has recognized the ... Cigar Makers' Union and ... adopted the union label ... this Council places itself on record as approving of such action, and requests all friends of labor in this city and province to patronize the above named concern, it being the first in the Maritime Provinces to adopt union principles and the use of the union label in manufacture.' But the local seems to have died an early death.[43]

Stratford had a strike between 6 and 15 May 1900 of 27 workers. It succeeded, at a cost of $160 to the union, which paid strike benefit of $5 a week. Berlin had a successful strike of 11 workers between 11 and 25 August 1900, which cost $110.[44]

George Warren, the Montreal Cigar Makers' witness before the Royal Commission on Capital and Labor in 1888, put the number of cigar makers in the city at that date at 1264; but the employers' figures for several of the same firms suggest that the total may have been nearer 1700. The largest firm had 600 or 700, the second largest about 350, the next four a few over 100 each. The remaining 200 worked in 11 small establishments, of which 6 had only 1 or 2 employees, and only 2 had more than 30.

Warren testified (and the largest employer concurred) that in the preceding decade the average earnings of Montreal cigar makers had been cut in half. He traced this to the introduction of the cigar mould in 1873. Before that there had been some children in the factories working as apprentices. But from 1873 on an increasing number were employed as ordinary workers, because they were cheaper than men. The union tried to meet this threat by demanding a law to fix the minimum age of employment and to regulate the number of apprentices, and by pushing the use of the union label. Neither worked. Warren told the commission: 'We have expended thousands of dollars in making the Union trade mark known, and in similar matters, but it seems as if people would rather smoke child labour cigars than any other.' The only shops using the label were among the small ones.

Some of the evidence before the commission is almost unbelievable. The second largest factory was the one which made the most use of child labour. It imposed fines for misbehaviour and deducted them from the children's meagre wages. The children were also frequently beaten and, on occasion, confined in a small, dark room, as further punishment. The proprietor of this factory himself gave this evidence of how he treated one girl of 18:

I asked her to make one hundred cigars. It was in the afternoon or in the morning before the quitting hour, and she said she was not going to do it; and she spoke in a very impertinent manner. I had had several troubles with the same young lady previous to that, and I had seen her mother, and her mother had prayed me to do the best I could. So after receiving these instructions, and as I had three or four of her brothers working for me at the time, I took a great interest in the girl – the mother being alone and supported by the children – to see that the children were properly attended to. I took this young lady by the arm to have her sit down. She would not, so I turned her around and tried to sit her down. She would not. I took the cover off a mould and tried to sit her on my knee, but she was too heavy and fell on the floor. I held her on the floor and smacked her on the backside with the mould. I asked her if she would do it, and after a couple of strokes she said 'I will.' She got up and sat down at her table and made her one hundred bunches and went off quietly. She never lost one hour, and I think she is very glad to-day to have received the lesson she did, for she has been a very obedient girl ever since then.

Q. Do you believe it is decent for a man to place a girl of eighteen in that position?

A. When she is very disobedient and there are about fifty or sixty other girls there, I think it is only right that she should be taught a lesson when she deserves it.

Q. By a stranger?

A. ... She was bound to me, and I was to represent her father. It is important you should know that these boys and girls are bound to me. They are engaged by indentures, and, of course, under the engagement the mother and father must help me along as much as they can ... I must say that ... most of the parents who could not get along with their children, because they were in bad order and were bad boys, came to me as a cigar manufacturer and put them in my hands. They had seen my name so often before the Recorder that they knew if there was great trouble with them I would put them into the Reformatory.

This was an extreme case; but the more respectable employers had to cope with this kind of competition. The biggest factory gave its children or young people special piece-work payments and said it would have liked to do away with child labour, but could not. Its preference was for European cigar makers, of whom it brought in some 200 at a time when many Montreal workers in the trade were leaving for higher wages in the United States.[45]

Montreal Local 58 struck on 27 June 1883. The excise tax on cigars had been cut by $2.60 per thousand cigars, and the workers wanted $1 of this. The strike started at Davis but soon spread. On 6 July three firms gave in, and on 21 July three more. Davis kept going with girls and boys.

There was a lockout in 1893.

On 7 June 1894, both locals (58 and 226) struck at Davis, against a wage reduction. This strike lasted 13 weeks, cost the union $4481.37, and was completely successful; 2 months later the men were out again, for 10 days, and again they won. In the same summer, both locals struck successfully against a wage reduction at

Tassé-Wood. In the summer of 1895 there was a fresh and prolonged strike at Davis against a wage reduction. The Toronto Trades and Labor Council denounced the 'disreputable conditions' imposed on 'our Brothers ... compelled to look to these Shylocks for employment,' and the $4 per week wage that permitted of a bare subsistence (the Montreal newspapers put the wage at $5 to $9). In the fall of 1896, there was a strike at Blackstone.

In January 1898 new methods at Davis produced a union demand for piece-work. The workers organized only after the strike had broken out. In March the union struck L.O. Grothé against a wage reduction, and in December against J.M. Fortier, alleged to be paying less than the agreed rate. This latter strike continued into 1899, when the union also struck, briefly, against a wage cut at Hirsch.

In March 1900 there was a one-day strike at Grothé, and in April a six-day strike at Hirsch and Grothé for an eight-hour day and observance of the rule governing the number of apprentices. Two days after the strike broke out, two other firms told their employees either to leave the union or to force it to call off the strike. The workers refused and went out themselves. Hirsch gave in on the apprenticeship question.[46]

None of these strikes could compare with the great struggle which began 19 April 1901 and lasted for 17 months. The union wanted to get union rates and conditions accepted by every one of the 32 factories. Fourteen were already in line. Eight more accepted the demands. The other 10, employing 600 of the union's 872 members, refused. The strike petered out. By June 1902 the employers claimed that all the strikers' places had been filled. The international is said to have spent $1 million fighting sweatshops in Quebec.[47]

While the big strike was on the independent Spanish and Cuban Cigar Makers' Union reached an understanding with the international and informed the Davis firm that it must meet the CMIU's demands and take back the men it had dismissed. Davis refused and 29 members of the independent union then walked out. This strike also petered out.[48]

On 22 June 1901 the Quebec City cigar makers, whose wages were described as the lowest in Canada, struck for a 25 per cent increase. Twenty-four men in two factories were involved. The employers at first refused even to negotiate, and at the end of August both plants were reported working, with no settlement. By the end of the year, however, John Flett, AFL organizer, was able to report that he had settled with 1 of the 2 for a 20 to 40 per cent increase.[49]

Winnipeg Local 414, organized in July 1898, ran into trouble by November. It had presented a bill of prices slightly above the Toronto rates and a demand for an apprentice-journeyman ratio of one to five (the apprentices had actually been out-numbering the journeymen). It thought the employers had accepted the demands, then found they had not. It organized a co-operative cigar factory. The results must have been disappointing, for by 20 September 1901 we find that the local had been again reorganized a week before.

A year later the Havana Cigar Factory had been organized, which made three union factories in the city, and negotiations were in progress with the fourth and largest. By the end of November another factory had adopted the union label.[50]

THE AMALGAMATED ASSOCIATION OF STREET RAILWAY EMPLOYEES

The Amalgamated Association of Street Railway Employees formed its first Canadian division, No 30, in Toronto, on 28 September 1893. Three others followed in 1898, three more in 1899; Toronto was reorganized in June 1899 as Division 113. Two new divisions were added in 1900, two in 1901, and one more in 1902.[51]

London Division 97 had two strikes in this period, the first short and successful, the second long and disastrous. Both assumed the proportions of national struggles.

The London Street Railway was far from popular with London citizens. The *Industrial Banner* said it had 'long been looked upon as a soulless and grasping corporation that has broken every agreement that it has entered into. It has been in constant conflict with the city engineers and civic officials. It has systematically reduced the wages of its employees and subjected them to many and grievous annoyances, and has shown an utter disregard of public opinion in any shape or form.'

The workers' discontent had been mounting. The company had been charging exorbitant rates for breakages, unless the men could produce evidence that the damage was not their fault. It had also cut the maximum wage from 15 cents to 12½ for new men. The last straw came when it switched the hours of regular and relief employees. Most of the regular men had been working a 10-hour day at 15 cents an hour, and relief men a 7- or 7½-hour day at 12½ cents. The company now put the regular men on the shorter day and the relief men on the longer.

Twice, earlier, the Trades and Labor Council had tried to get the men to organize, but each time those who attended any meeting 'were quietly informed that they had better not attend another,' and the hint had been effective. This time, the would-be unionists were smarter: they met at the house of one of their number, formed a union, elected officers, and applied for a charter from the international union. When it arrived, the new Division 97 held a meeting in the Labor Hall. It was addressed by members of the Trades and Labor Council, and by Rezin Orr, international treasurer, who had come, that very day, 22 October, to help get the new division 'into proper working shape.' He found all the employees but three were charter members. 'The men had been receiving very cruel treatment and were working for wages as low as twelve and one-half cents per hour, and while the company from time to time had been making promises of increases, instead they were decreasing ... Organization ... had been ... an absolute secret ... until the majority of the men had been brought into the organization and ... demands ... had been ... agreed upon ... About the first knowledge that the company received of the organization was on October 21st, and they at once began to suspend the men who they thought were leaders ... On the 22d the committee presented their demands for better conditions, but the general manager refused to receive their proposition and discharged the entire committee.'

The demands were in the form of a petition:

1 16⅔ cents an hour for regular men, and a nine-hour day, 'with a lee way of as near 2½ hours as the time table will allow,' and with relief men getting 'the remaining hours ... [not] less than eight,' and overtime at 10 cents an hour;

2 only London residents to be employed, and before starting work, to pay the union initiation fee and get a union work permit; after 60 days' experience, to join the union;

3 all regular employees to get seniority, spare work to be divided equally among the spare men;

4 all conductors and motormen to report for work 15 minutes before their runs went out, otherwise their runs to be taken by spare men; any regulars who failed to report within 4 hours of starting time to lose next day also;

5 no charge for breakages unless proved to be the men's fault;

6 no conductor or motorman to lose time looking up accident reports, and conductors and motormen suspended for violation of rules or wrongdoing to have their cases investigated, and if they were exonerated, to be reinstated with back pay;

7 disputes not mutually adjusted to go to an independent board of arbitrators, one chosen by the company, one by the union, the third by the other two;

8 all employees to have free transportation over the company's lines;

9 union officers and committee men who had to take time off for union business to have their places back when they returned.

These conditions were to be embodied in a six months' agreement.

Three hours after the meeting which drew up the demands, the company discharged George Pickell, the union president, on the ground that he was not a citizen of London and his employment was therefore breaking a city by-law; this though the company had previously refused a request by the city engineer for Pickell's discharge on precisely this ground, stoutly maintaining that Pickell was in fact a resident!

The manager flatly refused even to meet the union committee or look at the petition; and when the members went back to their cars they were told they were discharged for absenting themselves without leave. Orr himself tried unsuccessfully to see the manager. He then called on the mayor, who 'took a determined stand in behalf of the men, a position ... he never wavered from during the entire contest.' The mayor tried to see the management but was turned down. He then called a meeting of the city council. Orr appeared and presented the men's demands. The council was unanimous for the men. It 'instructed the mayor and city solicitor to use all their influence to bring about a settlement, and, if that was impossible, to allow no foreigners or outsiders to operate street cars in ... London if a strike should follow.' The company ignored the council, and next day the union ordered the men to take their cars to the barn. All did, except two, who soon caved in. Next day the company brought in men from Hamilton, at $8.50 a week for a start and promising a raise in the near future. When the Hamilton men found there was a strike, they refused to work. The company then brought in others, but the citizens objected, and almost every store window in the city displayed 'We walk to protect Labor' placards in its front windows. Four cars got out, but they were hissed and hooted and showered 'with choice epithets'; one found its way blocked by a rig across the tracks, two others were pelted with rotten eggs and their windows smashed, the company manager had his hat knocked off by a rotten egg, and one of the conductors 'came in for some rough handling.'

Orr boasted that 'Public sentiment was unanimous for the men.' That very evening there was ample proof: one of the greatest mass meetings ever held in London. The strikers marched from the trades council headquarters headed by the leading bands of the city. 'Long before they got near the Princess Rink thousands of people were in line. Accommodations had been arranged at the rink for 5000 people. The rink was crowded to its full capacity and full that many more were turned away.'

The mayor presided and 'announced in opening the meeting his position in favor of the men in no uncertain terms. Colonel Leys [MP], the first speaker, said that he had gone on strike with the street railway employees, and for the people not alone to walk, but not to let any cars run until this strike was settled in favor of the men, that to deny a committee a hearing was not British fair play and contrary to the Bill of English Rights ... Prominent ministers also addressed the meeting, also International President Mahon. Resolutions endorsing the men in their position were unanimously passed.'

On 29 October more strikebreakers were brought in, from Montreal. The police escorted them to the car barn by back streets. Before the cars were due to go out, one of the strikebreakers appeared at a window brandishing a revolver. The crowd retaliated by throwing rocks and stale eggs at the barn and so frightened the strikebreakers that they asked to be sent back to Montreal. The company refused, and the men had to remain in the barn. Merchants refused to sell them food. The next day they took the train home.

By this time the city council was getting alarmed by the condition of the streets, which were littered with broken crates, rubbish, and the remains of rotten eggs, which gave off a terrible stench. Next day the Riot Act was posted, and things quieted down a bit; and the Trades and Labor Council distributed a further 20,000 'We walk' cards to be worn in hat bands. The cards were soon all snapped up.

On 1 November the company told the union it wanted to see the committee. Nine days later a final settlement provided for a starting rate of 13 cents, rising to 15⅓ cents after 1 year; a 9-hour day with 2½ hours' leeway; permission for the men to join the union, with no requirement to sign any document abridging the right; seniority; reinstatement of all strikers; and acceptance of the other demands in the petition.

Meanwhile, however, union supporters were taking no chances. The Trades and Labor Council had begun by printing tens of thousands of cards with the legend 'We walk' and the slogan 'No surrender to monopoly.' It followed this up with a circular addressed to 'Organized Labor throughout the Dominion.' This recited the 'vain and fruitless attempts' of the men to lay their grievances before the company; declared, 'This battle is the battle of organized labor throughout the entire Dominion'; and wound up by announcing that 'In order to raise contributions to the defence fund, it has been determined to issue a magnificently illustrated 8-page strike edition of the INDUSTRIAL BANNER, the oldest labor paper in Canada, to be retailed at 5 cents per copy, all proceeds to go towards this fund. 100,000 copies will be printed. It will contain handsome half-tone cuts of the men on strike; the stirring scenes that have been and are yet occurring; photographs of the speakers at the immense Mass Meeting held in the Princess Rink, and local labor men who have taken a prominent part in the struggle.'

The Toronto Trades and Labor Council promptly subscribed for a hundred copies.[52] But there was scarcely time for the appeal to have much effect before the company gave in.

The company's unpopularity had evidently taken the management by surprise and temporarily knocked it off balance. But it soon showed it had learned nothing and forgotten nothing. Within months the union was charging systematic breach of the clause in the agreement conceding the employees' right to join the union and not to have to sign any document: the company was asking applicants whether they thought they could be loyal to both company and union and giving job preference to those who promised not to join. One man, dismissed for chronic drunkenness on the job, was immediately rehired when the union expelled him. The company also issued a new rule book containing provisions which ran headlong into others made a year earlier and accepted by the union.

By 15 May 1899 the union had had enough. The members struck and set up pickets to persuade the rest of the men to join the strike. Early in June the union had a highly successful parade, in which many citizens joined. Overwhelming public sympathy was again forthcoming and encouraged the union to believe it could repeat its former triumph in short order.

This hope, however, proved a wandering fire. The strike dragged on and on. The union did its best, and with considerable success, to keep its members within the law, but it could not control its sympathizers, who resented the importation of strikebreakers who taunted and jeered at the strikers. As a result there were several riots during the summer and fall: in one case, union men had to rescue the strikebreakers from an angry crowd. Even children got into the act by obstructing the tracks.

On 22 August 1899 there was a big demonstration, with Frank Morrison, AFL secretary, as star speaker. London had 'shown to the world a moral boycott fought out on the highest lines. If I know the Anglo-Saxon people, the citizens of London can never be crushed, and every man, woman and child will walk until spring comes again if their rights are not secured. "The Union prevents strikes and does not cause them ... There have been more strikes among the unorganized than amongst organized labor. The workers are opposed to strikes except when it would be cowardly not to strike" ... Organized labor had the highest code of ethics known to mankind; honesty, mutual confidence and loyalty were its cardinal principles. There [sic] warfare was a ... mental warfare; bloodshed and riot were the products of unorganized labor. Every tenet of organized labor prohibited violence towards persons and property.'

Labour Day, the international president reported, 'saw another monstrous demonstration and the greatest industrial parade ever witnessed in London. All the trades unions of the city are contributing to the support of our Canadian brothers, and throughout the entire Dominion the trades organizations are raising funds to assist them. At Toronto the Trades Council is giving a band concert on the 9th ... at which they expect to clear $1,000.' (The concert duly took place. So did a second, on 22 February 1900, arranged by the union's Toronto division, the Toronto council, and the Musical Protective Association. They seem to have netted $1019.)

The international president claimed the company had probably not done $200 worth of business in the whole 4 months since the strike broke out. 'The cars pass up the street empty, the only passengers ... are the wives and families of the employees who ride upon passes and the Pinkerton thugs ... hired to trample upon the rights of honest labor. They have ... even found it impossible to keep scabs in line; ... [last reports showed] they did not have enough men to fill all their runs.' London, he said, would soon take over the line and operate it as a municipal utility.

When the Western Fair took place, the union got buses from Toronto and Windsor and transported people to and from the exhibition grounds. The company countered by offering free tickets to farmers and others; but the union buses were full, the company cars almost empty. The company sued the city officials for $20,000 for granting a special licence for the union buses and got an injunction to prevent the union from operating them. But the magistrate allowed the buses to run on payment of one dollar and on condition that they charged no fixed fares. The public were very generous, and the company's cars were very poorly patronized, even during the Christmas rush, when they carried less than a fifth of their normal number.[53]

Meanwhile, the TLCC, in September 1899, had passed a resolution of 'hearty sympathy and appreciation of the splendid battle so heroically waged against a grinding monopoly,' and had instructed its executive to issue an appeal to organized labour throughout Canada for financial aid. This produced a total of $229.65. Three trades and labor councils (Montreal Federated, Vancouver, and Victoria), the Winnipeg Independent Labor party, and 15 local unions (7 in Winnipeg and 1 each in Montreal, Toronto, Ottawa, Hamilton, St Catharines, Victoria, Nanaimo, and Rossland) contributed.[54] A couple of months later the international reported the London situation 'very little changed ... The boycott stands as firm as ever. The men are now making arrangements for a complete bus system during the winter ... and have secured from the Cleveland Herdic Company six herdics, which had been forwarded to the London boys to use during the winter.'

In January 1900 the Everett Trust, which controlled the company, published advertisements in all the large newspapers of the United States and Canada, claiming the strike had been called off. The purpose of this was to stop the flow of funds to the union and end sympathy strikes on a number of other lines controlled by the trust. The union at once denied the claim in a manifesto which thanked the people of London for their 'marvellous co-operation,' and announced a mass demonstration and parade for 1 May.

The demonstration lived up to the advance billing. Almost every trade unionist in the city turned out, and the parade was a mile long. Orators attacked the company in rousing speeches and enlisted public support to such an extent that, in spite of the union's declaration that the public was entitled to use the streetcars when and where it saw fit, fewer and fewer in fact did so.

The trust now tried new tactics. First, it approached individual strikers, urging them to come back, and promising better treatment. All refused; at least one spat in the face of the company agent. Second, a trust representative approached Joseph Marks, editor of the *Industrial Banner* and one of the most prominent union men in London. He had handled the money from the TLCC appeal. The agent asked if the removal of the local manager, who was particularly obnoxious to the men, and the reinstatement of strikers as positions became available would be enough to end the strike. Marks replied that the strikers would go back 'at the top of the list.' The agent then asked if Marks was getting any pay for his part in running the strike. Marks said no. The agent then offered to pay him to work for the company. Marks replied that the only pay he wanted was a fair agreement for Division 97, and that the Everett Trust did not have enough money to buy him.

Marks published all this in the *Industrial Banner* 29 June 1900, but there were widespread insinuations that he had in fact taken money from Everett and then 'laughed at him.' Marks accordingly asked the Trades and Labor Council to appoint an investigating committee to go into all the financial transactions related to the strike. He said it would find that, far from having taken money from Everett, he had in fact spent $500 out of his own pocket to aid the strikers.

The council was reluctant to appoint the committee. The delegates thought it 'hideous' that Marks' character should be called in question, and that the charges should even be dignified by a formal investigation. But one delegate thought otherwise: 'There are people who cannot imagine a man giving time and money to aid a cause and while they can insinuate behind his back, they cannot face him.' That did the trick. The committee was appointed and found exactly what Marks had said it would.

Meanwhile, in July, the company offered what it was pleased to call terms of settlement. It would take back on its extra list, at once, 10 men, on their personal application, with seniority according to their former positions. It would take on its list for employment any others who made application and give them first preference. The strikers would be hired as individuals, but without prejudice to any man who belonged to, or might wish to join, any association. The strike and boycott would then be called off, and resolutions to that effect printed in the daily papers and the *Industrial Banner*. Finally, the terms would not be made public: all that would be published would be a statement that the strike had been settled satisfactorily to all concerned. Naturally, the union flatly refused what amounted to unconditional surrender plus an official lie that it was pleased with the surrender.

In September 1900, when the TLCC met, the strike was still on, and the congress passed another resolution calling on all central labour bodies, local unions, and the TLCC provincial executive committees to make every possible effort to support the London union.

Eighteen months after it had begun the strike was called off. In spite of strong local support, in spite of the TLCC's national appeal, in spite of the widespread and substantial response to that appeal, the company had won total victory. It was so cock-o'-the-hoop about the whole thing that in the summer of 1902 it sent a number of its employees to Toronto to help break the streetcar strike there. This fraternal gesture was not successful, and the strikebreakers returned to London ingloriously, after getting something of a trimming from the Toronto workers. The London Trades and Labor Council was so furious that it served notice that if the company ever tried the same game again the council would take immediate and drastic action.[55]

The Street Railway union was in the forefront of the battle at the turn of the century. Its mere existence seems to have infuriated the companies, doubtless because they were wealthy local monopolies which had been accustomed to having things all their own way. When their men organized, they seem to have felt much as the early bird would have felt if the worm earmarked for its breakfast had turned and snapped at it. The wrath of the London company was repeated elsewhere, more than once.

While the London strike of 1899 was in progress, Division 121 of St Thomas found itself up against a company attempt to discharge all union members. The chairman of the union's international executive, with the Trades and Labor Council, called on the general manager 'to see if an adjustment could not be had but when he learned who they were he went into a fit of hysterics and ordered them from the office, and declaring that he would discharge every union man in the service.' The division then held a meeting and ordered a strike. The men were out only 'some forty-eight hours when an agreement was reached and the union men returned to work, but before going to work they were treated to a fine supper by the manager, the hatchet was buried and the members of Division 121 are now feeling prouder than a little boy with his first pair of red-top boots.'[56]

The Toronto division ran into trouble in August 1900. The men wanted an increase from 16⅔ cents an hour to 20. A committee of union and non-union employees secured a compromise: 15 cents for the first year's service, 16⅔ for the second, 17 for the next 3 years, and 18 from then on.[57]

In October 1900 the international president had reported that every street railway employee in Kingston was a member and that Division 150 had reduced their hours from 12 and 14 to 9 hours per day, with the same rate of pay. Not unnaturally, every one of them was 'an enthusiastic union man'; but the company was evidently less pleased. When, in the spring of 1901, the union asked for a 15 cent wage increase, to bring the motormen's rate to $1.40 a day, the conductors' to $1.15, and the night watchmen's to $8.50 for 7 nights (this for 4 months), the company refused. The union then withdrew the demands for motormen and night watchmen. The company still refused to consider even the increase for conductors, and the union struck on 8 June. On 15 June the company asked every employee to sign an agreement to desist from further demands for wage increases; to give 48 hours' notice of leaving; and, in default, to consider himself discharged. The men refused to sign individually, but offered to have the union officers sign for them collectively. The company refused, and discharged the lot.

The union appealed to the international, and the chairman of the executive board hastened to the scene. The company then offered to take back all employees, with a five cent increase for four months 'if receipts warranted.' The union refused, but offered to submit the matter to arbitration. An agreement was reached on 22 June. All the men were to be taken back; the company was to recognize the union and establish a grievance procedure; and it was verbally agreed that motormen would continue at their old rate, 'middlemen' would get $1.15 (a 15 cent increase), and conductors $1.10 (a 10 cent increase).[58]

Toronto had a short but bitter strike in June 1902. On 31 May the 900 men involved adopted a set of demands: union recognition; reinstatement of James McDonald, a union member; a 9-hour day (as nearly as the runs shall permit); 25 cents an hour for conductors and motormen and time-and-a-quarter on Sunday; pay for time lost by employees unjustly suspended; leave of absence for men on union business; and provision for cleaning the cars. (The existing rates were 18 cents an hour for regular conductors and motormen and 15 cents for 'extras.')

The company refused to meet the union, notably because it was an international body with headquarters in the United States: 'If this foreign intervention with Canadian concerns is to be tolerated, then, so far as I can see [said the president], there is nothing to prevent a few American labour leaders from tying up every Canadian street railway, steam railway, and factory whenever it suits them to do so.'

The union then asked the manager to meet a committee of the employees and, if this failed to produce a settlement, offered to submit the dispute to a tripartite board of arbitration. Meanwhile, the company had been bringing in, and training, men to take the places of its regular employees if they struck. The union demanded that these men be taken off and sent back whence they had come. A Toronto Board of Trade committee persuaded the company to take off the spares and to meet a committee selected by the employees. Further efforts by the board of trade narrowed the gap between the two sides. The company offered a wage increase: first year rate, 15 to 17 cents an hour; second year, 16⅔ to 18; third, fourth, and fifth years, 17 to 19; sixth to tenth years, 18 to 20; after the tenth year, 21; with Sunday rates sufficient to bring earnings up to the weekday level. It was also ready to agree to the desired provision for cleaning the cars, and to give aggrieved employees a right of appeal to the general manager. The union cut its wage demand to 18 to 20 cents for the first year and 20 cents thereafter, dropped McDonald, and virtually withdrew its demand for recognition, though it still insisted on a grievance committee. Beyond this, however, neither side would go, the company even refusing to accept arbitration. The president of the board of trade, at the eleventh hour, dangled before the union's nose an offer to pay $10,000 into its pension fund if there were no strike before the end of the year; but in vain.

Three days of industrial war followed. The company tried to find strikebreakers in the city and outside, and the men tried to find buses to run a competing service. On 22 June the company tried to bring cars out of two of its barns, but a crowd of union sympathizers had assembled and, in spite of the presence of 'a considerable detachment of police, volleys of stones were thrown at the first car ... smashing all of the windows and making it necessary for those in charge to abandon the car when only a short way out. Four other cars were sent out, and in every case the windows were smashed and those handling them driven away. One or two persons were also struck and more or less severely injured by flying missiles.' Similar scenes took place at the other barns, and the company gave up for the day. It also asked for more protection, and the civil authorities invoked the aid of the militia: 700 cavalry from Niagara and 700 from city regiments. That evening the car barns were seriously damaged by union sympathizers.

Next day, before the militia had been distributed about the city, the board of trade committee had managed to get from the company a fresh proposition, which the union accepted. It did not concede union recognition, but it did stipulate that the wage rates in the company's previous offer should stand till 1 July and that if, after that, the men voted, by ballot, for 18 cents the first year and 20 cents after that, the company would accept the decision. It also provided for a grievance procedure by appeal to the general manager, giving the aggrieved employee the right to bring with him fellow-employees or other witnesses who might have knowledge of the circumstances. It further explicitly recognized the rights of the employees to organize under any form of constitution. The men went back on 24 June and on 25 June unanimously voted for the 18- and 20-cent rates.[59]

When the Ottawa division was formed, its president was told to leave it or be dismissed. All the officers but one thereupon resigned. The other unions rallied nobly to the division's aid: the Allied Trades and Labor Association (Trades and Labor Council) supplied a president and a secretary from the Machinists, a vice-president from the Sheet Metal Workers, and a chairman of the executive. But the council and its members were not prepared to handle any of the division's funds; so the treasurer, Thomas Willcox, a conductor, stayed on: the one member of the executive the company could get at. Early in October he was dismissed for absenting himself from work without permission (he had apparently been off for one day, doing his job as treasurer). The company superintendent said he did not know Willcox was a union member. The union did not believe him and regarded the dismissal as the beginning of a fresh attempt to destroy the union. If it was, it failed.[60]

Hamilton Division 107 seems to have led a rather tranquil life. In September 1899 the international president was able to report that every street railway worker was a member, that there was an agreement, and that 'the best of feeling prevails between the company and the association.'

In the spring of 1900 the division reported that the company had changed hands and a new manager had been brought in. To show its good feeling for the retiring manager, the union presented him with an address and a portmanteau. 'The ex-manager replied in a touching manner, thanking us for our kindness.' The new manager the division found 'a very reserved and painstaking man' who ran a tight ship. But the division's discharged men 'have all been given work building a new machine shop, so they are not left out in the cold entirely. Conductors Laing and French are assisting in the blacksmith shop, the company being busy building eight new cars ... [On] April 1, 1900, the initiation fees are switched to two dollars.'

In June 1900 a new agreement provided for, among other things, a 15 cents an hour wage, a proper grievance procedure, and the employees' right to buy their own uniforms, subject to the company's approval of style and cloth.[61]

The 1903 international convention had interesting reports on some of the Canadian divisions. Winnipeg wages had got up to 15 cents an hour for the first 6 months, 17 for the next 6, 18 for the second year, 19 for the third, and 20 from then on. Vancouver, Victoria, and New Westminster had 20 cents for the first year, 22 for the second and third, 23 for the fourth, and 25 from then on. Hamilton had 15 cents for the first year, 16 for the second, 17 for the third, and 18 from then on. Toronto had 18 cents for the first year and 20 from then on. Windsor had a straight 16 cents.[62]

The metal and clothing trades unions

The Amalgamated Society of Engineers (ASE) grew only very slightly in this period. Its 1902 membership, 296, was only 31 higher than 21 years earlier. It seems on the whole to have led a fairly quiet life till towards the end, when it found itself confronted by the International Association of Machinists, notably in the Kingston Locomotive Works strike of 1902–5, which the ASE at first declined to join. It continued to pay sick benefits and superannuation benefits (introduced in 1879), and to make 'donations.' The sick benefits per member ranged from about 9s. 3d. in 1879 to about 13s. 8d. in 1887. Superannuation benefits per member ranged from 10s. 2½d. in 1881 to £1 6¾d. in 1902, rising pretty steadily over the period. Donations, of course, varied widely. In 1882, they were a modest 9s. 6½d. per member; from 1884 to 1888 inclusive, they ranged from £1 4s. 7¼d. to £1 17s. 11¾d.; in 1889 and 1890, they were about 10s. 8d.; from 1892 to 1895, they ranged from £1 9s. 7¾d. to £1 17s. 6¾d. After falling back to 18s. 4½d. in 1896, they rose to an all-time high of £4 9s. 4d. in 1897, dropped back to £2 1s. 8½d. in 1898, and from 1899 to 1902 ranged from 10s. 5d. to 19s. 2½d.[1]

The second oldest international union, the Iron Molders, had plenty of 'trouble,' in spite of the unpropitious economic climate. Professor Creighton says 'The brief trade revival which had accompanied the introduction of the National Policy and the commencement of the Canadian Pacific Railway faded away in the gloom of renewed failures and disappointments. The slump deepened ... For over twenty years, the depression continued virtually unrelieved.'[2] The records of the Molders provide ample support for what he says. In 1881, 62 per cent of the reports from locals reported trade 'good,' and 32 per cent 'fair.' By 1883, the percentage of good had dropped to less than 9, the fair had risen to just under 48, and poor had risen from 6 to 34. From 1884 to 1895 inclusive, out of some 1850 reports of locals, only about 8 per cent reported conditions good, and about 33 per cent fair. About 38 per cent reported poor, and nearly 21 per cent bad.[3]

In these circumstances, it is astonishing that the union was able to put up any fight at all, especially as conditions in the United States also were generally poor. But in fact, until 1894, strikes and lockouts were numerous, and sometimes very extensive and prolonged.

There were four small stoppages in 1881 (and one wage increase without a strike). In 1882 Oshawa got a wage increase without a strike. But Montreal and Brantford had strikes, and Hamilton a two-month-long lockout. London had a major strike, at McClary's, for a wage of $2.25 a day, a 25 per cent increase in piece-work rates, and a proper number of apprentices. The employer jibbed at the two latter demands, imported strikebreakers, and called in the police. The chief of police told him to have his watchmen and some other employees sworn in as special constables. The strike seems to have been lost within six weeks, but was not officially called off till about a year later. It cost the international some $590.[4]

From January to July 1884 Brockville was locked out. The April report gives a vivid picture of the situation: 'As war has been declared in this town ... we are not fighting on anything like even terms. While our men are all walking around with a detective force at their heels, the scabs are boarding and sleeping behind a heavy stone wall.' A Mr Marshall, a new superintendent, had arrived the summer before, and had commenced 'getting ready for his life-long trade of running a first class scab shop ... He has secured the services of eleven or twelve of these *famous* Massachusetts scabs, who, according to all accounts, are more fit to use a shovel or pick on a railroad or in a State prison than they are to work in a foundry.' In spite of this, and bad trade conditions, new members kept coming into the Brockville local as late as June, but the fight seems to have been lost. In November 1884 the Quebec stove molders had to accept a reduction of 12½ per cent.[5]

In August and September 1885 Oshawa had a strike which may have lasted till March 1886. In 1886 Montreal had two strikes, the second in the Grand Trunk shops; an 1887 Quebec strike was probably lost, as the Quebec local disappeared in April 1888. In 1888 Montreal struck against a five-cent-an-hour-wage reduction at Clendennings (where the rates ran from $2 to $2.50 a day). The international sent $300 for this strike, $200 to Brantford and $100 to London. Guelph won an increase without striking.[6]

1889 saw no less than seven strikes: Montreal, Victoria, and five others, each of some particular interest. On 17 February the Ayr local (organized 19 January) struck because the whole membership had been discharged for being members and for asking for an increase from their existing rate of $1.50 a day. The employer had refused to meet a union committee; instead, he paid the men their wages and locked them out. The strike got international sanction and aid, but in vain. The men all got work elsewhere, but the local died.[7]

Sackville, organized 12 March, struck the Sackville Foundry on 11 April. The firm was trying to cut wages to the rates paid apprentices in other foundries 'in Nova Scotia' [sic]. The strike lasted a little over two months, and the union won. Meanwhile, on 10 May it had struck the Enterprise Foundry against a 10 per cent wage cut. Again it won, this time after only three weeks. The two strikes cost the international $471.38.[8]

On 27 April the local in Galt, where trade was good, struck to bring wages up from the existing $1.75 a day to the $2.25 being paid in surrounding towns. One employer settled in September; the other three held out till March 1890, when dull trade forced the men back on the employers' terms. The strike cost the international $4562.68.[9]

On 12 October the Ontario Malleable Iron Co locked out six members of the Oshawa local. The union had had an agreement, running to 31 July, terminable on 30 days' notice. On 26 July the company suddenly gave notice of an immediate 10 per cent reduction in piece-work rates. Trade being very dull, the union was willing to accept a 7½ per cent cut, though it declined to make a new agreement with an employer who had flagrantly broken the old one. The firm then put in new men at a reduction of 17½ per cent. The union set a fair price, which the employer rejected, and the union members were discharged. The union won, apparently in short order, for the stoppage cost the international only $88.[10]

In 1890 there were four stoppages, three very prolonged. On 24 February Gurney's in Toronto demanded that the 35 men in its radiator department work 'bucks.' The local refused and sought and got international sanction. The men were locked out till 28 May 1891. On 11 October H.A. Massey and Son's demanded that the moulders in its agricultural shop work bucks, and at a 12 per cent wage cut. The men refused, and were locked out till 10 July 1891. In January 1891 the international president went to Toronto to try to get a settlement. He met both Gurney and Massey. Gurney simply refused to budge. Massey, in a long interview, demanded the introduction of the 'Berkshire system' (which the union opposed) and a 12½ per cent wage cut. Both employers refused the union's proposals for settlement. They might have done well to act otherwise, for, according to the Ontario Bureau of Industries, the union finally won in both cases.[11]

It was less fortunate in Hamilton where, in November 1890, the men in the Sawyer, Massey plant had refused to work on patterns from the struck Massey plant in Toronto and had gone out. They stayed out till July 1891 and lost.[12]

In November 1890 the Sackville, New Brunswick, local was having trouble in Fawcett's; it probably lost, for in December it reported 'shops closing down.' Sackville seems to have contributed the only internationally sanctioned stoppage in 1891, at Fawcett's. The Smith's Falls, Ontario, local had an unsanctioned grievance against a speed-up in Frost Malleable Iron.[13]

There were seven stoppages in 1892. The first, 1 January to 15 August, was in Kingston. Some firms wanted to put their men on an eight-hour day, at $1.84 per day and under 'very obnoxious rules.' The international president visited Kingston in March and got a favourable settlement in some shops. In others the stoppage continued, and the union lost: the men came back at $2 (which was some gain), but without a union agreement. The second dispute was a lockout in Sackville, at the Enterprise Foundry, which was trying to cut wages by 15 per cent.[14]

Much the biggest stoppage was a lockout in Hamilton, from January 1892 to March 1893. It involved 166 men in six shops and cost the international $26,038.28. There were also generous donations from locals in Brantford, Toronto, London, and Quincy (Illinois), and from Hamilton well-wishers. But, except in one shop, the union lost. The local's reports say that it all began with the employers demanding a 10 per cent wage cut. The union was willing to accept this for the moment, but balked at signing an agreement for the whole year. It believed the employers were trying to break up the organization. By the time it was all over, one foundry had accepted union rates and was employing union men; most of the other strikers seem to have left the city, though some 40 were employed in shops which had not been involved in the stoppage.[15]

The fourth stoppage was a lockout by Chown and Cunningham, Kingston, from March to July. The local's own trade report in February had read, 'The bottom has fallen out'; and the firm evidently decided this was a good moment to try conclusions with the union. The firm accordingly proposed to suspend it, to make its men liable to lay-off on two weeks' notice, and also to make them pay for all breakages and losses. The local of course refused, and the men were locked out.[16]

In March and April there was trouble in Saint John, where trade was dull. In April and May six men were discharged from a shop in Moncton, at a cost of $550 to the international. In June there was trouble in a stove shop in Montreal.[17]

In 1893 the Moncton local was locked out from March to July.[18]

On 5 May 1899 Local 21 struck 13 shops in Montreal, including the Grand Trunk and the Canadian Pacific. No less than 596 men went out, paralysing the whole iron and steel industry in the city and putting about 2000 men out of work. The union was demanding recognition by the employers' association (which included all the shops) and the replacement of piece-work rates (which varied from shop to shop) by straight time. The employers said the wage question was of no consequence: the real issue was recognition, which they flatly refused. They declared that the union had 'made slaves of the employers in Toronto'; they themselves were not going to be forced to give 'inferior workmen the same wage as was paid to the best ones.' Thanks to its ample strike fund, the international was able to pay strike benefit almost equal to regular wages. The strike was directed by the international's second vice-president. Gradually, the smaller shops gave in, and, after holding out for a month, the Grand Trunk and the Canadian Pacific followed suit.[19]

On 20 February 1900, the Brantford Local struck Massey-Harris, chiefly because the company had introduced labour-saving machinery and refused to let the moulders operate the machines. The union offered settlement by conciliation or arbitration; the company refused; and pickets were set up around the plant. By the end of June, all the men had secured employment (though the strike was still officially on at the beginning of 1901); but the picketing went on, and led to a series of rows, in and out of court.

The company had lost no time in applying for an injunction against the picketing, and the union had by 14 April filed 63 affidavits against it. An injunction was granted, but the picketing continued. Early in July, as a result of trouble on the picket lines, the union asked the city council to take action against the strike-breakers, on the ground that they were carrying revolvers. The council replied that the matter was beyond its jurisdiction. On 12 July the company took proceedings to have three moulders committed for contempt of court for disregarding the injunction, even by peacefully persuading men not to work. Chief Justice Meredith ruled that the picketers had a perfect right to expostulate with strikebreakers, though not, of course, to intimidate them; in spite of this, before the strike fizzled out, 15 moulders had been fined a total of $150 for intimidation.[20]

Meanwhile, in March, 125 Toronto moulders had struck against the same company, 'being dissatisfied on account of the introduction of labour-saving machines and other conditions of their employment.' This strike seems to have been as ineffective as the one in Brantford; by January 1901 the *Labour Gazette* was reporting that nearly all the strikers had found employment elsewhere. Here also the company invoked the power of the courts by way of injunction, but it took so long to proceed with its action for a permanent injunction that the master at Osgoode Hall finally lost patience and threatened to dismiss the case. The company then settled by paying costs.[21]

In 1901 the Molders seem to have had three strikes: Brantford, Saint John, and Winnipeg: all lost. In December 1901 the Guelph Molders got, without striking, a minimum wage of $2.25 a day, an increase of 25 cents.[22]

On 29 April 1902 Toronto employers granted Local 28's demands for 27½ cents an hour (a 2½-cent increase), time-and-a-quarter from 6 pm to midnight, time-and-a-half after midnight, and double time on Sundays. Hamilton, in the same month, was less successful: day-workers in several foundries got an increase of 25 cents a day (bringing them to $2.25), but, in response to the employers' pleas that they could not stand the competition, the union dropped its demand for a 15 per cent increase in piece-work rates. On 1 May the London moulders in McClary's got an increase of 5 cents an hour. In May also, the CPR moulders in Winnipeg got an increase of 1 cent an hour, bringing their rate to 26 cents; but they pressed for more, and on 1 June got a further 1½ cents. But 1902 was not all plain sailing; there were strikes in Moncton, Sackville, Hamilton, Smith's Falls, Montreal, Toronto, Guelph, St Catharines, and Quebec, with varying degrees of success.[23]

The *Iron Molders Journal* gives us occasional glimpses of other sides of the life of the Canadian locals. In June 1881, for example, it notes that all trade unions in Montreal took part in the St-Jean-Baptiste procession, the Molders marching 200 strong with two wagons, from which they 'melted iron and cast throughout the line of March.' William Clendenning, employer of 75 to 100 men, and the union's antagonist of 1879, marched side by side with the union's grand marshal, the now thoroughly rehabilitated J.C. McEvoy, late 'thieving ex-treasurer of No. 23.' In August, there is an account of an Oshawa demonstration. Molders' locals 28, 189, 140, and 136 took part; so did about 1500 members of the Knights of Labor. Six days earlier Toronto had mustered 3000 demonstrators, from 23 unions (including a delegation from Oshawa Molders' Local 136). Oshawa was described as the best organized town in Canada.[24]

In January and February 1884 the *Journal* records attempts, in Toronto and elsewhere, to set up a purely Canadian moulders' union; but these seem to have fizzled out, like so many others, in various unions, since.[25]

In the United States, by this time, friction between the unions and the Knights of Labor was becoming evident, but it seems not yet to have spread to Canada. The July 1886 *Journal* reprinted from the London *Advertiser* an account of a labour demonstration in that city on the occasion of the Molders' international convention. Over 4000 workers paraded, the largest number ever seen at any such event in Canada. The affair was under the joint auspices of Local 37 of the Molders and the Knights of Labor and the various trade unions of the city. The 'Ladies of the Knights of Labor' rode in carriages; men from the Typos, Cigar Makers, Bricklayers, Bricklayers' Labourers No 2, and, of course, Local 37, marched with others from LAS 3305, 3558, 5099, 5172, and 7110. The ladies were presumably from LA 3502, a mixed assembly of women. The *Journal* adds that 'the law closing the saloons at 7 o'clock did not seem to trouble the delegates very much.'[26]

In the September *Journal* the Oshawa local reported on a Toronto demonstration of 11 September at the Toronto Exhibition. The Oshawa Trades and Labor Council had arranged an excursion to the exhibition, which delegates from Local 136 and LAS 2355, 4279 (iron moulders), and 4428 (Cedar Dale, agricultural-implement workers) joined. They were met by representatives of Local 28, the Toronto Trades and Labor Council, DA 125, and the Queen's Own Rifles Band. The demonstration was even bigger than the one in London: over 8000 marched, with all the city bands and Highland pipers as well.[27]

In 1886 the Molders set up a system of district unions, and the January 1887 *Journal* gives a list of the Ontario district officers. A year later there was a second district convention. It had been hoped that the district system would save time, lighten the work of the international office, and make the union generally more efficient. It did not, and my March 1888 it had been ended, by vote of the locals.[28]

From late in 1886 till early in 1891, and again from January to March 1892, the *Journal* carried long leading articles in which 'Member of 136' (Oshawa) surveyed mankind from China to Peru. One series dealt with Irish Home Rule and land monopoly that provoked a tart protest from Peterborough, exhorting the author to 'stick to trade topics.' Another was called 'Sketches of Our Organization.' One article was on trade unionism in contemporary Rome; three were on the arts and sciences of the ancients.

Canadian members took a prominent part in the work of the international during this period. At the 1882 convention there were twelve Canadian delegates from seven Ontario and one Quebec City local. John Dance was again elected second vice-president. He was chairman of the executive board from 1883 to 1886. At the 1886 convention there were fourteen Canadian delegates from nine locals (seven in Ontario and one each in Winnipeg and Victoria), and R.H. Metcalf, of Toronto, was elected trustee and member of the executive board. In 1888 there were fourteen Canadian delegates from ten locals (nine in Ontario and one in Montreal). Metcalf was re-elected a trustee. There was a motion to organize Halifax and Nova Scotia to protect Boston and lower New England, which was referred to the committee on the constitution. (That committee, incidentally, recommended printing the constitution in French and German.) The committee recommended appointing an organizer for the provinces of Lower Canada (presumably its term for Halifax and Nova Scotia), but the convention turned this down. At this convention Canadians were appointed to the committees on petitions and claims, the *Journal*, ways and means, mileage and per diem, the constitution, and the Federation of Labor.

In 1890 there were thirteen Canadian delegates from eleven locals (ten Ontario and one in Sackville). Canadians were appointed to the committee to investigate certain charges, and to the committees on claims, mileage and per diem, and the constitution. A Hamilton resolution to organize the coremakers was adopted. Metcalf was nominated for international president but declined. He and Walters and David Black, of Toronto, were nominated for vice-president, but all were defeated. Metcalf was again elected a trustee.

The May 1893 *Journal* recorded the death of John Dance, with a brief account of his career. He had held many union offices but had always refused to be nominated for the international presidency.

In 1895 there were only six Canadian delegates from six locals (five in Ontario and one in Vancouver). Canadians were appointed to the committees on beneficial features and on the shorter work-day (which successfully recommended a 10-hour day and a special fund to get it adopted). Metcalf was elected 'Financier'; two other Canadians were nominated for trustee but defeated.

The minutes of Local 191 (Peterborough), which survive for the period between 18 August 1882 and 15 January 1892, contain a number of interesting, and sometimes entertaining, entries.[30] In the spring of 1886, there are several dealing with a 'document' or 'Iron Clad,' evidently a yellow-dog contract, in the Sylvester and Brother Iron Foundries. Apparently, the Peterborough local had, or claimed, jurisdiction over Lindsay, where the Sylvester firm was discriminating against members of the Knights of Labor LA 5402. The Knights apparently struck the plant in March. Local 191 had at least one member in the plant (a Mr Britton), and perhaps two others. The Knights seem to have wanted Local 191 to call out its member or members, but the international wanted more information before it would sanction the grievance. This the Knights evidently supplied, and in May two men were paid lockout benefits for three weeks, and another was ordered sent to Cincinnati. Britton, however, was to stay in the shop till Local 191 called him out, which it must have done promptly, since he also, in June, drew three weeks' lockout benefit.

In August, Sylvester's fired John O'Brien, an apprentice who had almost served his term, for being a Knight and refusing to sign the 'Iron Clad.' Local 191 promptly admitted him to membership, but the international office warned it not to interfere with the Sylvester shop until it had more information. Once again, the Knights provided this, and Local 191 thereupon sent O'Brien's and LA 5402's letters to Local 136 in Oshawa, urging the members there to 'do what they can to stop his Marriables [Malleables] as you see by this letter what he his.' (This is one of several instances where the presence of an extra 'h' suggests a Cockney secretary.)

On 1 January 1887 the local set a minimum wage of $1.75 a day for its jurisdiction. On 11 March it entertained a motion, 'that we get spittoons for our room,' and an amendment 'that we change our room instead.' The amendment carried. On 9 December it dealt with the weighty matter of 'A Commocation from ... Toronto in regard to a Dead Beet.'

On 17 August 1888, the local appointed a committee to co-operate with the other labour unions in Peterborough for a demonstration. This took place on 3 September, starting from the Knights of Labor Hall (the Knights had by this time two Peterborough local assemblies). The Locals of four international unions paraded (Carpenters 375, Bricklayers 12, Molders 191, and Typos 248), besides six other organizations, either purely local or part of the Knights (Masons, Shoemakers, Tailors, Machinists, Hod Carriers, and Painters).

In February 1889 the local was asking for 20 cents an hour in 1 plant, and undertaking to 'Explane the 9 Hour movement' to Mr Brooks at the Lock Works. In March it was sending $1 per member to help the strike of Local 200 in Ayr; and it was being told by the international president to take no action on demanding a 9-hour day till notified by the international.

In April 1891 Local 191 reported its ball of 30 March an unqualified success. In May it was trying to establish a rule of one apprentice to each shop, and one to every eight journeymen, and was asking for a Saturday half-holiday. In June, by 'unamass voat,' it supported a proposal for a joint committee of the international union and the employers' organization to settle strikes. In September it set rates for apprentices, to finish out their time at $3.75 a week for three months and $1 a day for the year that followed. In January 1892 it decided to have another ball at the Opera House.

The International Association of Machinists entered Canada in July 1890 when it chartered Stratford Lodge 103. Another 45 Lodges followed, but, here again, many fell by the wayside. Eight were reorganized (one of them twice), and one of these had disappeared again before the end of 1902. Another 15 had also disappeared, some of them having lasted only a few months. By the end of 1902 therefore, the IAM had 30 Canadian lodges: 20 in Ontario, 3 each in Quebec and British Columbia, and 1 each in Nova Scotia, New Brunswick, Manitoba, and what is now Alberta. The bulk of them were in railway centres.

The Machinists had a Canadian vice-president from 1895 on: A.W. Holmes. He had been prominent in the Knights of Labor, and had served as a delegate to the TLCC conventions of 1888, 1889, and 1891 from DA 125 and in 1890 from LA 9005 (machinists), Toronto. As late as 15 January 1892 he was a delegate from the latter assembly to the Toronto council; by 19 August he was representing IAM Lodge 235. He served in the same capacity at the TLCC conventions of 1892, 1894, and 1895. Till 1903, he seems to have had sole responsibility for organizing IAM lodges in Canada, and must therefore have the credit for forming 26 new lodges and reorganizing 8 old ones, from Halifax to Victoria. During the same period, 14 lodges disappeared. But even so, Holmes could chalk up a net gain of 20.[31]

In the fall of 1899 the Machinists struck the western and Pacific divisions of the CPR. They had a long list of demands: elaborate apprenticeship provisions; grievance procedure (which did not specifically mention the union); seniority rules; a 55-hour week (5 10-hour days, and 1 5-hour); time-and-a-half overtime till midnight, double time from then till 7 am; double time for Sundays and legal holidays; pay for meal hours; 12 hours' pay for 10 hours' work by regular night machinists; minimum rates of 25 cents an hour from Fort William to Brandon inclusive, 27½ cents to Laggan, 30 cents west of Laggan, on branch lines as well as the main line; straight time, and a dollar a day for expenses while travelling; and miscellaneous provisions designed to ensure the recognition and effective functioning of the union.

The Vancouver Boilermakers and Blacksmiths struck in sympathy; the ASE promised its moral and financial support; so did the Trades and Labor Council. On 16 October the CPR met a subcommittee of the union's general committee and asked for an interview with the full committee, and the prospects of a reasonable settlement looked so good that the union declared the strike off, ordering all machinists, fitters, boilermakers, and blacksmiths from Fort William to the coast to return to work at once. By 24 October the parties had reached agreement. The agreement, which contained a complex set of wages and hours, also provided for seniority and a grievance procedure, and was to run from 1 November 1899.

Early in August 1900, however, the men went out again, alleging violations of the grievance procedure. In May 1900 the union had drawn up a new schedule, and wanted to discuss it with the responsible official in Winnipeg. He was in China, so the matter awaited his return on 26 July. Meanwhile, on 16 July the CPR had dismissed the president of the Vancouver lodge and vice-president of the general committee, Will MacClain, a rip-roaring socialist who had been making himself obnoxious to the employing class by taking an active part in the big fishermen's strike. The lodge threatened to strike forthwith unless he was reinstated the same day; but this did not come off. Instead, it sent MacClain as its delegate to Winnipeg to discuss the new schedule, and the company cancelled his pass before he had got any farther than Mission. The union then struck the whole line from Fort William west. The CPR said the strike was 'really an extension ... of the boilermakers' strike at Montreal' and a sympathetic strike at Winnipeg, though it acknowledged that 'local grievances may play their part in the future.'

On 3 August a joint meeting of the IAM and ASE Vancouver locals arranged to picket all incoming trains and boats, and set up a press committee. IAM headquarters in Washington provided strike pay of $6 a week. The Blacksmiths were ordered out by their international; on 15 August the Vancouver Boilermakers struck in sympathy; three days later the local Railway Carmen went out. By 30 August the schedules of the Allied Mechanics and of the Boilermakers had been agreed on. The Machinists' wage rates were to go to arbitration, with the IAM president representing his union. The strike was declared over on 1 September.[32]

The next strike was a small affair, in Dundas, where 65 men struck one firm, John Bertram & Sons, for a minimum rate of sixteen cents an hour and a ban on new apprentices till the number was reduced to one for the shop and one for every five machinists. After the strike started on 5 October the lodge also demanded a 10 per cent wage increase. The strike lasted till 25 January 1901, when it was settled by negotiation and the friendly intervention of the Dominion department of labour. The firm rehired the men who had not secured employment elsewhere, and the department said the understanding reached was satisfactory to both parties.[33]

The Victoria machinists staged a partial strike before they even got their charter. The Machinists, Boilermakers, and Molders of Seattle were on strike. A vessel they had been repairing was towed to Victoria on 18 May 1901 to get the job finished. The Victoria Boilermakers and Molders refused to work on the job; the machinists, most of them already members or former members of the IAM, took the same line and proceeded to organize a local union on 19 May which, eight days later, got its charter. The employer offered the three crafts everything the Seattle men were asking for. They replied they were willing to work if the internationals would lift the boycott on the vessel. This the Boilermakers, at any rate, refused to do, and the ship was towed back to Seattle.[34]

Almost at the same moment the Ottawa Machinists, 34 strong, struck 6 shops for a 9-hour day with 10 hours' pay. Most of the employers granted it (some had been paying the higher rate already). Many of the men got jobs elsewhere; the rest went back on 11 September with a 5 per cent increase but no shortening of hours.[35]

The Kingston Machinists began a strike on 30 April 1902 at the locomotive works which lasted till November 1905. They wanted shorter hours, higher wages, and a stop to the extensive use of handymen and apprentices on skilled machinists' jobs. One incident of the strike was the arrest of 3 members of the picketing committee, who were fined $50 each by the magistrate, with the extraordinary proviso that if the strike were called off in 10 days the judgment would not be enforced. The strike was envenomed by inter-union rows with the ASE and the Ironworkers and Helpers Union, AFL FLU No 8412, both of which had members in the plant and declined to take them out. The AFL withdrew the Ironworkers' charter; the IAM, in 1903, joined with the Pattern Makers and the Blacksmiths to have the ASE expelled from the AFL.[36]

In September 1902 the Vancouver Locals of the IAM and ASE signed a joint agreement with the local engineering firms. It provided for a 10-hour day and a 55-hour week; time-and-a-half for all time from 6 pm to 10 pm; double time from 10 pm to 7 am; double time for Sundays 'and all such holidays as New Year, Good Friday, Empire Day, Dominion Day, Labour Day, King's Birthday, Thanksgiving Day and Christmas Day.' There was to be a four-year apprenticeship, with at least one apprentice to each shop and one to every five machinists thereafter; men with dependants were to have preference in any reductions in staff; and there were various provisions for outside work.[37] Evidently the inter-union dispute at Kingston had not prevented co-operation between the IAM and the ASE on the west coast.

The International Brotherhood of Brassworkers (organized 1890, renamed, 1892, United Brotherhood of Brass Workers) had a Toronto local, No 23, from 1891 to 1894, and a London local, No 39, in 1893. In 1895 this union merged with the KOL's National Trade District 252 to form the United Brotherhood of Brass, Composition and Metal Workers, Polishers and Buffers. This, in turn, in 1896, merged with the Metal Polishers, Buffers and Platers Union of North America to form the Metal Polishers, Buffers, Platers and Brass Workers International Union of North America. Toronto Local 21 of this union dated itself from 1893; Brassworkers London Local 39 became Local 39 of the new union, which organized a second London local, No 32, in 1895, and Brantford Local 47 in 1896. By the end of 1902 there seem to have been three Toronto locals, two each in London and Montreal, and one each in Hamilton, Brantford, and St Catharines.

The Brantford local struck the Buck Stove Co in June 1899, and in August it was appealing to unions across the country for help. It asked union members to refrain from buying five specified products. The strike seems to have petered out.[38]

The Boilermakers, in 1881, had formed the National Boilermakers and Helpers Protective and Benevolent Union (renamed, 1883, the International Brotherhood of Boilermakers and Iron Shipbuilders Protective and Benevolent Union of the United States and Canada). In 1888 this merged with the National Brotherhood of Boilermakers, organized in 1883, to form the International Brotherhood of Boilermakers and Iron Ship Builders of North America.[39] The 1883 union had three Canadian lodges: Hamilton 21 and Toronto 22, both organized in 1884, and Winnipeg 58, organized 1892. Toronto Lodge 22 seems to have lasted till at least January 1894; there was a Montreal lodge from 1894 to 1897; and Toronto Lodge 128 figures in the Toronto Trades and Labor Council from 1895 to 1901.[40] Ten more lodges followed. By the end of 1902 there were five in Ontario, two in British Columbia, and one each in Quebec, Nova Scotia, and Manitoba.

During the Boilermakers' strikes in the west in 1900, Toronto also struck for three weeks, and got an increase. Montreal struck for 11 weeks, and lost.

The Victoria Boilermakers struck on 19 November 1901, asking for the American conditions (an 8-hour day and a $3.50 minimum wage) on vessels coming to Victoria from outside. The employer insisted on their working nine hours and got the work done by non-union labour. The union struck again early in 1902, refusing to work nine hours outside; most got work elsewhere. This union had of course been involved in the machinists' strike in May and June 1901, and had got a reduction in hours from ten and nine to nine and eight.

The Toronto Boilermakers went out again on 7 June 1902 in three firms, in sympathy with the Helpers, who had struck five days earlier for a wage increase. The Helpers went back on 14 June (under an agreement to submit the dispute to arbitration), and the Boilermakers the same day.[41]

The International Union of Bicycle Workers, Toronto Local 25, had been admitted to the Trades and Labor Council by 8 December 1898. It was still there on 9 November 1899. By that time the union had changed its name to Bicycle Workers and Allied Mechanics, and on 9 November 1900 this became the International Association of Allied Metal Mechanics.

Lodge 35 of this body was organized in Winnipeg on 6 December 1899 and still flourishing at the end of 1902. A Vancouver lodge was strong enough to get an agreement with the CPR in 1900 and another in August 1902 covering the railway's Pacific division. This last provided elaborate ranges of rates, from 15 to 23 cents an hour; a day shift of 10 hours for 5 days a week (9 hours on the sixth, from 1 October

259 The metal and clothing unions

to 1 April, changing to 5 hours from 1 April to 1 October); and a night shift of 11 hours for 5 days and 10 hours the sixth, the year round.

Another lodge seems to have been organized in Moose Jaw towards the end of 1900, and a St Catharines lodge in the spring of 1901; Brantford had a local of bicycle workers in 1902.

The Toronto Junction lodge must have started out with high hopes, for it contributed a third vice-president to the international union. But by the beginning of February 1901, to the great embarrassment of the international president, it had voted to disband. He called in the aid of the AFL. Its organizer, John Flett, was able to reorganize the lodge, which not only pleased the international union but brought Flett a letter of thanks from Samuel Gompers, the AFL president.[42]

The Stove Mounters and Steel Range Workers International Union came into Canada on 18 March 1899 with London Local 33. Four others followed. Locals of 'Stove Fitters,' perhaps the same union, were organized in Moncton, Sackville, and Amherst in October 1900, by John P. Frey of the Molders; but this is the last we hear of them.

The Stove Mounters held their 1901 international convention in Hamilton. They seem to have had only one strike during the period, in Toronto on 21 January 1902. An employer refused to recognize two men as members of the union. The company called them apprentices, the union journeymen. When they were dismissed, the union said it was for union membership. A union committee and an international officer tried in vain to settle the dispute (which seems to have involved 22 men). By the end of January the company claimed it had filled all the strikers' places; but the union was still reporting the strike at the end of April.[43]

The Coremakers came next, with Montreal Local 31 in March 1899. Four more followed.[44]

The Blacksmiths chartered their Brantford Local 115 in May 1899. Seven more followed. By the end of 1902 there were certainly four locals in Ontario, two in British Columbia, and one in Manitoba. Brantford may have disbanded by this time.[45]

THE CLOTHING TRADES UNIONS

The United Hatters of North America apparently had a Hamilton local by 20 March 1889. On 31 January 1896 delegates from the Hatters' union were admitted to the Trades and Labor Council, and a union of that name figures in the *Labour Gazette* list of December 1901. So does a Montreal union.

On 10 August 1902 eight members of the Hamilton union struck one firm which was employing a non-unionist; three days later the man had left town. On 8 November the same trouble recurred; this time, the firm dropped the union label and proclaimed its intention of running an open shop. At the end of the year the dispute was still officially unsettled.[46]

The Journeymen Tailors Union of America chartered its first Canadian local, Windsor 114, in December 1889. More than 40 others followed, but mortality was very high, though the Tailors usually ran to reorganizing old locals rather than organizing new ones in the old places.

Of Windsor 114 the *Tailor* reports that it started with 25 members, 'but they are made of the stuff that goes to make good union men. About a year ago [April 1889] the boss tailors signed an agreement with the union to abolish the "sweat" system, by which is meant the letting out of work to be done on contract by women who employ young girls at very low wages. Last week it was discovered that a firm were violating the agreement. The union investigated the matter and fined the firm $15. They refused to pay and on Monday the men walked out of the shop.' The union members were assessed enough to pay the strikers $4 a day; the firm weakened, and the men were back in 2 days, having won.

From July to October 1891 Windsor went through 'one of the most bitter strikes ever on this continent.' A number of members were arrested on charges of conspiracy, but the local remained solid. Three of those charged, including the local's president, were convicted and sentenced to one month in jail, a proceeding which moved the *Tailor* to comment: 'It seems as though enough of such lessons had been given the working people, to make them understand that they must take control of the law-making power themselves.' Seven other members, charged with conspiracy and assault against a non-union tailor, were acquitted. The strike cost the union $1410.[47]

Brantford started off by negotiating, under threat of a strike, a compromise settlement in May 1890, and was 'congratulated by the president of the master tailors for the very gentlemanly way we gained our point; and wishing our union grand success.' In January 1891 it reported: 'Everything is all straight now, thanks to the special organizer, Mr James Simms,' of Toronto. In August 1893, however, one employer locked out his men, and the dispute, which lasted into September, cost the union $165. In July 1895 Brantford had another strike which cost $30.[48]

Toronto Local 132 had three small strikes in the period 1892–94. Late in November 1895 the merchant tailors asked the local to agree not to interfere with non-union hands. The union of course objected and proposed arbitration, which the employers rejected. On 28 December 9 firms locked out their employees, about 140 strong. The international office issued a circular to all locals, dated 24 January 1896, appealing for help. On 3 February it issued a second circular, saying there had been no desertions and the prospects were excellent if the union could get enough money, whether by gifts or loans. When the local formally appealed for support, the international voted $1000 (the first instalment of what ultimately came to at least $2747, and perhaps as much as $5000). The Amalgamated Society of Journeymen Tailors of London, England, sent a message of sympathy and assurances of help, financial if need be. In spite of everything, the result was a disaster; by May 1897 the union was acknowledging defeat and drawing what little comfort it could from the fact that some of the employers had agreed not to discharge workers for belonging to the union.

By the fall of 1899 the local had recovered, and when it struck on 27 September some 250 workers came out, 100 new members joined, and in 2 days most of the employers had given in. Those who held out employed only about 60 men, but they were stubborn: the union was still paying strike benefit as late as October 1900 (though in that month the amount was only $12), and the total paid was $1361. The strike was still officially on in November.[49]

St Thomas 141 distinguished itself in several ways. In January 1891 it declared in favour of admitting 'tailoresses' to the union, a step which must have been taken promptly, since the very next month shows four Canadian locals reporting women members. From April to June 1891 St Thomas had a strike, evidently minor, since total strike benefit was only $90. In December 1892, when it was described as one of the banner branches, it had a short strike which it won. In December 1895 it entertained J.B. Lennon, the international secretary-treasurer, at a dinner with 40 present, and 5 toasts: the queen, the dominion, the JTUA, guests and sister societies, and 'Our Local Union.'

In February 1898, however, the local seceded from the international to become Local 1 of the Journeymen Tailors Union of Canada. In a letter sent to every local in Canada, it complained that it did not get enough financial help from the international: too much money went down to the United States, too little came back. Besides, with the passing of the American Alien Labor Law, what use was an international union?

Hugh Robinson of Hamilton, a JTUA organizer, replied that there were only 300 JTUA members in the whole of Canada (an average of 20 per local); that it would take 10 years for a national union to accumulate enough money to pay the funeral and strike benefits that had been paid to Toronto and St Catharines alone since they had joined the international; that the Alien Labor Law was no obstacle to the movement of tailors across the border; and that it might be well for the AFL to pay to the TLC the per capita the AFL received from Canadian members of AFL unions (an interesting anticipation of later events).

The secession did not last long. In May 1899 Thomas Sweeney of Toronto, another JTUA organizer, visited St Thomas and persuaded the sinners to return. It was agreed, incidentally, that 'Canada is a very fair place for tailors, very little sweating and a great number of free shops.'[50]

The Victoria local of the JTUA in July 1891 was in good order and its rates were recognized by every firm of any importance. It had by this time over 50 members, 35 of them men. In March and May 1892 it paid strike benefits of $12 and $24 respectively.

In August 1893 the scene changed. The master tailors took advantage of a continent-wide commercial panic and widespread unemployment to announce a wage reduction of 20 per cent. The union offered to accept 10 per cent, but the masters refused. The International office, though doubtful of the success of any strike, nevertheless sanctioned one, though warning the local that strike benefit must stop the first week in September. It paid $348.[51]

The Ottawa JTUA local had a strike in May and June 1891 which cost the international $185. From November 1892 to March 1893 it struck against the employment of non-unionists. In April 1893 it persuaded the international office to appoint an Ottawa member, George Power, to organize the Montreal tailors, which he succeeded in doing.[52]

The Owen Sound Local appointed two committees, one of men, the other of women, in January 1891 to draw up a bill of prices. The men's bill was ready by 17 March; the women were to put theirs in shape next day, with the same rates for coats. The work was done by May, but the local seems to have collapsed soon after.

The local's report in April had commented on the failure of a tailors' co-operative. Like the strikes which had perhaps given it birth, it was 'generally a loss to the men only, or more of a loss to them than to anyone else, and generally ends in quarrels and breakups, one of the number getting all or most and starting on his own account.' Women tailors must have been undercutting the men, and the organization of a union of both, with common prices, was perhaps an attempt to meet the problem.[53]

The Nanaimo JTUA local in both April and November 1892 asked international sanction for a strike against employment of non-unionists, and in September 1893 it declared an unsanctioned strike against a wage reduction for 13 of its members.[54]

In Vancouver, the master tailors tried to impose a 20 per cent wage cut in August 1893, and the JTUA local, in spite of a warning that the international could not afford a strike, went out. The strike was still on on 15 September, when the Tailors' delegate to the Trades and Labor Council declared his members 'could not live on less than they were receiving at the present time,' adding that the strikers intended to start a co-operative. The Local seems to have collapsed, but it was revived at the beginning of 1898. On 30 March 1899 it presented its bill to the employers: the 10-hour day, a small wage increase, and the union shop. The tailors had been demoralized for some years because of the absence of a union, and the local's only members now were in 'free back shops.' It held an open meeting, which was told that the employers had been unable to hold a meeting of their own, so there was no reply to the demands. A large number of non-unionists then joined up, converting the unionists from a minority of the trade to a decided majority. The master tailors then refused the bill and made a 'scandalously low' counter-offer which the union rejected: a strike broke out 6 April.

The union at once appointed committees to look after the trains, boats, and the respective shops. Two employers caved in almost at once; the rest stood fast. There were rumours, indignantly denied, that the masters would bring in Oriental labour. One employer said he would send to Montreal for men, another was reported to be looking for men in Seattle; still another sent his work to Victoria. The rest made do as best they could with one or two hands. The union was optimistic, because of the heavy orders on hand. By 10 April it had doubled its membership.

On 11 April, one master tailor, J.P. McPherson, was reported working his shop with strikebreakers from Seattle, whom he had succeeded in getting past the pickets on the docks. The union said he was breaking the Alien Labour Act, but two days later was speaking only of 'the alien tailor,' and was hoping soon to have him in the union. (It turned out he was a German, who spoke very little English; he refused.) More strikebreakers from Seattle were expected that afternoon and would be 'met by delegation which will instruct them as to the situation.' The Trades and Labor Council pledged its support, asked tailors' unions in other towns in the province to do no work from Vancouver while the strike lasted, and appointed a committee to interview the city council, which had given contracts for firemen's and policemen's uniforms to McPherson.

The city council held a hearing, at which both parties appeared. McPherson said that before he tendered for the uniforms, he had asked union men if they were thinking of bringing down a bill, and been told there would be no change. He had therefore bid on the basis of the old wage rates. The council referred the matter to the finance committee and the city solicitor.

By 24 April the union said four employers had now signed the bill, two more would do so that evening, and six others would soon fall in line. This turned out to be premature: only three new recruits to the union shop came in, and one of those only after the union had agreed to allow overtime if needed. Most of the big shops were still holding out, and two of them said they were going to get men from San Francisco.

On 28 April the union told the Trades and Labor Council there were 30 tailors at work and 23 on strike. The ASE had offered material assistance if necessary, but the union said it was getting all it needed from the international. Next day the Typos offered their support, and a day or two later the Painters theirs.

At the beginning of May, violence erupted. Two strikebreakers arrived from Seattle. The union offered them money to go home again. They refused. Next morning the union tried again, with the same result. The strikebreakers then tried to break through the picket line to Campbell's shop; the pickets resisted and the strikebreakers got 'cut.' Five of the pickets were arrested and charged with beating and conspiring to intimidate one of the strikebreakers. They were acquitted. Meanwhile, the Cigar Makers had offered their support, and one more employer had signed the bill.

McPherson and the union had another hearing before the city council, the union this time alleging that McPherson had undertaken to employ union labour, which he was not doing, so that his contract was void. The council, however, declined to take action. The last we hear of this strike is in the *Tailor* of June 1899, which reported that the employers were giving in, one after the other. Total strike benefits paid amounted to $888.[55]

The Winnipeg local of the JTUA, No 70, was asking for international sanction in resisting a wage reduction in March 1893. It got it, and struck. The strike lasted till May and cost the international $3414. There was another strike, from July to October 1900, which cost $1193.50.[56]

Montreal Local 219, organized in May 1893, disappeared in September 1894. In October 1896 C.W. Mowbray of Ottawa, a JTUA organizer, reported that three different tailors' unions had been formed in Montreal, and all had failed. He had tried unsuccessfully to organize a meeting there. However, a dozen men had told him they were willing to try to organize if he came back in the spring. In September 1897 E.S. Christophersen, another organizer, tried his hand. He held two meetings and got a fair number signed up, but prospective members jibbed at the fee. He advised getting 'a good union Frenchman' to work there, adding: 'That city is really a detriment to the whole Dominion of Canada. They either make up the work during strikes in other cities, or else furnish all the scabs required.'[57]

Peterborough Local 47 had a minor strike in May 1897, which cost $40, and a bigger one, from December 1897 to March 1898, which had cost $540 to 19 March, when the international had to cut off supplies.[58] The local disappeared soon after. St Catharines had a happier history. Hugh Robinson went there on 11 August 1896 and got a strong muster at a meeting. On 22 August he got word from the provisional secretary to come for another meeting on the 25th. He did, found the hall filled, and not only saw the local off to a good start but also urged it to organize a trades and labour council, which it decided to do. In May 1897 Christophersen was able to report that all the tailors in the town were members, and that the local had raised wages by 25 per cent over the year.

Next month, however, St Catharines had a strike, which lasted till October and cost the union $351. While it was on, Christophersen sent in a most enthusiastic report: St Catharines had 44 members and was 'the best local in Canada.' This was in strong contrast to his reports on some other locals: Windsor had started a local a year before, but had given up; in Chatham 'also, they had given up their sword and shield. I persuaded them to take them up again'; in Sarnia, he had not been able to get enough members to form a local; Ingersoll was no good; Hamilton was 'struggling along.' London, in contrast, was all right, and Woodstock, though its members were few, was in good shape.[59] The Brockville Local was in such poor shape in December 1897 that a 40 per cent wage reduction in one shop did not even evoke discussion! Small wonder the local disappeared.[60]

The *Labour Gazette* has notes of a few strikes not mentioned in the *Tailor* in 1901 and 1902 in Hamilton, Kingston, Ottawa, St Marys, Lindsay, and Guelph.[61] In February 1901 Vancouver tailoring was 'practically controlled by Japanese and Chinese.' Tailors worked long hours; men got $9 to $12 a week. Victoria tailors were discussing forming a union; Oriental competition had killed the old one, and only about 25 tailors were left. Kingston tailors had been reorganizing, and the master tailors seemed disposed to adopt the union label.[62]

Altogether, the JTUA organized locals in 38 places: 28 in Ontario, 7 in British Columbia, 1 each in Quebec, New Brunswick, and Manitoba. But some fell by the wayside, and some places the union felt should be organized, notably Belleville and Prescott, never were. In May 1896 the *Tailor* had said there were 32 places in Canada with over 8000 people where there ought to be JTUA locals. By the end of 1902 the union had 24 Locals in Ontario, 6 in British Columbia, and 1 in Manitoba. Four Ontario locals had disappeared; so had the single locals in Quebec and New Brunswick, and one in British Columbia. The union never got into Nova Scotia or Prince Edward Island in this period, though it sent organizers into both provinces.[63] The locals were often small. Winnipeg started with 31 members, Windsor with 25, Owen Sound with 24, Victoria with 23, Ottawa with 20, Vancouver with 13, Nanaimo with 10, and Peterborough with 9.

The Boot and Shoe Workers International Union, formed in 1889, had a Hamilton local from 1890 to at least 1893, a London local, No 85, in 1890, and a Toronto local, No 77, from 1890 till at least 1898. This international merged in 1895 with the Lasters Protective Union and the KOL's National Trade District 216 to form the Boot and Shoe Workers Union, which chartered Hamilton locals 228, 232, and 234 and Toronto 233 in 1900; Aurora in 1901; a second Toronto local, Berlin 206, and Galt in 1902.[64]

Much of the industry, however, was concentrated in the province of Quebec, where several local or regional unions already existed. Early in 1901 four of these in Montreal and two of the three regional locals in St Hyacinthe voted to join the international. Two St Hyacinthe locals may have been chartered in May; Montreal Local 249 perhaps even earlier; Montreal Local 266 on 12 June 1901; and Montreal Locals 251 and 267 before the end of the year. This tremendous coup, which was said to involve about 6000 workers altogether, was brought off by John F. Tobin, the international's president; it took in all the Montreal organizations except the Lasters. The international local or locals in St Hyacinthe had, by March 1901, succeeded in getting the Séguin & Lalime factory on a union label basis.[65] How many of these locals were still in existence at the end of 1902 is not clear; nor does there seem to be much information on their activities. There was certainly lively competition with regional and local organizations.

The Toronto locals of the successive internationals fought a series of battles with J.D. King & Co. That firm had borne its part in the defeat of the Female Shoe Operatives in 1882. At the beginning of 1894 it was locked in combat with what was probably still Local 77 of the first international union. On 2 February the Trades and Labor Council unanimously passed a resolution that, 'having heard ... from the proper delegates' that the firm had laid charges of intimidation against the strikers, male and female, and 'believing that the ultimate intention of the firm is to break up the union, and to lower wages to a starvation level,' it pledged itself 'to use every available means in its power in support of the employees,' and called on the members of every affiliate to do likewise. By 2 March 'a settlement had been reached.'

On 14 April 1898 a delegation from what may have been a local or locals of the second international union appeared before the TLC to 'state the facts' of a fresh strike at King's. King was up to his old tricks: 'several men had received summonses to the Police Court for intimidation & c.' On 2 July the Typos had a circular from the strikers asking for help.

This union seems to have lost this battle, but it refused to admit that it had lost the war. In November 1900 arrangements were started to place King's 'on a union basis, which, if accomplished, will put an end to a struggle which has lasted over two years.' The 'difficulty' was being 'arranged' by the international president, John F. Tobin, 'who had a long consultation with Mr. King on the 22nd ... The employees were organized as members of the local union that same evening. It is probable that an agreement will be arrived at ... under which none but members of the union are to be employed ... that the union stamp will be placed on all boots and shoes manufactured and that there shall be no strikes until recourse has been had to arbitration. The proceedings throughout the negotiations have been of a friendly and harmonious character.' Next month, the settlement had not been completed. But in January 1901 the firm became a union shop, with all the employees members of the local, which had a total membership of about 400.[66]

In September 1901, the union won a strike against the Ames-Holden Co, Montreal, which adopted the union label.[67]

The United Garment Workers of America seem to have entered Canada in October 1894 with the organization of Toronto Local 81. Twenty-three more followed, but the mortality was heavy. By the end of 1902, Toronto had had six locals, of which three survived; Montreal seven, of which five survived; Hamilton four (all gone); London two (consolidated by the end of 1902); Stratford two (one still there at the end of 1902); and Winnipeg, Victoria, and Dundas one each (all still there at the end of 1902).

In June 1899 the Hamilton local had a one-day strike. Calder and Co had imported 30 tailors from New York. About 50 members of Local 134 struck against this on 1 June. On 2 June the employer agreed to employ only union members and to reduce hours from 54 a week to 52, and the strikers went back.[68]

The Toronto Cloak and Mantle Workers' local struck against the T. Eaton Co in the summer of 1899. Eaton's brought in strikebreakers from New York. One, 'finding himself [said the Trades and Labor Council] the victim of the Co.'s misrepresentation, and being a stranger in a strange land, without means, and being refused return passage by the Co., in excess of despair drowned himself.' The Council was so roused that it passed a resolution declaring that Eaton's had shown its hostility to organized labour on many occasions and denouncing the company 'as an enemy to organized labor, and as being, by the use of fraud and deception, primarily responsible for the death of the man.' The council also denounced Eaton's as 'unworthy of the patronage of organized labor' and sent copies of the resolution to every trades and labour council, local union, DA, and Knights of Labor LA in Canada.[69]

Local 35 of the UGW was Winnipeg's first union of women workers. It started in February 1899 with nearly 50 members in Emerson and Hague's tent and overall factory. This firm had recently imposed a 20 per cent wage cut. The women objected so vigorously that the employer restored the old rate of $4 a week until the spring. But the threat remained. So the women asked the Trades and Labor Council for advice. Naturally, the council advised forming a union, and the women did. The employer then discharged three of the employees, without giving reasons. The council then succeeded in getting an interview with the employer, which resulted in an undertaking to recognize the union and a draft agreement, providing for a minimum rate of 12½ cents an hour, no out work, a 9-hour day with 5 cents an hour overtime, the union label, and other improvements. The company then balked, refused a union offer to submit the dispute to arbitration, and discharged the whole union committee. The union then struck. The *Voice* issued a special strike edition, recounting some of these facts, and congratulating the women on their 'manliness.' The council appealed to unions all across the country for funds, and got $688.10. A new company, Hoover Manufacturing, was organized, which was ready to accept the union, union conditions, and the union label. It apparently succeded so well that by November 1901 Emerson and Hague were actually asking for the label.[70]

Other international unions
and the American Federation of Labor

The Order of Railway Telegraphers chartered its first Canadian division at Wood-stock, New Brunswick, on 29 April 1888. The Order was at first a 'fraternal organization,' though one of its aims was the 'limitation of students.' It soon had to face in the United States a rival, militant, union, the Brotherhood of Railway and Commercial Telegraphers. This led to its reorganization in 1891 as the Order of Railroad Telegraphers, 'with provisions for calling a strike.' In two years, the total membership in both countries rose from 8000 to 15,000, and 'some 5,000 members received wage increases of about $350,000,000. However, there was a great deal of hasty and ill considered and confused action ... Union discipline was not good and when strikes were called the results were devastating.'

From this plight the whole organization was rescued by a successful strike, in the fall of 1896, on the Canadian Pacific Railway:

The Canadian Pacific Division 7 had been established in 1895 and within a year had more than 1,000 members. The General Committee took up a number of pending grievances along with a demand for certain improvements in working conditions and the restoration of wage rates which had been cut in 1895 ... After months of ... negotiations the Railroad attempted to compel the Train Dispatchers.to withdraw from the ORT. This was regarded as an overt act and countered with an immediate declaration of a strike on September 28, 1896.

Before October 1, the tie-up was complete from ocean to ocean so far as the movement of freight trains was concerned. Goods received at Vancouver ... from China and Japan were piled up awaiting shipment. Cattle were starving at different points along the road and the immense grain crop of the Northwest could not be moved forward to vessels waiting in port for their cargoes. For nearly nine days the affairs of the Great Canadian Railroad System were in a chaotic state ... [Then] Management authorized its five General Superintendents to enter into agreements and the strike ended October 11 and agreements were quickly established on each of the five operating regions.'

The eastern lines 'agreement of 1898 established a 12-hour day. It provided for an agent and operator, with a dwelling, fire and light found, a rate of $47.50 a month from Cartier to Fort William. From Chalk River, to Cartier, Sudbury, and Sault Ste Marie, the rate was $42.50; east of Chalk River, $40 on the main line and $38 on branch lines. For an agent and operator without a dwelling, the corresponding rates were $52.50, $47.50, and $45 and $43. For operators, the rates were $47.50, $42.50, and $40 and $38. Relieving agents from Cartier to Fort William were to get $50 a month; on the rest of the lines, just what they had been getting before.[1]

In 1898 the Order tackled the Grand Trunk, on 'an extended set of grievances, including wages and working conditions and union recognition.' The Grand Trunk responded by canvassing the individual operators to discover the union's strength. The results evidently staggered it, for 'an agreement to arbitrate was signed December 23, 1898. About a month later the award returned was favorable to the Telegraphers based on the Canadian Pacific schedule ... Inspired by these successes [in Canada], the Telegraphers on other roads became active once more, and during 1898 and 1899 at least sixteen new and revised contracts were signed.'[2]

In January 1902 the ORT got an agreement with the CPR for British Columbia, containing a long list of rates, ranging from $55 to $85 on the main line, and from $55 to $100 on branch lines.

In May 1902 after five days of negotiations, the ORT got an agreement with the Grand Trunk east of Detroit and the St Clair River. Agents had operators on the main line, with a dwelling, were to get $40 a month, on branch lines $37; without a dwelling, $45 and $42 respectively (a $2 increase for all). Relieving agents were to get $55 (a $5 increase). Overtime was to be 20 cents an hour (a 5 cent increase), with special rates for ticket agents on branch lines after 12 hours a day.[3]

The Bakers entered Canada towards the end of 1889. A Journeymen Bakers Friendly Society had marched in the Halifax Labour Day parade of 1888. It must then have joined the Knights of Labor, for towards the end of 1889 it is reported as having seceded from the Knights and joined the National Bakers' Union of the United States.[4] On 5 May 1890 this local asked for a wage increase of $2 a week, and a reduction of hours from 15–18 per day to 10. The men claimed that they had to go to work between 3 and 4 AM and work 4 or 5 hours, standing, before they had any breakfast. They had had to do this all their lives and could endure it no longer. They wanted to start work at 6 am with an hour's break for breakfast. Two of the small employers were willing to grant whatever the bigger ones did, and on 8 May the union committee met three of the leading master bakers. The union threatened to strike on 11 May if no satisfactory settlement was arrived at. On that date, all the master bakers but one agreed to grant the 10-hour day and pay $10 a week. The union struck the one dissentient.

On 7 February 1891 it was appealing to the Halifax Typos for help in a grievance against Moir's; it got a vote of sympathy. A month later, its president, Lewis Archibald (a veteran of the old purely local organization) again appeared before the Typos and made 'quite a lengthy speech on the grievances of the striking bakers,' winding up with a vigorous appeal for financial assistance. The Typos unanimously voted $30.[5]

The Winnipeg local demanded recognition in the spring of 1902, and 25 cents an hour for ordinary workers and 30 cents for foremen, an increase of 5 cents. Two employers agreed. The other 11 jibbed, and the union struck 1 May. By 9 May one more employer had accepted the demands; but the rest held out, and by 1 July the strike had collapsed. This, and a second strike in the Paulin-Chambers biscuit factory on 25 May, produced a co-operative bakery. It cost $4000 and was opened in November with a concert and much rejoicing. The Machinists had the honour of giving the first union social to serve co-operative pastries.

The Paulin-Chambers strike resulted from the firm's flat refusal to let its 40 women employees join a union at all. This roused Winnipeg unions to fury, and they collected a strike fund of $437.65. The strike none the less failed, and by early August the last strikers had been paid off.[6]

Hamilton had a lockout by one firm on 25 May 1902, against men who refused to work on Sunday. This seems to have petered out by the end of July. In the following month, however, the union got what appears to have been a city-wide agreement. It had asked for $18 a week for foremen, $11 for journeymen, $10 for day hands, and $8 for helpers; it got all these. It had wanted 25 cents an hour for jobbers, it got 20 cents. It had wanted apprentices to be classified as jobbers after two years' experience; it got them journeyman status after three years. It had wanted a closed shop; it got an undertaking to employ union men 'if competent.'[7]

The Victoria Bakers, on 1 October, got a weekly rate of $18 for foremen and $16 for journeymen, with $3 a day for jobbers. No members were to be required to work with Oriental labour; after 1 November all night work was to be abolished; board and lodging were not to be counted as part payment of wages. There was to be one apprentice to each shop, who was to get $4 a week the first year, $7 the second, and $10 the third.[8]

The Pattern Makers League of North America seems to have entered Canada in November 1891 at Toronto. Three other branches were added before the end of 1902. The Toronto branch had a prolonged, and apparently unsuccessful, strike in 1902.[9]

The Brotherhood of Railway Carmen of America was formed in 1891, by a merger which took in a Canadian brotherhood of the same occupation. It chartered Toronto Lodge 84 that same year, and 14 others before the end of 1902. By that time, the first four had disappeared.[10] On 1 November 1901, the Carmen signed an agreement with the CPR (Pacific division). It provided that from 1 October to 1 May hours should be from 7 am to 6 pm, with an hour for dinner, 5 days a week, and from 7 am till 5 pm on Saturdays; from May to 1 October Saturday hours were to be from 7 am till noon. It also set forth a detailed list of rates for Vancouver, Kamloops, Revelstoke, Nelson, Rossland, Smelter Junction, North Bend, Nakusp, Eholt, and Midway. This agreement was revised, with a new set of rates, at the very end of 1902.[11]

The Journeymen Horseshoers Local 49 was admitted to the Toronto Trades and Labor Council on 16 December 1892; it may have been reorganized in 1897. Local 72, Hamilton, was formed 13 April 1896; Local 71, Montreal, about the same time. The Journeymen Horseshoers Union in Halifax, formed July 1901, may have been another local of this international. There is also evidence of locals in Ottawa in 1895, and Brantford in November 1902.[12]

The Toronto local, in the summer of 1900, demanded a rate of $12 a week for firemen and $11 for floormen for 54 hours, instead of $10 for 57½, with overtime at 35 cents for firemen and 30 cents for floormen. After a strike on 27 August 46 out of 50 employers accepted the terms, except that hours were to be 55 per week.[13]

The Hamilton local, in the fall of 1902, demanded a $2 a week increase for smiths (to $12) and shoers (to $11). Two employers, with four employees, refused, and the local struck. At the end of the period there was no settlement.[14]

The Amalgamated Woodworkers arrived in Canada in 1893. Local 65 (varnishers and polishers), Toronto, was organized in February (it may have been reorganized on 8 May 1900); Local 19 (piano finishers) was admitted to the Toronto Trades and Labor Council on 17 March; and Quebec Local 129 was organized in June (perhaps reorganized in the summer of 1901). A Local 56 marched in the Montreal Labour Day parades of 1893, 1894, 1897, and 1899. Local 91 (piano and cabinet-makers) was admitted to the TTLC on 15 March 1895; Local 34 (pianomakers) was formed 24 September 1895.[15]

The Amalgamated Woodworkers seem to have organized 16 locals in 1900, 1 in 1901, and 6 or 7 in 1902. By the end of 1902 locals 19 and 91 in Toronto, and the Goderich and Seaforth locals, seem to have disappeared. The rest were apparently still in existence: 23 in Ontario, 2 in Quebec and 1 British Columbia.

The Woodworkers had a strike in Ottawa on 3 June 1901, when some 350 in 12 firms went out for a 9-hour day and a 20 per cent wage increase. The employers refused to negotiate, even repulsing department of labour offers of friendly intervention. Subsequent proceedings were as in the Carpenters' strike, and the union finally declared the strike off on 5 July. The men who had not obtained work elsewhere went back on the old terms.[16]

On 20 November 1901, the Woodworkers' Council of Toronto, representing 6 locals in the piano-making industry, served the Piano Manufacturers' Association with demands for a wage increase from a range of 18 to 25 cents to a new one of 20 to 27½ cents an hour, with 30 cents for piano-action finishers; abolition of the contract system; a 9-hour day with a Saturday half-holiday; and time-and-a-half for overtime. After a conference between committees for both sides, the manufacturers refused to recognize the union. The union then decided to try dealing with the companies individually. One firm accepted the demands; two others agreed to negotiate; the union struck the rest 23 December. About 480 men came out. Five days later, the union asked the dominion minister of labour to intervene. A joint conference on 30 December, with the minister present, reached an agreement. The employers granted a reduction in hours and a small wage increase, but refused to recognize the union.[17]

On 13 March 1902, the finishers' local in Berlin demanded that Lippert and Co, furniture manufacturers, dismiss an employee who had been expelled from the union. The company refused, and the union struck the finishing room. One or two men who had refused to join, or had left the union, stayed in, and a few came in from other departments. The union then demanded that the company stop all work in the finishing room till the dispute was settled. The company refused, and the union then struck the whole plant. The company then wrote to the minister of labour and Mackenzie King, the deputy minister, hastened to Berlin. As a result of his efforts, the company agreed to take back all the men, and the strike was over on 22 March. 'The other terms of the agreement,' says the *Labour Gazette*, 'were not made public' (this seems to have been a favourite device of King's at the time: the Toronto piano makers' agreement also was kept under wraps). The department claimed that it later received from both company and employees 'acknowledgements expressive of general satisfaction at the result of its intervention.'[18]

The Bookbinders had started off as part of the ITU. As a separate union they organized Toronto Local 28 in June 1893. Six others followed. One, the Toronto Women's Bindery Local 34, in October 1902 won a considerable victory without striking, before it was 18 months old: a wage increase averaging 10 per cent, with a reduction of 3 hours per week 'left optional with each employer to introduce, if it can be done, without interfering too much with business.'[19]

The Tin, Sheet Iron and Cornice Workers International Association had an Ottawa local in 1893 and 1894. It withdrew in 1894 and formed a Canadian Tin, Sheet Iron and Cornice Workers Union.[20]

The Upholsterers chartered Toronto Local 30 at least as early as January 1894; Guelph 41 on 14 March 1898; Berlin 42 probably soon after; and Montreal 78 in 1902.

The Toronto Upholsterers had a grievance against Eaton's in March 1897. They had a strike, against the Gold Medal Manufacturing Co and others, from April 1898 till February 1899. One firm in Berlin gave in in May 1898, and apparently some others did later, for the reports to the Toronto Trades and Labor Council in July and August 1898, and in January and February 1899, speak of the workers at Gold Medal being still out.[21]

The Railway Switchmen had a Montreal Lodge 94 in 1894. Hamilton Lodge 25 was formed 1 May 1899, and five others followed (four in Ontario, one in Quebec).[22]

The Barbers organized their first Canadian local, Montreal 34, on 18 November 1895, but it was suspended 28 August 1897. Ottawa 130 may have been started 30 May 1898; Winnipeg 69 was chartered in May or June 1897, but was gone a year later. Vancouver 120 was certainly organized 28 August 1899. By the end of 1902 there were 15 more, 13 in Ontario, 2 in British Columbia.[23]

The Sheet Metal Workers entered Canada in 1896, with the chartering of Toronto Local 30 on 23 November. By the end of 1902, there were 12 more.[24]

The Ottawa local struck on 1 June 1901, demanding a 15 per cent increase for all men getting 20 cents an hour or over, and a minimum wage of 20 cents; a union shop; prohibition of any apprentice of less than 4 years' standing doing journeymen's work; time-and-a-half from 5:30 pm till midnight, double time after midnight and on Sundays and holidays. One firm had accepted the demands; ten refused. By 13 June the employers had agreed to meet the strikers, though they still refused to recognize the union. In a day or two, they reached agreement, and the men went back on 17 June. They got a 10 per cent increase, and the overtime and apprenticeship provisions they had demanded. The employers also agreed to 'meet a committee of union grievance.'[25]

In the spring of 1902 the Toronto local tried to get a flat rate of 30 cents. In an agreement on 30 June most of the employers accepted a 25 cent minimum rate, a 2½ cent increase which also applied to those getting 25 cents and 27½ cents.

One employer, the Metallic Roofing Co, stood out, and 7 August 1902 saw the beginning of one of the most celebrated strikes in Canadian history. It involved only 15 men, but it started a legal case of vital importance to the whole union movement which dragged on for 6 years. This hinged on the fact that the members of other unions, especially in the Exhibition buildings and in Polson's shipyard, had refused to handle Metallic Roofing products. The company applied for an injunction to restrain Local 30 and certain of its members from unlawfully interfering with the company's business; it also sued the unions and their members for damages. The local retaliated by claiming that the company's work on the St Lawrence Market was defective because it was employing incompetent men, and tried to get the civic authorities to investigate the matter. The strike seems to have been a failure, but it raised the whole question of the legal position of trade unions. The case dragged on, inconclusively, till 1909, when it was settled out of court.[26]

The Montreal local, in February 1902, asked for a minimum rate of 20 or 25 cents an hour, a 9-hour day, and pay day every Saturday. The employers balked, the union struck 11 firms with 65 men on 1 May, and by 15 May all the principal firms had signed the schedule. The previous rates had been 14 cents and 17½ cents an hour, so the increase was substantial.[27]

The Steel and Copper Plate Printers organized their Ottawa Local 6, on 14 February 1897; it appears to have been reorganized in October 1900.[28]

The National (later International) Alliance of Theatrical Stage Employees came, or rather was dragged, into Canada in 1898. The Toronto stage employees seem to have organized a purely local union in 1894. This was admitted to the Toronto Trades and Labor Council on 15 February 1895, and soon afterwards must have taken steps to get into the National Alliance formed in the United States two years before. At any rate, the third convention of the Alliance, in 1895, was informed that its secretary had received the application money of the Toronto union, and that it would like to affiliate. The convention would have none of it: there was strenuous objection to changing the union's name to 'International,' and to the admission of Canadian organizations, and a motion to merge into an international body was defeated, 29 to 5.

Toronto tried again in 1897. The Alliance convention listened to a letter of thanks from Toronto for its recognition of a Toronto membership card. But a motion to take up the Toronto application for a charter was met at once with an amendment to take up only that part of the letter which contained the vote of thanks, and the amendment carried. A further motion to give the Toronto representative the floor to state his case was met with a motion to refer, which carried, 34 to 20.

The 1898 convention was faced with an application from Montreal, which had formed a purely local union in September 1897. The Alliance executive referred the application to the convention, which consented to hear a representative from Montreal. When he had spoken, the convention was faced with the straight question, 'Shall we merge into an international union?' (The question of becoming international seems to have been regarded rather as a merger of American and Canadian organizations than a mere matter of admitting Canadian locals into an American union.) The opponents of internationalism moved a motion to table the Montreal application till the convention had received the report of its committees on resolutions and laws, and an amendment simply to change the name to 'International' was declared out of order. This was followed by a decision to refer the Montreal application to the next convention. Then, suddenly, the majority of the delegates changed their minds: on 22 July the Montreal application was granted with one abstention.

The barriers against Canada were now down. Within a few months Montreal Local 56 had been followed by Toronto 58 and Winnipeg 63. Toronto may have been chartered before September, when the union was demanding a 50 per cent wage increase. The Grand and the Princess gave it, at once, but refused to sign an agreement till 'Mr Whitney' arrived from Detroit for negotiations. The Toronto Opera House refused the demand, and was struck on 5 September. By 22 September the strike was won. The two new locals did not send delegates to the 1899 convention, but Montreal did, and its representative, P.J. Ryan, took a most active part, including the preparation of the report on laws and resolutions.[29]

The 1901 convention had to deal with a Vancouver application. This had been refused by the executive because the local union had fewer than the minimum of 15 members required by the Alliance's constitution, but at the request of the AFL, and after Vancouver had sent in extra names, the executive referred the matter to the convention. The delegates endorsed the refusal.

In 1902 the convention unanimously applied to the AFL to change the Alliance's name to 'International.' This did not mean that it had gone soft on accepting Canadian unions. It had applications from Ottawa, Hamilton, and London, and granted none of them. The Ottawa application had arrived too late for the executive to act, and was referred to the convention which seems to have let it lie. The Hamilton and London unions were declared not eligible: Hamilton 'could not comply with a single law' of the Alliance. Both Ottawa and London, however, may have been admitted soon afterwards, for the 1903 list of Alliance locals contains Ottawa 95 and London 105, and the proceedings record a case from Ottawa 95 against the Painters, who were charged with poaching on Local 95's jurisdiction. Hamilton was again turned down: its application was not in due form.[30]

The United Brotherhood of Leather Workers on Horse Goods seems also to have entered Canada in 1898. Its Local 93 was admitted to the Toronto Trades and Labor Council on 4 October. (This local was apparently reorganized the next spring, again late in 1900 or early in 1901, and still again in March or April 1902.) Montreal Local 43 followed in 1899, a Winnipeg local early in 1900, and Hamilton 73 15 months later.[31]

The Hotel and Restaurant Employees International Union and Bartenders International Alliance organized its first Canadian local, Toronto 168, in January 1899, but this lasted only till October 1900.[32] By the end of 1902 there were eighteen locals in Ontario, four in British Columbia, and one each in Quebec, New Brunswick, and Manitoba.

There were two teamsters' organizations during this period: the Team Drivers International Union and the Teamsters International Union. The latter had broken away from the former early in 1902 because it objected to employer teamsters being members.[33] It is hard to sort out which Canadian local unions were locals of which international (sometimes, indeed, whether they belonged to either), or whether they shifted from one to the other, or when they were started. By the end of 1902 there were probably thirteen or fourteen locals of the Team Drivers (nine or ten in Ontario, two in British Columbia, and one each in New Brunswick and Prince Edward Island) and two of the Teamsters (one in Ontario, one in New Brunswick).

The Retail Clerks organized their first local in Vancouver on 1 April 1899. There is some indication of a Montreal local in October 1899, and of a St Thomas Local in May 1900. Another 18 followed.

There is evidence of other unions of retail clerks, and it is not always clear whether they were locals of the International Protective Association, purely local bodies, or federal labour unions (AFL or TLCC). There was a clerks' union in Nanaimo in April 1900, in Peterborough in the fall of 1902, and in Calgary in June 1902. The Retail Clerks' international convention report of 1903 lists a Calgary Local 642 formed since the previous convention but does not mention any of the others.[34]

Next came the Carriage and Wagon Workers, with London Local 46, on 10 May 1899. At least eight others followed. There were also carriage and wagon workers' unions in Halifax (formed in June 1901), Gananoque (probably formed in the summer of 1902), and Brockville (fall of 1902); whether they were locals of the international is not clear.

The Orillia local ran into heavy weather as soon as the company found out it had been organized. The company locked out its 35 employees on 13 September 1901. By December the men had 'gradually signed an agreement not to belong to any union and returned to work, the charter of the union being returned to headquarters.'

On 1 May 1902 the Toronto local, 175 strong, struck 22 firms, demanding a 15 per cent increase in wages and a 55-hour week. By 20 June it had won, except in a few instances.[35]

The International Longshoremen's Association also formed its first Canadian local in 1899: Hamilton 120, on 28 June. Another score or so followed. By the end of 1902 there were probably twenty-two locals: ten in Ontario, five in Nova Scotia, three in New Brunswick, and two each in Quebec and British Columbia.[36]

The Longshoremen had two strikes in Montreal in November 1901, both for a single day, and both successful. The first involved 56 men in one company, who wanted an increase of 20 to 40 cents an hour. They got it, for themselves and the men in several other firms. The second strike, by 32 men against another company, was for an increase in the number of men working in the holds of ships. The company increased the number from six to eight. On 29 October 1902 Montreal had another strike, of 800 men, for an increase from 20 cents to 30 cents an hour for day work and to 35 cents for night. The employers gave in on 30 November.[37]

A fourth strike was in Halifax in April 1902. In March the ILA had presented the steamship companies with wage and other demands, to take effect 2 April. Only one company replied at all, and that one only to ask for more time. On 31 March the union committee called on the companies, but was unable to negotiate a settlement. Between 600 and 700 men thereupon walked out, at midnight on 1 April bringing the port practically to a standstill. On 7 April the coal workers, some 200, refused to load or discharge coal on any struck vessel, and next day they were joined by 300 fish handlers and a considerable number of members of the Coopers' Union. On 7 April the deputy mayor got the union and the companies together, but without result. The union president then invoked the aid of the dominion department of labour, which promptly despatched Mackenzie King to the scene. He arrived 9 April and found the Freight Handlers (another ILA local) and other unions prepared to call out their members in sympathy at any moment. He strongly advised against this, and embarked on a series of meetings with the two sides, separately, followed by a mass meeting of over a thousand strikers, to which he presented draft agreements, which the men unanimously accepted. The men who had struck in sympathy were to be taken back without discrimination. The longshoremen were also to be taken back without discrimination (whether by employers against the strikers or by union members against non-members). They were also to get 20 cents an hour, day work, and 25 cents night work; double time for Sundays, Good Friday, Thanksgiving Day, Christmas Day, and Labour Day, unless otherwise arranged by mutual agreement; 25 cents an hour (and board) for work on stranded or wrecked vessels, with time to run from wharf to wharf; 25 cents an hour for all time after 6 pm till men were ordered home; provision for work not finished at ordinary quitting time; and a requirement of 30 days' notice of any change in the terms of the agreement, or of any strike or lockout. The strike was settled on 11 April.

In October, the Hamilton local got a new schedule of wage rates, with a 5-cents-a-ton increase, bringing the rate for handling anthracite coal to 22 cents and bituminous coal to 25 cents, with 3 cents extra for vessels with side hatches.[38]

The Tobacco Workers chartered their first local, Hamilton 48, on 30 August 1899, in the plant of George E. Tuckett & Son Co, one of the largest in Canada. It had figured prominently in the Cigar Makers' reports as a good, fair employer, and it promptly adopted the union label. Within a month or so of its organization the local's membership had grown to 100, and soon after it reached 300. Montreal Local 53 was chartered 27 December 1899 in the plants of the Globe Cigarette and the Dominion Tobacco companies, which signed union label contracts. Four more Locals followed in 1900: Joliette 60 on 15 October in the plant of J.U. Gervais and Co; London 61 on 24 October; Leamington 62 on 6 November in the plant of the Consumer Tobacco Co Ltd; and Toronto 63 on 10 December in the shops of William Blaney, McAlpin Tobacco, and the Globe Cigarette Co (which became union shops). Local 71, which covered Windsor and Kingsville, was chartered 16 April 1901 in the plant of the Erie Tobacco Co, which became a union label shop. Charlottetown 82 was chartered 1 February 1902 in the plant of the Riley Tobacco Co. The minutes of the Toronto Trades and Labor Council for 23 October 1902 also record a Local 64, but this may be a misprint for 63. The Joliette local seems to have disappeared by the end of 1902.[39]

Charlottetown had a strike of 12 workers in Riley's from 25 March to 1 April 1902 for a wage increase. They got a quarter-cent per pound. But on 11 June Riley refused to recognize the union. On 19 July his employees left it, and by October it was reported in danger of going under. It survived, though only by becoming in September a purely local body which lasted till 1905.[40]

The Amalgamated Meat Cutters and Butcher Workmen chartered three locals in 1899, beginning with Ingersoll 55, whose charter was revoked January 1900. Another three to five followed, of which two or three were still in existence at the end of 1902. The Stratford local seems to have been done in by a lockout.[41]

The International Wood Carvers Association came into Canada 24 October 1899 with a Local at Berlin. A Toronto local followed in September 1900.[42]

The Textile Workers seem to have formed a Hamilton local in the summer of 1899. They certainly formed their Brussels Carpet Weavers' Local 277 in Guelph on 16 August 1900. Toronto Local 360 was admitted to the Trades and Labor Council on 28 August 1900 and Guelph 340 was organized some time in 1902.

Guelph 277 struck within 15 days of its organization. The employer demanded a reduction of 25 per cent on piece-work and of 5 cents an hour on day work. The strike lasted from 31 August to 16 October, when the workers went back to work for a new management, accepting the reduction conditionally.[43]

A strike at the Toronto Carpet Manufacturing Company on 16 July 1902 involved some 300 workers. Their chief grievance was the introduction of a time clock, which, they said, cut considerable time from the 45 minutes allowed them for lunch. The employer gave orders that any worker refusing to ring up should be suspended. The weavers, followed by the carders and spinners, thereupon struck. Once out, they formulated a series of demands, including a wage increase of 10 per cent in most departments, a reduction of hours from 60 to 55 per week, abolition of ringing up on leaving at noon, and 5 minutes' dressing time for women employees. The strike, which had actually preceded formation of the local, lasted till 19 September. By that time about half the strikers had got work in Philadelphia. The rest went back unconditionally, but the company dropped the requirement of ringing up on leaving work, and the union survived.[44]

The International Brotherhood of Electrical Workers chartered Ottawa Local 93 on 20 December 1899. Thirteen other Locals followed. By the end of 1902 there were four locals in Ontario, two in British Columbia, and one each in Quebec and Manitoba.[45]

In June 1900 the Ottawa local demanded $2 a day (from a range of $1.25 to $1.60) and a 9-hour day from the Ottawa Electric Co. The company replied by discharging 45 men. The mayor tried to discuss the matter with the company, but the manager refused: he would talk to the men. Several aldermen also tried their hands, apparently without effect. The local was admitted to the Allied Trades and Labor Association; the members expected money from the international; some got jobs outside Ottawa.

Montreal Local 182 struck on 14 April 1902 against 2 firms with 260 workers, for a 25 cent wage increase and a 9-hour day. The mayor got the dispute referred to arbitration, and the men went back 25 April on the old conditions but with a promise of 'consideration individually.'

Toronto Local 114 struck, a hundred strong, on 2 June 1902 for a wage increase to 30 cents an hour and an 8-hour day. Some of the employers gave in early, but not till 19 July did they make a general agreement for 25 cents and an 8-hour day.

Meanwhile, the Hamilton local had struck on 17 June against 2 firms with 50 employees for a wage increase of about 40 per cent and shorter hours. The men went back 23 June pending settlement by arbitration. This proved to be only a lull: on 8 August some 35, in 1 firm, were out again because of a delay in the arbitration proceedings. They went back 29 August on the arbitration board being duly constituted. The award made no change in hours, but gave wage increases, varying from ½ cent an hour to 15 cents. For most of the workers the hourly rates remained at the level of 15 to 20 cents an hour, with some at $2 a day and some at $50 a month. It is not hard to see why some workers became disillusioned with arbitration.[46]

Towards the end of November 1902 Vancouver had a telephone workers' strike, settled 15 December by an agreement which established a closed shop; an 8-hour day; time-and-a-half for overtime to 10 PM, double time thereafter and on Sundays and holidays; one apprentice to every two repairers; an immediate increase of $5 a month; an elaborate scale for operators (beginning at $20 a month and rising to $30 at the end of 2 years); $3 a day for linemen; a union grievance committee; and miscellaneous concessions. The Victoria men struck in sympathy, but were not taken back when the Vancouver strike ended.[47]

Fourteen international unions had entered Canada in 1899. Another nine arrived in 1900.

The Meat and Pastry Cooks International Association formed Toronto Local 210 in January.[48]

The Composition Metal Workers Union formed its Toronto Local 11 in March.[49]

The International Broom Makers Union formed its Berlin Local, 7, on 2 April and Hamilton Local, 9, on 15 May. Three others, all in Ontario, followed, and there seems to have been a Broom Makers Union in Winnipeg in September 1902.[50]

The Architectural and Structural Iron Workers formed their Toronto local on 14 May 1900. Three more followed, of which one may have been gone by the end of 1902.[51]

The Shirt, Waist and Laundry Workers formed their Nelson, British Columbia, Local 68, on 26 July 1900. Six more followed: four in Ontario, one in British Columbia, and one in Quebec.[52]

The Wood, Wire and Metal Lathers chartered Ottawa Local 57 just after the 1900 TLC convention in that city. Locals in Toronto, Winnipeg, and Hamilton followed.[53]

The Trunk and Bag Workers Union, formed in Montreal on 15 March 1900 and still in existence in December 1901, reported in December 1900 that one of the largest manufacturers had 'signified his desire to adopt the union label.' Toronto Local 11 was organized in February 1902.[54]

As early as 7 November 1884 the Toronto Trades and Labor Council had had a letter from a Mr E. Amey, 'with a pamphlet Upon Farming & Farm Labourers asking assistance from the Council in organizing the Farm Hands.' All this produced was a mild puff for the book at the next meeting.

But on 13 September 1900 the council must have been startled by a report from its union label committee: a Farmers Union had been formed in Elgin County. The committee made the most of it: 'At last the farmers of Elgin County have discovered that their condition will not be improved by the promises of either political party and have organized upon the trade union plan for mutual benefit. The "National

Farmers' Union" have adopted a "Union Label," and it is now possible to get "union label" milk, poultry, butter and eggs; while the farmers in return are demanding the products of union mechanics. The union label is in truth gaining ground. Let the farmers and mechanics co-operate and it will solve many unsatisfactory conditions of the laboring class.'

The National Union was really an international. The Elgin local survived at least through 1901.[55]

The Amalgamated Association of Iron, Steel and Tin Workers re-entered Canada in 1900. A Hamilton lodge was in existence at least as early as 10 June 1882, and took part in the demonstration of 4 August 1884; but the Ontario Rolling Mill had knocked it out some time before 18 January 1888. By 6 February 1891, however, a reorganized, or new, Hamilton lodge was being invited to join the Trades and Labor Council. In the same year there was an Amalgamated Iron Workers Union in Ottawa and an Iron and Steel Workers Union in Montreal. This last may well have been part of the international, for in 1892 and 1893 lodges 2 and 3 of the Amalgamated Association marched in the Labour Day parade.

By December 1900, however, Belleville Lodge 1 was 'the pioneer lodge in Canada.' A Hamilton lodge seems to have existed by the summer of 1901, for a strike between 31 July and 8 August of six ironworkers, 'alleged to have been called out by order of the Amalgamated Association of Steel Workers of the United States,' was amicably settled.[56]

The American Federation of Musicians says its first two Canadian locals were Vancouver 145 and Toronto 149, both chartered on 3 June 1901. But a Musicians Local 62 marched in the Montreal Labour Day parades of 1898 and 1899. Also, the *American Federationist* of December 1900 says the Ottawa musicians had just organized as part of an international union. If so, it must have been either an AFL federal labour union, or else the AFM must have turned down the application; for the AFM says Ottawa Local 180 was chartered 8 February 1902 (and the *American Federationist* of May 1902 records the formation of an Ottawa local). Winnipeg 190 was chartered 31 March 1902; Peterborough 191 on 11 April; Victoria 241 on 1 November. London 279 presents somewhat the same problem as Ottawa. The AFM says it was chartered 10 February 1903, but the *American Federationist* of May 1902 says London had applied for a charter, while the June issue says both Winnipeg and London have their charters, a statement which is repeated (for London) in July. The *Labour Gazette* of March 1902 lists also a Local 94, Nelson, British Columbia, formed in July 1901.[57]

Two unions of highly skilled workers appeared in 1901. Of the International Watch Case Engravers Union in Canada it may be said: 'Brief life was here its portion, brief sorrow, short-lived care.' On 24 January 1901, it appeared before the Toronto

Trades and Labor Council. A deputation stated the facts of a grievance between the American Watch Case Co and the union. A member had worked piece-work and overtime, in violation of the union's rules. He was evidently disciplined by the union for the company proceeded to discharge the union's shop representative, whereupon the union struck on 18 January. The international general secretary hastened to Toronto and asked the company for an interview. The management refused. He then suggested arbitration. The company refused that also. The international was then able to place all, or most, of the strikers in jobs in the United States, and the strike ended 1 February.[58]

The International Jewelry Workers Union, chartered by the AFL in 1900, came into Canada in June 1901. On 23 May the Toronto Trades and Labor Council's organization committee reported that it had organized the jewelry workers, with about 50 members, and that the union had applied for an international charter. Local 7, formed 6 June, was admitted to the Trades and Labor Council on 14 November; it was still there on 13 November 1902. A Hamilton local was formed in May 1902.[59]

The Toronto local had two strikes in 1902. On 14 and 16 April about 90 men employed by Saunders, Lowe & Co and T.W. Capp & Co struck against the discharge of the union's president and secretary. The international at once provided strike pay, and the strike ended 2 June with the 2 firms recognizing the union and reducing working hours from 55 to 52.

This evidently whetted the local's appetite, for in the early fall it served several firms with a demand for a 9-hour day and a 49-hour week. Some of the employers agreed; 2 balked, and about 70 men struck on 26 September. They went back on 20 October 'upon the understanding that grievances would be investigated.'[60]

In the spring of 1901 John Flett, AFL organizer, organized the first Canadian local of the Steam Engineers, in Berlin. A Toronto local, No 152, was in existence by 13 November 1902; and a Moose Jaw local of stationary engineers was reported in November 1902.[61]

A new Coopers International Union had been organized in 1890, and in the fall of 1901 it seems to have taken in the old Halifax Coopers. It may also have taken in the Toronto Coopers at the end of 1902.[62]

John Flett, in 1901, was 'directed by President Gompers to take charge of [a] lockout at the International paper Mills at Niagara Falls. After the union [the United Brotherhood of Papermakers] had been out three weeks, the company ... agreed to a reduction of thirteen hours per week without any reduction in the men's pay, a very substantial victory.' The Papermakers organized three locals in 1902, all in Quebec:

at the Hull and Windsor mills in November, and in Sherbrooke in December. They also organized a St Catharines local.[63]

Some time in 1901 the Brewery Workers chartered their first Canadian Local, Victoria 282. Seven more followed in 1902, all in Ontario.[64]

The Brotherhood of Steam Shovel and Dredge Engineers Cranemen of America may have had a Thorold local at the end of 1901.[65]

Another 14 international unions made their appearance in Canada in 1902, but this includes 2 which had got out of the Typos and set up for themselves: the Photo-Engravers (whose Montreal Local 9 dated from 1898), and the Stereotypers and Electrotypers (4 locals, dating from 1893, 1897, 1900, and 1901).[66] The Marble Workers International Union Local 12 of Toronto was organized 24 March 1902; and in May the Marble Cutters Union and the Marble Polishers Union decided to amalgamate. It was the combined union which struck on 2 June for a wage increase: polishers to 25 cents an hour (from 14 to 16½ cents), cutters to 30 cents (from 20 cents). It was out 2 weeks, and won the increases, and a 9-hour day. There was also a Marble Cutters Union, apparently international, in Montreal in the summer of 1902.[67]

The Railway Clerks organized Local 32, Saint John, in April and their locals 58 (Saint John) and 59 (Lévis) in December.[68]

The Amalgamated Leather Workers organized Kingston Local 41 on 16 April 1902, Woodstock 48 probably in August, and Berlin by September.[69]

The Sawsmiths International Union organized three locals in 1902: St Catharines in July, Galt in August or September, and Toronto (precise date unknown).[70]

The Amalgamated Glassworkers Association, Toronto Local 21 (stained-glass workers), was formed 16 May 1902.[71]

The International Brotherhood of Marine Engineers organized a Quebec City local in June 1902.[72]

The Special Order Clothing Workers had Toronto Local 21, in August.[73]

The Stationary Firemen, formed their Local 24, Vancouver, in September.[74]

The International Brick, Tile and Terra Cotta Workers Alliance, Local 19, and the International Ceramic, Mosaic and Caustic Tile Layers and Helpers, Local 37, were admitted to the Toronto Trades and Labor Council on 13 November.[75]

The Piano and Organ Workers seem to have come in towards the end of the year, and to have promptly organized, or taken over from the Woodworkers, four locals: Guelph 34, Toronto 39 and 41, and Berlin 43.[76]

Besides all these locals of particular international unions there were also, by the end of 1902, probably some 46 FLUs organized and chartered by the AFL itself.

Until 1896 there seems to have been no formal contact between the AFL and the TLCC. But in that year the congress felt obliged to complain to the AFL about the application of the American Alien Contract Labor Act to Canadian workers, and the ensuing correspondence led to an exchange of fraternal delegates in 1899 and a growing AFL interest in Canada.

In the fall of 1896 an eccentric merchant in Sault Ste Marie, P.J. Loughrin, wrote Samuel Gompers, AFL president, asking for an organizer's commission. Gompers, at first dubious, finally sent the commission, and by the New Year Loughrin was hard at work. He organized the first AFL Federal Labor Union (FLU) in Canada, Sault Ste Marie 6779, early in 1897; but by May he had been dismissed. He had fallen foul of Gompers by attacking the TLCC leaders, by agitating for an export duty on pulpwood when he should have been organizing, and by effectively preventing a Canadian tour by Gompers himself.[77]

In the spring of 1899, however, the AFL began an organizing drive in both the United States and Canada. Before the year was out, it had twelve volunteer organizers, from various affiliates: three in British Columbia, eight in Ontario, and one in Quebec. Among these organizers were Louis Gurofsky from the Garment Workers, John Flett from the Carpenters, George Bartley and C.S.O. Boudreault from the Typos, J.H. Kennedy from the Allied Metal Mechanics, and Ryan from the Stage Employees. But early in 1900 Gompers appointed Flett general organizer for Canada, with a salary and expense account; and from then on the AFL cut a large figure in Canada.

Flett and his helpers organized locals for 50 international unions. Of the 155 or so international union locals chartered in 1900, about 80 seem to have been started by AFL organizers; in 1901, about 74 of 170; in 1902, probably over 60 of 280 to 295. In the four years 1899–1902, the total comes close to 230. The increase in international union locals in the Maritime provinces was very largely Flett's work.

The AFL organizers helped these international locals with their negotiations and strikes. They also organized trades and labour councils.[78] But there were occupations and industries where no established international union existed. In these the AFL organizers set up AFL Federal Labor Unions (FLUs): sometimes for a single trade or industry, sometimes for general unskilled labour.

The first AFL FLU in Canada was followed by Montreal Furriers 7116 on 22 June 1898. Another 9 followed in 1899, 24 in 1900, 20 in 1901, and 30 in 1902. Some later became locals of international unions; some became TLCC FLUs; some died. Of the grand total of 86, 46 or 47 still existed at the end of 1902.[79]

At one time or another, down to the end of 1902, there seem to have been AFL FLUs in thirty-six places in Ontario, four in Quebec, five in British Columbia, two each in Nova Scotia and Prince Edward Island, and one each in New Brunswick and what is now Saskatchewan. The fifty-one places included Montreal (six FLUs),

Toronto (eight), Hamilton (two), London (two), Quebec City (two), Saint John (two), Halifax (one), Vancouver (three), St Catharines (four), Berlin (four), Guelph (three), and Brockville (three). There were FLUs also in a variety of smaller places, from Charlottetown (two), Summerside (one), and Truro (one) in the east to Nelson (two), Nanaimo (one), Revelstoke (one), and Field (one) in the west.

The occupations covered were many and diverse: plumbers and tinners, builders' labourers, ironworkers and helpers, boilermakers' helpers, wire drawers, gilders, rubber workers, furriers, car repairers, florists, cork workers, ice cutters and drivers, aerated water bottlers, tanners and curriers, coal handlers, milkmen, harvest and tool finishers, quarrymen, metal workers, shingle weavers and bunchers, fishermen, miners, retail clerks, hod carriers, suspender and neckwear workers, and carpenters.

Both in organizing miscellaneous occupations and small places the FLUs clearly filled, to some extent, the gap left by the decline of the Knights of Labor. But the FLUs were by no means always small or unimportant. Valleyfield 7387, one of the earliest, organized Montreal Cotton mill workers. In October 1900 some 200 labourers digging foundations for a new mill complained that, at $1 a day, they were not getting the prevailing rate in the district, which they said was $1.25. Their demand was refused. They struck on 22 October, picketed the plant, and prevented the delivery of coal and the operation of the company's dredge in the tail race. 'These acts [says the *Labour Gazette*] were the occasion of more serious happenings,' and the company got the mayor to requisition troops to protect the company's property. The mill workers, some 3000, objected and walked out on 26 October. The minister of labour, in the middle of a general election, sent his deputy minister, Mackenzie King, to help achieve a settlement.

King arrived on 29 October, when many of the mill workers had already gone back, and some had been dismissed. He met the striking mill workers that evening and arranged a final settlement. The troops were to be withdrawn; there were to be no further dismissals; and the company was to reconsider the case of any employee who felt he had been unjustly dismissed. Absolutely nothing was said about the excavating labourers; the company had already settled their hash by simply stopping the digging.

The *Labour Gazette*'s concluding words on the affair are vintage Mackenzie King:

It is evident that little more than a proper understanding between the two parties was necessary to effect the settlement, but for many reasons this could not have been done without the intervention of some disinterested third party, whose duty it was to promote conditions favourable to a settlement. As matters stood, the willingness of both parties to have an understanding arrived at made it possible for a termination of the difficulties to be speedily brought about ...

Many of the labourers obtained work from the municipality almost immediately after the commencement of their strike, others received employment elsewhere; and at the time the settlement was arrived at between the mill operatives and the company, but few of the labourers were still out of employment.

The company's 'willingness ... to have an understanding arrived at' had been expressed, for King, by its statement to him that 'there is no dispute between the company and their operatives. They are not working, but for what reason we do not know ... There is nothing to arbitrate or settle between the company or any of their employees. The company appreciate your kind offer.' As Ferns and Ostry observe: 'Just as Thomas Wolfe spent his life re-writing *Look Homeward Angel*, so Mackenzie King spent his years re-writing Valleyfield, elaborating, refining, embellishing and adapting [it] to new media, but always adhering to the basic pattern.'

Clearly FLU No 7387 was no match for the Montreal Cotton Co and King. St Catharines Laborers' Protective Union 9030 was more fortunate: in August 1901 it was able to report that, partly thanks to its exertions, the street labourers had got a wage increase and a 9-hour day, and the teamsters a rate of $3.50 for a 9-hour day.[80]

Peterborough 9240 (Laborers) organized in the summer of 1901, reported in January 1902 a membership of three to four hundred. Peterborough had been 'one of the worst towns in Ontario from a union standpoint,' but things were now looking up. Unionism had 'taken a-hold of some of the ministers of the Gospel there, and one has joined the union and is taking a lively part in its work.'

Lindsay's FLU 9826, chartered 26 April 1902, had by July a membership of 300. In August it reported a strike of 60 members against the holding back of a percentage of wages till the end of the season. By January 1903 it was able to say it had won 2 strikes, and that in some other firms it had got wages up by 10 to 25 cents a day without any strike.[81]

Kingston 8412 (ironworkers and helpers) struck the Canada Locomotive Works on 16 May 1901. It had demanded recognition of the union, a wage increase for the 143 men involved, and the reinstatement of a discharged employee. Flett came in to help, and after 5 days the company signed an agreement, fixing the minimum rate for common labour (69 of the strikers) at $1.25 a day, and giving an increase of 15 cents a day to 2 of the more skilled men, 10 cents to another fifteen, and 5 cents to the remaining 57. The union also got a grievance procedure of sorts, and an undertaking by the company not to discriminate against any union member who had taken part in the strike. The union undertook not to make any further demands for a year, and acknowledged the company's right to 'retain in its service no [labourer] who was not willing to earn' the $1.25 a day, and its further right to 'discharge inefficient men at its discretion.' The highest rate under the agreement was to be $1.65.[82]

St Thomas 8329 apparently took in both city corporation labourers and labourers in the Michigan Central Railway shops and coal and lumber yards. In December 1900 Flett reported it had over a hundred members and was flourishing. In April 1901, with the Trades and Labor Council, it asked the city to raise the wages of its labourers from 12½ cents an hour to 15, and in May the city council agreed. In May 1901 also the union asked the Michigan Central to raise the wages of unskilled men from 12 cents an hour to 15, with 16 to 24 cents for various more skilled classes, and time-and-a-half for overtime. The company refused. The union had by this time grown to about 300 members, having doubled its membership in the single month between April and May. In August 1902 the union was presenting demands to the company, but nothing seems to have come of this.[83]

By the end of 1902 there must have been 748 to 766 Canadian locals of international unions affiliated with the AFL, and another 46 or so AFL FLUs. The major thrust of the organizing effort was coming from the AFL and its affiliated unions. So it is hardly surprising that at the September convention of the Trades and Labor Congress, the AFL unions were in a position to throw out rival organizations and to weld the mass of Canadian unionism firmly into the AFL international system.

PART THREE

Local, regional, and national unions, 1880–1902

Local unions in the Maritimes
and Quebec 1881–1902

The Knights of Labor and the international trade unions together dominated the Canadian labour movement in the last two decades of the nineteenth century. But plenty of purely local unions continued to exist, though towards the end they were often suffering a sea change into locals of international unions; there was also the powerful Provincial Workmen's Association, in Nova Scotia; and, though many of the attempts to establish national unions fizzled out, some did not.

Local and regional unionism was especially important in the Maritime provinces, where the Knights never made much impression and international unions comparatively little until almost the end of the period.

HALIFAX

The Halifax Shipwrights and Caulkers broke into two unions in 1884, though with the curious provision that members of eight might also belong to the other. By 1888 the Shipwrights had about 40 members, the Caulkers about 50. They seem to have marched as two unions in the Labour Day parades of 1890 and 1891; as one in 1892. They appear as one union in 1893, 1901, and 1902.[1]

The House-Joiners must have disappeared in the 1870s, for on 3 June 1881, the journeymen house-joiners of Halifax unanimously resolved to form the House Joiners Union of Halifax. Within a month, they 'respectfully asked for a ten per cent increase of the present rate of wages from July 1st next, which was readily granted.'

By March 1882 the union was going strong. Its regular monthly meeting was 'one of the largest and most enthusiastic meetings ever held in the city.' One of the members, 'with spirit and energy delivered an address on the progress of the organization and the state of the trade in general. [He] called ... attention ... to the high rate of taxation and the rate of living at present in Halifax, and the low rate of wages the joiners are receiving ... to meet so extortionate a demand. He also referred to the general increase of wages throughout the Upper Provinces, also to the great field for immigration to the Northwest Territory and the United States and finally concluded that unless the employers of the city of Halifax would further the interest of their journeymen ... they would have to leave their native province and seek a home on foreign soil. He also trusted that another month would swell the ranks of the organization with ... every carpenter and joiner in ... Halifax and Dartmouth.' The meeting unanimously resolved to demand an average wage of 18 cents an hour from 1 May, 'deeming this to be proportionately low in comparison with domains within the United Kingdom.'

The implication that 'the Upper Provinces' and 'the Northwest Territory' were foreign soil is interesting. So is the comparison with the United Kingdom.

The employers, notified through the public press, apparently paid no attention to the resolution of 6 March. For on 25 April the union met again, and unanimously resolved on a 10 per cent wage increase from 8 May. The employees signed the notification. They apparently did not fear victimization.[2]

This demand must have been granted. For in September 1882 the Carpenters' delegate to the Amalgamated Trades Union (the Halifax central labour body) reported that before the formation of the union wages had been varied and low, with few skilled carpenters receiving over $1.50 a day; but that 'at present ... after somewhat of a struggle ... we are receiving nearly 25 per cent more than in the spring of 1881.' This success must have been transitory. On 5 March 1883 John Saxon, recording secretary of the union, wrote that the rate of wages in Halifax was $1.40 to $1.65 a day. He added a series of rates for various other areas: Canada West, $1.75 to $2.50; Cleveland, $2.25 to $2.75; New Orleans, $2.25 to $2.50; New Mexico, $3 to $3.50; New Jersey, $2 to $2.25; Boston, $2 to $2.50; Chicago, $2.75 to $3; Yarmouth, Nova Scotia, $1.50 to $1.75. These figures had come from the secretaries of carpenters' unions throughout the United States and Canada. (Yarmouth evidently had a union.) These reports showed Halifax 'far behind the majority of large cities in America in this, to us, all important matter.'

Next day, the union's regular monthly meeting took place: 'one of the most interesting since the formation of that body, their neatly furnished meeting room [in the Mechanics' Hall] being crowded.' Several new members were initiated, and Saxon held forth against letting the mills use their own employees to construct and finish work. From 7 March, the union insisted, work in sash, door, and planing mills would be subject to the order of the builder, and Carpenters Union members would not work on other jobs. Halifax wages, Saxon said, had been shown to be below those in the upper provinces and in the United States, and the union was asking for a 20 per cent increase.

By 27 May 1884 the Carpenters were again demanding an increase, and waiting only till 31 May to see whether the employers would grant it. If not, they were resolved to strike on 2 June with the support of the other trade unions in the city. They were probably in a position to do so fairly effectively. For, a year before, 'only 75 out of 300 carpenters in the city remained out of the union.' The other trade unions comprised two international unions, the Typos, and the BLE, and at least eight purely local unions: Shipwrights and Caulkers, Painters, Labourers, Bakers, Masons and Bricklayers, Freestone-Cutters, Plasterers, and Truckmen. Moreover, in the spring of 1883 only 10 masons, and no painters at all had remained outside the unions of those trades.[3]

The Halifax Carpenters secured an international charter on 23 January 1885.[4]

The Typos who had fallen out of the international in 1879, carried on as a purely local body till they rejoined the ITU in 1883.[5]

The *Labour Gazette* suggests that the Coopers had a continuous existence from July 1870. But there is no sign of them in the 1888–89 Labour Day parades. They turn up in all the parades of the 1890s. In May and October 1895 they were appealing to the Typos for aid in a strike. They got $25.[6] The Coopers became a local of the international in 1901.[7]

Five or six local unions seem to have been organized in 1882.

A painters' association was certainly in existence by 8 April. By 8 January 1883 it was described as 'in a flourishing condition.' On 14 April 1884 nine Journeymen struck to enforce the rule of not more than three apprentices to an establishment.[8] A witness before the Royal Commission on Capital and Labor in 1888 said the Painters had had a strike 5 or 6 years earlier to get a uniform wage of $10 a week. This had meant bringing some men up from $8 and others down from $12. There had been no trouble since.[9] The levelling down of the $12 men is something as rare in trade union history as the Shipwrights and the Caulkers toleration of double-headers.

In August 1885 there was a strike over the apprentice question. The 1884 strike had apparently been settled on the basis of allowing each shop three apprentices and two shop or errand boys. Two employers had violated the settlement, so their men struck.[10] From September 1891 till March 1892 the Painters were again on strike. In September and October the Typos contributed $80 to help them.[11] The Painters appeared in the 1888–99 Labour Day parades; in 1901 they became part of the international union.[12]

The Ship Labourers Union Society was certainly in existence on 8 April 1882, but may have been absorbed by the Labourers Association (ship and other labourers) formed 13 April. Both 'Labourers' and 'Ship Labourers' paraded in 1888.[13]

One of the first acts of the Labourers Association was to pass a resolution prohibiting any sectarian or political discussion. Any officer who violated this rule would automatically be removed. The union also 'agreed to an uniform tariff in regard to coal shovelling, pledging the members to employ only each other in contracts of this nature.' At the end of three months, the union's financial secretary reported 325 members, receipts of $213.38, expenditures of $75.29, a balance on hand of $138.09, and badges on hand worth $21.52, making the total assets $159.61.

On 20 August the Longshore Labourers Association paraded through the streets, headed by the St Patrick's Band and a drum and fife corps, and then embarked for McNab's Island to enjoy their first annual picnic: 'The best of order and good nature prevailed.'[14]

By January 1883 the membership had dropped to 315, but by April it was up to 518. During the year the union had paid out $80 in funeral benefits, and $130 to members who were in need of assistance. By 30 April balance on hand was $394.66.[15]

Early in May 1884 the Labourers notified the 'Merchants, Stevedores and other employers of transient labour' in Halifax that from 12 May the rates to be paid to labourers would be: 'Store work. Labour per day, $1.50; per half-day, 75 cents. Work required after 6 o'clock p.m. to be 25 cents per hour. To be no quarter or three-quarter days, as formerly, and Sunday work to be 50 cents per hour. Stevedore work. Work on sailing vessels, per day, $2.00; half-day, $1.00. To be no quarter and three-quarter days, as formerly. Work on steamships, barges and tugboats to be by the hour and at the rate of 25 cents. All Sunday work to be 50 cents per hour.' The union also stipulated that its members would not work with non-unionists, and that 'where private labour is employed it will have to be dispensed with.'

These demands irked the employers, and a brief strike took place. Every member got a badge with the letters 'L.U.' and his number on the union books. Over 150 new members were enrolled, and by the middle of the month the strike was over. There was a brief flurry on 16 May when the *Caspian* arrived, because union members refused to work with non-unionists, but the non-unionists joined the union. Altogether about 200 men were employed discharging the steamers and loading the cars, at 25 cents an hour. 'It is considered that there are very few non-union men in the city now.'[16]

The Labourers took part in the 1888–99 Labour Day parades.[17]

By the summer of 1900 there were two societies of ship labourers. One or both had struck in July, unsuccessfully it would seem, for the *Labour Gazette* says the September rate was 33 cents on sailing vessels and 40 cents on steamers, while the old rate had been $3 per day of 9 hours on the former, and $4 per day on the latter.[18]

The Journeymen Bakers' Society was reorganized on 22 April 1882. By August 1884 it was invoking the aid of the Amalgamated Trades Union (ATU) against Moir, Son and Co. The Bakers' letter to the ATU said: 'Some sixteen years ago the journeymen bakers, by combined action, succeeded in changing the work-commencing hour from two o'clock a.m. to four a.m. This hour remains the hour in all soft bread shops in the city except Moir's, who compel their men to go to work at half-past two a.m., and keep them at work just as long as they please, not infrequently until eleven o'clock at night, and always until long after the men in other shops are away from their work. All this for one day's pay and small pay at that ... The system conducted by the Messrs. Moir [is] degrading to honest labour, destroying the independence of the working man and gradually but surely sapping the foundations of legitimate trade.' The ATU appointed a committee, which waited on Moir. He 'declined to be dictated to by anyone.'

The Bakers then instituted a boycott, which apparently was less than successful, for on 13 November the ATU called a meeting of workingmen to strengthen the Bakers' hand. There was a large attendance. John Saxton, of the Carpenters, president of the ATU, was in the chair. He thought the questions to be considered were: 'Are we workingmen or slaves? and Do we govern ourselves or not?'

Lewis Archibald, President of the Bakers' Society, explained that the late 'boycotting' had originated with that society, and was the result of the fruitless negotiations which the society had attempted to conduct for the purpose of making the rate of wages and hours of bread in the soft bread bakeries uniform all over the city ... He appealed to the audience to enforce the boycott on Messrs Moir and all the shops supplied by them.

Peter Martin, president of the Painters' Society, narrated the story of the painters' strike, and closed by asking why Mr Moir did not deny that he worked his men eighteen hours a day.

Mr Drummond (Editor of the *Trades Journal*, Stellarton) spoke for some time on the general principles of labor, and did not think that any man had a right to work his men eighteen hours a day. He might have a legal right to get all he could out of them, but he had no moral right. He considered if there was no other way to remedy this evil the workingmen's unions had a right to get legislation on the subject.[19]

The Bakers took part in the 1888 Labour Day parade.[20] They must have joined the Knights of Labor soon after. By the end of 1889 they had become a local of the American National Union.

The Barbers met on 19 May 1882 to form a union, and planned another meeting when the organization was completed.[21]

The Masons and Bricklayers were already organized by 6 June 1882 and trying to get a wage increase. Their rate was 15 cents an hour, and, as they averaged not more than 6 months' work a year, their average daily pay over the whole year was reckoned to be about 83 cents. By the beginning of May 1883 they had got the hourly rate up to 25 cents for a 10-hour day, and were considering asking for 30 cents. They decided not to ask for an increase, but to enforce the 25 cent rate by fining members who worked for less. The question of an increase was to be brought forward again in June; but the rate seems to have stayed at 25 cents till 1887, when some employers granted a 5 cent increase.[22]

In August 1883 this union got into a curious wrangle with a prominent local contractor, one Brookfield, who had imported workers from England. When the union protested, Brookfield replied that in 1882 wages had been increased from $2 to $2.50 a day; that much of the money had been spent on liquor; that he had dismissed a boy who had carried liquor to men on the job; that 8 men had quit work, ostensibly in protest, though really because they wanted to go to Moncton for higher wages; that he had then put the boy to work elsewhere; that some of the men had come back; that this year the union had demanded $3; that all the contractors had refused; that his men had then accepted $2.50, till an employer came from Moncton offering more, whereupon they had left; and that since no local workers were then available he had got in Englishmen. The union replied at length, contradicting some of Brookfield's statements, and accusing him of having organized a secret society of employers to resist the union's demand for $3 a day. Brookfield denied having organized the society: several of his fellow-employers had asked him to call a meeting of the Builders' Association. A number of the contractors had met, and seven of them wrote the union asking it to reconsider. Brookfield and the union disagreed on the relative competence of Halifax and English workmen, and Brookfield suggested a competition on the job for $100 or more a side. The union accepted the challenge, and double the amount was subscribed, but when the union wanted to have the stakes placed at the disposal of the winner, Brookfield jibbed, and the match was off.[23]

On 16 January 1888 the Masons and Bricklayers Union became a local of the BMIU, and, in accordance with that body's rules, asked for 30 cents an hour and a 9-hour day, and got them.[24]

The next union, the Freestone-Cutters, formed in July 1882, is listed in the 1901 *Labour Gazette*. A branch of the Journeymen Stonecutters of North America took part in the 1888 Labour Day parade. A Stonecutters Union was certainly active in August 1896 and again in November 1902. A Stonecutters Union took part in the 1899–1902 Labour Day parades.[25]

A Plasterers Union was in process of formation at the end of March 1883. By May 15 it was a going concern. It took part in the 1888–92 parades.[26]

There was a functioning Truckmen's Union in March 1884, and a Truckmen's Union marched in the 1891–1902 parades.[27]

The Coal Handlers (later ILA Local 274) are said to have been organized on 7 May 1887.[28]

The Licensed Trackmen's Union of Nova Scotia (freight handlers), organized in August 1889, figures in the *Labour Gazette*'s January 1902 list of labour organizations.[29]

The Halifax Boot and Shoe Workers Union is reported to have been organized in January 1889; Boot and Shoe Workers paraded in 1890, and a Boot and Shoe Workers Union in 1899 and 1901. This union was also listed in the December 1901 *Labour Gazette*.[30]

A Carriage Builders Union marched in 1889, about 50 strong; so did a Cabinet Makers and Upholsterers Union, some 100 strong.[31] Next year the Masons' Labourers marched, and in 1891 they were joined by the newsboys: neither is described as a union.[32]

A Woodworkers Union marched in the 1890 parade. So did a recently formed Metal Workers Union.[33]

The Metal Workers Union had lost no time in getting to work. On 19 May it asked the employers of Halifax and Dartmouth to grant a nine-hour day 'as is now granted to the other unions of the city,' to come into effect 1 June. A meeting of 200 on 30 May was informed that 30 employers had agreed to the demands.[34] The Metal Workers marched in the 1890–99 parades.[35]

A Pressmen's Association took part in the 1891–92 parades.[36]

A Builders' Labourers Union marched in 1891, a Masons' Labourers Union in 1892, and a Builders' Labourers Union in 1893; probably all the same union.[37]

The Journeymen Plumbers Union was organized, 23 March 1899. It marched in the parades of 1899, 1901, and 1902.[38]

The reports of the parades usually give an estimate of the number of marchers from each union. The Shipwrights and Caulkers turned out about 100 strong in 1889, but from then on varied from 20 to 68. The Painters ranged from 40 to 90, with an average of about 60. The Labourers started off with about 350. They fell as low as 100 in 1893, but averaged around 200. The Plasterers started in 1889 with 65, and by 1892 were down to 35; they averaged about 40. The Truckmen kept pretty steady from 100 to 150. The Coopers ranged from 20 to 50. The Metal Workers Union, which expected to have 200 members in the 1890 parade, had 175 in 1891, and in the period 1892–99 ranged from 50 to 150, with an average of about 110. The Carriage Builders, in their one appearance, had about 50, and the Cabinet Makers and Upholsterers about 100. The Builders' Labourers ranged from 24 to 90, with an average of around 70. The Plumbers in 1899 had 40. The Boot and Shoe Workers had 60 in 1899 and 25 in 1901.

It is interesting to compare the figures for international unions. The Typos varied from 40 to 70, an average of about 55, the Carpenters from 80 to 300, with an average of about 175; their best year was 1890, over 300, and their worst probably 1899, about 80 to 115. The Bakers started at 50 in 1889; rose to 60 in 1890; fell to 30 in 1892; and to 18 in 1893. The Bricklayers and Masons started at 75 in 1889; dropped to 30 by 1893; got back to 60 in 1895; may have touched 80 in 1899; and were back to 60 in 1901. They averaged about 60. The Stonecutters paraded 35 strong in 1889, 26 in 1890, and about 15 in 1899. The Boilermakers in 1901 turned out 70 of their 75 members.[39] All these figures should probably be taken with a grain of salt, for in 1899 the two Halifax newspapers, the *Chronicle* and the *Herald*, differed sharply on the numbers.

ELSEWHERE IN NOVA SCOTIA

As already noted, there seems to have been a Carpenters Union in Yarmouth in 1883. On 4 July 1896 the Halifax Typos received a Pictou man with an expired travelling card, and on 3 July 1897 a travelling card from Yarmouth;[40] so there may have been a Printers Union in both places.

In the first few months of 1887 a 'tight little union' at Trenton was making contributions to the strike fund of the Pictou County lodges of the PWA.[41]

At the beginning of 1889 the Mechanics and Engineers Association at the Drummond Colliery, Westville, was on strike against an attempt by the management to introduce the 12-hour day, instead of the 10 usually worked. The 'little, young, Association' was out for two days and won. At the end of May it struck again. Most of the men had been out of work for three months; then a vacancy occurred, and was given to a non-union man. The miners went out in sympathy, and by 5 June the strike was settled, apparently on the Association's terms. By 29 September 1897 the PWA Grand Council was noting the failure of the men at the Trenton steel works 'to stand by the union they had formed.'[42]

A Barbers Union was formed in Pictou County in March 1901.[43]

SAINT JOHN

In 1881 Saint John probably had local unions of carpenters, painters, bakers, tailors, ship carpenters (or shipwrights), sailmakers, cabinet-makers, caulkers, boilermakers, and ship labourers. All of these had existed before 1880, and all were on hand at the time of the 1883 procession celebrating the coming of the Loyalists.[44] The Riggers Union also was probably still in existence.[45]

By 30 September 1882 a Cartmen's Protective Society was functioning.[46]

In the procession of 2 October 1883 the following purely local unions marched: Cartmen, Tailors, Painters, Tinsmiths, Bakers, Masons and Plasterers (organized in 1883), Cabinet-Makers, Ship Labourers, and Carpenters. The procession also included cotton spinners, plumbers, brass finishers, safemakers, and blockmakers, who may or may not have been organized. The Ship Carpenters refused to take part. The Sailmakers and Caulkers Unions were certainly in existence, but did not march. There seem also to have been organizations of moulders and boilermakers. This would make a total of 14 local unions. The newspapers in the summer and fall of

1883 mention also blank-book binders, carriage workers, furniture workers, black-smiths, car builders, bolt and nut makers, nailmakers, edge-tool makers, machinists, millmen, confectioners and upholsterers, but it is impossible to tell whether these trades were organized or not.[47]

On 9 August 1887, the Saint John City and County Barbers met and elected officers.[48]

A Stonecutters Union was in existence in March 1888, and was reported as having had no trouble for the past two or three years. A Raftsmen's Association had existed some years before, and had got the price of work raised from $1.40 to $2 a day without a strike; but this body had now disappeared. There was also in March 1888, a scowmen's organization, to which, however, the employer reported that only a few belonged. Another witness before the 1888 Royal Commission on Capital and Labor said that the Masons and Builders Union had had trouble two or three years before.[49]

There was another trades procession on 22 July 1889, to celebrate the union of Saint John and Portland, but only the Cartmen, Painters, and Tailors turned out. The Ship Labourers refused; the Tinsmiths at first said they would, then reversed their decision.[50]

A Plumbers Union was organized on 3 April 1890, the tinsmiths were apparently reorganized on 16 April, and the millmen formed a union on 29 May.[51]

The Ship Labourers seem to have split in two in 1890 along denominational lines.[52] The local Carpenters Union had either gone into the United Brotherhood or been superseded by it on 18 April 1881.[53]

A short-lived labour paper, the *Workman*, gives a list of Saint John unions on 26 November 1892. Besides the four international unions (Typos, Bricklayers, Carpenters, and Molders), there were the Shipwrights, Painters, Millmen, Ship Labourers (only one of the two unions was apparently recognized by the movement generally), Tinsmiths, Cartmen, Stonecutters, and Ship Carpenters; a total of nine local organizations.

In the Labour Day parade of 1894, four international unions (Typos, Molders, Bricklayers and Masons, and Carpenters) all marched, along with the Cartmen, Tailors, Carriage Workers, Millmen, and the Ship Labourers Union.

The 1895 procession was a meagre affair. The Molders' Local 277 had been suspended in June, but a local Molders Union marched. So did the Cartmen, as well as the two remaining international unions, the Typos and the Bricklayers.[54] The two Ship Labourers' organizations were, of course, still in existence; so were the Caulkers, and perhaps the Shipwrights and the Sailmakers.[55] At the end of January the stenographers had met and decided to form a union.[56] By September 1900 the only organized trades in Saint John were the Typos, the Bricklayers, the Caulkers, and the two ship labourers' organizations; but an Association of Shoe Clerks was formed in January 1901.[57] By November 1901 the old association of Ship Labourers had gone into the ILA.[58] By 1902 Saint John once more had enough unions to muster a parade of a dozen; but only two or three of them, the surviving local Ship Labourers and the Masons and Plasterers Protective Union, and perhaps the Woodworkers, seem to have been purely local bodies.[59]

By the spring of 1882 the Ship Labourers Union had evidently recovered from the disaster of 1875, for on 5 June it decided to increase the Labour rate on sailing vessels from $2.50 to $3 per day from 6 June. The employers agreed. The rates on steamers were now 50 cents an hour for 9 hours and $1 per hour for overtime.

This easy victory evidently hotted the union up; for in November it was once more in battle array. It forced 1 employer to pay a 50 per cent increase for unloading a steamer. He retaliated by giving the job of reloading to a boss stevedore whose employees were supposed to be non-union but turned out not to be. They struck, apparently without success.

A further strike in April 1883 evidently failed, for on 17 March 1886 the union had been 'practically reorganized,' after being dormant for some months past. It first set out to reinstitute the $5 and $3 rates. A strike for this purpose failed, perhaps partly because in March the scowmen had left the Ship Labourers Union to form their own union, which seems to have lasted till 1888.

By January 1887 the Labourers must have recovered a good deal of their old power, for a board of trade committee taking evidence on the labour question heard detailed lamentations on the subject. First, a letter from Scammell Bros:

The rules and regulations of the laborers' Association ... are to say the least arbitrary – especially the cessation of work on all ships to rectify a supposed grievance, is an outrage. The preventing steamers from using their steam winches loading and the high rate of wages charged this class of vessels, is something that should be remedied; also the arbitrary claim that they should appoint any certain number of men to do the work – instead of permitting the man who pays the hire to select those he chooses, and sundry other rules that are obnoxious.

Two days later, one from R.A. and J. Stewart:

Now supposing you are questioned by the capitalist, seeking to establish a steamship line from here, as to what wages he will have to pay in loading his steamers ... you have to tell him that during the busiest portion of the season he can have nothing to say as to the wages he must pay ... in the selection of the men ... or in the number of hours per day his men shall work. This is all arranged ... by the Ship Laborers' Union. And supposing that some vessel in which he is not interested at all dares to act contrary to the regulation of the union, or the commands of its secretary not acceded to, his vessel, in addition to every other vessel in the harbor, has to stop working immediately until this little difference is satisfactorily arranged, his steamer lying idle in the mean time under an expense of from £15 to £20 per day. Upon resuming work, he may very likely be informed the union has directed its members to have $5 per day of nine hours, and if asked to work longer than five o'clock in the evening, $1 per hour. But when you have to admit that such labor-saving machinery as steam winches are not to be thought of for a moment, you cap the climax, and cause him to ask, is St. John going back to the dark ages?

In March the union cut its daily rate to $2, but stuck to its rule that 2 or 3 hours' work must count as a quarter of a day. This, of course, helped men who had to work broken time, which was common; but the employers naturally disliked it, and seized the opportunity to try to introduce payment by the hour. The union struck, and after a few days won a compromise daily rate.

Almost at once, however, the Labourers were out again, demanding their old $5 rate. According to an employer witness before the Royal Commission on Capital and Labor, the men had gone on to one steamer 'by hundreds ... terrorizing our men.' The union had 420 men on its roll, but in the trouble its members and supporters had 'congregated by hundreds, perhaps 600 or 750 on the wharf, watching and talking,' to prevent a vessel from being loaded by outsiders. This was a form of intimidation in the face of which strikers were afraid to come back to work, and there should be a law 'to prevent the men massing together in such large numbers.'

The union quickly got a written agreement, its first, with one of two principal steamer agents, and then with a second. This provided for a closed shop, and rates of $3 a day from 1 April to 1 October 1887 and $2 from 1 October 1887 to 1 April 1888. This was well short of the $5 demanded; and the union had to give up its established rights to select the gangs for each job, to limit the use of the ships' own men in loading or unloading cargoes, and to forbid the use of steam winches. In return, it got maintenance of the system of paying wages by the day. The rest of the agents soon signed up, though for sailing vessels the union had to cut the summer wage to $2.50.

Rice comments: 'The contractual approach to negotiations with employers resulted in two highly important advances. First, the agreement gave formal recognition to the existence of the Ship Laborers' Union. Second ... a practical and forceful basis for the continued status of the Union was ensured ... The wage guarantee obviated the need for the constant struggle on the part of the Union to extract the highest rate possible during periods of peak harbour activity. At the same time, it reduced the temptation of agents to take advantage of a labour surplus situation to force wages below reasonable levels. Previously, the existence of the Union was often in jeopardy. Now, the Union no longer had to fight for its life several times a year.'

In 1888, the agreement was renewed for another year, with a $3.60 rate on steamers the year round, but no increase for sailing vessels. The differential between steamers and sailing vessels widened further in 1889. The palmiest days of the unions, and of Saint John itself, were over. None the less, in Rice's words, the organization 'was still generally able to provide safer and more remunerative work for its membership than that of longshoremen in any of the competing ports in Canada and along the north-eastern seaboard of the United States.'

In the spring of 1896 the union was on strike again, and appealing to the Montreal Central Trades and Labor Council to take steps to prevent the employers bringing in strikebreakers from Montreal. Within a week of the first appeal the council was able to report that victory had been won.[60]

The Cartmen, in the fall of 1882, heard a formal appeal to support the work of the Society for the Prevention of Cruelty to Animals, notably the provision of drinking fountains for horses. The union had then about 100 members.[61]

The Masons and Plasterers, in 1886 and 1887, struck for a wage increase of 50 cents a day, and got it, bringing their rate to $2. They struck again to secure the discharge of four apprentices. The employer refused, but sent two away. In 1889 they got the nine-hour day.[62] This had the incidental effect of stirring up the Carpenters, who were irked to see the Masons and Plasterers knocking off work a solid hour ahead of them. In March 1890 they threatened to strike on 1 April unless they also got the nine-hour day. At the eleventh hour, the employers, by a vote of 27 to 7, gave in.

This was the signal for almost every occupation in the city to follow suit: ship carpenters, plumbers, tinsmiths, street labourers, boilermakers, quarrymen, iron moulders, brass moulders, carriage workers, gas house workers, cabinet-makers and upholsterers, brushmakers, and millmen. Some got the nine-hour day, some did not. The Common Council referred the question to the board of works, where it slumbered for 13 years. McAvity's, the brass founders, offered its striking moulders the choice of the nine-hour day or a Saturday half-holiday, and they took the half-holiday. This was a blow to the nine-hour movement, as McAvity's was one of the large employers. The newly organized Tinsmiths stuck to the nine-hour demand. Some of the iron moulders got the nine-hour day in the spring of 1890, but either some did not, or those who had lost it; for in April 1892 Local 277 struck to get it. The Millmen must have got it, and then have been faced with an attempt to take it away from them, for in July 1891 they struck to keep it.[63]

We have fragmentary information on the size of some of the unions. The Ship Labourers Union in 1883 mustered for the Labour Day parade about half its strength of 800 or more; in 1894 it was down to 300 or more. The Cartmen, in 1883, were variously estimated at 40, 50, and 150; and at 94 in 1894. The Tinsmiths had 55 in the 1883 parade; the Tailors 90, the Painters 60, the Bakers 30 (they had expected 100), the Masons and Plasterers 60. The Carpenters expected 100. In 1894 the Tailors had 65, the Carriage Workers 30.[64] There were two international unions in the 1883 parade. The Typos had exactly 66 members; the Crispins, about 10 days before, expected to have about 200.[65]

In 1902, when practically all the marchers were international, the Teamsters mustered about 140, the Bricklayers about 40, the Carpenters about 54, the Painters about 50, the Cigar Makers about 15, the Ship Labourers about 400, the Molders about 40, the Freight Handlers (ILA 276) some 60 to 70, the Shingle Weavers and Bunchers (AFL) over 40.[66]

ELSEWHERE IN NEW BRUNSWICK

A ship labourers' association was formed at Chatham some time before 16 May 1882, when it set a rate of $2 a day for loading or discharging vessels. The ship labourers struck on 16 May 1901, for an increase of 25 cents a day, but went back next day at the old rate.[67]

There was a Granite Cutters Union in St George in the summer of 1902; it struck 1 June 1902 for a 9-hour day and 10 hours' pay, and won after 15 days.[68]

ST JOHN'S

The Seal Skinners Union survived throughout the period. It won one strike and lost another in 1901 on the use of machinery.

The Shipwrights also survived throughout the period.

The printers appear to have organized a union in 1883 which appears to have survived throughout the period. The *Evening Herald* locked the union out in 1895 to enforce a 50 per cent wage cut (the union was prepared to take an IOU for 40 per cent). The *Herald* won.

The moulders had formed a union by July 1886 which lasted well into the twentieth century.

The retail clerks formed their third union, the United Assistants Association, in March 1892. Within six weeks this union had agreements with most of the St John's mercantile houses. It won a closing hour of 6 pm till 15 October and 9:30 pm till the end of the year. By February 1892 the union had 189 members.

The drapers may have formed a union in 1891.

The coopers formed their union in September 1891. By the end of the year it had 240 members and had won a wage rate of $1.50 per day, with 10 per cent overtime. In 1895 the Coopers sued several of the employers for payment in cash instead of truck, and won; but the employers retaliated by replacing as many coopers as possible by handymen, to whom the court's decision did not apply. In 1897 the union got incorporated and persuaded the employers to adopt the union label. Early in 1900 the Coopers struck twice against the introduction of machinery; they finally had to accept the machinery and content themselves with insisting on a union shop.

1896 was a banner year for organization: the Bricklayers, Masons and Plasterers in January; the Sailmakers and the Tinsmiths (including plumbers) in September; the Boilermakers and the Tanners in October; and the Blacksmiths, the Tailors, and perhaps the Cabmen at various dates in the year. The Bricklayers Union was gone by 1901. The Sailmakers Union lasted not quite 14 years, the Tinsmiths 6. The plumbers formed their own union about the middle of 1902. The Boilermakers struck against employment of non-unionists in May 1902. The strike seems to have been lost and the union disbanded. The Tanners lasted till at least October 1900. The Blacksmiths lasted till at least May 1897; a new union was reported in the making in 1903. The Tailors lasted two years. The cabmen formed a new union in September 1898.

The Boot and Shoe Factory Employees Union may have been formed in January 1897; in May 1900 there is word of a new union forming. The bakers also organized in 1897; but 1904 they were forming a new union. The truckmen formed their union in September 1898 (there may have been a union in 1896). The wheelwrights had a union by 1898; it was gone by April 1901. The stenographers formed a union in 1898.[69]

QUEBEC CITY

Quebec City was a stronghold of local unionism. In 1881 it had the five branches of the Ship Labourers, the Bargemen, and the Plumbers and Tinsmiths Union. The Ship Labourers lasted throughout the period, the Plumbers and Tinsmiths till after 1900 at least. The Bargemen may have disappeared in 1884, but a union of the same name appears in 1893 and 1895. The Bakers appeared in 1882, 1886, 1893, and 1895. In 1885 we find the Shoe Lasters (still there after 1900), Bricklayers and Masons (also still there after 1900), Carters (who appeared also in 1891; new union in 1901). In 1886 unions of carpenters, leather cutters (which lasted till after 1900), tawers (1893, 1895, 1898), shoemakers (1893, 1895), butchers (which lasted till 1895), painters (which lasted till 1898), and merchants' clerks (1893, 1895, 1896, 1898) and a Société de bienfaisance des ouvriers all made their appearance. In 1888 there is a Barbers Union (1891, 1893, 1895); in 1890, Stone Cutters (till after 1900); in 1891, Woodworkers (which went international in 1893 and may have gone local again by 1895), Tanners and Curriers, and Machine Shoemakers (both lasting till after 1900). In 1893 we have unions of tailors and moulders (1893, 1895, 1900); in 1893 of labourers (perhaps the same union which lasted till after 1900), horse-shoers, roofers, coopers, and compagnons-boulangers. In 1894 there is a union of grocery clerks (again in 1895); in 1895 a Union commerciale (also in 1898). In 1898 we find the Stadacona Labourers and a Machinists Union; in 1899 the Lévis Molders (international in 1900); in 1900 a Union secourable of shoemakers; in 1901 a Brotherhood of Labourers; in 1902 a new Longshoremen's Union.[70]

Even at the end of the period the local, regional, and national unions far outnumbered the internationals. There were also the Knights of Labor LAs. It is not surprising that the expulsion from the TLCC in 1902 of all rivals to AFL organizations killed the Quebec Trades and Labor Council and, for a time, pretty well knocked the stuffing out of the labour movement in the city and district.

The accounts of the Labour Day parades give numbers for the various organizations. In 1891 the Painters expected to have 300. In 1899 the Labourers had 450. In 1900 9 LAS had 1280; the Shoemakers of the Dominion of Canada 1800; a regional Shoemakers Union 20; and a regional Barbers Union 3. Four international locals had 154 (Typos 35, Molders 30, Woodworkers 44, Electrical Workers 45); Ship Labourers 1000; Labourers 450; Stadacona Labourers 150; Bricklayers 130; Tanners and Curriers 80; Plumbers and Tinsmiths 50; and Butchers 5. In 1901, the Shoemakers of the Dominion had 400; the regional Mechanical Engineers 10; 3 international locals 62 (Typos 12, Cigar Makers 10, Carpenters 40); Labourers 300; Stadacona Labourers 50; Brotherhood of Leather Cutters 75; Tanners and Curriers 40; Stone Cutters 30; and Bakers 10.[71]

The local union we have most information on is the Ship Labourers, complaints of whose behaviour take up an impressive amount of space in the evidence before the Royal Commission on Capital and Labor and in the House of Commons debates. As in Saint John, the union was powerful, and at least some of Quebec's 'better classes' felt that 'there ought to be a law.' In fact they tried to get one, and to some extent succeeded.

Professor Cooper says the Knights of Labor tried unsuccessfully to get the Ship Labourers into the Order. He adds: 'The later history of the Society is one of increasing quiet. The decline of the trade in square timber, and the eclipse of the port of Quebec were body blows. They were accompanied by the draining away of the Irish population itself.'[72]

The increasing quiet was not very evident in 1887. A brief strike in June which succeeded in spite of police intervention,[73] stirred Dr Amyot, MP, to introduce a bill for the protection of labourers on board vessels. He said:

Everybody knows the fearful state into which the harbor of Quebec has been brought by the action of the Ship Laborers' Society, in preventing anybody from working at loading or unloading vessels there, who does not belong to their society, and in compelling everybody who works to work at certain wages, which are very high. The consequence is that ships have ceased to come to the harbor, to the prejudice of the commerce of the country in general, and more especially of Quebec. This Bill is framed ... to make the act of preventing or trying to prevent anybody from working on board or near vessels, a misdemeanor, and any gathering of more than three people near a vessel before the shore will be a misdemeanor, and the penalty ... very severe. Those who know the state of Quebec harbor, and the large organisation of these ship laborers, who have caused almost the ruin of Quebec, know that a strong remedy must be applied.

Amyot's bill did not get past first reading, but he and his backers evidently kept up their pressure on the government. A few days before the session ended the minister of justice, Sir John Thompson, introduced a bill to amend the existing law on threats and intimidation. He described it as being merely to remedy technical defects in the law, since the penalty and the procedure were to remain the same. In fact, the bill would have done much more. Where the existing law specified that the 'threats' must be 'of violence,' the bill said simply 'threats' in the case of ship labourers. It also forbade the use of 'other means' to attain the ends specified.

The bill drew the vociferous support of Peter Mitchell, the former minister of marine and fisheries, who said that when he was minister, 'the rowdy element of Quebec had obtained the mastery to such an extent that they had actually gone on board vessels and turned men out of the forecastle, and in one case had shot a man, so that it was necessary to bring in a very stringent law.' His own act, 15 or 16 years earlier, had been aimed at the Quebec crimps, who had evidently survived the pre-Confederation legislation against them. Dr Amyot praised Mitchell's act. Before its passage, 'we had Quebec crimps, who went on board ships and stole seamen.' Under the act, two men were sentenced to the penitentiary: 'Since then there has been no crimping.'

Telegrams and letters against the bill poured in: from the Toronto and Oshawa trades and labour councils, DA 138 (Woodstock), and 27 LAS of the Knights of Labor. Several members also took strong objection, and succeeded in getting minor amendments. In committee, Amyot entered the lists again. Once more he professed his friendship for workingmen. But the ship labourers, 'or some 60 of them, were incorporated under the pretence of being a mutual benefit society. Now that they have got the subscriptions of a large class of people and have become powerful, they have passed by-laws imposing a high tariff on ship captains, and the captain has no right to move his ship an inch without paying them enormous wages. He is bound to employ a certain number of men, and if he does not submit his cargo is ruined. The ship laborers are there, they do not kill people, but they gather by hundreds on the wharf, and those who dare to go to work against their will, know what is likely to befall them that evening or the next day, when they happen to be alone or when darkness overtakes them.' The Labourers wished to earn 'a month's wages in two or three days' time, working eight or nine hours a day.' He was clearly far from satisfied with the government's bill, and would have preferred something lingering with boiling oil in it; but he seems rather grudgingly to have accepted what Thompson offered. The bill was passed on division.

In March 1888 Amyot renewed his attack, moving for copies of the rules of all trade unions registered under the Trade Unions Act, 'with a list of designation of their several officers.' He wanted 'to draw the attention of the minister of justice to some of the by-laws passed by the trade unions.' His particular target was the Quebec Ship Labourers, from whose by-laws he proceeded to quote at some length. The society's act of incorporation in 1862 had said its purpose was to assist the distressed families of sick members. But in the current by-laws he found 'a number of "practical by-laws," which show a very different purpose.'

He cited 11. They set wages ($4 a day for holders and swingers, $3 for winchers and watchmen, $2 for stagers); regulated the size of work gangs; set an 8-hour day; prohibited work where a donkey engine was used for loading or unloading timber; forbade work with a non-union foreman, or on any vessel where sailors were used for loading or taking in broken stowage; prohibited loading a vessel which had been unloaded by non-members; boycotted any shipmaster who used his own crew to load or unload; and protected members 'discharged without a fault' by requiring all other members employed on the same vessel to stop work till the victim was reinstated. Penalties for breach of these rules varied from fines of $5 to $10 a day to loss of a day's pay for each day illegitimately worked. Amyot went on to blame the decline in the number of ships coming to Quebec, in the revenues of the harbour, and in the population of the city on these by-laws. He was not opposed to the organization of workers or to the protection of their wages and of working women and children. But he did not believe 'in these coalitions, combinations, and associations, which in spite of law, rule by force and violence ... This association has ruined the harbour of Quebec, and I ask the minister of justice to come and give us help.'[74]

In its hearings in 1888 the Royal Commission heard some 10 witnesses on the Ship Labourers' activities. After Amyot's horror tales, the evidence is rather an anticlimax. Several of the commissioners were union members or sympathizers, and kept asking the employer witnesses highly inconvenient questions until they got precise answers, generally very lame ones. The charges against the society usually turned out to be, in the Irish phrase, 'big offers and small blows.'

It was established that the decline in exports was largely due to such factors as the exhaustion of forests within reasonable distance of Quebec, the development of steam navigation, the deepening of the channel to Montreal, and the building of railways (all of them running into Montreal). The employer witnesses contradicted each other on important points. One said the high wages were the only difficulty; another said no, it was the restriction on the size of work gangs; a third blamed the eight-hour day; a fourth had no complaint of that; one complained of the overtime after 5 pm; another said no overtime was paid. None of the specific complaints seems to have stood up to examination.

The 'enormous wages' Amyot complained of were, of course, earned only for the six months the port was open. In the winter the men got various local jobs or went to the United States. There was general agreement that the Quebec longshoremen were quick, efficient, and hard working; in Quebec, said one witness, 'you pay more [than in Montreal], but you get more work for your money.'

One employer complained of the union's refusal to allow the use of steam winches, but had no answer when asked why the merchants had not used them before the prohibition. Others admitted that the union allowed steam winches for certain work, but that for other work the machines were too dangerous: hand loading was both safer and quicker. The cost of loading had been cut in half and was lower than when the union was formed. One boss stevedore flatly denied that the union had increased the cost, or was in any way responsible for the loss of trade: 'My opinion is that no matter what the ship laborers might do, if they were to tear up their by-laws and pitch the pieces into the fire, it would make no difference to Quebec.'[75]

In the whole story, four things stand out. First, Amyot's sweeping charges against the union were mostly wild nonsense. Second, the merchants were ready to blame all their woes on the union; but the facts did not bear them out. Third, even though the port of Quebec may have been past its heyday, the Society was still much too strong for the employers to dare to fight it. Practically every longshoreman in Quebec and Lévis was a member;[76] so if the merchants wanted their cargoes loaded or unloaded, they had to accept the society's terms. They grumbled; they complained; they wailed; they invoked the aid of Parliament; but they seem to have made not the faintest attempt to break the union, or even force it to change its rules, by a lockout or by bringing in non-union labour. Fourth, the 1887 act must have had little or no effect, for none of the witnesses seem even to have mentioned it.

The Ship Labourers made the news again in 1901. The men had been getting $3 per 8-hour day, which was higher than at other ports. The union justified it on the grounds that the members got work for only a few hours at a time, had to wait long hours for the arrival of ships, and lost time and money going to and from ships loading at distant ports.

On 17 April 1901 the manager of the Great Northern Railway, the president of the board of trade, a representative of the Leyland Steamship line, and members of the union met for three hours and discussed the interests of the port. As a result, the Great Northern Railway Company addressed a letter to the president of the Ship Labourers' Society, stating that the railway 'had decided to employ a regular staff of men at the company's new elevator, freight sheds and steamships; that they were prepared to engage about 100 men at $2 per day of 10 hours work, with overtime when required at 20 cents per hour. In consideration of these rates being accepted it was intended to give full employment during the whole season of navigation, and the staff so employed would have preference of any winter work that might be required on the railways. Grain trimmers would be paid 30 cents per hour. The men employed would be insured against accident ... free of cost, and the agreement would apply only to steamers loading full general cargoes ... in connection with the Great Northern Railway.' The Ship Labourers Society was offered the preference of engagement on these terms, and an answer within three days was requested. The company claimed that the rates offered were those paid at other St Lawrence loading places, and that the success of their new lines from Quebec depended on stevedoring being paid at Montreal rates. The company's letter was endorsed by the mayor and the acting chairman of the harbour commission.

The union did not even reply. The company then advertised for men, and on 29 April a gang was hired and set to work to unload the Leyland liner *Belgian* and get her ready to load grain. 'A crowd of ship labourers and others gathered around the harbour, and demonstrations ... caused the men to stop.' Fears of violence brought a large force of police which caused the crowd to disperse. The union repudiated all responsibility for the demonstrations, but it claimed the company's action was a breach of an understanding reached at an interview in the mayor's office the week before, according to which the first shipment of grain was to have been made at the Society's rate and under its rules as an experiment to test whether, even at the higher rate of wages demanded, it would cost more to load cargo in Quebec than in Montreal, the Society contending that its members did the work quicker and better.'

On 30 April some 25 men came to work under the protection of city and provincial police, and behind a high board fence around the elevator. The railway and the Leyland line then issued a statement saying they had no desire to cut wages but were only anxious to load as cheaply as at Montreal. They said that after the *Belgian* was loaded, they would submit to a committee of the men cost figures, and if these showed the total was less than it would have been in Montreal, the company would make up the difference. Members of the Ship Labourers Society and representatives of the railway and steamship companies then held two meetings, an agreement was arrived at, and the labourers resumed work the following morning. The agreement provided for a continuance of the existing wages and hours, unless, after a fair trial, it was proved that the cost of handling cargo (except grain) was higher at Quebec than at Montreal. If it was, wages would be reduced proportionately. Any disputes were to be settled by a board of arbitrators consisting of Archbishop Bégin, Father McCarthy, the president of the board of trade, the chairman of the harbour commission, and H.M. Price. The non-union men who had been employed were engaged to work around the elevator.

By the spring of 1902 the Great Northern, Leyland, and the Ship Labourers were at it again. The steamship company complained that Quebec rates were much higher than those at other ports: 37½ cents an hour day work, 47 night, compared with 22 to 25 for day work and 30 for night in Halifax, Saint John, Portland, and Boston. Leyland demanded that the railway carry out its agreement to arrange for loading Leyland ships at the same rates as in Montreal. It was agreed to have two ships loaded under the supervision of an experienced boss stevedore to see what the real cost was. A month later the mayor wrote the union president that the excess at Quebec was $729.14. The union still insisted that Quebec rates were lower; the Great Northern asked for arbitration to fix future rates. Leyland then refused to pay union rates and tried to get non-union longshoremen to load its *Iberian*. When none could be found, it put the ship's crew on the job. The union longshoremen working on another Leyland ship thereupon struck, on 4 July. The strikers, 190 strong, stayed out till 19 July when, thanks to the intervention of William Power, MP, and the harbour commissioners, they went back at the regular union rates. The harbour commission contributed to the cost of shed labour, enabling the stevedores to pay the full union rate.

During the strike, the unorganized men in the freight sheds had refused to handle cargo worked by non-union men. On 9 July they formed a new union, 300 strong, the Quebec Longshoremen's Society, and demanded 25 cents an hour (instead of 20) for a 10-hour day, 31¼ cents for overtime, and 40 cents for Sunday. As part of the general settlement, they got what they asked.[77]

The Shoe Lasters had a sensational strike in June 1891. The union wanted a uniform rate of wages and an incrase. The employers refused to negotiate and announced that no union members would be employed after 12 June. Anyone who wanted work would have to sign a document undertaking not to belong to any union. Twenty-eight workers at Polley's factory refused and walked out. Fifteen firms joined in a lockout; only three refused. The stoppage, which had become general by 15 June, was still continuing on 3 July, despite the employers' efforts to get the clergy to intervene. The introduction of new machines forced the workers back on the employers' terms, but in October three lasters sued Polley's for blacklisting them after the trouble was settled.

The Lasters struck a single factory against a 10 per cent wage reduction in June 1894. The employer hired strikebreakers; there was a riot; the police intervened; the workers lost.[78]

A Muff Makers Union, organized early in 1899, struck in August for a wage incrase and the abolition of the sweating system. It won increases of $4 to $6 a week.[79]

The Protective and Benevolent Building Labourers, in January 1902, asked 70 employers for an increase of 2½ cents an hour (to 15 cents), effective 1 April. Six employers agreed, 6 refused, 58 did not reply. On 21 April the union struck against the recalcitrant employers; six caved in, and eight got outside men. In June the union struck again, 450 strong, to force the remaining low-wage employers to pay the increase. It lost.

Early in 1902 also, a newly organized Painters and Decorators Union asked for 17½ cents an hour for a 54-hour week. Its members had been getting about 15 cents an hour for a 60-hour week. The union asked for an inquiry by the Quebec board of arbitration. The board sent circulars to the employers, which they ignored. The union then asked the mayor to intervene; he agreed, and most of the employers accepted the union demands.[80]

MONTREAL

In 1881 at least three local unions survived from the previous period: the Stone Cutters, the Cabmen, and the Bricklayers.

The Stone Cutters appear in every Labour Day list from 1886 on. In 1893 there was also a Progressive Union of Stone Cutters. In October 1893 the two merged, and the new union joined the international, probably in or before 1898.[81]

The Cabmen's Union of 1870 seems to have lasted till 1894. A Cabmen's Union appears also in 1895 and 1896, and an Independent Cabmen's Society in 1898–99. Another union was organized in July 1900. It was probably this last which marched in the 1902 Labour Day parade.[82]

The Bricklayers Union lasted till it went international in 1896.[83]

In the 1881 St-Jean-Baptiste parade nine local societies marched: Nailmakers, Upholsterers, Carpenters and Joiners, Butchers, Coach Makers, Shoemakers, Bookbinders, Stone Cutters, and the Bakers of Ste-Brigide. In 1882 the Nailmakers, Coach Makers, Shoemakers and Bookbinders appeared again, along with two barbers' societies, and organizations of tanners, painters, plumbers and tinsmiths, newspaper carriers, saddlers, longshoremen, merchants' clerks, grocery clerks, bricklayers, and Compagnons-boulangers.[84] In this year the Shoemakers had five sections, or else five sister associations, of which the Lasters claimed to be the head.

A Nailmakers Union appears again in 1892 and 1893. In 1892 it struck, 150 strong, at the Montreal Rolling Mills, for a wage increase of $1.10 a day (from a rate of $1.40). The men were out nearly three weeks; they won a compromise. In 1893 they struck again, at Pillow and Hersey, against the importation of 13 American workers. Seven of the 13 went back to the United States. A Horseshoe Nailmakers Union appears in 1894. The Knights of Labor had a horseshoe nailmakers' LA in 1893 and 1894, and a nailmakers' LA in the years 1894–96. A Nailmakers Union reappears in 1899.[85]

An Upholsterers Union appears in 1889–90, and there was an upholsterers' LA in 1894–96.[86]

An independent Carpenters Union appears in 1894, and the Association of Joiners and Carpenters of the Province of Quebec in 1895.[87]

A Butchers 'Assembly' appears in 1887, 1889, 1890, and 1893. An Association of Compagnons-bouchers was formed in 1889. There was a Butchers Association from 1893 to 1899.[88]

The Coach Makers appear in 1890–94, 1897, and 1899.[89]

The Shoemakers paraded in 1886, and again in 1888 (800 strong); in 1889 they became LA 6023 (Co-opérative), which lasted till 1896.[90] In 1897 they became part of the United Shoemakers of the Dominion of Canada.

A Bakers Union, in October 1882, had almost 400 members, mostly French Canadians. It opposed Sunday work and any reduction from the current wages of $6 to $12 a week. It was considering asking the legislature for a charter. A second Bakers Union, organized in July 1885, appears in 1886, 1889–91, 1893–95, 1897, 1899, and 1900. This may have been the Compagnons-boulangers who in May 1887 struck Trudel's bakery unsuccessfully for a wage increase. In 1893–94 there were two bakers' unions (one 'Co-operative'), and on 15 February 1902 a new independent union was formed, competing with international Local 55, organized in 1898.[91]

The Shoe Lasters seem to have continued till November 1893, when the union gave place to an LA which lasted till early in 1896. The union then reappeared. In 1898 it became part of the United Shoemakers of the Dominion of Canada.[92] The Lasters in 1882 had some 300 members. Soon after the union's formation in April, it had presented the employers with a demand for an increase of 75 cents to $1.50 weekly (roughly 15 to 17 per cent). The employers did not even reply. The union then cut its demand to 10 per cent. The employers countered with an offer of 5 to 7½. The union thereupon reverted to its original demand, and won it without a strike (except at Linton's and Slater's, where the Knights of St Crispin are described as having been out for about two months, and, later, briefly, at Rolland's); they won at Linton's and at Rolland's. The employers evidently felt they had been caught unprepared. In July, the time of the Rolland strike, they formed an association of their own.

The more highly skilled men at Cochrane, Cassell & Co, one of the larger firms, who were already getting more than their fellows in the other factories (though the union said they also worked harder), had not even asked for an increase. In the fall the group working on men's brogans were handed a cut of 25 cents a case. Two lasters of 20 to 25 years' experience, whom this reduced to $6 or $7 a week, declared they could not live on such wages, and left. 'As no member of the Union wished to work for such wages [the secretary reported], the foreman took a labourer from the docks and endeavoured to make a laster of him. His work, though bad, was always taken and the other lasters forced to do their work better if possible. Each week a new labourer was taken under instruction and as places became vacant they were filled by these men. The lasters fearing they would be discharged, sought an interview with the employers in order to explain matters, but they refused to listen.' Some of the men also had grievances against certain foremen; and on 20 November 11 men walked out in an unauthorized strike.

The union alleged that the employers' association had 'resolved that on the first demand for an increase ... they would shut up their factories.' In the event, they did not even wait for a demand. On 22 November they presented the union with an ultimatum: get the 11 strikers back to work by the 25th, or face a general lockout. The union protested, but the association did not even reply and on 25 November the lockout began.

It was not quite as general as the association had said it would be: 13 of the biggest factories shut down, but 18 did not. None the less, by 29 November 356 union members were locked out, along with about 600 workers in other trades in the industry. Needless to say, the other four unions, or sections making up the general union of shoemakers, supported the Lasters.

By 1 December three members of the employers' association had given in and taken back their men with a written agreement. But this still left about 200 Lasters and some 500 other shoeworkers locked out. At this point, the Toronto Trades and Labor Council began to take an interest. On 1 December it decided to write to Montreal for information and lay it before the next meeting.

The information came in full measure. Having set forth some of the facts noted above, the Lasters' letter proceeded: 'For the past month [the employers] have actually closed and cut down prices contrary to their agreement ... "You will have to work," say they, "after we have taken stock, provided the lasters will return to work for Messrs Cochrane, Cassels & Co., and renounce the Union" ... Lying and the most wicked means have been used against us. They have endeavoured to stamp us as a secret organization [this, of course, would have brought the union under the ban of the church] and when they did not gain the public favour they accused us of hindering them from employing whom they wished. "Pass a resolution," say they ... "that we can employ whom we desire; expel the lasters from Cochrane, Cassels & Co. from your Union; send us a copy of resolutions passed to this effect and we will give you work."' The union replied that it had no by-law preventing employers from hiring whom they pleased; that it had no report from the men at Cochrane's; and that 'as the employers had treated us rather unceremoniously we would not render ourselves amenable to the law.' It added that if the employers would accede to its former conditions, its members were willing to work, and that they 'awaited justice in [their] case with patience.'

The employers remained adamant, and the union, convinced that 'they have but one aim in view, ... to destroy our Union,' implored fellow-unionists to aid them materially. 'We are the head of five sister associations in our trade, and they desire to conquer us, knowing well that a body without a head is of little use. We ask you in the name of justice, and in our misfortune, to aid us ... with your funds to alleviate our sufferers from hunger and cold.'

The employers had not only locked out the lasters: they were trying to get the members of the 'sister associations' to take their places. 'If we submit [said the union's secretary], we do not deserve to live, for then we would prefer to be slaves rather than free men ... The sufferings of our members ... can only be relieved by the generous donations of the friends of the workingman and the grand cause in which we are engaged – the fight of Labour against Capital.'

This stirring appeal did not fall on deaf ears. Delegate Meredith moved that the Toronto council send $200. 'If the wages in Montreal were reduced the natural result would be that a corresponding reduction would be made here. There was no doubt that the object of the lock-out in Montreal was to burst the Union, and if that were accomplished the same game would be tried on here.' The Typos, Meredith said, were prepared to go down in their 'dip' and support the lasters, but they wanted the council to act first.

Some delegates objected that the proceeds of the demonstration were to be divided among the member unions. Mr Heakes, soon to be the council's candidate for the Legislature, replied heatedly that 'the money belonged to the Council, and if they were not to support Unionism with it far batter throw it out in the street.' Two delegates 'spoke against French Canadians, who, they said were opponents of Unionism and good wages. Mr Meredith referred to a Union in Montreal of French Canadians who he asserted were as staunch Union men as could be got ... Mr Crowe spoke in favour of French Canadians ... Mr Heakes strongly deprecated any slur being cast upon the French Canadians.' After a good deal of discussion, the motion carried and the $200 was sent off next day.

Meanwhile, the lockout had been continuing, with a futile deputation from the union to the employers on 4 December and the usual series of charges, counter-charges, rumours, and denials.

About the middle of December, a letter in the *Witness* from the employers' side countered union charges of low wages by asserting that 6 lasters, working only 5 days a week over a period of 5 months, had averaged $16 a week. Elzéar Ayotte, the union's secretary, promptly challenged the employers to produce any lasters who had made as much as $10 a week working 6 days a week for a period of as much as 2 months. An employer countered with a list of 4 who had averaged $11.30 to $11.55.

About 17 December the employers offered to settle on the basis of a uniform wage rate for a year, with employment guaranteed, but with the union recognizing their right to employ anyone they saw fit. This seems to have been ignored, or turned down, but on 23 December the employers announced that the lockout was over: Cochrane & Cassels was now provided with lasters, who had signed a document undertaking not to contest the right of the employers to hire apprentices or any other persons as they saw fit. On 27 December Ayotte indignantly denied that the lockout was over. True, there were six lasters at work at Cochrane & Cassels, but they were ex-members of the union 'which they had purified by leaving it.'

On 17 January 1883 the union was still holding out, after nine weeks, and had lost only seven members. Two factories had taken back their men without conditions. The union secretary added that, 'before starting a Trades Assembly we wish to prove that, in spite of our misery, we can still hold out.' It seems likely that they did hold out for a while longer, for on 2 February the Toronto Council received a letter from Montreal asking for information on forming a trades and labour council.[93] The Lasters were defeated.

The Tanners and Curriers were probably another of the sister organizations of 1882. A Tanners and Curriers Union appears in 1895, 1899, and 1902.[94]

There was a Heelmakers (or Heelers) Union in 1882 and 1883.[95]

The leather cutters appear in 1882, 1883, and 1886. In 1893 they formed an LA; in August 1894 this gave place to a union which paraded in 1894–99. A Leather Workers Union marched in 1901.[96]

A Painters Union paraded in the years 1888–90; two international locals replaced it.[97]

A Barbers Association was formed in 1889. In May 1894 there is word of a new society, and in November of another. In 1896 this last, with the Quebec City Barbers, may have gone into a provincial association formed in 1889. It may have been the Montreal local of this body which was noted as 'something new' in the 1896 Labour Day parade. A Montreal Barbers' Union was dropped from the TLCC in 1902 as 'purely an association of employers.'[98]

A Plumbers and Steamfitters Union existed from 1888 to 1894. It was gone by May 1896, when the plumbers 'were thinking of reorganizing.' They evidently did, for a new union appears later in 1896. It probably became international Local 144 in September 1898. The Plumbers', Gas, and Steamfitters' Helpers Union appeared in 1898 and continued till after 1900.[99]

The Saddlers appear in 1891. In the period 1892–95 they were LA 3745 (Espérance).[100]

The Montreal Longshoremen (Ouvriers de bord) struck for 3 days in June 1881 for a wage increase, from $1.10 to $1.25 per day. The harbour commission brought in strikebreakers from Sorel, and the men went back on a promise that the commission would examine their case and do them justice.

The Ship Labourers also struck, a thousand strong, 20 June 1881 and stayed out till 14 July. They wanted an increase of 10 cents an hour (to 27 cents for day work and 30 cents for night). The nine shipping companies involved gave the strikers four days to return to work or be discharged. Strikebreakers began to come in from the Maritime provinces; there were instances of violence. On 8 July 700 strikers paraded along the wharves, there was a confrontation with the police, and the Riot Act was read. Four policemen were injured and some strikers arrested and they were severely punished. A second parade went off peacefully. The union finally advised the men to go back to work for all the companies which were willing to pay the higher rates except the Allan Line, which had to sign a formal agreement.

On 26 August 1882 the union heard the president of the Boston Longshoremen urge formation of an international organization for all the Atlantic ports. This may have been a sequel to a fortnight's unsuccessful strike in May for the Portland rate (25 cents an hour, 5 cents more than Montreal). The union appears again in 1883, 1886 (when there was a small and unsuccessful strike against one company which was paying substandard wages), and 1888. The Royal Commission on Capital and Labor was told that the Montreal longshoremen were partly organized but not thoroughly.[101]

The Knights of Labor organized the English-speaking longshoremen into LA 7628 (River Front), which existed from 1886 to 1896, and LA 1711 (Black Diamond), which existed from 1890 to 1902. They also organized the French-speaking longshoremen into LA 7906 (Grande Hermine), which lasted from 1886 to 1896.[102] In June 1901 the Union of Port Workers was organized. It seems to have gone international in 1902.[103]

The Merchants' Clerks appear again in 1885, 1889, 1890, 1893, 1898, and 1899. In 1885 the union was involved in the Early Closing Movement (which appears again in 1889), along with an Association of Wholesale Clerks in Leather, Supplies, and Shoes (formed in September 1885), and an Association of Druggists' Clerks.[104] A new union of grocery clerks, formed in 1894, appears in 1895, 1896, 1898, 1899, and 1901.[105]

A Coopers Union seems to have survived from the 1870s and lasted till the end of the period, though it may have been a Knights of Labor LA in 1885.[106]

There was a Stenographers Association in 1881.[107]

A Co-operative Union of Plasterers appears in 1892, 1899, and 1900. There is some evidence of an international Local 144, formed in 1882, which went local, rejoined the international in 1896, and went local again in 1897. There were strikes by a Plasterers Union in 1883, 1890, 1898, and 1900, but exactly what union was involved is not clear.

The 1890 strike, involving about 250 men, arose from the union's demand for an increase of 50 cents a day (to $3) and the enforcement of the 1888 agreement's limit of 2 apprentices per establishment. The workers claimed they could work only 9 or 10 months a year for a total of about $450. The employers said good plasterers could work the year round and make $600 to $655. The union struck, 6 February. By about the middle of the month, 10 or 15 employers, mostly French Canadians, had given in. The rest balked, till 5 March, when the men went back for a compromise rate of $2.75 and some easing of the apprenticeship clause.[108]

An Early Closing Association appears in the Labour Day parade lists, 1888–89, 1891, 1894, and 1896; a Quarrymen's Union in 1888–90, 1893, 1897, and 1899; a Watch-Case Makers' Union in 1888–93 (though this may have been a Knights of Labor LA).[109] A Carters Union appears in the years 1889–91, 1893–94, and 1896, as does a union of Carters of 'Grosse Voitures' in the period 1897–1900. The Knights of Labor had a Carters Assembly in the years 1892–96, an English-speaking Carters Assembly in the years 1893–94 and 1897, a Truckers Assembly in 1896, as well as LA 339 (carters of 'gross voitures'), between 1893 and 1896, and LA 525 (carters and freight employees), in 1897 and 1899. A Truckers Union appears in 1897 and 1899.[110]

A Tailors Union appears in 1889, 1892, and 1893; a Cutters and Trimmers Union in 1889–92; a Wholesale Clothing Tailors Union in 1890, 1899, and 1900; a Tailors and Cutters Union in 1891; and an Independent Tailors Union in 1900–02. There was also LA 44 (English-speaking tailors) in the period 1892–95, and LA 849 (clothing cutters) in the period 1893–95.[111]

A Builders' Labourers Union appears in 1889–91; a Labourers Union marched in the 1893 Building Trades parade, and appears in 1894–96; and another Labourers Union in 1902.[112] The Glass Bottle Blowers Association appears in 1889–91; by 1892 it was international Local 18.[113]

A Horseshoers Union marched in the 1890 Labour Day parade. A Horseshoers' LA existed in 1889–90.[114] The Copper (or Brass) Workers appear in 1890 and 1891; they appear to have gone into LA 8120 (Phoenix) in 1886–93, and reorganized as an independent union in May 1894. They appear also in 1895.[115]

A Tinsmiths and Roofers Union appears in 1891 and 1892, and a Roofers Union in 1899.[116] A Railway Porters Union appears in 1891–93. An Iron and Steel Workers Union appears in 1891; in 1892 and 1893 it was lodges 2 and 3 of the international Amalgamated Association.[117]

A Stone Masons Union appears in 1893–97, and in 1899–1900. By the end of the latter year it had probably become Local 2 of Quebec in the Bricklayers and Masons International Union.[118]

There was an Electric Pole Climbers Union in 1894.[119]

A Musicians Union appears in 1895; a Musicians Protective Union 62 in 1898 and 1899; and a Musicians Alliance in 1899–1902. (There were also two Musicians' LAS: 'La Harmonie' (1889) and 'Musicians' (1894).[120]

The Association canadienne des bonnes (apparently nurse-girls) was formed in 1895.[121]

The Theatrical Stage Employees Union, formed in September 1897, became international Local 56 in 1898.[122]

A Muff Makers Union appears in 1898–1902.[123]

The 1899 Labour Day parade had five newcomers: Hardware Clerks, Barbed Wire Makers, Steel Stove Workers, Granite Cutters, and Pattern Makers. The Pattern Makers went international on 25 June 1901; the Granite Cutters seem to have collapsed, with a new union taking their place in 1901, and still there in 1902.[124]

A Protective Association of Civil Employees (apparently postmen), formed in January 1899, seems to have fizzled out. In the same year, one of the four branches of the provincial United Shoemakers, the Cordonniers en turns, became independent. A union of this name appears in 1901, but was probably an international local.[125]

A Lathers Union, organized in July 1899, appears again in 1902.

A Fruit Peddlers Union, organized in October 1899, appears also in 1900 and 1901.[126]

Unions of Coremakers and Car Wheel Moulders appear in 1899.[127]

A Bread Deliverymen's Union existed from 1900 till the beginning of 1902.[128]

A Ship Carpenters Union, formed in June 1901, seems to have joined the United Brotherhood of Carpenters in November 1902. Two other unions of ship carpenters were organized in 1902.[129]

A Federated Association of Street Railway Employees, organized in March 1902, probably became Division 328 of the international union, chartered on 23 February 1903.[130]

A Divers Union was formed in September 1902, and a Bootblacks Union in December.[131]

ELSEWHERE IN QUEBEC

St Hyacinthe had a Labourers Protective Union, organized 15 April 1899. It was still there in the spring of 1902. It seems to have been made up of workers in the Canadian Woollen Mills.

On 7 March 1901 the cutters in these mills struck against a wage reduction. They went back on 9 March, 'the manager having accepted their price list for one year and dismissing the two parties who had the misfortune to take the place of some old employees who were members of the union.'

On 2 September 1901 the company announced a 10 per cent wage cut. The union protested and demanded arbitration. The company agreed. The award decreed that employees getting from $6 to $7 per week were to take a cut of 5 per cent; those getting $7 to $10 per week, 10 per cent; those getting $10 to $18 per week, 12 per cent; those getting $18 and over, 15 per cent. The Manager's salary was cut 25 per cent. The men were reported satisfied.

In April 1902 the union demanded that the August 1901 wage rates be restored, claiming this had been agreed to when the cuts were made. The company complied for those who had lost the 5 per cent, but said it could do no more. The union countered by proposing restoration of half the cut imposed on the rest.[132]

The St Hyacinthe Leather Cutters, formed in August 1896, struck Séguin and Lalime in May 1899 to get a demoted foreman reinstated. The union's Montreal headquarters ordered the workers back. In September 1900 the union asked for a wage increase. Two months later they got 10 per cent, bringing their time rates from $9 to $11 per week, and from $11 to $14 on job work. The union was still there in December 1901.[133]

A local Barbers, Hairdressers and Wigmakers Protective Union, was formed in St Hyacinthe 29 August 1900. It was gone by December 1902.[134]

By the summer of 1902 St Hyacinthe seems also to have had local unions of moulders and of machinists and engineers, though these may have joined the AFL in August 1901.[135]

A Hull Labourers Protective Association, formed on 10 October 1899, was still there in the summer of 1902.[136]

Sherbrooke had a local Carpenters Union in the summer of 1902.[137]

Shawinigan Falls had a Benevolent and Protective Union, formed in August 1902.[138]

Valleyfield had a Benevolent Assembly of Barbers (formed 1 August 1899) which lasted till after the turn of the century.[139]

13

Local unions in Ontario and the West 1881–1902

Kingston had a local Carpenters Union in June and July 1896. The Tanners and Curriers Union which became an Amalgamated Leather Workers' local on 16 April 1902 may have been started as a purely local body on 1 April 1901.[1]

OTTAWA

A Hackmen's Union was formed about the beginning of 1885 and lasted till at least 1896. A Cabmen's Union was formed in December 1902.[2]

A Plumbers and Steamfitters Union was represented at the 1886 TLCC convention and a Plumbers and Tinsmiths Union at the first meeting of the Ottawa Trades and Labor Council, 20 February 1889. The latter union probably became Local 71 of the United Association, 30 September 1891.[3]

A Coopers Union and a Workingmen's Association existed in 1887.[4]

The Painters and Decorators Union which took part in the first meeting of the Trades and Labor Council probably went international in 1890; the bookbinders at that meeting were probably part of the Typos.[5]

Other Ottawa local unions during this period were:[6] Blacksmiths (1889), Blacksmiths and Horseshoers (1895), Blacksmiths (1897); General Labourers (1890–91, and 1898), Labourers ('Union Cecil') (1898–1900), Labourers Association (1899), Labourers Union (1900); Butchers (1890–92), Butchers' Association (1898); Cabinet Makers and Machine Woodworkers (1891–93); Amalgamated Iron Workers (perhaps international) (1891); Carpenters (1893), Carpenters and Joiners No 28 (1898); Barbers (1894); Lathers (1899) (groups of lathers and of brewers, perhaps unions, marched in the 1894 Labour Day parade); Musicians ('Union

Musicale') (1895); Plasterers (1896–98, and 1900); Commercial or 'Clerks Commercial' (1897–98, 1900–1902); 'Federal' (1897); Waiters (1899); Plumbers' Apprentices (1899).

In 1898 there was a local union of street railway employees, the Ottawa Electric Railway Protective and Benevolent Association. Early in May it asked for shorter hours and more pay. The men were working 11 hours a day for $1.50. The superintendent offered $1.40 for a 10-hour day, which the men seem to have refused. Early in July the company alleged that many of the signatures on a petition presented to it had been obtained by false pretenses, and the vice-president and managing director offered to meet any of the company's old employees privately to settle any differences. He claimed shorter hours could be granted only with a reduction of wages. By this time the company was refusing to deal with the employees except on the basis of $1.34 for a 9-hour day. By 19 August the employees were claiming that the company had used the evidence of 'certain domestics' to find excuses for dismissing some employees, and that these domestics had now left the city. The union was reported, at the end of August, as being expected to march in the Labour Day parade; if it did, this seems to have been its last appearance.[7]

In June 1901 a Servant Girls, or Household Workers, Association was organized with about 225 members. It created a considerable dust-up. 'A number of servant girls [were] said to have left at 7.00 p.m. while their employer was entertaining cabinet ministers.' Employers had said they would employ men, and threatened to employ Chinese. The organization was still in existence in the summer of 1902.[8]

In the fall of 1902 J.W. Patterson (former Typos' organizer, former president of the Ottawa Council, and labour candidate for Parliament) was charged with having organized a dual Musician's Union, in opposition to international Local 180.[9] Patterson was later to go over to the National Trades and Labour Congress, after the 1902 split.

PETERBOROUGH

Peterborough had in 1882 a Journeymen Harnessmakers Protective Society, and in 1888 local unions of printers, machinists, painters, and hod carriers (or contractors' labourers). In the fall of 1902 there seem to have been organizations of tinsmiths and 'outside workers.'[10]

LINDSAY

Lindsay in 1902 seems to have had organizations of plumbers, brewery workers, and team drivers (this last may have been an international local).[11]

Toronto in 1881 had at least 13 local unions: Bricklayers, Painters, Plasterers, Friendly Carpenters, Stone Cutters, Labourers, Tinsmiths, Tailors, Machine Shoemakers, Hand-Sewed Shoemakers, Bakers, Longshoremen, and Brakesmen.[12] The Bricklayers became Local 2 of the international union 21 November 1881.[13] The Machine Shoemakers probably became LA 2211 in September 1882.[14] All the rest, except perhaps the Friendly Carpenters, seem to have been still there at the end of 1882. During that year another 16 local unions seem to have been organized: Stone Masons, Plumbers, Lathers, Woodworking Machinists, Wood Turners, Varnishers and Polishers, Pianomakers and Cabinet Makers, Coopers, Brass Finishers, Horseshoers, Silversmiths (or Goldsmiths) and Jewelers, Gilders, Hackmen, Saddle and Harnessmakers, Female Shoe Operators (or Fitters), and Boot Blacks.[15]

The Painters Union collapsed late in 1881; a new one, organized in March 1882, seems to have lasted till the organization of Local 3 of the international, 9 April 1887.[16] The Plasterers Union became Local 48 of the international 30 March 1889.[17]

The Labourers appear in 1883;[18] Builders' Labourers in 1883, 1885–88, 1890–93, and 1897 (in 1888 and 1897 they seem to have been an international local);[19] and United Labourers in 1883 (two branches) and 1884, with a new union in 1885, 1886, and 1890.[20] Bricklayers' Labourers appear in 1883, Plasterers' Labourers throughout the period,[21] and General Labourers in 1892.[22]

The Tinsmiths lost a strike in May 1882 for a wage increase of 25 cents a day, and became 'disorganized.' They were apparently reorganized in 1883 but gone by the end of 1884.[23]

The Tailors became, in August 1886, LA 8527 of the Knights of Labor and, in June 1890, Local 132 of the Journeymen Tailors Union of America. The Hand-Sewed Shoemakers, still there in March 1886, probably became, in April, LA 6250, which lasted till at least July 1893.[24]

The Bakers, on 8 February 1898, became international Local 204.[25]

The Longshoremen appear in 1883 and 1885, and may have become, in April 1886, LA 6564, which was still there at the end of 1902.[26] The Stone Cutters had gone international by January 1889. The Stone Masons seem to have done the same in 1884.[27]

The Plumbers were gone by 13 May 1883. The Lathers seem to have lasted till 1886. The Woodworking Machinists were reported in March 1883 about to enter the American Carpenters. The Wood Turners may have become LA 3684, which existed from March 1885 till 1893.[28] The Varnishers and Polishers appear in 1883, and may have become in May 1884 LA 3181, which was still there in February 1891, and may itself have become Amalgamated Woodworkers' Local 65 in 1893.[29] The Pianomakers and Cabinet-Makers appear in 1886 and 1890–92 and may have become Woodworkers' Local 19 in 1893. The Coopers appear in July 1882. They are described as an international local in January 1883 and February 1884; they appear again in 1885, 1886, 1889, and 1892.[30]

The Horseshoers appear in 1887; they went international in 1892. The Gilders appear in 1883. A new union appears in 1895, and on 27 March 1901 it became AFL FLU 8980.[31] The Hackmen appear in 1883–84. A Coach and Cab Drivers Union, 1897–99, was succeeded by the Licensed Cab and Express Association in November 1899. The Association was still there in 1902.[32] The Saddle and Harnessmakers (perhaps part of a regional union) were still there in April 1883, and in August probably became LA 2782, which lasted till 1889.[33] The Female Shoe Operators were still there in April 1884.

A short-lived Maltsters Union was organized in 1883; a new one appeared in 1894.

The Boilermakers, organized in March 1883, probably became international Lodge 22 in 1884, which may then have become LA 6724 (1886–89).[34] The *Telegram* newsboys were organized in the spring of 1883.[35] The Stove Mounters appear in 1883 and December 1885. A United Workmen's Union marched in the 1883 demonstration.[36] The Expressmen appear in December 1883; a Teamsters Union in 1887, 1889, and 1893;[37] a Carters Union in 1895, 1896, 1898, and 1899 (probably the same as the Carters and Teamsters, who paraded in 1899).[38]

A rival bakers' union (Journeymen Bakers, No 1) tried unsuccessfully to get into the Trades and Labor Council in 1884, 1887, and 1888. It included members expelled from LA 3499 (1884–93).

A Barbers Union appears in July 1885. It may have become LA 4538 (1885–87). A Barbers Union appears also in 1894 and 1899.[39] In December 1885 the Brewers' Employees Association was writing to the Trades and Labor Council.

As far back as March 1883 the TTLC's organizing committee had tried to organize the coal drivers and teamsters, but this attempt fell through. Not till 19 February 1886 could the committee report the success in organizing the coal carters. The next union we hear of in this occupation is a Coal Deliverers Union, in 1897. This union (also known as Drivers No 1, Coal Drivers, Coal Drivers No 1, and Coal Drivers 27 (this last suggests a TLCC FLU), seems to have existed from early in 1897 till at least January 1901.[40]

There may have been an upholsterers' union on 16 April 1886, when 'the Upholsterers of the City had a request before their Bosses for a shortening of hours, and a minimum rate of wage.' It seems probable, however, that the organization was LA 3490 (1884–89).

Very few local unions seem to have been organized in the period 1884–86, and only one in 1887, doubtless because the Knights of Labor were doing most of the job. In 1888, however, at least one new union did appear: the Corset Stitchers. The

Trades and Labor Council, on 6 July, turned down a motion to give them $10 in support of their strike. The only local union organized in 1889 seems to have been the United Excavators, admitted to the Council on 19 July. It appears again in 1890 and 1891. The Pick and Shovel Men's Association of 1892 was probably the same organization. It may have been a continuation of LA 5087 (January 1886 till at least February 1889).[41]

In 1890 a Marble Workers Union was organized. It reappears in February and March 1891. On 21 August it asked for the attention of the council's organizing committee because of the disorganized state into which it had fallen. The Switchmen's Mutual Aid Association appeared in February 1891, the Consolidated Glass Workers Union in December, and the Toronto Orchestral (or Musical Protective) Association in April. The Orchestral Association reappears every year till, on 3 June 1901, it became Local 149 of the international.[42]

On 20 May 1892, the Trades and Labor Council seated delegates from three branches of the Brickmakers' Employees' Union, and all three branches marched in the Labour Day parade. There had been a brickmakers' LA 7210 from May till at least October 1886.[43] The Amalgamated Journeymen Slaters Society seated three delegates in the council on 13 April 1892. One was Joseph Henry. As a man of that name had been a Builders' Labourers' Union delegate on 15 January, it seems possible that the Slaters had broken away from the BLU. The new society marched in the Labour Day parade and was represented at the 1892 TLCC convention. A Slaters Union also marched in the 1896 parade.[44] The Blacksmiths and Helpers Union No 1 appears in 1892 and 1893.[45] The Wood Carvers marched in the 1892 Labour Day parade.[46]

The Working Women's Protective Association was on strike in February 1893; on 21 April it seated three delegates in the Council. It appears again in July, and in January 1894. One of its delegates was the Council's vice-chairman.[47] The Waiters were admitted to the Council on 16 February 1894, and appeared again on 20 December 1895. There was a letter from the Waiters Association on 6 December 1898; this was probably the beginning of Local 68 of the international, organized in 1899.

The Pavers appeared in the Council on 20 April 1894, and on 4 May the municipal committee was trying to bring about an amicable settlement of a wage dispute with the city. The Theatrical Stage Employees appeared in the Council 15 February 1894. They continued as a local union till they became Local 58 of the international towards the end of 1898 or at the beginning of 1899.[48]

Civic Employees No 1 was admitted to the Council on 6 December 1895, and Civic Employees Benevolent Association No 2 on 20 December. No 1 appears again in 1896, 1899, 1901, and 1902. No 2 appears in 1896–99, 1901, and 1902.[49] Both unions marched in the parades of 1896, 1899, and 1900; 'Civic Employees' in the parades of 1897, 1898, 1901, and 1902.[50]

A Window Shade Workers Union appears in December 1898, and again 1899 and 1900. An Electrical Workers Union, organized early in 1899, appears in the Council on 9 March. It probably became Local 114 of the international on 1 April 1900.[51]

The bread drivers, organized in LA 3499 from November 1884 till at least January 1893, formed a Bread Drivers Union No 1 in 1899. This appears in the Council minutes in 1899, and on 27 March and 25 July 1901 (when it was trying to get a Bakers' charter). It marched in 1899, and in 1902, by which time it had become TLCC FLU 33.[52] The Furriers appeared in 1899. A Furriers' Union marched in the 1901 parade, and probably became on 16 April 1902 AFL FLU 9791.[53]

Toronto had a Stenographers' Union in the summer of 1902. In December the cloth cap makers and the city firemen organized.[54]

Two local unions were involved in strikes in the spring of 1882. The end of the old Painters' Union was followed by a gradual fall in wages. In March 1882 a mass meeting organized a new union, with about 150 members, which promptly asked for an increase of 2½ cents an hour. The employers refused, and the men struck, 15 April. After two weeks the employers granted a two cent increase and agreed to recognize the union.[55]

Meanwhile, the Female Shoe Operatives (otherwise the Female Boot and Shoe Fitters Association and the Ladies Boot and Shoe Fitters Association), under the presidency of Mr Armstrong, had been engaged in a struggle with five shoe manufacturers: Kings & Co, Childs & Charlesworth, Hamilton & Co, Damer, and Cooper and Smith. On 3 April the girls in the first three firms struck, since their repeated requests for a wage increase had not been met. They had already formed a union, 'and this was one of the chief objections made by the bosses, as they preferred dealing with their employees individually, instead of collectively.' A few days later the girls in the other two factories also struck, because 'all the girls were not working on the same basis.' The strike continued for some time, and the wholesale boot and shoe makers struck in sympathy. On 23 April the employers met the women strikers and agreed to prepare, within a month, a uniform bill of wages, 'which would include in it certain advances.' The girls accepted this, 'but with the express understanding that they would not abandon their Union.' They, and the wholesale shoemakers, then went back to work.

The settlement turned out to be no settlement at all. The very issue of the *Trades Union Advocate* which announced it carried also a flat refusal by one of the manufacturers to 'allow Union principles to be introduced into his shop.' Subsequent issues of the *Advocate* described various oppressive measures by other manufacturers, and kept recording the non-appearance of the bill of wages which had been promised for May. It also hinted at a guilty liaison between Cooper and his forewoman, a Miss Allegate, 'a full-grown Allegate-or, [who could] lounge at leisure in her spacious arm chair, decked with jewels and gold bracelets presented by her employer ... languidly sawing the air with her varied coloured fan, like an Oriental princess, while the female operatives are compelled to sit on seats without backs ... [and who ordered that] the windows must be shut down and the blinds fastened on the plea that the young ladies waste their time looking at the clerks in the opposite establishment.'

Finally, the union lost patience, and on 7 October a deputation, consisting of Armstrong and four members, waited on Charlesworth (who seems to have been one of the less openly anti-union employers) to ask when they might expect to get what had been promised them. Charlesworth said the bill was at the printers', and would be issued shortly. 'Now Mr Charlesworth,' said Armstrong, 'let us come down to hard pan. These young women have waited so long for this uniform bill of wages that patience has ceased to be a virtue. They have a perfect right to receive each a copy of the bill, and fully discuss its merits, and say whether they will accept it or not, or work under the rates they are receiving. Reform in politics, like charity, should commence at home. However, Mr Charlesworth, I believe you said the bill was in the hands of the printers, and you will see that it is presented as soon as possible.' Charlesworth replied: 'I will do all that lays in my power to have the bill completed as soon as possible.' The deputation then withdrew.

This ought to have presaged the happy ending. But on 19 October the *Advocate* asked 'Are the female [b]oot and shoe fitters ... going to wait for their uniform bill as long as Jacob did for Rachael? ... It seems so. Much longer delay may cause the historic last straw to drop.' In early November the uniform bill had not yet appeared, and the *Advocate* wondered if the employers were 'waiting for Gabriel's trumpet to herald the fact?' They may well have been, for it seems the uniform bill expired without ever seeing the light of day. It is amazing that the union was still alive and kicking as late as 18 April 1884.

Meanwhile, J.D. King had been incurring the wrath of the *Advocate*. He had hired a male Jew for less than the current wages, and the girls had objected. King had accused them of being prejudiced against men and Jews. The *Advocate* of 14 December 1882, after recalling the broken promise of the uniform bill and noting that King had since instituted two reductions on the price for buttonholes in his shop, said:

The young women would have had no objection to this Israelite had he been engaged at the same rate as they are receiving. But no, Jew-like, he offered his services at a much less rate, and when he was not button-holing, he proposed to tinker round the machines, do chores, and make himself generally useful about the house ... Six dollars a week is an outside figure for a first-class hand on button-holes. Some twenty operatives make this statement, and they are to be believed in preference to a man like King, who is interested and steeped to the lips in prevarication of this kind. His whole life is permeated with a species of grinding tyranny upon his employees. Even when in Reid's peddling whiskey and cigars, the cloven hoof of the would-be capitalist protruded far beyond the limits of discretion ... Sinister and shrewd ... J.D. King seems to play upon the trusty nature of his female employees by penetrating their thoughts and intentions. A few of the weak-minded place confidence in him, and therefore unravel their mind to him ... By this means he is capable of finding out who are the spirited union girls and who are the ones that would toady to his blandishments ...

His female employees do not object to a man working in their department, but they do object to a thing, in the garb of a man, working under the starvation prices which they are receiving. It also speaks very little for the manhood and unionism of the men in King's factory, to fiddle away, as it were, while Rome was burning, to sit pegging away with the knowledge that the young women on the next flat of the same shop were struggling for union principles, without receiving a helping hand from men who boast of their independence of character and pronounced unionism in certain quarters where they know their statements cannot be successfully contradicted.[56]

The Painters also faced at least one attempt to whittle away their victory of April 1882. In March 1883 William Elliott, a master painter employing some 60 men, confessed to the daily press that he had had, even the previous summer, 'grave doubts as to the practicability of carrying out the arrangements made then between the master painters and their men.' Experience had confirmed his doubts. Many of the union men were not worth even $1 a day, let alone the agreed standard rate. The men should be paid according to their ability. Rather inconsistently, he proceeded to cut wages all around, except for paperhangers, by one cent per hour effective 10 March. The union held a meeting with the Master Painters' Association on 12 March to try to settle the difficulties with Elliott. The association was sympathetic. Its president regretted Elliott's action, first, because the increased cost of living meant that journeymen painters were not getting 'higher wages that would make them feel comfortably independent,' and second (he implied) because Elliott's wage-cutting would enable him to engage in unfair competition with other master painters. The president's own men were getting 20 cents an hour, 'and he did not think he would get a fair day's work from them at a lower figure.' Another master painter expressed similar views. The meeting ended with the president expressing sympathy with the union but telling the men that 'the remedy could only come from themselves.'

The union struck, 19 March and provided strike pay at $5 a week for married men and $3 for single. On 29 March the *Wage-Worker* quoted the union's president, J.W. Carter: 'The Union is now fully determined to fight the matter out if it takes all summer. There is lots of funds, good pickets, and any amount of pluck, and with right and justice on their side they are bound to succeed.'[57]

In March 1883 the male Shoemakers found themselves faced with a request by the Master Shoemakers Association for a wage reduction. The employers were the same cast of characters that had figured in the earlier play with the Female Shoe

Operatives: the employers' meeting had been held in the offices of W.B. Hamilton, who moved the motion to ask for the reduction; the seconder was James Cooper; and the letter to the union was signed by H.G. Charlesworth. The scenario was somewhat different. The employers recognized the union, and their letter was couched in mild, even respectful, terms. This, however, did not prevent the *Wage-Worker* from describing it as 'sublime impudence and cool cheek ... evidently intended as an offset to the expected demand for an increase of pay.' The letter had said that the advances which had been granted the previous few years should, in view of the depressed state of the boot and shoe trade in Canada, be reduced. On this the *Wage-Worker* commented that it would 'convey the impression' that the employers had granted increases 'of their own free will and real good nature. Fiddlesticks – they never conceded, other than what was forced from them, and never more nor near as much as what the business owed to the workmen.' It noted that Hamilton was treasurer of the Sick Relief Society lately organized in his factory, and had 'graciously donated $50 to its funds,' adding caustically that 'now he is anxious to recoup himself by reducing the wages of those who craved his acceptance of the treasurership.'

A union mass meeting, 31 March, bluntly told the employers 'that in place of a reduction we ask for an advance of 10 per cent all round,' plus various changes in the McKay Finish Bill. A week later the *Wage-Worker* reported that it understood the employers had withdrawn their request for a reduction and had 'acceded to the "demand" for a 10 per cent advance on certain work.'[58]

On 20 April 1883 the Longshoremen's Union reported to the Trades and Labor Council a breach of agreement by a dock owner named Bailey. The Council set up a committee to obtain a settlement. Bailey pops up again on 16 May 1884, when the Longshoremen asked the Council for a deputation to Bailey 'requesting him to employ only Union Men.' A committee waited upon Bailey who said he would 'see the men again next week and thought the trouble could be amicapably [sic] settled.'

The Plasterers, towards the end of March 1883, received a letter from J.J. Kennedy, president of the National Plasterers Union in the United States. Kennedy had worked in Toronto in 1879 and was delighted to hear his trade was now organized there. He exhorted the Toronto union to help organize the plasterers in Hamilton, London, Ottawa, and Montreal, and hoped all Canadian plasterers' unions would come into the NPU.

Nothing seems to have come of this. But by 15 October the Toronto union was on strike. The employers' association had tried to impose a wage cut, and the union had struck. Apparently some employers had shown signs of caving in, for their association had decided to levy a fine of $25 on any of its members who employed a striker. The Trades and Labor Council sent its organizing committee to 'visit the Plasterer Bosses with a view to settle by Arbitration if possible, if not to call a Public Meeting at as early a date as possible to discuss in Public the grievance of the Plasterers.'

The committee met the employers, but failed to get a settlement. The 'Carpenter and Bricklayer Bosses and Architects' were supporting the master plasterers. The Council voted $100 to the union; then, when the employers took out an injunction against 4 of the leaders, and the union won its case, another $200 towards the court costs. It was not till March 1884 that the strike was satisfactorily settled. Two years later the union settled for nine hours and a pay raise starting in June.[59]

The Builders' Labourers told the Council on 19 June 1885 that they had decided to strike next day, 'on account of the Bosses not agreeing to advance their wages to 18 cents an hour, and to be paid every week.' The council promptly appointed its officers a standing arbitration committee to act if necessary. Some 500 labourers struck, and a mass meeting in Queen's Park rallied 1000 workmen. The strike lasted for some time and was settled by arbitration. But the settlement came unstuck. On 16 October the union told the Council that the employers had given notice of a wage reduction, 'in contradiction to the agreement of the arbitrators, those gentlemen had been interviewed by the Officers of the Union, and they had expressed themselves annoyed at the action of the employers, and would make it their business to look into it.'[60]

The Bakers held their annual concert and social 8 November 1882. The audience received a treat, 'not of poundcake and gingersnaps, but one which suited the intellectual palate, even of the most fastidious, in the shape of a well-selected programme.' John Armstrong, president of the Trades and Labor Council, presided and made the opening speech, in which he set forth the origin of the trade union movement: 'It was the outgrowth of the crushing power of capital, and the monopoly which followed in its wake. This fact can be traced back to time's earliest recollection. Even from the time when our great progenitor received that solemn decree, "by the sweat of they brow shalt thou eat bread," you will find that capital has always been antagonistic to labour.' He traced the history of the emergence of unions from the mediaeval guilds, and argued the increasing necessity of unions 'on account of the enormous amount of labour-saving machinery ... which was unquestionabl[y] the product of the mechanic's brain, and he should receive the benefit of that production by shortening the hours of labour.' He urged working-class representation in Parliament, and 'ended a neat and stirring speech by making a strong appeal to wage-workers present, whether male or female, to form and join Trades Unions. He was happy to inform them that there were two highly skilled branches of female industry already formed in this city, and he hoped to see the day, and that in the near future, when the dressmakers, the furriers, seamstresses, and tailoresses would all be formed into Trades Unions.' The speech was followed by a series of songs and a dance.

In February 1884 the Bakers Union started a co-operative bakery.[61]

The Working Women's Protective Association, early in 1893, struck A.R. Clarke & Co's glove factory, and on 3 February appealed to the Council for co-operation and got it. The executives of the Council and the Knights of Labor District Assembly issued a joint appeal for funds to all labour organizations, and the Council president and the district master workman, with members of the union, collected $568. By 7 April the strike was over, and the union was setting up a co-operative glove factory. It asked the Council to help it get factory law reform and votes for women.

On 11 February 1897 Drivers Union No 1 asked the Council to take steps in its trouble with Pat Burns & Co. The request, referred to the organizing committee, seems to have died there.

HAMILTON

A Hamilton local Bricklayers Union was formed on 14 February 1881. It went international 7 July.[62] A Shoemakers Union existed in 1881 and 1882. In August 1882 it probably went into the Knights of Labor LA 2132, which was still there December 1888.[63]

On 4 May 1881 the bricklayers' and plasterers' labourers, trying to get their wages raised to $1.50 a day, formed a union. The Bricklayers' and Masons' Labourers' Union was represented at the dinner which celebrated the Bricklayers' affiliation with their international union. A Labourers Union (probably the same body) marched in the 1883 demonstration. A Builders' Labourers Union, by July 1884, was asking the master builders to raise wages to $1.60. A Builders' Labourers Union was represented in the Central Labor Union in February 1886; and Builders' Laborers Union No 3 was represented at the 1886 and 1887 TLCC conventions and in the 1887 demonstration. This union was the centre of the great 1888 building trades lockout. It survived that contest; was represented in the Trades and Labor Council in November and December 1888 and January 1889; and was apparently still in existence at the end of 1889.[64]

In May 1881 the Brickmakers organized a union, and this body took part in the demonstration of 3 August 1883.[65]

By 27 August 1881 a new Bakers Union had been formed, with about three-quarters of the journeymen as members; by January 1882 this had become Branch 3 of the Ontario Union. A Bakers Union was represented in the Central Labor Union in February 1886.[66]

The harness makers held a supper on 25 October 1881; there is a report of a Hamilton Journeymen Saddlers and Harness-Makers Association 8 April 1882; and by 12 October 1882 this was among the 'branches' being circularized by the Toronto Harnessmakers on the subject of affiliating with the national union in the United States.[67]

On 17 February 1882 the painters began a rather hectic career of organization and reorganization by forming a Protective Society 'for the purpose of regulating wages for the ensuing season.' This union took part in the 1883 demonstration, when it reported a membership of 80. On 3 May 1884 a new union was formed, which took part in the 1884 demonstration of 4 August, but had died by 23 April 1885. This second Painters Union seems to have fallen foul of the Knights of Labor, for, when it complained to the employers of insufficient wages, the *Palladium of Labor* came out against the union. It said that when the union members were idle, they did contracting on their own, and at rates 20 to 30 per cent below the going rates. So the master painters were unable to fix their prices, unable to get assurance of sufficient work, and hence unable to raise wages. By 24 July 1886 the painters had organized a third union, and on 15 March 1887 Local 27 of the international union came into existence.[68]

On 13 March 1882 the boilermakers', blacksmiths' and moulders' helpers set up a temporary organization to ask their employers for a wage increase. On 17 March the machinists' helpers joined to form a permanent union, which started with 90 members. The lathers formed a union between 27 March and 3 April 1882 and agreed to demand an increase of half a cent per yard, to 2½ cents. A Lathers Union appeared in the Trades and Labor Council, 3 December 1888 and 27 January 1889. The Tinsmiths and Sheet Iron Workers Union met on 19 April 1882.[69]

On 3 May 1883, about 25 policemen met to discuss forming a benevolent association, to provide for the wants of the widows and families of deceased members. Unlike the firemen, who in June 1880 had formed a benevolent association, the Policemen's Benevolent Association, by 17 July, had got to the point of threatening to strike if the policemen did not get higher pay and better conditions. The policemen wanted to work less than 365 days a year for shorter hours and with compensation for injuries. They secured some concessions so promptly that they called off the threatened strike next day.[70]

In the 3 August 1883 demonstration unions of hatters (40), plumbers, carters (21), brushmakers (60), and longshoremen appear for the first time. The hackmen had just formed a union.[71]

The Hatters on 21 March 1884 were stirring up the Toronto Council to begin its prolonged inquiry into the Toronto Straw Hat Works. They also marched in the 1884 demonstration.[72]

The plumbers and steamfitters held their second and third annual picnics in July 1884 and 1885. It is possible that their organization was actually LA 2586 (plumbers and tinsmiths), which existed 1883–89. But by 29 September 1887 this assembly was being described as a railroad assembly. So the Plumbers Union involved in the 1888 building trades lockout was probably a new union – perhaps the Steamfitters Union mentioned in the Trades and Labor Council minutes of 28 February 1889. This last, however, may have been a local of the international which preceded the present United Association.[73]

The Longshoremen's Union may have become, in June 1886, LA 7822 (longshoremen and teamsters), which was still in existence in June 1888. Longshoremen marched in the 1895 Labour Day parade.[74]

Before 1883 was out, unions of cotton operatives, car-builders, toolmakers, and sewing-machine hands had been organized. The Cotton Operatives marched in the 1884 demonstration, though by that time the union may have become LA 3040 (cotton workers), which existed 1884–86. This had certainly disappeared by May 1890 when the Trades and Labor Council was considering helping the Ontario Cotton Co weavers to organize. The weavers were to affiliate with a British organization; the spinners were to be organized later. Meanwhile, the weavers' committee was asking the Council to send a committee to see the company and try to settle the strike, which the Council agreed to do. The company's response was evidently unsatisfactory, for on 2 June the Council was urging all labour organizations to support the strike. Faint yet pursuing, it was also asking the Ministerial Association and the Women's Christian Temperance Union to help get a settlement. The Ministerial Association agreed to help as far as possible, and the WCTU made an appointment to meet the manager. But when the ladies arrived they were told the meeting had been held in the morning. The Council, 7 July, voted thanks to the Ministerial Association and the WCTU.[75]

A Builders' Labourers Union was formed in the summer of 1885, and in January 1886 the wine clerks organized.[76]

The Plasterers were represented in the Central Labor Union 24 February 1886 and appear in the Trades and Labor Council, 12 November 1888. They were involved in the 1888 building trades lockout. The Council's minutes for 13 September 1895 record a letter from the Plasterers Association.[77]

A Stonecutters Union appears in 1888, 1889, 1891, 1897, and 1902.[78]

A rather pathetic attempt to form a street railwaymen's union was quickly snuffed out in the fall of 1892. On 3 September the men formed 'an association for their mutual benefit and protection.' Fifty-one of the company's eighty employees joined. The association insisted that it was not originally 'intended to deal specifically with the question of hours and wages, but one of its primary objects was to form a sick benefit fund.' At a second meeting, on 5 September, however, it decided to ask to have the hours of work divided 'more equally ... The men could not stand the present system of fifteen hours a day for two days and then four hours the next day.'

Next morning, six of what the company persistently called the ringleaders were told that there was no work for them. When the association's delegation went to see the superintendent, Mr Griffith, he refused to listen to them because they were 'no longer employees.' The leaders, headed by George Sharp, a Methodist local preacher and active temperance worker, reported back to a meeting that evening. The members decided that unless they could get a hearing, they would strike. Next morning the men on the first cars due to go out refused to start. Griffith got men from the other cars, and the first cars went out to the accompaniment of jeers and hoots. Within 10 minutes about a dozen cars had gone out, but some were later deserted by their crews. By three in the afternoon nearly all the cars were moving. Some of the strikers had already gone back, and the company had succeeded in getting some new men, whom the strikers tried unsuccessfully to persuade to join the strike.

On 8 September all but three or four cars were running. Griffith had already declared that the dismissals had been decided on before the association's deputation came to see him. The company would never take back the dismissed men, but it would give 'favourable reception to the application of any of the strikers who will declare that they have not been actuated by any hostile motive.' He also played a game which was to become familiar by announcing that the company was putting into effect a new timetable which would distribute the hours more equally.

Meanwhile, on the evening of 7 September the association had held a mass meeting. Sharp, aldermen McAndrew and Stewart, and Rev Dr Burns spoke. McAndrew, one of the founders of the Trades and Labor Council, said he 'did not consider this a strike at all: the men had merely thrown up their positions for a principle.' The company was breaking a city by-law. Stewart called a 15-hour day white slavery. Dr Burns felt that there was a misunderstanding, which he hoped a discussion with the company would clear up. The meeting voted to send McAndrew, Stewart, and Burns as a deputation to see the management. McAndrew had to decline, since he was due to leave for the TLCC convention in Toronto, but the other two accepted. Alderman Moore, who had heard of the meeting too late to be present, went to Griffith on his own to protest against the company's behaviour.

Griffith told Moore that a new timetable had been in preparation before the dispute broke out. Mr Charlton, the company's president, admitted that the existing hours were 14½ for 2 days, then 4 for the third. He said there were now to be 6 men for every 2 cars, with 2 days of 10½ and 11½ hours respectively, each day to be divided into 3 sections. On reinstatement of the leaders and the strikers, he repeated Griffith's earlier statements, adding: 'We have reason to believe that the real object of the association was to furnish material for designing demagogues by which they could further their own interests. The company has determined that its employees are not to be made the tools of self-seeking agitators.' He thought it was 'in the interests of the men themselves ... to show our determination now ... rather than wait until the organization had time to grow and strengthen.'

At noon on 8 September George E. Tuckett, a company director, arranged a conference with the men's deputation. The management explained the new timetable, which the men approved, admitting that a 10-hour day was impractical. The men insisted the association was not hostile to the company: it was set up 'merely for mutual assistance in case of sickness.' Tuckett suggested 'it would have been well if the men, in organizing such an association, had consulted the officers of the company. No doubt Mr Charlton and Mr Griffith would be glad to co-operate with the men and help them if their objectives were such as those described.' Charlton said he would have been glad to attend a meeting: but he would not now. There would be no reinstatement for the five discharged leaders (Sharp had got employment elsewhere); as to the rest, he would not say. He declined to answer a question about company informers within the association. A union delegate said the men thought that all should get the same wage rate. Griffith said no; experienced men should get more. The men said the strike had not been authorized; the men had gone out on impulse, on hearing of the discharge of their committee.

The 20 men who had struck then decided not to go back unless the 5 leaders were reinstated. The company refused. It also declined to give reasons for dismissals. These often took place for such reasons as drunkenness, and to give the reasons would make it hard for the dismissed man to get another job. It did make one further concession: the employees were to get 25 cents an hour overtime.

On 9 September the mayor intervened. He proposed that the company pay the 5 leaders 1 month's pay, and reinstate the 20 strikers. The company agreed, with the proviso that it would not dismiss any of the new men to make room for strikers: these would have to take their turn as vacancies occurred. On 10 September the men accepted the mayor's terms and, said the Hamilton *Spectator*, 'peace, harmony and good will were restored ... Last night nearly all the men called at the company's offices, expressed regret at the hasty action into which they had been led, and asked to be reinstated.' Nothing was said about the fate of the company's electrician, dismissed on 7 September for his refusal to help in a sudden emergency.[79]

This play had been enacted before. It was to be re-enacted many times. But there is smoothness, a finish, a polish, an unctuousness, about this particular performance which makes it a classic. It is not surprising that when the men organized again, the 'ringleader' was not a company employee, but a printer, Philip Obermeyer.

The 1897 Labour Day parade included local unions of barbers (newly formed), butchers, marble workers, and slaters and unions of tailors, cutters and trimmers, and garment workers. The last four were apparently about to become locals of the United Garment Workers. It also included *Spectator* route and news boys and city employees.[80]

The Barbers probably became Local 131 of the international chartered 20 October 1900. The Butchers took part in the 1900 Labour Day sports; by Labour Day, 1902 they had become Local 228 of the international. The civic employees (apparently organized) took part in the 1900 Labour Day sports; by February 1902 there was certainly a Civic Employees Union, which seems to have been still there at the end of the year.[81]

In November 1900 the carters and cabmen formed a union (still there in 1902), and in August 1902 the theatrical stage employees.

There was a Teamsters Association No 1 in 1902.[82]

LONDON

In August 1881 there was already a Bakers Union which, in 1882, became a branch of the Ontario union. By 1882 there was also a Journeymen Harnessmakers Protective Association, which may also have been part of a regional union. The bricklayers organized in February 1882 a union which struck in March for $3 a day, and got $2.50. In October this union applied for membership in the international union and became Local 5 of Ontario.[83]

The hod carriers may have organized a union in 1885; the plasterers almost certainly did. The painters had a local union from 1887 to 1890. The tailors had a union in 1889, which probably became Local 30 of the international the next year. There was a Labourers Union in 1888, and a Switchmen's Union in 1889.[84]

A Barbers Union was organized in 1893 and marched in the Labour Day parades of 1893, 1895, and 1896. This may have lasted till the chartering of Local 366 of the international union, 17 December 1901. The retail clerks had an organization before 1895, but 'never anything more than a union in name,' and it collapsed in that year. A Grocery Clerks Union was organized in 1898, and marched in the 1899 parade.[85]

The plumbers had a union by 1895, which may have become Local 64 of the United Association in or before 1897.[86]

The Trades and Labor Council organized the Builders' Labourers Union in 1895. This, at some stage, became Local 8 of an international union; it marched in the parades of 1896–1902.[87]

A local union of brickmakers marched in the 1896 parade, and a local Coopers' Union in 1897–99. A General Labourers' Union marched in 1897; Railroad Teamsters (organized in or before 1898) in 1899 and 1901; Draymen in 1899 and 1900; Newsboys and Electricians in 1899 (the latter became international Local 120 on 20 April 1900). The Railroad Teamsters were still on hand in 1902.[88]

The harness and trunk makers who marched in 1899 were probably members of a purely local organization. A Hackmen's Union was organized in 1898 or 1899 and marched in 1900 and 1901. It was still on hand in 1902. A Carriage Workers Union, 1898, became international Local 46. There was a Linemen's Union in 1902.[89]

The Coopers struck in the spring of 1899 for an improvement in their conditions of employment. They complained that, after being placed on a job, they often had to wait hours for materials. As they worked by the piece, this meant no pay. They also complained that it was often hard to make out who was really boss of a job. The union won the strike, gaining recognition, a 10 per cent increase in wages, the use of the union label, and a guarantee that materials would be on hand when the men were placed on the job. The strike lasted long enough to get the men thinking about a co-operative cooperage, but this idea evaporated with their victory.[90]

BRANTFORD

Brantford's second trades and labour council (21 January 1887) included a Builders' Labourers Union and a Plasterers Union. By July the Builders' Labourers were sending delegates to a Toronto conference on forming a national union. A Barbers Union was organized in May 1887, and a fresh one in 1893 which lasted till 1901, when it probably became international Local 298.[91]

The weavers in the Craven Cotton Mills struck, 16 June 1887, and formed a union on 20 June. They wanted a return to the rates of three or four years before, three cents per cut higher. They complained they were getting 10 to 20 per cent less than weavers in other Canadian cities. The company said the existing state of the trade would not permit such an increase. Many of the workers went back on 17 June and many others on 28 June. The strike failed, and the union probably collapsed.

A second union of weavers in the same plant, The Wage-Earners Society, was formed in 1900. It was said to be affiliated with some larger body. Its president, John Smith, was dismissed by the company, and the union struck, 23 April, for his reinstatement. When Smith got a job in Hamilton, he advised the men to go back to work, which they did, 26 April.[92]

There was a Carpenters Union in May 1889, probably Local 280 of the United Brotherhood gone purely local some time in 1888.[93] There was a Tailors Union at the same time; this became, in March 1890, international Local 117.[94]

Unions of painters and of tinsmiths were organized in August 1894. There was a Painters Union in August 1899, which probably became, in March 1901, international Local 113. The Tinsmiths may have been part of the international Tin, Sheet Iron and Cornice Workers. The Horseshoers Protective Association, organized in March 1897, seems to have lasted till 1904. The bricklayers formed a local union on 4 March 1898; on 23 March 1899 this became international Local 9 of Ontario.[95]

ST CATHARINES

The St Catharines barbers organized a union 1 October 1886. On 10 October 1894 it expressed sympathy with the carpet weavers in their strike; in May 1897 it took part in a labour rally; by 23 November 1898 it was able to report that all the barbers in the city were members. It was still in existence in 1902.[96]

A Builders' Labourers Union and a Ship Carpenters and Caulkers Union appear in 1887 and 1889. In 1889 there were unions of painters, plumbers, and forkrake makers (though this last may have been a Knights of Labor LA).[97]

The painters reappear in April 1897: international Local 407 was not chartered till 8 August 1901. The plumbers took part in the 1897 rally. Local 244 of the United Association was not chartered till 13 April 1901.[98]

Early in October 1894 the handloom weavers at the Garden City Carpet Works struck. They were working a 14-hour day and getting less than $9 a week. The company brought in strikebreakers, but the strikers persuaded them not to work. After the strike had been on for some time, the workers organized as the St Catharines Carpet Weavers' Union No 1, with a charter membership of 35. They also passed a resolution urging all the carpet weavers of Canada to form a union. Large delegations from the Cigar Makers and the United Carpenters were present at the organization meeting, and the various unions of the city contributed cash to help the strikers.[99]

A new Builders' Labourers Union was organized in April 1901.[100] A Retail Clerks Protective Association, organized in April 1897, took part in the May labour rally. It stated its intention of affiliating with the international. But the Retail Clerks National Protective Association had no Canadian locals till 1899. Perhaps St Catharines was turned down for want of jurisdiction. It was not till November 1902 that St Catharines Local 703 was chartered.[101]

ELSEWHERE IN ONTARIO

Belleville had a local Barbers Union at some unknown date before December 1902, when the *Labour Gazette* chronicled its demise.[102]

St Thomas had a Tailors Union in 1885, a Builders' Labourers Union in 1887, and a Carpenters Union on 31 July 1902, probably a survival of the United Brotherhood's Local 220, suspended in 1900.[103]

Guelph had a Tailors Union till at least 1887, a Labourers Union 1886–88, a Carpenters Union in 1888 and 1889, unions of stonecutters and masons, and of plasterers, in 1889, and an Ontario Agricultural College Employees Union in November 1902.[104]

Stratford had a Labourers Union in 1887. Berlin's Steam Engineers Union, formed in 1887, was still listed in October 1901. There was also, in 1902, a Glove Workers Union, probably AFL FLU 8900 gone local. St Marys had a Delivery Boys Union, formed in November 1901, and still in existence in February 1902. Merritton's LA 5933 had disappeared by 6 March 1896, when the workingmen of that town met 'to consider ... re-organizing the Knights of Labor or other Labor Association.' But the United Wage Earners of Canada (Pioneer Assembly) was not organized until November 1898. This union had ambitions: in July 1899 it was reported that a movement was on foot to organize a branch of the Wage Earners in St Catharines, to include all unorganized workers. Nothing seems to have come of this, however. The Merritton Assembly, in March 1899, heard several ministers explain the Lord's Day Alliance and impress on the members 'the moral right of all workingmen to a day of rest.' In June the Assembly presented a small purse to Rev T.J. Parr, 'whose charming entertainments, public and private lectures, were chiefly instrumental in obtaining for us the success by which our efforts are crowned.' The report adds: 'We feel certain that many brother Wage Earners in Hamilton' would benefit by Parr's presence – which suggests that there may have been a Hamilton Assembly.[105] The Merritton Assembly, on 5 March 1901, became AFL FLU 9661.[106]

A Millmen's Union, formed in Rockland in the late summer of 1898, paraded in the Ottawa Labour Day parade. It arose out of a strike at the W.C. Edwards' mill which began 17 July. The men had been working an 11-hour day for less than $1, and getting paid in truck once a month. They wanted shorter hours, fortnightly payment, and $1.25 a day. Edwards, a prominent Liberal MP, was an exponent of the theories of Henry George, which had enjoyed a considerable vogue in the labour movement. But his progressive views did not prevent him from refusing the demands, and the men went out. About 12 Dominion Police then came to Rockland from Ottawa on a tugboat. They fired their revolvers into the air to frighten the strikers, who replied with volleys of rocks, and the police beat a hasty retreat. Edwards then offered a little more pay and shorter hours, which the men refused. Rumours that the militia would be brought in proved unfounded. Two of the main causes of the trouble seem to have been differing rates of pay for the same class of work, and the payment of wages in goods at company stores. By 22 June Edwards had caved in, granting a 10-hour day at $1 a day, with fortnightly payment in cash. The union was formed during the strike.[107]

Rockland also had a Stonecutters Union, in 1902.[108]

A Brotherhood of Woodsmen was organized in Sault Ste Marie in November 1902 and lasted till 1906. Collingwood had a Longshoremen's Union in 1889. Welland seems to have had a Switchmen's Union in 1891.[109]

WINNIPEG

In 1894, when Winnipeg formed its third Trades and Labor Council, it seems to have had at least 10 local unions: Hod Carriers, Icelandic Labourers, Tinsmiths, English-speaking Labourers, Painters, Freight Handlers, Butchers, Lathers, Plumbers, and

Bakers. The Icelandic Labourers, the Tinsmiths, the English-speaking Labourers, the Painters, and the Butchers all appear again in 1896, and the Lathers in 1895 and 1896. The Bakers go right through to 1898 (by July 1899 international Local 34 had arrived).[110]

A second Painters Union, organized in 1898, appears also in 1899 and 1900, and in 1902 probably became international Local 739. A second Lathers Union was organized in 1898, and a third in April 1902 (this last, in October, probably became international Local 147). A second Plumbers Union, organized in April 1898, by May had apparently got a union-shop agreement with every firm in the city. By September it had become international Local 62.[111]

About 30 city blacksmiths took part in the 1895 Labour Day parade, and a Blacksmiths Union in the 1896 sports. A Retail Clerks Union appears in 1896; a second, organized in April 1899, lasted right through to 1903 at least. The barbers formed a union in May 1897; in June it became international Local 69, which collapsed early in 1898.[112]

The list for the 1896 Labour Day sports includes boilermakers, teamsters, harness makers and brewery workmen. Organizations of laundry workers and woodworkers appear in 1897, brickmakers in 1898, photographers' employees in 1899. There had been a Teamsters Union in 1897 or 1898, but its life had been neither long nor peaceful. In March 1899 both the teamsters and the draymen (team owners) organized unions, with provision for joint action. The Teamsters Union was still there in January 1902; the Draymen's Association appears throughout 1902 and marched in the 1903 Labour Day parade.[113]

A Western Carpenters Union, formed in August 1901, was still there in 1903. A Quarrymen's Association, already in existence in July 1901, continued through 1902. A Civic Workers Union appears in 1901 and throughout 1902. A Deliverymen's Union, organized in July 1902, appears in the 1903 Labour Day preliminary list. A Women's Protective Union ('workers by the day') was organized in November 1902.[114]

There were apparently two Sheet Metal Workers Unions in the summer of 1902. (International Local 31 was closed in 1901 and not rechartered till 1903). A Builders' Labourers Union, organized in July 1902, lasted till 1905.[115]

ELSEWHERE ON THE PRAIRIES

Brandon had a Threshers National Protective Association from July 1891 till some time in 1904. Moose Jaw had a Draymen's Union (Teamsters and Owners) in 1902. The Calgary retail clerks organized a union in June 1902. Some time between then and August 1903 this probably became international Local 642.[116]

VANCOUVER

The earliest local union in Vancouver seems to have been Stevedores No 1, formed in the spring of 1888. In July 1892 it became LA 677. In December 1896 it left the Knights and became the Stevedores and Freight Handlers. By March 1901 this seems to have become international Local 211. There may have been a secession on 1 April 1899, with the chartering of TLCC FLU Vancouver Freight Handlers No 4, though this was more probably the Railway Freight Handlers Union, or Brotherhood of Freight Handlers, which appears in the Vancouver Trades and Labor Council's minutes in April, July, and October 1902. By December this had gone into the UBRE, which again suggests FLU No 4, since that body's charter was surrendered about this time.

The Stevedores had a prolonged strike in 1900. The union's delegate had always been responsible for assigning jobs. In February 1900 the Pacific Coast Steamship Co suddenly jibbed, and insisted that one of its own officers should be responsible. Some 80 union men then refused to work for the company, which, on 20 February, got its *Union Queen* unloaded by 31 men from Seattle and Everett, Washington. Of these, however, 26 walked off when they found out about the strike, and the union paid their way home. On 22 February the company brought in 50 Japanese strikebreakers. The union turned back five, and the Japanese members of the Canadian Pacific Freight Handlers Union dealt with the rest by striking till the Japanese strikebreakers withdrew. The union tried to get the San Francisco Seamen's Union to call out the men on the *Union Queen*, but the Seamen's Union refused, since it had a contract with the steamship company.

Next day, the union offered a compromise: it would pay its own delegate, who would take orders from the ship's mate. The company refused, and the union charged it with trying to break the organization. It also alleged that the company's behaviour was a scheme by James J. Hill, president of the Great Northern Railway and the dominant figure in the steamship company, to get business away from the CPR for the Great Northern. On 6 March the company announced that it was 'done with' the union. Meanwhile, the Trades and Labor Council had taken a hand. It asked the city to charge the company's imported strikebreakers poll tax and to have the company pay for police protection. The captain of the *Union Queen* was summonsed to court, but he got off, as the court ruled that poll tax was payable only if the men had been in service for at least a week.

On 10 April the company announced that about 20 non-union men would be put to work next day. This cannot have been very successful, for on 19 April it was reported that freight was piling up, and that though the *Umatilla* had taken 34 cars that morning, 189 were still waiting, while 90 more were on their way to North Portal. By 13 July it was nearly five months since any Pacific Coast Steamship Co ship had been unloaded by the union. Large quantities of freight for California were arriving daily, and the ships' crews had to cope with it as best they could.

At this point, Mr Bremner, of the Dominion department of labour, intervened. He visited the company's Seattle agency, and secured from a new agent an offer of 35 cents an hour for day work and 40 for night, and an undertaking to let the union delegate list the men for work, with a company official superintending the assignment of jobs. This was accepted.[117]

A second local body was the Plasterers' Protective Society, one of the founders of the Trades and Labor Council, 21 November 1889. It was still in existence on 13 February 1891, but by 17 June 1892 the Council is recording that active steps are to be taken 'to organize the Plasterers.'[118] Another union in existence when the Council was started was the Bricklayers and Masons. This became on 19 February 1890 international Local No 1 of British Columbia. There seems to have been a rival Bricklayers Union in November 1902.[119]

The Lathers Protective Union was represented at Council meetings in 1890 and 1891. By 17 June 1892, however, it was in the same state as the Plasterers.[120]

On 8 August 1890 the Council appointed a committee to organize the building labourers. On 19 September the Hod Carriers Protective Union made its appearance. It was represented again on 10 October, when it approved a Knights of Labor resolution on street cars and against Sunday labour. On 3 April 1891 it figured in the discussion of the Bricklayers' resignation from the Council. 'The laborers, instead of the sliding scale in force of $2.25 to $3.00 had adopted a uniform rate of wages of $2.50. The bricklayers said they were asking too much. The opinion of the meeting was that the bricklayers had nothing whatever to do with regulating the wages of the hod carriers.'

It seems likely that the Hod Carriers were the same union which appears later in the Council's minutes as the Building Labor Union and as the Builders' Laborers Union, from October 1891 to January 1895, when their delegate regretted 'that his union the "Deay Labourers" was compelled to withdraw for a time.' The Council, however, on 1 March, wrote the union asking it to resume sending delegates without, for the time being, paying per capita tax; on 15 March the delegate was back.

This union must have collapsed by September 1899, when the Council's organizing committee reported that the labourers had been organized, and an international charter sent for. The new union must have had a short life, for in 1902 the TLCC chartered its FLU 32, later described as Builders' Labourers. This was already active in June 1902, and it survived till 1911.[121]

A Plumbers Union was formed in October or November 1890, but it lasted only till May or June 1892. Local 170 of the United Association was not organized till the fall of 1898.[122]

A Tinners and Cornice Makers Union, perhaps an international local, was admitted to the Council on 24 April 1891. On 22 May the Council assured the local of support in its demand for a rate of $5 per day. On 17 June came the glad news that, with one or two exceptions, the employers were willing to grant the demand, and that no serious trouble was expected. The victory may have been too easy, for, though the Tinners appear again on 11 March 1892, by 23 September their union had 'gone out of existence.' The Council tried to reorganize it but apparently failed.[123]

In April 1899 there was a Vancouver Stenographers Union.[124]

The Vancouver and New Westminster Shipwrights and Caulkers Association was formed on 11 September 1900, and a Ship Carpenters Union in December. Both appear in the *Labour Gazette* 1901 and 1902 lists. The Ship Carpenters and Caulkers Association started off with 25 members, who promptly adopted a wage scale of $4 a day for new work and $4.50 for old, with double time for Sundays and statutory holidays. This was to come into force 1 October. Trouble followed in one yard, Cates', which refused to recognize the union. By 22 April 1901 Cates had brought in nine men from Seattle, and the union had complained to Mr Bremner of a breach of the Alien Labour Act. On 3 May the union struck for a wage of 90 cents an hour for a 9-hour day on the reconstruction of river steamers (the men had been getting 60 cents, with no overtime). This was accepted on 6 May. By 22 May the Cates yard had been unionized.[125]

The Musicians organized a union in April 1901, and became Local 145 of the international on 3 June. A Vancouver Boilermakers' Helpers Union was formed 25 October 1902, but this may have been or become international Lodge 49.[126]

VICTORIA

The Shipwrights and Caulkers Association seems to have flourished right through the period 1881–1902.[127]

A Bricklayers and Masons Union was among the founders of the Victoria Trades Assembly in June 1889. It became international Local 2 of British Columbia on 1 May 1890. A Painters and Decorators Union seems to have been formed soon after the Trades Assembly. International Local 5 was not chartered till 8 May 1901.[128]

There was a Musicians Union in July 1890, and a Plasterers Union in January 1891. On 6 January 1899 the Victoria *Colonist* said that unions of carriage workers and horseshoers were to be organized that week by the organizing committee of the Trades and Labor Council.[129]

The Marine Firemen's Association was probably formed in the late summer or early fall of 1900; it went international in February 1901.[130] Local 65 of the Hotel and Restaurant Workers, chartered 3 September 1901, 'never reported' to the international office, but seems to have continued as a local union till at least July 1902. There was a Victoria Civic Employees Union in July 1902. A Boilermakers' Helpers Union was formed in September, but is later reported as a Boilermakers' lodge.[131]

NANAIMO

The coal trimmers formed a union in November 1889; a Longshoremen's Union is mentioned in January 1890. In February 1890 the Trimmers were writing the Miners for support, and in September the Nanaimo *Free Press* was reporting that Coal Trimmers No 1 would be organized from and after 1 October. In July 1891 there was a Coal Trimmers Protective and Benevolent Association. The Coal Trimmers were among the founders of the Nanaimo Trades and Labor Council.[132]

A Carpenters Union seems to have been formed 15 September 1890, chiefly to get an eight-hour day. On 21 March 1891 this became Local 755 of the United Brotherhood.[133]

An Engineers Protective Association No 1 was formed 27 September 1890, in the New Vancouver Coal Co. It had over 20 members. It was among the founders of the Trades and Labor Council.[134]

A Teamsters and Expressmen's Union, formed 12 April 1899, was still there in July 1902. A Carriage Builders and Blacksmiths Union, formed 15 April 1899, is listed in the *Labour Gazette* of October 1901. The Nanaimo *Free Press* of 4 May 1899 mentions a Merchants' Employees Association.[135]

The *American Federationist* of May 1900 reports the chartering of a Barbers Union in Nanaimo, and in February 1901 says it has all the shops but one. This union is not listed in the *Labour Gazette* of July 1902. The *American Federationist* in April 1900 had reported the formation of a new Nanaimo Trades and Labor Council, with the Miners, Tailors (international), Teamsters, Clerks, and 'Artizans' as members. The *Labour Gazette* of May 1901 explains that the Artisans Club, which it says was then taking steps to make itself a union, was 'composed of surface and shop hands employees' of the New Vancouver Coal Co. The *Labour Gazette* of March 1902 lists, among general labour unions, a Nanaimo 'Amalgamated Association of M. and I.' There was a Blacksmiths Union listed in 1901 and 1902.

ELSEWHERE IN BRITISH COLUMBIA

Nelson had a Cigar Makers Union, formed 28 November 1899; international local 432, was formed in June 1901. There was also a Stonecutters Union in July 1902.[136]

Rossland had a Carpenters and Joiners Union No 1, formed 28 December 1897. By July 1900 it had 120 members, and was considering joining the United Brotherhood. But it apparently decided not to, and in July 1902, was still in existence. Greenwood had a purely local union, with 60 members in July 1900, which soon joined the international union.[137]

Rossland seems also to have had a local Barbers Union in March and July 1902. So do Greenwood and Phoenix. Phoenix had also a Local 155 of the Western Labor Union, chartered 5 May 1901, and still there in July 1902.

Maywood had a Street Railway Employees Union in January 1902. Ashcroft had a Labourers Protective Association in May 1902.[138]

THE YUKON

In June 1902 unions of tinsmiths (or sheet metal workers), carpenters, cooks and waiters (or hotel workers), bakers, and painters, and two federal labour unions, were formed in Dawson City. By July unions of miners, stenographers, a second painters' union, and a third labour union had been added.[139] This last, the Yukon Labour Protective and Improvement Union, in September 1901 addressed a long appeal to the TLCC. The union had established a wage of $5 a day with board. But work was possible only 9 months of the year at most. When a man was not working, board cost him an average of $20 to $30 a week. Boots cost $10 to $12, rubber boots $14 to $20, shirts $2.50 to $4, tobacco $1.50 to $2 a pound, cigars 25 to 50 cents each, whiskey, 'etc.' 25 to 50 cents per glass, beer the same, stage fares 50 cents per mile, laundry 25 to 50 cents apiece, picks $4 and up, shovels $5 and up, and 'Lawyers' fees – All you are worth; absolutely no limit. Do not for a single moment imagine that $5 is easily obtained for a day's work. The banks, large mercantile companies and English mining companies all endeavour to obtain men at less than the going wage, and as it is only for a short time in the spring that men are scarce, the difficulty in keeping up wages is easily understood.'

Wages were ordinarily paid in gold dust, 'which runs from 50 cents to one dollar and a half less per ounce than what it is taken at, namely, $16 per ounce. Every amusement is more than double outside prices, and the comforts of life are entirely absent. Canned goods and bacon, with the staples of life, constitute the food ... Now, with banks, English capital and grasping Shylocks as the principal operators of large groups of claims, the richest ground is fighting with characteristic capital methods to grind the wages down to less than a living rate, hoping, apparently, thereby to either enslave the white labor or force it from the country and then resort to Chinese. But the price of foodstuffs is maintained.'

The Chinese labourers had not yet appeared, but the union was mortally afraid of their coming, and appealed to the Congress and unions generally to do everything possible to 'prevent even a starting of this course in the Yukon.' It also appealed to the merchants who supplied the Klondike not to spoil their market by letting the Orientals in.

The union also complained of interpretations of the common law that swindled the workers, and of a paternalistic government exacting 'a license of $10 a year for the privilege of having to submit to such treatment. Things have now reached such an unhappy pass that in the matter of the right of the wage-earner to seek redress against an employer who defrauds him of his wage, a state of absolute anarchy exists.'

The appeal wound up: 'Again wishing for the millennium, as far as labor is concerned, to come in our time, we remain, Yours in the brotherhood of man.'

D.H. Dick, one of the signatories, was also secretary of the Grand Forks Labour Union, and 'a member of the Wait-Upon-The-Minister-of the Interior Committee.' He added a letter of his own, which emphasized that the appeal was based on petitions and resolutions of mass meetings, and declared that in the Yukon workers had 'no preference for wages under the Territorial Court ... and this has worked more hardship on wage-workers here in the past three years, to my personal knowledge, than I ever noticed in the whole course of my life. Shop-keepers, bankers, gambling debts – in fact any old claim was given preference to wages ... The question of giving us a Dominion representative at once, and of giving us what might be called a lay delegate for this winter, I think, touches the pith and germ of the questions.'

The convention responded unequivocally, endorsing the petition and promising to do all it could to secure redress of the grievances.[140]

In March 1902 there were also labour unions in 'Cariboo, Dominion Creek,' Grand Forks, 'Hunker, Hunker Bruk,' and '30 below Lower Discovery, Dominion Creek.' All four were still there in July.[141]

The total number of purely local unions at the end of 1902 was probably about 112 to 134. Of these, something like 12 to 15 were in the Atlantic provinces, about 35 to 39 in Quebec, about 24 to 34 in Ontario, 10 or 11 in Manitoba, 1 each in what are now Saskatchewan and Alberta, about 14 to 18 in British Columbia, and 15 in the Yukon.

14

Regional and national unions 1881–1902

Nova Scotia

Of the regional unions, far the biggest and most successful was the Provincial Workmen's Association. It entered 1881 with seven lodges, all on the mainland, and all in coal mining and coal shipping. In the course of that year it organized twelve more, three on the mainland, nine in Cape Breton.[1]

On the mainland the PWA undertook its first two ventures outside the coal industry. A glass works had been started in New Glasgow, apparently in the summer or early fall of 1881. By 2 November the *Trades Journal* was reporting the chartering of Our Rights, No 18, in the New Glasgow Spike and Foundry Co, and was commenting that the glass workers had set the example for non-mining lodges. The example was short lived. By the end of the year, another new mining lodge, Progress, Chignecto Mines, Maccan, had been chartered with the number 17, which must have belonged to the Glass Blowers. In September 1892 the grand secretary said the Glass Blowers' lodge had 'been forced to leave the Association as the rules of the society in the States made it imperative that a lodge in affiliation with the society there should be organized.' No 18 was about as short lived: organized in October 1881, the last mention of it is on 9 November. No 17 lasted till October 1884, when work stopped at the mine.[2]

The expansion in Cape Breton was swift and spectacular. At the grand council's half-yearly meeting on 7 April 1881, 'Brother Gray thought the Association might find a footing in Cape Breton this summer.' He commented on the low wages and said the men were bound down. Brother Wilson said 'Cape Breton needed to be helped as much as ever Nova Scotia required ... There are good men and true in Cape Breton, men who would stand up manfully for their rights, but [they] had been so crushed down of late that they have very little spirit in them. But the spirit is still

there and needed only to be stirred by this Association to make it burn brightly.'
The council sent the grand secretary and an agent to the island.

They found at least one employer ready to give them a hot reception. The manager of the Gowrie Mine, Cow Bay, threatened to dismiss any men who attended PWA meetings, and forbade owners of halls to rent them for such meetings. A newspaper charged that Drummond had left Lingan and Little Glace Bay years before with a pile of unpaid debts. Drummond repled that he had indeed left debts behind him, but with one exception, debts owing *to* him, not by him. The one exception, for $2, a Mr McDonald had assured him he would do his best to collect and pay, and Drummond thought the whole thing had been settled.

Threats and slanders alike seem to have produced no effect. The *Trades Journal* of 13 July 1881 recorded the formation of four lodges: Drummond, No 8, Sydney Mines; Island, No 9, Bridgeport; Unity, No 10, Reserve; and Equity, No 11, Caledonia. The 20 July issue had four more: Banner, No 12, Gowrie; Eastern, No 13, Block House; Keystone, No 14, Little Glace Bay; and Coping Stone, No 15, Lingan. By 19 October Wilson, No 16, Big Glace Bay, had been added. Drummond and Island were still there at the end of 1902. Unity seems to have lasted till the end of 1888; it was reorganized in the fall of 1893, and was still there at the end of 1902. Equity and Keystone led a revolt in the summer of 1897 and were expelled; Equity was reorganized in 1901 and was still there at the end of 1902. Banner lasted till the end of 1898. Eastern was suspended in 1886 because of the closing of the mine. Coping Stone probably lasted till the summer of 1887, when the mine closed down. Wilson seems to have disappeared by the end of 1883.

By 10 August 1881 there was a sub-council for Cape Breton, which lasted till 1891.[3]

Three new lodges were formed in 1883: Brunswick, No 18, Joggins Mines, in February; Cape Breton, No 19, Sydney and Lousibourg Coal and Railroad Co, Sydney, by 30 May; International, No 20, International Pier, Sydney, by 12 September. Brunswick enjoyed the distinction of being named after the mine manager, who was so enthusiastic about unions that he wanted to be a member of the new lodge. Membership rose within a week from 71 to 93. This, however, turned out to be a false dawn. The lodge had a series of little strikes, irritating the grand council, which on one such occasion ordered the men back to work. Then, in June 1884, the lodge struck again, without the council's authority, because of non-payment of wages. It was out only a few days when the company announced no one would be taken back unless he renounced the union. Most of the men did, making this mine the only non-union mine of any size in the province. The charter was then suspended.[4]

By September 1883 the 11 Cape Breton lodges had a membership of about 1250. By February 1884 this was down to 940, and by September had recovered to 952.

The 7 mainland lodges had 963 members in February 1884, and 908 in September. Around 600 members were in arrears.[5]

Garfield Junior Lodge (boys), a branch of Cameron, Westville, was organized in March 1884, but seems to have fizzled out almost at once. Steadfast Junior Lodge, at Reserve, appears in April 1887 and February 1888, then disappears till 1901. In February 1888, Rock, No 21, Spring Hill, was organized; it seems to have disappeared within a year. It was followed by Victoria, No 22, Victoria Mines, Cape Breton, in April 1888, which survived till the fall of 1897.

In October 1890 the PWA chartered Mechanics' Lodge, Spring Hill. This disappears from grand council minutes in September 1892, and reappears only in 1894; by December 1898 it is listed as defunct.

A Juvenile Lodge at Spring Hill made a brief appearance in January 1891.[6] In January 1891 also the PWA made a fresh sally into industries other than coal mining, with the chartering of Concord, No 24, Amherst. The boot and shoe workers there, in October 1890, having 'discerned that the PWA was for all classes of workmen,' put out feelers about affiliation, and soon 'abandoned another society and cast their lot with us.' This lodge certainly lasted till 1899, and reappears in September 1901 and 1902, though not in January 1903.[7]

Cadegan Lodge, Gardener Mines, Cape Breton, was organized by September 1893; so was Progress, Old Bridgeport. A year later, the Gardener Mines had been closed, and Cadegan had suspended its meetings. Progress lasted till September 1897.

In 1894 Maple Leaf Lodge, Westville, was organized, but promptly became inactive; in the fall of 1895 it had 50 members, but a year later it seems to have been gone. Holdfast, No 27, Joggins Mines, chartered 16 February 1894, was still there at the end of 1902. Golden Rule, at Dominion No 1, Cape Breton, organized 14 February 1895, lasted throughout the period. Power, New Victoria, organized in 1896, apparently lasted only till September 1897; Neptune, No 30, Louisbourg, also organized in 1896, was defunct by the end of 1898.[8]

In April 1888 the grand secretary had reported 3000 men in the mines 'who claim a connection with the Association,' but added that 'a large number of them are apparently content to be nominal members.' By October 1891 the enrolled membership was 2000, with 1350 in good standing. In 1893 the members in good standing, in 15 lodges, averaged only 1100, fewer than in the 9 mainland lodges 10 years before. In 1894, still with 15 lodges, the membership in good standing was 1173. In 1895, with 16, it had risen to 1416; but the nominal membership was not short of 2000. By 1896 the number of active lodges was 16; of inactive, 3.[9]

In 1896 Drummond, the grand secretary, had won a unanimous vote of confidence in the grand council. But within a few months the attacks on him had been renewed. On 13 May 1897 representatives of 10 Cape Breton lodges met in Sydney to hear formal charges. Drummond had offended many of the members by his attitude on the company store question. After some 'sharp firing,' a majority report exonerating Drummond was adopted, 12 to 5, with Unity Lodge abstaining. A further motion, giving Keystone and Equity lodges (which had made the charges) 30 days to accept the decision was carried by 16 to 4.

When the council's September meeting took place the two rebel lodges had been suspended for four months, beginning 1 July. Delegates from 13 other lodges, however, were present, and heard Drummond boast that the PWA was the strongest, single labour organization in Canada, and that, in contrast with the United States, Canadians had 'reason to be thankful that we know nothing of "government by injunction" or ... the bullets of braggarts or panic-stricken deputies.' The grand secretary seemed to be firmly in the saddle. But the majority of the lodges had not accepted his proposal for dealing with company stores (he admitted he had not favoured the late agitation against them), and there were rumours of the formation of a rival organization.

This, of course, materialized in DA 35 (Glace Bay) of the Knights of Labor, under the leadership of A.B. McGillivray, who in March 1889 had been elected to the Cape Breton Island committee, and since 1894 had been its secretary. The revolt was formidable enough to produce Drummond's resignation, 30 June 1898, and it killed eight of the lodges. When the council met again 28 December 1898 with John Moffatt as grand secretary, Keystone and Equity, by now expelled, had shown no sign of repentance and had even become aggressive. The Victoria, Mechanics (Glace Bay), Banner, Progress, Pioneer, Mechanics (Springhill), International, and Neptune lodges were gone also. Only Holdfast, Concord, Golden Rule, Unity, Island, and Drummond remained, though several others were seeking reorganization.[10]

On 16 October 1898, Ladysmith Lodge, Westville, was organized.[11] So by September 1899 there were seven lodges. By September 1900 there were five more: Buller, Stellarton, on 14 March; Kimberley (Mechanics), Dominion No 1, and Strathcona, Westville, on 14 April; Mafeking (mechanics), Reserve, probably about the same time; and Pioneer was back. By the end of the year, there were a further four: Roberts, No 35 (Mechanics), Sydney Mines, 30 October; Olive, No 36, Dominion No 3, at the end of November or beginning of December; Queen, No 37 (Mechanics), Glace Bay, 30 November; Powell, No 38 (Mechanics), Bridgeport, 3 December. Fidelity and McBean had been back in April, but do not appear in the September list; neither does Concord. By the end of the year there must have been at least 16 lodges. Of these, Powell lasted till at least October 1902; the others were all still there in January 1903.

By September 1901 Equity and Steadfast had been reorganized; Concord was certainly now operating; and six new lodges had been organized: Liberty, No 40 (coal trimmers), Whitney Pier, Sydney, and Star, No 41, Broad Cove, Inverness, in January; Kitchener, No 42, Thorburn, and a new Banner Lodge, Port Morien, in February; Sampson, No 44, Louisbourg, in April; and Seaside, No 43, Port Hood, in September. Of the six new lodges Kitchener seems to have been gone by January 1903, but the rest were still there.[12]

At the September 1901 council meeting the grand secretary was able to report not only the 12 new or reorganized lodges since the previous meeting but also a membership of 5000 to 6000 in the 24 lodges. Yet 1902 was to witness new advances: 11 new lodges, and organization in a new industry. There were already five mechanics' lodges and one of boot and shoe workers. To these were now added four of railway workers: Consolidation, at Stellarton; Gibraltar, at Mulgrave; Eden, at Point Tupper; and Coronation, at Sydney. All these, and Ironside (or Ironsides), Glace Bay, had been organized by September 1902. Between then and the end of the year, six more appeared: Chignecto No 54, 25 July, and Ingot, Thistle, Onward, Ironclad, and Marble at various dates uncertain.[13]

By the end of 1902, therefore, the PWA had 33 lodges in three different industries and covering a variety of occupations. It had, in the five years 1898–1902, organized 26 new lodges and reorganized 3 old ones, a record unequalled by any international union except the Trackmen. It had more locals than any international union except the Trackmen, the Locomotive Firemen, the United Carpenters, the Railroad Trainmen, the Locomotive Engineers, and the ITU; that is, more than any international outside the railway industry, except the Typos and the Carpenters. Its total membership must also have put it among the first seven or eight organizations in the country. Moreover, it had a notable list of achievements.[14]

Its objects can scarcely be described as revolutionary. It wanted 'to improve the condition of workingmen morally, mentally, socially and physically ... [and] to foster habits of thrift, industry, economy and sobriety among its members.' Its history gives ample proof that it took all this very seriously. It had also, of course, more mundane aims, but they were modest and stated with Scots caution. It wanted to make sure that the miner got the true weight of his output at the pit head, and 'to assist in abolishing all illegal stoppages at pay offices.' (All of these cast a lurid light on what at least some of the employers must have been up to.) It also wanted to secure compensation for injuries received at work, but was careful to add 'where the employers may be liable.' It also wanted higher wages, but only 'by promoting such improvement in the mode of remuneration as the state of trade shall warrant or allow.' Naturally it wanted to shorten the hours of labour. It also wanted better legislation; but this was qualified by the significant words, 'whereby the more efficient management of mines and other works may be effected – thereby securing the health and safety of the workmen.' And it wanted better enforcement of such legislation as already existed.

Its list of objects did not even mention strikes. It recognized that disputes and stoppages might take place. But it labelled them, firmly, employer trouble. The association would 'extend support to lodges and their members who may be locked out by their employers or forced into discontinuing work on account of insufficiency of wages, or from any unjust cause whatsoever.' Nor was this merely words: from a very early stage the PWA consistently discouraged strikes and, in the teeth of employer opposition, pressed for compulsory arbitration. None the less, strikes it had; a fair number, and some of them big and prolonged.

Westville in 1881 had a strike (small and successful) and a lockout. Stellarton in 1882 struck for a 12½ per cent increase, and got it. Spring Hill and three Pictou County collieries got increases in 1882 without striking.[15]

Lingan, Cape Breton, was less fortunate. From its beginning in July 1881 till 5 December of that year, Coping Stone Lodge had had no difficulties. Then Mr Lynk, the manager, told the employees that the owners, the General Mining Association in England, 'would have no connection with unions or union men,' and demanded that the members renounce the union. They refused. The GMA then showed it meant business: the engineer of the tugboat and the locomotive found himself 'knocked idle' for the first time. He was told to quit the union; he refused and was discharged; and the management refused to take him back. A lull followed, while the mine was shut down for the usual two months' winter idleness.

The mine reopened early in January. Lynk refused to take on some 15 regular employees, and refused to see the union committee. He announced, however, that there was work for the 15 if they would leave the union. Four did and got work. The rest were replaced by men who, in the union's words, 'could have no claim on the manager.' The members of the lodge then asked to be allowed to share work and pay with those who had not been re-employed. The manager refused. The lodge protested and said it would strike unless he gave way. It also demanded the discharge of the new workers, including one or two non-unionists. Lynk again refused, and on 8 March the strike began.

Drummond was more than usually anxious to avoid a strike or, at worst, to end it quickly. The GMA was well established, rich, and powerful; Coping Stone Lodge was small. Drummond accordingly telegraphed the lodge to withdraw the demand for the discharge of the new employees, which it did. The lodge then proposed arbitration on the other issue. The manager refused, adding that he had work for all but five of the strikers. Drummond asked for the names so that the union could 'assist in their removal to another locality, and thereby end the strike.' The manager refused this also.

Early in April Lynk announced that miners living in company houses would be evicted on 1 May. On 6 May he brought in 35 miners from Scotland, who were met by himself, R.H. Brown, agent-general for the GMA, some 14 Sydney constables, all notoriously anti-union, and (doubtless marring the harmony of the occasion) a delegation of union members. The Scots, on learning there was a strike, promptly joined the strikers.

Late in June, Mr Swan, the GMA secretary, said he was willing to agree to the union's other demands, but he would not take back six of the strikers. The union would have none of it. In July Drummond and the lodge committee met Swan, and again offered to submit the whole dispute to arbitration, and were again refused. Swan made a counter-offer: to have the men return to work, subject to discharge on 14 day's notice of any he chose. The union refused to accept this unless he would tell it the names of those he meant to get rid of, which he refused to do.

The strike dragged on through the fall and winter of 1882, with the mine shut down for the customary two months in November and December. Then, in January 1883, Lynk threatened to close it permanently. By 5 January a few pairs of non-union cutters had gone to work; on 17 January 40 or 50 union members from the International, Reserve, and Glace Bay mines visited Lingan at 4 am, interrupted the men on their way to work, and tried to persuade them to come out. According to the manager, they succeeded only with a few newcomers. A week later, the union reported a few pairs of cutters at work, but only one local union man, who had been compelled to go back. One union member from Spring Hill and one from Stellarton were also working; but nine men brought in from Low Point had joined the strikers.

By 27 January, so the manager said, 26 cutters were at work. Union men from other places had appeared again, and 'succeeded in capturing six men whom they carried off'; the number of cutters then rose to 28. The *Trades Journal*, however, said only nine pairs were at work. About the middle of March, according to one union member's story, 'some anti-union men began to beat the few union men that were left around Lingan.' There followed what the Halifax *Chronicle* called a riot.

According to the union, a deputation from all the Cape Breton lodges went to Lingan to try to persuade the men who were working to come out. It chose to attempt this on a railway bridge, described by the manager as private property. A constable ordered the deputation off the bridge, and the management ordered the strikebreakers not to speak to the deputation. The deputation then barred the way. 'One of the leaders of the workmen [strikebreakers], it is asserted, [says the grand secretary,] at this time drew a revolver, and then the heather was on fire. There was a little muss, a scuffle, in the course of which several were knocked down but none hurt. The manager and his men then proceeded on their way.' The management story of the affair is substantially the same, down to the 'none hurt.' The GMA says that 'many were struck, some were knocked down, others were kicked'; that one man had some teeth knocked out; that Lynk was struck on the head; and that the engineer received a savage kick in the groin.

Some of the deputation decided to go farther. According to the union, they went to the houses of one or two of the strikebreakers and badly beat two men. They also stopped two others, and after someone had drawn a pistol, beat them also. 'We need not say [Drummond added], how sorry we are that some of the delegation so far forgot themselves.' The GMA account says the unionists broke the windows of houses and kicked in the doors, and caught two men, of whom one escaped and one was forced to join the union under threat of being thrown into the channel. Next morning, over 40 men (named) broke in the front and back doors of the carpenter's house, beat him in the presence of his wife and 10-day-old baby, splashed her bed with his blood, dragged him out by his feet, and escaped.

A third account, by the union member already quoted, says the deputation crowded around the doors of some of the strikebreakers' houses and 'burst one or two of them in, with no bad intention,' until they were met by anti-unionists and struck. Then some of the inmates of the houses were struck a few times, but no one was badly hurt. The union men then went into a couple of houses, 'and the men talked to them civilly, and everything was quiet ... At 10 a.m. all the union delegates had gone home, and Lynk then made a great fuss, sent word to have the schools closed and everything stopped idle, and the constable made a great fuss over nothing. Then the union men that remained at Lingan couldn't stir out, as the anti-union men would beat them as sure as they would meet them, but this was nothing for the poor union men.' A week later the same writer said there were not two dozen unionists in Lingan.

Still another account, violently anti-union, calls the events of 19 and 20 March a 'reign of terror.' It says the Cape Breton sub-council ordered the lodges to send 135 delegates to Lingan (but puts the actual delegation at 60 or 70), a 'half drunken crowd of ruffians,' and says they stopped the colliery; it adds that only about half a dozen people were badly injured.

At this point, the GMA got three magistrates to requisition the militia. The county warden was ready to provide constables but the management wanted troops, and got them, since the dominion had no power to refuse a request from any civil authority. The Cape Breton Volunteers were called out, and the martial ardour of Halifax was aroused. A hundred or so men of the Prince of Wales Own Yorkshire Regiment were mustered, with 5500 rounds of ball, and stores for 4 or 5 weeks' campaign; their baggage was actually put aboard the steamer *Newfoundland*. Then the authorities decided it would be better to wait and see if they could not get enough militia to handle the situation. They did, and the regiment of regulars was sent back to barracks.

On 28 March there wee 25 non-commissioned officers and men of the Sydney militia in Lingan. The county constable and his assistant had arrested two of the rioters. Next day a magistrate, seven volunteers, and seven constables had been overpowered at Little Glace Bay trying to arrest rioters. The county constable had retired to the Glace Bay lock-up for safety!

By the beginning of May the militia were getting restless, and the *Trades Journal* reported, with some glee, that the volunteers were on the verge of striking for better rations! By this time, however, their presence had become, even for the employer, superfluous. For on 17 April the GMA had asked the lodge committee to meet it, and on 24 April 1883 the parties reached agreement. The *Trades Journal* reported the terms as: recognition of the union, reinstatement of all strikers not convicted of a breach of the peace, company houses to be provided for the men on their return to work, coal to be provided the men at once, winter wages of 40 cents a ton or 80 cents a running yard, and provision for 14 days' notice of discharge or quitting.

This version of the agreement as a union victory nettled the Cape Breton Colliery Association (employers), whose secretary promptly published some further details: that there should be no dictation by the union as to whom the manager should or should not employ (though he was to furnish the union with lists of both), and there were to be no reasons given for dismissals or quittings. The Colliery Association formally approved the agreement.

Two subsequent events may be noted: Drummond was able to report that the GMA had promised to stop all further court proceedings, as far as it was able to; and the County of Cape Breton refused to pay the expenses of the troops, whose presence it had never requested and considered unnecessary, and was sued by the dominion government for $4000.[16]

In March 1884 the management of the Vale colliery (Pictou County) demanded a wage reduction, and the lodge agreed, against the advice of the grand council. The Cape Breton mine managers then tried the same game (at Reserve and International the demand was 10 per cent), but the Cape Breton lodges resisted. By the end of May the managers had given up the idea, except at Gowrie, where the manager was reported to be still trying. Even he must eventually have caved in, for the grand secretary in October reported that Cape Breton wages had been adjusted without the interference of the council.

In May 1885 Cameron Lodge accepted a 10 per cent reduction at the Drummond colliery. Visatergo, at Granton Wharf, refused to take a 10 per cent reduction from a wage of $1.10 a day. It struck with the reluctant sanction of the grand council, which had urged using every other means to secure a settlement. The strike was lost; the men went back on poor terms; and the lodge's charter was revoked.

In April 1886 the grand secretary expressed his gratification that whereas before the PWA was organized, labour had waged 'a sort of gorilla warfare,' industrial relations were now conducted in an orderly manner. He also expressed his hope that before long disputes would be settled by arbitration. At the October meeting of the grand council, however, he was obliged to sound a less optimistic note. One Cape Breton lodge was gone because the members had been 'gently and by degrees forced from the locality ... In some quarters in Cape Breton the spirit and temper of the middle ages abounds.'[17]

But it was on the mainland that the next trouble arose. About the middle of December 1886 the management of the Albion mines (Pictou County) notified the miners that at the end of 14 days their terms of service would expire. The men took this as warning of a wage reduction. Sure enough, along it came: 20 per cent or more. Two years before, they had had to take a reduction of 10 cents a ton; in October 1886 a further reduction. To accept this new one would, they said, mean semi-starvation. Men who, at the old rate, were getting a net wage of $1.15 per shift would drop to 83 cents; men who were getting $1.14 would drop to 81 cents; men who were getting $1.04 would drop to 75 cents.

The Albion men accordingly struck, 31 December 1886; those at Vale and Acadia followed, 29 January 1887. In February the Albion men offered to arbitrate on the basis of a half-cent reduction from the former maximum rates. Mr Poole, the manager, refused, unless they would agree to forfeit 14 days' wages and to abide by the arbitrator's decision for the whole of 1887. The men refused. Poole also met the men at Thorburn, and urged them to go back to work, offering to guarantee that their wages would remain unchanged for the whole year. They replied that they were ready to go back when the Albion dispute was settled.

Both sides now dug in for a long struggle. The Acadia mines had been supplying coal to the ironworks at Londonderry, and the question now arose whether the men at the Drummond colliery and Spring Hill would mine coal to fill the gap. They decided that if their employers sent any coal to Londonderry, the lodges would demand a wage increase. This seems to have scared the Drummond and Spring Hill companies out of trying anything. For the next thing we hear is that the Steel Co had leased the McBean seam about the middle of April and was trying to work it with 'all manner of nondescripts and New Glasgow loafers, niggers and white blacklegs.' So far, added the *Trades Journal*, 'an utter and expensive failure.'

Meanwhile, the strikers had been getting what was, for those days, massive financial aid from the other lodges and from the independent labour union at Trenton. Cameron Lodge alone contributed a total of $1274, Pioneer $846, Island at least $200, and Keystone, Equity, and Banner unstated amounts. The Trenton union sent at least 11 weekly contributions of 50 cents per member.

Towards the end of March Poole made a further offer to the strikers: 38 cents per cubic yard for 'big boards,' 42 cents for 'bords,' 47 cents for balances. The union said the proposed rates were very low, and would in fact amount to accepting the full reduction proposed at the beginning of the year. Late in April Poole raised the figures to 42, 47, and 52 cents per cubic yard; the union committee demanded 43,

50, and 55. Poole replied with an offer of 42, 50, and 55, but with the top coal left on. The men wanted it down, and held out for this. There was also the question of what was to be done with the blacklegs at the Vale colliery. Would the Steel Co be prepared to discharge them? At the beginning of May the strike was still on, and Poole was saying that there would be no places for some of the Acadia men, who would have to go to Vale. Finally, about the middle of May, the strike was settled on terms reasonably satisfactory to the union.[18]

But scarcely was this trouble out of the way when difficulties began at Spring Hill. Some time before October, the Spring Hill miners had accepted a reduction of three cents a box, with the labourers' wages remaining unchanged, and with the understanding that the miners' old rate would be restored when trade permitted. Pioneer Lodge thought this time had now come; but it was willing not to ask for full restoration of the old rate for miners if the company would give the labourers 10 per cent, instead of the proposed 5 per cent all round. The matter apparently was settled without a strike, though in April 1888 there were complaints that the increase granted was not really as big as it looked: the company had made certain reductions.

The spring of 1888 saw a series of reductions at Albion which the union was evidently too weak to resist. By October Gladstone Lodge was reported 'all but lifeless,' Cameron 'once more in a comatose condition,' Fidelity feeble but improving, and McBean at the same level as in the spring but not as good as it should be. In Cape Breton, however, things were better. Towards the end of May 1888 Banner Lodge was asking for a wage increase. The mine manager said the request was reasonable, but he would have to ask the Mine Managers Association. Apparently the increase went through, probably because the Cape Breton lodges, in contrast to those in Pictou, were in a strong position. Drummond told the Grand Council in October that not since 1884 had the Cape Breton returns been so favourable. In April 1889 he was able to add that Cape Breton was holding its own well, again in contrast to mainland Nova Scotia, where there was no 'gratifying increase.'[19]

In 1887, the PWA had drawn up a bill for compulsory arbitration of labour disputes, and had got it passed by the legislative assembly. But it had been blocked in the legislative council, 'through the influence of capitalists and mine owners.' By April 1888 a second bill had got through the Assembly and as far as the report stage in the council. By April 1889 it had become law, and the grand council decided to ask to have it applied in Spring Hill, where the company was trying to cut wages. The application was duly made. The company raised technical objections. Pioneer Lodge then got close to 750 names on a second application; the company applied to the courts for a writ of *certiorari*, and capped this by stopping a fortnight's pay, under the terms of the Arbitration Act whose application it was protesting![20] Arbitration or no arbitration, Spring Hill had a strike in 1890 which succeeded in getting rid of what the union called the 'illegal and unjust docking system' (company deductions from wages).

In April 1891 the Cape Breton sub-council was considering demands for a wage increase of 3 cents ton for miners and 10 cents a day for other workers; and Island Lodge raised the question of the three-quarter-time winter wages. This last was referred back to the lodges.[21]

At the September 1893 grand council meeting Drummond congratulated the association on having had, during the year, no strikes. He hoped there would be less and less reliance on the strike 'as more modern and less crude methods are being resorted to.' In 1894, however, he was obliged to report two short strikes at Spring Hill (unauthorized, and adjusted by conference), and a successful strike at Joggins. In 1895 Drummond reported that he had done a lot of adjusting of differences with favourable results. In 1896, against the grand council's advice, the Joggins men struck for three months against a wage reduction. They lost.

During the late summer of 1900 the employees of the Dominion Coal Co (which in 1893 had amalgamated most of the mines south of Sydney harbour) heard that the price of coal had gone up from $2 to $3 a ton. In September the PWA decided to ask for a 10 per cent wage increase for all mine workers of the province on 1 November. (Kimberley and Mafeking lodges wanted increases of 60 cents a day for mechanics, and 30 cents for helpers; but this was referred to a committee.) The company replied that it had a December 1899 agreement running till the end of 1900. The union appears then to have held two successive meetings. The result was a demand upon 14 collieries for a 12 per cent wage increase for all their employees except mechanics and helpers; for the mechanics (carpenters and blacksmiths), 50 cents a day, for the helpers, 25 cents; all to come into force 1 January 1901. It also wanted a further 10 per cent on 1 May.

At Springhill (as it was now generally spelt), the company granted the January increases. At Westville and the Acadia mines, the employers refused to grant anything. The men struck 1 January about 1500 strong. On 4 January the Intercolonial Coal Co (Drummond mine) agreed to the 12 per cent, and the men went back, but 'because of a misunderstanding as to the increased payment to ... mechanics and their helpers,' they struck again that afternoon. On the 5th, however, the management of both companies agreed to pay the 50 cents and 25 cents to the mechanics and helpers, and the men went back. The mainland miners also got the May 10 per cent.

At Sydney Mines the union applied for the conciliation services of the Dominion department of labour. The Nova Scotia Steel and Coal Co agreed, and Mackenzie King arrived on the scene. He got the parties to agree to accept whatever rates were arrived at for Dominion Coal, with special provisions in regard to the bonus paid at Sydney Mines, and to refer all contract disputes to a conciliation procedure, with final and binding arbitration. This resulted in some slight advances in wages.

Dominion Coal, which owned most of the mines south of Sydney harbour, granted its mechanics and helpers some increases on 1 January. Some of these were more than the union had asked, some less. The union was not satisfied, but the Cape Breton lodges (which complained that Cape Breton was being undercut in the markets by Cumberland) thought the circumstances unfavourable to a strike, and decided to go to arbitrarion under the provincial act. A board was appointed, and reported on 25 April. It denied all the increases demanded. It said the company had given its miners an increase on 9 May 1900, and while the published prices and local prices for coal showed a considerable increase, this was illusory. Most of the company's sales came under long-term contracts at low prices, and increased costs further reduced the company's apparent gains, so that its average net price per ton was 'not one half cent in excess of that of the preceding financial year.' As for the mechanics and their helpers: the increases granted in January were fair, and no further increases were warranted.

By September 1901, however, the union seems to have got some increases in Cape Breton, for machine rates there were up 30 to 40 per cent, mechanics' wages 40 to 100 per cent, day labour rates 40 to 50 percent, and winter banking rates had been abolished. Against this, the price of house coal to the miners had gone up from 50 cents per ton to 75.[22]

The PWA had, of course, fought for other things besides wage increases and compulsory arbitration. As early as 1890 Pioneer Lodge had suggested the union should try to get a law establishing an eight-hour day underground and a nine-hour one on the surface. This was referred to the committee on legislation, with instructions to have a bill framed and presented to the legislature. It was also suggested that no boy should be allowed to work underground unless he was 'capable of undergoing an examination in the seventh standard.' The grand secretary agreed in October that it was necessary to keep uneducated men out of the mines. But it would be enough if they were able to read, write, and count as far as fractions, and if there were proper certification of miners (which would also take care of the troublesome problem of immigrant miners coming in with foreign certificates). It was agreed that no boys under 12 should be allowed into the mines, and no one over 12 unless he could meet Drummond's standards.

The 1891 grand council was informed that on the questions of shorter hours, prohibition of boys underground, foreign certificates, proper certification for miners generally, fire-bosses, and other matters, the Mines Act 'had been amended in the direction indicated.' Further, any 12 workmen could now sue an employer for infringement of the Mines Act, and they were granted the right to choose their own checkweighmen, and fortnightly payment of wages. The legislative advance in the matter of hours must, however, have been inadequate, for in September 1897 the grand council was directing that the question of an eight-hour law should be discussed in the lodges with a view to a ballot.

The question of hours came up again in the railway lodges in 1902. The railway workers' main concerns seem to have been hours and seniority. They objected to the night shift of 13 hours, and day shift of 10. They succeeded in getting the council to appoint a committee on railways, which reported that the council should ask the minister of railways and canals (the railway concerned was the government-owned Intercolonial) to establish an eight-hour day, and ensure an equitable distribution of positions on the Sydney and Oxford division, keeping politics from infringing on seniority.

The PWA had also pressed for, and got, the check-off of union dues by the employers. Pioneer Lodge had wanted it in February 1888, and the company had been willing, provided the union would give up sub-pays (evidently the fortnightly payment of wages). In 1893 the grand council formally decided to try to get union dues stopped in the office by the various employers. In 1894 Drummond reported that this had been secured in most of the Cape Breton mines. In 1900, however, Buller and Drummond Lodges were still trying to get the check-off.

It was rather hard for the companies to refuse to check off union dues, because they checked off so many other things. Even in 1880 many companies were deducting rent (for company houses), doctor's fees (for the company doctors), household coal charges, and school fees or taxes. Two or three years later the men were taking so much time off for holy days and saints' days that serious losses were occurring because vessels were held up waiting for shipments. Drummond suggested to one company that it should offer the clergy deduction of church dues from the men's pay. The manager tried it; the clergy willingly agreed; and the arrangement worked so well (from the employer's point of view) that other companies followed suit till the practice became general.

The effect on take-home pay was appreciable. In 1880 the average coal cutter's annual earnings were about $272.60; the check-off (which did not include union dues) was $33.60. By 1888 a coal cutter's annual earnings seem to have been about $300 (the figures vary from $150 to $350). The average annual deductions were about the same as in 1880. On the mainland work was steadier and annual earnings correspondingly higher; there deductions (again excluding union dues) ran close to $60 a year. PWA dues meant only a modest addition to the deductions: 25 cents a month. The PWA seems to have been a pioneer in the checking-off of union dues.[23]

The PWA tried to encourage benefit societies to insure the workers against sickness and accidents. As early as October 1886 it was trying to get the legislature to pass a sick and accident fund law, which would allow companies and workers to set up societies to which both, and also the government, would contribute. In April 1889 Drummond reported that a bill on the subject had been introduced; in 1896 he listed relief societies among the achievements of the PWA which had given Nova Scotia better mine legislation than any other part of the English-speaking world.

The union also exerted itself to see that the men had some say in the choice of company doctors, for whom they paid. In 1893 it demanded that the doctors should be nominated by a meeting of the employees, and that if the company did not appoint the men's nominee, it should be obliged to say why. In 1896 the grand council spent some time on the question of doctors for Dominion Coal employees. It decided that at any mine where there were not over 300 employees, the majority should choose the doctor, and his charges would be checked off. Where there were more than 300 employees, but not less than an extra 100, there should be 2 doctors; and a committee of the men with the doctor should define the limits of his district.

A thornier problem was the company stores, the 'pluck-me's.' The truck system had caused trouble very early, and the General Mining Association, which then held a near-monopoly, had given it up about 1831. It did not reopen any company stores till about the time the PWA was founded. There was some reason for reopening them then. Cape Breton had no rail connection with the mainland until 1890; drift ice often blocked the harbours, and brought the people near starvation; and the local merchants freely took advantage of the situation. The company store was probably less oppressive, if not a real boon.

By 1858 the GMA monopoly had come to an end, and some of the companies in the south Cape Breton coal field were re-establishing the truck system. 'The winters and ice-infested springs then cut off the collieries for months, and the necessity of banking coal for the opening of navigation imposed peculiar burdens upon the less wealthy operators. They doubtless found it more convenient and profitable to defray the cost of labour during these months by paying wages in goods, and the system probably proved useful in financing the mines especially in the depression after 1866.' In other words, the men were indeed plucked, swindled out of part of their pay.

Until the coming of Dominion Coal, there was very little winter work; prices at the company stores were certainly excessive; and by the beginning of May each year nearly all the men were from $100 to $200 in debt. To some extent, 'the system placed a premium on idleness; for industrious men were at times denied work during slack seasons in order that the less thrifty, who had incurred debts at the company store, might liquidate them without delay. The Royal Commission on Labor, in 1888, found that the system induced carelessness, extravagance, and dependence; that its ill consequences extended to the farmers, who often had to take payment in goods; and that it enabled the employers to make double or more than double profit out of their workmen's labour.' The commission recommended a dominion anti-truck act, but nothing was done (perhaps because of doubts about dominion jurisdiction). Dominion Coal extended the store system and profited from it during its early years of large initial expenditure.

In 1893 the grand council considered the question, but opinion was so divided that it reached no conclusion. One ardent co-operator seized the opportunity to say that the solution to the problem was for the men to join the co-operatives, of which there were already several, both in Cape Breton and on the mainland. By 1895 Drummond was calling the company stores a premium on beggary, and the council had a long discussion on the subject. The majority totally opposed the stores and the check-off of store debts. The matter was referred to the legislative committee, which recommended that a grand council committee meet a Cape Breton merchants' committee and 'lay the matter in all its bearings before the government at an appropriate time.' A.B. McGillivray, who was later to lead the breakaway to the Knights of Labor, was on this committee, and it seems probable that his differences with Drummond, who had become more favourable to the company stores system, had a good deal to do with the split.

At the 1896 council meeting, however, the differences were papered over by a compromise resolution. A committee was appointed to 'draw up desirable modifications' in the store system, and recommended that: the men should be given the right to stop dealing at the company stores if they wished; that after an agreed date there should be no check-off of more than 10 per cent of the debtor's net earnings to clear up what he had owed; and that if the company refused to accept these proposals the lodges which were opposed to the check-off of store debts should seek legislation. In 1897 the trouble burst into the open again. The resident managers fought hard to keep both the stores and the check-off. But in 1899 a provincial anti-truck act put an end to the worst abuses, though the stores and the check-off of store debts survived for nearly a generation.[24]

The co-operatives make frequent appearances in the *Trades Journal*, and their very names often indicate a close conection with the PWA.[25]

The PWA gave a high place to education, especially technical, notably, of course, for miners. The October 1888 grand council minutes note that the provincial government is going ahead with technical education; those of April 1889 comment on the success of these efforts. In 1896 Drummond listed night schools and free mining schools among the Association's main achievements.

Political action was an important part of the PWA's activities from a fairly early date. In June 1882 it supported the Conservative candidates in Cape Breton, on the ground that the Liberal candidates were prominent company men. In November 1885 grand council committees were set up to consider choosing workingmen candidates for the legislature. They decided to nominate in Cape Breton, Cumberland, and Pictou. In Cape Breton, they won; in Pictou and Cumberland, they lost. Drummond told the Council that in Cumberland the workers in Springhill had supported the labour candidates, but the rest of the electorate had given them less support than expected; in Pictou it had been the other way around. Some brethren evidently doubted the value of the effort even if it succeeded, for Drummond felt it necessary to answer the question, how much use would a mere four MLAs have been anyhow. His reply was: 'Take, for instance, the French in Canada. For a number of years they have been masters of the situation and able to dictate to governments.' He said the same of the Irish in Britain.

By the beginning of 1887 A.C. Bell, one of the Pictou MLAs, had resigned to run for the House of Commons as an Independent Conservative, and Drummond, who had run, and been defeated, as a Liberal in Pictou the previous June, announced that he was running again. The PWA backed Bell for the House of Commons; he lost.

At the council's April 1889 meeting, the grand master recommended the formation of workingmen's political associations; in October Drummond expressed the hope that, with the wider franchise, there would be renewed political action in the summer. In December the men in Little Glace Bay formed a Workingmen's Political Association under the leadership of the redoubtable A.B. McGillivray. Workingmen's candidates were nominated in the 1890 provincial election in Cumberland and Cape Breton. The Cumberland candidate was defeated, but in Cape Breton the 'workingmen's nominee was returned by a handsome majority ... and his colleague also was carried to success' (evidently an old-party candidate endorsed by the PWA). Drummond himself ran as a Liberal in Pictou in 1890, and was defeated by a small majority.

In 1893 Drummond told the council that apathy in unions was partly the result of banning any discussion of politics at union meetings. He was happy to note, however, that unions were outgrowing the idea that their sphere of action was 'confined to discussion of questions directly bearing on wages.' He instanced as others which required political action, and which unions ought to deal with, the eight-hour bill, employers' liability, and the franchise. (Later he returned to the subject of apathy, and said that 'the brother should be presented with a gold-headed cane who could give a solution to the problem.') Various proposals for direct representation of Cape Breton County in the assembly were sent to a committee for study; the council subsequently decided to ask the lodges whether there should be labour candidates in the provincial election. If the answer was yes, then they were asked to make the nominations and report them to the grand secretary, who would then announce them as PWA candidates. In 1896 the council passed a resolution favouring nomination of workingmen's candidates for the legislature in the mining counties.[26]

Unlike unions in the central and western provinces, the PWA did not pay much attention to immigration, except on the rare occasions when an appreciable body of immigrants turned up in the mining districts.[27] But it was not by any means uninterested in other countries, notably Scotland. In 1888 Drummond spent two months' leave of absence in Britain. On his return he gave the council an account of his tour among the Lanarkshire miners, of whose organizations he complacently observed that, after much sad experience of other ways of doing things, they were now proceeding along the lines of the PWA!

A few other features of the PWA and its activities are worth noting. First, it believed in getting itself and all its individual lodges incorporated by act of the legislature, and did. Second, it was broadminded enough to admit women, though with careful safeguards. As long as the PWA remained almost exclusively a miners' organization the matter did not arise. When it branched out into other industries, the situation changed. In 1895, accordingly, it was faced with the question of admitting women into certain lodges. The delegates recognized that in some other industries there were women workers. The council decided to admit them to lodges made up of workers from industries where women were employed, but they were not to have anything to say about mining.

Third, the PWA was strongly temperance. The *Trades Journal* has a good deal on this subject, as early as the spring of 1884. Fourth, it always tried to have an official paper. The *Trades Journal* originally belonged to the union itself. But in October 1884 it was handed over to Drummond, to be conducted in the interests of the association. He paid $500 for the press and the council's financial interest, and was to receive a subsidy of $50 per half-year. This must have lasted till Drummond's resignation as grand secretary. In 1901 the grand council adopted the *Searchlight* as its organ. This paper must have collapsed almost at once, for in 1902 the council resolved to set up a paper in Glace Bay.[28] Finally, the PWA, though not unsympathetic with other labour organizations, never even considered joining the Knights of Labor, and resisted the occasional wooing of the TLC and the AFL.[29]

British Columbia
The British Columbia miners, in 1881, still had the Miners Mutual Protective Association. The Wellington miners, on 4 August 1883, faced the Dunsmuir interests with demands for a straight wage increase of 25 cents a ton; the calling of places every 3 months; an undertaking that no one would be discharged for belonging to the union; and reinstatement of miners who had already been discharged. The union gave the owners till 8 August to reply; if no satisfactory reply was received by then, the men would strike. Actually, they seem to have gone out on 10 August. The company thereupon served notice that employees would have to get out of their company-owned houses by 10 September and advertised for 300 strikebreakers. It got 14; but when they arrived 9 October and found a strike was on, they refused to work. In November the union withdrew its wage demands, but insisted that all Chinese miners should be discharged. The strike collapsed 14 November.

This probably killed the union, though it held a regular quarterly meeting on 28 November or 1 December 1883, and at least gave notice of a regular monthly meeting on 2 January 1884.[30]

The miners seem then to have gone into the Knights of Labor. But in February 1890 they organized another regional union, the Miners and Mine Laborers Protective Association of Vancouver Island. The decision to form this body was taken at a meeting of over 1000 miners in the Nanaimo Opera House. The meeting had been called to consider the company's proposed wage reduction at Wellington, and the advisability of forming a union. There were two Knights of Labor LAS in the area at the time, but some of the men did not like the Knights, and some the Order would not accept. So it was decided to form an open union, and at an even larger meeting 14 February the new association was definitely established, with headquarters at Nanaimo and branches there and at East and North Wellington. By 20 February it was reporting rapid progress, and hoped that within three months every miner in the three collieries would be enrolled.

On 19 May 1890 the association was nominating candidates for the coming election, and demanding an eight-hour day from bank to bank. Dunsmuir refused to have any dealings with the association. It tried to organize the miners at Comox, the main issues raised being the use of Chinese workers underground, and the high prices at the company store.[31]

The union sent a delegate to the 1890 TLCC convention, where he chaired the committee on standing orders and resolutions, seconded a resolution to prohibit Chinese labourers in mines (carried), and was placed on a committee to interview the dominion government on Chinese immigration. The union was represented again at the 1896 TLCC convention, this time by Ralph Smith. In 1897 Smith was the delegate of the 'Nanaimo Miners Union'; in 1898 of the 'Nanaimo Miners Trades Union'; and in 1899 of the 'Nanaimo Miners Union.' This, and the Congress's chartering in 1901 of FLUs 15 and 20 (Miners and Mine Laborers Protective Associations, Extension and South Wellington), suggest that the original association may have dwindled to a single local. So does the fact that on 12 January 1900 the Nanaimo union secured an AFL charter as FLU 8098, which it appears to have surrendered later that year for a TLCC charter.[32] In effect, however, something like a regional union survived or was recreated.

The 1896 TLCC convention proceedings have an account of the use of Chinese and Japanese labour in the Union Mines at Comox, and the lesser use of Chinese in 'the more liberally managed mines of the New Vancouver Coal Company at Nanaimo.' Smith was put on the committee on standing orders and resolutions. He moved a resolution to increase the head tax on Chinese labourers and to provide stricter measures for naturalization of Japanese immigrants (unanimously adopted), and was elected vice-president by acclamation. In 1897 he was again on the committee on standing orders and resolutions. He moved an elaborate resolution on gold mining in the Yukon (carried), moved a further resolution expressing dissatisfaction with the government's reply to the 1896 resolution on the poll tax on Chinese immigrants, and was again elected vice-president by acclamation. In 1898 he seconded a resolution asking for prohibition of the employment of Chinese and Japanese on coast steamships 'in the capacity of stokers and other responsible positions' (carried), and was elected president by acclamation. He was again elected president in 1899, 1900, and 1901.[33]

Almost immediately after its formation, the Miners and Mine Laborers Protective Association struck for the eight-hour day. On 14 November 1890 the lockout at Wellington was still in progress, and the Vancouver Trades and Labor Council was raffling a watch in aid of the strikers. The raffle brought in nearly $80, and on 13 March 1891 the Wellington miners acknowledged a further contribution of $5. Other labour organizations also contributed, but 'the aid proved to be of little help against the company which was backed by a battery of artillery sent in by the premier.' The strike was 'long, bitter and unsuccessful.' James Dunsmuir, who had succeeded his father in the control of the family empire, was just as anti-union, and the next dozen years were a tale of intermittent warfare between him and the association.[34]

In spite of its preoccupation with the strike, the MMLPA managed to take a prominent part in the organization of the first British Columbia provincial central organization, the Federated Labor Congress, which elected three MMLPA members to its executive.[35]

When the 1890 strike failed the MMLPA asked unions throughout the province to boycott Dunsmuir coal. In November 1892, however, the Nanaimo Trades and Labor Council informed the Vancouver council that 'the union miners of Nanaimo had decided to try and make a union mine of the Dunsmuir mine and consequently would not push the boycott.'[36]

In 1890 the Nanaimo miners had joined with the farmers to elect two MLAs. By 1894, evidently discouraged by the ill success of industrial action, the MMLPA, like so many unions before and since, was deciding to switch its emphasis, for the moment at any rate, to politics. It was 'still not strong enough after the clashes with the employers to operate politically on its own.' Hence it united with other organizations to form the Nanaimo Reform Club, which nominated three candidates. All were defeated. In 1898 the Nanaimo miners had another go at politics, and elected Smith on an independent labour ticket. Smith and two other labour or pro-labour members held the balance of power in the assembly, and managed by 1900 to get through, among other things, a new coal mines regulation act prohibiting the employment of Chinese underground.[37]

Meanwhile, the union had got into a fresh trial of strength with Dunsmuir. That potentate had refused a wage increase, and the union had struck; in the middle of March 1899 he was announcing that the men could return at the former wage of $2 a day, or see the mine closed indefinitely. He claimed he was paying 25 cents an hour for an 8-hour day while mines on the Sound were paying 15 cents an hour for 10 hours. The miners nevertheless stayed out.[38]

In the summer of 1900 the union asked a very different employer, the New Vancouver Coal Co, at Nanaimo, for a 10 per cent wage increase. At this mine all the 875 employees, except officials, were union members. On 10 August the negotiating committee reported that the manager said he could not grant the increase, and had invited a union committee to examine the company's books. Some of the members were satisfied, and ready to let the matter drop. But, after long debate, the majority voted to give the company 30 days' notice of a demand for the 10 per cent increase and, if it said no, take a strike vote. A two-thirds vote was necessary to sanction a strike, and the old-timers were said to be against it. No strike took place. At the same time the Extension miners, who had contemplated demanding 'equalizing' wages, decided simply to try for a regular pay-day. Apparently, according to the Vancouver *Province*, 'the men never know when they are going to be paid': an almost incredible indication of the state of industrial feudalism at this mine.[39]

In October there was a fresh battle with Dunsmuir at Wellington. He had brought 'a lot of miners from Scotland to fill the places of Chinamen who are employed in some of these mines. The first lot who arrived were divided up, some going to work in the Extension Mines, and about 40 going to the Union Mines. Those going to Union Mines were dissatisfied when they got there, and claimed that the contract under which they came was not being carried out, and therefore refused to go to work [4 October]. They all started out to walk to Nanaimo, a distance of about 70 miles. When they arrived there their case was taken up by Mr. Ralph Smith, MPP, the miners' agent, who saw Mr. Dunsmuir, and in conjunction with Mr. Bremner [of the dominion department of labour], the case was satisfactorily settled, and the men went to work at the Extension Mines' on the terms they had originally agreed to.[40]

For once, Dunsmuir had climbed down. Indeed, even before this he had shown signs of being a changed man. At the 1900 TLCC convention the British Columbia executive committee had reported: 'The employment of Chinese in the coal mines of our Province ... has suddenly taken on a new aspect. The Dunsmuir Corporation, which has for years been the only offender in this respect, and the strongest enemy that organized labor has had to contend against, has evidently underwent a complete change of heart and mind upon this all important question ... This company has at last arisen to a full sense of its true duty to the people of this Province and discharged all Chinese and Japanese employed in their mines and withdrawn its objections to the organization of its employees.'

But it must have been a case of: the Devil was sick; the Devil a saint would be – The Devil was well; the Devil a saint was he! For by 18 December 1900 Dunsmuir had shut down South Wellington and offered some of the men work at a reduction: the same pay for 2800 pounds of coal as they had formerly got under an agreement for 2352 pounds, and no pay now for 'turning off stalls.' This would have amounted to a 20 per cent reduction; so the men struck. They were ordered to take out their tools, and did. Two months later they were still out, 'although some of them [were] feeling it badly, as they had invested their savings in building houses.' In March 1901 the company offered the men work at $3 a day for diggers, but the union secretary and one other were not to get work. The union refused these terms and stayed out, though a good many of its members 'left the Island or got work elsewhere.' Not until 10 June 1901 was the dispute settled. Dunsmuir met the committee and agreed to open the mine and to pay the old wages. He refused to recognize the union, but promised not to discriminate against union men.[41]

Meanwhile, in March 1901,[42] the men at the New Vancouver Coal Co had renewed their demand for a 10 per cent wage increase, and the manager had again refused and given his reasons. The union then laid the matter over till 6 April when it accepted the manager's position and explanations.

On 4 May the Extension miners held a mass meeting at which they drafted an agreement with a wage scale. It was presented to Dunsmuir, who refused to accept the scale, and countered with one of his own, 'which involved quite a reduction.' The men refused this, but decided to continue working until the committee could have another try at getting an agreement. The attempt was made, and the committee and Dunsmuir arrived at a compromise for one year.

In November 1901 the management of the Alexandria Mines, South Wellington, made contracts with six groups of miners, with six men each, to mine coal at agreed rates, but with no provision for stringing timbers in the mines. After some of the men had started work, they were told they would get 80 cents apiece for stringing timbers, a reduction of 20 cents. They objected; the union met; the men decided that this reduction was simply the prelude to a general wage reduction; the superintendent refused to meet a committee; and on 25 November all 260 or so employees struck.

Mackenzie King was already in British Columbia, and Ralph Smith, MP, asked him to intervene. By the time he reached South Wellington the company was offering to pay $1 for the timbers, if the men would agree to deduct the extra 20 cents from the agreed price for cutting coal! This piece of cheap generosity met the fate it deserved, and poor King found the parties at a deadlock. He ingeniously suggested scrapping the whole contract and starting over again. Both sides agreed, and accepted a new arrangement under which the men who had entered into the original contracts were to have the opportunity of making specific agreements with the manager, receiving meanwhile $3 a day. They were to get $1 for stringing timbers, and the union committee was to be recognized. If the individual miners could not make satisfactory agreements, then new tenders were to be called for and the work awarded on the basis of these. The strike ended 30 November.

In April 1902 a new seam was being opened at the New Vancouver Coal Co's mine. The company proposed to pay the same rate as on the old workings. The men said they could not make a living at that rate and struck. The manager said he could not pay more and still make money on the new coal. The matter was settled by dropping work on the new seam till the market improved, and letting the men take their turn on the old workings.

On 15 May 1902 a strike was in progress at South Wellington, for the Vancouver Trades and Labor Council had a letter from the South Wellington Miners acknowledging receipt of $50 from affiliated unions. On 3 July the council's secretary announced that a balance of $20 had been withdrawn because the union had become defunct. This, however, proved incorrect, and on 17 July there was a letter from the Wellington Miners acknowledging receipt of the other $20.[43]

By this time the Vancouver Island miners were getting tired of the mild liberal-labourism of Smith and his friends, and turning to the new, socialist Western Federation of Miners. Smith very unwisely chose the fall of 1902 to go to Europe. He did not realize that, in Sir Winston Churchill's phrase, 'When the mouse is away, the cats will play.' His own Nanaimo union joined the WFM, and the Extension and South Wellington unions surrendered their charters.[44]

The British Columbia fishing industry had what were in effect several regional unions. The first was the Fraser River Fishermen's Protective and Benevolent Association, organized at New Westminster in May 1893. Most of the men fished about two months a year. Their chief reason for organizing was to protect themselves against an influx of Americans, native Indians, and Japanese. The union got the Vancouver Trades and Labor Council to back it in asking the dominion government to reduce the number of licences to Orientals.

The canners, on 8 July, with 1 firm dissenting, set a price of 6 cents per fish. The fishermen demanded 10 cents, and $3 a day (an increase of 50 cents), for men on day wages, who made up about a third to half of the 2350 men involved. The union asked each canner to meet the union committee, 14 July. The canners refused, and the union struck.

The canners tried to replace the strikers by Indians and Japanese. They got officials of the department of Indian affairs, together with the governor of the provincial jail and several special constables sent by an obliging provincial government (whose minister of finance was a canner), to tour the Indian camps. They told the Indians they were free to work and should make private arrangements with the canners. Most of the Indians refused, but a number were persuaded or intimidated into going back 16 July. The Japanese stepped into the breach.

The canners offered $50 reward for information leading to the arrest of anyone committing acts of violence or intimidation or damage to property (they used the text of the Criminal Code, omitting the crucial word 'unlawfully'). Several union members were arrested, though the union made no attempt to interfere with non-strikers. By the end of the week all the Indians and some others were fishing; on 23

July the strike collapsed, leaving as an incidental legacy a strong Indian distrust of white fishermen, who, the Indians said, had abandoned them and made the best deals they could with the canners.

The union survived long enough to apply for membership in the Vancouver council in August and to march, 300 strong, in the Labour Day parade. In December 1896 there was an attempt to form a new one, but it came to nothing.[45]

New government regulations in 1898 met most of the fishermen's demands on licences, but pressure by the canners produced undesirable amendments. Late in 1899 the canners formed a combine to control selling prices, limit production, and fix prices for raw fish. This evoked in December a TLCC union at New Westminster, and in March 1900 an AFL union at Vancouver.

By this time many of the white fishermen had gone to the Klondike and been replaced by Japanese, who in fact used most of the licences granted to the canners. In spite of strong labour feeling against the Japanese, the Vancouver union declared itself open to all; New Westminster, however, refused. In fact, efforts to get the Japanese into the Vancouver union failed. The Indian agent apparently tried unsuccessfully to block the Indians joining. The Japanese formed their own organization.

Both unions now demanded 25 cents per fish for the whole season. The canners' executive met union delegates 3 July 1900 and promised to call a canners' meeting to consider the matter. On 7 July the Canners Association announced they would pay no more than 20 cents per fish, subject, as usual, to reductions and limits on what the canners would take as the season advanced.

This promptly produced meetings of the white fishermen at Steveston and Eburne. A representative of the Indians said they would back the union, but warned of trouble if the whites went back on the Indians as they had done in 1893. The Japanese union said its members would not fish. Next day, however, a large group of them did. Union patrol boats soon swept the river clean. There were reports that every Japanese carried a revolver; that the whites had forced the Japanese to hang up their nets and threatened to smash any Japanese boats which went out; that the whites were threatening to burn the Japanese hospital. A huge union parade wound its way through the Japanese bunkhouse areas, explained the situation, and warned the Japanese not to fish. Two canneries cut off their men's supplies of food; the cannery stores were closed.

There are no reliable reports of actual violence. But the union had to take down unauthorized posters threatening death to any Japanese who took his boat out; there were rumours of strikers being armed; and two of the most prominent strike leaders, Frank Rogers (of the Longshoremen) and Will MacClain (of the Machinists), were militant socialists. The canners, accordingly, not only issued the same misleading posters as in 1893, but wired the provincial government for extra police protection.

The provincial police arrived under the chief constable, who reported all quiet. But he began hiring special constables and arranging to have them patrol the fishing grounds in cannery tugs. The president of the Vancouver union was arrested and charged with intimidation; the charge was dismissed, but he had been got off the scene. The CPR dismissed MacClain from his job.

By 13 July the Japanese were complaining that they needed to fish for food. The white unions said they would be allowed to catch 500 to 700 fish per day under protection of a white flag. The Japanese said this was not enough, but agreed to wait a little longer before taking any action. By 16 July the heavy run of fish had started, and the Japanese were fishing only for the permitted food allowance. A big parade and meeting in Vancouver had produced some $225 to $300; union bakers had sent a wagon-load of bread, and the unions were feeding several hundred men daily.

The canners now agreed to meet a union committee of 'bona fide fishermen.' The meeting took place 18 July with Mr Bremner present. Meanwhile, the Japanese union's secretary had said they might settle for 22½ cents or even 22. Despite this, the white unions stuck to 25, and the canners to 20 (to drop to 15 in a heavy run, and for no more than the canneries could can; between 15 cents and 20, price to be governed by the state of the market). When the parties met again, 20 July, the unions offered to take a fixed price for the season, with a month's notice of change; equal limits on quantity for all fishermen; no discrimination against strikers; and freedom for men with their own gear to deliver fish to any cannery. The canners countered with a straight 18 cents; the union insisted on 20. Negotiations broke off. That evening in Vancouver, the New Westminster and the Japanese unions were willing to take 20; Vancouver, Steveston, and the North Arm wanted 25.

Before the unions had turned down the 18 cent offer, a canner sent out 2 boats, with 10 special constables in 3 cannery tugs, to test the strikers' attitude. Union patrols seized one boat, towed it ashore, and manhandled its boat-puller. The special constables, perhaps because of hope of a settlement, did not interfere.

The employers thereupon appealed to the dominion and provincial governments for military protection, but neither would act, yet. The canners then offered 20 cents for the first 600 fish, 15 cents for the rest, with equal limits for each boat. The whites refused by a large majority, but the Japanese accepted. The canners then got three justices of the peace (one a foreman, one a former cannery partner) to requisition troops. Such a requisition was mandatory. One hundred and sixty soldiers arrived with orders that, if necessary, they were to shoot to kill. Union patrols became largely ineffective, but most of the whites and Indians and about 600 Japanese stood firm.

The run of fish had generally stayed light, and the canners needed more fishermen. Moreover, debates in the assembly had cast a lurid light on their behaviour. After some manoeuvring on both sides, Bremner got the parties together again on 28

July. The union asked for 20 cents and union recognition. The canners refused both. The union, next day, offered to take 19 cents for the whole season, waiving recognition. The canners agreed, and the strike ended on 30 July.[46]

The unions had won a single price for the full season and an end to discrimination against individual fishermen. Otherwise, the settlement was a defeat. The men apparently felt one reason for this was insufficient organization, which they promptly set about remedying. On 25 August a meeting in Vancouver decided to organize a province-wide grand lodge. Unions already existed at Vancouver, New Westminster, Canoe Pass, Eburne, Ladner, and Port Simpson. The grand lodge seems to have been set up in January 1901. New Westminster, Vancouver, Canoe Pass, and Eburne became locals by February 1901, Port Simpson somewhat later, and Cowichan at the beginning of 1902. There was also a local at Port Guichon, an Alaska Fishermen's Union at Bristol Bay January 1902, a Marine Fishermen's Union at Victoria March 1902, and a TLCC FLU 24 (fishermen) at Duncan late 1901 or early 1902. The grand lodge probably lasted till March 1903. The 1903 TLC convention was informed that the New Westminster, Eburne, Port Guichon, Port Simpson, and Duncan unions had surrendered their TLCC charters.[47]

In February and early March 1901 the various locals held a series of meetings to work out proposals to submit to the Canners Association, which, it was rumoured, had already decided on a price of around 12½ cents per fish. The union wanted 15. In June the association offered 12 cents for July, 10 for the rest of the season. The grand lodge is said to have been inclined to accept this, but the locals were against it, about 80 per cent voting to stick to 15 cents for the season. A grand lodge committee met the canners. It got a new offer, precise terms unknown. The men rejected it, and demanded 12½ cents. The canners were willing to pay this from 1 July to 3 August, and to meet all the other union demands. But the union, having come to an agreement with the Japanese, refused this also, whereupon the canners withdrew all their offers. The grand lodge suggested that whatever price was fixed should apply only to fishermen who signed agreements on or before 5 July, after which a new agreement at a lower price might be necessary. This olive branch seems to have brought no response.

The men struck, 1 July, and stayed out till 20 July. The pattern of the previous year was pretty much repeated, with the Japanese acting as strikebreakers and six fishermen arrested on charges of intimidation. Bremner again intervened, and by his efforts and those of a number of business men the parties agreed on a compromise: 12½ cents for the first quarter of the pack, and 10 cents for the rest, with no discrimination against union fishermen.

In June 1902 the canners offered, for the first 200,000 cases, 20 cents per fish; for the next 100,000 cases, 16 cents; for the next 100,000 cases, 13 cents, for the next 100,000 cases, 11 cents; for the next 100,000 cases, 10 cents. The fishermen turned this down, but their own investigating committee later found the canners' contention that they should pay only 16½ cents correct, and a sliding scale was mutually agreed on at the opening of the season.[48]

British Columbia had several regional (or local) unions of seamen. The Mainland Steamshipmen's Benevolent and Protective Association of British Columbia was formed 15 November 1892. It appears under various names right down to the end of 1902 in the minutes of the Vancouver Trades and Labor Council, and, in 1893, in the minutes of UBC's Local 617. Some time in 1900 or 1901 it appears to have become TLCC FLU No 6; in September 1902 it officially changed its name, by order-in-council, to the British Columbia Steamshipman's Society; in 1903 it was incorporated, surrendered its charter, and was dissolved. In April 1902 it had reported having got firemen's wages up by $50 a month, and coal passers' wages up to $40.[49]

An International Coast Seamen's and Sealers Union of British Columbia was said to have 1000 members on 8 October 1892. A week later, the membership had grown to 1400, and a branch was to be organized in Vancouver the following week.

In April 1901 unions of steamboat firemen and of steamboatmen were formed at Victoria. The June 1903 *Labour Gazette* shows two unions of steamboatmen in Vancouver, and three in Victoria at 31 July 1902. The third in Victoria may have been the Shipmasters Association, formed in December 1901. In March 1902 it was reported campaigning vigorously against aliens 'who have been in the habit of making false declarations of citizenship in order to secure masters' certificates entitling them to ply their calling on Canadian waters.'[50]

There are signs also of a regional organization of teachers. On 9 January 1901 'a [mainland] teachers' union was formed by a number of teachers ... with the same objects for which trades' unions are formed.' On 10 May the Victoria teachers unanimously resolved that the time seemed ripe for 'the formation of a teachers' union in British Columbia,' and that the Victoria Teachers Institute was 'heartily in favour of a teachers' union, and ... prepared to resolve itself into such or to enter a British Columbia union.' They appointed a committee to draft a constitution for a Victoria teachers' union and communicate with other 'Institute and educational centres of the province and urge forward the formation of similar unions elsewhere, with a view to the ultimate formation of a Provincial Teachers Union.'[51]

Quebec

In Quebec, the names of organizations are not always a reliable indication of whether they were local, regional, or national. Some that called themselves provincial may in fact have been purely local; some that called themselves national may have been provincial, or even purely local.

A case in point is the barbers. The Association des Barbiers de la Province de Québec, formed in 1896 and chartered by the Quebec legislature, had the power to license barber shops, examine candidates for the trade, and make sanitary regulations. By the end of 1899 it claimed to have locals in every city and town in Quebec with 5000 or more people. This would mean Montreal, Quebec City, Sherbrooke, Trois-Rivières, St Hyacinthe, Sorel, Valleyfield, Hull, Lévis, and the Montreal suburbs of St-Henri and St-Cunégonde. The relationship, if any, to the provincial body of the Valleyfield Benevolent Assembly of Barbers, the Association Bienveillante des Barbiers of Quebec City (formed 2 April 1888), the Montreal local of the Union Protectrice des Barbiers du Canada (formed in September 1894), and the St Hyacinthe Union Protectrice des Barbiers, Coiffeurs et Perruquiers is obscure. All four were still in existence in July 1902.[52]

The boot and shoe union situation is both more complicated and more important, because the industry was a major one in Quebec. In September 1898 Montreal had a Fraternité des Cordonniers Unis de la Puissance du Canada (Brotherhood of United Shoemakers of the Dominion of Canada), which included locals of cordonniers-monteurs (lasters) and of coupeurs de cuir (leather cutters), and which had a joint council. The lasters apparently dated from 21 December 1896. This 'national' body, with 1800 members, boasted itself the biggest and strongest of the trade in Canada. It seems to have taken part in the Montreal Labour Day parade of 1899. In the 1900 Quebec City parade, the United Shoemakers had two locals from the city (machine shoemakers, with 1200 parading, and lasters, with 600) and two from St Hyacinthe (also machine shoemakers and lasters). The four locals paraded again in Quebec in 1901 (though the machine shoemakers were down to 300 and the lasters to 100). The December 1901 *Labour Gazette* lists the Quebec City Shoe Workers Fraternity, and a Union Protectrice des Cordonniers Monteurs du Canada, formed in 1885. Both may still have been parts of the nominally national union. It also lists, for St Hyacinthe, the Fraternité des Cordonniers Unis du Canada, formed 23 March 1898, and a Union Protectrice des Cordonniers Monteurs du Canada formed 17 December 1896. These were doubtless the two survivors of the three United Shoemakers Unions it had mentioned in February 1901.[53]

The United Shoemakers seems to have disappeared from Montreal by 1901, and to have been succeeded by the Canadian Federation of Boot and Shoe Workers, formed 14 November 1901 with at least eight locals. Three Montreal locals were represented at the 1902 TLCC convention from which the federation was expelled.[54]

Neither the United Shoemakers nor the Canadian Federation of Boot and Shoe Workers seems to have had any locals outside the province of Quebec. There had been a Federated Boot and Shoe Workers Union of Canada, with Hamilton and Toronto locals, in 1895, but it seems not to have lasted out the year.[55]

The United Shoemakers of Canada were having difficulties with the Slater Co in Montreal in the fall of 1898. Slater locked out the union; it was willing to accept arbitration, but not the closed shop. The Tailleurs de Cuir, who apparently did not then belong to the United Shoemakers, unanimously backed the United locals, one of which was strong enough to pay strike pay equal to regular wages. The lockout was still on at the beginning of March 1899.[56]

The Lasters Union had a series of disputes in Montreal in 1898 and 1899. They struck Linton's in January 1898 for a wage increase, which two other firms had accepted; Lafleur's for two weeks in May 1898; Fontaine's for a wage increase in July; Bell's, also in July; Brouillet's in December 1898 and January 1899 against a wage reduction; Lynch's in March 1899 against the employment of non-unionists from the United States; Whitman's (apparently a wildcat) in May, against a dismissal; and Vinet's in December, when that firm refused a uniform wage rate agreed to by all the other manufacturers.[57]

The Montreal Lasters struck Ames-Holden 25 February 1901 for a new scale of wages on the recently introduced machines. The company brought in strikebreakers, but the union persuaded most of these to leave. The company then brought in more strikebreakers, and the strike apparently fizzled out in May.[58]

The St Hyacinthe shoemakers in February 1900 won a closed shop in a one-day strike. In March 1901 they got a 10 to 15 per cent wage increase without striking.

The Cordonniers Unis (machine shoemakers and lasters) and the Brotherhood of Leather Cutters were involved in the great lockout of 1900 in Quebec City, which helped lay the foundations of the Roman Catholic trade union movement in Quebec.

In 1899 there had been a boot and shoe strike which, the employers said, ended with their granting a 20 per cent wage increase and with the employees 'binding themselves to no longer belong to any union.' But the workmen stuck to their unions, and 'hardly two months had elapsed before they forced the manufacturers to further increase their wages, after the latter had contracted for large orders ... causing thereby serious loss to the manufacturers.'

Then the unions had made exaggerated demands, notably the closed shop. In W.A. Marsh's factory, when he 'wished to replace one of his employees at a machine by another ... the other employees quit work.' When Vermette and Thivierge dismissed 'an incompetent employee' and put their foreman in his place, the men struck and forced the reinstatement of the dismissed man. When Alfred Poirier & Co dismissed an employee, the rest struck. Their position, the employers said, had become intolerable, so, on 25 October 1900, they posted notices of a lockout in 21 factories, effective 27 October. On 30 October another factory closed, leaving only four in operation.

The employers said the lockout affected 5000 employees, whose wages would amount to $20,000 a week; it would also affect manufacture of leather, machinery, and wooden and cardboard boxes. The *Labour Gazette*'s correspondent said the stoppage threw out of employment 3850 people (2390 males and 1150 females over 18 years of age, and 205 boys and 110 girls). It affected also engine drivers, machinists, packers, and others.

The employers' association said the sole issue was 'whether the operatives will continue to run the factories as they like, or ... the employers, who have invested their capital in this industry, will have the right to administer their establishments as they wish and employ what operatives they desire whether they belong to unions or not ... The manufacturers are decided not to reopen their doors until they have checked the intervention of foreign labour unions ... seeing that these unions are trying to take trade elsewhere.'

Nothing further happened till 14 November, when the association stated the terms on which the factories would reopen. Every employee would have to sign a judicial declaration that he belonged to 'no labour union intended to interfere between the workingmen and their employers'; that he did not intend to join any such union; that he had withdrawn from any such union to which he had formerly belonged; and that he would 'take no part in any difficulty that may arise between my employer and one or more of his employees.' He would also have to sign a contract embodying these terms, giving his employer the right to dismiss him if he did not strictly comply with what he had promised, and waiving all claims against his employer in this condition. The advertisements further announced the creation of a grievance procedure. An aggrieved workman would have the right to confer with any two fellow-workmen in the same factory, and, if they thought his cause just, they would notify the secretary of the Manufacturers' Association, who would immediately call a meeting of the committee of the association. The committee would act as a board of arbitration, and its decision would be final and binding.

This incredible document produced a reply, two days later, from the secretary of the unions' joint committee. It was, of course, a resounding no. The unions drew attention to the outrageousness of an association of employers denying their employees' right of association. They pointed out also that the proposed contract imposed no obligations whatever on the employer, and left the employee without even the right of notice of dismissal. They called the proposed board of arbitration 'a grotesque parody of justice, ... a simple farce.' ('"I'll be judge, I'll be jury," said cunning old Fury.') They wound up by saying they were willing to accept their old wages, willing to negotiate, willing to accept 'with joy and eagerness a Board of Arbitration, equitably constituted.'

The employers, 20 November, refused to budge. The workers could negotiate individual contracts. They would be free to join any association other than those prohibited ('Hang your clothes on a hickory limb, But *don't* go near the water'). They could appeal to the courts from any decision of the board of arbitration. A few employees, mostly foremen, signed the documents and went back to work. Most refused.

The employers, four days later, decided to ask Archibishop Bégin to act as arbitrator. The archbishop said he would if the unions agreed. They did at once, saying that the employers' action had 'anticipated' their own wishes. They also wrote the employers that they were ready to go back to work at the old wages while the arbitration was going on. The employers said yes, if the men would sign the documents. The unions refused.

On 10 December the archbishop asked the employers to reopen the factories, and the men not to attend union meetings till he had given his judgement. Both agreed, and after the reopening, but before any decision by the archbishop, the leather cutters were given an increase of $1 per week, simply, so the *Labour Gazette*'s correspondent says, because 'the supply is scarce.'

On 14 January 1901 the archbishop handed down his decision, an elaborate document, with a long quotation from the papal encyclical on the condition of labour. It found the constitutions of the unions objectionable in certain respects and, if literally applied, 'sure [to] greatly injure personal liberty, freedom of conscience and justice.' The unions must therefore revise their constitutions. The workers were to appoint a board of complaint, with three members, the employers a board of conciliation, also with three members. The two boards would sit jointly to consider any grievance. If they could not agree, the grievance would be submitted to a court of arbitration, made up of three members, one chosen by the board of complaint, one by the board of conciliation, the third by the other two, or, failing agreement, by the archbishop himself or a judge of the superior court. The decision of the court of arbitration would be final and binding. The lockout cost the trade $750,000 and the workers about $200,000 in lost wages.

There was a sequel, pregnant with consequences. On 28 June 1901 the parish priests of Saint-Roch, Saint-Sauveur, and Saint-Malo asked the shoe workers to come to a meeting in Saint-Roch church, and 1800 came. They had to listen to a letter from Archbishop Bégin asking the unions to revise, immediately, the rules of their organizations, 'in conformity with justice and charity,' or, if they could not do this, to form another organization whose principles would be based on these lines, and to 'abstain from objectionable and reprehensible principles.' The new rules should make strikes impossible for any reason, and should provide for settlement by conciliation and arbitration. The workers decided to lay the whole question before the three unions.

In July the Lasters and the Cutters submitted their constitutions to the archbishop. On 9 October the employers posted notices that the archbishop had relieved the manufacturers of their 'engagements with the machinists [machine shoemakers] who had ... refused to abide' by the terms of the settlement, and that, accordingly, from 12 October the manufacturers would employ only 'non-unionists or workmen belonging to associations having similar by-laws to the new by-laws which concern the cutters and lasters who have conformed to the award.' The Machine Shoemakers thereupon submitted their constitution also to the archbishop, who apparently, duly emasculated it.[59]

In March 1901, the United Shoemakers' Machine local in St Hyacinthe got, without striking, a 10 to 15 per cent increase, at the very time that the international union was getting its label adopted by Séguin & Lalime.[60]

The Canadian Association of Mechanical Engineers began in Montreal, 16 February 1892, as the Union (or Association) St-Laurent des Ingénieurs Stationnaires. This figures regularly in *La Presse* from June to November 1893 (in October as part of the Trades and Labor Council) and at intervals in 1894. The regional body was formed 24 October 1894. The Montreal 'Cour St-Laurent' appears regularly in *La Presse* throughout 1895; in *La Patrie* and *La Presse* fairly often in 1896; and in *La Presse* in the first half of 1899. It marched in the 1900 Labour Day parade, and what appears to be a new local union of the same name was listed for the 1902 St-Jean-Baptiste parade. The Quebec Cour Champlain was formed 16 April 1895, had a delegate at the 1896 TLC convention, and marched in the Labour Day processions of 1895, 1900, and 1901.[61]

Ontario

The only Ontario regional union of any consequence was the Industrial Brotherhood, and even this was regional more in intention than in fact. The only directory (local) outside London seems to have been in Woodstock. But the Brotherhood played a part, in London, in Ontario, and even in the national movement, out of all proportion to its numbers.

It was organized in London in August 1891 by Joseph T. Marks and others. It seems to have been partly an attempt to fill the vacuum left by the decline of the Knights of Labor. Like the Knights, the Brotherhood was ready to take in all kinds of workers. It devoted itself to organizing the unorganized, both the unskilled and mechanics who had no craft union available in their neighbourhood. Like the Knights, it emphasized education and the co-operative movement. Marks was to become one of the leading figures in labour political action in Ontario. Like the Knights also, it included people who were at the same time members of particular unions.

The headquarters was called the general directory. There seem to have been at least nine directories. Directory No 1, London, lasted from August 1891 till January 1903. There were at least three others in London: No 4, which was there in 1897, and nos 7 and 9, which marched in the 1893–95 Labour Day parades. The general directory and nos 7 and 9 were represented at the 1895 TLC convention. Some directory or directories marched in the London Labour Day parades of 1896, 1897, and 1900–01. In the fall of 1900 John Flett, the AFL organizer, approached the Brotherhood in an unsuccessful attempt to get it to affiliate with the AFL. Directory No 3 was in existence in Woodstock in 1897. Nos 2, 5, 6, and 8 may well have been in other western Ontario towns, for in 1895 steps were being taken to organize in

1896 a district directory for western Ontario, to include London, Woodstock, St Thomas, Stratford, Ingersoll, Strathroy, and other places. In February 1897 Marks made a tour of the region, and workers in many towns are reported to have expressed interest in joining.[62]

The Brotherhood organized the London general labourers in February 1897. It adopted, and promoted, a union label of its own. It set up sick benefit branches. It established a regular Sunday afternoon open forum, where workers could meet 'to discuss our difficulties in a calm and reasonable manner.' This was expected to (and did) appeal to all 'lovers of intellectual liberty,' and it lasted as long as the Brotherhood itself. The Brotherhood also tried to set up libraries and educational branches in every place where it organized. It distributed free literature on social problems. It provided free lectures to all organizations which asked for them. It founded, early in its career, the *Industrial Banner*, which soon became and long remained one of the most influential labour papers Canada has known. In 1896 the Brotherhood inaugurated what it called a labour revival, whose main aim seems to have been to teach workingmen that the 'greatest duty of the citizens was to use the ballot properly. Too much time had been wasted in idle talk about social reforms – Their motto was action.'

In June 1897 Directory No 1 called a meeting for 18 June to make 'final arrangements for the instituting of the co-operative factory. The Directory having granted money for a start, all members desiring to go to work will do well to report at this meeting. Everything is now ready to commence.' This enterprise, like so many others, seems to have failed.[63]

The Brotherhood played a very large part in the London Trades and Labor Council. Marks was the council's secretary in 1895, and one of its three delegates to the TLCC convention. He was its sole delegate to the conventions of 1897 and 1900, and one of its three in 1899, 1901, and 1902. In these last three years, one of the other two delegates was a member or supporter of the Brotherhood (in 1899 Frank Plant of the Typos, and in 1901 and 1902 William Burleigh of the Builders' Labourers). Marks and Plant were two of the council's five candidates for alderman in 1896.[64]

Marks succeeded in 1895 in getting the TLCC constitution amended to provide for representation of directories of the Industrial Brotherhood and of the general directory. In 1900 this was rescinded. (The Brotherhood had sent no delegates after 1895.) In 1902 Marks was elected to the Ontario executive committee of the TLCC. Other Brotherhood delegates took a prominent part in the 1895 convention.[65]

In June 1899 there was an attempt to form a Provincial Firemen's Association of Ontario. A meeting of delegates from Toronto, Niagara, St Catharines, and Kew Beach took place at Merritton and resolved to hold a convention at Toronto at the time of the Exhibition to complete the organization. The Merritton meeting appointed a commitee of delegates from Toronto, St Catharines, Niagara Falls, Merritton, and Welland.[66]

We have already noted efforts by seceders, or would-be seceders, from international unions to set up purely Canadian national unions.[67] None of these succeeded. In July 1887 delegates from the Brantford Builders' Labourers went to Toronto to a convention to set up a national union of that occupation.[68] This also seems to have come to nought. Slightly more successful was the attempt to organize a National Brotherhood of Bookbinders, whose first (and perhaps only) local appears in the 1897 Ottawa Labour Day parade. The following month the Ottawa Allied Trades and Labor Association was discussing whether the national union should be represented, since there was already an Ottawa international local. The national union seems to have marched again in 1898, 1900, and 1901; but in September 1902 the international announced it would admit members of the national for an initiation fee of $2.50, and this seems to have been the end of the national.[69]

In May 1896 David Gibson of the International Bricklayers and Masons visited Montreal to get the Montreal Bricklayers to help form a Canadian Federation of Bricklayers.[70]

A Canadian Federation of Labour, or Canadian Trades Confederation, existed in Ottawa in September and October 1896 and marched in the 1896 and 1897 Labour Day parades. *La Presse*, in November 1895, had reported that several Montreal unions were proposing to leave their internationals and join this body.[71]

In the fall of 1901 some disgruntled and enterprising railway men in North Bay tried to organize a Canada (or 'National') Union (or 'Association' or 'Order') of Railwaymen, to include engineers, firemen, conductors, brakemen, and telegraphers. The promoters sent out a letter to all Canadian railwaymen, and succeeded in getting representatives of the older orders to meet in Ottawa 20 November to discuss the idea. The meeting was unimpressed by arguments that a single Canadian union would be cheaper to run than Canadian branches of five international unions, and that, being purely Canadian, it would 'have more weight in proposing legislation,' and, after a lengthy discussion, 'the meeting adjourned *sine die*.'[72]

Three other national organizations actually came into being and lasted, though one of them seems scarcely to have been a real union. The Federated Association of Letter Carriers was formed in 1891. The first charter seems to have been issued to Branch 4 (London), 9 October 1891. This was followed by Branch 2 (Ottawa) and Branch 7 (Winnipeg), which got theirs on 19 October; Branch 6 (Saint John), 23 October; Branch 1 (Toronto), 2 November; Branch 9 (Halifax), 7 November; Branch 3 (Hamilton), 17 November; Branch 10 (Montreal), 13 January 1892;

Branch 5 (Quebec), 11 November; Branch 12 (Vancouver), 15 May 1901; Branch 11 (Victoria), 11 June; and Branch 13 (Brantford), 3 December. The *Labour Gazette* says Branch 8 (Kingston) was chartered in November 1891; but the union headquarters says 12 February 1908. The explanation seems to be that there was a branch organized in 1891, which was dissolved in 1903, and evidently reorganized in 1908.[73]

The Letter Carriers, being dominion government employees, in the days before collective bargaining in the public service relied on the method of legal enactment, or variants of it, to get improvements in pay and working conditions. For instance, in February 1893 Branch 9 (Halifax) petitioned the postmaster-general and the prime minister for a salary increase. They said that their salaries were low; it took them 8 or 10 years to reach their maximum of $600; their wages had not kept pace with those of other workers; letter carriers were 'especially liable to sickness through constant exposure to all changes of weather, as well as ... to early and permanent disability or death by reason of the incessant long limit of walking daily.' They therefore asked for a minimum salary of $450, with an annual increase of $50 for each of the succeeding 6 years.[74]

Halifax, after the manner of the Maritime provinces, had more modest ideas on the subject than the TLCC which, in 1892, had already passed a resolution for a $600 minimum salary. The congress returned to the charge in 1898. Its resolution said that the letter carriers and other postal assistants had 'frequently appeared before the different Trades Councils ... and complained' of bad conditions of work, and that the councils had investigated, and found that the men 'received insufficient wages, had no set hours of labor and ... no definite system of promotion.' It asked for a minimum wage of $2 per 8-hour day, and a system which would ensure promotion for steady service.

In 1901 the congress noted that the Letter Carriers had petitioned the postmaster-general for a 20 per cent increase, and had had no reply; it instructed the incoming executive committee to draw the minister's attention to the fact that 'the increased prices of the various necessities of life, rent and fuel, render it necessary that this urgent and important question should receive immediate and favorable consideration and settlement.'

The response to this was an amendment to the Post Office Act in 1902, dividing the employees of the post office into five groups, with salaries of $1.25, $1.50, $1.75, $2, and $2.25 per day respectively. The amendment also provided that after six months' probation, employees in the first group might be transferred to the second; after a further two years, to the third, after another two years, to the fourth; and for work of 'a specially arduous and responsible nature,' to the fifth. This fell so far short of the union's demands that the 1902 congress convention instructed the executive to tackle the government again forthwith. The act had 'not received the approval of the men affected' by it; the cost of living was higher; and the government 'should recognize the justice of the claim of the Letter Carriers with as little delay as possible.' The demand for the 20 per cent increase was duly presented to the government 6 April 1903, but the postmaster-general would not budge.[75]

A second national union, established during this period, and lasting long after it, was the National Association of Marine Engineers. An Association of Marine Engineers appears in the Toronto Trades and Labor Council's minutes on 1 March 1889. The National Association appears from March to July 1902. On 24 April it reported that the Niagara Navigation Co, the White Star, and the Richelieu and Ontario Navigation Co were 'unfair,' and asked the delegates to 'remember this when getting up excursions.' On 8 May it mentioned the Niagara Co and the Oakville Co as employing non-union marine engineers, and the council's secretary was instructed to write both firms. The association complained that, in spite of its request, labour bodies had been booking excursions on unfair boats; the practice was denounced by all the delegates. On 22 May the council heard the cheering news that the Oakville Co's non-union engineer had joined the association; that the White Star boat was now on the fair list; and that the Niagara Navigation Co's boats, and other boats running out of Toronto, were now fair to the Marine Engineers.[76]

Kingston Council No 4 of the NAME was organized 21 January 1900; Montreal No 5, 11 January 1900; Victoria No 6, 5 January 1901; Sorel No 9, March 1902. The 1903 TLCC convention was informed that the NAME had affiliated its 10 subordinate councils on 30 July 1903: Toronto No 1, Saint John No 2, Collingwood No 3, Kingston No 4, Montreal No 5, Victoria No 6, Vancouver No 7, Lévis No 8, Sorel No 9, and Owen Sound No 10. There were 574 members. All of these branches, except perhaps Owen Sound, were probably in existence at the end of 1902.[77]

The Canadian Association of Stationary Engineers was incorporated in 1887. Its claim to be a real union is doubtful. The preamble to its constitution said: 'This association shall at no time be used for the furtherance of strikes or in any way interfere between its members and their employers in regard to wages. It shall recognize the identity of interests between employer and employee, and shall not countenance any project or enterprise that will interfere with perfect harmony between them ... Its meetings shall be devoted to the promotion of educational, professional and mechanical knowledge.' In September 1893 this organization had locals in Montreal, Toronto, Hamilton, Ottawa, London, Guelph, and Dresden (Ontario). It had been listed for the Montreal Labour Day parade of 1890.

That the Toronto Trades and Labor Council did not consider the CASE a union is amply clear from its educational committee's comments on 5 October 1894. The *Evening Star* had published an interview with the association's secretary, in which that worthy had ardently disclaimed any connections with the Knights of Labor or any other labour body, insisting that 'the society was formed for an educative purpose. By meeting together and discussing the subject of engineering one gains the knowledge of the rest. That is the only object we have in meeting. We are the only society that wishes to be taxed ... We ask for it and we advocate it. We want the profession licensed. Then there would be less danger to life and property, and insurance rates would come down.'

The TTLC educational committee observed:

That the society was formed for an educational purpose we were interested to learn, but of what character this education partook we were at a loss to comprehend when we considered the sapient remark, 'By meeting together and discussing the subject of engineering one gains the knowledge of the rest.' Perhaps if we were to refer the passage to the ... machinists they might be able to explain when called in to rectify errors occasioned by the engineers having obtained their education in so pleasant and perfunctory a manner. No wonder that with so much education they should desire to enter the licensed professions. It is on record that this Council is of the opinion that for safety to life and property only duly qualified and licensed men should have charge of stationary or other engines. We assert that if their intense desire to be taxed and employers to be thus relieved from a portion of their insurance rates is acquiesced in that not class privileges be accorded them. Their significant admission that 'we have no connection with the Knights of Labor, nor with any other labor body' is a fatal give away to the efficiency of their educative purpose.

The CASE seems to have confined its activities, such as they were, mainly to Ontario. It is not represented in the *Labour Gazette*'s 1901 and 1902 lists of unions.[78]

PART FOUR

Central organizations 1880–1902

15

Local central organizations 1881–1902

ORIGINS

The Canadian labour movement entered the year 1881 without a single functioning local central labour organization. But on 23 July delegates from the various trades in Toronto met in Dufferin Hall 'with a view to reaugernise a Trades Council.' The unions represented were the Tailors, Stone Cutters, Bakers, Bricklayers, Plasterers, Longshoremen, Amalgamated Society of Carpenters, Cigar Makers, Labourers, Seamen, Typos, Shoemakers, and Molders. Of these, only five (Carpenters, Cigar Makers, Seamen, Typos, and Molders) were locals of international unions. The only delegates with power to do more than discuss and report to their union were the Bricklayers. None the less, the meeting unanimously agreed that it was advisable 'to form ... a Trades and Labour Council for Mutual protection and that it be non-partisan or Political.'

On 13 August there was a second meeting, with 13 unions represented (this time, they included a Shoemakers Association and a 'Hand sewed Shoemakers' Union). It elected officers and empowered the president, William Todd of the Cigar Makers, to appoint a committee to draw up a constitution. It also elected an organizing committee.[1] This council lasted till it was absorbed by the present Toronto and District Labour Council.

The second local organization was the Hamilton Trades and Labor Assembly. The Toronto council, on 16 December 1881, had instructed its secretary to correspond with the (presumed) Hamilton council. But on 6 January 1882 he reported that 'they had made enquiries at Hamilton but found there was no Trades Council or Assembly inorgerated there as yet but the Trades themselves were moving they had left several coppies of our constitution there with the expectation they would be acted upon.'

They were. On 24 March 1882 the various unions held meetings to consider forming a council, 'whereby all branches of labor could act unitedly on all questions which affected any one branch ... in this or any other locality.' This meeting appointed a committee to correspond with all labour organizations in the United States on the plans they had adopted and how well they had succeeded. It also invited all local labour organizations to a mass meeting 6 April. This must have formally set up the Trades Assembly, for on 28 April we find that body holding its regular meeting, with deputations from the Cigar Makers and the Tinsmiths asking about the conditions of affiliation.

The Hamilton assembly seems not to have lasted long. It was succeeded by the Central Trades and Labor Council, or Central Labor Union, the exact date of whose formation is not clear. The later Trades and Labor Council in 1897 said the CLU was formed in 1883 'under the auspices of District Council No. 61, K. of L.' The *Palladium of Labor* of 6 December 1884 said the first meeting had just taken place, 3 December, with all the labour organizations in the city represented. The Hamilton *Spectator*, in February 1886, said the CLU had just had its first annual supper. The organization was certainly still in existence in December 1887.[2]

Some time in 1888, however, it evidently disappeared; for on 12 November of that year three Knights of Labor LAS (2132, 2225, and 2307) and eight unions (ASE, Typos, Machinists and Blacksmiths, Bricklayers, Plasterers, Painters, Molders, and Builders' Labourers) met to consider forming a trades and labour council. On 3 December a second meeting heard that three LAS (2225, 2307, and 8915) and five unions (Machinists and Blacksmiths, Bricklayers, Molders, Builders' Labourers, and Carpenters) favoured forming a council, while the Typos had taken no vote on the question, and the Glass Blowers and the Lathers no action. On 16 December delegates were present from LAS 2225, 2307, and 8915 and from the Machinists and Blacksmiths, Bricklayers, Carpenters, Typos, Painters, and Flint Glass Blowers. This meeting elected officers. This council lasted till it was absorbed in the present Hamilton and District Labour Council.[3]

The third local central body to appear in the 1880s was the Halifax Amalgamated Trades Union, formed 22 August 1882 by the Carpenters, Painters, Bricklayers, and Bakers. It lasted till at least 1895, perhaps till 1897, though there was, in 1891 and 1892, a Trades and Labour Council.[4] In August 1898 a new council was formed, which lasted till it was absorbed by the present Halifax, Dartmouth and District Labour Council.[5]

London had a meeting, 2 December 1882, to form a Trades Assembly or Trades and Labor Council. The Toronto council sent the chairman of its organizing committee, Thomas Moor, to help. Moor addressed a meeting of union representatives, pointing out the advantages of a central delegate body like the Toronto council, and his speech is reported to have been unanimously endorsed. But the result was just an attempt to breathe new life into the moribund Canadian Workingmen's Association of London, formed 12 August 1882. The attempt failed, and about the middle of

1883 the London unions seem to have formed a Legislative Council, of which very little is known. A London *Free Press* article on 31 August 1946 says it consisted of delegates from all organizations which were willing to affiliate. Another writer says it was made up of three delegates from each Knights of Labor local assembly.[6] (This is nonsense. In 1883 there was only one LA in London.) Whether or no, the Legislative Council did not last long.

Before the end of 1884 the various organizations formed a Trades and Labor Council. This council's existence may have been interrupted by 1894, for on 16 March of that year the minutes of the Toronto council record a letter from London asking for information on the constitution of trades councils.[7] However, there is no doubt that there was a London council from 1895 on, and that it was both active and powerful.

The TLCC convention of 1883 passed a resolution calling upon all towns and cities to form 'trades' councils, where practicable, these councils to communicate with one another ... and consider all subjects of importance to the interests of the working community, and to carry out their best endeavours to attain the object in view, whether socially or otherwise.'[8]

This does not seem to have produced any immediate results. But a council was organized in Guelph in 1885 which was still in existence in 1888. This probably disappeared some time between then and 16 March 1894, when Guelph was asking for the same information as London. In March 1898 a new council was formed, which was still there at the end of 1902.[9]

Another four councils appear in 1886: Montreal Central Trades and Labor Council, formed in February on the initiative of LA 3484; Oshawa, formed by 18 June; Brantford, 7 August; St Thomas, by 14 September.[10]

The Montreal Central Council lasted till after the 1902 split in the TLCC, when, on 18 September, it gave place to a National Trades and Labour Council.[11] A second Montreal council, the Federated Trades and Labor Council, was organized in 1897. A meeting was held, 20 April, in the Hebrew Social Hall, with the object of reforming the central council or seceding from it. The rebel unions were the Plasterers, Typos 176, United Carpenters 134 and 376, and Barbers 34. They founded the new council, which held its first meeting 28 July. This council later became the Montreal Trades and Labor Council, and lasted till it was absorbed into the present Montreal Labour Council.[12]

The Oshawa council appears in the Toronto council's minutes several times in 1886 and on 8 February 1887. It was represented at the 1887 TLCC convention, and was still in existence in 1889.[13]

The Brantford council was reorganized 21 January 1887, when credentials were received from the Typos 51, Molders 29, Bricklayers 6 of Ontario, Cigar Makers 59, Plasterers, Builders' Labourers, and LAS 2491 and 2817. The *Labour Gazette* says it was disbanded 4 March 1893. But there is evidence that in fact it had disappeared before 3 April 1890. Late in October 1892 a meeting was held 'for the purpose of discussing the advisability of organizing a trades council or an Association of Federated Trades Unions.' This meeting led to another, 7 November, which resolved to form a council; and on 10 December a new council came into existence. The *Labour Gazette* further states that a new council was organized in February 1897.[14]

The St Thomas Council was represented at the 1886 TLCC convention. It was still in existence in February 1887. A second council was organized in 1899 or 1900, and was still there at the end of 1902.[15]

Winnipeg formed its first council in 1887, though it does not seem to have lasted long. In March 1890 the building trades organized a council, which soon afterwards was expanded to take in all the trades in the city and became the Manitoba Trades Council. According to one source, this lasted till June 1891; according to another, till the end of 1892. A third council, formed in 1894, lasted till it was absorbed in the present Winnipeg and District Labour Council.[16]

The first St Catharines council was organized by 3 August 1888. The town had fifteen labour organizations (seven LAs, four international unions, and four local). In 1889 it still had thirteen, and the Council was represented at the TLCC convention by three delegates, one of whom, J.T. Carey, was elected president. Some time between then and August 1896 this council must have faded out. For in September 1896 we find Hugh Robinson, a Tailors' international organizer, reporting that he had visited St Catharines on 25 August and had urged the workers to establish a trades and labour council, which they had decided to do. They seem actually to have done it on 25 January 1897, and it was still there at the end of 1902.[17]

Five new councils were formed in 1889: Ottawa, 20 February; Victoria, in June; Peterborough, probably also in June; Vancouver, 21 November; Quebec City, 29 December.

Organization of the Ottawa council seems to have been under way as early as the first week in January, when the Hackmen's Union appointed three delegates to 'the ... Council being organized.' On 20 February delegates from this union, and the Typos, Bookbinders, Pressmen, Bricklayers and Masons, Painters and Decorators, and Plumbers and Tinsmiths – the last two purely local – and two LAs (5222 and 1034), elected officers. This council lasted till the summer of 1897, when it was reorganized into the Allied Trades and Labor Association, which lasted till it was absorbed into the present Ottawa and District Labour Council.[18]

The Victoria council was originally called the Trades Assembly. It lasted till it was absorbed into the present Victoria Labour Council.[19]

The Peterborough council must have been in existence before 5 July 1889, for on that date the Toronto council considered 'an invitation from the Trades & Labor

Council of Peterboro' to take part in a demonstration. None the less, the Peterborough *Examiner* of 26 December says that at an adjourned meeting of unions the night before the Bricklayers, Carpenters, and Knights of Labor had established a Trades and Labor Council. It was to 'deal with matters of municipal and national politics, discussion of which is prohibited in individual unions, and labor interests in general.' The 25 December meeting elected officers and a committee to appoint legislative, municipal, and organizing committees. This council does not seem to have lasted long. A new one was organized in 1902. A meeting to discuss the matter was held on 20 March with delegates from the Carpenters and FLU 9240 present. A further meeting, with more unions represented, was arranged for 2 April. FLU 9240 had already asked the Bricklayers and Masons to send delegates, and on 1 April that union appointed two. Apparently, when the 2 April meeting was held, only the delegates from the Teamsters turned up, and they asked for a postponement. The council, however, was already in being by 15 April when the Bricklayers tabled a letter from it.[20]

The first steps to organize the Vancouver council were taken at a meeting in Sullivan's Hall, 21 November 1889, with delegates from the Knights of Labor, the Amalgamated Carpenters, a local Carpenters Union, the Typos, the Painters, and the Plasterers. This meeting issued a call to all labour organizations in the city to send delegates to a further meeting on 5 December, when the council was formally established. This council lasted till it was absorbed by the present Vancouver and District Labour Council.[21]

The Quebec City Trades and Labor Council was formed 29 December 1889 by eight LAS of the Knights of Labor (713, 1007, 4003, 10061, 10123, 10581, 10829, and 10879) and five unions (Typos 159 and 160, Leather Cutters, Lasters, and Barbers). As a result of the expulsion of the Knights of Labor and dual national, regional, and local unions by the TLCC in 1902, the Quebec council ceased to exist in that year. It was succeeded first by the National Trades and Labour Council (formed in 1902, and affiliated with the new National Trades and Labour Congress of Canada) and then by the Federated Trades and Labour Council (formed in 1903, and affiliated with the TLCC).[22]

Three new councils were formed in 1890: New Westminster, Saint John, and Windsor.

On 28 February the Vancouver council considered a letter from two unions in New Westminster 'who intend working to secure a Trades and Labor Council.' At the abortive conference to set up a provincial congress, the only two delegates present had been two from the New Westminster council. This council was still in existence on 3 June 1892. It was gone by September 1901.[23]

The first Saint John council was formed 28 May 1890 by the Typos 85, Carpenters 397, Bricklayers and Masons 1 of New Brunswick, and the Ship Labourers,

Cartmen, Tailors, and Tinsmiths. By 11 July 1891 it had not held a meeting for two months, and only the Typos and the Bricklayers were showing any interest.

On 1 March 1893, on the initiative of the Bricklayers, a second council was formed. The Bricklayers, Typos, Carpenters, Molders, and the local Painters were the original members. In April the council was trying to get the Ship Labourers Union to join, in May the Caulkers, in June the Shipwrights and the Cartmen (but the Painters had disbanded). By September only two unions were unaffiliated. By 3 January 1894 the Labourers had come in; in February, the Shipwrights came in; in March, the Sailmakers came in and the Shipwrights went out; by July, the Carriage Makers were in. Rice says this council had the continuous and active support of the Typos, Molders, Bricklayers, and the Ship Labourers Union, with the Sailmakers affiliated for over a year. He mentions the Cigar Makers 394 and the Letter Carriers Branch 6 as other affiliates. The Caulkers, Tinsmiths, Stonecutters, Scowmen, Cartmen, and the Ship Labourers Society were apparently never members.

A third council was organized 11 December 1901, with eight unions (Painters and Decorators, Molders, Machinists, Carpenters, Typos, Cigar Makers, Hotel and Restaurant, and Longshoremen). It lasted till 1908, when it had to be reorganized; this fourth council came to an end in 1909.[24]

Windsor's first council was organized some time before September 1890. It must have been a rather ramshackle affair, for, though it sent a delegate (John Barnett) to the 1890 convention of the TLCC, his bona fides was, to say the least, very dubious. Just over a month after the convention, a committee appointed by LA 3281 reported to the TLCC secretary that Barnett had never been elected or appointed a delegate at all: there had not even been a meeting of the council 'on the night or day on which he claimed he was elected, nor for two weeks before or after,' and the council president had never signed his credentials. In fact this council seems to have met only irregularly, and petered out some time before 1894. It could make no headway against hard times and anti-union public feeling.

A second council was established in 1894. The founding meeting, 5 February, had a large attendance. It appointed several committees. There is one newspaper report of a further meeting, 1 April, which condemned the action of the board of education in recognizing day labour. This council also seems to have faded out, some time before 1900.[25]

A little before Labour Day 1901 the Windsor Carpenters met with the Bricklayers and Masons to try to organize activities for that occasion. Someone suggested forming a new council, and in December seven unions (Bricklayers, Carpenters, FLU 8019, Teamsters, Tailors, Electrical Workers, and Street Railway Employees) decided to do it, and appointed a committee to draw up a constitution and by-laws. On 9 July 1902 the council was formally established. This was the third council to get a TLCC charter (20 August 1902, just 12 days after Toronto).[26]

Nanaimo formed a council in 1891. There was a preliminary meeting 5 December with representatives from the Miners, Tailors, Carpenters, the Engineers Protective Association, and the Coal Trimmers present. By December it was in full swing. This council appears in the Vancouver council's minutes down to 17 July 1902. It seems to have survived till at least 1904.[27]

Kingston had a council in September 1894. A second Kingston council was organized in December 1899 and lasted till at least 1904.[28]

In St John's, Newfoundland, by early September 1896, the Mechanics Society was transforming itself into what was, in effect, a trades and labour council. By December, 12 to 14 unions, with some 1200 members, were said to be considering affiliation; by February 1897 8 unions had joined. This body organized Labour Day parades in 1897 and 1898, formed an apprenticeship branch, and did some lobbying for tariff reductions and the appointment of trade inspectors.[29]

The Rossland council was formed 11 April 1897. It was represented at the TLCC conventions of 1898, 1899, and 1901, and appears in the Vancouver council's minutes in 1899, and the Toronto council's in 1901 and 1902.[30]

The Revelstoke Trades and Labor Assembly was organized on 10 October 1899, by D.J. Stamper, AFL organizer, and got an AFL charter on 17 October. It was listed in the *Labour Gazette* of September 1901.[31]

The St Hyacinthe council was organized 8 or 9 September 1899, and lasted till 3 December 1906. It had one feature which must have been unique: the December 1900 *Labour Gazette* reports that '*The Merchants Union*, having desired to go hand in hand with the union workmen, has allied itself with the Central Trades and Labour Council. This union wishes to show that trade and organized labour have united together to help each other.' In the summer of 1901 St Hyacinthe had seven affiliated local unions.[32]

Seven new councils appeared in 1900: Nelson, probably in January; Berlin in March; Greenwood, British Columbia, in June; Stratford, 21 July; Brockville, 15 November; Phoenix, British Columbia, 14 December; Moncton, probably in December.

Nelson was the first council to get a TLCC charter. It appears in the Vancouver council's minutes in February 1901, and was represented at the 1901 TLCC convention. It is listed in 1904 among the councils not chartered by the congress. In the spring of 1900 it seems to have had 12 unions.[33]

The Berlin Twin City Trades and Labor Council was represented at the TLCC conventions of 1901 and 1902, and in 1904 was listed among councils chartered by the congress. The *American Federationist* of April 1902 noted that whereas in 1900 Berlin had had only two unions, it had, by that date, a large council and 23 unions.[34]

The Greenwood council is listed in 1904 among those not having a TLCC charter.[35] The Stratford council lasted till 1911.[36]

The Brockville council got its AFL charter on 19 November 1900. The original member unions were the Typos, Masons, Carpenters, Moulders, and FLU 8656. This council lasted till at least 1908.[37]

The Phoenix council was represented at the TLCC convention of 1901. In 1902 it made history. During the year it had withdrawn from the congress, because, as it explained in a letter summarized at the convention, it 'believed that as at present constituted the Congress is rather an appendage of a capitalist party than a body devoted to the advancement of the interests of the working people of Canada.' This charge applied 'somewhat largely to the rank and file of accredited delegates, but more especially to the executive officers and leading spirits.' Specifically, the council charged that Ralph Smith, MP, the congress president, 'had acted as a Liberal partisan in the House of Commons, and that he took the stump in the Liberal interests;' that he 'carried a pass from the CPR [and] a man who debauches himself in this way is not likely to be a disinterested champion of labor;' and that he was Dunsmuir's brother-in-law, and that Dunsmuir had checked off union dues for his benefit. The congress secretary summed up the charges in these words: 'President Ralph Smith is a henchman of a capitalist party, who accepts favors which may be classed as bribes from a corporation, and who tries to identify the interests of capital and labor.' Smith replied that the Phoenix council had offered not one word of evidence to support the charge that he was a Liberal; that he had not taken the stump for the Liberals in the Ontario elections (he had spoken in two places, on the invitation of the local council presidents); that he had accepted the CPR pass on instructions from his own union; that, on the identity of the interests of capital and labour, he had taken the same position as Samuel Gompers, president of the AFL; that Dunsmuir was not his brother-in-law, and that, so far from having checked off union dues for Smith's benefit, Dunsmuir had 'never had the moral courage or sufficient brains to allow his miners to have a union.' The congress, after investigation by a committee, unanimously exonerated Smith and presented him with an elaborate testimonial, which was ordered to be engrossed. It need hardly be added that Phoenix figures in the 1904 list of councils not chartered by the congress.[38]

The *American Federationist* of January 1901 reported a Trades and Labor Council in existence in Moncton. But this cannot have lasted long, for a second council was organized in March 1902. It was listed in 1904 among the councils chartered by the TLCC.[39]

The Calgary council may have been organized in 1901. It wrote to the Toronto council in May and August 1902, and is listed in 1904 among those not chartered by the TLCC.[40]

Eight more councils were organized in 1902: Charlottetown, in February; Kamloops, in February; Dundas, in May; Dawson City, in June; Smith's Falls, 1 July; Galt-Preston, 24 July; Woodstock, about the same time; and Sarnia, 13 November.

The Charlottetown council was the centre of a far-reaching controversy. The TLCC in 1898 or 1899 had chartered a Prince Edward Island Railway Employees Federal Labor Union No 10, Charlottetown. In 1901 its delegate to the congress convention urged that body to send an organizer to the island. It did not, but the AFL did, in the person of John W. Flett, a congress vice-president. Flett organized five unions, and a second AFL man three more, all eight in Charlottetown. Before the last of these had been chartered, FLU No 10 set about organizing a council, to which it appointed five delegates. When they presented their credentials, they found that the council had been 'advised by the Secretary of the A. F. of L., not to admit representatives from unions chartered by your Congress. We have therefore,' said the congress provincial executive committee, 'knocked at their door in vain.'

FLU No 10 did not take this lying down. It was strongly of the opinion that Canadian trades and labour councils should be chartered by the TLCC. The congress general executive (of which, of course, Flett was a member) felt the same way. It told the 1902 convention that 'each and every Trade and Labor Council in Canada should be chartered by this Congress.' It noted that there were 35 such councils in existence, from Charlottetown to Dawson City, Yukon Territory, not one of them, apparently, with a congress charter. In May 1902 the congress had circularized them all, asking them to take out charters. The Toronto District Labor Council, the Montreal Central Trades and Labor Council, and the Windsor council, did. The other 32, apparently, had been like the deaf adder which stoppeth her ear.

The general executive was not pleased. After all, it was at this very convention taking steps to throw out of the congress all unions dual to AFL unions. The least it could expect was some recognition, by the AFL and its affiliates, of the congress's status, and concrete proof of it in this very matter of chartering councils.

The executive's report devoted a whole section to the subject. It said in part: 'While dealing with this question of charters, we desire to state that the time has arrived when the powers, rights and privileges of this Congress, as the national organization for legislative purposes of the Canadian wage-earner, must be defined. It is almost useless to expend further time and energy in an attempt to operate its business with any degree of success. The operation of the movement in Canada, particularly during the past twelve months, has demonstrated this fact more clearly than ever. The Constitution is of such an experimental construction, we are forced to the conclusion that a change must be made at this Convention to meet the situation.' Charlottetown, the executive said, was a case in point.[41]

The proceedings of the 1903 convention of the TLCC record a compromise reached between the congress and the AFL on the chartering of councils. The AFL agreed that, from then on, any charters it issued to councils in Canada would carry the condition that such bodies affiliate with the congress, and that AFL councils already existing in Canada would be instructed to affiliate. The congress was not altogether happy with this, but felt it was the best that could be accomplished. The Charlottetown council seems never to have obeyed the instruction to affiliate.[42]

The Kamloops council does not appear in the 1904 TLCC lists.[43] The Dundas, Ontario, council appears in the list of those not chartered by the congress. So does the Dawson City council. The Smith's Falls council lasted till January 1905.[44] The Galt-Preston council started with three affiliated unions: Typos, Machinists, and Retail Clerks. It was organized by O.R. Wallace, a part-time AFL organizer. It is listed in 1904 among those chartered by the congress.[45] So are Woodstock and Sarnia.[46]

At the end of 1902, therefore, there were probably 36 to 38 Trades and Labor Councils in existence: 19 in Ontario, 6 to 8 in British Columbia, 4 in Quebec, 2 in New Brunswick, and 1 each in Nova Scotia, Prince Edward Island, Manitoba, the Yukon, and what is now Alberta. In 1890 there had been only 11 or 12: 4 or 5 in Ontario, 3 in British Columbia, 2 in Quebec, and 1 each in New Brunswick and Nova Scotia. In 1897 there had been 15: 6 in Ontario, 4 in British Columbia, 3 in Quebec, and 1 each in New Brunswick and Manitoba.

On the activities of most of these councils little information is available except by minute scrutiny of the local newspapers, and not always then. For others, about a dozen fairly ample records exist.

THE MARITIMES

In Halifax the formation of 'an amalgamation of the various trade unions' had been agitated for a long time before the mass meeting of 22 August 1882, which actually set up the Amalgamated Trades Union of Halifax and Dartmouth. The unions had already appointed a committee to secure a hall, and they now reported that Revere Hall, Barrington St, was being prepared and would be 'furnished as a club house for the Amalgamated Union.' (The organization meeting was held in the Reform Club Hall.) The Bricklayers and Masons seem to have taken the initiative; one of their members, Mr Mooney, was in the chair. John Saxon, of the House Joiners, spoke at some length on the advantages of union organization. He spoke bitterly of those 'who had reaped the advantages of the work of the unions, yet were not present at the meeting. He deprecated militia drill, or anything which would prevent the mechanics attending a meeting of such importance to themselves. He concluded by exhorting all to stand by the motto, "United we stand, divided we fall."' James Fultz, of the Typos, spoke of the 'mutual improvement from the formation of a union where the mechanics might be better acquainted with their fellows and aim to elevate and educate their class. He wanted it distinctly understood that the meeting was not called for the purpose of a strike. The trade he followed ... were receiving a fair remuneration for their labor, and if others were not they should ask for it and he had no fear they would get it if their demands were reasonable.' The ATU was then formally established.

The ATU's Revere Hall contained a general meeting room, waiting, committee, and reading rooms, and janitor's apartment. The opening took place 29 September 'by a mass meeting of carpenters, the officers of the four labour associations interested being on the platform.' Edward Melvin occupied the chair, and addresses were delivered by Saxon and Arthur C. Lessel. The meeting heard a letter from the BLE requesting its 'sympathy with them in their trouble. This was readily accorded.' After business was disposed of, 'the members were invited to inspect the reading and recreation rooms, and surprise was freely expressed at the results of the committee's work. The room was tastefully decorated with pictures, the gift of two gentlemen, friends of wage-workers of this city. In a neat book case were to be seen some valuable books, also presented by well-wishers, which we hope to supplement by different additions at no distant day. On the tables were periodicals and papers and games of all sorts, which afforded instruction and amusement to many during the evening. It was indeed a fine sight to see the neat hall, well lighted, filled with brothers of four different branches of industry enjoying themselves in such a rational manner. This room will be kept open day and night all winter.' The reporter proudly added a description of the rooms from a local paper, which notes that the premises had been entirely renovated, painted, whitewashed and furnished, and that the front windows were decorated with gilt-bordered grey blinds. The general meeting room had seats for 'about one-hundred and seventy-five or two hundred persons, with a neat oil clothed platform filled with tables, chairs, etc., for the officers. The room is well lighted with gasaliers. The next floor contains a spacious reading room, committee room, clothing room and other conveniences. The reading room is plainly but neatly furnished with chairs and tables, on which are checkers, dominoes and other games, and current periodicals ... The efforts to keep mechanics' institutes afloat in Halifax have not heretofore met with continued success, but now that such comfortable quarters have been secured, and so many of the trades Unions have combined, it is to be hoped their efforts to cultivate each other's acquaintance and enjoy mutual improvement away from the influences of the tap room may result more happily.'[47]

The ATU held regular business meetings 18 January and 22 February 1883. On 22 March it was informed that only 75 out of some 300 carpenters remained not unionized, only 10 masons, and no painters at all. A week later there was another meeting, to consider petitioning the city to impose a tax on outside builders and others who came to Halifax to work without paying anything into the city revenue. A committee made up of the chief officers of the member unions was appointed to draw up a petition.

On 20 January 1884, the ATU's rooms were crowded to hear again P.J. McGuire, the New York lecturer. McGuire spoke chiefly on 'the most efficacious and practical method of organizing and maintaining trade unions, so as to obtain the greatest practical benefit from them and gave much good advice and many feasible recommendations. Mr McGuire has won golden opinions among the workingmen of Halifax.' At the ATU annual meeting, 26 February 1884, McGuire was elected an honorary member, and the union sent him a letter of sympathy on the death of his wife.

The Typos had been among the founding unions of the ATU, but they must have seceded almost at once. On 2 February 1884, however, they received a request to join, and by 10 May they had. On 7 June they appointed a member to the ATU executive committee, and on 5 July two delegates to its meetings. On 1 November the Typos paid their share of the deficit on the ATU picnic and ordered their ATU per capita to be paid at once.

In 1887 the ATU sent delegates to a committee arranging for a procession to celebrate the Queen's jubilee. From 1888 to 1891 it arranged the Labour Day parades, which took place towards the end of July or the beginning of August. In 1890 six unions (Bakers, Bricklayers and Masons, Stonecutters, Painters and Decorators, Plasterers, and Coopers) are explicitly stated to have been members. Early in 1891 the ATU decided it would like to build a hall of its own, at a cost of $25,000, to be financed by $5 shares, with a maximum of 10 shares to any 1 holder. The scheme fell through.

By the summer of 1891 the ATU must have been in difficulties, for the Typos' minutes for 5 September record a request from the 'Trades and Labor Council to send representatives to the council and to confer with a council committee 'as to the desirability of forming a Halifax federation of labor.' The Typos evidently joined, for in October, November, and December they had reports from their delegates. This council, however, cannot have been much of a success, for at the Typos' 5 December meeting their president suggested 'that it would be just as well for our union to withdraw.' But no action was taken. On 4 June 1892, however, the Typos did withdraw.

The council had not knocked out the ATU. In November 1891 and February 1892 the Typos had ATU bills for rent, and in March there was an ATU letter asking for the appointment of a Typos' committee to discuss with the ATU the advisability of procuring a new hall. But the ATU was not strong enough to undertake the arrangements for the Labour Day parade, which the Typos took the initiative in organizing. However, by the spring of 1893 the ATU was showing signs of renewed vitality. It held a meeting on the question of buying a new hall, and appointed a committee to arrange for the Labour Day parade.

On 13 July 1895 the Typos were informed that a committee had been formed by various unions to celebrate Labour Day, and the union appointed its own committee to co-operate. A week later it was told that some unions were not financially able to carry on the celebration of the day, but would co-operate in the picnic (which usually followed the parade). The president explained that 'the great expense attached to turning out, with no way of meeting said expense, was a great obstacle in the way of the trades union.' None the less, the Typos agreed to 'hand over our rights of holding pic-nic on that day to the Trades union,' and to take an active part in the celebration of Labour Day. Apparently, however, the ATU proved unable to handle the affair.[48]

A *Labor Journal* article on the history of the Halifax labour movement embodying the recollections of a veteran unionist, says that internal dissension caused the disbandment of the ATU in 1897. It also says that men from the Typos, the Coopers, the Shoeworkers, the Shipwrights and Caulkers, the Painters, and the Metal Workers had taken a prominent part in ATU affairs. How far this account can be relied on, however, is doubtful, for it also states that the ATU was organized in 1889.[49] Whatever the date the ATU ended, there is no doubt that the second Halifax Trades and Labor Council was formed in 1898, though the *Labour Gazette*'s August may be a little early. The *Labor Journal* article says the council was formed in November, but this is plainly too late, for the Typos on 5 November voted to contribute $1 to the 'T. & L. Council.'[50]

The new council, in February 1899, was insisting on the 'necessity of celebrating Labor Day, claiming that the lack of doing so [there seem to have been no parades 1896–98] was largely responsible for the decay of unionism in Halifax.' It looked after the celebrations in 1900, 1901, and 1902.

In 1901 the council gave the TLCC the first report it had had from Nova Scotia. The council had waited upon the Nova Scotia government and asked for a factory act, and got it. While the bill was under discussion, the council had been invited to suggest changes; when it became law the council was invited to submit a list of names from which the government might appoint an inspector or inspectors. It reported the success of several Halifax unions in getting the nine-hour day, and the success of the council itself in organizing six new unions during the year, and reorganizing an old one which had not existed for two years. There were now 14 unions, and several other organized bodies, affiliated with the Council. The council urged the appointment of an organizer for the rest of the province, notably Sydney, where not one union had been organized in the past two years. The congress responded by setting up a provincial executive committee for Nova Scotia, with the council's secretary, Daniel A. Wilson, as vice-president for Nova Scotia. It was probably the council's appeal that brought Flett into Nova Scotia in August, and prompted the AFL to appoint Kempton McKim, of the Halifax Typos, a deputy organizer, with spectacular results. The 1902 report of the provincial executive said the Halifax council had 20 affiliated unions, even though several of the new unions had not affiliated.[51]

From 1890 till 1910 the important developments in Saint John's labour movement were either initiated or channelled through its various trades and labour councils. In February 1894 the Saint John Trades and Labor Council declined an invitation to join the Saint John Board of Trade, and gave unanimous support to the Ship Labourers in refusing to accept a wage reduction from Mr Schofield. It also pledged its support to the fishermen of Pisarinco (Lorneville), who had petitioned Parliament on the subject of enforcing the law prohibiting drifting for salmon in the Bay of Fundy. In March it provided for committees on statistics, grievances, and education, and dealt with petitions from the TLCC and with the Tax Reduction Association's ticket for the civic election. In April it established a committee to study the influx of labour from outside the city (reported to have taken jobs needed by local workers). It asked the mayor not to give city printing to non-union offices, deplored the 'discontinuance' of the *Workman* and declined the *Daily Telegraph*'s offer of a column. It handled all the arrangements for the Labour Day parade.

In January 1895 it received an appeal from the American Railway Union to help defend Debs and his executive in the courts. This was referred to the unions. Only the Ship Labourers seem to have replied, and they only to say that dull times precluded any contribution beyond an expression of sympathy. From February to April the council repeatedly debated the question, 'Of what benefit has the present Common Council [city council] been to St John?' On 3 April the council's representative on the Tax Reduction Association reported most unfavourably, and the council decided it could not support the TRA ticket as a whole, but thought there should be a special meeting of all unions to choose candidates from the two tickets then in the field. In May the council was already starting to prepare for the Labour Day parade. In June it appointed a committee to interview the attorney-general on the abolition of the post of queen's printer; the appointment of a practical printer to superintend the printing of the *Royal Gazette*; the possibility of farming out the printing of the *Gazette*; and the printing of the law reports. In August it asked the city for a grant for the Labour Day parade.

In 1897 the council sent a delegate, Thomas Killen (Ship Labourers), to the TLCC convention. He was elected (along with William Coates and George Swetka of the Typos) to the newly established New Brunswick legislative committee. He carried a resolution for the appointment of inspectors of gear and tackle used in longshoring. He seconded a motion on following up congress resolutions which involved legislation, to which governments had apparently been paying scant attention. The congress now proposed to put pressure on them by having local labour organizations bombard them with copies of the resolutions and demands for action, and to reinforce this by having the organizations appoint deputations to see their local MPs and MLAs, and generally (in the phrase of a later congress president), 'put a bonfire under them.' This resolution also passed.

The Saint John council was not again represented at a congress convention till 1903. Meanwhile, the provincial executive, in 1901, had reported that the New Brunswick labour movement was in a dormant state; in 1902, in strong contrast, it reported rapid strides, with the organization of Trades and Labor Councils in both Saint John and Moncton, as well as a series of unions, most of them the fruit of organizers' trips. The new Saint John council in 1902 co-operated with the Fabian League in sponsoring labour candidates for the provincial House, and successfully promoted a workmen's compensation act and a factory act.[52]

QUEBEC

The Quebec council began its career with a declaration of principles under five heads: education, justice, work, public health, and political rights. It wanted to have employers forced to give child employees who could not read or write time off for school. It also wanted night schools and public libraries. It demanded laws to protect workmen's goods from seizure for debt; creation of a court of arbitration for labour disputes; replacement of the Master and Servant Act by 'regulations more in conformity with modern civilization,' and enforceable by a court of arbitration, not police magistrates; and a new factory act. It wanted abolition of labour by children under 15 in factories; an 8-hour day for women and children; intervention by the court of arbitration in all apprenticeship contracts; abolition of prison labour competing with free labour; and an end to assisted immigration, except agricultural.

It wanted enforcement and improvement of laws dealing with conditions of work in factories; construction and maintenance of houses and sewers; qualifications for municipal candidates made uniform with those for candidates for the House of Commons; abolition of statute labour and of poll tax. It campaigned against lotteries and taverns and against the employment of outsiders on public works. It fought hard for abolition of the property qualification for the municipal franchise. It succeeded in getting night schools established and the Factory Act improved. During the 1894–95 depression it got the city council to vote large sums for public works, notably a new city hall. It set up a colonization committee to encourage a back-to-the-land movement as a remedy for unemployment. In 1896 it gave its support to particular municipal candidates in three wards.

It seems to have started off with 9 affiliates, all KOL LAS. In 1891 this had risen to 18. In 1892 it seems to have dropped to 12. From 1893 to 1899 it varied from 14 to 18; in 1900 it was 21; in 1901 it rose to 26 and in 1902 to 28. Till 1901 the Knights of Labor usually predominated.[53]

The Quebec council had delegates at every TLCC convention from 1890 to 1902, except 1898, and they took a prominent part. Patrick J. Jobin was elected vice-president in 1892 and 1893, and president in 1894 and 1895. He was on the Quebec executive in 1890 and 1896: in 1890, 1896, and 1897, Quebec council delegates won two of the three seats on this committee. In 1899 and 1900, John Scott, one of the council's delegates, was Quebec vice-president.[54]

Three other things about the Quebec council's participation in the congress are worth noting. The first is the number of 'English' names among its delegates: Jackson, Fox, Guthrie, Schryburt. The second is the number of Knights: 7 out of the 15 names in the lists from 1890 are Knights, and till 1900 at least 1 of the 3 delegates was always a Knight. The third is the much smaller part the Quebec council delegates seem to have taken after 1897. This is doubtless partly a reflection of the declining influence of the Knights in the whole Canadian labour movement.

The Montreal Central Trades and Labor Council included most of the unions of the city till 1897, except, perhaps, for the years 1892–95, when the Bricklayers, Painters, Plasterers, Stonecutters, and United Carpenters formed the Building and Constructions Trades Council and held themselves somewhat aloof from the central council (they had separate Labour Day parades in 1893 and 1894).[55]

The central council organized Labour Day parades in 1886, 1888–90, 1898–99, and 1901. It strongly opposed the property qualification for the municipal franchise.[56] It repeatedly denounced certain factory inspectors for their incompetence. In the years 1894–96 it established an unemployment committee which tried to find work or provide relief for the unemployed. It also tried to get the city to embark on vast public works programmes. It got the municipal franchise widened to give the vote to some 13,000 more workers. It succeeded in getting a steep increase in the water tax repealed, saving the workers some $100,000 a year. It established committees on dominion-provincial affairs, on legislation, on municipal affairs, organization, statistics, grievances, and the union label.[57]

The central council was represented, and active, at every TLCC convention from 1889 to 1902. One of its delegates, Urbain Lafontaine, was elected vice-president in 1889 and president in 1890 and 1891. In 1895 another central council delegate, P.J. Ryan, was elected to the Quebec executive committee; in 1896 another; in 1898 and 1900, a third; in 1901, a fourth.[58]

After the organization of the federated council in 1897, the central council went down hill. In 1898 its Labour Day parade had only 9 organizations represented, while the federated council's had 15. In 1899 the central council recovered some ground: it mustered 28 organizations to the federated council's 21. In 1900 the central council does not seem to have had a parade at all, while the federated council brought out 35 unions. In 1901 the central council had 10 organizations, the federated council 37.[59]

Of the twenty-four names in the central council's lists of delegates to the TLCC, nine were Knights. In 1890 both delegates were Knights, in 1896 one of the two, in 1897, 1899, 1901 and 1902, two of the three, and in 1900 all three. Five of the twenty-four names were English. In nine of the fourteen years there was one English delegate, and in two of the fourteen, two.[60]

The Montreal Federated Trades and Labor Council arose out of the dissatisfaction of the international unions with the central council, in which, in their opinion, the Knights of Labor were grossly overrepresented. In the central council every organization, regardless of size, had three delegates. The Knights, so the unions alleged, had a habit of subdividing their assemblies to create new ones, each, of course, endowed with three delegates. Besides, the membership of the assemblies was open to pretty well all comers, so that their delegates might not be workingmen at all. The unions repeatedly tried to get the central council reorganized on the basis of the size of affiliates. But any change in the constitution required a two-thirds vote, so the Knights were always able to defeat these efforts. Finally, when the membership of the affiliated assemblies had sunk to only about one-tenth of that of the unions, most of the latter seceded and formed the federated council.[61]

Not all the international unions left the central council in 1897; in 1899, there seem to have been seven or eight of their locals, and in 1900 three, still in it. But the federated council soon got most of them, and became much the more important of the two bodies. In 1898 the 2 seem to have had about the same number of affiliates; in 1899 the central council had about 24 to the Federated Council's 20; but by 1901 the central council's affiliates had shrunk to 10 and the federated council's had risen to 38. In 1902 the numbers were 11 and 40 respectively. Both councils, however, continued to be recognized by the TLCC; both claimed to represent the workers of Montreal. Right down to the expulsion of the Knights and other dual organizations at the 1902 congress convention, they fought each other vigorously, running rival demonstrations and organizing drives, and backing rival candidates for municipal office.[62]

The federated council began by setting out a declaration of principles. In view of the 'continually growing encroachments of centralized and consolidated capital,' it was absolutely essential for the working classes to have a central body for their mutual protection, education, and social advancement. The council proposed not only to back existing unions but to help organize the unorganized; to promote education, the discussion of public questions, the free exchange of ideas on social reform, especially the shortening of the hours of labour, as formulated by the AFL; and to observe strict neutrality in dominion, provincial, and municipal politics. It favoured legislation to shorten hours of work for public employees, women, and children; to prohibit labour by children under 16; to raise the school-leaving age to 16; to abolish the contract system on public works; to provide for the initiative and referendum; to regulate prison labour in order to reduce its competition with free labour, to establish employers' liability for accidents to workmen; and to guarantee equal pay for equal work for men and women.

In pursuit of these objectives, it took action in the fields of municipal, provincial, and dominion politics. Municipally, it demanded improvement in the system of tax collection; advised termination of the franchise of the Mountain Railway and its acquisition by the city; and supported the city council's tax on machinery which replaced men in manufacturing. It also demanded a municipal subsidy to preserve the city's employment office; no city subsidy for the Grand Trunk Railway; an increase in the number of school commissioners to provide for labour representation; and a halt to speculation in coal and city arrangements for citizens to buy the fuel at a reasonable price. Provincially, it asked for a law to allow workers to get damages for injuries sustained at work, and to give the factory inspectors full power to enforce this law and to prevent children under 16 from working in dangerous jobs, and to provide for registration of factories. It protested against the tax on wages under $500, and asked for the repeal of the Masters and Servants Act, which had been condemned by the dominion Royal Commission on the Relations of Capital and Labor. In dominion affairs, it protested against the inadequate Alien Labour Act and demanded the expulsion of all alien workers; asked the Montreal representative in the Senate to vote in favour of the union label bill; protested against subcontracting by contractors for the department of militia and defence; and demanded an increase in the headtax on Chinese immigrants from $100 to $500.

Miscellaneous activities included a condemnation of the Quebec College of Physicians and Surgeons for preventing doctors from practising on salary; a demand for a royal commission to inquire into charges against aldermen and heads of civic departments; numerous campaigns against lotteries and taverns and for the improvement of public transport in rush hours; a protest against the Grand Trunk's having bought a stonecutting machine; a proposal to tax country tailors who took work away from Montreal tailors; and a protest against the CPR's employing unqualified Italians.

Politically, the federated council followed the Gompers policy of endorsing individual candidates favourable to labour. Usually, it formed an election committee which scrutinized the policy of each candidate and then issued a list of preferred candidates which it sent to all affiliates. Even when the council's own president ran in 1900 for the House of Commons against J.I. Tarte, all the council's members but two disavowed his candidature. The federated council also, of course, consistently campaigned for the union label; sent money to unions on strike, both in Canada and the United States; boycotted goods made by struck firms; helped organize new unions; and mediated between employers and their workers, as, notably, in the 1899 dispute between Her Majesty's Theatre and its employees.[63]

The federated council was represented, and active, at the TLCC conventions of 1899–1902. In 1899 one of its delegates was elected to the Quebec executive committee; in 1900, a second; in 1901, a third; and in 1902, a fourth. Alphonse Verville, delegate in 1902, was to become congress vice-president for Quebec in 1903, and president 1904–08. He also became an MP.[64]

As might have been expected, the federated council was highly indignant that the congress continued to recognize its rival, and made repeated efforts to put an end to this. In 1900, according to a series of articles in *La Presse* in 1902, the federated council's delegates to the TLCC convention strongly urged the congress to inquire into the state of affairs in Montreal. This was equally strongly opposed by the central council, by all the delegates of the Knights of Labor except some from Quebec City, and, astonishingly, by almost all the delegates of international unions, except those from Montreal. (The author of the articles in *La Presse* explains this by saying that the congress was so much in the habit of letting itself be directed by a few Knights that it could not, on this occasion, escape from the established custom.) Three-quarters of the delegates seem to have agreed with Daniel O'Donoghue, of LA 2305 (Toronto), who called upon the labour organizations of Montreal to 'wash their dirty linen at home.' So thoroughly was this advice heeded that the convention proceedings contain not one word of the whole affair.

After this the federated council seems to have been on the verge of withdrawing from the congress, but a few determined opponents of this drastic step managed to prevent it, and one delegate went to the 1901 convention. This time, according to the *La Presse* articles (the convention proceedings again are silent), J.A. Rodier (Typos 145) moved for an inquiry into the Montreal situation, but could get no support, even from Félix Marois (Quebec Typos 302) who seconded the motion for the purpose of getting it discussed.

The federated council then, on 1 May 1902, decided to withhold its per capita payment to the TLCC while its legislation committee drew up a circular letter to all the international unions in Canada, which was duly sent, and also published in various newspapers, English and French.[65] This got home to the international locals, and their delegates to the 1902 convention, already thirsting for the expulsion of the Knights of Labor, arrived with a determination to settle the hash of the central council.

ONTARIO

One of the first things the Ottawa Trades and Labor Council seems to have concerned itself with was the provincial election of 1890.[66] Early in April it held a mass meeting to draw up a platform. J.T. Carey, TLCC president, was present. So were representatives of the Carpenters, the Bricklayers, and the Hackmen. The platform was a curious mixture: an eight-hour day on government works, a minimum wage on government contracts, a first lien on the produce of work for wages, irrespective of ownership, an end to land grant subsidies to railways, abolition of immigration, and a demand that candidates seeking labour support should vote for all pro-labour legislation. This was sent to all three candidates, who duly replied. What they said, the newspaper report does not state. But it must have been unsatisfactory, for on or about 15 May the council chose Alderman F.J. Farrell as its own labour candidate. The alderman, however, declined, whereupon the council decided to remain neutral.

By February 1891 the council represented seven LAS of the Knights of Labor (5222, 1034, 193, 1619, 2806, 2966, and 2676 – this last from Hull) and seven unions (Typos, Carpenters, Painters, Tailors, Pressmen, Bookbinders, and General Labourers). Faced with a dominion election it decided that, though it favoured representation of workingmen by workingmen, the time was inopportune to bring out a labour candidate. A minority felt otherwise and nominated the council's president, J.W. Patterson. He was defeated.

From then on the council, and its successor, the Allied Trades and Labor Association, occupied much of their time with political action, mainly municipal. At the beginning of November 1891 the council protested the grant of an annuity of $1000 to the former city clerk and demanded that all encroachments on city property (notably by four of the lumber companies) be removed. It drew up municipal platforms; endorsed or ran municipal candidates; wrangled over certain delegates' participation in Liberal or Conservative politics; nominated a candidate for the House of Commons and initiated proceedings for the nomination of two others.

Late in May 1892 the council set up a committee to consider forming a local federation of building trades. (By mid-June 1893 it was established and flourishing.) In December a meeting accepted the affiliation of LA 525, listened to a report on negotiations between the city and the street railway company, and heard several unions endorse an early closing by-law.

In January 1893 the council listened to a lecture by Professor Adam Shortt on the origin of labour unions. In February the organizing committee recommended placing on file the question of organizing bartenders and waiters.

Like many other labour organizations at this time the council was inclined to favour the Single Tax. But there were dissenters. J.G. Kilt called the theory a myth: if the tax on a valuable building was removed from a building owned by a rich man and tax applied simply to land the poor man would pay more and the rich less. In 1893 the president, Mr Connell, admitted he was not enthusiastic about Single Tax outside municipal affairs, as it would mean an end to all protection. A little later, two questions were disturbing the council: participation of delegates in party politics, and double representation on the council itself. Patterson carried a motion that delegates be forbidden to work for a candidate or a party or to attend a convention until the council had decided not to take part in the election concerned. Walsh objected to the fact that some unions, in effect, popped up twice on the council, through their own delegates and through members who appeared as delegates of Knights of Labor LAS.

By 15 March 1894 the Liberals seem to have got control of the council. There was a motion to condemn the Conservative government for freeing Connolly and McGreevy from prison, and this opened the way for a general discussion of the council's involvement in politics. Delegate Macdonald felt the members should take the opportunity to get in a whack at the government whenever they could, as a matter of principle. It was the only way they could get justice. Kilt felt that politics could not be avoided: they were involved in every issue the council had to deal with. President Choquette felt the council had every right to make political comment but did not think it wise to do so. Delegates Patterson and Dorion succeeded in getting a motion passed condemning the government for releasing prisoners before the end of their term except in case of sickness.

In July 1895 Delegate St Pierre moved a resolution calling for federal national schools. He said Catholic and Protestant children should be taught together. Not surprisingly, in view of the furious battle then being waged over separate schools in Manitoba, the resolution got the six months' hoist. The wonder is that it was moved at all, and especially by a French Canadian.

By August the council had become the Allied Trades and Labor Association, which admitted to membership the Ottawa and Hull branches of the Canadian Federation of Labour (or Canadian Trades Federation), which had marched in the 1896 Labour Day parade, and did so again in 1897. Patterson, who had for some time been showing marked signs of nationalism, was active in the Canadian Federation, and in September 1897 moved to have the ATLA instruct its delegates to the TLCC convention to ask for the formation of a Dominion Federation of Labour. He noted antagonism in Canada against the United States because of the American Alien Labor Law, and the growing national spirit in Canada. He said Canadian unions got no benefit from their international affiliation, though they had paid dues to the American unions for years. The motion carried, but only by the president's casting vote. At the same meeting the ATLA voted to ask the congress to expel the Patrons of Industry, on the ground that the congress was supposed to be non-political.

The congress turned down the Patterson proposal, but the question of national unionism continued to plague the ATLA. In October 1897 it discussed the problem of admitting the National Bookbinders, since there was already a Bookbinders Union in the city. In November, when Macdonald moved to have member unions pay per capita tax to the TLCC, Patterson openly attacked the congress, saying it did nothing to further the interests of labour. The motion was lost, ten to four. Within seven months Patterson was out.

At the same meeting the ATLA set up a committee to report on the adoption of the union label throughout the city. The municipal committee reported that the Granite

Co, working on a municipal contract, worked its employees ten hours a day, contrary to the civic nine-hour by-law, but that the city said the nine-hour clause had been left out of the contract by mistake and promised it would not happen again.

In December 1898 the ATLA asked the city council to petition the legislature to reduce the property qualifications for mayors and aldermen from $1000 to $500, and to give the vote to everyone 21 years of age and with a yearly income of $200. In May 1899 the ATLA decided to send organizers to Rockland, Arnprior, and Buckingham to form unions. In July 1899 it denounced the city council for permitting Sunday streetcars, and promised to get even at election time. The same meeting discussed a mysterious proposal, said to have come from the AFL, to form a labour trust, to counter an alleged capitalist anti-labour trust.

Patterson had got back into the fold in 1901, though he had failed to get elected as a Typos' delegate to the TLCC convention, and by September 1902 he was organizer for the ATLA. His repentance, however, must have been only skin deep, for towards the end of September 1902 he had to stand trial for organizing a dual musicians union. He was still a member of the Typos, where, a few months later, he got into hot water as a result of an election row with C.S.O. Boudreault. On the night before the Typos' elections Patterson issued printed cards attacking the Boudreault faction in the union. Boudreault replied with a long attack on Patterson, distributed in the Government Printing Bureau where Patterson worked. It called him, among other things, 'The peerless fakir, unequaled front-office intermediary and unique behind-the-back apologist – the most contemptible and disagreeable apology for a labor man.' It also accused him of having ruined the old Trades and Labor Council through maladministration. Patterson then charged Boudreault with criminal libel.

Some ATLA members deplored the TLCC's expulsion of the Knights of Labor, and two delegates moved a motion to say so. Another motion, to recognize only one union in any trade, carried.

The Ottawa Council and the ATLA were represented and active at the TLCC conventions of 1890, 1892–97, and 1899–1902. P.M. Draper, ATLA delegate in 1900, was elected secretary-treasurer in that year and continued to hold the office for many years. An ATLA delegate was elected to the Ontario executive in 1893, 1895, 1897, 1899, and 1901.

On the activities of the Toronto council we are faced with an embarrassment of riches. All the minutes are there: five solid volumes, not to mention the record of the Toronto council's delegates to the TLCC conventions. Moreover, it was the Toronto council which summoned the Canadian Labor Congress of 1883; that body expressly charged the Toronto council with the calling of a second convention; and accordingly it was the Toronto council which summoned the convention of 1886.[67]

The council cast its net almost as wide as the old Toronto Trades Assembly. Certain subjects, of course, were hardy perennials: immigration, education, and political action. Chinese immigration figures prominently from 1882 till ca mid-1885. Prison labour got a good deal of attention till the end of 1892. Factory bills and acts and shop acts, and their enforcement, occupy much space till ca 1886. The union label, though it came up as early as 18 November 1881, entered into its own only after 1894, when the council set up a committee to deal with it, from then on it was one of the main subjects of discussion. Municipal affairs naturally took up much time, especially from 1885 on.

Some subjects were carried over from the TTA. The Lien Law was discussed four times in 1881, thrice in 1882, and twice in 1884, often at some length, but only once in 1886 and 1892, and in later years not at all. Moreover, the Council discussions were at least once the result of months of 'hardues' labour by the legislative committee. The Criminal Law Amendment Act also came in for a good deal of discussion in the earlier years, especially in 1887. After that, it almost disappeared from the proceedings till 1900, when further amendments aroused strong resistance and resulted in the organization of an Organized Labour Defence Association, to which the council sent two delegates. However, the council was hospitable to new ideas: the Single Tax (1889–1902); proportional representation (1881–82 and 1891–1902); the initiative and referendum (1893, 1895, 1899, 1902); and the eight-hour day (in the 1890s – much less on this than might have been expected).

In one respect the council differed markedly from the TTA: after the mid-1880s it seems not to have done much organizing of new unions till 1902, and even then it served as a mere adjunct to Flett of the AFL, whom it begged the AFL president 'not to call ... hence to work in another portion of God's vineyard for another week.'

The range of public questions on which the council pronounced is amazing: free water for horse fountains; ice-cutting in Toronto Bay; seats in the public library reading room; congratulations to Jarvis Street Church for paying taxes, and to Lord Aberdeen for 'timely, sensible, sympathetic ... democratic and advanced remarks' at a concert for the unemployed; pool rooms ('an unqualified evil'); use of the streets for horse-racing and the need of regulating the speed of 'scorching' bicycles; use of heat from crematoria; laying telephone wires underground; civil marriage; public swimming baths; the St Lawrence deep waterway; the Georgian Bay Ship Canal; trading stamps; the street railway; telephones; Toronto Island; health and safety; and minimum wages on city and school contracts.

To two major questions, education and political action, the council devoted on immense amount of attention. On education, it began by setting up an educational committee in the spring of 1886. In 1887 it successfully opposed the Toronto Medical School Bill. It called for a levelling up of women teachers' salaries and for shorter summer holidays. It endorsed school scholarships and condemned Upper Canada College as a class institution. It urged free school books, playgrounds, a college of domestic science, and the teaching of typewriting and commercial training. It denounced trustees who wanted to abolish kindergartens. It suggested teachers should form a union to get their salaries up and strongly supported the Women Teachers Association's efforts. It condemned the expulsion of a pupil because of his fondness for dime novels and scalping stories and rejected a motion to abolish high schools. It refused to endorse one national unsectarian school system, but objected to the use of the Bible as a textbook and to dogmatic and sectarian religious teaching. It made a blistering attack on the celebrated inspector J.L. Hughes. It opposed manual training in the schools, but favoured technical schools; manual training would give employers a pool of semi-skilled strikebreakers, but technical education would improve the knowledge and skills of artisans. It called for a better class of teachers in the night schools and attacked the lowering of the library board's estimates and the lowering of high school entrance standards. It objected to the teaching of French and German in collegiates. It supported a generous superannuation plan for teachers. It sponsored lectures and concerts.

In the spring of 1896 the University of Toronto decided to confer an honorary degree on Goldwin Smith. There was vociferous opposition, but not from the Trades and Labor Council. On the contrary, despite the fact that Smith and the council (or, indeed, the labour movement generally) by no means saw eye to eye, the council strongly supported the granting of the degree, and wrote both Smith and the president of the university to say so. It got replies from both, and was so pleased with them that it ordered them spread upon the minutes, where they were accordingly neatly glued in. President Loudon said he was 'glad to observe that the Council apparently sympathises with the efforts of those who desire to make the University a home of learning, where there will always be a warm welcome, not only for scholars, but for all members of the community, including politicians, if they will only leave their party weapons at the door.' Smith asked the secretary to 'present to your Council my best thanks for your kind expression of approbation and sympathy ... The value of your sympathy ... is enhanced by the conscientious difference of opinion which, as you say, exists between us on economical questions.'

On political action, the council's activities took many forms. At various times it drew up a list of questions to candidates and noted the replies; sometimes it used the replies to divide the sheep from the goats; sometimes it distributed questions and replies on dodgers across the city; sometimes it issued a manifesto; sometimes it endorsed candidates; sometimes it set up committees to defeat obnoxious aldermen; sometimes it drew up a blacklist.

In 1883 it nominated provincial candidates in East and West Toronto, and worked hard for them, but in vain. The main result was a substantial debt. In

1886–87 it tried again, this time joining with DA 125. Again the candidates were defeated, and again the effort left a substantial debt. The legislative committee, however, while regretting the defeats not only in Toronto but also in Hamilton and London, recommended renewed activity in the future and energetic lobbying in the meantime. In April 1894 the council appointed a committee to arrange for a convention to nominate one or more provincial candidates. The result was an invitation to the Single Tax Society, the Social Problems Association, and the Socialist League to a joint convention (a motion to include the Prohibitionists was turned down). The convention nominated a candidate, who was defeated.

By March 1898 zeal for independent political action had cooled considerably. The council defeated a motion to forbid its officers from appearing on the platform of any party unless the party or candidate had been officially endorsed. In December the Socialist Labour Party nominated aldermanic candidates in four wards; but the council held aloof. In 1900, however, it called a convention of labour and social reform organizations which nominated labour candidates in Centre and West Toronto; by February 1901 the council was paying per capita dues to the People's Party; and in July it was granting $5 to the Canadian Socialist League for a travelling organizer.

Between the bursts of election activity, the council kept up an incessant bombardment of dominion, provincial, and municipal governments on a variety of issues. In dominion, and to some extent provincial, politics one of the main issues was immigration. Here the council's position can be summed up in Calvin Coolidge's historic words on his pastor's attitude to sin: He was against it. The reports of the legislative committee are replete, year after year, with accounts of unemployment and distress, alleged to be at least partly the result of government immigration policy; with attacks on assisted immigration and the importing of waifs, strays, and ne'er-do-wells; garnished, in the later years, with virulent attacks on Dr Barnardo and on the Salvation Army and General Booth and his family. In 1894 the council gave a representative of Dr Barnardo a chance to reply; the Salvation Army had to wait many years for a similar opportunity before the TLCC.

In December 1901 the legislative committee fired a broadside at another target: the capitalists' use of the protective tariff to raise prices and of immigration policy to cut wages. The committee had not 'the slightest objection to suitable immigrants who come of their own accord; but they do most emphatically object to the taxation of labor to flood the labor market against the wage earner and to favor the protected capitalists.' On Chinese immigration the council simply echoed the ferocious opposition of the rest of the North American labour movement.

Other issues of dominion politics on which the council pronounced were the franchise, redistribution, and the abolition of the Senate; safety on railways; railway passenger rates; the Railway Disputes Bill; the Seamen's Regulation Act; safety of ships; the Combines Act; an insurance bill; the Bankruptcy Act; the Copyright Act; employers' liability; fair wages on government contracts; letter carriers' wages; postage on newspapers; the tax on coal; the duty on flour; and the duty on cigars. It also found time to register a 'funny money' protest against the congratulations of the government organ to the government on the floating of the 1892 dominion loan in London; to protest against the Grand Trunk's double-tracking; to protest against the release of McGreevy and Connolly from prison in 1894; to table, without a dissenting vote, an 1896 resolution for a Canadian republic; and to condemn 'a proposed sub-military expedition to the Klondike' in September 1897.

In provincial politics, the council dealt not only with the Lien Law and provincial immigration policy but also with redistribution; qualifications for municipal office; employers' liability; the use of scab labour on the legislative buildings; and an apprenticeship law. Particularly interesting are the protests against a subsidy for the development of the Sudbury nickel deposits (1893) and against abolishing all royalties on mining claims taken up or to be taken up before 1900 (1894); and the representations on the inadequate training in the Brantford Institute for the Blind (1893 and 1894, and jointly with the London council in 1896).

The question of a labour paper came up repeatedly. In January 1882 Eugene Donovan approached the council about what became the *Trades Union Advocate*, to be published under the council's auspices. The *Advocate* was established, but not under council auspices: most delegates seem to have been afraid it would involve the council in Liberal or Conservative politics. By April 1883 the paper's successor, the *Wage-Worker*, was in financial difficulties, and wanted the council to take it over. After investigation, it regretfully but emphatically declined.

A new labour organ, the *Labor Record*, started in the spring of 1886, lasted a little over a year. In October 1889 affiliates were being urged to support the *Canadian Labor Reformer*, which had reappeared after the lapse of a few months. In August 1890 DA 125 was trying to get the council to help start a new paper, and by April 1891 the *Labor Advocate* was in being. At the end of 1895 the council accepted George W. Wrigley's offer of a page in his weekly *Brotherhood Era*; three years later it accepted the same from his *Citizen and Country*. An 1899 project for a daily fell through, and the council accepted instead extra space in *Citizen and Country*. By the end of 1900 the council's own paper, the *Toiler*, had been launched. In the fall of 1901 financial troubles had forced the council to hand over the paper to a company, but with labour control assured; at the end of the period the *Toiler* was still publishing.

During these two decades the council seems to have been reasonably representative of Toronto organized labour, though it probably never included all the unions or assemblies. There was a tussle, at first, about whether the Knights of Labor should be let in at all. LA 2305 was admitted on 18 January 1884. But the Typos, United

Carpenters, Stonecutters, and Molders all objected, even while more assemblies were being admitted. But by the end of 1884 11 assemblies were in, and the objections had ended.

Between 1881 and February 1888 54 bodies had affiliated, of which 14 had withdrawn. On 15 November 1895 there were 34 affiliates, and on 7 February 1896, 36. In December 1901 the city had 67 trade unions and 17 'railroad bodies'; how many were in the council is not stated. The railroad bodies generally held aloof, though the BLF were represented in 1891 and 1892, and the Railroad Trainmen in 1899 and 1902. Unity Association No 2213, of the Patrons of Industry (a farmers' organization), was admitted in November 1894 and seems to have remained till September 1896.

The Toronto council of course played a very big part in the TLCC.[68] At the first convention it had two delegates and at every later one, three. Charles March, a council delegate in 1883, 1886, 1887, 1891, 1892, 1895, 1896, 1898, 1900, and 1901, was chairman of the first convention, and he and O'Donoghue were both elected to the first executive committee. March was also president in 1886 and 1887. George W. Dower, a council delegate in 1889, was elected secretary-treasurer in 1888, and held the office, with one short break, till 1900. David A. Carey, a council delegate in 1895, 1896, 1900, and 1901, was elected president in 1896 and 1897, and to the Ontario executive in 1895. George T. Beales, a council delegate in 1889, was elected president in 1892 and 1893. March was elected to the Ontario executive in 1891, 1897, and 1898, and Ontario vice-president in 1900 and 1901. Robert Glockling, a council delegate in 1889, 1890, 1892, and 1893, was elected to the Ontario executive in 1890, 1892, and 1893. O'Donoghue was a council delegate to every convention from 1883 to 1896 inclusive, and again in 1898, and in those 11 conventions moved nearly half of all the resolutions moved by council delegates in all 18 conventions.

The prominence of the Knights of Labor in the council is indicated by the fact that men who at one time or another were Knights made up the whole council delegation in 1883, 1889, 1892, 1893, 1895, and 1896, and two-thirds of it in 1886, 1887, 1890, 1891, 1894, 1898, 1899, and 1900. It seems safe to say that down to 1896 the Knights wielded very considerable influence in the council. Small wonder, for by the end of 1886 some 32 or 33 LAs had sent delegates to it. In 1887 it seated delegates from at least 24 LAs; in 1888 from at least 14; in 1889 from at least 12; in 1890 from at least 13; and in 1891 from at least 10. Even in 1892 there were at least 9 LAs represented, though in 1893 the number fell to 6, and in 1894 to 4.[69]

The Oshawa council during its brief existence played a rather more important part than might have been expected.[70] In June 1886, apparently impatient with the delay in calling a new labour congress convention, it wrote the Toronto council 'requesting a unity of trades organizations throughout the Country in connection with all questions relating to the interests of the wage earner.' It also sent a resolution of sympathy with the Toronto streetcar strikers, which called for the resignation of Frank Smith from 'the executive committee' of the dominion government. In September it had negotiated with the Dominion Grange with a view to a closer relationship with the farmers, and asked the Toronto council to carry out future such negotiations. The Toronto council's legislative committee asked its own council to appoint a committee for the purpose, which it did. That committee reported that 'the Granger's was of the opinion that trades organizations were antagonistic to themselves inasmuch as they were struggling to raise their wages at the expense of the farmer's. This the committee set to work to remove and at the same time show them where our interests were identicle, and that by a unity of action our interests would be served, and the Country benefitted. The committee was pleased to state that there was a much better feeling existing through the interview; and they expected further developments after the meeting of the Grange which will take place shortly.' How contemporary it all sounds.

The Oshawa council sent James R. Brown to the 1886 TLCC convention. He was appointed to the committee to meet a committee from the Grange, and elected to the executive committee for the Oshawa to Cobourg district. In 1887 the Oshawa council's delegate, Lewis Allchin, took an active part.

On the Hamilton central organizations the information is spotty, the only official records which survive being the minutes of the Hamilton Trades and Labor Council for 1888–96.

The Central Labor Union, in February 1886, had a membership of 11 unions, the Hamilton DA, and 8 LAs. This was probably about half the total number of organizations in the city. In 1885 it included a lodge of the BLF.[71] The CLU passed resolutions on a variety of subjects. It repeatedly opposed Chinese immigration and cheap European immigration under contract. It required labour candidates for the city council to sign an oath that they would oppose the granting of any contract to any person, persons, or company that refused to bind themselves to employ only city residents. In March 1885 it started a movement for weekly payment of wages. In April it petitioned the Ontario government to amend the income tax law by raising the exemption from $400 to $800, and in December raised the figure to $1600. It also opposed current procedures for collection of debts, citing many cases where the bailiff was sent to the wage earner's door 'to sell him out because he was unable to pay the tax which he never earned.' Some men were out of work and had either to pay the amount or see their household effects sold 'to satisfy an unjust and outrageous claim.' It said the wealthy capitalists were assessed far too little, and so taxed less than they should be: the absence of a capital gains tax was reflected in the unjust burden placed on workingmen. In March 1886 it was agitating for adoption of the eight-hour day by the city administration. In December it endorsed the Conservative candidate for the House of Commons.[72]

The CLU had three delegates at the 1886 TLCC convention. One, M.W. Conway, was elected a vice-chairman, was narrowly defeated for the presidency, and was elected vice-president by acclamation. All three delegates took a prominent part. At the 1887 convention held in Hamilton itself, the CLU as such had no delegates.[73]

The Hamilton Trades and Labor Council minutes are very voluminous and are concerned mainly with local issues.[74] Occasionally the council went farther afield, as when its legislative committee pronounced against the 'importation of European waifs and strays' or against assisted immigration of skilled artisans and mechanics; or when it extended sympathy to the victims of the New York Central lockout of 1890; or when it supported the Taylor Alien Labour Bill of 1890 or urged the TLCC to use its influence with the AFL to get the American Alien Labor Law repealed, or asked candidates for the House of Commons whether they favoured a similar act here; or when it endorsed Sunday observance bills. Occasionally, also, it patronized lectures. On 15 February 1895 it listened to a paper by R.T. Lancefield on ideals and idealism. It accepted, in November 1890, an invitation to attend the annual sermon of the Women's Christian Temperance Union. In May 1892 it accepted 12 complimentary tickets from the Knights Templars to an illustrated lecture by J.W. Bengough, and chose 12 delegates to attend. But in November 1893 a motion to attend in a body a lecture by Mr Farming, the Labor Prohibitionist, was tabled on a tie vote, even though he was persuasively described as having been a labour man who had become a prohibitionist 'as a result of his study of economic questions.' On 26 January 1891 it had a paper and discussion on the co-operative movement, and on 18 December 1892, a few remarks on the same subject from Mr Davis. On 17 July 1896 it charged its organizing committee with the task of acquiring information on co-operatives.

Within the local community, however, the council dealt with almost every aspect of civic life, including representation on the library and public school boards; taxation; bonuses to industry; and health and safety of citizens. Wages and working conditions in city employment and on city contracts naturally occupied much of the council's attention. In April 1889 it discussed injustices and anti-union discrimination on municipal work and considered a petition to the city council to reduce city employees' hours. In May it asked for a nine-hour day and in July for an eight-hour day. In September it arranged a meeting on the eight-hour day. In March 1891 the city board of works advised the city council to inaugurate the nine-hour day, with a minimum wage of fifteen cents an hour, on city work. The Trades and Labor Council of course endorsed this, but apparently without effect, for in June it was again expressing its dissatisfaction that the nine-hour day was not yet in force. In April 1895 it was asking for a minimum-wage clause in city contracts.

For some unknown reason, the council at first had a scunner against the city firemen. In September 1889 a motion to petition for a salary increase for the fire department was defeated. But in October 1891 the council expressed pleasure at the firemen's getting an increase. In November the executive recommended that the firemen's time off should be increased from 42 to 84 hours a month, and a month later noted that this had been granted. On 18 January 1895 the council went so far as to ask for better equipment for the fire department and more and better hydrants. Retired city employees were another group for whom the council felt no sympathy. On 17 March 1893 it unanimously resolved 'That this Council enters a decided protest against any proposal to superannuate employees of the corporation, or grant a retiring allowance when they cease to be able to render efficient service, believing that all have received full compensation in salary for the services rendered during the term of their employment, and often more than they were worth, and also that if they are no longer useful the money of the taxpayers should not be used to maintain them in idleness.'

A notable resolution, 17 March 1893, dealt with the city's refusal to abolish its tax on water for baths. The Council suggested, as an alternative source of revenue, a tax on lawn sprinklers, adding: 'As cleanliness and good health generally follow each other, we trust our city fathers will show their interest in the health of all our citizens to the extent of making it possible for them to get water to wash themselves without a special tax being levied upon them.'

On education, the council had a good deal to say. On 20 October 1890, while asking for appointment of a truant inspector, it wanted also to have prepared a list of children under 12 years of age working in factories. On 16 October 1891 it was again asking for the appointment of a truant officer, demanding a minimum age of 14 for employment in factories and prohibition of employment of children in canneries during the July–October season. Just over a month later it was noting with pleasure that a truant officer had at last been appointed. In September 1891 it set up a committee to get artisans to take a greater interest in the Art School; in October a committee report recommended asking employers to make it compulsory for their 'improvers' or apprentices learning a trade to take at least two lessons a week each term in geometry and mechanical and freehand drawing. It also wanted the city council to make a grant of $200 a year towards students' fees, with no individual fee more than $10, and one scholarship to each firm. This report was referred to the executive committee, which suggested that the council itself should encourage the school by presenting a gold medal for proficiency. The council also favoured the teaching of domestic science in the schools. Perhaps one should include also under the heading of education its support for the hiring a piano for the nurses at the City Hospital.

On temperance, we have already noted some of the council's actions. A very specific instance of co-operation between the council and the WCTU occurred in November 1889, when a WCTU deputation asked the council to help distribute temperance literature and election sheets, pledging in return the WCTU's 'support and influence to such candidates as we may suggest for municipal Honors who are strictly Temperance.' The council resolved that 'Whereas The members of the Trades & Labor Council of the city of Hamilton recognize the wide spread evils of intemperance and welcome any efforts to encourage soberiety and temperance among the Working Classes, Therefore ... we cordially accede to the request of the Ladies of the Christian Woman's Temperance Union, and pledge ourselves to do all in our power to distribute any Literature they may forward to us to forward the Causes.'

The council was much interested in the welfare of women and girls, especially those at work in local industries. On 8 April 1889 it welcomed 'the steps being taken by the sympathetic Ladies ... to provide a suitable institution for the better protection of young girls and women in our city.' At the same time, however, it felt bound to call their attention to what it thought the greatest single factor causing 'young girls to depart from the paths of rectitude and propriety, ... The small pittance doled out to the working girls and women ... [which was] not sufficient to keep up presentable appearances.' On 5 May 1893 the council endorsed giving married women the vote in municipal elections 'as a step in the direction of universal suffrage.' On 21 June 1895 it asked the city council to appoint inspectors for shops where girls and women were employed. On 17 January 1896, in response to an invitation from the Local Council of Women, it appointed a delegate to that body. Four weeks later it referred back to the LCW a petition calling for inspection of schoolchildren's teeth. Curiously, it seems to have got round to considering the organization of women workers only on 31 July 1896, when it referred the matter to its organizing committee.

On political action, the Hamilton council in these years was cautious. It supported the referendum in 1892 and proportional representation in 1893. It twice drew up election platforms. But this was about as far as it was prepared to go. It interviewed MPs in 1891. It compiled records of municipal candidates, both in 1891 and 1895, and endorsed those who passed muster. It drew up in 1892 a list of questions to be put to civic candidates. But, both in 1892 and 1893, it refused to run candidates of its own.

How representative was the council? The three LAs and six unions whose delegates elected the first officers added to their numbers, 14 January 1889, the Molders (who seem to have stayed in) and the Builders' Labourers (who, by 1 April 1892, seem to have left). The accession of the Lathers, 27 January 1889, brought the total of affiliates to 12; but the Amalgamated Carpenters, Tailors, Plasterers, Stonecutters, Steam Fitters, LA 2847, and the 4 railway running trades unions were apparently still outside. The BLE came in 11 February 1889 and stayed. The Flint Glass Blowers, one of the originals, left in March 1889, seem to have been back by June 1890, gone again by April 1892, and finally back again in August 1896. The BLF came in in March 1889, but were gone again by 14 October. The Tailors came in in

April 1889, were out by September 1891, back by May 1892, then out again, then back in March 1893. The Amalgamated Carpenters came in in May 1889 and apparently stayed. The Shoe Workers, Local 31, came in in April 1890, the Canadian Federation of Boot and Shoe Workers in February 1895. LA 6931 joined in May 1890. The Railroad Trainmen came in in October 1891 but seem to have been out by 1 April 1892. The Cigar Makers, Local 55, joined in March 1892, and seem to have stayed. At the end of 1889 there may have been fourteen unions and four LAs in the Council. By 1 April 1892 there seem to have been only nine unions and one LA. On 20 May 1892, there seems to have been one extra union, the Tailors.

After that, there seem to be no more lists. But the Metal Polishers joined in July 1895, the Hatters in January 1896, and the Horseshoers in March 1896. The Plasterers, Stonecutters, Steam Fitters, Railway Conductors, Amalgamated Iron and Steel Workers, and the Stationary Engineers seem never to have been members, though most of them were asked.

The Hamilton council had a delegate, D.R. Gibson, at the 1889 TLCC convention and he was elected to the Ontario executive. At the 1892 convention it had three delegates: Gibson, William McAndrew (one of the council's founders) and Fred Walters. At the 1895 convention the council had two delegates, John Flett and David Hastings. Flett was elected to the Ontario executive. He was there again in 1896, with Philip Obermeyer, and was again elected to the Ontario executive. In 1897, when the convention was held in Hamilton, the council had three delegates – Hastings, Hugh Robinson, and Edward Williams – and they took an active part. Flett represented the Hamilton council in 1898 and 1899 and in both years was elected vice-president. In 1899 he moved a resolution favouring independent political action which carried by a large majority, in the teeth of a contrary recommendation from the committee on standing orders and resolutions. He also moved the resolution supporting the London street railway strikers. In 1900 the council's delegates were Flett and Henry Obermeyer. Flett was again elected vice-president, and Obermeyer member of the Ontario executive. In 1901 the delegates were Flett, Robinson, and Thomas Monogue, and Flett was once more elected vice-president. In 1902, when the council had three delegates, Flett was elected president.[75]

The London Trades and Labor Council is said to have exerted great influence for several years after its organization, but to have gradually declined in prestige and numbers, partly because its officers 'made a practice of appearing on the platforms of political parties.' Many unions withdrew; the Typos, the Knights of Labor, and the Brotherhood of Carpenters alone remained. When the Knights disbanded, apparently in 1890, the Industrial Brotherhood took their place; but then even the Carpenters disaffiliated, leaving, for a short time, only the Typos and the Brotherhood. By 1895, however, the council was on a firm footing again.[76]

One of the council's earliest activities was an attempt in September 1886 to get the police to close hotels on Saturday nights and Sundays. This led to an acrimonious dispute with the Cigar Makers, who claimed the measure would hurt their organization. The council replied briskly that it could not see that much harm was being done, since of 275 cigar makers in the city only 35 were members of CMIU Local 19. Later, it added that 'If the Cigar Makers have to depend on men breaking the laws of the country to give them employment, the sooner they found another trade the better.' Besides, observed Delegate Wright, the platforms of both the council and the Knights of Labor fully endorsed temperance, and he was sorry to see some of the men going back on this to pander to some hotel-keepers because they boycotted some of their handiwork: 'The workingmen looked for prosperity and they would never prosper until temperance was universal.'[77]

In August 1886 the council organized the Builders' Labourers; in 1895 it organized the Brass Workers and the Metal Polishers.[78]

During these early years the council passed the usual resolutions against immigration under contract and Chinese immigration. There were also hot disputes over the protective tariff, and over the CMIU's and the Knights of Labor's respective union labels on cigars. In 1895 the council came out for election of school trustees, and in September of that year for the establishment of a technical school for girls.[79]

But the most notable feature of the council's activities before 1896 was its persistent, and ultimately successful, campaign for a public library. Victory came in 1893, but several years before this, and thanks partly to the council's campaign, the electors had voted on the proposal. But they turned it down. The council thereupon decided to start a library of its own. It was too poor to build a new hall, let alone a library, but it bought an old house. The various trades gave their services free to repair it and, when it was decided to have a library, to convert two anterooms for that purpose. All union men were requested to donate a few books, and Joseph T. Marks and Harry Keene canvassed leading businessmen to get others. The council also put on several concerts to raise funds. The result was the Workingmen's Free Library, consisting mainly of books 'of a mechanical nature ... intended to assist the craftsmen.' It issued a catalogue, and was open to the public. But this library was open only on Saturday evenings from 7:30 till 9:00, and it rapidly outgrew the Dufferin Hall premises. So the council decided to have another go at trying to get a public library. This time the by-law was approved, and two years later the London Public Library was opened, and the books of the Workingmen's Free Library were transferred to it.[80]

Until 1896 the council's political action was confined to compiling records of civic candidates and supporting those who seemed to deserve it. But in 1896 it put up labour candidates for aldermen and for water commissioners. It continued to do this regularly and in 1899 succeeded in electing an alderman. In 1900 it nominated candidates for mayor, aldermen, water commissioner, and hospital trustees, and issued a municipal programme. This included public ownership of public utilities, abolition of the ward system, abolition of the contract system on public works, enforcement of compulsory education (with free textbooks), the union label on all municipal supplies where a union label existed, compulsory arbitration of all labour disputes in public utilities, an eight-hour day on all municipal work, and abolition of aldermanic patronage on such work.[81]

In May 1896 the council was rent by a dispute over the activities of its president, M.J. Donohue, who was charged with being in league with one of the parties to sell the prestige of the council in the dominion election. An investigating committee acquitted Donohue of ill intent, but held that his actions would inevitably throw disrespect on him and 'possibly cause the Council to be held in contempt by the public if the matter was not speedily settled.' It therefore suggested he resign, but the council expelled him.

In spite of this row, the council proceeded during the year to demand union wages on school construction, legislation against personal canvassing in elections (which, it held, led to bribery and corruption), and public ownership and develop-ment of a newly discovered Algoma coal deposit and all minerals. In March 1897 it called for public ownership of the Crow's Nest Pass Railway, endorsed a propor-tional representation bill, and pushed its campaign for day labour on public works as a measure against unemployment. It also tried, vainly, to organize the street railway employees. In 1898 it again came out against Chinese immigration.[82]

The London council played a surprisingly small part in the TLCC. It was not represented at all till 1888; it missed altogether the conventions of 1889, 1891–93, 1896, and 1898; and to those of 1894 and 1900 it sent only a single delegate, J.T. Marks. Furthermore, in 1890, 1894, and 1900 its delegates seem to have said or done nothing important enough to get into the proceedings. In most of the other years down to 1902 they were pretty quiet.

In 1895 the council had three active delegates. In 1899 one of its delegates was elected to the Ontario executive. In 1901 and 1902 it had three delegates. In 1902 Marks was elected to the Ontario executive. He moved the constitutional amend-ment to exclude the Knights of Labor; a resolution that all trades and labour coun-cils and federal labour unions should be under the jurisdiction and control of the congress (and instructing the executive to work this out with the AFL); a motion to support the Berlin Broommakers' co-operative factory; and a motion of strong sup-port for the striking Montreal Cigar Makers. All carried.[83]

The comprehensiveness of the council in later years is indicated by the fact that in 1899 it had 19 affiliates: the Street Railway Employees, Cigar Makers, Metal

Polishers, Molders, Typos, Carriage Workers, Painters, Tailors, Railroad Train-men, Garment Workers, Stove Mounters, Boot and Shoe Workers, Coopers, Hack-men, Grocery Clerks, Industrial Brotherhood No 1, Builders' Labourers, Railway Team Drivers, and Draymen.[84]

The first, short-lived Brantford Trades and Labor Council called a mass meeting for January 1887 to discuss violations of the Factory Act, notably the provisions dealing with time allowed for lunch and those covering employment of women and children. It was this meeting which reorganized the council. The constitution was a rather curious one: the executive consisted of one delegate from each organization, and there was no president, merely a chairman elected afresh at each meeting. This last, and the council's endorsation of a party candidate, were later given as the cause of its early demise.

This first council's municipal committee in May 1887 produced a report on the local postal system. It condemned the existing facilities (box and wicket delivery) and wanted named streets, numbered houses, and regular delivery at the houses. Rather oddly, many delegates objected; one, K. Halloran, said the whole thing was not a matter for the council at all but for the board of trade. The committee's report was rejected. This council had one delegate at the 1887 TLCC convention.[85]

In 1887 Brantford had had a labour alderman, accused, however, of following a straight Tory line, but apparently absolved, as he was elected an honorary member of the council. The new council, organized in 1892, promptly called a meeting to consider the various candidates for municipal office. This meeting decided to endorse only candidates known to have been identified with, and interested in, union labour and labour interests. This turned out to mean endorsing Halloran, of the earlier council, who was elected.

This council endorsed the sales ladies' early closing movement in 1893, estab-lished a hall in 1897, and appealed to unions across Canada in 1901 for aid in getting the Trade Mark Act amended to legalize union labels. It was represented at the TLCC conventions of 1900–1902. In 1902 it had 18 affiliated unions.[86]

The first St Thomas council was represented at the 1886 TLCC convention by George Wrigley, who took an active part.[87] The second St Thomas council was represented at the conventions of 1901 and 1902. The first St Catharines council had three delegates at the 1889 convention. One, J.T. Carey, was re-elected president. The second council was represented in 1902. The second Guelph council had a delegate at the conventions of 1901 and 1902.

The Guelph and St Catharines councils, together with several unions in Guelph and Brantford, petitioned the 1900 convention to appoint a solicitor to keep watch on all legislation likely to affect workers' interests (a step actually taken some years later). The convention appointed a special committee to consider the question. The committee reported that, while it would be a good thing, it would be under the circumstances, unwise. It recommended instead that affiliated organizations 'in their various localities co-operate in the establishment of a law defence fund.'

The first Windsor council's 'fraudulent' delegate at the 1890 convention seconded a resolution against the contract system of public works which carried. The Berlin council was represented at the 1901 and 1902 conventions: three delegates each year. By April 1902 it had 23 affiliates. The Stratford council was represented at the 1902 convention.

THE WEST

The third Winnipeg council had been formed by the Bricklayers and the Carpenters. By September 1897 it had 14 affiliates, including the 4 railway running trades; by the end of 1898, probably 18; by February 1899, probably 20, though 2 of the running trades seem to have dropped out.[88] By 5 July 1901 the council had 32 affiliates, and the 23 August list of unions expected to march in the Labour Day parade showed 31, though not all of them actually marched. Of the 31, 6 were local, 1 national, the rest international. Before the year was out the Quarrymen seem to have affiliated; in January 1902 the Draymen followed; in April the Allied Metal Mechanics; in August the Stereotypers and Electrotypers. By the end of the year there were 38 affiliates.[89]

The Winnipeg council organized the barbers in May 1897 and the brickmakers in June 1898 and probably had a hand in organizing a number of other bodies. It published the *Voice*. It took a lively interest in co-operatives, and of course in independent political action, though this was in the later years mainly entrusted to the Winnipeg Labour Party. In 1898 it collected some $450 from all across western Canada for the ASE strike in Britain.[90]

The Winnipeg council was represented at the TLCC conventions from 1895 on. Its 1895 delegate, C.C. Steuart, was elected to the Manitoba committee; so was its 1896 and 1897 delegate, John Appleton, who in 1898 became vice-president, with Steuart on the Manitoba committee. John Mortimer, delegate in 1899 and 1900, was elected vice-president in both years. Alfred Gossel, delegate in 1901 and 1902, was elected to the committee in both years; Albert G. Cowley, 1902 delegate, in that year. All these delegates took a prominent part in the proceedings.[91]

The Vancouver council soon added to its six original member organizations.[92] The Stevedores came in on 10 January 1890, the Lathers three weeks later, the Bricklayers in May, and the Hod Carriers in September. The Stevedores, in successive organizations, stayed. The Lathers and the Plasterers had disappeared by June 1892. The Bricklayers left the council in the spring of 1891, were back by January 1892. Disbanded in April 1895, the union reappeared in 1898. The Hod Carriers (or Builders' Labourers) left the council in January 1895. The Tinners and Cornice Makers joined in April 1891 but had collapsed by September 1892. The Plumbers were admitted in July 1891, but had disbanded by June 1892. The Knights of Labor (probably LA 5506) left the council in July 1891 but were back within a year. The Molders and the Stonecutters joined in July 1891 and the Tailors in December. By the end of that year, therefore, the council seems to have had 13 affiliates.

In 1892 the number of affiliates seems to have held steady at 10 to 12. In 1893 the Steam Shipmen came in. Early in 1895 they were out, and by the fall in again. The American Railway Union affiliated in January 1896, but had collapsed by July 1897. The Railroad Trainmen joined in March 1896 and were still there in the spring of 1899.[93] By that time the Council had at least 18 other affiliates, including the BLE. By 30 September it had added the Barbers; by March 1900 the Retail Clerks; by April the Fishermen and the Quarrymen. In January 1901 the Ship Carpenters and Caulkers affiliated, and in March, the Fishermen No 2 and the Waitresses and Cooks No 28. A year later, the Woodworkers and the Electrical Workers were in. The Laundry Workers were in the council in May 1902, the Blacksmiths and the Bakers in June, the Team Drivers in July, the Firemen's Protective Union in August, the Civic Workers in September, the Musicians and the Stationary Firemen in October, and the UBRE in December. By the end of the year there must have been over 30 affiliates.

The Vancouver council, like the Toronto one, interested itself in an enormous range of questions, and no doubt for much the same reason: that it was far the biggest council in the province, and to some extent filled the place of a provincial central organization. There are, however, significant differences. The most obvious, of course, is the amount of attention devoted to the Oriental question, on which the Vancouver council harped constantly. It demanded exclusion of Chinese workers from the sugar refinery, the graving dock, the railways, and the experimental farm. It complained of the Chinese piggeries and washhouse. It demanded total exclusion of Chinese immigrants. It denounced Chinese 'ignorance, superstition and vice.' In 1899 it urged the legislature to put the Japanese on the same footing as Chinese and Indians in voting rights; endorsed the act forbidding employment of Japanese on work carried on under franchises granted by law; and urged re-enactment of the disallowed labour regulations and tramways acts forbidding employment of Japanese.[94] The council also repeatedly, and at length, brought the whole Oriental problem before the TLCC.

Sheer prejudice undoubtedly played a part in all this, but so did the unmistakable fact that the real threat to British Columbia workers' standard of living came from the Orientals, who were willing to accept meagre wages and poor working conditions at which even European pauper immigrants would have turned up their noses. This helps to explain why the Vancouver council had so little to say about European immigration. It did, on 26 February 1892, hear a report from its parliamentary committee on surplus labour which said that the poorest class of European immigrants was 'directed to Canada, as it is closer to Great Britain and Europe than Australia, South Africa or Brazil.' It made the familiar denunciation of the dominion government for 'spending thousands of dollars of public money encouraging and enticing the poor of foreign countries to come to the Dominion and enter into a life struggle competition with our people in a market always overcrowded as long as Canada is open to all and every class of emigrant,' and this in the face of the government's restrictive and protective trade policies. The committee recommended removing all tariff restrictions which tended to increase the cost of living, and having the Government 'stop spending money to entice outsider labour ... ultimately to prohibit landing on our shores of anyone not showing means enough to enable them to live on their own resources for a given time.' It also recommended total exclusion of the Chinese, and a land allotment system, as well as labour bureaux, for the surplus immigrants already here. But any such statement of comprehensive immigration policy was altogether exceptional.

On 16 June 1893 the Vancouver council unanimously voted for absolute free trade between Canada and Australia, and on 2 December 1893, for free trade, neat. By 15 February 1895 it was putting a little water in this Cobdenite wine; but even the diluted beverage was still pretty strong. A committee report on that date declared that the dominion customs tariff was founded on the principles of protection rather than of public needs, and that, based on such principles, it had 'developed monopolies, trusts and other combinations ... hindered the promotion of agricultural pursuits ... oppressed the masses to the enrichment of the few ... retarded desirable immigrants who would attain the full stature of citizenship ... failed to exclude from our shores Chinese and other undesirable classes who would never become citizens to the detriment of enfranchised working men ... caused great loss to our population and ... impeded commerce ... occasioned great public and private injury, all of which evils must continue to grow in intensity, so long as the present Tariff system remains in force.' The committee accordingly proposed that 'the tariff should be reduced to the needs of honest economical and efficient government and ... so adjusted as to render free of taxation the necessaries of life, and ... to promote freer trade with the whole world, more particularly with Great Britain, Australia and the United States.' It added that the principle of protection was 'radically unsound and unjust to the masses of the people and ... any tariff changes based on that principle must fail to afford any substantial relief from the burdens under which the country now suffers.' The highest interests of Canada, the committee wound up, demanded 'the repeal of its present system of protection as an obstacle to the Dominion's progress and the adoption in its stead of a sound fiscal policy which, while not doing injustice to any class would promote domestic and foreign trade.' Clearly British immigrant workers had brought with them the prevailing British devotion to free trade; clearly, also, Vancouver was already looking westward across the Pacific for markets in the antipodes.

The first of the council's stated purposes when it was founded had been support of the nine-hour movement. While demands for shorter hours and legislation to enforce them were common ground all over the continent, the presence of Oriental immigrant competition lent an extra edge to the movement in British Columbia, where, in fact, it became one of the favourite proposals for coping with the Oriental. Force the employer to work all his employees only at North American hours and, if possible, at North American wages, and the incentive to employ the 'Chinaman' or the 'Jap' would disappear.

In 1890 the council asked for a nine-hour day for city labourers. By February 1895 it had succeeded. In January 1891 it demanded an eight-hour-day clause on all provincial public works and, for dominion public works, 'a clause observing the trade rules in the locality where such work is being carried on.' In 1896 the civic committee recommended the introduction of a provincial eight-hour-day bill that session. In February 1899 it approved a bill to establish an eight-hour day on public works of the province, districts, and municipalities. A year later it passed a resolution urging the provincial government not to interfere with the eight-hour-day law in the metal mines, and a second condemning the Vancouver board of trade for urging the opposite.

It is a depressing commentary on the slow progress of the movement for shorter hours that, as late as 4 December 1902, the Vancouver Molders were reporting to the council, amid applause, that they were asking for the nine-hour day which Ontario unions had been fighting for thirty years before, and expected no trouble in getting it.[95]

Both the Oriental question and the legal regulation of hours of labour figured prominently in the council's various essays in political action. These had a modest beginning: a resolution, 14 February 1890, to canvass workers to get themselves on the voters' lists. But only a month later a delegate raised the question of a labour candidate or a platform suitable to workingmen. Another delegate thought 'the best way was to co-operate with the business men'; the matter was laid over. It came up again on 25 April, with a letter from the Workingmen's League of New Westminster inviting the council to send delegates to a conference in view of the coming dominion election. The council appointed a committee of five for the purpose. It also arranged for each affiliate to send one representative to a meeting to consider the coming provincial elections. After the dominion and the province, the city: on 26 September 1890 the council appointed a committee of two to get the names of 'gentlemen of the city who would be suitable and willing to run for the mayoralty and the council for next term in the interests of the working classes of Vancouver.' On 14 November it was decided that Dr Carroll should be asked to run for mayor.

Meanwhile, the British Columbia Federated Labor Congress had drawn up a platform. The first plank called for a reduction of the provincial government's printing bureau's hours from nine to eight; the second and third were for an eight-hour day on provincial and dominion public works; the fourth urged additional restrictions on the Chinese. It also endorsed a draft employers' liability bill, and weekly payment of wages, and empowered its executive to devise ways and means to nominate labour candidates in the dominion election.

In December 1891 the council adopted a municipal platform which it handed to the affiliates for their action, and in January this was presented to the candidates in five wards. In April it resolved to select an 'eligible workingman candidate and provide funds and devise means to represent' the workers' interests in the dominion House. In December 1892 the council was again considering a labour platform, and then receiving reports from five wards on the candidates for aldermen and one from the mayoralty committee. In January 1893 it endorsed one candidate in Ward I, two in Ward II, one in Ward IV, and one (Delegate Towler) in Ward V.

In November 1895 the council approached the Nationalists for co-operation in the election of aldermen and school trustees who would favour 'much needed reforms such as the clearing and maintenance of a Public Park, and the establishment of evening schools and other matters.' The Nationalists agreed, and in December the two organizations produced a joint platform. In April 1896 the council appointed a committee to see the Nationalists and find out what could be done about running a labour candidate for the dominion House. The committee reported that the Nationalists recommended that all members interested should attend the ward meetings, 24 April, and try to elect delegates who favoured nominating a man who would represent the labour interests.

In December 1896 the council adopted a municipal platform similar to the one adopted a year before. In December 1899 the council's parliamentary committee discussed the nomination of aldermanic candidates, and decided that under existing conditions it was not advisable. Instead, it sent questions to the candidates (notably on Sunday labour and the union label), and endorsed the three aldermanic candidates who returned satisfactory replies.[96]

In February and March 1900 there were rumours and talk of labour candidates in the provincial election. In April the council resolved to ignore the old parties and request unionists to act up to the independent political action resolution passed by the 1899 TLCC convention. On 3 April the affiliated unions were faced with three very pointed practical questions: did they want independent labour candidates, how much money would they put up if they did, and had they any suitable names to propose? Fourteen unions replied, and the secretary was told to write the rest. Meanwhile, the parliamentary committee recommended a 12-point platform.

On 10 May the council decided to nominate two candidates; on the 16th it named Joseph Dixon, its president, and Francis Williams, its treasurer. On 2 June it also endorsed Will MacClain (Machinists) and repudiated the Martin government. All three candidates were defeated, but the council, undaunted, promptly called a meeting to prepare for the next election. This meeting decided to form a labour party, and Victoria, Nanaimo, New Westminster, and many other cities and towns were expected to follow suit. Ralph Smith, MLA, it was announced, would call a meeting of delegates from local organizations, in Vancouver or Kamloops on or about Labour Day to draw up a platform for the next provincial election.

On 21 September the council instructed its parliamentary committee to work with the Vancouver Labour Party in drawing up a platform for the dominion election. The committee submitted its report, which was adopted, on 5 October. It called for government ownership of all public services which were by their nature monopolies; the Single Tax; government issue and control of money; abolition of the contract system on public works; the eight-hour day; an end to all assisted immigration and all Asiatic immigration, and regulation of all other immigration by an educational test; abolition of the Senate; direct legislation; and the union label on all manufactured goods supplied to the government, where practicable. The same meeting endorsed Ralph Smith's candidature for the House of Commons. Two weeks later, however, the council disclaimed all political connection with the Vancouver Labour Party.[97]

Other measures the council fought for would have had the incidental effect of raising further barriers to Oriental labour. It supported an alien labour act. It advocated, as early as March 1890, Sunday observance legislation (and it kept at this with a resolution against Sunday streetcars, 26 September 1890); demanded enforcement of the Sunday closing by-law; and urged (with particular reference to 'saloons' which 'close[d] their front doors on Sunday and open[ed] their back ones') appointment of a committee 'to try and arrange for a universal closing of shops on Sunday.' It supported the Lord's Day Alliance's stand against Sunday traffic on the railways. The council also backed the early closing of stores, and, especially from 1899 on, the union label in all its forms.[98]

The council was prepared to take in unions from places outside Vancouver where there was no local central body: on 21 June 1895 it actually invited the Kamloops BLF to affiliate. But where there were councils or trades assemblies, it was always ready to co-operate with them, though as a rule it seems to have been the bodies in other places which took the initiative.

British Columbia was the first part of Canada to try to set up a provincial central organization. The first attempt came in the fall of 1890. New Westminster had apparently summoned a convention of delegates from the different labour assemblies of the province, but only its own turned up. None the less, these proceeded to consider the establishment of a provincial Trades and Labor Congress or Federated Trades Congress, whose organization meeting should take place in New Westminster, 24 September. To this meeting the Vancouver, Victoria, and New Westminster councils each sent two delegates, who proceeded to form the British Columbia Federated Labor Congress. The meeting set up a committee to draft a constitution, and set a date for a second meeting in Nanaimo the first Saturday in November. This time fog kept the New Westminster delegates away; but Vancouver sent seven, Victoria three, and Nanaimo ten. They elected an executive and drew up the platform already noted. Tully Boyce (Nanaimo Miners) was chosen president; Thomas Howell, Victoria, vice-president; Arthur Dutton, Victoria, secretary; W. Pleming, Vancouver, treasurer; J.V. Nicholls, East Wellington, sergeant-at-arms; and Thomas Salmon, Northfield, and George Irvine and George Pollay, Vancouver, executive members.

By 17 July 1891 Dutton and Boyce both thought the congress should dissolve, as they considered its usefulness gone. The Vancouver council disagreed, and on 2 July 1892 we find it appointing a committee to take steps 'towards the formation of a provincial Trades Assembly.' In April 1893 the Victoria council favoured resuscitating the BCFLC provided all cities in the province were willing to take part; in October it suggested that when the delegation from the mainland was in Victoria would be a good time to do it. This was accepted, and on 2 December the Vancouver council's secretary reported that a committee of two from each city had been appointed to take steps and had met and slightly amended the old constitution.

From 1895 on the TLCC regularly elected a British Columbia executive committee, which, with the election of Ralph Smith to the congress's vice-presidency in 1896, may have taken the steam out of any further agitation for a provincial federation.[99] It did not, however, prevent at least two more efforts to get the various local councils together for concerted action. On 8 May 1896 Ralph Smith suggested a convention of delegates from Vancouver, Victoria, and Nanaimo. Vancouver said it would be willing, and suggested inviting the Patrons of Industry. On 5 November 1897 the Vancouver council itself tried to start the ball rolling, by appointing a special committee to take the necessary steps. In December 1899 Nanaimo suggested, and Vancouver agreed to support, 'a conference of the labor people of the province to discuss the subjects involved.' Delegates were to come from Vancouver, Victoria, Nanaimo, South Nanaimo, Kamloops, Nelson, Ymir, Sandon, and Revelstoke, and the meeting was to take place in Vancouver.

It did, and devoted itself mainly to discussing the eight-hour day and compulsory arbitration. The shorter work day, the Vancouver *Province* reported, met with unanimous favour, and after thorough discussion 'a strong resolution upon this question was carried.' The other question was more contentious. Everybody supported it theoretically, but some felt it was not clear that at the moment it would be 'very workable in this province.' True, it had been a success in New Zealand, but there 'the working men controlled the government.' Here, there was 'always the chance of the third member ... the nominee of the government, being an enemy rather than a friend of labor.' To make the existing optional arbitration compulsory might do more harm than good. The meeting also recorded its opinion that 'an annual labor conference would be an important factor in the success of solving the labor problems.'[100]

The Vancouver council sent delegates to the TLCC in 1890, and a long letter in 1891, but by 20 November 1891 it must have fallen out, for on that date it formally accepted the congress's request to affiliate. It sent two letters to the 1892 convention, but must again have let its affiliation drop, for on 18 November 1892, the congress again asked it to affiliate. In 1893 and 1895 it sent further long letters. It was represented again in 1898.

In 1892, it was twice asked to send delegates to the 'Pacific Coast Council, Trades and Labor Federation,' and again in 1893. On this last occasion, the request got as far as the organization committee.[101]

The council did a certain amount of organizing, though it is not very clear how much.[102] It devoted a good deal of attention to pleading the cause of the unorganized or even of unfortunate individuals. In 1899 it appointed a committee to investigate the grievances of city postal workers. On 10 November this committee submitted a strongly critical report. The 3 permanent carriers got $40, $45, and $47.50 per month. They were entitled to 3 weeks' annual vacation, but 2 of them had in fact got less, and 1 none. The 4 temporary men got $42.50 to $45 a month, and the 6 or 7 day labourers $1.31 per day; these classes were not entitled to any vacation. The carriers were supposed to work a 7½-hour day; the official records showed they had been regularly working 7¾- to 8½, and the men themselves were unanimous in saying they averaged 10, this because 13 or 14 men had to do the work of 15 or 16. There was supposed to be a superintendent for every 12 men; actually, 1 man had been acting supervisor for some time but had never got superintendent's pay. Another man had passed the examination and been appointed to the permanent staff, but his salary had been reduced from $42.50 to $38.50. It was also claimed that men appointed by the late Conservative government got $2.50 more than the Liberal appointees. The Vancouver rates were the same as Winnipeg's (employees from Winnipeg to the coast got a 40 per cent living allowance), though rent, clothing, and food were from 10 to 20 per cent higher in Vancouver than in Winnipeg. Further, the statutory yearly increase had not been paid in Vancouver.

The sorters had similar grievances. They were classed as day labourers at $1 a day with a living allowance. They often had to get up at three or four in the morning.

Sunday work was a little lighter, but holiday work was heavier. They got no vacation or sick leave. They had been promised an increase, but it had never come, and their repeated appeals both to the local postmaster and the department had been ignored.

The committee recommended a memorial to the postmaster-general, setting forth the facts about the cost of living in British Columbia and especially Vancouver, and asking for a minimum salary of $50 a month. The memorial was sent; the post-master-general sent an investigator; and just before Christmas the *Province* reported that the postal workers were to get an increase of $5 a month. The article added that 'the letter carriers ... appear to receive about the same pay as teachers in the lower grades of Vancouver's ... schools. They were not satisfied, however, and demanded ... $60 per month.' The office staff started at $43 per month, and got regulated increases. They complained that they got less than employees in the customs depart-ment, whose work was 'often but mechanical copying,' and whose responsibility was much less.[103] It is hardly surprising that the post office workers organized not long afterwards.

In December 1895 the council took up the case of single unemployed men (it wanted to have them work for any relief they got). In March 1899 it concerned itself with a CPR conductor who had lost a leg while uncoupling a car on a siding. A jury awarded the conductor $6,000 in damages, but the council thought this too little, and set to work to raise funds for an appeal – which failed. Its next notable piece of knight-errantry was on behalf of drunken sailors 'Shang-Haied' on board ships. In May 1899 it protested against the practice of certain saloons which, for a payment of $10 per man, herded drunken sailors to the docks, where they were 'bundled aboard ship to awake next day and find themselves on the ocean.' The city council ordered the police to 'keep special watch, in order to suppress shanghaiing.'[104] In December of the same year came the case of W.B. Ross, committed to the New Westminster Insane Asylum because, so a delegate alleged, 'he knew too much about the ways of the police force.' The council demanded that the case be thoroughly investigated.[105]

In March 1902 the council took up the cudgels for working girls. J.H. Watson, afterwards TLCC organizer, told the council that 'the Millinery House, on Cordova Street, had offered a girl, who had worked there as an apprentice ... for a year without wages, 50 cents a week, and later, after a protest ... by him [Watson], this proposed stipend had been increased to a dollar. Mr. Watson said that the head milliner had told him that this was the prevailing wages, and he replied that in this country people breathed the fresh air of heaven and wanted something to eat. Young women clerks received $2 a week. Mr. Watson contended that this was a deplorable state of affairs, right under our noses. No young woman could live a virtuous life on $2 a week. The Council ... instructed the delegates to bring the matter before their respective unions.'

The Vancouver council seems to have taken less interest in education than some of its fellows. In February 1897 it passed a resolution favouring the submission to the people of a by-law establishing a free library. Two years later it heard a representative of the University Association, and passed a resolution 'urging delegates to lay the matter before their respective unions, favouring the proposed educational scheme.' In April 1899 it wrote to the TLCC endorsing technical schools, and also to the secretary of the school board asking him to move in the matter. In November it called the attention of the city council to Sir William Macdonald's offer to equip one school for manual training education in each province, and asked the city to do all it could to get the British Columbia school for Vancouver. In April 1900 the parliamentary committee was instructed to look into the proposals of the Ottawa Allied Trades and Labor Association and the Ottawa board of trade on the subject. In November 1900 the council asked the council of public instruction to veto the school board's resolution 'regarding teachers taking an active part in politics.' In May 1902 a delegate called attention to the rumour that the school board was considering charging fees for high school pupils; a few weeks later a committee reported that the rumour was false.[106]

The Vancouver council in the years 1890–95 gave some support to the co-operative movement. In August 1890 it listened to a speech in favour of the early establishment of a co-operative society. In December 1894 the ASCJ and LA 677 (stevedores) reported that they were in favour of starting a co-operative store, and in March 1895 the council appointed a committee to report on the matter. In April the Typos added their support, and in June LA 677 reported that it had 'placed about twenty shares of the co-operative store stock.' Later that month the council suspended its regular business to hear Mr Dodds of the Canadian Co-operative Commonwealth, who asked for its help in establishing a newspaper in Vancouver. He thought publication costs for the paper would run between $40 to $50 a month, and that 500 subscribers would be enough to sustain the paper for 4 to 5 months.

This last was not the only proposal for a labour paper. In October 1892 Mr Trythall had made similar proposals to the council, and in February 1893 the minutes mention 'the reporter from the Peoples Journal.' By February 1899 Victoria had its own labour paper, the *British Columbia Workman*, but the Vancouver council resolved to have nothing to do with it. But by 27 May it had changed its mind to the extent of asking the proprietor, W.M. Wilson, to address the meeting. He offered to transfer the paper to Vancouver if the Vancouver council would help support it. On 9 June a committee reported that, 'although the paper was in the interests of the working men, and Vancouver was the natural headquarters, yet it could not recommend that the Council assume responsibility, as it thought energies should be directed towards the building of a hall.' In February 1900 there was a fresh attempt which resulted in the establishment of the *Independent*. George Bartley resigned from the council to become editor.[107]

As early as September 1892 the council manifested its hostility to militarism in the not very formidable shape of a movement to establish and equip a battalion of volunteer riflemen in Vancouver. It strongly objected 'to the establishing or enlarging of an army in our fair and peaceful Dominion of Canada whether as a militia or volunteer corps of any class or grade of arms,' and it specifically stated that it thought the proposed battalion 'would entail an unnecessary expense, and ... would become at most unexpected times the tools of a few greedy, avaricious and domineering citizens.' In August 1900 the question recurred in a new context: the calling out of the militia during the fishermen's strike. A delegate raised the question whether a man could be a consistent unionist and belong to the militia. A long discussion followed, ending in a mere emphatic protest against the use of the militia at Steveston.[108]

The council's delegate at the 1890 TLCC convention was George Bartley. He moved two motions, one to prohibit Chinese immigration, one to appoint a committee to interview the dominion government on the question. Both carried. He also seconded a motion to prohibit employment of Chinese in mines, with a penalty of $500 for each offence.

The council's 1891 letter to the congress dealt mainly with the all-absorbing Chinese question. The continual influx of these immigrants was bound, in the council's view, to lead to 'the ultimate degradation and ruin of the dignity of white labor on the ... Coast ... British Columbia capitalists too freely encourage this kind of immigration. The immorality of this class of people should not be slighted. It will never be possible to elevate the Mongolians as a race to the level of the Caucasians.' The letter went on to charge that the Chinese had taught many white youths the habit of using opium; that the new CPR boats were bringing in far more Chinese than even the existing law allowed; and that some of the Chinese were suffering from leprosy.

The council also took occasion to warn all and sundry that the coast labour market was overcrowded. Local workers suffered from the competition of arrivals from eastern Canada who knew nothing about unionism because they came from numbers of good-sized towns in Ontario, Quebec, and the Maritime provinces where 'a union is almost unknown except by name.' It hinted that the congress might well do some organizing in these benighted regions. The letter wound up with a prophecy that the Dominion Trades and Labor Congress would soon 'possess a weight in public affairs equal to our parliaments and legislatures,' and a fraternal invitation to hold the next convention in Vancouver.

The 1892 letter takes up almost three pages of the congress proceedings, and deals with a long list of questions. First, it complained that mechanics working on building construction in Vancouver for the CPR and the dominion government ('which are looked upon here as one and the same') were being worked a ten-hour day, instead of the prevailing nine hours, and that the minister of public works said he could not interfere. The council said the railway and its patron 'appear[ed] to be bent upon breaking up the trade unions.' Second came dissatisfaction with the way the voters' lists were made up. In the 1890 provincial election nearly 2000 people had been able to vote; but in the 1891 dominion election, on the separate dominion franchise, only about 960 had been eligible.

Finally, it complained about Chinese immigration. According to the council, the Chinese were 'nothing better than filthy harbingers of disease. Morality they have none. Christianity they cannot conceive of except as a huge joke.' As domestic servants, they stole, and adulterated food with 'drugs almost unknown to white men, thus placing the female members of the household at their disposal and unscrupulous will,' and causing many divorces. They took on extra Chinese servants whom they kept in virtual slavery. They had harems, which they maintained as houses of assignation and gambling dens 'of squalid infamy ... frequently visited by thoughtless and intemperate men and by rural tenderfeet from the East. ... Leprous Mongolian viragoes [and] even China*men*' stood on the streets at night, soliciting. The city was still suffering from smallpox 'introduced and fostered by the Chinese.' This section of the letter ended with: 'But enough, it is impossible to do the subject justice without wearying you.'

The letter then urged independent political action, adding that 'if the rapid and effectual concentration of the wealth created by the toilers into the hands of the few, who, by their cunning, backed by unscrupulous politicians ... be not checked, this fair Canada of ours will soon become a land of serfs.'

The council then declared its support for the initiative and referendum; for total exclusion of the Chinese, or, failing that, a $500 head tax on arrival and an annual tax of $200; for refusal of naturalization to 'persons of Mongolian origin'; for a legal eight-hour day; for abolition of the contract system on public works, and, pending this, local trades' rules clauses in all contracts; for using the provincial voters' lists for dominion elections; for a right of appeal for seamen convicted under the Seamen's Agreement Act; for a proper admiralty court to hear such appeals; for an alien labour act; for prohibition of foreign sailors doing longshoremen's work; for abolition of the Senate; and, finally, for using the preamble and platform of the Knights of Labor (which the council had adopted) as a guide in framing a congress platform.

The special committee appointed to consider all this reported that most of it was already covered by congress policies, and recommended concurrence in the rest, except for the bit about the sailors doing longshoremen's work, which it considered a matter for the local labour organizations.

The council's 1893 letter returned to the Chinese question and complained that 'those highest in authority at Ottawa remain hand-in-glove with the very individuals who have everything to do with the dumping of the obnoxious vermin on our soil.' It went on to recite the growth of unionism in British Columbia ('Even Indians are taking to unionism'), the province's dependence on foreign capital, and several resolutions of the council during the year, and enclosed a long petition to the minister of marine and fisheries on the fishing industry.

The 1895 letter took a whack at the immigration of 'Government-assisted foreign paupers ... like those proposed for settlement by General Booth, of the Salvation Army.' It favoured instead having the government lease land to bona fide settlers and grub-stake citizens desiring to become so. It objected to the employment of Orientals on CPR boats, and wanted government subsidies stopped till the company mended its ways. It called attention to the wiping out of the white tailoring shops by the Chinese, and suggested that the Chinese might be taxed for all they made. It wanted two separate sections in the government department of labour statistics, one for the employers, one for the employees. It reiterated the call for independent political action. It wanted the congress to charter local trades and labour councils. It declared for the eight-hour day. It demanded an end to patronage in the Vancouver post office. It endorsed municipal ownership of electric light plants, a fair-wage clause on public works, payment of aldermen, free trade, public ownership of telegraphs and railways, and some other measures.[109]

The Victoria council's records for this period are unfortunately lost. But the Vancouver council's minutes have a number of references which indicate how prominent and active a part Victoria played. In August 1890 it addressed a circular to the clergy. In February 1892 it asked the Vancouver council to join in petitioning the legislature to ask the dominion to raise the Chinese head tax. In the spring of 1893, and again in November, as already noted, it discussed reviving the provincial congress. In February 1894 it agreed to work with Vancouver for an eight-hour-day clause on provincial public works. In July 1897 it was asking Vancouver to back its efforts to have Mr Templeman appointed lieutenant-governor. In April 1899 it complained that work on the construction of a certain steamer violated the Alien Labour Act. In August 1899 it negotiated with the street railway for reduced fares in rush hours. In May 1902 it asked Vancouver to send a delegation to Victoria on the Workmen's Compensation Bill.[110]

The Victoria council sent a letter to the 1890 TLCC convention denouncing the influx of Chinese, and describing the strike in the Wellington coal mines. In 1892 it sent another, enclosing a petition on Chinese immigration. The council complained that the provincial government steamer *Quadra* was being built on the Clyde, when local shipbuilders could have built a better and more suitable wooden steamer for less. The letter also urged immediate attention to the eight-hours question. The special committee appointed to consider this and the Vancouver letter endorsed the Victoria council's views.[111]

In 1898 the Victoria council sent its first delegate to a congress convention: William McKay. He was elected to the British Columbia committee, and seconded a motion on the Crow's Nest Pass Railway by Wilkes, which carried. In 1899 the council wired its regrets at being unable to send a delegate, and its best wishes.[112]

The Nanaimo council also makes fairly frequent appearances in the Vancouver council's minutes. Some of these we have already noted; but there were more. In October 1892 the Nanaimo council undertook to send names of dealers selling non-union coal to the Vancouver council. In October 1893 it sent word that the Caledonian Society was employing Chinese on its grounds, and asked Vancouver to make this known. In June 1900 it wanted a copy of the Vancouver petition on the Oriental question. In November it wrote about the royal commission on Oriental immigration. In May 1902 it wanted the commission's recommendations enacted into law. In July 1902 it regretted it could not sign a Vancouver open letter on the Chinese question, as it had always held out for total exclusion.[113]

The Nelson and Phoenix councils each had a delegate at the 1901 TLCC convention, and both were elected to the British Columbia executive.[114]

The Rossland council had one delegate at each of the conventions of 1898, 1899, and 1901: James Wilkes in the first two years (when he was elected British Columbia vice-president), and Chris Foley in 1901. In 1899 Wilkes seconded a motion by Flett asking for a referendum of congress affiliates on independent political action. The committee on standing orders and resolutions reported against this. After a long and animated discussion, the motion submitted by Flett and Wilkes was carried by a large majority. The Flett-Wilkes motion declared that the time-honoured method of interviewing governments had accomplished nothing; that henceforth 'members of labor organizations found on the platform and advocating the interest of the old political parties be regarded with suspicion, as decoys of the wage earners, and ... opponents of the advanced labor movement'; and that, if the majority favoured independent action, the local central bodies should proceed to name candidates wherever warranted.[115]

The conventions of the
Trades and Labor Congress
of Canada 1883–1902

Canada's second national central labour organization, like its first, originated with the Toronto local central body.[1] On 17 August 1883 T. Moor gave notice of a motion 'That the Council take the necessary steps towards holding a Labor Congress in the City of Toronto in December of the present year, to be composed of duly accredited representatives of all organized Bodies of Working men in this Dominion for the purpose of deliberating and determining upon such Legislation or other action as may be deemed Essential in the interest of the Whole.' On 7 September this was handed to the legislative committee. On 21 September the committee reported that it 'had communicated with a great number of Towns throughout the Dominion and would report further at the next meeting.' On 5 October the committee said it had 'received a number of answers from different parts of the Province in sympathy with a labor Congress being held at the close of this year.' On 2 November the committee finally reported that it endorsed the holding of the congress, 'after receiving so much encouragement in answer to enquiries made ... all over the Dominion.' It was accordingly empowered to 'take all necessary steps in the premises.'[2]

Several points are noteworthy. First, the initiative came from Moor, of the British Amalgamated Carpenters. Second, the congress was plainly intended to include both skilled and unskilled workers. Third, it was to accept affiliation from every kind of labour organization: local, regional, national, international, British, American, trade unions, Knights of Labor.

The convention call, signed by Charles March, president of the Toronto council, and John Aldridge and D.J. O'Donoghue, chairman and secretary of its legislative committee, was addressed to the 'Officers and Members of the various Trades' and Labor Organizations and Assemblies of the Knights of Labor, throughout the Dominion.' It set the basis of representation at 2 delegates for every union or LA with 100 members or fewer, 3 for those with 200 and upwards. It asked organizations to submit resolutions, and added a warning that practical work would be one of the main objects, so that there would be 'no time for holiday enjoyment.'

The Canadian Labor Congress met 26–28 December 1883. Like the Canadian Labor Union, it consisted entirely of delegates from Ontario. The Toronto council had 2 delegates, and Toronto another 38 or 39; 3 each from the Bricklayers, Builders' Labourers, Longshoremen, and Molders (1 from Local 28, 2 from Local 140); 2 each from the Typos, American Carpenters, Amalgamated Carpenters, Tailors, Plasterers, Maltsters, Stone Masons, Stove-Mounters and Pattern-Makers; 1 each from the Bakers, Plasterers' Labourers, Stone Cutters, Seamen, perhaps the Sailors;[3] 2 each from LAS 2305, 2622, and 2782. St Catharines had 1 from the Sailors Union and 2 from LA 2056. Oshawa had 2, from LA 2355; Belleville 1, from LA 2900; Port Dalhousie 1, from LA 2513. Of the 48 delegates, 12 were from the Knights, 14 or 15 from international unions, the rest from purely local unions (all in Toronto), and 2 from the Toronto Council (both later to represent LAs of the Knights).

Charles March opened the proceedings, and appointed a committee on credentials. When this had reported, March was elected chairman and proceeded to address his 'Fellow workers from all parts of the Province' (something of a gloss on the facts!). He drew attention to 'the disturbed condition of trade matters, coupled with strikes, always detrimental under any phase,' and the need for common defence and protection. He emphasized that the call had included both trades unionists and Knights of Labor, between whom 'antagonism should not, and ... does not, exist.' With the two types of body, 'no section or class of wage-earners need be without organization ... and consequent protection. In the perfection of organization lies education, and a consequent raising of the masses to a thorough realization of their own power under our present advanced system of government – although yet a system capable of many improvements.' He hoped the convention would consider the extension of the franchise, 'the Chinese immigration curse, pauper and assisted passage immigration from Europe, the necessity for factory and sanitary legislation,' dominion legislation to protect the 'wages of mechanics and laborers involved in insolvent estates; a protest against placing the product of convict labor in an open market in competition with the product of honest men,' and employers' liability.

The congress elected a standing orders committee, to which all resolutions were to go, and which was to decide on the order of their presentation. It also elected a ways and means committee and adopted the procedural rules of the Toronto council as far as applicable.

The standing orders committee, next day, reported an order of business. This was adopted, and the convention proceeded to deal with a resolution, moved by John Rooney (LA 2622, Toronto), and seconded by J.R. Brown (LA 2355, Oshawa), calling for total exclusion of the Chinese. Rooney said the Chinese could not be civilized, or assimilated. To let them in did not benefit them, and injured Canadians. The Chinese were 'idolatrous,' and if they were allowed to keep coming in, 'in the course of a century' the people of Canada would be affected by this. The Chinese were immoral. They brought with them neither skill nor money; when they went back to China, they took a great deal of money with them. By the 'cheapness of their labor ... they forced the working-people out of industries ... The agitation against the importation of Chinese was not a weakness ... of the laboring classes, as they were simply looking to self-preservation and self-defence.' Brown concurred, and added his own two pennyworth: that Chinese immigration was like Coolie immigration to the West Indies; that the Chinese in Canada were nothing less than slaves; and that they were 'brought out by monopolists who were looking for cheap labor.' A series of other delegates added other charges which were to become familiar, and the resolution was unanimously adopted.

The subject came up again at the next convention, 1886, which passed a resolution for 'much more stringent legislation, in the direction of prohibiting the importation of Chinese labor.' After that, it slumbered till 1890, when motions for total exclusion of Chinese immigrants, and a $500 penalty for employing any Chinese worker in mines, were carried. In 1891 the convention demanded total exclusion; in 1892 total exclusion of Chinese immigrants, and a $100 head tax on Chinese residents; and in 1893, total exclusion of Chinese immigrants or, failing this, a $100 head tax on both Chinese and Japanese immigrants. In 1895 the resolution called for an increase of the head tax on Chinese immigrants from $50 to $500. In 1896 the convention reiterated its demand for the increase in the head tax and stricter administration of the naturalization law for Japanese, and in 1897, 1898, 1899, and 1901 once more asked for the $500 head tax.

A second resolution in 1883, on shorter hours, was the forerunner of many more. It condemned 'the present system' of a 10-hour day in summer and 7½ in winter, and wanted a straight 9. Everybody favoured this in principle. The difficulty, several delegates pointed out, was that workers wanted to get more money by working overtime, or an extra day or half-day. One delegate even said it would be 'insane' for the congress to commit itself to the nine-hours' movement. Others, however, strongly supported the resolution (Alfred Jury said a depression was beginning, and the workers should share the work); and in spite of verbal opposition and misgivings, the resolution was 'declared unanimously carried.'

In 1886 the convention came out for the eight-hour day as 'the only means by which the large amount of surplus labor at present in the market of the Dominion can be employed and a fair amount of remuneration ... received.' (One delegate favoured no work on Saturdays, another full time; and Jury objected to any legislation at all.) It also asked for eight hours for employees of 'the State, public bodies and companies obtaining contract or concession from Parliament,' and an eight-hour-day clause in all government contracts. In 1887 it adopted a motion for an eight-hour-day clause (with five hours on Saturdays) in government contracts, though not without opposition. In 1888 a motion for general eight-hour-day acts was amended in favour of 'a general refusal to work more than eight hours.' In 1889, after much discussion and reference to a committee, the same motion was amended to one 'strongly advocat[ing] eight hours as a day's work, and urg[ing] that all Government and Municipal work be done on the same basis.' In 1890 the convention strongly urged workers to do all they could to get hours shortened and asked for an eight-hour day on all public works. In 1891 it called for a dominion act gradually shortening the workday to eight hours. In 1892 it repeated the 1890 resolution, and considered a motion to limit the railway running trades, switchmen, and railway telegraph operators to 48 hours a week. Amazingly, this produced an amendment to make it 60, moved by, of all people, the one railway union delegate present: Crowhurst, of the Toronto Locomotive Firemen. A subamendment, for 8 hours in every 24, carried.

In 1893 the convention plumped for a straight eight-hour day; in 1894 and 1895, it reverted to the eight-hour day in public works contracts, adding, in 1895, a call to trades and labour councils to co-operate with Local Councils of Women to get shorter hours for women; in 1896 it declared in favour of the eight-hour movement and asked for eight hours in all workshops and on all other works of the dominion government. In 1897 it again asked for eight hours on all dominion government contracts, and in 1901 for an eight-hour day on government railways.

The third subject taken up in 1883 was immigration. The convention passed a long resolution denouncing assisted passages, which overcrowded a labour market 'already more than amply provided for by the surplus working population.' After a long discussion, this was unanimously adopted. To make assurance doubly sure, the convention also passed a resolution condemning the 'systematic shipping to this country of the pauper population of Great Britain or of any other country.' Resolutions to the same effect were adopted at almost every subsequent convention during the period, and were sometimes accompanied by denunciations of 'people in the old countries who made a fat living out of' the immigration system, and got occasional trips across the Atlantic to boot; also of the big salaries paid to immigration agents in Britain.

The 1895 convention unanimously passed a furious resolution inspired by reports that General Booth, of the Salvation Army, was trying to get a grant of 100,000 acres 'whereon to establish a colony of so-called reformed criminals, sinners, and others, under such conditions and regulations as would preclude any person in the so-called colony from ever becoming the owner or occupier of any part of said colony.' The convention said this would establish 'to a most unjustifiable extent, a tacit union of State and Church, an iniquitous condition not to be tolerated in Canada.' It accordingly entered 'its strongest protest against the granting of any of the public lands of Canada to General Booth or any other persons, corporations or associations for monopolistic purposes, or under any other conditions than those governing ordinary settlers.'

In 1896 the convention struck a more positive note: the immigration system should be remodelled to bring in only the proper class of people,' who should be settled on vacant lands by 'a very liberal system of colonization.' In 1897 it approved an Ontario act to regulate the immigration of children, and wanted to bracket with the abolition of assisted immigration a 'co-relative [system] of emigration under which people already in Canada should receive more special opportunities to go upon the public lands of the country.' In 1899 came an abortive attempt to deal with the problem by a legal minimum wage and maximum day.

The fourth subject on the 1883 agenda was a factory act. The dominion government had introduced a factory bill into the Senate in 1882, but withdrew it because of the 'very considerable amount of correspondence' coming in almost daily from employers. In 1883 it introduced a revised bill, which, in its turn, was withdrawn later in the session, for amendment, with the promise of a new bill in 1884. This was duly introduced, but dropped without debate, apparently because of representations by the Manufacturers' Association. In 1885 Sir John A. Macdonald said the government was considering bringing in yet a fourth bill, but it never did.[4]

All this meant, however, that the congress, in 1883, was perfectly justified in thinking that a dominion factory act was constitutionally possible; and a dominion factory act it accordingly requested, unanimously.

By 1886, however, the whole subject wore a new complexion. In 1884 the Ontario legislature had passed a factory act of its own; but for some reason or other the government chose to leave it in a state of suspended animation. The 1886 convention accordingly appointed a committee to see the government and urge it to proclaim the act, and passed several strong resolutions on the subject. It also passed one informing the government that no factory act would attain the end sought unless the inspector or inspectors appointed had the confidence of the various labour organizations, and asked 'the Dominion and Local Governments to pass a Workshop Regulations Act,' with competent inspectors enjoying the confidence of the labour organizations.

By 1887 the congress seems to have decided that perhaps the dominion had jurisdiction after all. It noted that the passage of stricter laws by some provinces than by others put the manufacturers in the former at a disadvantage, and therefore asked for a uniform dominion act. It added that, if it turned out that the dominion had no power to legislate, the constitution should be amended to give it such power. It also asked for dominion and provincial workshops acts, again with competent inspectors, enjoying the confidence of labour.

In 1888 the convention asked to have the Ontario act amended to cover all factories, regardless of size. It also wanted local inspectors for cities, and for groups of towns and villages, and a workshops regulation act.

Till 1889, the conventions were exclusively Ontario affairs, except for the presence of one Quebec City delegate, R.H. Leahey, LA 4003, in 1886. So the legislation requested was exclusively dominion and Ontario. In 1889, however, the convention met in Montreal, with almost half the delegates from Quebec. Resolution after resolution, therefore, asked for action by the provinces, or specifically mentioned Quebec. One of them was for workshops regulation acts.

In 1890 the convention, reciting the need for uniform factory and workshop legislation, asked the dominion government to take steps to determine the question of jurisdiction. It evidently had little doubt of the answer, for it proceeded to ask for dominion acts, adding that till such acts were passed, or the jurisdiction settled, it wanted legislation by all the provinces. In 1891 it repeated the workshop acts resolution, and demanded stiffening of the Ontario Factory Act. In later years, doubtless because it was now clear that factory legislation came under provincial jurisdiction, the congress usually confined itself to pressing for amendments to the various provincial factory and workshops acts.

The fifth subject on the 1883 list was 'Seamen's Act.' J.D. Murphy (Seamen's Union, Toronto) moved, and J.T. Carey (Seamen's Union, St Catharines) seconded, 'That we do earnestly and respectfully request the Dominion Government to protect life and property on our inland waters; that the hulls of sailing vessels, as well as steamboats, should pass proper inspection, and if not found seaworthy, condemned; that the sanitary conditions of the sleeping apartments of the crews should be looked after; that all vessels are manned with crews according to their tonnage; that vessels should not be overloaded with shifting cargoes; that a duplicate of ships' articles be left in Custom House on every voyage.'

Carey said that 'many of the vessels now afloat were not fit to sail across Toronto Bay in bad weather'; that there were no life-saving stations along the lakes; that some vessels were improperly manned; that steamboats sometimes had 'not a man aboard who knew how to handle the boat' if the machinery gave out, or how to launch a lifeboat in bad weather; that the rigging was often rotten; and much else to the like effect. Since the sailors had formed their union, 'they had derived a great deal more benefit from their labours'; for one thing, they had got hours down from 14 or 15 a day to 10. The government, however, had done nothing for the sailors (except to compel masters and mates to pass an examination by examiners of doubtful competence), 'and he thought that the prospects were that they would not amount to anything unless some influence was brought to bear upon them.' The resolution was unanimously carried.

In 1887 Carey moved for 'a law compelling all vessels ... to carry competent crews of seamen ... making it necessary to have hulls and rigging inspected by competent men appointed for that purpose; and ... to stop the loading of vessels below a certain mark, to be designated by said inspector.' This also was adopted unanimously. J.F. Keefer (DA 207, St Catharines) moved to amend the Seamen's Agreement Act to give sailors the right to trial by jury and an appeal. This was adopted.

The safety resolution of 1887 was readopted in 1888, 1889, and 1890; by 1891 Parliament had acted. The Seamen's Agreement Act resolution was readopted in 1889, 1890, 1891, and 1892.

The sixth 1883 item was property qualifaction for municipal office. The convention unanimously asked the Ontario legislature to lessen the amount of property qualification. It did the same in 1886 and 1887, and for all provinces in the years 1890–94, 1897, 1898, 1901, and 1902.

The next question was manhood suffrage. The convention 'respectfully' petitioned Ontario to grant a qualified manhood suffrage. In 1886 it raised its sights to manhood suffrage. It repeated this in 1887, along with a demand for household suffrage in voting on municipal money by-laws. In 1890 and 1893, it asked for manhood suffrage in municipal elections for all the provinces; in 1891 for Quebec, in 1892 for Ontario. In 1890 it also asked Quebec to give the provincial vote to people getting salaries of $300 and up, as a step towards manhood suffrage. In every year from 1890 to 1894, it asked that all municipal voters be allowed to vote on money by-laws. In 1893 it asked Quebec to reduce the money qualification for the vote in cities from $400 to $200. In 1891 and 1893, it called for votes for women on the same terms as men. In 1897 a motion to ask Ontario to give the municipal vote to every male subject, aged 21 or over, was amended to read 'every citizen of Canada, both male and female.'

The final item on the original 1883 agenda concerned the land question. These were the great days of Henry George and his Single Tax, and year after year the congress gave its support to the proposal.

In 1898 it restated its Single Tax faith in resounding terms; but plank number 7 in the platform of principles adopted at the same convention says only: 'Tax reform by lessening taxation on industry and increasing it on land values.'

By 1902, though plank 7 still remained, the congress was apparently beginning to have doubts, for on a resolution calling on 'the labor unions and friends of justice everywhere' to do all they could to get legislatures 'either to remove taxes from improvements or to give municipalities the power' to do it, the committee on standing orders and resolutions reported that, 'without expressing any opinion upon the economic principles involved,' it recommended 'the principle of the right of any municipality to determine their own system of taxation;' and the congress concurred.

By the morning of its third day the 1883 convention had almost finished its original agenda. So it adopted a second list of 16 further questions to be considered.

The first was organization of trades' councils. The second was the extension of magistrates' powers respecting employees' wages, on which it asked that magistrates should have primary jurisdiction in all cases of non-payment of wages. The third was the Insolvency Act; there it wanted a priority of at least 30 days for claims of wages. In 1886 and 1887 the convention passed the same resolution with the substitution of 60 days for 30. In 1887 it adopted also a resolution that in all cases of insolvency employees be paid in full from the assets, and that landlords be placed on the same footing as all other creditors. In 1894 it asked to have piece-work wages brought under the legislation.

The fourth item was the accumulative vote. The working class would never get full justice till it was represented in the legislatures by men of its 'own class and opinions,' and this 'would be best obtained by grouping constituencies with an accumulative vote.' This was the first of a long series of resolutions favouring proportional representation: in 1886, 1887, 1894, 1896, 1897, 1898 (when the proposal was put into the platform as plank 14), and 1901.

Land grants came next. Jury moved to stop all grants, replacing them by leases to actual settlers, with a limit of 320 acres. In 1886 and 1887 the convention merely condemned 'the monopolization of public lands by corporate companies and individual speculators.' In 1897 it repeated this, with special reference to railway companies, and coupled the condemnation with a call to the government to promote colonization by 'the surplus labor.'

Tax exemptions were roundly condemned in 1883, 1886, and 1887 (twice), and 1888. In 1899 the convention asked for provincial laws making it illegal for any municipality 'to offer bonuses, bribes, or exemptions to manufacturers or employers of labor to settle or move into aforesaid places.' In 1900 it asked Quebec to forbid the granting of bonuses 'to manufacturers who are desirous of establishing private industries with the money of the people.'

Government aid to colleges was next. A motion against grants to denominational colleges and universities and for 'a non-sectarian university ... free to all who desire to avail themselves of its advantages,' produced a variety of opinions. Three delegates wanted the University of Toronto's proposed additional grant given to the common schools: 'the laboring classes were not interested in the dead languages.' One wanted the grant money spent on free school books. One said higher education 'at present was, comparatively speaking, a failure. It fitted men to become teachers ... but for practical purposes it was a dead letter ... Schools or colleges should be instituted for the education of the children of the people in practical callings.' An amendment against grants to any college or university was defeated. A second amendment, against any further grants to universities or colleges and for free school books, carried.

In 1886, 1887, 1888, and 1889, the convention asked Ontario to transfer the allowance for universities and colleges to the public schools, and to use part of it to provide free school books. In 1890 an amendment, 'That this Congress, while believing in a liberal expenditure ... on colleges and universities, desires to have the grants ... for primary education ... increased materially,' carried.

Next came piece-work. Here the 1883 convention was terse and forthright: 'We recommend that all the Assemblies and Trades' Unions enforce, where applicable, upon their respective trades the necessity of doing away with contract or piece-work among tradesmen and laborers.' In 1889 a motion to amend the factory acts to make piece-work for apprentices unlawful, except in the last year of their apprenticeship, was amended to: 'that the piece-work system be totally abolished.' In 1890, however, the milder proposal was adopted.

The ninth item was boards of arbitration. The convention unanimously resolved 'That this Congress approves of the appointment of a Board of Arbitration to which all disputes between workmen and their employers shall be submitted.' J. Strachan (Toronto Tailors) 'did not think it would be wise to appoint any outside persons on such a board,' but no one else went even this far.

In 1886 R.H. Leahey (LA 4003, Quebec), the single Quebec delegate, moved, seconded by O'Donoghue, 'That this Congress approves of the appointment by law of Dominion and Provincial arbitrators, to which all disputes between workmen and their employers shall be submitted for settlement, and that their decision be final.' After 11 delegates had spoken, Jury moved in amendment 'That this Congress approves of the principle of arbitration, and petitions the various Governments to pass a law giving legal and binding effect to the decision of any Board of Arbitrators mutually agreed upon by both parties to any labor dispute.'

George Wrigley was 'opposed to the arbitrators being permanently appointed by the Government. There would be too many opportunities to buy them up. He thought the arbitrators should be appointed by the men' *ad hoc*. He moved an amendment, in effect, striking out government appointment. After discussion by another eight delegates, this was carried.

At the 1887 convention R.J. Whitten moved almost precisely the same resolution. This time, however, a voluntary arbitration amendment carried. In 1888 a long resolution for voluntary arbitration carried unanimously. The 1889 and 1890 conventions went back to compulsory arbitration. In 1891 the congress called for a Dominion board of arbitration, whose decisions would be binding for 'railway companies and other corporations holding public franchises,' but apparently not for others. This carried.

In 1892 the congress went back to voluntary arbitration. A special committee recommended that the unions and assemblies in each locality should elect two representatives of each trade, and invite the employers to do likewise, and that these four should choose an outside chairman. These 'conciliation boards' (the name is significant) should 'tender their services' and keep a record of their proceedings.

Luc Routier moved in amendment: 'That in the event of a strike or lockout, if not settled in fifteen days, a board composed of two members from the trade or calling affected, two from the employers, and two judges of the Superior Court, be appointed to settle the dispute, the decision of the board to be final.' This was too strong for other delegates. After discussion by no less than 14 delegates, an amendment for a government board of arbitration and conciliation (voluntary) carried.

In 1893 the congress swung back to compulsory arbitration. In 1898 it wrote into its platform plank 13: 'Compulsory arbitration of labor disputes.' In 1899 it reinforced this by resolving 'That this Congress petition the Dominion Government to establish a Board of Arbitration to adjust all disputes between employers and employees.'

In 1901 Ralph Smith, MP in his presidential address, referred to the long strike of coal miners on Vancouver Island, the serious strike of fishermen on the Fraser River and the strike of the CPR trackmen, and went on to say that, though there was 'some difference of opinion' among labour leaders on the wisdom of compulsory arbitration, and though President Gompers of the AFL had come out strongly against it (in American circumstances not without some reason), he (Smith) nevertheless thought that in Canada 'the compulsory principle of settling these grievances is worth a trial. Both capital and labor have a legal right to insist upon what each considers its due; but when the enforcement of these claims brings stagnation and danger to the public, they ought to be compelled to submit to the decision of impartial arbitrators appointed by the Government. I am convinced that this would be a great advantage to this country, and I am persuaded that there is not any single question that labor unions ought to concentrate their energies to bring about of so vast importance as this.'

The convention resolved 'That in view of the recent disastrous Trackmen's strike, ... the ... Congress should formulate some practical scheme of compulsory arbitration, and press the Government for its adoption.'

Blithely ignoring both this resolution and plank 13 of the platform of principles, the committee on the president's address reported that it was 'not prepared to recommend a dogmatic pronouncement ... in favour of Compulsory Arbitration or its exercise in such strikes' as those mentioned by the president. It submitted 'as an alternative, that your body approve of a trial of Compulsory Conciliation.' This section of the report was duly adopted. So, at the end of 1901, the congress was officially in favour of compulsory arbitration; committed to formulating a practicable measure for carrying it into effect, and to pressing it on the government; and simultaneously 'not prepared to make a dogmatic pronouncement in favor of ... Compulsory Arbitration,' but rather to 'approve a trial of Compulsory Conciliation!'

In 1902, however, the congress was faced with what it called a compulsory arbitration bill for railways. Horrified by this attempt to put into practice one of its own two contradictory principles, it decided that it did not really believe in compulsory arbitration at all. J.H. Hall (Order of Railway Conductors, Division 245, Toronto), moved that 'whereas [the Bill], if enacted, would rob the employees of their constitutional rights, destroy their organizations and place them absolutely in the hands of the railway companies, at the same time depriving them of that citizenship which is so dearly prized, and which is the inherent right of all free-born British subjects,' it be resolved 'that this ... Congress ... denounce said Bill, and instructs their legislative committee to use every effort in their power to defeat this measure; and ... that the labor organizations of the entire Dominion be instructed to use every effort in their power to assist the legislative committee in bringing about the defeat of this measure.' This was adopted. Next day 'voluntary' replaced 'compulsory' in plank 13.

The 1883 convention next took up the organization of female labour. John Armstrong moved 'That this Congress do strongly recommend the organization of female labor wherever possible [for] better wages and shorter hours.' His speech went a good deal farther: 'If the men of the country worked under the same disabilities as the working women there would soon be a revolution. He could not for the life of him see why a woman should not receive the same rate of wages as a man, if she was capable of performing the same amount of labor ... and many times it had come under his observation that their work in some lines was accomplished with more neatness and dispatch. In his estimation the small pay women receive[d] in many branches of trade was one of the greatest incentives to crime. As one presiding over the only women's union in the city, his experience was that they were just as able to conduct the business of a union as most men.'

The same resolution carried in 1886, 1887, and 1888. In 1889 the convention requested employers 'to pay the woman the same wages as the man for the same class of work properly done.'

Meanwhile, in 1888, the congress had been tackling the question of female labour from another angle: the administration of the factory acts. Two Knights of Labor moved that 'female inspectors of factories and workshops be appointed ... and that in order that the duties of female inspectors ... shall not be performed in a merely perfunctory manner, the wishes of the various labor bodies should be consulted in making such appointments.' A letter from Hope Assembly, No 7629 (ladies), of Toronto, supported the motion, and a 'somewhat irregular discussion followed,' dealing mainly with the shortcomings of factory inspection generally. Someone got the debate back on the track by remarking that the appointment of a female inspector was necessary 'owing to the many delicate questions that required to be asked female workers.' One delegate mentioned 'alleged slanderous statements reflecting upon the morality of certain manufacturing establishments in Montreal. Many people, from a sense of mistaken modesty, did not believe in exposing such a state of affairs. If such existed, he held that they should be thrown open to public scrutiny. The women themselves were not wholly responsible for their downfall, but it lay principally with the proprietors, who paid them such a meagre allowance as to almost compel the sacrifice of virtue. There were potent reasons why female inspectors should be appointed, and only those who were qualified to fill the positions by experience gained as wage earners.' The resolution carried unanimously.

The congress had its first woman delegate in 1888: Mrs Elizabeth Wright, LA 4650, St Thomas. In 1889 it had its second, Miss Emma Witt, DA 125, Toronto. She moved the 1888 resolution at the 1889 convention: 'There were many instances in which a woman among women would insist upon a closer observance of the law than would ever suggest itself to a man. She would ... be in a position to make inquiries and obtain information which is now practically a closed book. Notwithstanding the limitation of hours which Parliament had imposed ... in Toronto at any rate there were a large number of children employed under age, and this was specially a case in which the services of a woman would be of the utmost value.' The resolution carried.

The resolution was repeated in 1890, 1891, and 1892. In 1891 and 1892 there were resolutions asking for the appointment of both male and female factory inspectors in Quebec outside the cities. In 1896 the president observed that 'This body owes a deep debt of gratitude to ... Her Excellency Lady Aberdeen, to whose energetic efforts we owe that reform so long sought for by this body: The appointment of Female Factory Inspectors in the interests of women workers in the Province of Quebec.' By 1901 the women inspectors were a fact; the next step was to get them the same pay as their male colleagues. The convention noted that, though women inspectors' work was 'as important and onerous as that of the Male Inspector, her salary [was] only one-half that paid to her male colleague,' and demanded equal pay.

The 1883 convention asked for the establishment of dominion and provincial bureaux of labour statistics. The 1889 convention asked for provincial bureaux. In 1896 the congress asked the dominion, the provinces, and the municipalities 'to aid and establish as soon as possible, in all cities of the Dominion, Labor and Statistical Bureaus, for the benefit of the workingmen at large.'

Nowadays, temperance is about the last thing any labour convention would be expected to pass resolutions on. It was not always so. The 1883 convention unanimously resolved that 'any practical legislation tending to reduce the consumption of intoxicating liquor will meet with the hearty approval of this Congress,' and several delegates 'dwelt strongly upon the evils of drunkenness.' In 1886 delegates from the prohibitionist organization, the Dominion Alliance, addressed the convention at length and were warmly received; the 1883 resolution was repeated (with the substitution of 'effort' for 'legislation'); the congress appointed a delegation to confer with the Alliance for 'closer relations ... on all matters looking to the elevation of the

working classes, and adequate representation of their interests in our legislatures;'
and the congress executive was empowered to co-operate with the alliance 'in their
respective localities.' In 1887 a motion for a plebiscite on prohibition was tabled. In
1888 the convention repeated the 1886 temperance resolution, defeating a prohibition amendment. In 1889 a delegation from the alliance's Quebec branch addressed
the convention, which passed a resolution calling on all labour organizations 'to use
their influence ... [in] promoting and encouraging temperance.' In 1890 the WCTU
sent a fervid telegram of greetings, urging the convention to declare for woman
suffrage and to say a word in favor of temperance to 'cheer the women who work for
God, Home and humanity.' The convention ignored the woman suffrage part, and
turned down prohibition, 30 to 23. The question was then ignored till 1898, when
Mr Small, seconded by Mr Large, moved a prohibition resolution, which was
tabled.

The 1883 convention asked the Ontario legislature to adopt the Torrens system of
land transfer. In 1886 it endorsed the system. In 1889 it asked to have it applied in
Quebec.

Employers' liability came next in 1883. The convention wanted the dominion
government to 'assimilate the law of Canada with that of Great Britain.' By 1886
Ontario had passed an act; but, according to the congress, it contained a provision
depriving some workers of its full benefits. This the convention wanted wiped out at
the end of a year. In 1887 it asked for a dominion act, in 1889 for provincial acts,
and in 1890 for a dominion act or, failing that, provincial acts in all the provinces. In
1892 and 1893 it asked for a Quebec act modelled on the Ontario one.

The 1883 convention left the calling of a new one to the Toronto council. That
body considered calling a convention in 1884 but decided against it. The legislative
committee recommended instead that the council should 'rather take up with energy
those questions passed at the last congress and which are laying dormant up to the
present time,' notably 'the emportation of Chinese cooly labor.' The council also
invited the British Trades Union Congress to hold its next meeting in Toronto.[5]

The question of a second convention came up again in the spring of 1886, and the
council issued the call in July, specifying representation on the same basis as in
1883. It was expected that the attendance would be much larger, delegates being
expected as far east as Quebec City.[6]

The number of delegates was indeed much larger: 109 against 48; and there was
1 delegate from Quebec City. Local central bodies had eight delegates: Toronto and
Hamilton three each, Oshawa and St Thomas one each. Toronto (including Parkdale) had also forty delegates from the Knights of Labor (three from DA 125, the
rest from sixteen LAs) and sixteen from trade unions (three Typos, two Bricklayers,
two Cigar Makers, one American Carpenters, three Builders' Labourers, two

Painters, one each from the Stonecutters, the Plasterers, and the Lathers). Hamilton had five delegates from three LAs, and three from Builders' Labourers No 3. St Thomas had three delegates from three LAs; London five, from four LAs; Oshawa three, from two LAs; Guelph three, from two LAs; St Catharines three, from LA 2056; Belleville three, from LA 2900; Merritton three, from LA 5933; Thorold three, from LA 6798; Ottawa two from LA 5222, and one from the Plumbers and Steamfitters; Uxbridge two, from LA 5331; Windsor two, from LA 3281; Port Perry, Amherstburg, Port Dalhousie, and Ingersoll one each, all from LAs. Of the 109 delegates, 81 were from the Knights, 8 from international unions, 8 from local central bodies, and 12 from local or regional unions. The predominance of the Knights is unmistakable, especially as several of the delegates from central bodies were almost certainly Knights. So is the much wider distribution of the delegates across Ontario, compared with 1883: 17 places, against 5, and from Ottawa to Windsor, instead of Belleville to St Catharines. Toronto, however, still had an impressive majority of the total.

March again opened the convention. The standing orders committee again drew up an agenda, this time of 10 items. Five were repeated from 1883: manhood suffrage, proportional representation, the property qualification for aldermen, the Single Tax, and the Torrens system of land transfer. The new ones were political action, amendments to the municipal acts, publication of municipal assessment lists, raising the income tax exemption from $400 to $800, and abolition of the municipal income tax.

The most important and durable of these was political action. The resolution on this declared that 'the working classes of this Dominion will never be properly represented in Parliament or receive justice in the legislation of this country until they are represented by men of their own class and opinion,' and called on the delegates to 'pledge themselves to use their utmost endeavors to bring out candidates at the ensuing Local and Dominion elections.' Michael O'Halloran, the seconder, strongly advocated 'the formation of a third party on a Labor Platform.' John Nott supported the motion: 'When there was nothing to divide the parties he voted Conservative, but he wanted to vote for men who would give labor fair consideration ... The parties should be given to understand that the workingmen would no longer be bound by party ties in view of their own interests. He advocated the casting of blank ballots ... which would show their strength, and serve as a protest against the existing state of things.' O'Donoghue 'thought they would waste time by discussing the matter in the present shape,' and moved to refer it to a special committee to report, 'with a view to political action.' The amendment carried. The special committee reported back the original resolution almost word for word, except for the significant addition of the words 'where practicable.' George Wrigley and Bryan Lynch moved to add: 'And where it is not deemed advisable to nominate labor candidates ... all labor organizations be advised to act unitedly in support of the candidate who pledges himself to vote for most of the planks of the platform of this Congress.'

This produced a long argument. Some delegates wanted a straight platform. Some took Parnell as an example. One emphasized the expected union with the farmers. One said they should vote for the best candidate in the field. The amendment carried, and the resolution as amended.

The 1887 convention brought the 1886 committee's resolution, the Wrigley amendment, and a subamendment to add the words, 'Where the past record of the candidate is not in direct opposition to his pledge.' After a lively discussion, the subamendment and the amendment were both defeated, and the original motion adopted unanimously.

In 1889 two Montreal Knights moved for a committee to consider forming an independent political party, with a platform 'based upon the inalienable right of man to life, liberty, and the pursuit of happiness.' This echo of 1776 won some support. Patrick Jobin (Quebec) wanted 'an independent party which would make it fashionable to be honest ... The old parties ... always appealed, not to intelligence but to ignorance. The people put them in, and then when the people wanted anything they had to go ... with humble petitions ... There was not a labor candidate in the Legislature in Quebec. There were lawyers, doctors, and merchants. These men were rich.' William Darlington (Montreal) said 'They had been made tools of by both parties. This third party would be the lever which would compel the carrying out of ... reform ... Thousands of good men had left ... labor societies because they were sick, sore and tired of coquetting with both parties, who cared nothing for their interests.' Urbain Lafontaine favoured a third party, but not yet: they would first have to find 'honest men.' M.H. Brennan (Montreal) said the one labour MP had never uttered a word for labour. A.T. Lépine, MP, warmly defended his course as a representative of 'all classes ... not simply the working classes,' and strongly opposed a third party. S. St Pierre (Montreal Typos) said a third party could accomplish nothing without a majority, and if there was a majority, there was no need for a third party. They should support 'measures ... rather than parties ... The mass of the people were not intelligent enough to thoroughly appreciate the great political questions of the day, and to attempt to break down the existing parties would be madness.' Jury said that if the workingmen were honest, they could elect their men, but they voted as Catholics, Protestants, and so forth, not labour men; and when a man got in he became simply a party member. An amendment recommending action along the lines of the 1887 resolution, and the main motion, were both carried.

In 1890 Bartley (Vancouver) moved for a committee to consider framing a labour platform for the dominion election. An amendment to make the report of the convention the platform carried. In 1892 two Quebec delegates moved that the congress consider forming a labour party, and this carried.

In 1893 the executive committee reported that it had taken part in a meeting with representatives of the Patrons of Industry, the Dominion Grange (both farmers' organizations), DA 125, the Toronto Trades and Labor Council, and the Social Problems Conference, which had agreed on a platform. The planks were reservation of public lands for the actual settler; purity of administration and absolute independence of Parliament; rigid economy in every department of the public service; simplification of laws and general reduction in the machinery of government; abolition of the Senate; effectual legislation to protect labour from monopolies; prohibition of bonusing of railways; preparation of dominion and provincial lists by municipal officers. This smacks rather of the farm than of the factory. It probably reflects both the survival of the old individualism in the unions, and the necessity of winning the support of the farmers, who were, of course, far more numerous and influential.[7]

A change seems to have set in with the decline in the influence of the Knights of Labor. In 1894 Beales, in his presidential address, said: 'It behoves us to again and again knock at [the dominion government's] doors until our just and reasonable demands are granted.' The committee on this address disagreed strongly: 'The time has come to stop knocking at the Government doors and ... to take such independent political action as will leave the doors open to us all the time through the formation of an independent labor party.' O'Donoghue moved to strike this out and concur in the president's recommendation; and this carried.

In 1895 there was a reaction. A resolution approved various trades and labour councils' actions in 'fostering and encouraging the spirit of independent political action on the part of the toiling class,' and hoped that 'the day is not far distant when organized labor will go to the polls in one compact body in support of men from its own ranks.' The committee on the president's address and executive committee's report said 'labor organizations should now unite for independent political action,' and this carried.

In 1897 there was a resolution 'that this Congress is strongly impressed with the urgent desirability of labor being directly represented in our Legislative halls, and urges the importance of labor candidates being nominated in all electoral districts where a possibility exists of securing their election.'

By 1899 the congress had again tired of knocking vainly at government doors, and passed the Flett-Wilkes resolution for a referendum of the affiliates on independent political action.

Forty-three organizations replied: 7 councils, 32 international local unions, 2 Congress FLUs, and 2 purely local unions. Their total membership was 2932. Of these, 1424 voted yes, 167 no, and 1341 did not vote at all. Of the councils (400 members), 59 per cent did not vote at all, 33 voted yes. Of the international unions (2206), over 40 per cent did not vote and over half voted yes. In Ontario, for all organizations, 43 per cent did not vote, and just over half voted yes; in British Columbia, less than 40 per cent did not vote, and almost 60 per cent voted yes. Victoria was the only council where all members voted (13 yes, 1 no). In Toronto, Hamilton, Montreal Federated, and Revelstoke, the majority did not vote. Montreal voted no, 14 to 8. The 4 Ontario councils voted yes, 101 to 16, the two British Columbia councils voted yes, 23 to 1.

One international union local, the Winnipeg Bricklayers (175 members), did not vote at all. The rest, with 2031 members, showed a marked contrast to the councils: less than 39 per cent not voting, and almost 55 per cent voting yes. In the building trades, almost 51 per cent did not vote, and just over 43 per cent voted yes. In the metal trades less than 25 per cent failed to vote, and almost 74 per cent voted yes. Of the Typos, who had 668 members (more than either the building trades or the metal trades), 45 per cent did not vote, and almost 41 per cent voted yes. The other 6 international locals, with 290 members, showed 34 per cent not voting, and 65 per cent yes.

Of the 4 purely local unions' 326 members, 153 did not vote and 173 voted yes.

The report of the vote was referred to the committee on the president's address. Not surprisingly, it reported that it did not feel justified in making any recommendation. Mortimer (Winnipeg council) and Flett promptly moved an amendment, that the result of the vote was 'of sufficient strength to justify the Congress in taking such steps as may be deemed advisable to further the progress of such action.' This carried, 38 to 22.

Analysis of this vote is interesting. Of the nine local councils represented, seven voted for. Montreal Federated split: two for, one not voting. Montreal Central also split: two against, one not voting. Of the nineteen delegates from councils, fifteen voted for, two against, and two did not vote.

Delegates from international unions numbered thirty-two, from twenty-four locals and the Toronto Printing Trades Council. The Printing Trades Council and delegates from fifteen locals voted solidly for, delegates from four locals solidly against. The Ottawa Typos split, one for, one against, one not voting. Delegates from four other locals did not vote.

Purely local unions were split. The Ottawa Builders' Labourers and the Nanaimo Miners voted for, the Montreal Coopers and the Charlottetown and Moncton FLUs against.

The Knights of Labor voted heavily against. Their one Toronto delegate (O'Donoghue) and nine of their ten Montreal voted against; the other Montreal delegate and two from Quebec City did not vote.

Toronto voted seven for, two against, one abstaining; Ottawa, ten, one, three; Montreal eleven, sixteen, three. Ontario voted twenty-three, three, four; Quebec thirteen, sixteen, five. Of the French-Canadians, nine voted for, seven against, four abstained.

The opponents of the Mortimer-Flett amendment evidently took their defeat as decisive, for next day two of them moved 'that no candidate other than a member of organized labor for at least a year be selected or endorsed by this Congress'; and this carried. So did a motion that, since Labour candidates were generally unable to bear the expense of an election the Congress should issue a circular urging affiliates to contribute money 'when in their opinion such candidates are members of organizations in good standing with this Congress and ... [have] received a sufficient endorsation by organizations in good standing.'

The 1900 convention also formally asked the Nanaimo Miners Union to take the initiative in nominating Ralph Smith for the House of Commons. In 1901 the executive committee's report expressed satisfaction at Smith's election and the re-election of A.W. Puttee (Winnipeg) to the House of Commons.

The municipal act amendment which the 1886 convention wanted was to abolish voting 'in other wards than that in which the voter resides.' This was repeated in 1887. Publication of municipal assessment rolls was demanded in 1886, on the ground that some business men were getting assessments so low as to enable them to evade their due share of taxes. The demand was repeated in 1887, 1888, and 1889.

On the municipal income tax, we have already noted the resolution passed in 1886. In 1888 the convention unanimously asked the Ontario legislature to abolish all personal taxes.

Part way through its second day, the 1886 convention had finished its agenda. But it was far from finishing its work. It proceeded to pass a large number of resolutions.

First, prison labour: the Toronto council had a resolution already placed before the provincial government, which had promptly asked what it would substitute for the existing system. The council had promised to propose a scheme, and wanted suggestions. It got them: send the convicts to the Northwest and the wild lands of Ontario to open up the country; set them to work breaking stones on the country roads; have them make goods for the inmates of public charitable institutions. Each of these provoked objection. So the matter was referred to a committee, which reported that 'this Congress disputes the right of Governments to sell convict labor, and place it in competition with the labor of honest workingmen, and ... would recommend that, where it is not deemed advisable to keep [the convicts] in solitary confinement, they be profitably employed ... on public works ... [or] in new countries, improving the lands and roads for intending settlers.' This pleased no one. It was replaced by a terse 'protest against the employment of prison labor in any way by which it will come into competition with free labor.'

This was repeated in 1887, with two additions: that governments should not sell convict labour to contractors at rates which would compete with free labour, and that prison-made goods should be plainly marked.

From 1889 to 1892 the convention was concerned with labour not only in prisons, but also in religious institutions. In 1889 it asked that the products should be used only for the immediate use of such institutions, and should not receive government grants or subsidies. In 1890 it wanted reformatories put only in the country, to teach agriculture, and the inmates to be so employed that their products should enter as little as possible into competition with free labour. In 1891 it wanted all prison products exported. In 1892 it appointed a committee to look into the abolition of convict labour in reform schools.

In 1892 it appointed also a second committee, to report on the state account system. This reported in favour of giving prisoners work; against selling their labour on contract; against the government providing machinery, and private interests the raw materials, with the State getting payment for the product; and for the state furnishing both machinery and materials and selling the products in the open market. It also favoured giving the prisoners pay, to be handed to them on their release or given to their families in case of need. The convention adopted the report.

In 1893 the convention asked for prohibition of the manufacture of tinware in provincial prisons or private reformatories getting provincial grants. In 1895 it requested labelling of all prison products. In 1896 it wanted the Montreal reformatory to drop apprenticeship in printing and teach the inmates farm work. In 1897 a special committee reported against manufacturing in prisons products to be sold in competition with free labour; in favour of more education for prisoners; for using prisoners to build roads, clear lands, and so forth; and against using them to make a variety of products for government use. The last part was struck out, the rest adopted.

In 1897 the convention refused to adopt the cumulative sentence system for offenders, and the indeterminate sentence and parole system for first offenders. It asked provincial governments to discourage production of prison goods for the open market; commended the congress executive's efforts to get labour-saving machinery out of the prisons; and demanded the labelling of all prison-made goods. It also asked the executive to instruct all labour organizations to work for the defeat of the governments which did not take steps to abolish prison labour, and put a prison labour plank into its platform. In 1901 and 1902, it again asked for the prison-made label.

Weekly payment of wages in cash was another hardy perennial: the Congress asked for it in 1886–87, 1889–91, 1894 (for Quebec), 1895, 1897, 1900, and 1902.

So was support of the co-operative movement: 1886, 1887, 1893, and 1900 (twice).

The next business was endorsation of the label of the Knights of Labor Shoe and Leather Workers Council. An attempt to get the Cigar Makers International Union label endorsed raised the rival claims of the CMIU and the Knights; the convention backed the CMIU label as *a* (not the only) reliable guarantee of union-made cigars. In 1888, after noting the royal commission's revelations of conditions in the cigar factories, it passed two similar resolutions. In 1889, 1890, 1892, 1893, 1895, 1896, 1897, and 1902, it endorsed union labels generally, sometimes also mentioning particular unions. In 1894, 1896, 1897, 1898, and 1899, it demanded union label legislation. In 1898 it put the label into the platform of principles. In 1900, the Commons having passed the Toronto council's Union Label Bill, the convention urged the executive to direct its energy to getting the measure through the Senate.[8]

The next item in 1886 was an exhortation to district assemblies or trades and labour councils represented at the convention to get up 'a course of winter lectures in their respective districts, for the purpose of improving the moral and mental condition of the working classes, so as to better qualify them for the discharge of their increased and important duties as citizens.'

The next resolution, for the abolition of the Senate, was repeated in 1887 and 1893, and in 1898 embodied in the platform of principles. In 1886 it provoked an amendment, to make the Senate elective, but, after a series of blistering speeches by the abolitionists, this was defeated by a large majority.

Then came monetary reform. In 1886 and 1887, the convention demanded that the dominion government issue all money; adding, in 1887, that it stop granting charters to banks. In 1888 it repeated the 1886 resolution, adding that the volume of money should be sufficient to meet the needs of the country, and that public works should be financed by such money. In 1890 it again objected to the issue of bank charters. The congress in 1891 repeated the 1888 resolution in more elaborate form; in 1893, called for revocation of all bank charters; in 1895, moved a further variant of 1888; in 1899, added a demand for a national bank.

A series of resolutions (1886–89, 1896) demanded that yellow-dog contracts (contracts which obliged an employee not to belong to a union) be outlawed.

The next 1886 subject was the contract system on public works. The congress demanded that these be 'carried on under the direct supervision of the National, Provincial and Municipal Governments, thus saving the people that large proportion of public revenue now absorbed by middlemen and non-producers of the capitalistic class.' This was repeated in 1887, 1888, and 1890. In 1891 the convention, noting that recent investigations by committees of the Senate and the House of

Commons (into the McGreevy and Baie des Chaleurs Railway scandals) had 'demonstrated that the system of constructing public works by contract is the cause of flagrant and deplorable corruption, resulting in enormously increasing the cost of such works,' demanded that the contract system be abandoned in favour of doing the jobs by day labour. In 1892 it specifically applied this to Quebec, in 1897 to the dominion. In 1898 it again asked for it on both dominion and provincial works, and put it into the platform of principles.

Resolutions on railway safety legislation failed in 1886 and 1887, but passed in 1888, 1889, 1892, 1893, 1896, and 1902. Resolutions on wage increases for ICR workers were passed in 1890 and 1902, and for an eight-hour day on government railways in 1901. In 1895 the congress wanted railway workers to have the right to take legal action to recover wages after three months of arrears.

In 1896 the Railway Employees' legislative board (represented for the only time) asked support for no less than 11 demands, including not only various safety measures but also legislation making wages a first lien on all railway contracts and to prevent arrears on employees' pay; submission of all railway rules to the REB before approval by the government; dominion adoption of the Ontario Arbitration and Conciliation Act; protection against partisan dismissals from the ICR; higher pay for ICR trackmen and telegraphers; and, grand climax, appointment of E. Williams (BLE) to the Senate. The committee on the president's address and the executive's report said the congress had already approved most of the proposals and recommended that the convention give impartial consideration to two specific safety bills, the placing of two men on electric locomotives, the submission of railway rules to the REB, and the two proposals on the ICR. It said it esteemed Williams, and thought that while the Senate existed labour should be represented in it, but declined to support any individual.

In 1897 O'Donoghue and March vainly tried to get a special committee on the Toronto Grand Trunk freight handlers' grievances. Another motion, to have the executive, with the Running Trades Brotherhoods, see the minister of railways and canals about a seniority system on the ICR, passed.

The 1886 and 1887 conventions demanded a dominion act prohibiting 'armed and uniformed private detectives or detective bodies.' The 1890, 1891, and 1892 sessions simply demanded prohibition of private detective agencies of any kind.

Three 1886 resolutions of some interest were tabled: one deploring the dissension between the Knights of Labor and the trade unions, urging them to remove all causes for it, and recognizing 'the right that both bodies have in the elevation of labor'; the second, urging the Toronto building trades to amalgamate; the third, to have all commissions of inquiry made up of MPs or MLAs, so that the public could hold them accountable for the reports. The convention wanted to have a variety of public officials, from the governor-general to sheriffs, elected by popular vote. The 1887 convention also wanted to abolish the lieutenant-governorships. A fresh motion for the election of the governor-general carried, in 1890, by 89 to 14; but in 1895 the convention tabled a motion to abolish the lieutenant-governorships and in 1897 one for a Canadian governor-general.

The 1887 convention was a much smaller affair (45 delegates), partly, no doubt, because it was held in Hamilton. It had no delegate from outside Ontario. The Toronto council had three delegates, Brantford and Oshawa one each. Toronto had also twelve delegates from the Knights of Labor (three from DA 125, nine from eight LAs), and nine from trade unions (three from the Builders' Labourers, two each from the Typos, and the Plasterers, one each from the Amalgamated Carpenters and the Painters). Hamilton, curiously, had only seven delegates: four from three LAs, two from the Builders' Labourers, and one from the Typos. St Catharines had four: one from DA 207, two from LA 2056, one from LA 7025. London had one from LA 3558, Merritton one from LA 5933, Thorold one from LA 6798, Amherstburg one from LA 4139, Port Dalhousie one from LA 2513, St Thomas one from LA 4069, Uxbridge one from LA 5331, and Guelph one from LA 2980. Of the forty-five delegates, twenty-eight were from the Knights, four from international unions, five from local central bodies, and eight from local or regional unions. The predominance of the Knights is again unmistakable. Only ten places were represented, and none east of Toronto and Uxbridge. Toronto had a bare majority of the total.

The 1887 convention abandoned any attempt to draw up an agenda, and from then on, the delegates always faced a lush jungle of resolutions, old and new.

This convention, besides the resolutions already noted, passed one favouring government night schools (with which it coupled shorter hours). It also urged 'all organized bodies to form in all localities night schools or assemblies of male children of 14 years and upwards, to be instructed in the principles of Labor progress and all questions necessary to enable them to take their places when of age in the Labor Party.'

Both the 1887 and 1888 conventions voted for stronger patent laws, and for drastic amendment of the debt-collection laws. (In 1887 Garson and J.T. Carey tried, unsuccessfully, to have such laws abolished.)

The 1887 convention passed the first of many resolutions on public education, asking Ontario to enforce its compulsory education law. In 1888 it asked Ontario school boards to appoint truant officers. In 1889 it voted for free schools in Quebec, similar to those in Ontario. In 1890 it voted for free and compulsory education in all provinces. In 1892 it tabled a motion for free and compulsory denominational education in Quebec, but demanded free schools and free school books, and in 1893 voted for free, though not compulsory, education in that province. In 1895 it refused to come out for a 'free, compulsory and non-sectarian school for all classes.' In 1898 it put compulsory education into its platform of principles, and demanded free school books and supplies, in all provinces.

The congress favoured technical education (science classes in 1887, and technical education in 1888 and 1889) and agricultural courses (1898), but strongly opposed manual training, which it denounced in 1888, 1889, 1896, and 1900. It reaffirmed its support of technical education in 1900 and 1901. The unions seem to have felt that manual training would produce 'bunglers ... willing to work at low wages' (a pool of strikebreakers), while technical education would help improve craftsmen's skills.

Resolutions in favour of prevailing (later union) wage rates in public contracts were passed in every year from 1887 to 1895 inclusive; and in 1898 the convention listened to a long and learned oration on the subject by J.S. Ewart, QC.

In 1887 also came the first of the resolutions on inspection of stationary engines and boilers, repeated in 1888, 1889, and 1890, with variations in 1895, 1896, 1897, and 1898.

The 1886–89 conventions asked for the immediate appointment of the necessary officers to give effect to the Trade Unions Act of 1872, so that labour organizations could incorporate under its protection. In 1891 and 1892, the congress asked the provincial legislatures to amend their incorporation laws 'so as to facilitate the incorporation of trades' unions and labor societies,' which it thought entitled to equal recognition with any other body. The obstacle was the high fees charged. It repeated the demand for Ontario in 1892 and for Quebec in 1893 and 1894.

In 1887 and 1888, the congress called for dominion ownership of railways and telegraphs and municipal ownership of gas, telephones, ferries, and street railways. In 1890 telephones were transferred to the dominion list; in 1891, electric light and water works to the municipal. In 1892 the convention voted for municipal ownership of franchises, monopolies, and public utilities, and for a postal telegraph system; in 1893 the main resolution of 1892 was reaffirmed. In 1897 there were two resolutions for public ownership of the Yukon gold claims. In 1898 public ownership of all franchises, such as railways, telegraphs, and lighting, went into the platform of principles.

The 1887 and 1888 conventions declared for government life assurance; and in 1893 the congress asked the dominion to set up a system of state insurance to be directly connected with the post office savings department.

The 1887 convention adopted the first of the series of resolutions againstd moonlighting by government employees, passed in three succeeding years and again in 1892.

The 1887 convention also called for a regular apprenticeship system, in all trades where this was practicable. This was repeated in 1888 and 1889.

In 1887, 1890, 1891, and 1892, the congress asked for amendments to the Ontario Mechanics' Lien Act; in 1889, for lien acts in all provinces; in 1892 and 1893, for a Quebec act.

The 1888 convention in London, was another small, purely Ontario, affair, with forty-one delegates from eight places, from Cornwall to St Thomas. The Toronto and London councils had three delegates each. The Knights of Labor had twenty-one: three from DA 125, one from DA 207, seven from six Toronto LAS (including Parkdale), three from three Hamilton LAS, two from two in St Catharines, one each from London, St Thomas, Stratford, Clinton, and Cornwall. Trade unions had fourteen delegates: five from the Typos (three Toronto, one Hamilton, one London), three from the Bricklayers (Toronto), one from the ASCJ (Toronto), one from the Molders (London), one from the Painters (Toronto), and three from the Builders' Labourers (Toronto). Again, there was a majority of Knights, and a majority from Toronto. London, the host city, sent only six delegates.

This convention asked the dominion to amend the conspiracy laws 'to prevent their application to labor disputes, where no actual damage is done to person or property.' In 1889 the congress asked for a specific amendment to prevent prosecution for refusing to work for an employer, or doing or causing to be done any act for the purpose of a trade combination, unless such act was punishable by statute.

The 1888 convention passed a resolution for inspectors of scaffolding in Ontario. In the years 1889–93, this was generalized. In 1894 and 1901, it was asked specifically for Quebec.

At the 1883 convention, John Rooney had wanted the congress to protest against Sunday labour. But nothing happened till 1888, when the convention passed, unanimously, its first resolution on the subject, most emphatically condemning the dominion government for opening canals on Sunday, 'thereby compelling lock-tenders and sailors to work during a time they should be resting to prepare for the following week's work.' Later the same day the convention unanimously instructed the executive to stir the dominion government against railway companies which were flagrantly violating 'laws against Sabbath desecration.'

Two years later came the first demand for legislation: 'a Sunday observance law, compelling all employers to close their factories and workshops during ... the Sabbath, except in cases of absolutely needed repairs.'

In 1894 an attempt to ask the provinces to authorize Sunday streetcars produced a counter-resolution for acts to prohibit any Sunday traffic not shown to be absolutely necessary. This carried.

In 1897 O'Donoghue and March carried a strong resolution against Sunday work of any kind: 'The labor people demand ... as a right, that they should have the Sabbath for their own use ... [therefore] we urge upon our members to continue their warfare against Sunday work, remembering that ... any time six men work Sunday they are taking the bread out of the mouth of one fellow workman.'

Next year there was an instruction to the British Columbia executive to ask the province to ban Sunday work in the metal mines.

In 1899 the congress reaffirmed its stand for one day's rest in seven and instructed all its affiliates to co-operate with any and all associations to get legislation for the purpose.

The 1901 convention received a deputation from the Lord's Day Alliance, whose field secretary urged the Congress to join hands with the alliance 'in an effort to preserve the Sabbath.' He received a unanimous vote of thanks, and next day the convention appointed a standing committee to act with the alliance.

In 1902 there was another alliance delegation, whose spokesman thanked the labour organizations for the help they had given, advocated a Saturday half-holiday, and looked forward to a five-day week.

In 1888, also, the congress asked for a stringent law to prevent adulteration of food and potable liquors. In 1899 it wanted the date clearly placed on all canned goods.

The last two 1888 resolutions of importance were for an alien contract labour act, and for establishment of a Labour Day as a national holiday.

The alien contract labour question came up again in 1890, 1891, 1892, and 1895. By 1898, an act had been passed, but the congress found it entirely unsatisfactory and inoperative, and pressed for a better. In 1899 it complained that the act was not being enforced. By 1901 it had got several amendments, but wanted more.

The 1890 convention repeated the 1888 resolution on Labour Day. In 1892 and 1893 the congress specifically asked for the first Monday in September, which it got in 1894.

In 1889, for the first time, the convention met outside Ontario: in Montreal. This had a marked effect on its composition. The number of delegates more than doubled, to 83, and Quebec had nearly as many as Ontario: 38 to 45. Toronto, with 23 delegates, yielded first place to Montreal, with 30. Ottawa came third, with 11; Quebec City fourth, with 8. The Knights of Labor, with 40 delegates, though no longer a clear majority, remained by far the largest single group, the international unions mustering only 22 delegates. Delegates came from as far east as Quebec City and as far west as St Catharines: two places in Quebec, seven in Ontario. Five councils sent twelve delegates: Toronto, Montreal and St Catharines three each, Ottawa two, Hamilton one. Of the Knights' delegates, DA 125, DA 236 (Uxbridge), and sub-DAS 1 and 2 (Montreal) sent three each, DA 207 one, LA 7628 (Montreal) and LA 10123 (Lévis) three each, LA 4003 (Quebec) two; eleven other Montreal LAS, three Toronto, three Quebec, one Ottawa, and one Cornwall one each. The Typos had three from Toronto, three from Ottawa, two from each of the Montreal locals, one from Hamilton and one from London, a total of twelve. The Pressmen had one (Ottawa). The Bricklayers had three (one Toronto, two Ottawa), the Plasterers the same (two Toronto, one Montreal), the Cigar Makers two (Montreal), the Bookbinders one (Ottawa). The Toronto Builders' Labourers had the largest single delegation (eight), the Ottawa Hackmen one.

The 1889 convention took up the question of calling in the militia in case of riots. It wanted the power vested solely in lieutenant-governors and mayors. The 1898 convention strongly protested sending 'special contingents to the Klondike or elsewhere to act as police or soldiers. The 1901 convention was so incensed by the use of the militia 'to aid monopolies against organized labor' in strikes in Vancouver, London, and Valleyfield that it urged all union men not to join 'military organizations excepting when the country is invaded.' In 1902 the committee on standing orders and resolutions seems to have recommended non-concurrence in a resolution to vest in the minister of militia alone the power of calling out the militia in civil disturbances, and the convention seems to have agreed; but it reaffirmed the 1901 resolution.

In 1889 also the congress urged safety measures on wharves and floating booms at Quebec and Lévis, with penalties for neglect, and compensation for accidents.

Another 1889 resolution complained of the great injury done to organized labour by the Combines Act, and instructed the executive to seek new legislation to give labour 'at least a legal status, of which it has been deprived by the Act referred to.' In 1890 the congress asked for outright repeal of clause 6, which, it alleged, virtually cancelled section 22 of the Trade Unions Act. In 1900 the convention asked to have the Combines Act applied to the American Tobacco Co.

The 1889 and 1892 conventions asked for a Quebec early closing law. The 1893 convention asked Ontario to make repeal of early closing by-laws as hard as adoption. In 1895, the convention asked all members of affiliated organizations to do their buying before six pm.

The 1890 convention, in Ottawa, had ninety delegates, and was notable for the appearance of the first representatives from outside Ontario and Quebec: two from Vancouver, one from Nanaimo. Ten Ontario towns and cities were represented, from Cornwall to Windsor, and two Quebec (Quebec City and Montreal). There were fifteen delegates from councils: three each from Toronto, Ottawa, and Quebec City, two each from Montreal and London, one each from Vancouver and Windsor. The Knights of Labor had thirty-six delegates: three each from DAs 125, 138, 207, 18 (Montreal), one each from DAs 19 (Montreal) and 20 (Quebec City), three from three Toronto LAs, three from three Ottawa LAs, four from four Montreal LAs, five from five in Quebec City, and one each from LAs in London, Windsor, St Thomas, St Catharines, Prescott, Cornwall, and Port Perry. The Knights were still the largest single group, for the international unions had only thirty delegates. The Typos had thirteen delegates: five Toronto, two Ottawa, one Vancouver, one London, one Quebec City, two from Montreal 176, one from Montreal 145. The United Carpenters had three (one each from Toronto, Ottawa, and London), Bricklayers three (two Ottawa, one St Thomas), Cigar Makers three (Montreal), Plasterers two (Toronto and Montreal), Molders two (Toronto and Smith's Falls), the Pressmen and the Bookbinders one each (both Ottawa), Boot and Shoe Workers one (London), Tailors one (Windsor). There were nine delegates from local or regional unions: three Ottawa General Labourers, two Toronto Builders' Labourers, one Ottawa Hackmen, one Quebec Leather Workers, one Montreal Carriage Makers, and, of course, the Nanaimo Miners and Mine Labourers. Toronto had 19 delegates, Montreal 18, Ottawa 17, Quebec City 11, London 6, St Thomas 5, St Catharines 4, Windsor 3, Vancouver 2, and Smith's Falls, Prescott, Cornwall, Port Perry, and Nanaimo 1 each.

Several new issues came up in 1890: the Quebec Master and Servants Act, the Ontario Landlord and Tenant Act, colonization, child labour, the tariff, ensuring that government printing went to Typo shops.

The Quebec and Lévis council moved to ask outright repeal of the Quebec Master and Servants Act of 1881, but the convention adopted an amendment to ask for modifications favourable to the working classes. In 1891 the convention asked to have the Quebec Municipal Act amended to place the power to regulate relations between masters and servants in the province, not the municipalities. In 1893 and 1894 it condemned 'the barbarous and inhuman ... Master and Servants Act as applied in ... [Montreal and Quebec] which permits a brutal employer to assault and inflict bodily punishment without affording any legal protection to the servant.' In 1896 it reverted to a demand for outright repeal.

An 1890 resolution called for further amendment of the Ontario Landlord and Tenant Act to render null and void any agreement intended to evade or prevent the carrying out of its provisions. This was repeated in 1891. In 1892, some amendments had been passed, and the congress wanted them repealed. It renewed this demand in 1893.

Another 1890 resolution asked Quebec, which was paying a bonus to 'strangers' to settle on Crown lands, to give the same privilege to 'workingmen of the province to facilitate their settlement on said lands.' The congress then asked the dominion to consider increasing the rural population by granting residents free lands within reasonable distance of a railway and advancing money at low interest to cover expenses for the first year of settlement. This was repeated in 1891. In 1892 came a motion to have the dominion and the provinces provide money to enable agricultural labourers and others now in Canada and suffering from enforced idleness to work on the land.

As the depression persisted the congress became more specific. In 1884 two Quebec City delegates moved to substitute for the existing system of immigration a system of dominion 'military agricultural schools, with the design of colonizing the still vacant public lands ... with farmers trained to their calling.' This was referred to a special committee, which reported a substitute: to abolish the existing system of immigration and replace it by 'a scheme of unemployed citizen colonization ... in specified sections of the Dominion under which direct financial assistance from Dominion resources could and would be advanced to each settler under certain defined and liberal conditions.' This carried.

In 1895 the president's address advocated this plan, and the 1896 resolution on immigration urged also a very liberal system of colonization. Another 1896 resolution endorsed Hon. E.H. Bronson's proposal to place the Ontario unemployed on the vacant lands of the province; a third reaffirmed the 1894 resolution.

The congress's repeated demands for compulsory education had implied restrictions on child labour. Now it began to be specific on this also. In 1890 2 Montreal Cigar Makers moved to prohibit boys under 16 and girls under 18 in cigar-making, since the trade was injurious to health. The convention referred the matter to the executive. Next year the motion added tobacco manufactories, and the convention added match factories and unanimously adopted the whole thing.

In 1891 the congress had asked Quebec to limit women's hours to nine per day in workshops, shops, and factories. In 1892 the motion added children, and an amendment changed nine to eight. The amended motion carried. In 1893 the convention asked Quebec to prohibit employment of children unable to read or write, except deaf and dumb children. It asked both the province and the city of Montreal to stop the employment of children under 14 on public works, because it was bad for the children's health and unfair competition to workingmen. It asked Quebec to prohibit children under 14 in factories from carrying or dragging loads of over 25 pounds, and women from carrying or dragging more than 160 pounds and from drawing trucks. It also wanted the factory inspector empowered to insist on factories keeping on file birth certificates or sworn declarations by parents 'to dispel all doubt as to the reports of parents who wish to set their children to work before ... the age required by law.'

In 1894 the congress asked Quebec to prohibit manual labour by children under 14; the dominion to make it an offence for parents to send such children to work in shops or factories; and Ontario to prohibit the employment of boys under 14.

In 1898 the congress wrote into its platform 'Abolition of child labor by children under 14 ... and of female labor in all branches of industrial life, such as mines, workshops, factories, etc.' In 1900 it returned to the question of proof of age, this time asking that certificates of age bear the signature of the last schoolteacher.

In 1890 the Cigar Makers wanted a higher tariff on cigars so that 'child or non-union labor on cigars may be lessened, or removed entirely.' An amendment leaving out the reference to child or non-union labour carried.

In 1891, however, the Cigar Makers carried their resolution, and the Typos one for a duty of three cents per square inch on all stereotype plates and matrices used in the printing or publishing of newspapers. This convention also passed a resolution that 'whenever the employers in any line attempt to destroy or prevent the organization of their employees, it is the duty of organized labor to use its power politically' to have the kind of goods concerned put on the free list. In 1893 an attempt to get a heavy tax on the exportation of saw logs failed. A motion that the incoming executive, in co-operation with the Patrons of Industry, ask to have coal oil, binder twine, wire for fencing, and agricultural implements placed on the free list was amended to a straight declaration for free trade.

In 1902 the convention, noting the Manufacturers' Association's declared intention of seeking an increase in the tariff, said the injury and oppression of industry came from 'the extortions to which labor is subjected by the holders of the land, the forests, the mines and other natural opportunities.' It therefore condemned any increase in the tariff and urged 'that taxes be removed as soon as possible to those values which now enable non-production to impoverish industry' – a neat blend of anti-protection and Single Tax.

Efforts to make sure that government printing went to Typo shops began in 1890. Identical resolutions covering the dominion, the provinces, and the municipalities were passed in 1890 and 1891, and in 1892 the convention added school boards. Coupled with this was a demand that Quebec stop subsidizing institutions which were competing in the printing trade and other industries. This also was adopted in 1890, 1891, 1892, and 1894.

An interesting anticipation of a later method of political action is an 1890 resolution urging members of affiliates to write personal letters to their MPS and MLAS to support or oppose pro-labour or anti-labour legislation.

A remarkable feature of the 1890 convention was the adoption of a report of a committee on census statistics. This requested the dominion government to ask detailed questions, more than 50 of them, on matters of interest to labour.

The 1891 convention, meeting first in the city council chamber of Quebec, and then in the legislative chamber, was, numerically, a come-down from 1890: only 56 delegates. There were eight from councils: three Toronto, two Montreal, three Quebec. There were thirty Knights of Labor: two from DA 125, three each from DAS 207 and 20, one from DA 19; one from each of nine Quebec City LAS, one from each of five in Montreal, one from each of two in Toronto, one each from Ottawa, St Catharines, Cornwall, Peterborough, and Hull. The international unions had eleven delegates: eight Typos (three Toronto, two Ottawa, two Quebec, one Montreal), one Cigar Makers, one Plasterers (both Montreal), one Railway Conductors (Quebec City). Local or regional unions had seven delegates: four from Quebec City, three (Builders' Labourers) from Toronto. Three places in Quebec were represented (Quebec City, Montreal, and Hull), and five in Ontario (from Cornwall to St Catharines). Quebec had 34 delegates; 25 (including 2 from Ottawa) had French names.

The 1891 convention asked the Quebec government to establish a free public library in Montreal. In 1892 the Quebec executive reported that the library formerly existing had been closed because of the withdrawal of the usual government grant. The convention resolved that the Quebec organizations should try to get the municipalities to set up libraries, and the province to pass any legislation necessary to empower them to do so.

The 1891 resolution on manhood suffrage in Quebec and Ontario municipal elections also asked for a legal half-holiday on election days (dominion, provincial, municipal; this had been asked for municipalities in the 1890 resolution on municipal elections), and compulsory voting. In 1893 the convention reiterated the demand for compulsory voting.

The 1892 convention, back in Toronto, had 77 delegates. Ontario had 51, Toronto alone 38. Only five other places in Ontario were represented: Hamilton (five delegates), St Catharines (four), Ottawa (two), and Guelph and Cornwall (one each). Montreal and Quebec City had 13 each. For the first time, the international unions had the largest single group: 28, to the Knights' 26. Of the Toronto delegates half were from international locals: three Typos, two Masons, two Plasterers, two Tailors, and one each from the ASCJ, United Carpenters, Painters, Plumbers, Stone Cutters, Machinists, Molders, Boot and Shoemakers, Cigar Makers, and Locomotive Firemen. Only three of Montreal's were international (one Typos, two Plasterers) and only two of Quebec City's (one Typo, one Railway Conductors). Of the twenty-six Knights, DAS 125, 207, and 18 supplied three each, DA 20 two, DA 19 one, six Toronto LAS one each, three Montreal LAS one each, three Quebec City's the same, and Guelph and Cornwall one each. The Toronto, Hamilton, Montreal, and Quebec councils sent three delegates each, Ottawa one. Local and regional unions had ten delegates: seven from Toronto, three from Quebec City.

The 1892 convention dealt with a number of new issues.

It wanted a two-cent-a-mile passenger rate on railways (repeated in 1893), and the postage on letters reduced to two cents (with the one-cent rate on drop letters restored). In 1893 it repeated the demand for a two-cent general rate, with a one-cent rate in cities. It asked for a whole day off for elections (repeated in 1893). It wanted the dominion to abolish all tolls on ship canals, and Quebec all tolls on public roads.

It passed a resolution asking all cities and towns to pass a plumbing by-law similar to Toronto's. In 1897 it wanted Ontario to compel all municipalities of over

12,000 to appoint qualified plumbing inspectors. In 1899 this was broadened to cover the whole country. In 1900 a similar resolution was defeated, but in 1901 a demand for plumbing inspectors in all cities of 30,000 and over carried.

Another safety measure demanded in 1892 was prohibition of the use of dynamite by any but experienced men. This was repeated in 1893 and 1900, with specific provision for inspectors and certificates of competency.

The 1892 convention also instructed all delegates to do their best to get their organizations to assist, morally and financially, the circulation of wholesome labour literature.

The same convention also launched into discussions of two of a series of questions which indicated a fresh wind of radicalism, political and economic, blowing.

First, it carried a resolution for the initiative and referendum, reaffirmed in 1893, 1897, 1898, and 1899 (when it went into the platform of principles).

Next, a resolution favouring complete autonomy, domestic and international, and the establishment and recognition of the independence of Canada, produced a motion to table the proposal and send it to the affiliates to vote on. A subamendment asking the dominion government to hold a plebiscite on 'maintenance of our present colonial status; Imperial Federation; Canadian independence; Political Union with the United States' carried, 25 to 23, after a long discussion by 17 delegates. A motion to send the resolutions to the affiliates to vote on then carried.

By 1893 no replies had been received. But a motion for a plebiscite on the 4 questions carried, an amendment declaring the congress preference for independence being defeated, 29 to 17.

The 1893 convention, in Montreal, had seventy-five delegates, of whom forty-one were from the Knights of Labor: three each from DAS 18 and 19, two from DA 20, one each from DA 6 (Ottawa) and 125; nineteen from seventeen Montreal LAs, four from three Quebec City, four from four Ottawa, one each from Toronto, St Catharines, Hull, and Prescott. There were twelve delegates from councils (three each from Toronto, Montreal, Quebec City, and Ottawa). International unions had fourteen: four Typos, four Cigar Makers, two Boot and Shoe Workers, and one each from the Railway Conductors, Machinists, Stone Cutters, and Woodworkers. Regional and local unions had eight. Eight places were represented: Montreal, Quebec City, Hull, Toronto, Hamilton, Ottawa, St Catharines, and Prescott. Of the fourteen international delegates eight were from Quebec, six from Ontario. The predominance of the Knights and of Quebec (51 delegates) was unmistakable. Of the 75 delegates 34 had French names.

At the 1893 convention the winds of change were still blowing strongly.

An amendment to the initiative and referendum resolution directed the executive to poll the affiliates on four questions: '(1) Are you in favor of the present industrial system? (2) Are you in favor of the so-called co-operative system of productive distribution and exchange? (3) Are you in favor of the communistic system of government? (4) Have you any other system better than the above to suggest?'

Only 5 organizations out of some 300 replied at all. The Toronto and Guelph Molders, and LAs 2966 (Ottawa) and 2676 (Hull), were dissatisfied with the present industrial system or existing conditions, but neither the Toronto Molders nor LA 2966 had any specific changes to suggest. The Guelph Molders were in favour of the co-operative system and also of the communistic system. The Hull LA favoured the co-operative system, and also 'a communal system of government with rigid laws against corruption.' The Toronto Bakers, silent on everything else, favoured the co-operative system.

The radicals in 1893 succeeded in carrying a resolution to abolish the high commissionership and one for abolition of the sweating system (on which the 1895 convention asked for a royal commission). But a resolution for state socialism was tabled. A less ambitious demand for inspection of electrical apparatus carried, and was reaffirmed in 1894 and 1899.

The 1894 convention, in Ottawa, had only 53 delegates, and was again restricted to Ontario and Quebec. The Knights of Labor had much the largest single group of delegates: 26. DAs 6, 18, and 19 sent three each, DA 20 two; four Montreal LAs sent four; three Ottawa, three; two Hull, three; two Toronto, two; two Quebec City two; Prescott one. The Toronto, Montreal and Quebec City councils sent three delegates each, London one. International locals sent ten: seven Typos, one Machinists, one Molders, one Bricklayers. Two of the international unions' delegates were from Quebec (as were seventeen of the Knights'). Seven places were represented: three in Quebec (Montreal, Quebec City, and Hull) and four in Ontario (Toronto, Ottawa, London, and Prescott). Ottawa had 15 delegates, Montreal 14, Quebec City and Toronto 9 each. Ontario had a bare majority, 27 to 26. Nineteen of the delegates had French names. The Quebec delegates were overwhelmingly Knights.

This convention produced a resolution in favour of death duties, which it called 'a step in the direction of justice' and wanted it followed by a progressive tax system for real and personal property.

The Socialists, undaunted by their 1893 defeat, tried again in 1894, this time avoiding the word 'socialism': 'Whereas, through the perversion of democracy to the ends of plutocracy, Labor is robbed of the wealth it alone produces, is denied the means of self-employment, and by compulsory idleness in wage slavery is ever deprived of the necessities of life; Resolved, that private property in the natural sources of production and the instruments of labor is the obvious cause of our economic servitude and political dependence.' The motion was lost on a vote.

More to the convention's taste was a motion asking for appointment of letter carriers in all cities of over 5000.

The 1895 convention, in London, was the smallest in the whole period: 39 delegates. Of these, one was from Winnipeg, eleven from Quebec (Quebec City six, Montreal five), the other twenty-seven from Ontario (London twelve, Toronto eight, Ottawa five, and Hamilton two.) There were sixteen delegates from councils (three each from London, Toronto, Ottawa, and Quebec City, two from Hamilton, one each from Montreal and Winnipeg), and two from the Toronto Building Trades Council. There were only six delegates from international locals: two Typos, and one each from the United Carpenters, the Bricklayers, the Machinists and the Cigar Makers. There were ten Knights: three from DA 18, one each from DAS 6 and 20, two from two Toronto LAS, two from three Quebec City LAS, one from Montreal. There were five delegates from local and regional unions.

This convention's resolutions did not, on the whole, break new ground.

In 1896 the Congress was back in Quebec City with 54 delegates: 38 from Quebec, 12 from Ontario, 1 from British Columbia, 1 from Manitoba , and 2 from the Railway Employees' Legislative Board of Canada. Exactly half the delegates had French names. The Knights of Labor had the largest single group: sixteen (three each from DAS 18 and 20, nine from seven Quebec City LAS, one from Montreal). There were fourteen from councils: three each from Quebec City, Montreal and Ottawa, two each from Toronto and Hamilton, one from Winnipeg. There were twelve from international bodies: seven Typos, two Woodworkers, two Railway Employees, one Cigar Makers. There were also 12 from local and regional unions. Eight places were represented: two in Quebec (Quebec City and Montreal), three in Ontario (Ottawa, Toronto, and Hamilton), two in British Columbia (Nanaimo and Vancouver), and one in Manitoba (Winnipeg).

The 1896 convention also contented itself in the main with resolutions on well worn subjects. It also saved time by giving a blanket endorsement to 'all acts done and measures passed upon at previous sessions ... not inconsistent with the action of the present session, and not dealt with in detail.' It specifically recorded its approval of the fast line of transatlantic steamers with the cautious amendment 'without any financial aid from Government funds.' It referred to the executive a motion to ask the dominion and Quebec governments 'to encourage the destruction of seals and porpoises in the River St. Lawrence, which destroy every year the small fish and thus starve the fishermen who have to be brought up with their families, into our cities.'

It asked the executive to watch the Copyright Bill, which would have allowed books to be printed from imported type or stereotyped plates, and to prepare an amendment to have the type set in Canada and the plates made from such type. In 1897 the convention drew the government's attention to the flagrant violation of the Copyright Act by the Presbyterian Hymnal Committee, and urged this as another reason for a new act. In 1898 it instructed the executive to present the congress's 1896 proposed amendment, this time to a new bill.

The 1897 convention, in Hamilton, had 51 delegates, including 1 each from Saint John and Winnipeg (councils) and 1 from Nanaimo (Miners). There were 34 from Ontario: Toronto, 15; Hamilton, 12; Ottawa, 5; and London, 2. From Quebec came 14: 7 each from Montreal and Quebec City. There were 16 from councils: 3 each from Toronto, Hamilton, Montreal, and Quebec City and 1 each from Ottawa, London, Winnipeg, and Saint John. The international union bodies' delegates, at twenty-four, formed the largest single group: seven Typos, two each from the Molders and the Cigar Makers, one each from the United Carpenters, Bricklayers, Tin Workers, Machinists, Horseshoers, Sheet Metal Workers, Flint Glass Workers, Tailors, Garment Workers, Street Railway Employees, the BLF, the Toronto Union Label League, and the London Blue Label League (cigars). One of the internationals' delegates came from Quebec, all the rest from Ontario. The Knights of Labor had dwindled to eight: three from DA 18, one from DA 20, one from Montreal LA 2436, one from Toronto LA 2305, two from two Quebec City LAS. There were three delegates from local or regional unions.

The only significant novelty in resolutions in 1897 was a recommendation to organizations 'in the several centres of population' to set up a legal fund for the purpose of 'asserting and ascertaining the value of such laws ... said or presumed to be for the protection of the working classes.'

In 1898, for the first time, the convention was held outside Ontario and Quebec: in Winnipeg. This cut attendance to 44. Winnipeg contributed 17, Ontario and Quebec 11 each, British Columbia 5. Montreal had seven delegates, Toronto six, Quebec City four, Ottawa three, Vancouver two, Hamilton, Victoria, Rossland, Nanaimo, and Rat Portage (Kenora) one each. The international unions sent the largest single group: 20. There were five Typos, two Bricklayers, and one each from the Pressmen, United Carpenters, ASCJ, Painters, Moulders, Machinists, BLE, BLF, BRT, Trackmen, Railway Carmen, Tailors, and Bakers. Councils had fourteen: three each from Winnipeg, Toronto, and Montreal, two from Vancouver, one each from Hamilton, Victoria, and Rossland. The Nanaimo Miners and the Rat Portage FLU (TLCC) had one delegate each; so had the Winnipeg Labor Party. There were only seven Knights of Labor: three from DA 18, one from DA 20, two from Quebec City LAS, one from Montreal LA 2436.

This convention concerned itself largely with reaffirming old stands and adopting the platform of principles.

The 1899 convention met in Montreal with 70 delegates: 39 from Quebec (29 from Montreal, 9 from Quebec City, 1 from St Hyacinthe). But there were some significant changes from 1896. The Knights of Labor were down from 16 to 13. The international unions up from 12 to 24, council delegates up from 14 to 21; and most of the increase was in councils dominated by international unions. TLCC FLUS, which in 1896 had no delegates, now had 5; local and regional unions had dropped from 12 to 7. In 1896, 16 of the 38 Quebec delegates had been Knights; now only 12 of 39.

12 had been from local or regional unions; now only 7. Of the 23 Ontario delegates, 10 came from Toronto, 9 from Ottawa, 3 from London, 1 from Hamilton. Winnipeg had three; Moncton two; Vancouver, Nanaimo, and Rossland one each. The largest single group of delegates was from the international unions: 24. There were eleven Typos, three Cigar Makers, two Machinists, two Street Railway Employees, one each from the United Carpenters, the Painters, the Plumbers, the Sheet Metal Workers, the Glass Blowers, and the Bakers. The next largest group, twenty-one, came from the councils: three from each of the two Montreal councils, three each from Toronto, Ottawa, London, and Quebec, one each from Hamilton, Winnipeg, and Rossland.

The 1899 convention passed almost no new resolutions.

In 1900 the congress met in Ottawa, with 67 delegates. Ontario had 29: 14 from Ottawa, 9 Toronto, 2 each Hamilton and London, 1 each Brantford and Brockville. Quebec had 32: Montreal 28, Quebec City 4. Winnipeg had two, Charlottetown, Moncton, Vancouver, and Nanaimo one each. The twenty-nine international union bodies' delegates were the largest group: nine Typos, one each from the Pressmen, Bookbinders, Bricklayers, Masons, Builders' Labourers, Stonecutters, Painters, Plumbers, Metal Polishers, and the Toronto Printing Trades Council; two each from the Molders and the Sheet Metal Workers; and three each from the Machinists and the Cigar Makers. There were nineteen from councils: three from each of two in Montreal, and from Toronto and Ottawa; two each from Hamilton and Quebec City; and one each from Winnipeg, London, and Brantford. There were fourteen Knights of Labor; three from DA 18, eight from seven Montreal LAs, two from two Quebec, one from Toronto. There were two from congress FLUs (Charlottetown and Moncton), and two from local or regional unions (Montreal and Nanaimo). All the provinces except Nova Scotia were represented, and thirteen cities and towns.

The 1900 convention also produced a few new resolutions.

The 1901 convention, in Brantford, showed a spectacular increase to 93 delegates, much the largest number since 1886. This time also international union bodies' delegates, at 38, were much the largest group: Typos, 11; Woodworkers, 4; Tailors, 3; Printing Trades, 3; United Carpenters, Sheet Metal Workers, Cigar Makers and AFL FLUs 2 each, Machinists, Broom Makers, Hotel and Restaurant, Barbers, Molders, Plumbers, Bookbinders, Bakers, and Street Railway 1 each. Trades and labour councils had 31 delegates: Toronto, Hamilton, Ottawa, London, Berlin, Quebec, and Montreal Central 3 each; Brantford, 2; Winnipeg, Brockville, Guelph, St Thomas, Nelson, Phoenix, Rossland, and Montreal Federated, 1 each. Of these, all but about half-a-dozen were probably international-dominated. There were two delegates from two Congress FLUs, and three from local and regional unions. The Knights of Labor numbered nineteen: three each from DAS 18 and 20, one from DA 180 (Toronto), six from four Montreal LAs, two from two Quebec, three from three

Toronto, one from Ottawa LA 2422. Of the 60 Ontario delegates, 34 were from international union bodies; of the 25 from Quebec, only 2; while 14 were Knights. British Columbia had five delegates, Manitoba two, Prince Edward Island one.

The 1901 convention contented itself mainly with reiterating its established opinions on much the usual subjects.

The 1902 convention, in Berlin (Kitchener), was an AFL man's dream. It had 152 delegates (nearly half as large again as the previous record high of 1886), and of these 79 were from international union locals or councils of unions (Printing Trades, Woodworkers, Boot and Shoe), 1 was from an AFL FLU, 8 were from Congress FLUs, and 33 from trades and labour councils, nearly all of them international-controlled. (Actually, in the first decisive vote, the expulsionists got 66 votes from international unions, 22 from councils, and 1 unidentified; while the opposition got 9 from international unions, 8 from councils, 4 from congress FLUs, and 11 from Knights. In the second decisive vote, the expulsionists got 64 from international unions, 21 from councils, 1 from a congress FLU, and 2 unidentified. The opposition got 11 from international unions, 9 from Councils, 4 from Congress FLUs, and 11 from Knights.) There were 13 from national, regional and local unions, and 18 from the Knights: 3 each from DAS 18, 20 and 180; 5 from four Montreal LAS, 2 from two Toronto, 1 from Ottawa, and 1 from Trenton. Ontario had 97 delegates: Toronto, 27; Hamilton and Berlin-Waterloo, 19 each; Ottawa, 7; London, 5; St Thomas, 4; Brantford and Guelph, 3 each; Stratford, St Catharines, and Hawkesbury, 2 each; Brockville, Galt, Niagara Falls, and Trenton, 1 each. Quebec had 48: Montreal, 37; Quebec City, 10; Valleyfield, 1. Winnipeg had 3, and Charlottetown, Saint John, Victoria, and Duncan had 1 each.

The chief innovations at the 1902 convention (apart from the constitutional changes) were three.

The first was procedural: the committee on standing orders and resolutions went through all the resolutions submitted and recommended concurrence or non-concurrence. This became standard practice.

The second was two resolutions on Indian rights, proposed by Rev. C.M. Tate, Duncan Fishermen's Union (Congress FLU 24). The first was to ask the dominion government to administer or amend the fishery laws so that the Indians could use their own method for catching fish, 'and thus assist the Indians of British Columbia to become an independent people.' The second, after reciting that the Cowichan Indians formed 'an industrious and progressive community of farmers and fishermen,' but found their land encroached on so that they had not enough room for their horses and cattle and enough land to grow their food, asked for a dominion royal commission on the subject. Both these resolutions passed. (Tate had less luck with a third, asking the dominion to fix the price of fish each year, high enough to give the fishermen a living wage and the cannery proprietors a fair profit.)

The third unusual feature in 1902 was an uncommonly large number of resolutions backing particular strikes: Berlin Broom Makers, Berlin FLU 17 (Builders' Labourers, who complained of Bricklayers' strikebreaking; referred to the Berlin Council); Winnipeg UBRE; Toronto Stove Mounters against Gurney's; Toronto Typos against Eaton's; Toronto Sheet Metal Workers against Metallic Roofing (non-concurrence, because *sub judice*); Montreal Cigar Makers; Textile Workers against Toronto Carpet; Machinists against Kingston Locomotive.

The institutional development
of the Trades and Labor Congress
# of Canada 1883–1902

The previous chapter's survey of resolutions passed by congress conventions is by no means complete; but it is enough to show the extraordinary number and variety of subjects dealt with, and something of the development of congress opinions on many of the subjects. In later years it leaves out a great deal, because, especially from 1896 on, and increasingly, more and more matters were dealt with in the president's address and the reports of the general executive and the provincial executives (there were no provincial federations, except for the short-lived attempts in British Columbia). To see how this came about, and what it involved, we must look at the development of the congress's constitution.[1]

At the outset, of course, it had none. But the 1886 convention adopted one, brief and simple. The Trades and Labor Congress of the Dominion of Canada was to consist of trades unions and Knights of Labor assemblies; it was to meet annually; its objects were to be 'the better consideration and carrying out of the measures most suited for the advancement of the wage-earners and the cementing more closely of the various industries throughout the Dominion'; and it was to be financed by per capita assessments on affiliated bodies. The affiliated unions and LAS were to have 1 delegate for every 200 members and under, 2 for 200 to 400, and 3 for over 400; trades and labor councils, district assemblies and central labour unions were to have 3 delegates each. The officers were to be a president, vice-president, secretary-treasurer, and an executive committee of 10, elected by districts (1 in Quebec, the rest in Ontario).

This was changed a year later.

March, in his 1887 presidential address, lamented that during the year the executive had had no power to act on the legislation which had come up in Parliament and the Ontario legislature. He therefore recommended appointment of a standing parliamentary or legislative committee, with adequate funds. The convention authorized an assessment of six cents per capita on each affiliate. There were 5300 members, which would give a revenue of $318, which, with the $74 balance on hand, would, it was thought, pay all expenses. An amendment to the constitution – that the executive should consist of the three officers and a special parliamentary committee of five members – was adopted.

In 1888, for the first time, there was a report of the executive and parliamentary committees. This had consisted largely of meetings, the circulation of petitions to Parliament and the Ontario legislature, and the appointment of a subcommittee to look after Ontario legislation. The subcommittee wanted to interview the Ontario cabinet, but got only as far as the commissioner of public works. The real job at Ottawa, as we have seen, was done by the Knights of Labor.

The report also recommended doing away with the parliamentary committee; and the executive had prepared a new constitution, which was adopted. This changed the name of the congress to Dominion Trades and Labor Congress, which remained its official title till 1892, when it took the name by which it was known for the rest of its life: Trades and Labor Congress of Canada. Its object was stated to be: 'To unite all the labor organizations of the Dominion so as to secure the enactment of new laws or amendments to the existing statutes in the interest of wage-earners, and to further, by every honorable means, the welfare of the working classes.' The conventions were to be made up of delegates from trades councils, central labour unions, trade unions, and district and local assemblies of the Knights of Labor. Local trade unions and local assemblies were to have one delegate for each hundred members, and one additional delegate for every extra hundred or fraction thereof. Councils, CLUs, national unions, and provincial and district assemblies of the Knights of Labor were to have three delegates each. Two or more local unions or LAs whose aggregate membership did not exceed 150 could send 1 delegate. There was to be no proxy representation, and delegates had to be members of the bodies which sent them (joint delegates of one of the two or more which sent them). Per capita dues were not to be more than 10 cents per year. The executive was to consist of the president, a vice-president, a secretary-treasurer, and four additional members. It was to watch the provincial legislatures and dominion Parliament, and 'endeavor to further the legislation decided on by the Congress at each session, or such other legislation as shall by them be deemed advisable.'

In 1889 the president's address recommended that the executive should consist of the three officers, plus three members from Ontario and three from Quebec, these trios to form the local legislative committees for the two provinces; and this was adopted. A French secretary and translator was appointed immediately after the preliminary proceedings.

The executive reported that the president had seen the minister of marine and fisheries on the Safety of Ships Bill, on which Tupper declined to accept the congress's proposed amendments. He had also appeared before the committee on immigration, and entered the congress's protest against the entry of paupers, indigents, and orphan children and waifs.

The Ontario executive had had 'invariable courtesy and kind attention,' and reported passage of acts amending the Workmen's Compensation for Injuries Act, the Factories Act, the Shops Regulation Act, the Municipal Act and the Free Libraries Act, and an Act for the Enforcement of Orders under the Master and Servant Act.

There were no changes in the constitution in 1890.

The secretary-treasurer reported that the number of organizations contributing to the income of the congress stood at 61, compared with 47 represented at the 1889 convention. The president recommended, and the committee on standing orders and resolutions agreed, that the congress should have an accredited representative at Ottawa during the parliamentary sessions.

The dominion executive reported having met with the minister of justice and three other ministers on 15 February, and with the prime minister, the minister of justice, and two others on a later date. Parliament had amended the law on conspiracy along the lines the congress had suggested, but the amendment to the Seamen's Act was unsatisfactory. The Act on Labour Statistics was reasonably satisfactory. The executive had impressed on Sir John A. Macdonald and his colleagues the necessity of stopping assisted immigration, and of doing various other things the congress had asked for.

The Quebec and Ontario committees also reported. The Quebec committee had met the provincial cabinet, and noted some favourable legislation. The Ontario committee gave a long list of acts of interest to labour passed from 1873 to 1890.

In 1891 the dominion executive had the first of the interviews with the government as a whole which were to become a regular feature of congress activities. This historic meeting took place 18 May 1891. Because of Macdonald's sudden death, very few of the measures the congress had asked for had become law; and some of the legislation passed had serious shortcomings. The executive had drawn up petitions on a variety of subjects and circulated them to the various labour organizations. Very little legislation had been secured in Ontario.

The 1892 executive reports contained nothing remarkable. The convention made several amendments to the constitution, the most notable being specific provision for amendment, and the re-establishment of the parliamentary committee of three members each from Ontario and Quebec, with the convention empowered to elect three more from any or every other province. Proposals to make Single Tax Associations eligible for affiliation, to require that all delegates must be bona fide wage earners, and to bar civic or civil employees as delegates were defeated. (The last two proposals were probably aimed at the Knights of Labor.)

In 1893 the president lamented lack of progress, the result, he said, chiefly of the exodus of members to the United States because of the depression in trade. He emphasized the importance of the consultations which had taken place between the Ontario executive and the various farmers' organizations. 'The interests of the farmer as relating to the monopolistic tendencies in our commercial system are identical with the artizans of our cities.' He also noted the existence of the Ottawa Council's paper, the *Wage-Earner*, and of the Saint John *Workman*, and deplored the disappearance of the Montreal *Echo*, because of lack of interest.

An attempt to amend the constitution to permit affiliation of the Patrons of Industry, Grangers (both farmers' organizations), and Single Tax Associations was referred to a vote of the affiliates.

In 1894 the results of this vote, and of those on the various systems and the initiative and referendum, were in. Only about a dozen of some 300 organizations had voted; so a motion to admit the Patrons was met with an amendment that the returns did not justify action. A subamendment to welcome a delegation from the Patrons, elected from their executive, upon the same basis as district assemblies and councils, carried, 31 to 5.

The reason for making flesh of the Patrons and fish of the Grangers and Single Taxers appears in the president's address: 'the splendid fight' of the Patrons in the Ontario election, and the grand results achieved. The farmers of Ontario, Beales said, presented 'a lesson of the effect of united action that I trust will have a salutary effect on, not only the rural residents of other Provinces ... but also with our urban population.' The question of closer co-operation with the farmers was commended to the delegates' consideration. What it got, we have just seen.

The president and four other members of the executive had had the annual interview with the dominion government, which had promised earnest consideration of the congress's requests. Various petitions circulated by the congress had had a poor time of it, few of them reaching the House of Commons. The ones on compulsory arbitration and on the future of Canada had fared particularly ill: 'hardly any were presented, our membership refusing to sign them for various reasons. Many of the bodies do not believe in compulsory arbitration and for that reason would not present the petition. The few that were sent in regarding the future of Canada would not be presented to the House by those members who received them on the ground of disloyalty to the country.' Parliament had passed only three acts of interest to labour: one establishing Labour Day; one for suitable and sufficient shelter for employees on electric cars; and one for better inspection of gear and tackle used in loading and unloading vessels. The executive regretted that Lépine had not reintroduced his eight-hour bill.

The Quebec executive had been refused an interview with the provincial government, though it had later appeared before the committee on amendments to the Factory Act without 'obtaining one single modification or amendment that might be remotely considered as of direct benefit to the worker.' The Quebec executive had done what it could, though 'with all but a negative result,' to help the Montreal and Quebec councils on amendments to their city charters.

The Ontario executive had had several meetings with its provincial government, and was able to report passage of several acts 'of very great importance and benefit to wage-earners generally, and especially ... organized labor.' The Conciliation and Arbitration Act had amongst its provisions some of 'the best and most practical to be found in the laws of Great Britain, Australasia and the United States'; the Benefit Societies Act would enable labour organizations 'to secure incorporation and consequent legal status'; the Municipal Amendment Act provided for payment of aldermen; an amendment to the Landlord and Tenant Act afforded certain relief to tenants.

The 1894 convention had charged the executive to consider amendments to the constitution. In 1895 it produced a draft new one. This proposed four major changes.

The first would rename the congress 'The Canadian Federation of Labor.' This was defeated.

The second would give it power to form organizations 'in localities where none at present exist.' These could be either LAs or Federal Labour Unions chartered by the congress itself. This protected the Knights of Labor; and the clause went on to specify that no charter should be granted where there was already an international or national union in existence. Further, if a new international or national union was chartered in the trade or calling concerned, the congress officers were to see to it that the chartered FLU became a local of the international or national. That protected the international unions, while still leaving room for purely national unions. These provisions were adopted.

Third, the draft proposed to strike out the provision for representation of state and provincial assemblies of the Knights, and to admit sections of the 'Socialistic Labor Party, and the Executive of the Patrons of Industry.' This ran into heavy weather. The London section of the Socialist Labor Party had actually sent a delegate to the convention, 'Comrade' Robert Healy, but the credentials committee had of course turned him down. An attempt to get this part of the proposals expunged was defeated. An amendment to admit the Industrial Brotherhood then carried.

Fourth, the draft proposed a fixed per capita of 12 cents from councils, DAs, and the Patrons, 8 cents from trade unions, LAs, and sections of the SLP, and 16 cents from Congress FLUs (which were to pay also a charter fee of $25). This carried.

The executive apparently had no interview with the dominion government in 1895, and it reported that none of the bills labour wanted had even reached third reading. It thanked the Montreal *Saturday Times*, the Ottawa *Free Lance*, the London *Industrial Banner*, and the Winnipeg *People's Voice* for the 'great assistance' they had rendered organized labour, and asked the 'hearty support' of union members for these papers.

The Quebec executive had had an interview with the provincial government, but the ministers had been non-committal, describing some proposals as 'too early,' others as 'too late.' One important bill, to incorporate benevolent, national trades unions and labour associations had passed the assembly, but 'we are sorry to state that one too many of those "anti-labor mummies" are still living and sitting in the Legislative Council, as he got our bill rejected by one vote.'

The Ontario executive, as usual, reported a series of provincial acts, generally in line with labour's wishes. It reported also a successful effort to block an amendment to the Assessment Act desired by 'certain interested and unscrupulous land speculators and large property owners' and caught, at the eleventh hour, by the watchdogs of labour.

The 1895 convention elected executive committees for Manitoba and British Columbia.

In 1896 the president's address directed the convention's attention to five questions: the eight-hour movement; abolition of the sweating system; work for the unemployed; exclusion of Chinese immigrants and 'the Barnardo protégés'; and the organization of women workers.

The dominion executive had not even visited Ottawa as a committee let alone met the government. It had sent ministers typewritten copies of resolutions, all officially acknowledged; and it had helped to get the eight-hour day adopted in the printing bureau and the Quebec Cartridge Factory.

The Quebec executive had a good deal more, and better, to report. It had had an interview with the government, which had reeled off a list of the reforms it had passed in line with labour's requests. The executive had protested against the repeal of an act giving mechanics and labourers a first mortgage on the product of their labour. It reported also that, with the help of Lady Aberdeen and the Local Council of Women, it had succeeded in getting two women factory inspectors appointed.

The Ontario executive listed five progressive acts passed, and noted the success of its efforts to have the staff of factory inspectors changed around.

The Manitoba executive listed six important problems 'at present engaging the attention of workingmen all over the world'; shortening hours; getting the worker a larger proportion of the product of his toil; 'freeing the land from all existing impediments to its being used by the people for the people'; 'a Government Currency based not upon either ... gold or silver ... but upon ... the credit and wealth of the whole nation for its redemption'; 'abolition of private ownership of Mines, Fisheries and all other natural resources'; 'the substitution at as early a date as possible for the present competitive system of a co-operative system business, based upon the closest possible relations between producer and consumer.' To do all this, it was first necessary to rouse the workers to political action. The executive had met with some considerable success in getting better laws passed, and labour had elected one alderman and only just failed to elect a second.

The British Columbia executive had not met, but William McKay submitted a report from Victoria and George Bartley one from Vancouver. McKay's was short. He said the legislature had passed no acts favourable to labour, but the city was now having nearly all its work done by direct day labour instead of on contract. The depression had resulted in a very marked decrease in the labour organizations of Victoria; it had been impossible to reorganize any of the disbanded unions, and very hard even to keep the rest going, except for the Stonecutters, Typos, and Cigar Makers, who had held a grand Labour Day celebration, Victoria's first. Bartley's report was the familiar tale of the horrors of Oriental immigration.

The only notable change in the constitution in 1896 was the exclusion of the Socialist Labor Party, by 36 to 6. The parliamentary committee became the legislative committee.

D.A. Carey, opening the 1897 convention, cast a glance back over the past, the progress achieved since the Toronto Trades Assembly was organized. He also looked to the future:

Let us ... be steadfast and persevering in seizing ... every opportunity of furthering our ideas and principles, and hastening on the time when the workers may all join in saying, 'There is nothing better for a man than that he should eat and drink and make his soul enjoy good in his labor.' Unfortunately too many of the toilers ... fail to get either enough to eat or to drink and thus have no enjoyment of life. This too in the face of the fact that year by year our country grows richer and richer. No doubt, much of this is due to defects in our present social customs, and directly traceable to the old feudal system, with the reverence, the hommage, and the servility which had to be paid to the lords of the soil by the toilers.

[But] the spread of education – the educating and new power of the press, properly described as the library of the workingman and the reception of political power, have infused new ideas, new principles and new aspirations into the heads and hearts of the workers. No longer are they mere hewers of wood and drawers of water.

[Let] our local bodies [strike] out anew, by an organizing crusade among the unorganized – by the discreet use of political power – by the advancement of social and labor questions on all local or municipal boards – by our trade unions and labour organizations practising more carefully all the doctrines they preach, and by the development of co-operation in all our undertakings.

Carey went on to advocate proportional representation, citing its success in Tasmania. He also urged the congress to refrain as much as possible from the introduction of new legislation, concentrating rather on getting existing laws fully carried out, notably the factories and shops acts. He emphasized the importance of getting the eight-hour day extended till it became the universal law of the land, and put in a strong plea for the union label.

Some new legislation, however, was required: to keep out Orientals; to establish free employment bureaus; to make the Alien Labour Act more effective.

The dominion executive had interviewed the government and laid before it various requests for legislation. Laurier had been 'candid and outspoken,' but he guaranteed nothing.

The executive had given consideration to organizing the vast number of unorganized men in Canada. The trouble was lack of money. A proper charter and outfit would cost about $200, apart from the organizer's time. The formation of a few large unions would more than pay the first cost, but this would take time.

The Ontario executive's report was mainly the usual chronicle of acts passed, with an underlining of Carey's plea for concentrating on better enforcement of existing laws. The Quebec executive had had a long interview with the provincial cabinet, but with very little result. The Manitoba executive's report was mainly an account of conditions in the Prairie west. British Columbia reported at length on the Oriental question, with special attention to the fishermen.

The executive in 1897 had pointed out that every international union in America was a member of the AFL, which accordingly got per capita dues from all of them, including money paid in by the Canadian members. The congress was in no such happy position. No international or national union was affiliated as such; individual locals affiliated (and disaffiliated) as they saw fit; so did trades and labour councils. (In 1901, only 133 or 135 local unions of all kinds were affiliated with the congress, though the total number of labour organizations was 871 or 873.) The executive accordingly had strongly urged affiliated locals of international unions to ask their parent organizations to turn over to the congress 'for legislative purposes the amount of the per capita tax now paid the Federation on their Canadian members.'

This was more than the AFL international unions were prepared to concede; but in 1898 the secretary-treasurer was able to report an AFL grant of $100 for legislative purposes. This was repeated in 1899, increased to $200 in 1900, and to $300 in 1902, when the United Hatters and the Amalgamated Woodworkers also made grants of $25 each, and the Street Railway Employees of $10.

In 1897 Carey had urged the creation of local law funds for testing acts already on the statute books. In 1898 he returned to the subject; but, noting that the 1897 resolution had been almost forgotten, he now suggested that the congress itself set up such a fund. He again demanded legislation against the Chinese, and backed the union label; he also denounced manual training.

The dominion executive reported an interview with four members of the dominion cabinet (which had put union wages clauses in the contracts for the post office and the department of militia and defence). The president had already mentioned the chartering of the first congress FLU, in Moncton; the executive added that the union had been formed by employees of the Intercolonial Railway, and took the opportunity to suggest that all the trades and labour councils be asked to take out congress charters. It thought this would make them organizing centres and would 'tend to bring into the fold of your Congress many local organizations now holding aloof.'

The Ontario executive had had an interview with the provincial government, and had concentrated on getting better enforcement of the laws, with results so meagre that it wound up by saying: 'The time has arrived ... [when] we must be independent at the ballot box, irrespective of whatever political party is in power. As the capitalistic lobyist [sic] controls and corrupts our Government it is imperative that more attention should be given by the toilers to the selection of representatives who will at least voice their rights on the floors of our legislative halls.' Manitoba and British Columbia submitted brief reports.

Smith, in his 1899 presidential address, declared that 'the representation of this Congress comprises the labor interests of the whole Dominion,' that the congress had 'a larger national representation than any organization in the Dominion (except-ing the Dominion Parliament),' and 'anticipate[d] that before long our provincial representation to this Congress [would] be equal to that of the National Govern-ment.' He affirmed that there was 'the greatest necessity for a National Union, yea, and I may add, for an International Union [meaning a federation] ... [since] the rapid introduction of factories and railroads' was 'multiplying cities, and making all rural regions their suburbs,' 'the power of electricity' was 'narrowing the world by increasing the rapidity of both production and distribution,' and 'our competitors' were 'not only near at hand across our streets, but everywhere, thus every single employer's contract with a single employee or local union is governed not by the local conditions, but by national and international competitions and combinations.'

He complained of lack of enforcement of the Alien Labour Act, and the failure to deal adequately with Chinese immigration, and urged education for political action.

The dominion executive's report was largely concerned with its interview with Sir Wilfrid Laurier and his very frank observations on Chinese and Japanese immigra-tion. He had declared that there was 'a great ethical difference' between the two. Also, the Chinese Empire 'was going to pieces, but Japan, healthy and progressive, was an ally of Her Majesty, and ... if the Japanese Emperor should make representa-tions against a Japanese exclusion bill there might be strong remonstrances that could not be passed over. The Chinese and Japanese could not be treated on the same level, and members of the labor organizations should be acquainted with their different conditions.' Sir Wilfrid was, however, ready to extend the day labour sys-tem on public works, and would consider a copyright act on the lines recommended by the congress. The Alien Labour Act was before the Anglo-American Commission, and for the present would therefore not be enforced.

Five more FLUs had been chartered; it was high time to provide these organizations with constitutions, by-laws, ritual, stationery, and supplies.

The Ontario executive had met the provincial government, which had made it quite clear that it had no sympathy with the unions 'and did not want to be bothered listening to what the Committee had to say, and ... had simply granted the interview because it is customary ... never intending to do anything asked by the Committee.'

The most noteworthy feature of the Manitoba report was the account of the spate of organization in Winnipeg following the 1898 convention: 'Garment Workers, Cigarmakers, Railroad Employees, Laborers, Teamsters, Retail Clerks, Tinsmiths, Street Railway Men, Stage Employees, Bakers, Boilermakers and Pressmen.' There had also been a substantial increase in the membership of many of the older organizations. The Winnipeg Council and the Winnipeg Labour Party had taken a referendum on political action, and the mandate being for action, had nominated Arthur Puttee for the dominion House. The executive felt similar action was needed all over Canada.

The British Columbia executive was all smiles. 'A great deal of legislation of a valuable character and of permanent ... benefit ... to the working people' had been passed. Metal mining hours had been reduced to eight per day, and conditions greatly improved. Contracts to bring in non-British Columbia labour had been outlawed. The franchise had been widened. The coal miners had got legislation giving them pay according to the actual weight of the coal they mined. The Chinese had been got out of the coal mines (by enforcing an earlier act), and when the employers had replaced them by Japanese, the legislature had promptly passed a new act prohibiting their employment also. The Judicial Committee of the Privy Council had declared the provincial Chinese Exclusion Act *ultra vires*; but the obliging provincial government had passed an order-in-council forbidding employment in coal mines of anyone unable to read and understand and explain the provisions of the Coal Mines Regulation Act. The Semlin government had redeemed every pledge given to labour. The executive added that the growth of unionism in British Columbia during the year had been phenomenal.

Smith's presidential address in 1900 struck a note of high economic orthodoxy:

The economist and the statesman especially are watching us ... They will judge the great movement of Trades Unionism, not by its results in improving the position of any particular section of workmen at any particular time, but by its effects on the permanent efficiency of the nation ... If any of the methods ... result in the choice of less efficient factors of production than would otherwise have been used; if they compel the adoption of a lower type of organization than would have prevailed without them; and especially if they tend to lessen the capacity or degrade the character of either manual or brain workers, that part of Trades Unionism, however advantageous it may seem to particular sections of workmen, will stand condemned. But if it promotes the selection of the most efficient factors of production, whether capital, brain or labor; and brings these factors into better organization, thereby increasing the activities and improving the character of all, it must then be approved by these critics; this is what we claim for it and are constantly trying to demonstrate in every effort of the great movement.

Smith went on to call the congress, repeatedly, the national union of Canada, a sign, one suspects, of some uneasiness over the growing strength and influence of the AFL in Canada. He also noted with satisfaction the good works of the Liberal dominion government; the fair wage clauses; the appointment of O'Donoghue as commissioner to enforce them; the passing of a Conciliation and Arbitration Act; the establishment of the *Labour Gazette*; the backing of the Union Label Bill; the existence of the Alien Labour Act; the appointment of a commission to investigate grievances in connection with its enforcement in British Columbia; the appointment of Alfred Jury as immigration agent and of E.P. Bremner for the settlement of labour disputes in British Columbia; the increase in the Chinese head tax; and the prospect of a royal commission on the Oriental question. In a somewhat different vein, he hailed the election of Puttee to the House of Commons as 'a delightful achievement.'

The dominion executive, accompanied by Puttee and Bremner (then a representative of the Western Federation of Miners), had met Laurier and been cordially listened to. (Its report is largely a rehash of Smith's address.) The Ontario executive's report contained nothing of moment.

The Manitoba report expatiated on Puttee's election and his subsequent services in the House, which showed 'the immense benefit of experienced labor representation' there. It also noted the passage of a provincial factories act, the organization of several new unions (notably the Allied Metal Mechanics), and strikes by the Leather Workers, Plumbers, Painters, Tailors, Bakers, Machinists, Metal Mechanics, Blacksmiths, and Boilermakers (these last four against the CPR).

The Quebec executive (minus the Montreal members, on whose absence it commented satirically) had met four members of the provincial cabinet. It had got some good amendments to the Industrial Establishment Act, and the appointment of Jobin as factory inspector.

The British Columbia report lamented the overthrow of the Semlin government, which had 'placed more legislation in the interest of the laboring people on the statute books ... in the single session of 1899 than all the governments that have held power since this province has been a constituted commonwealth.' Surprisingly, it also noted some good legislation from the new Dunsmuir government, though it censured the defeat of a bill which would have barred Chinese from almost all employment. The report also recorded the settlement of the Kootenay miners' strike on favourable terms and the compromise settlement in the fishing industry.

In 1901 Smith, now himself an MP, told the national congress not to despair because progress was slow, and not to play into the hands of labour's opponents 'by manifesting a disposition of mistrust of those who are the elected leaders of the movement all over the country' (a slap at the Socialists). 'There are no trades unions that would not assist to a considerable extent in the bringing about of the nationalization of certain industrial enterprises. We are all socialists to some extent, but I find a great deal of denunciation against trades unionism emanating from professional socialistic societies. Surely the aim is one, even if we disagree as to the method.'

Smith noted that there had been some improvements in the Alien Labour Act but found it still inadequate. The CPR had imported aliens to take the place of the striking Trackmen, but the government had thought it too costly to put the law in motion against the company. What was necessary was to give the department of labour the power to investigate, and to deport, at the expense of the guilty employers, those whom they had illegally employed.

Smith wound up by stressing the 'vast importance that this Congress should adopt some method of increasing its own usefulness. There ought to be a Canadian Federation, for, whilst I believe that unionism ought to be international in its methods to meet the necessity of combatting common foes, this usefulness is only assured by the strength of national unions. A Federation of American union[s] represented by a national union and a Federation of Canadian unions represented by a national union, each working with the other in special cases, would be a great advantage over having local unions in Canada connected with the national unions of America ... I do not reflect on any American officials who have handled our labor troubles ... but I am certain ... that there are such distinctive differences in the condition of each that a presentment of Canadian matters by Canadian leaders ... would lead to a greater success and would not in any way prevent a Federation of the national bodies.'

This was a declaration of war on international unionism, only slightly mitigated by Smith's adding that he only just mentioned it 'as preliminary to a complete reconstruction of the constitution and powers of this Congress,' and that he would be 'pleased and satisfied if a condition of greater usefulness could be provided in the machinery of our Congress.'

Smith can hardly really have expected that his call for purely Canadian unions in a purely Canadian congress, co-operating on equal terms with purely American unions in a purely American AFL, would be heeded. Ever since 1898 the election of congress officers had been presided over by the AFL fraternal delegate. The congress's national vice-president was the AFL's Canadian general organizer, and the congress's secretary-treasurer was a member of the International Typographical Union. All the members of the Ontario and Manitoba executives were from international unions; so were at least half of the British Columbia executive, and probably of the Quebec and New Brunswick. The PWA was not in the congress at all and the Knights were dwindling to a very small, weak minority. There was no power base for an anti-international movement.

Moreover, the disproportion in the size of the AFL and the congress made any notion of co-operation between equals ludicrous. The congress, in 1901, had only 8381 members in affiliated and federal unions; the AFL, in 1900, had had 10,457 in Canada alone. And the 1901 report of the dominion executive rubbed it in. Before seeking the annual interview with the government the president and the secretary-treasurer had met to consider how many of the executive the congress could afford to bring to Ottawa. They decided to ask Flett, March, Scott, J.S. Fitzpatrick, and J.A. Rodier (two Knights, three international unionists). Then 'it was decided also to communicate with Samuel Gompers, President, American Federation of Labor, and request him to allow Mr John A. Flett, Canadian General Organizer of the A.F. of L., to come to Ottawa one week prior to the interview, for the purpose of helping the other two members of the Executive to prepare our side of the case. We are pleased to state that President Gompers acceded to this request forthwith, in a very nicely-worded letter, conveying his best wishes to the Congress and concluding with the hope that our projected interview with the Government would be highly beneficial to the Canadian wage-earners.' The deference on the one side and the patronizing condescension on the other could hardly have been made plainer.

This year, for the first time, the dominion executive's report was subdivided into nine clauses.

The first celebrated the election of Smith and the re-election of Puttee to the House of Commons as independent labour members.

The second was devoted to the annual interview with the government. This presented several novel features. Smith and Draper, the new secretary-treasurer, had a preliminary meeting which went over the 1900 convention resolutions, picked out those intended for presentation to the dominion government, and found that 'eleven resolutions and two subjects (namely, The Trade Marks and Design Act and the dismissal of Messrs Murray Fleming and Allan McDonald from the Intercolonial Railway service) would comprise the bill of fare.'

Next, they printed 200 copies of a 4-page circular, and mailed copies to every minister, the leader of the opposition, and 'any members of Parliament known to be favorable to organized labor, thereby giving them ample time and opportunity, if they so desired, to peruse and study the demands submitted, and likewise precluding the possibility of the deputation receiving an answer to the effect that these matters were new – in fact had never been thought of before – and that time would be required to seriously consider these complex labor issues.' The congress officers were becoming wise in their generation.

Copies of the circular were sent to all provincial executives; and the Ontario and Quebec executives got also copies of the convention resolutions affecting those provinces, 'with instructions to lay them before their respective legislatures.'

Then, having decided who should make up the deputation, and secured the services of Flett, Smith, and Draper (with Puttee), the executive decided at once that two questions need not be brought before the whole cabinet, but could be dealt with by a committee seeing the individual ministers concerned. Accordingly, Smith, Flett, and Puttee were authorized to see the minister of railways and canals on the one matter, and the minister of marine and fisheries on the other.

The first was the dismissal of the two members of FLU No 1 without a fair and impartial investigation. (The union had at first demanded Fleming's and McDonald's reinstatement, but, on finding that the two had taken an active part in the 1900 election, had dropped this, and was asking only that 'no further unnecessary dismissals would take place until an employee had been heard before the management of the Intercolonial.') The three labour men met the minister, and got a written promise to instruct the railway management 'to afford every reasonable opportunity for the Grievance Committee of the Trades Union with which the men in our workshops are identified, to lay before the management any complaints which they may now have to make, or which may hereafter arise.'

The second question was union representation on the Saint John Pilotage Board. This turned out to be a damp squib: the pilots were not organized, and the minister persuaded the committee that it was best to leave the matter to the MP from the constituency. The executive added an exhortation to the pilots to organize.

The committee divided up the remaining ten resolutions so that each would be presented to the cabinet by the man considered most competent to deal with it.

Of the ministers, only Laurier and Mulock turned up.

Smith dealt with the naturalization of Japanese immigrants, Scott with Crown payment of costs for people acquitted by the courts, March and Henderson with the grievances of the Toronto Musical Protective Association against militia bandsmen, Fitzpatrick with the demand that the government give no more clothing contracts to Mark Workman of Montreal (who had been violating the fair wage clause and replacing union members by 'a newly arrived shipload of Europeans to work at scandalous wages'). Flett and Puttee presented the demand for amendments to the Criminal Code to allow peaceful persuasion by pickets and to stop injunctions 'forbidding men on strike or lockout from doing perfectly legal acts.' Puttee presented the resolution for weekly payment of wages, urging the government to set an example. In the absence of Rodier, resolutions on tracklaying by the Montreal Harbour Commissioners, on the American Tobacco Co, and on the handling of dynamite by incompetent persons were not dealt with at all. Smith had wound up with a plea for reform in the alien labour law.

Laurier's reply seems to have dealt only with this last (on which he said 'everything possible would be done for the Canadian workingman consistent with the rights of the rest of the country') and with the naturalization of the Japanese, on which he was stiff. Mulock contented himself with asking for a synopsis of the arguments in writing.

The congress's representatives were highly displeased. They had taken unprecedented pains to do their job thoroughly, but the government had been casual and offhand. Smith especially, who had assured Laurier of his strong sympathy for the liberal cause, and had in turn received Laurier's 'sincere congratulations on your splendid victory as well as my thanks for the same,' must have felt that he had received a poor reward for his labours.

The executive summed up:

The interview was not considered satisfactory ... there being no disposition to discuss the points or weigh the arguments.

Bearing in mind the merely perfunctory methods of the past and the almost utter uselessness of formal and always very brief interviews with a Premier and only one or two of his colleagues ... interviews always too limited in time to allow of thorough elucidation and discussion of matters of direct interest to our working people, your Executive believes there should be a complete change in this particular. It is therefore

RECOMMENDED, that hereafter, when requesting an interview with ... the Government, your Executive make it clear that the intention is to secure opportunity to discuss ... such measure and matters as are within the scope of their duties and in the direct interest of the working people of Canada, so that members of the Government may thoroughly comprehend what is sought.

Clause c of the report recommended that all bills asked for by the congress be legally prepared, and proposed the appointment of 'a well-informed and capable representative at Ottawa during each session of Parliament.' Large corporations had a solicitor, and often several lobbyists, there and usually got the measures they wanted. At election time, especially in cities and towns, where the labour vote was a factor, MPs were profuse in expressions of sympathy with the working man. But it was not 'merely friendship and sympathy the toilers require, but measures and public Acts which will better their condition.' With a permanent representative in the capital, the congress 'could at least keep a record of some of these members who say they are in favour of labor measures, when they are looking for votes, but when elected do little or nothing in that direction.'

The executive's next recommendation was to adopt the British Trades Union Congress's procedure on resolutions: submission to the secretary-treasurer a specified time before the convention met, after which the standing orders committee should go over them and present them in the order of their general or special importance.

Clause E chronicled the Senate's defeat of the Union Label Bill, 'because of bitter and unjustifiable prejudice, as well as hostility to organized labor and anything savoring of advantage to the working elements of Canada.'

Clause G praised the Conciliation Act, and explained that it could not provide for compulsory arbitration because property and civil rights fell under provincial jurisdiction. It suggested, however, that the government might put into government contracts a clause providing that when disputes between the contractor and his employees could not be otherwise settled, they would have to be referred to 'either a conciliator or a board of arbitration, to be appointed by the Minister under the Act. This especially where the dispute had existed for a longer space of time than, say, one week, and there were indications that the public were in any way being embarrassed or injured in consequence.' The same proviso should be attached to all grants or bonuses. The act should also provide for compulsory reporting of every dispute, the reports 'to be inserted in the annual blue books of the Government and in the Labor Gazette.'

Clause H contained a detailed report of the operation of the fair wage schedules in government contracts, and asked to have the system embodied in legislation and applied to all contracts.

Clause I was a Victoria Typos' resolution asking for an effective check on 'Asiatic Coolie labor, which is continually increasing and thereby coming into greater competition with the workers in all lines of industry.'

The convention committee on the report was against having all bills legally prepared, and said the congress hadn't the money to pay for the parliamentary representative. It was doubtful about the proposed procedure on resolutions, and wanted it referred to the executive for report at the next convention. In general, it approved the rest of the recommendations. The convention adopted the committee's report, except for its recommendations on the legal preparation of bills and the appointment of a parliamentary representative, which it left to the discretion of the executive.[2] J.G. O'Donoghue, solicitor, was appointed three years later.[3]

The reports of the provincial executives took up more space than the whole *Proceedings* for 1899. British Columbia led off with eighteen pages of small print; Ontario had nine; Quebec four. At the other end of the scale, New Brunswick had only about half a page. So did FLU No 10, which reported for Prince Edward Island. The Halifax Trades and Labor Council took nearly two pages, the Manitoba executive three-and-a-half.

The British Columbia report had three parts: 'Oriental Labor,' by George Bartley, Vancouver; 'Mining and the Interior,' by James McLaren, Rossland; and 'Legislation,' by Thomas H. Twigg, Victoria.

The first made up about 90 per cent of the whole. Bartley had a robust faith and no doubts: 'The Anglo-Saxon race is one with which the world conjures. It is the most successful of all the races in the history of mankind. Then, if we are to maintain our present standard, it behooves us to still further the well-being of our own people, and to this end we must at all costs make Canada a distinctly white man's country, and this can only be accomplished by the enacting and carrying out of an improved and strict immigration policy. For the industries of British Columbia that should belong to our people are fast becoming monopolized by Orientals.' British Columbia was 'the most desirable part of the whole Dominion for poor white citizens, as well as others of our race, to locate in; but ... the white workers are being driven hither and thither to make room for aliens who are degrading to civilization.'

It was all the fault of the government at Ottawa, 'which listens to and heeds too much the wishes of capitalists.'

The province had 3000 'mechanics and bosses,' 3000 whites who 'already glut the market in the higher spheres of labor,' and 14,000 'Mongolian laborers replacing a similar number of whites.'

Where could the displaced whites go? To the United States. 'The best blood of our country [is] leaving it because our West is not a place for them to come to, the most resourceful part of Canada, as it is already overstocked with a coolie class ... It won't be long before Eastern Canada is invaded, as well as the Western portion ... by this cheap coolie labor.'

Bartley then proceeded to make the convention's flesh creep with some choice excerpts from the evidence before the Royal Commission. Rev Canon Beanlands had looked upon 'the coming here of Chinamen as a wise dispensation of Providence ... My idea would be to establish a coolie class here, similar to the Athenian system that made Athens the schoolhouse of the world. There a system of slavery was adopted applying to half the inhabitants. This gave the upper class leisure to cultivate the arts and sciences and thus obtain a degree of civilization that has never been surpassed.' Major Dupont, mine promoter, was less elegant: 'I formerly worked whites, but they asked for more pay, and not deeming it wise to permit my help to run my business I dismissed them and employed Chinese.'

Having cited statistics of 10 establishments where the Chinese and Japanese outnumbered the whites by 1306 to 969, and the Oriental unskilled the white unskilled by 1306 to 69, Bartley sounded the note of patriotism, with a special word for the French Canadians, who 'were engaged in the Transvaal a short time ago fighting their country's battles. Our forefathers bled and died on the frontiers of Canada in 1812, repelling the foreign invader in order that the Union Jack should float over this broad country. Now these industrial pirates refuse employment in the land that gave us birth. Will the Mongol fight for our country the same as Canadians? We think not. "Tommy Atkins" and "Bessie Jones" will do well to give British Columbia a wide berth if such people are to have their way regarding the employment of Chinese and Japanese.'

Bartley even suggested exclusion of 'Italians and other Latin races. I ... venture to give it as my own opinion that the Latin and Slavonic races of Europe are not wanted here. With the Teuton and the Scandinavian we assimilate. Each merges into the land. They are of our own type. It is from them we sprung. They become in every sense of the word good citizens and loyal Canadians.' But against the Orientals let the government impose 'such a head tax as to amount to exclusion ... to preserve one of the fairest portions of the earth's surface for the Canadian people, and not to allow it to be wrested from them ... by engulfing us in the rising tide of Oriental immigration.'

After this, Twigg's account of provincial legislation (largely attempts to get around dominion disallowance of anti-Oriental acts) comes as rather an anticlimax. So does McLaren's tale of conditions in the interior, mainly strikes of CPR trackmen and bridge carpenters, the Rossland miners, carpenters, blacksmiths, and helpers.

The Ontario report began with a slightly satirical note on the chorus of 'bankers, manufacturers, merchants, land speculators, railway promoters, professional men, farmers, statesmen, and even petty politicians, as well as the public press' who had been holding forth on the country's prosperity and progress. The Ontario executive agreed that that province had shared in the prosperity: 'Rents went up promptly and the cost of living along all lines increased very considerably.' It added that 'the wage-earning elements – the mass of the people – being consumers as well as producers, were made to acutely realize the changed conditions and were forced to meet them by seeking more pay – and never secured it without organized and aggressive effort. The improvement has been fairly general, however, except in classes of labor lacking proper organization and collective power of persuasion.'

Another striking feature of the year had been 'the effort in many trades and callings to secure a reduction of the working-day, especially from 10 to 9 hours' (nearly 30 years after the great nine-hour movement of 1872!). Here, though success had not been complete, there was much cause for congratulation.

The rest of the Ontario report was a detailed commentary on eight acts of the previous session. An apparently harmless-looking amendment to the Master and Servant Act was in fact very dangerous. The rest of the legislation represented improvements; and the committee, which had interviewed the premier, had hopes of more.

The Quebec executive had met the provincial cabinet, and presented 28 demands. Of these, it reported sixteen under consideration, one under promise of serious consideration, one under promise of consideration, one promised but not yet executed, two deferred, three deferred until next session, three granted, and one granted in part.

The Manitoba executive, of course, noted first the election of Puttee and the good work he had done in the House. It deplored the amendment to the Alien Labour Act, which took its enforcement out of the hands of the department of labour and thus, 'for large sections of labor, destroyed the usefulness of the law.' Individuals and unions often had not the means to proceed by summary conviction. The committee also complained of the ineffectiveness of the dominion department of labour and its Conciliation Act, and said the time had come for the congress to formulate some definite proposal for legislative enactment of compulsory arbitration. Enforcement of the fair wages clause in government contracts had also been very unsatisfactory. The provincial legislature, on the other hand, had passed a good factory act, though the premier had not carried out his promise to appoint an inspector satisfactory to the unions. A workmen's compensation act was needed, and steps were being taken to prepare one. Organization in Winnipeg had progressed moderately. The need for it had been dramatically illustrated by the experience of the carpenters. In 1899, after an extensive strike, hours and wages had been settled by arbitration; but 'the award was not respected four weeks by some of the contractors, and the carpenters not being sufficiently well organized to insist on observance, the trade is in a more chaotic state than ever, and this season or another the whole disturbance will be experienced again.'

The New Brunswick executive reported the movement there dormant, though the Saint John Molders had managed to get a 25 cent increase in some shops, and the grocery clerks, clothiers, tailors, barbers, and butchers had secured early closing, and the drug clerks were asking for it. The report also noted the organization of the Fabian League.

From Prince Edward Island, FLU No 10 reported it was the only union in the province, and there was little labour legislation except mechanics' lien acts. What was needed was a good organizer.

The Halifax council's report we have already dealt with.

Smith's 1902 presidential address opened with a tribute to Draper, to whose 'energetic, enterprising and intelligent work' the congress's present improved condition was almost entirely due. In two years, Draper had doubled the revenue, provided a complete set of books, furnished an office, and 'placed the business of the Congress before each session in ... a plain and intelligent manner.'

Next, Smith turned to the activities of 'so-called reformers' who attacked the union movement. He commented briefly on dominion legislation, and noted the railway unions' opposition to the Railway Labour Disputes Bill, which provided for the compulsory arbitration the congress had so long demanded. It would be necessary to get a very plain decision from the convention on this. He expressed his disappointment at the government's failure to act on the report of the Royal Commission on Oriental Immigration, and then discussed at some length the Taff Vale case in England. He wound up by emphasizing the necessity for putting a paid organizer in the field at once.

The report of the general executive was again an elaborate document. The president and secretary-treasurer had again held a preliminary meeting at which they went over all the 1901 resolutions and selected those calling for dominion action. These were forwarded at once to the parties for whom they were intended, and in some cases Smith had followed this up by interviewing the ministers himself. The next step was to name the vice-presidents for each province 'special organizers' and send them each 200 official letter-heads and envelopes, with a view to stimulating these functionaries to increased efforts on behalf of the congress. Next, out went a circular to all labour organizations in Canada, some 1200 in number, urging them to affiliate: this appeal resulted in several new affiliations. More important was a circular to every AFL international union 'calling their attention to the fact that a large number of International Trade Unions in Canada were unaffiliated with the Congress,' and urging the international offices either to make a grant or request their locals to affiliate. 'In many cases prompt replies were received expressing regret at their inability to contribute owing to lack of funds and constitutional enactments which debarred them from making grants for such purposes.' Three unions had made grants. The suggestion about affiliation had apparently been ignored. Undaunted by the meagre results of all these efforts, the officers then sent out 5000 copies of a 6-page folder, in 2 colors, and 4000 blank forms for affiliation, to the secretaries of trades and labour councils and all labor organizations throughout the dominion that could be reached. To cap it all, a special circular in French went to all organizations in Quebec, with 'a strong appeal to our French-Canadian fellow-workers and brothers in this Province to affiliate with our national legislative body. A few new affiliations resulted.'

The next section of the report dealt with trades and labour councils and their relation to the congress. The executive felt strongly that all such bodies should be chartered by the congress. It had accordingly sent a letter to every one of the 35 councils then in existence asking them to take out a congress charter and to appoint, each, a committee of 3 to wait on the local unions and ask them to join the congress. The result of this had been that the Toronto, Montreal Central, and Windsor councils had taken out charters.

Then, the annual interview with the dominion government. This year, for the first time, the congress had managed to have representatives on hand from every one of the seven provinces. The government had been represented again by the premier and the minister of labour. Smith and Draper had prepared, and sent to every minister beforehand, an eight-page leaflet setting forth what the congress wanted to say. It dealt with 10 specific subjects which, as in 1901, were parcelled out among the various representatives.

Smith presented the demand for a $500 head tax on Chinese immigrants, others the resolutions asking for a 20 per cent wage increase for letter carriers, public ownership of public utilities, the 8-hour day on government railways, the establishment of a system of technical schools, prohibition of moonlighting by government employees, the fair wage clause, the working of the Conciliation Act, and the Alien Labour Act.

Laurier's reply is printed in full in the *Proceedings*. He regretted that more ministers could not attend, owing to departmental duties, but the representations made would be placed before them. On Oriental immigration he said the government wanted to give people in eastern Canada time to digest the report of the royal commission. He was glad Smith had said he would take the matter up in the House. Public ownership of public utilities was 'a question of such deep magnitude and involving such a change in ... policy ... that he could not say he could consider it. Public opinion was not prepared for such a change.' He saw no reason why the Intercolonial should not adopt the eight-hour day, and he would present the matter to the minister. 'He was not prepared to agree with all that was said about immigration. If other than agricultural immigrants were coming out, it was against the orders given to the agents of the department.' On the Alien Labour Act, he objected to the proposal to restore the former practice by which an immigrant could be deported 'on the *ex parte* examination of an officer of the Labor Department. It would be a dangerous principle to say that either a British subject or an Alien who was on Canadian soil should be removed from the country before he was tried.' However, he would refer the matter to the minister of labour.

He had left it to Mulock to deal with the question of letter carriers' wages, but the minister appears to have restricted himself to extolling the achievements of the fair wages clause.

The executive was still far from satisfied. Laurier had 'dealt with the questions submitted separately, and expressed his views in a more pronounced manner, either in favor of or against the several propositions.' It remonstrated against the absence of all the ministers except two, especially as 'the questions submitted dealt with the majority of the employing and spending departments.' It thought the practice of having all provinces represented should be repeated, and that the congress should 'retain ... a legal representative and a well-informed trade unionist, as a lobbyist, at each Session.' These two would be 'able to do a great deal for Canadian wage-earners ... both in introducing new legislation and watching its progress; as well as opposing and stopping, if possible, undesirable and hostile legislation.' To induce more ministers to be present for the interview, the executive urged 'the more active co-operation of the Trade and Labor Councils ... both as to interviewing the Ministers who are representing the constituencies in which these ... Councils are situated, and the sending of a member of each provincial executive ... to these annual interviews, at the expense of the Provincial ... Councils.'

The report printed in full Smith's bill to amend the Alien Labour Act, and Puttee's to amend the Conciliation Act, and summarized Smith's bill for safety appliances on trains. None of the three had reached second reading. A private member's bill to allow importation of skilled labour for any business had also not been proceeded with; the congress had been prepared to oppose it. Guthrie's bill to prevent railway companies from escaping liability for injury to their employees had also fallen by the wayside. Puttee's eight-hour day amendment to the Post Office Bill had been defeated, with some other amendments the congress favoured: the new act set a higher maximum salary but was in general decidedly unsatisfactory.

The Toronto council's special committee on union label legislation, observing the fate of Smith's and Puttee's bills, very reluctantly had decided that it was no use trying for legislation in 1902.

The Ontario executive reported 'general employment at increasing wages and decreasing working hours,' though 'rarely ... without combined and aggressive effort on the part of the workers.' It also reported some 80 or more new local organizations, with good reason to believe the increase would continue in a like ratio. The executive had had an interview with the premier and the registrar-general, and the legislature had passed acts generally favourable to labour.

The Quebec executive had presented to the legislature the resolution for appointment of an inspector of scaffolding, and had tried, unsuccessfully, to get a bill passed providing for a three years' apprenticeship for barbers and a sanitary inspection for barber shops. Its efforts to amalgamate the Canadian Federation of Boot and Shoe Workers and the international union had failed, but it had got the Canadian Federation to affiliate with the congress.

British Columbia did not submit a report, but J.H. Watson, special organizer for the province, did. He had got Draper to appoint two district organizers. He found three or four unions in Nanaimo without a charter, and carpenters' unions in the Kootenays which refused to have anything to do with the international union; he accordingly wanted the prohibition of dual unionism removed from the constitution. He was disquieted by the fact that, in the absence of a congress organizer, the Victoria Marine Firemen had got a charter from the international Longshoremen's Union instead of a congress charter like the Vancouver men. This underlined the urgency of taking up the question of organization. 'If we are to do anything for the Trade Union movement in Canada, we must do it at once, or else all our organizations will become American organizations, which I, for one, do not wish to see.'

Watson also raised again the question of getting the per capita tax of international unions in Canada paid to the congress. He added a bitter complaint from the Vancouver Council that Flett, though a congress vice-president, had been organizing AFL unions in Canada. The Vancouver Freight Handlers had got a congress charter and had been trying to get the rest of the men on the line to do likewise. Along had come Flett and put the Freight Handlers under the Longshoremen. The Vancouver Freight Handlers thought Flett 'should resign his Vice-Presidency, as he cannot serve the interests of both the American Federation of Labor and the Dominion Trades Congress at the same time.'

The legislature had passed the Workmen's Compensation Act introduced by J.H. Hawthornwaite, labour representative for Nanaimo, which was nearly a facsimile of the British act, and Joe Martin's bill protecting union funds, outlawing injunctions against unions for persuading workmen not to work, and preventing injunctions for suits for damage against unions for boycotts. Smith Curtis' bill to prevent misrepresentation by newspaper advertisements or otherwise for procuring men, and allowing the victim to sue for damages, had also been passed. On the other side of the ledger was the dominion disallowance of provincial anti-Oriental acts. Watson wound up with a brief account of the formation of the Provincial Progressive Party and of a Vancouver council proposal that Chinese immigrants should enter Canada only at Ottawa and that the immigrants, and the existing Chinese population, should be distributed across the country in proportion to the population of each province.

The Manitoba report was concerned mainly with the UBRE strike but it had other things to say as well.

The province, and the territories, had been enjoying unprecedented prosperity in every line, but the benefits falling to the working classes had not been in proportion 'to those accruing to classes more fortunately placed.' Wages had risen about 10 per cent during the year, and employment was steadier; but rents had gone up 30 to 50 per cent in 2 years, food fully 20 per cent. There had accordingly been an exceptional number of strikes. The real cause of low wages was the constant influx of immigrants.

The working people of Manitoba were in favour of compulsory arbitration, and the UBRE strike had confirmed them in this opinion. Manitoba labour also warmly supported Smith and Puttee against 'the insidious attacks of fractious discontents who traitorously clothe themselves in honored names. Our greatest weakness has always been dissention, and just as this is suppressed will the chances be good of re-electing our present labor representatives, who, so far, have acquitted themselves ... in an irreproachable manner.'

Finally, the work of organization had been actively and successfully carried on in Winnipeg, and a footing had been obtained at 'points both in Manitoba and the

Northwest Territories. In Winnipeg a great progress can be recorded, and the Trade Council has a larger list of affiliated bodies than ever before.' All this, however, was merely subsidiary to the main work of the 1902 convention, which was the purging of the congress of all organizations dual to international unions. To understand this, it is necessary to go back and survey the congress's relations with unions not only in the United States but elsewhere.

In 1887, O'Donoghue and Whitten had carried a resolution that, as the British TUC had decided to hold an 'International Convention in London ... it be an instruction to the Parliamentary Committee to take such steps as may be deemed expedient in seeking recognition by representation or otherwise.' No action seems to have followed. In 1889 the convention had cabled the 'leaders of the great labor movement in London, England, expressing the sympathy of this Congress' with the striking dockers. Also, as we have seen, there had been resolutions of sympathy with various American strikers, and with Debs. And of course a large number of congress affiliates were locals of international unions or LAs of the Knights of Labor.

With the American Federation of Labor, however, the congress's relations were, until nearly the end of the century, very slight. The federation had generally been busy enough in the United States, and the congress resolved to remain all-inclusive. The presence, and the strong influence, of the Knights had made anything else very nearly impossible.

The federation, three years after it was founded, had indeed issued invitations to the organized workers of the world to an international congress under AFL auspices in Chicago, in 1893. But the international Socialist Congress, supported by most continental European unions, had refused and the meeting was cancelled. Gompers, the AFL president, thereupon decided to build a purely trade union international, and for this purpose set out to win the co-operation of the British TUC, with which the AFL began exchanging fraternal delegates in 1894. Two years later the Americans again suggested an international congress, but the British were lukewarm, and nothing happened.[4]

At this point, Dower, the TLC secretary-treasurer, wrote the AFL to complain about the American Alien Contract Labor Act. The congress had apparently been disagreeably surprised to find Canadians treated by the United States as foreigners. Gompers replied, soothingly, that the act had not been primarily directed against 'our fellow workers of Canada.' But large numbers of Chinese, having got into Canada, crept across the border, and also large numbers from European countries. If Canada and the United States alone were concerned, he was confident they could arrive at an agreement; but the 'most favored nation' clause prohibited the United States from giving one nation privileges denied to another. He was apparently uneasy at the news that the question was to be discussed at the TLC convention, and hoped that no ill-advised action would be taken. He suggested an exchange of fraternal delegates.

The TLCC, in its reply, did not even mention this proposal, and paid no attention to fresh appeals from the same quarter. Meanwhile, Gompers had been telling his own executive that he hoped the exchange of fraternal delegates between the AFL and the TUC, and the German unions and the TUC, and between the TLC and AFL, would develop into 'bona fide International Trade Congresses every few years.'[5]

At the TLCC convention of 1897, the executive noted that Gompers had been very anxious to have a fraternal delegate, but the committee could not see its way clear to send one. With this, it passed at once to its desire to get part of the international unions' per capita; and again no exchange of delegates took place.

Gompers, however, refused to be discouraged. He told the 1897 AFL convention that the federation's aim 'should be to unite the workers of our continent and to strive to attain the unity, solidarity, and fraternity of the workers of the world.' The convention appointed a fraternal delegate to the TLCC, and on 29 April 1898 Gompers suggested to the AFL executive council a $100 grant to the TLCC for legislative purposes. The council agreed to put this to the convention.

So Thomas A. Kidd, of the Woodworkers, the first AFL fraternal delegate, arrived at the TLCC 1898 convention bearing word of possible gifts. As a result of his conversations with the president and secretary-treasurer, and his observation of the convention proceedings, he concluded that the congress was not going socialist, and was able to report to the next AFL convention that it was not really a rival, since it did not deal with jurisdictional disputes but only with legislative matters and organization. For these purposes it needed more money. The convention voted the $100. Meanwhile, the TLC had elected its first fraternal delegate to the AFL, David Carey.

Carey attended the AFL 1899 convention, and in 1900 made an ecstatic report to the congress convention. His statistics of AFL membership and expenditures must have impressed the delegates: 73 affiliated national and international unions, 11 state federations, 118 city central labour unions and trades assemblies, 595 local unions (where no national or international unions existed), and 202 FLUs; total membership of affiliates, 144,282; total expenditure, $39,148.55. The contrast with the congress's total expenditure of $618.79 must have been painful.

American industry was spreading into Canada. So were American employers' associations. The American National Founders Association, formed in 1898, enrolled 600 firms in the United States and Canada, and proceeded to sign a continent-wide contract with the Iron Molders Union. The National Metal Trades Association, formed in 1899, took in 325 firms in both countries, and in 1900 signed an international agreement with the Machinists. Where the employers led, the AFL followed.

Till the middle of 1899, the federation was spending only about $50 a month on organizing. Then the executive council decided to branch out. It appointed the federation's first full-time walking delegates, and by October it had voluntary organizers in Canada, and from February 1900, a full-time Canadian organizer with many voluntary assistants. The effects were spectacular. Even the AFL FLUs, the least of the organizers' work, soon far outnumbered the congress FLUs. At the time of the 1899 congress convention, these latter numbered seven, against six AFL. But by the end of 1902, congress FLUs seem to have numbered 37, AFL at least 46.

Gompers himself spent three days in 1900 making speeches in London and Toronto, where he argued, with considerable effect, that when the 'Yankee capitalist' came in, 'it was but natural that the Yankee "agitator" should follow' (the London street railway strike of course lent point to his words).[6]

In 1901 Carey delivered another enthusiastic report. The federation, during 1900, had chalked up a net gain of 3300 unions and its total income had risen to nearly $80,000. Carey had been particularly impressed by the absence of politicians from the platform (which he went out of his way to commend as an example for the congress) and the resounding defeat of socialism.

Comparing the respective numbers and resources of the AFL and the TLC, one might wonder why the federation thought it worth while to spend so much time, money, and energy on Canada, and especially why it felt it necessary to purge the TLCC of what had, by 1902, become such feeble rivals of the international unions. Part of the answer undoubtedly is that the federation, and its unions, were afraid that, if Canadian workers were left unorganized, American employers would take jobs across the line where labour was cheap; and it was perfectly clear that local, regional, or national Canadian unions, and the TLCC itself, in general simply did not have the resources to organize the unorganized. Some of the individual international unions had enough workers within their jurisdiction in Canada to make it possible for them to send in their own organizers; many did not. If the task was to be performed at all, the AFL itself had to do a large part of it.

There was, however, a second reason for the federation's interest: what Professor Babcock has called 'the rise of political unionism in Canada' between 1895 and 1902. The Canadian labour movement of the 1890s was swept by all the winds both of American and British radicalism. A large proportion of Canadian labour leaders were of British birth and upbringing; the traditions of the British working-class movement were part of the baggage they took with them to the new world; and they retained a keen interest in, and close contact with, the developments in working-class organization and politics in the Old Country.

This was one reason for the growth of socialism in Canada, and in Canadian unions. Branches of the Socialist Labor Party sprang up in Toronto, Hamilton, Ottawa, Brantford, Halifax, Winnipeg, Vancouver, and, surprisingly, three in Montreal. Most of them did not last long;[7] but, as we have seen, in spite of the SLP's policy of denying membership to union officers, and its virulent criticism of the unions and their leaders, it was, briefly, actually admitted to the congress. Then there was the Canadian Socialist League, which tried to get in in 1900, and, along with the Socialist Party, was formally thanked, in 1901, for urging its members to join unions. There was the series of socialist resolutions at congress conventions, year after year. There was the election of socialist and labour candidates to the House of Commons and the British Columbia legislature.[8] There were the resolutions for independent political action.

What was not less significant, by 1900 there were signs that the Liberal Party was anxious to capture the congress. It established a department of labour. It passed the Conciliation Act. It put a fair wages clause into government contracts. It appointed O'Donoghue fair wage officer, Edward Williams alien labour officer, Frank Plant staff clerk in the department of labour, and a phalanx of labour men to be the *Labour Gazette*'s local correspondents.[9]

A third reason for the AFL's activity in Canada was the threat of dual unionism: the Western Federation of Miners, the Western Labor Union, the American Labor Union, the United Brotherhood of Railway Employees, Smith's proposal for a Canadian federation of Canadian unions, the persisting (if declining) influence of the Knights of Labor in Quebec. The question of who should charter trades and labour councils also entered into this, for the AFL looked to such bodies to help it enforce its jurisdictional decisions. But if the councils held charters from a hostile, or even indifferent, congress, the AFL's decisions might be largely frustrated. Most of the councils in Canada had set themselves up without benefit of a charter from any central body. By the end of 1902, Nelson, Toronto, Windsor, and Montreal Central had congress charters, while Revelstoke, Victoria, Brockville, Galt-Preston, Charlottetown, and Montreal Federated had AFL charters. The rest were fair game for either the congress or the AFL, or, in British Columbia, the ALU.

Weak as it was, therefore, a congress which was ready to accept any kind of labour organization, in the traditional manner; which had leanings towards independent political action; and which had the power to charter both local unions and councils could at least have made itself a considerable nuisance to the AFL and its affiliates. The threat became greater as Draper proceeded with his energetic internal reorganization of the congress. It was not, indeed, until 1902, when the congress's revenue had reached the dizzy height of $2342.41 that he took the epoch-making step of buying a typewriting machine and supplies, engaging the services of a stenographer and typewriter, and fitting up a small office with two desks and a chair. But even in 1901 the congress's official book showed an unprecedented list of affiliates; and this before Gompers' letter to Canadian locals of international unions, requesting them to affiliate with the congress, could have taken effect.

There were 18 trades and labour councils (including the AFL-chartered Victoria, Brockville, and Montreal Federated councils); 13 Typos' locals; District 6 of the WFM; 8 each of the Molders and the United Carpenters; 7 of the Tailors; 6 and a council of the Woodworkers; 6 of the Cigar Makers; 3 each of the Bricklayers, the

Machinists, and the Sheet Metal Workers; 2 each of the Barbers (international), the Railway Carmen, and the Stonecutters; 1 each of the Painters, Plumbers, Builders' Labourers, Allied Printing Trades, Pressmen, Steel and Copper Plate Printing, Bookbinders, Boilermakers, Metal Polishers, Broommakers, Bakers, Tobacco Workers, Hotel and Restaurant Employees, Street Railway Employees, and Glass Bottle Blowers. Even a very few locals of the railway running trades were affiliated: the Hamilton BLE, Toronto BLF, Winnipeg BRT. There were also two AFL FLUs. This made a total of 88 internationally chartered bodies. Two purely local Barbers' unions, the Montreal Coopers, and the Nanaimo Miners were also affiliated, and, naturally, the 22 Congress FLUs; so were 3 DAs and 11 LAs of the Knights of Labor. The grand total was 143; and several of these represented a number of locals. Montreal had 17, Toronto 15, Vancouver 13, Brantford 10, Ottawa 9, Winnipeg and Hamilton 7 each, Nelson and Berlin 6 each, Quebec City 5, London and Guelph 4 each. By provinces, the score was: Prince Edward Island 1, Nova Scotia 2, New Brunswick 2, Quebec 22, Ontario 74, Manitoba 7, and British Columbia 35.

A year later, the number of international affiliates had grown by 39 to 127, and the total number of affiliates by 61, to 204. The most notable gains came from the appearance of 4 new international unions (Boot and Shoe, 8 locals; Barbers, and Boilermakers, 3 each; Longshoremen, 2), with 5 extra locals from the United Carpenters and 3 of the Street Railway Employees; the affiliation of the Canadian Federation of Boot and Shoe Workers (with its 3 locals), and 14 extra Congress FLUs. Prince Edward Island now had 3 affiliates; Nova Scotia 3; New Brunswick 4; Quebec 32; Ontario 105; Manitoba 9; Alberta 2; British Columbia 46. Once again, some of the affiliates represented more than one local. The Toronto Council, for example, had 67 affiliates, Brantford 16, Guelph 15, St Catharines 14, and Brockville 9.[10]

W.D. Mahon, the AFL fraternal delegate to the 1900 TLCC convention, thought of the congress as a state federation of labor perhaps slightly glorified. Draper, nearly a year later, wrote of it as standing to the working people of Canada in the same relation as the TUC to those of Britain and the AFL to those of the United States: 'equally independent ... and necessary.'

By March 1902 Gompers seems to have made up his mind that dual unionism in North America had to be stopped. Canada was obviously the danger point; so he suggested to the AFL executive council that Draper be invited to attend its April sessions. The council agreed. Draper came; reported splendid progress in Canada, thanks to Flett and the international union organizers; admitted there was a small element opposed to international unions; and recommended that Gompers himself, or Frank Morrison, the AFL secretary and an ex-Canadian, attend the next congress convention. But, as Professor Babcock suggests, the expulsion of the dual organizations from the congress may well have been decided at the April meetings in Washington.

The 1902 convention opened with a bitter struggle over the credentials of the Montreal Central Council, the Montreal Barbers Protective Association, the Montreal Protective Coopers Union, FLU No 36, and the Canadian Federation of Boot and Shoe Workers. The credentials committee recommended seating the delegates of all but the Barbers ('purely an association of employers'); but it also recommended setting up a committee to do a complete revision of the constitution, notably to prohibit dual councils; and it urged the congress officers to get FLU No 36 and the Coopers to join the international unions of their trades. It clearly regretted that the existing constitution did not allow it to bar the Canadian Boot and Shoe Workers: the rival international union had no less than 13 delegates, buttressed by their international president.

The report of the committee was adopted, and its members were promptly reconstituted as the committee to revise the constitution. The result must have been a foregone conclusion. Of the nine members only two were not members of international unions; and one was a close friend of the AFL secretary, while another was a bitter enemy of the Montreal Central Council.

The committee came back with a set of drastic amendments, notably: the Knights were to be excluded; no national union was to be recognized where an international union existed; there was to be only one central body in any city or town, and it was to be chartered by the congress; and the executive was to be explicitly authorized to use congress funds for organizing purposes.

The committee turned down a proposal to give fraternal delegates the full privileges of the convention, except for AFL and TUC delegates. It also recommended that the Montreal Federated Council be recognized as the one Montreal council, but that it must take out a congress charter, under the name of the Montreal Trades and Labor Council.

All the changes were to go into effect 1 January 1903. This would give the officers of the Congress 'an opportunity of using conciliatory means in endeavoring to bring together the conflicting elements.'

Sam Landers and O.R. Wallace tried to have the committee's report adopted *en bloc*; but an amendment, by Robert Glockling and D.J. O'Donoghue, for consideration clause by clause, carried.

The clause providing for organization of FLUs where no national or international union existed (striking out the provision for congress organizing of LAs), and barring national unions except where no international union existed, produced an amendment to allow DAs to be represented. Around this raged a furious debate.

William Horan (FLU No 36, Montreal Waiters) said the committee's proposal would destroy the labour movement in Quebec. The Hotel and Restaurant Workers would never get a foothold there. T.J. Griffiths said the exclusion of the Knights would divide the movement, in flat contradiction to the congress's declared aim of uniting all the labour organizations of Canada. William Annable said the exclusions 'would shut out some of the ablest representatives in the Congress,' no doubt referring to the veterans O'Donoghue, Beales, and Jobin, two of whom were delegates from KOL DAS and one from an LA. Joseph Marks suggested that the Knights amalgamate their membership and apply for FLU charters (which would, of course, have forced many of them into international unions). J.S. Fitzpatrick replied that the Knights would not be forced even into FLUs: they would 'go forward as they had in the past, because they held the key to the situation in Montreal and Quebec Province'; they refused to 'come sneaking into the Congress under another name.'

O'Donoghue said decisions by majorities were not always right or just. He had represented the Knights at congress conventions from the very beginning; he had also held an ITU card for 37 years. The exclusions 'would be disastrous to the interests of labor, and would practically shut Quebec Province out of the Congress.' Edward Little said the exclusions would leave Quebec City, now well organized, with only one recognized union local.

Landers said the existing situation, which permitted dual union labels, confused consumers. Rodier underlined this for the boot and shoe trade. E.S. Jackson said he had received instructions from his international union (Typos) to vote against dual organizations (this was contested by a Toronto Printing Trades Council delegate). The amendment to the committee's proposal was defeated, 87 to 32.

The next battle was over the exclusion of the Knights and the prohibition of dual councils. O'Donoghue played a leading part in this also. He pointed out that the proposed amendments would not only exclude the Knights but also prevent the affiliation of the PWA. Proderick, a delegate of the Ottawa local of the Plumbers (international) the year before, attacked the international unions generally, and his own in particular, which, he said, had not paid striking Canadian plumbers one cent while they were out. A.L. Garneau (LA 2436, Montreal) ridiculed the arguments based on the confusion of union and Knights' labels and charged that one international union in Montreal had actually allowed an unorganized shop to use its label. Landers replied to Proderick's charges by citing cases in which international unions had helped Canadian strikers. The previous question then carried, 89 to 33.

On the revised clause on basis of representation, F.X. Boileau and Omar Brunet tried to get DAS allowed in, provided they were affiliated with a trades and labour council chartered by the congress. This was defeated, 88 to 35.

The defeat of the attempt to get the Montreal Central Council recognized as *the* Montreal council we have already noted. This was followed by a motion to concur in the report as a whole, to which O'Donoghue and Fitzpatrick moved an amendment to strike out the new clause which would bar the Knights from membership in the congress. This also was defeated, on division.

Draper and Annable then moved an addition to the constitutional revision committee's report. This would have added, after the name of the congress, the words:

'and shall consist of such Trade Unions, Federal Unions, Trade and Labor Councils and National Trade Unions, as shall conform to its regulations.' It would also have deleted the whole clause setting forth the object of the congress, thus neatly disposing of the now embarrassing words, 'to unite all the labor organizations of the Dominion,' but also eliminating any statement whatever of the reasons for the congress's existence. This carried.

In Professor Babcock's words, 'the triumph of the craft internationals at Berlin was sealed by the election of John A. Flett, the AFL's salaried organizer, to the presidency.'

Some of the delegates from organizations which were now to be ineligible for membership in the congress (mainly French-Canadian Knights) promptly withdrew from the convention and set up a rival body: the National Trades and Labour Congress of Canada. Others remained (as of course they had a perfect right to do, since the amendments were not to come into force till the New Year).

Two subsequent decisions of the convention reflected both the dominance of the AFL influence and, ominously for the future, an east-west division.

The first was on Marks' motion to strike out compulsory arbitration from the platform of principles. The AFL was strongly opposed to compulsory arbitration, and Marks got the support of W.V. Todd, of the Cigar Makers, of which Gompers was president and Todd, his close friend, a vice-president. He was also supported by J.H. Hall (Railway Conductors, Toronto), and Peter Sharkey (ILA, Saint John). In contrast, as we have seen, the Manitoba executive had come out strongly for compulsory arbitration, and Robert Thoms, of the Winnipeg Typos, said the Winnipeg delegates had been sent to the convention to demand it. In New Zealand and Australia, under compulsory arbitration 'increased wages and shortened hours had been obtained, and the condition of the working classes generally advanced.' Another delegate protested against the congress abandoning a policy it had supported for seven years. Draper moved to substitute voluntary for compulsory, and this carried.

The second decision reflecting AFL influence and revealing east-west division came on a motion by A.M. Gossel to give all MPs and MLAs who had been elected as '*bona fide* labormen ... all the privileges of the Congress,' provided they were paid-up members of their unions. Western delegates, who said they expected to have 20 labour men elected to the next Manitoba legislature, strongly supported Gossel. The AFL constitution forbade representation of political parties at federation conventions; and the congress now, in effect, followed suit by defeating Gossel's motion.

It is hardly surprising that Gompers, in November 1902, asserted that the relations between the AFL and the TLCC were now substantially the same as between the AFL and its state federations.[11] There were in fact important differences, notably the congress's power to charter trades and labour councils and FLUs, which it continued to exercise, though within limitations subsequently worked out with the AFL executive council. But that the congress had been brought effectively within the AFL orbit, and was now powerless to admit any union dual to an AFL union, there could be no doubt. Draper, in his report to the 1903 convention, dwelt upon the fact that as a result of the amendments made to the constitution at the Berlin convention, 20 more councils had taken out congress charters, covering the whole country from Halifax to Victoria. He said this established 'our Congress beyond question in its rightful position as the supreme head and parent in this Dominion, for legislative purposes, of the legitimate international trade union movement, and effectively answers on the one hand those who would place it in the same category as State Federations of Labor, and on the other hand administers a crushing rebuke to those in Canada, professing to represent labor, who state that it is an appendage of the American Federation of Labor and that its policy is dictated from Washington ... It makes Congress the legislative mouthpiece of nearly two hundred thousand organized wage-workers.' But the fatal words 'for legislative purposes' and 'legitimate inter-national trade union movement' reveal the weakness of the congress's position and the limitations under which it operated.

Opponents of the 1902 constitutional decisions continued to wage a rearguard action within the congress in some places, notably Toronto, where the District Labor Council refused by a large majority to unseat the Knights' delegates (in fact they continued to sit in the Council throughout 1903).[12] But this was only a vestigial remainder of the old, free days of the congress, when the door was open to every labour organization, local, regional, national, or international, craft or industrial or mixed. The distinctive international character of the congress had been fixed, and remained so for more than half a century.

Canadian labour was split, but not as badly as might have been expected. Draper, in his 1903 report, noted that 23 congress FLUs had surrendered, or been deprived of, their charters during the year: 14 in British Columbia, 4 in Ontario, 2 in Quebec, 2 in Prince Edward Island, and 1 in New Brunswick. Of these, probably 5 were the result of the Berlin decisions; it seems unlikely that most of the rest had anything to do with the constitutional amendments. Besides, 18 new congress FLUs had been chartered: 4 in British Columbia, 8 in Ontario, 3 in New Brunswick, 2 in Quebec, and 1 in Manitoba. The Vancouver council had disaffiliated, but it had gone over to the ALU, not the new national congress. Draper put the loss of independent unions and Knights of Labor Assemblies as a result of the Berlin convention at 23, with a total membership of 2287. The largest losses were in Quebec: the Montreal Central Council, the Quebec Council, five LAs in Montreal and two in Quebec City, four Canadian Boot and Shoe locals in Montreal, two Fraternities of Shoe Workers in Quebec City, one independent Barbers and one independent Coopers union. The total was 17, with 2136 members. Total membership for the whole country had risen from 13,465 in 1902 to 16,108 in 1903. The biggest gain had been in Ontario (from

6214 to 10,384), and this had been only partly offset by losses in Quebec (down from 3993 to 2300) and the West (down from 2823 to 2463). There had been a small gain in the Maritimes: from 435 to 508. By 1904 the Quebec membership had reached 6179, to Ontario's 12,018.[13]

The new national congress rallied most of the organizations from Quebec which had been expelled, and a few others, but very few from outside that province. Isaac H. Sanderson, DA 180, Toronto, former president of the Toronto council, became the new congress's vice-president, but seems not to have stayed long, for we find him continuing to sit in the Toronto District Labor Council. P.J. Jobin, former president of the TLCC, was a delegate to the first regular convention of the National Congress; so were a number of former Montreal and Quebec City delegates to TLCC conventions.[14] It soon became clear, however, that the national movement was likely to be little more than a nuisance outside Quebec. None the less, schism there had been, and in French Canada it was serious. (A much stronger and more lasting rival to the TLCC, the Roman Catholic union movement, had yet to be born.) The year 1902 was a watershed for Canadian labour. On one side lay the spontaneity, the variety, the eccentric idealism, the haphazard organization and methods, the penury, and the nationalism of the nineteenth century; on the other the system, the discipline, the ordered jurisdictions, the business-like approach, the big unions, the large funds, and the continentalism of the twentieth.

Number of international locals in Canada 1880–1902

A note on the tables: There are several reasons why I have put down, for certain unions, in certain places, at certain times, two figures. First, it was not always possible to discover whether the particular union was simply a local union, a local of an international union, or part of a regional or national union. Second, it was sometimes difficult to establish whether a union formed in, for example, 1895, was still in existence in 1897. Finally, there was at times evidence of equal validity on any side of each of these questions.

These tables are compiled from the research notes on which this book is based. There are far too many sources to include in any reference. Those interested in them may consult chapter VIII of the manuscript of this book in the Public Archives of Canada.

TABLE 1

Number of locals of international unions in Canada 1880–1902

Union (year of entry)	1880	1890	1897	1902
Machinists and Blacksmiths	1	0	0	0
Sailors (Lake Seamen) (1877)	3	0	0	0
ASE	6	7	8	7
Molders (1859)	10	20	14	28
BLE (1865)	9	27	37	44
ITU (1865)	7	17	18	35
CMIU (1867)	5	7	11	20–21
ASCJ (1871)	5	10	8	10
BLF (1877)	3	30	39	48
Flint Glass Workers (1879)	1	1	1	2
ORC (1880)	1	18	26	28
Bricklayers and Masons (1881)	0	13	10	32
Iron and Steel Workers (1882)	0	1	0	2
UBC (1882; American Brotherhood till 1888)	0	19	8	46
Boilermakers (1883)	0	1	2	10
Stonemasons (1884)	0	1	1	1
Railroad Trainmen (1885)	0	29	42	46–47
Painters (1887)	0	5	5	29
Building Labourers (1888)	0	0	2	6
Journeymen Stonecutters (1888)	0	4	8	13–20
ORT (1888)	0	2	8	13–15
Plumbers (1888)	0	1	4	16
Bakers (1889)	0	1	0	18
Plasterers (1889)	0	2	4	8–9
Printing Pressmen (1889)	0	6	8	12
Journeymen Tailors (1889)	0	11	13	31–33
United Hatters (1889)	0	1	1	2
Boot and Shoe Workers (1890)	0	3	0	11–14
IAM (1890)	0	3	9	30–31
Pattern Makers (1891)	0	0	1	4
Railway Carmen (1891)	0	0	1	11
Glass Bottle Blowers (1892)	0	0	3	3
Horseshoers (1892)	0	0	3	4–5
Amalgamated Woodworkers (1893)	0	0	6	25
Bookbinders (1893)	0	0	2	6
Street Railway Employees (1893)	0	0	0	12
Railway Switchmen (1894)	0	0	0	7
United Garment Workers (1894)	0	0	4	13
Upholsterers (1894)	0	0	1	4
Barbers (1895)	0	0	1	17
Metal Polishers (1893)	0	0	6	10
WFM (1895)	0	0	1	23–24
Sheet Metal Workers (1896)	0	0	2	14–15
Steel and Copper Plate Printers (1897)	0	0	1	1
Allied Metal Mechanics (1898)	0	0	0	6–7
NATSE (1898)	0	0	0	3–5

TABLE 1
(continued)

Union (year of entry)	1880	1890	1897	1902
United Brotherhood of Leather Workers on Horse Goods (1898)	0	0	0	4
Blacksmiths (1899)	0	0	0	7–8
Carriage and Wagonmakers (1899)	0	0	0	10–13
Coremakers (1899)	0	0	0	5
Hotel and Restaurant Workers (1899)	0	0	0	25
Electrical Workers (1899)	0	0	0	8
Longshoremen (1899)	0	0	0	22–23
Meat Cutters and Butcher Workmen (1899)	0	0	0	2–3
Railway Trackmen (1899)	0	0	0	109
Retail Clerks (1899)	0	0	0	19
Stove Mounters (1899)	0	0	0	5
Team Drivers (1899)	0	0	0	13–14
Tobacco Workers (1899)	0	0	0	6
Textile Workers (1899)	0	0	0	3
Wood Carvers (1899)	0	0	0	2
Architectural Iron and Steel Workers (1900)	0	0	0	3–4
Broom Makers (1900)	0	0	0	6
Composition Metal Workers (1900)	0	0	0	1
Meat and Pastry Cooks (1900)	0	0	0	1
Musicians (1900)	0	0	0	8
Shirt, Waist and Laundry Workers (1900)	0	0	0	7
Trunk and Bag Workers (1900)	0	0	0	4
Wood, Wire and Metal Lathers (1900)	0	0	0	4
Brewery Workers (1901)	0	0	0	8
Coopers (1901)	0	0	0	2
Farmers (1901)	0	0	0	1
Jewelry Workers (1901)	0	0	0	2
Papermakers (1901)	0	0	0	4
Steam Engineers (1901)	0	0	0	3
Amalgamated Glassworkers (1902)	0	0	0	1
Amalgamated Leather Workers (1902)	0	0	0	3
Brick, Tile and Terra Cotta Workers	0	0	0	1
Ceramic, Mosaic, etc (1902)	0	0	0	1
Marble Workers (1902)	0	0	0	2
Marine Engineers (1902)	0	0	0	1
Photo-Engravers (1902)	0	0	0	1
Piano and Organ Makers (1902)	0	0	0	4
Railway Clerks (1902)	0	0	0	3–4
Sawsmiths (1902)	0	0	0	3
Special Order Clothing Workers (1902)	0	0	0	1
Stationary Firemen (1902)	0	0	0	1
Steam Shovel (1902)	0	0	0	1
Stereotypers (1902)	0	0	0	4
Teamsters (1902)	0	0	0	2
United Metal Workers (1902)	0	0	0	1
UBRE (1902)	0	0	0	5

TABLE 2
International union locals in Canada 1880–1902

	1880		1890		1897		1902	
	Number of locals	Number of places	Number of locals	Number of places	Number of locals	Number of places	Number of locals	Number of places
ONTARIO	42	16	147	35	192	33	615–635	101–3
Toronto	9		28		47		106–107	
Hamilton	7		17		19		45–46	
London	6		11		19		37–39	
Ottawa	1		9		20		37–39	
St Catharines	3		3		5		20	
QUEBEC	10	4	30	7	47	9	111–116	22
Montreal	5		19		31		59–62	
Quebec City	3		3		4		14	
NEW BRUNSWICK	0	0	12	5	17	7	43	15
Saint John	0		4		5		16	
NOVA SCOTIA	0	0	10	3	13	4	46–50	10
Halifax	0		5		6		20–24	
MANITOBA	0	0	11	1	17	2	48	10
Winnipeg	0		11		15		36	
BRITISH COLUMBIA	0	0	25	7	27	6	137–39	37
Vancouver	0		10		11		35	
Victoria	0		7		7			
(SASKATCHEWAN)	0	0	1	1	3	1	11–12	4
Moose Jaw	0		1				8–9	
(ALBERTA)	0	0	4	1	4	1	16–17	7–8
Medicine Hat	0		4				6	
PRINCE EDWARD ISLAND	0	0	0	0	0	0	—	4
YUKON	0	0	0	0	0	0	1	1
Total Canada	52	20	240	60	320	63	1037–1070	211–14

TABLE 3
Number of Locals of railway running trades unions,
by union and by place, in Canada 1880–1902

	1880	1890	1897	1902
Union				
Brotherhood of Locomotive Engineers	9	27	37	44
Firemen	3	30	39	48
Order of Railway Conductors	1	18	26	28
Trainmen	0	29	42	46–47
Total Canada	13	104	144	166–67
Place				
Ontario	11	62	86	93–94
Quebec	2	15	19	23
New Brunswick	0	7	12	12
Nova Scotia	0	5	8	12
British Columbia	0	6	6	10
Manitoba	0	4	6	8
(Saskatchewan)	0	1	3	4
(Alberta)	0	4	4	4
Total Canada	13	104	144	166–67

TABLE 4
Number of locals of building trades unions,
by union and by place, in Canada 1880–1902

	1880	1890	1897	1902
Union				
ASCJ	5	10	8	10
Bricklayers and Masons	0	13	10	32
United Carpenters	0	19	8	46
Painters	0	5	5	29
Journeymen Stonecutters	0	4	8	13–20
Plasterers	0	2	4	8–9
Plumbers	0	1	4	16
Building Labourers	0	0	2	6
Masons	0	1	1	1
Sheet Metal Workers	0	0	2	14–15
Electrical Workers	0	0	0	8
Lathers	0	0	0	4
Marble Workers	0	0	0	2
Brick, Tile and				
Terra Cotta Workers	0	0	0	1
Ceramic, Mosaic, etc	0	0	0	1
Place				
Ontario	5	29	31	125–31
Quebec	0	6	6	17–18
New Brunswick	0	2	1	4
Nova Scotia	0	3	2	8–9
British Columbia	0	12	6	22–23
Manitoba	0	3	6	10
Prince Edward Island	0	0	0	1
Saskatchewan	0	0	0	1
Alberta	0	0	0	1

TABLE 5
Number of locals of metal trades unions, by union

Union	1880	1890	1897	1902
Molders	10	20	14	28
ASE	6	7	8	7
Boilermakers	0	1	2	10
Iron and Steel Workers	0	1	0	2
IAM	0	3	9	30–31
Horseshoers	0	0	3	4–5
Blacksmiths	0	0	0	7–8
Metal Polishers	0	0	6	10
Allied Metal Mechanics	0	0	0	6
Stove Mounters	0	0	0	5
Coremakers	0	0	0	5
United Metal Workers	0	0	0	1
Sawsmiths	0	0	0	3
Jewelry Workers	0	0	0	2
Architectural Iron and Steel Workers	0	0	0	3–4
Composition Metal Workers	0	0	0	1
Total Canada	16	32	42	124–128

TABLE 6
Number of locals of transport unions (other than railway), by union

Union	1880	1890	1897	1902
Street Railway Employees	0	0	0	12
Team Drivers	0	0	0	13–14
Teamsters	0	0	0	2
Total Canada	0	0	0	27–28

TABLE 7
Number of locals of printing and publishing trades unions, by union

Union	1880	1890	1897	1902
ITU	7	17	18	35
Pressmen	0	6	8	12
Bookbinders	0	0	2	6
Photo-Engravers	0	0	0	1
Stereotypers and Electrotypers	0	0	0	4
Steel and Copper Plate Printing	0	0	1	1
Total Canada	7	23	29	59

TABLE 8
Number of locals of woodworking trades unions, by union

Union	1880	1890	1897	1902
Pattern Makers	0	0	1	4
Woodworkers	0	0	6	25
Upholsterers	0	0	1	4
Carriage and Wagonmakers	0	0	0	10–12
Wood Carvers	0	0	0	2
Coopers	0	0	0	2
Papermakers	0	0	0	4
Broom Makers	0	0	0	6
Piano and Organ Makers	0	0	0	4
Total Canada	0	0	8	61–63

TABLE 9
Number of locals of clothing trades unions, by union

Union	1880	1890	1897	1902
Hatters	0	1	1	2
Garment Workers	0	0	4	13
Tailors	0	11	13	31–33
Special Order Clothing Workers	0	0	0	1
Total Canada	0	12	18	47–49

TABLE 10
Number of locals of leather working unions, by union

Union	1880	1890	1897	1902
Boot and Shoe	0	3	0	11–14
Leather Workers on Horse Goods	0	0	0	4
Amalgamated Leather Workers	0	0	0	3
Total Canada	0	3	0	18–21

Notes

CHAPTER I

1 Sidney and Beatrice Webb, *Industrial Democracy* (London and New York, 1902), 246–76

CHAPTER 2

1 MacNutt, *NB: A History*, 157; PAC, Ward Chipman Papers MG23, VI, Chipman to Jonathan Odell, 16 May 1814
2 *New Brunswick Courier*, 26 Sept. 1835; J.C. Ward, 'Old Times in Saint John,' *Globe* (Saint John), 27 April 1907
3 *New Brunswick Courier*, 20 March 1841; *Morning News* (Saint John), 28 May 1849
4 Rice, 'History of Organized Labour in Saint John,' 85
5 *New Brunswick Courier*, 1 April, 1, 29 July, 2, 30 Sept., 28 Oct., 2 Dec., 1837; 3 March 1838
6 Ibid., 1, 8 April 1837; 18 Aug. 1838
7 *Morning News*, 17 July 1840
8 Ibid., 29 May 1840; *New Brunswick Courier*, 30 May 1840
9 *Morning News*, 17 July 1840; *New Brunswick Courier*, 25 July 1840
10 Saint John, TLC, *History*, 29
11 *New Brunswick Courier*, 17 Sept. 1853; *Morning News* and *New Brunswick Railway Advocate*, 15 Sept. 1853
12 *New Brunswick Courier*, 7 April 1849; 'Old Times in Saint John,' *Globe*, 19 March 1912; Saint John TLC, *History*, 15
13 Population returns for New Brunswick in 1851 are in NB, Legislative Assembly, *Journals*, 1852, appendix, xxii; Canada, *Census, 1870–71*, vol. IV, 178, 202.
14 MacNutt, *NB: A History*, 329–30, 333, 338–9, 374
15 *Daily News* (Saint John), 1 May 1875; *Morning Chronicle* (Halifax), 3, 4 May 1875

16 *Morning News*, 3 Sept. 1858; 'Old Times in Saint John,' *Globe*, 9 March 1912; Saint John TLC, *History*, 39

17 The Printers, in 1865, became Local 85 of the ITU; the Millmen certainly existed in 1873, the Carpenters in 1875, the Painters and the Tailors in 1883; and the Cordwainers probably became Lodge 171 of the KOSC in 1869.

18 *Miramichi Gleaner*, 26 May 1940; 'Old Times in Saint John,' *Globe*, 4 Dec. 1909

19 Fergusson, *NS Labour Movement*, 11, 14, 42. The Act was repealed in 1851.

20 Lawson, *Reminiscences of Yarmouth County*, 582

21 ITU, *A Study of the History of the International Union*, 133

22 *Morning Post and Shipping Gazette* (St John's), 3 March 1855, recording the 28th annual meeting; information from Mr J.A. Gibbs, QC, St John's, whose father organized a large number of unions in St John's in 1903 and later; Hattenhauer, 'History of Nfld Labour,' 225–6

23 H.M. Mosdell, *When Was That?* (St John's, 1923), 116; Hattenhauer, 'History of Nfld Labour,' 225–6

24 *Evening Herald* (St John's), 29 April 1913, letter from James Murphy

25 J.J. Fogarty, in *The Book of Newfoundland*, ed. J. Smallwood, I, 100; Hattenhauer, 'History of Nfld Labour,' 94–5

26 Coats, *Labour Movement*, 292. The union concerned itself with music and drama as well as wages and sick benefits.

27 *L'Evénement* (Quebec), 3 sept. 1895

28 Ibid.; Logan, *Trade Unions in Canada*; Lipton, *Trade Union Movement*; TTU, Minutes, 2 April 1845

29 Information from Fernand Ouellet; see also his *Histoire de la Chambre de Commerce de Québec, 1809–1959* (Quebec, 1959), 24, and his *Histoire économique et sociale du Québec, 1760–1850* (Montreal and Paris, 1966), 501.

30 *Gazette* (Montreal), 4 Oct. 1841

31 Alfred Hawkins [?], *Remarks upon the Desertion of Seamen at the Port of Quebec, 1852*; Canada, *Statutes*, 10–11 Vic., c. 25, esp. s. 7. The *New Brunswick Courier*, 31 July 1847, says the sailors at Quebec are asking the 'exorbitant wages' of £13 to £14 a month.

32 Appleton, 'Sunshine and Shade,' 53–4

33 Cooper, 'The Quebec Ship Labourers' Benevolent Society,' 336

34 Coats, *Labour Movement*, 293

35 Ibid., 292; Lipton, *Trade Union Movement*, 3–5; *Globe* (Toronto), 1 May 1854; *Gazette* (Montreal), 19 May 1854; *Observer* (Lambton), 20 Nov. 1856

36 Logan, *Trade Unions in Canada*, 24; Lipton, *Trade Union Movement*, 3–4; Conner, 'The Labour and Socialist Movement in Canada,' mentions a Montreal Letter Press Printers' Society in 1836; *Globe* (Toronto), 9 Feb. 1854; Appleton, 'Sunshine and Shade,' 57.

37 Lipton, *Trade Union Movement*, 4–5; Bélanger et al., *Les Travailleurs québécois,* *1851–1896*, 212; *Observer*, 20 Nov. 1856; *Morning Chronicle* (Quebec), 25 July 1858; Appleton, 'Sunshine and Shade,' 96–7

38 Lipton, *Trade Union Movement*, 5; *Globe* (Toronto), 1 May 1854; *Gazette* (Montreal), 6 May 1854; *Observer*, 20 Nov. 1856

39 *Labour Gazette*, II, 246; *Report on Labour Organization in Canada* (1938), 234; *Pilot* (Montreal), 17 May 1854

40 AEW (England), AEW, Records

41 Logan, *Trade Unions in Canada*, 24–5; Lipton, *Trade Union Movement*, 7; Hamilton and District Trades and Labor Council, *Diamond Jubilee Programme* (1948); TTU, Minutes, 5 Aug. 1846, 6 March 1849; *Gazette* (Hamilton), 2 Aug. 1852; *Spectator* (Hamilton), 31 July 1852

42 *Spectator*, 7 March 1857; TTU, Minutes, 6 March 1860

43 Appleton, 'Sunshine and Shade,' 48–50, 52, 73; Commons, *History of Labor*, I, 623; *North American* (Toronto), 13 May 1853; for the Carpenters in 1864, see chapter 5.

44 Appleton, 'Sunshine and Shade,' 57–9

45 AEW (England), ASE Records

46 Lipton, *Trade Union Movement*, 6; *Recorder* (Brockville), 20 Dec. 1833; E.G. Firth (ed.), *The Town of York, 1815–1834*, xxxiii, 77–8, 87–8

47 Logan, *Trade Unions in Canada*, 23–5; J.M. Conner, 'Trade Unions in Toronto,' in J.E. Middleton, *Municipality of Toronto: A History*, II, 555; Armstrong, 'History of No. 91,' ITU, *Proceedings*, 1905; Lipton, *Trade Union Movement*, 10; Armstrong, 'Reformer as Capitalist,' 191

48 Armstrong, 'Reformer as Capitalist,' 191–5; Armstrong, 'History of No. 91'

49 The preceding account of the years 1845–51 is based on TTU, Minutes, vol. I.

50 *Globe* (Toronto), 8, 12 June 1854; J.M.S. Careless, *Brown of the Globe*, II, 289–90; Armstrong, 'History of No. 91'; Appleton, 'Sunshine and Shade,' 103–18

51 The following account of the years 1859–60 is based on TTU, Minutes.

52 The following account of the Tailors is based on the *Tailor* (New York), the organ of the Journeymen Tailors' Union of America, 4; June 1890, 7; Oct. 1895, 4; Conner, 'Labour and Socialist Movement'; Appleton, 'Sunshine and Shade,' 44–5, 118–24.

53 Appleton, 'Sunshine and Shade,' 50–1, 91, 93; *North American*, 8 April 1853; *Globe*, 26 May 1853, 18 June 1857. The 1857 union may have been a new one.

54 Appleton, 'Sunshine and Shade,' 60; *North American*, 29 April, 22 July 1853; Conner, 'Labour and Socialist Movement,' 'Trade Unions in Toronto,' 558.

55 *Globe*, 16 Feb. 1854; Appleton, 'Sunshine and Shade,' 67; C.B. Robinson, *History of Toronto and County of York*, I, 409

56 For this and following paragraphs, see *Globe*, 17 June 1854; *Leader* (Toronto), 12, 13, 25, 26 Jan. 1858; Commons, *History of Labor*, I, 623.

57 Conner, 'Labour and Socialist Movement'; AEW (England), ASE Records

58 Orlo Miller, *A Century of Western Ontario*, 96; *Free Press* (London), 12 Feb. 1856; *Observer*, 12 Feb. 1856

59 Miller, *Century of Western Ontario*, 98; Davis, 'History of the Early Labour Movement in London, Ontario,' 3–4, says the union was organized in 1859 by William Beck. There is some evidence, however, of a purely local union of moulders in 1856 or 1857: Ontario, Bureau of Labor, *First Report*, 23, *Eighth Report*, 87, *Ninth Report*, 108, *Tenth Report*, 116. The union organized by Beck was more probably Local 37 of the National Union of Molders: NUM, *Convention Proceedings*, 1859. Beck was a member of the Brantford Local of the NUM, no 29, for some years.

60 Coats, *The Labour Movement*, 293; *North American*, 3 May 1853

61 *Leader*, 4 March, 3 May 1854; AEW (England), ASE, Records; *Daily Expositor* (Brantford), 18 April 1908; Guelph, *City Directories*, 1882, 1887

62 *Gazette* (Victoria), 20 Jan. 1859

CHAPTER 3

1 Commons, *History of Labor*, I, 623

2 Lescohier, *Knights of St Crispin*, 7, 33; KOSC, *Annual Meeting*, 1869, 16, 26, 32; 1870, 21, 24, 39, 42; 1872, 18; *Ontario Workman*, 20 Feb. 1873, 4; Pryke, 'Labour and Politics,' 41; *Evening Express and Commercial Record* (Halifax), 15 Nov. 1869. A list of the lodges as of 1 Dec. 1870 was furnished by the State Historical Society of Wisconsin: PAC, E.A. Forsey Papers.

3 *Spectator*, 24 Aug. 1863, 7 Aug. 1866, 24 Aug. 1867; *Evening Times* (Hamilton), 22 Aug., 21 Sept. 1867; *Daily Advertiser* (London), 15 July 1865

4 KOSC, *Annual Meeting*, 1869, 16; Lescohier, *Knights of St Crispin*, 51, 60

5 KOSC, *Annual Meeting*, 1869, 26; Hamelin, *Répertoire des grèves*, 24–5, 27

6 KOSC, *Annual Meeting*, 1870, 16, 19, 21; Lescohier, *Knights of St Crispin*, 87; Hamelin *Répertoire des grèves*, 26

7 For this and following paragraphs, see KOSC, *Annual Meeting*, 1869 and 1870, and Lescohier, *Knights of St Crispin*, 87.

8 For the following account, see Kealey, 'Artisans Respond to Industrialism: Shoemakers, Shoe Factories and the Knights of St Crispin in Toronto,' 145–9; *Workingman's Advocate*, 22 April 1870; TTU, Minutes, 18 Feb., 4 March 1871.

9 KOSC, *Annual Meeting*, 1872

10 *Morning Chronicle* (Halifax), 18, 24 Jan., 14 Feb. 1872

11 *Ontario Workman* 6, 27 March 1873; CLU, *Congress Proceedings*, 1873, 15; TTA, Minutes, 6 June 1873

12 Kealey, 'Artisans Respond to Industrialism,' 149–50

13 Ibid., 150; Lescohier, *Knights of St Crispin*, 56

14 AEW (England), ASE, Records; CLU, *Congress Proceedings*, 1876, I, 61; 1877, 79, 89–91; *Post* (Thorold), 10 March 1876

15 NUM, *Convention Proceedings*, 1859, 1861, 1864, 1865; list of locals with dates of formation from the international office of the union, 9 Nov. 1966: CLC Collection, MG28I103; the locals got their numbers in 1861: *Iron Molders International Journal* (hereafter *Molders Journal*), 28 Feb. 1874, 258

16 NUM, *Convention Proceedings*, 1865; *Molders Journal*, 11 April 1864, 4

17 *Molders Journal*, 31 Oct. 1871, 4–5; 31 Jan. 1872, 1–2; 31 May 1872, 16

18 Ibid., 28 Feb. 1873, 17; 30 June 1873, 29; CLU, *Congress Proceedings*, 1873, 15.

19 The preceding paragraphs are based on monthly reports in the *Molders Journal*, 1864, 1866–69, 1874–76, 1878–80; *Quarterly Report* of the international, 1868–70; and NUM, *Convention Proceedings*, 1863, 7, and 1866, 47.

20 See monthly reports in the *Molders Journal*, 1864, 1866–67, 1871–72, 1874–76, 1879–80; NUM, *Convention Proceedings*, 1861–82.

21 Unless otherwise noted, this and the following account of the Molders is based on information in the *Molders Journal* and in the NUM, *Convention Proceedings*.

22 As well as sources listed in ibid., see NUM, *Quarterly Report*, March 1870, 1; and United States, House of Representatives, *Congressional Record*, 43rd Congress, 1st Session, vol. II, pt 6, 5162.

23 Information regarding dates and places of chartering of divisions from the Assistant Grand Chief Engineer of the international, 24 Aug. 1966: CLC Collection

24 The following account is based on Ayer, 'The Locomotive Engineers' Strike on the Grand Trunk Railway in 1876–1877,' supplemented by the *Molders' Journal*, 10 Jan. 1877, 209, 242, 250.

25 Information from a list of lodges, with dates of chartering, from the BLF, 20 Aug. 1965: CLC Collection

26 Information from a list of divisions, with dates of chartering, from the ORC, 21 April 1966: ibid.

27 In this section, information concerning the chartering of locals comes from a letter from the ITU, 6 May 1966: ibid.

28 As well as ibid., see Tracy, *History of the Typographical Union*, 285, 296; *Molders' Journal*, 10 Sept. 1875, 436; TTU, Minutes, 6 Oct. 1877. For Halifax and Saint John, see Saint John Typographical Union, Minutes, 10 March 1883; Letter Book, 77; *Morning Chronicle* (Halifax), 11 July 1881; 9 Jan. 1882; TTU, Minutes.

29 *New Brunswick Almanac*, 1866, 111; 1867, 32; 1868, 56; *Saint John Directory*, 1869–70, 1871–73; *Workingmen's Advocate*, 9 June 1866, 2; Tracy, *History of ITU*, 269, 266–7

30 Except where otherwise noted, the following account of the TTU is drawn from its minute books.

31 For the Ottawa Typos, see various references in ibid.; see also *Times* (Ottawa), 15 April 1867; 9 Dec. 1872; 6 Jan., 17–18 March, 5–9 Aug. 1873; 18 May 1875; *Citizen* (Ottawa), 18 Aug. 1880; *Molders Journal*, 30 Sept. 1873, 114; Tracy, *History of ITU*.

32 Tracy, *History of ITU*, 251–2, 259, 266–7, 272, 277; *Ontario Workman*, 9 May 1872, 4; TTU, Minutes, 8 Sept. 1869, June 1875

33 Davis, 'History of Labour in London,' 5–7; interview with a son of one of the members; TTU, Minutes, 5 June 1880

34 TTU, Minutes, 23 April 1869; 12 Jan. 1870; 7 July 1877; 6 July 1878; *Workingman's Advocate*, 15, 29 May 1869; Hamelin, *Répertoire des grèves*, 22–3, 45–6.

35 Tracy, *History of ITU*, 264, 292–4; L'Union typographique Jacques-Cartier, *Programme-souvenir du cinquantième anniversaire* (Montreal, 1920)

36 *Workingman's Advocate*, 14, 28 June, 5 June 1873

37 Ibid., 12 July, 30 Aug. 1873

38 Ibid., 16 Nov. 1872; Tracy, *History of ITU*, 272; *L'Evénement*, 3 sept. 1895

39 CMIU, *100th Anniversary Journal* (Washington, DC, 1964); Logan, *Trade Unions in Canada*, 30; *La Presse* (Montreal), 16 juillet 1889

40 *Evening Times*, 18 Nov. 1865, 27 July 1868; *Spectator*, 27 July 1868; *Daily Expositor*, 2 Sept. 1899

41 *Workingman's Advocate*, 14 Sept. 1867; CMIU (Washington, DC), Convention Proceedings, 1869

42 *Workingman's Advocate*, 28 May 1870; 19–26 Sept., 28 Nov. 1874; 30 Jan., 13 Feb., 20 March, 25 Sept. 1875; 13 Oct. 1876; *Spectator*, 28 Jan. 1884; *Palladium of Labor*, 19 Jan. 1884; B. Scott, *The Economic and Industrial History of the City of London, Canada*, 103

43 The following account of the Toronto local in the 1870s is based on TTU, Minutes; and on information in the *Workingman's Advocate*.

44 *Spectator*, 27 July 1868; *Evening Times*, 27 July, 5 Dec. 1868; but the union had struck in Nov. 1865: *Evening Times*, 2 Nov. 1865

45 For this and following paragraphs, see monthly reports in *Workingman's Advocate*, at appropriate dates.

46 For the following account, see monthly reports in ibid., and Hamelin, *Répertoire des grèves*, 49–50.

47 *Workingman's Advocate*, 25 Nov.–2 Dec. 1871

48 Ibid., 15 Nov. 1873; 20 June 1874; 13 Feb., 30 Oct. 1875

49 Pryke, 'Labour and Politics,' 40

50 *Workingman's Advocate*, 21 May 1870; 28 Oct. 1871; 22 March 1873; *Labour Gazette*, II, 320; *Daily Advertiser*, 4 July 1873; CLU, *Congress Proceedings*, 1873, 15; TTA, Minutes, 16 May, 15 Aug., 5, 19 Sept. 1873

51 *Post*, 28 Jan. 1876; CLU, *Congress Proceedings*, 1875, 43; TTA, Minutes, 17 Feb., 22 April 1875; TTLC, Minutes

52 *Daily Advertiser*, 9 Nov. 1869; 4 July 1873

53 Amalgamated Woodworkers, ASCJ Records; *Evening Times*, 1 June 1864

54 TTA, Minutes, 1 March 1872; *Ontario Workman*, 6 Feb. 1873; Logan, *Trade Unions in Canada*, 31; *Free Press*, 31 Aug. 1946; Davis, 'History of Labour in London,' 10–11

55 TTA, Minutes; *Workingman's Advocate*, 1, 18 Feb. 1873

56 Goldwin Smith, 'The Labour Movement,' *Canadian Monthly* (Toronto), II, 530

57 Information in a letter from the secretary of the Bricklayers, Masons and Plasterers International Union of America, 3 Nov. 1965: CLC Collection

58 *Workingman's Advocate*, 22–29 Aug. 1874; *Post*, 19 Nov., 17 Dec. 1875; 25 Feb., 5 May 1876; 23 Feb. 1877; 25 Jan., 8, 15 Feb., 8, 15 Nov. 1878; 28 Feb., 9 May 1879; 19 March 1880.

59 TTA, Minutes, 4 Aug. 1871; *Workingman's Advocate*, 13 Oct. 1877; *Spectator*, 19, 25 Jan. 1872; 9 April 1879; CLU, *Congress Proceedings*, 1873, 16

60 *Post*, 7 May 1880; 11 March 1881; *Recorder*, 24 April 1879

61 *Spectator*, 19 April 1881

62 Hamelin, *Répertoire des grèves*, 46–7

CHAPTER 4

1 Fergusson, *NS Labour Movement*, 23–4; Pryke, 'Labour and Politics'; *Evening Express and Commercial Record*, 10, 12 April 1872

2 Fergusson, *NS Labour Movement*, 29; Pryke, 'Labour and Politics,' 34, 38; *Acadian Recorder* (Halifax), 6 June 1870; *Evening Express*, 15 June 1870

3 Fergusson, *NS Labour Movement*, 30; *British Colonist* (Halifax), 30 May 1868; E.J. Shields, 'A History of Trade Unionism in Nova Scotia' (unpub. MA thesis, Dalhousie University, 1945), 7

4 *Evening Express*, 20 March, 8 April 1868; *Acadian Recorder*, 24 April 1882; *British Colonist*, 4 April 1868; *Morning Chronicle*, 22 April 1868; Pryke, 'Labour and Politics,' 40

5 Pryke, 'Labour and Politics,' 38; *Acadian Recorder*, 6 Feb., 5, 8, 10 April 1869; 8 April 1882; *Morning Chronicle*, 9 April 1869

6 *Labour Gazette*, II, 320; Pryke, 'Labour and Politics,' 38; *Evening Express*, 12 Aug. 1873; 31 March 1874; *Morning Chronicle*, 31 March 1874

7 *Morning Chronicle*, 16 March 1872; 31 May 1873; *Acadian Recorder*, 8 April 1882; 30 March 1883; 19 March 1884; *Evening Express*, 27 Feb., 20 June 1873; Pryke, 'Labour and Politics,' 38

8 See *Morning Chronicle*, Jan.–June 1872, for details; Pryke, 'Labour and Politics,' 40.

9 *Evening Express*, 26, 27 Jan. 1874; Pryke, 'Labour and Politics,' 48

10 Fergusson, *NS Labour Movement*, 18–21, 24; E.A. Forsey, 'Economic and Social Aspects of the Nova Scotia Coal Industry' (unpub. MA thesis, McGill University, 1926), 76

11 Fergusson, *NS Labour Movement*, 25–8; Pryke, 'Labour and Politics,' 34–5, 42–3; Forsey, 'Nova Scotia Coal Industry,' 76; *Daily News*, 10 April 1875

12 P.W. MacEwan, 'The PWA,' *Cape Breton Highlander*, 8 Dec. 1965; E.A. Forsey, *Economic and Social Aspects of the Nova Scotia Coal Industry* (Toronto), 15

13 PWA, Grand Council, Minutes, 1–6; *Trades Journal* (Stellarton, NS), 25 Feb. 1880; Forsey, *NS Coal Industry*, 15

14 PWA, Grand Council, Minutes, 8; see also reports in appropriate issues of *Trades Journal*, 1880.

15 MacEwan, 'PWA'

16 Saint John TLC, *History*, 39; Rice, 'Organized Labour in Saint John,' 86–7; New Brunswick, *Statutes*, 30 Vic. c. 39; *Daily News*, 6, 7 May 1875

17 For the caulkers, see Saint John, TLC, *History*, 39; Saint John Caulkers' Association, *Act of Incorporation and By-laws* (Saint John, 1866), 13; New Brunswick, *Statutes*, 30 Vic. 3. 38.; *Daily News*, 5–8 May 1875; *Morning Freeman*, 6, 8 May 1875.

18 *Daily Telegraph*, 2 Aug. 1872

19 Saint John TLC, *History*, 73; Rice, 'Organized Labour in Saint John,' 48; see also May 1875 issues of the *Daily News*, and the *Morning Freeman*, and the *Morning Chronicle* (Halifax).

20 Rice, 'Organized Labour in Saint John,' 26, 88–9; *New Brunswick Courier*, 16 May 1840

21 *Morning Freeman*, 28 July 1870; 5 Nov. 1874; *Daily Telegraph*, 4, 5 June 1872; *Morning Chronicle* (Halifax), 6 June 1872; Rice, 'Organized Labour in Saint John,' 89

22 This and the following account of the millmen are based on Rice, 'Organized Labour in Saint John,' 65–70, and on accounts in appropriate issues of *Daily Telegraph*, and *Evening Express* (Halifax). For 1875, see *Daily News*, 5 April, 17 May 1875.

23 *Daily News*, 5 May 1875.

24 For the preceding account, see Rice, 'Organized Labour in Saint John,' 56–9, and June 1870 issues of *Daily Telegraph* and *Morning Freeman*.

25 *Daily Telegraph*, 6, 8 Oct. 1870

26 *Evening Express* (Halifax), 12 June 1873

27 *Morning Freeman*, 5, 10 Nov. 1874; *Saint John and Its Business* (Saint John, 1875), 188

28 Unless otherwise noted, the following account of the 1875 strike is based on reports in the *Morning Freeman, Daily News, Morning Chronicle*, and *Daily Telegraph*.

29 For the scowmen in 1878–79, see Rice, 'Organized Labour in Saint John,' 93.

30 *Watchman* (Saint John), 8 May 1875.

31 Rice, 'Organized Labour in Saint John,' 70–83; *Evening Reporter* (Halifax), 17 April 1876

32 Rice, 'Organized Labour in Saint John,' 94–5; *Daily Telegraph*, 13 Jan. 1880

33 *Morning Freeman*, 15, 22 July 1875; *Daily Telegraph*, 7 Oct. 1872; 17 July 1875

34 *Evening Express* (Halifax), 12 June 1869; 11 May 1874

35 Hattenhauer, 'History of Nfld Labour,' 114–15

36 The following account of the Ship Labourers is based on J.I. Cooper, 'The Quebec Ship Labourers' Benevolent Society,' *CHR*, xxx, 339–43; *Labour Gazette*, ii, 430; Hamelin, *Répertoire des grèves*, 16–17, 25–6

37 *Weekly Citizen* (Halifax), 29 Oct., 9 Nov. 1867; Hamelin, *Répertoire des grèves*, 19–20

38 Canada, Royal Commission on the Relations of Capital and Labor in Canada, 1889, *Quebec Evidence*, i, 951–2, 1001; Hamelin, *Répertoire des grèves*, 28–9

39 Logan, *Trade Unions in Canada*, 31; Bélanger, *Les Travailleurs québécois*, 204, 206, 208–13, 215

40 *Gazette* (Montreal), 10–13 June 1867

41 Ibid., 8, 10, 12 June 1867; Hamelin, *Répertoire des grèves*, 17–18

42 *Gazette*, 8, 12 June 1867

43 Ibid., 11, 12, 25 June 1867; *Weekly Citizen* (Halifax), 22 June 1867; Bélanger, *Les Travailleurs québécois*, 204

44 Hamelin, *Répertoire des grèves*, 21, 38–40

45 Ibid., 39, 57, 59; *Workingman's Advocate*, 28 July 1877

46 Hamelin, *Répertoire des grèves*, 50, 57–8

47 *British Whig* (Kingston), 4, 21 Oct. 1872

48 *Union* (Ottawa), 4 July 1863; 17, 19 May 1864

49 *Labour Gazette*, ii, 90; *Ontario Workman*, 6 Feb. 1873; *Times* (Ottawa), 25 April, 2 May 1872

50 *Times*, 17 May, 26, 30 July, 4 Sept. 1872

51 Ibid., 23 Jan. 1873; *Ontario Workman*, 5, 12 Dec. 1872; 2 Jan. 1873; clu, *Congress Proceedings*, 1873, 16

52 *Times*, 30 March 1874; 1 April, 2 May 1876

53 Ibid., 9 Dec. 1872; 9 June, 23 July 1873; 12, 14, 20–21, 23 Jan., 5 Nov. 1874; 14, 19 Jan. 1875; *Daily Citizen*, 10 Sept. 1878; *Ontario Workman*, 2 Jan. 1873; clu, *Congress Proceedings*, 1873, 20; Tracy, *History of ITU*, 272

54 Kealey, 'Artisans Respond to Industrialism,' 150; TTU, Minutes, a loose printed sheet headed 'appendix,' and marked 1868–69

55 *Workingman's Journal* (Hamilton), 18 June 1864; *Fincher's Trades Review*, 27 Feb. 1864

56 *Globe* (Toronto), 20 May 1886; TTU, Minutes; TTA, Minutes. The following account of Toronto unions is based on information in the minutes of the TTU and the TTA; only *additional* sources are cited.

57 *Workingman's Advocate*, 25 Jan. 1873; 25 July 1874

58 *Molder's Journal*, 10 June 1875, 340; *Labour Gazette*, II, 246; *Labour Organization in Canada* (1958), 71; TTA, Minutes, 5 May, 16, 21 June, 7 July 1875

59 The *Workingman's Advocate*, 14 March 1874, says a Painters' Union had been recently formed in Toronto. This must have been a rival organization, for the TTA minutes, Jan.–June 1874, provide indisputable evidence of the continuous existence of the 1872 union.

60 Rice, 'Organized Labour in Saint John,' 43–4, 87–8; *Daily Union* (Ottawa), 22, 25 April 1865; *Times*, 4 Oct. 1872

61 *Ontario Workman*, 9, 16 May, 11 July 1872; 30 Jan. 1873; *Daily Advertiser* (London), 11 March 1878

62 Toronto Musicians' Association, Minutes; *Workingman's Advocate*, 7 March 184

63 *Spectator*, 24 Aug. 18763; 23 July 1864; 7 Aug. 1866; 24 Aug. 1867; *Evening Times*, 25 June, 2 July, 22 Aug., 21 Sept., 1867; 18 Jan., 6 May 1868

64 *Spectator*, 25 July, 15 Aug. 1862; 24 April 1869; *Evening Times*, 30 June, 24 July, 12, 27 Aug., 10–11 Sept. 1862

65 *Workingman's Journal*, 18 June 1864; *Workingman's Advocate*, 25 May 1872; *Spectator*, 1 July 1867; 14 Nov. 1868; 22, 27 Feb. 1872; 20 April 1882; *Evening Times*, 8 Nov. 1867; 12 Nov. 1868

66 *Spectator*, 15 July 1946 and 26 Feb. 1952, suggests that this body existed as early as 1860. For 1864, see *Evening Times*, 30 May, 1 June.

67 *Spectator*, 16 Nov. 1866; 12 Dec. 1867; *Evening Times*, 7, 15, 22 Nov. 1866; 11 Dec. 1867; *Workingman's Advocate*, 25 May 1872

68 Ontario, Bureau of Industries, *Report*, 1892, 7; *Workingman's Advocate*, 25 May 1872; *Tailor* (NY), August, December 1891; January 1892; *Spectator*, 4, 6 March 1872; 24 Oct. 1873; 21 Aug. 1874

69 *Evening Times*, 16 July 1867; *Spectator*, 29 June, 3 Aug. 1869; 20 Jan. 1872; Ontario, Bureau of Labor, *Report*, 1908, 100

70 *Workingman's Advocate*, 25 May 1872; *Spectator*, 20 Jan., 6 March, 4 April, 10, 15 May 1872

71 *Spectator*, 17 Dec. 1874, 27 Dec. 1875; 2 April 1880; *Daily Advertiser*, 11 March 1878

72 Davis, 'History of Labour in London,' 10–11; *Daily Advertiser*, 12 April 1865; 15 July, 3 Oct., 9 Nov. 1869; 27 April 1870; 23 Feb. 1872; 23 May, 2, 7 July, 30 Sept. 1874; 11 March, 30 Sept. 1878; 29 Jan. 1880; *Workingman's Advocate*, 21 June 1873; *Ontario Workman*, 16, 23 May 1872

73 *Workingman's Journal*, 18 June 1864; *Daily Expositor*, 22, 29 Dec. 1871; 18 July 1873

74 *Workingman's Advocate*, 5 April 1873; CLU, *Congress Proceedings*, 1873, 16; 1874, 35; 1875, 43, 47; 1876, 61–62; 1877, 91; *Journal* (St Catharines), 13 June, 11 July 1861; 6 Jan. 1868; 25 May 1871; 23 April 1872; 3 April, 6 June, 27, 31 Dec. 1873; *Weekly News* (St Catharines), 6 March 1873; *St Catharines General and Business Directory*, 1874; *Post*, 10 March 1876

75 *Journal*, 18 April 1872; *Post*, 8 Nov. 1878; 28 Feb., 9 May 1879; *Ontario Workman*, 25 April 1872

76 *Labour Gazette*, II, 252; Victoria TLC, *Labor Annual*, 1948, 41; British Columbia Archives, Shipwrights and Caulkers Association, Constitution and By-Laws; Victoria Typographical Union, Constitution and By-Laws, 31

77 Phillips, *No Power Greater*, 2; Griffin, *People's Story*, 44–5; *Journal of United Labor*, 10 Oct. 1884, 813; *Free Press* (Nanaimo), 28 Feb. 1877; 8, 15, 18 Aug., 13 Oct., 28 Nov., 29 Dec. 1883; 8 March 1884

CHAPTER 5

1 Lipton, *Trade Union Movement*, 3–6; *Spectator*, 21 Dec. 1863

2 *Evening Times*, 1 June 1864; *Spectator*, 10 Nov. 1864; 14 July 1872; 2 Oct. 1873; 27 Feb. 1875

3 TTU, Minutes, 10, 24 Aug. 1867; 12 Aug., 9 Sept. 1868; *Fincher's Trades Review*, 27 Feb. 1864

4 TTA, Minutes. Unless other or additional sources are cited, all the information in this chapter is drawn from appropriate entries in the TTA minute books.

5 TTU, various entries; Toronto Trades and Labor Council, Minutes, various entries

6 Sidney and Beatrice Webb, *The History of Trade Unionism* (London and Toronto, 1950), 313–17

7 Careless, *Brown*, II, 288. The *Ontario Workman*, 23 Jan. 1873, says the Hamilton league was organized 'twelve months ago'; Logan, *Trade Unions in Canada*, 39, says the spring of 1871.

8 This, and the following account of the nine-hour strike, are based on the TTA minutes, as well as on TTU, Minutes; Careless, *Brown*, II, 288–98; D.G. Creighton, 'George Brown, Sir John Macdonald and the "Workingman,"' *CHR*, XXIX, 366–75; and on accounts in the *Ontario Workman*, April–May 1872.

9 Canada, House of Commons, *Journals*, 1872, 88–9, 315, 330–1, 334; Bernard Ostry, 'Conservatives, Liberals and Labour in the 1870s,' *CHR*, XLI, 99, 109–11

10 *Ontario Workman*, 8, 15 Aug., 5 Sept. 1872

11 Canada, *Statutes*, 38 Vic., c. 9

12 Ontario, *Statutes*, 38 Vic., c. 20

13 Ostry, 'Conservatives, Liberals and Labour in the 1870s,' 117–19; *Ontario Workman*, 5 Sept. 1872

14 TTA, Minutes; *Ontario Workman*, 2 Jan. 1873; CLU, *Congress Proceedings*, 1874, 35; *Times* (Ottawa), 6 Feb., 23 July, 6 Dec. 1873; 26 Feb., 5 March, 17 June 1874; 11 Jan. 1876

15 CLU, *Congress Proceedings*, 1875, 43

CHAPTER 6

1 Unless otherwise noted, all material in this chapter is drawn from Canadian Labor Union, *Proceedings of the Congresses, 1873–77* (Montreal, 1951).

2 Logan, *Trade Unions in Canada*, 32

3 See chapter 7.

4 (1899), 2 *Juridical Review* (London), 279–80

5 TTA, Minutes, 20 Feb. 1878

CHAPTER 7

1 See following chapters.

2 Foner, *History of the Labor Movement in the United States from Colonial Times to the Founding of the American Federation of Labor* (New York, 1947), 433; Brooks, *Toil and Trouble: A History of American Labor* (New York, 1964), 56

3 *Journal of the Knights of Labor*, 25 Sept. 1890

4 Garlock, 'A Structural Analysis of the Knights of Labor' (unpub. PHD thesis, University of Rochester, 1974), computer printout of LAS, with years of first and last appearance in any records (hereafter cited as Garlock, 'Structural Analysis'); *Journal of United Labor* (Philadelphia), 15 May 1880, 6, 15

5 Kennedy, *Knights*, 35; *Journal of United Labor*, July 270; August 287, 290; October, 1882, 322

6 Eugene Forsey, 'The Telegraphers' Strike of 1883,' Royal Soc. of Can., *Trans.*, ser. 4, IX, 245–59

7 *Journal of United Labor*, 1886; Garlock, 'Structural Analysis'

8 Kennedy, *Knights*, 83–97; V.O. Chan, 'The Canadian Knights of Labor with Special Reference to the 1880s' (unpub. MA thesis, McGill University, 1949) 20–23, 160–202; Greg Kealey, 'The Working Class in Toronto in the Late Nineteenth Century' (draft PHD thesis, University of Rochester), chap. 6, says D.J. O'Donoghue took an active part in getting the condemnation lifted.

9 The figures in this paragraph and in Table 1 are based on *Journal of United Labor*; *Journal of the Knights of Labor*; Garlock, 'Structural Analysis'; for Toronto, especially, on Kealey, 'Working Class in Toronto,' chap. 6; for Winnipeg, especially, on David Spector, 'The Knights of Labor in Winnipeg' (unpub. undergrad. thesis, University of Winnipeg, 1974); for Trois-Rivières, see *La Presse*, 16 mars 1893. The

figures for Montreal and, to a lesser extent, Quebec City, may be understatements. For Montreal, *La Presse* and *La Patrie* mention some 40 LAS by name or occupation only, without a number. Some or all of these may be LAS for which we have the numbers but not the names or occupations; but some may be additional to those for which we have the numbers. In Quebec City there are at least three similar cases.

10 The KOL figures here and in Table 2 are based on KOL, GA, *Proceedings*, 1883–96, 1898–1902, 1906, 1908.

11 *Daily Mail* (Toronto), 19, 24 July 1883; KOL, GA, *Proceedings*, 1883

12 The figures for Table 3 are taken from KOL, GA, *Proceedings*, 1883–88, 1891–94.

13 *Journal of United Labor*, 3 Sept. 1887, 2484; *Journal of the Knights of Labor*, 26 April 1894

14 This paragraph is based on figures drawn from KOL, GA, *Proceedings*, 1883–87.

15 G.N. Grob, 'The Knights of Labor and the Trade Unions,' *Journal of Economic History*, XVIII, 177

16 *Journal of United Labor*, 27 Aug. 1887, 2480; Kennedy, *Knights*, 74; KOL, GA, *Proceedings*, 1884, 652

17 *Wage-Worker* (Toronto), 22 March 1883

18 The following section dealing with the Toronto Knights is based on TTLC, Minutes, Oct., Dec. 1885; May–July 1886; KOL, GEB, *Report*, 1887, 1286–7; Canada, Royal Commission on the Relations of Capital and Labor, *Report*, 1889, Ontario Evidence, I, II, 120–1, 128, 263, 312; *Globe* (Toronto), 19 April, 10–12, 15–16, 20 May, 15, 19, 30 June 1886; *Daily British Whig* (Kingston), 12 March, 12 May 1886; *Journal of United Labor*, 10 March, 10 June, 10 Aug. 1886; Kealey, 'Working Class in Toronto,' chap. 6; Chan, 'Canadian KOL,' 66–7; and Kennedy, *Knights*, 44–5, 71–4.

19 *Spectator* (Hamilton), 19, 22, 29 April, 14 May 1886; *Palladium of Labor*, 24 April 1886

20 KOL, GEB, *Report*, 1889, 14; Canada, Royal Commission on the Relations of Capital and Labor, *Report*, 1889, Ontario Evidence, 1060, 1066–7, 1083–4, 1088, 1092

21 Canada, Royal Commission on the Relations of Capital and Labor, *Report*, 1889, Nova Scotia Evidence, 320. The Coal Cutters Union was doubtless the PWA. The Knights had tried to do something in Nova Scotia in 1888. Three members of the Order at Acadia mines were discharged for taking part in a strike. The PWA's *Trades Journal*, 21 Nov., commented: 'We are afraid the Knights of Labor is not exactly the right society for the men of Acadia Mines. Londonderry is too far removed from the head quarters of that body.'

22 Saint John Typographical Union, Minutes, 12 July 1890; PWA, Grand Council, Minutes, Oct. 1891; PAC, Sir John Thompson Papers, CVI

23 He turns up repeatedly in the *Trades Journal* from 1888 on, and in the Grand Council minutes, ibid. See also Coats, *Labour Movement*, 313.

24 KOL. GA, *Proceedings*, 1898–1901. *La Presse*, 24 juin 1895, reported that Richard Kerrigan, of the Knights of Labor, was in Nova Scotia to organize LAS.

25 The following account is based on Edward McKenna, 'Unorganized Labour versus Management: The Strike at the Chaudière Lumber Mills, 1891,' *Social History*, V, 186–211; Ontario, Bureau of Industries, *Report*, 1892, 34; TTLC, Minutes, Sept.–Nov. 1891; *Citizen* (Ottawa), 15–19, 23–24, 28 Sept., 1–2, 5–6, 9–10, 15 Oct. 1891. In 1893 DA 6 was trying to get a 10-hour day in the mills; the employers refused to compromise or arbitrate; and the Trades and Labor Congress pledged its support to the DA: TLCC, *Proceedings*, 1893, 25.

26 KOL. GA, *Proceedings*, 1884, 728; *Journal of United Labor*, April 1884, 683; KOL. GEB, *Report*, 1887, 1295; R.H. Babcock, 'The AFL in Canada, 1896–1908' (unpub. PHD thesis, Duke University, 1968), 37. For other Knight strikes, see TTLC, Minutes, 24 June, 22 July 1897; 26 April 1900; 14 Feb. 1901; *La Presse*, 3 août 1887; *Journal of United Labor*, 21 March 1889, 2808.

27 Kennedy, *Knights*, 55; TLC, *Proceedings*, 1887, 45; 1888, 8, 11–12, 28, 33; 1889, 7–8, 10, 19; 1890, 8–9; *Journal of United Labor*, 31 Jan. 1889, 2779; report of the Canadian Legislative Committee, KOL. GA, *Proceedings*, 1889–90

28 TLC, *Proceedings*, 1887, 11; 1890, 3; Richard Desrosiers et Denis Héroux, 'A.T. Lépine: premier véritable député ouvrier (1888),' *Le Travailleur québécois et le syndicalisme* (Montréal, n.d.), 58–9, *Can. Parl. Guide*, 1968, 335

29 Kennedy, *Knights*, 51–2; *Can. Parl. Companion*, 1885, 220; 1887, 206; *Labor Union* (Hamilton), 3 Feb., 3 March 1883

30 *Journal of United Labor*, 11 Oct. 1888, 2713; Desrosiers et Héroux, *Le Travailleur québécois*, 53, 58–61; Desrosiers et Héroux, 'Les Chevaliers du Travail,' *Recherches Historiques*, XLIII, 303; Canada, House of Commons, *Debates*, 31 Jan., 1 Feb. 1889; *Can. Parl. Guide*, 1968, 419; *Canadian Directory of Parliament, 1867–1967* (Ottawa, 1968), 335

31 Kennedy, *Knights*, 53–4; *Citizen*, 24 Feb. 1891; *Can. Parl. Companion*, 1891, 192

32 Phillips, *No Power Greater*, 15; Griffin, *People's Story*, 68–69; *Colonist* (Victoria), 16 June 1886

33 *Palladium of Labor*, 3 July 1886

34 Kennedy, *Knights*, 17; Phillips, *No Power Greater*, 14

35 *Journal of the Knights of Labor*, 2 July 1892; 8 Feb. 1894. Note also DA 125's co-operation with the Toronto Trades and Labor Council in 1892 and 1893: TTLC, Minutes, 5 Feb., 15 July 1892; 3 March 1893.

36 Kennedy, *Knights*, 43; *Journal of United Labor*, 24 Sept., 2495; 10 Dec. 1887, 2539; 7 April 1888, 2608; KOL. GEB, *Report*, 1887, 1342; 1888, 93, 102; KOL. GA, *Proceedings*, 1888, 52; *Palladium of Labor*, 28 Feb. 1885, 7; Spector, 'KOL in Winnipeg,' 35–6

37 Kennedy, *Knights*, 46–7; Phillips, *No Power Greater*, 15; Kealey, 'Working Class in Toronto,' chap. 6; Spector, 'KOL in Winnipeg,' 6–8, 10; Hamilton and District Trades and Labor Council, *Diamond Jubilee Programme* (1948), 5; R.G. Hann et al., *Primary Sources in Canadian Working Class History, 1860–1930* (Kitchener, Ont, 1973), 109–10; PAC, TTLC, Minutes, MG28I44, 18 Oct. 1889

38 Martin Robin, *Radical Politics and Canadian Labour, 1880–1930* (Kingston, Ont, 1968), 21, citing the *Voice*, organ of the Winnipeg Trades and Labor Council, 11 Dec. 1903; Kennedy, *Knights*, 46–7; Spector, 'KOL in Winnipeg,' 11

39 The following account is based on Kennedy, *Knights*, 37, 55–7; *Labor Union* (Hamilton), 10 Jan. 1883, 6; TLC, *Proceedings*, 1886, 1888, 1890; and, especially, KOL, GA, *Proceedings*, 1883–92, 1894–1902, and on KOL, GEB, *Report*, 1887–88.

CHAPTER 8

1 Machinists and Blacksmiths: *Gazette* (Montreal), 2 Aug. 1882; Sailors: TTLC, Minutes, 19 Dec. 1884; Flint Glass Workers: TLC, *Proceedings*, 1897, 4; Bélanger, *Les Travailleurs québécois*, 216; *La Presse*, 31 août 1891; 2 sept. 1899; 2 sept. 1902

2 *Labour Gazette*, II, 558

3 Florence Peterson, *Handbook of Labor Unions* (Washington, DC, 1944), 244; Phillips, *No Power Greater*, 28

4 The preceding paragraphs are based on Phillips, *No Power Greater*; *Labour Gazette*, II, 362–5, 376; *American Federationist* (Washington, DC), Jan. 1900, 45; *Province* (Vancouver), 13 June, 31 Aug., 20, 29, 30 Sept. 1899; 3, 12, 17 Feb., 3, 17 March, 6 April, 10 June 1900; 9 April 1901; WFM, Can. District 6, Proceedings, 1901, 1903.

5 WFM, Can. District 6, Proceedings, 1899; *Labour Gazette*, II, 364

6 *Labour Gazette*, I, 480–1; *Province*, 19 Feb., 6, 30 March, 4 April 1901.

7 Phillips, *No Power Greater*, 34, 38; Vancouver TLC, Minutes; TLCC, *Proceedings*, 1902; Griffin, *People's Story*, 77–9; Robin, *Radical Politics*, 56–60.

8 For District 7, see Phillip, *No Power Greater*; Griffin, *People's Story*; *Labour Gazette*, II, 399, 477; III, 675; IV, 828; WFM, Can. District 6, Proceedings, 1901.

9 Vancouver TLC, Minutes, 17 Jan. 1896, 16 July 1897; TTLC, Minutes, 11 June 1896; *Voice*, 19 June 1897, *Daily Tribune* (Winnipeg), 5 Feb. 1894; 13, 16 July, 30 Aug., 3 Sept. 1895 (supplement); *Morning Free Press* (Winnipeg), 8 Sept. 1896; Davis, 'History of Labour in London,' 26

10 Vancouver TLC, Minutes, 4 Dec. 1902; Winnipeg TLC, *Souvenir Programme*, 51; Phillips, *No Power Greater*, 39; *Labour Gazette*, V, 884

11 TTLC, *Proceedings*, 1902, 43, 45–7, 72, 108

12 *Labour Gazette*, III, 48–9, 89–90, 110–12, 144

13 Winnipeg TLC, *Souvenir Programme*, 51, 55–6; *Labour Gazette*, IV, 130–1, 133–4

14 D.W. Hertel, *History of the Brotherhood of Maintenance of Way Employees, Its Birth and Growth* (Washington, 1955), xi, 30–4, 44–51. By March 1901, the Canadian Brotherhood had over 7000 members: *Labour Gazette*, I, 398. See also Hamelin, *Répertoire des grèves*, 150–1.

15 *American Federationist*: January 1900, 22, 45; March, 77; May, 147; July, 223; March, 1901, 90; February 1902, 84; June, 329

16 George Parkin, *The Great Dominion* (London and New York, 1895), 214

17 TTLC, Minutes, 15 Sept., 6 Oct. 1882; *Trades Union Advocate*, Aug.–Nov. 1882, various issues; *Acadian Recorder*, 26, 29 Aug. 1882; *Morning Chronicle*, 29 Aug. 1882.

18 David Spector, 'The 1883 Locomotive Engineers' Strike in the Canadian North West' (unpub. ms, University of Winnipeg, 1976); *Daily Sun* (Winnipeg), *Daily Times*, Dec. 1883 issues; *Commercial*, 5 Feb. 1884

19 TTLC, Minutes, 14 April, 5 May 1882; *Trades Union Advocate*, 4 May, 10, 17 Aug. 1882

20 Amalgamated Woodworkers, ASCJ Records

21 Ontario, Bureau of Industries, *Report*, 1888, pt. IV, 15–16; *American Federationist*, Feb. 1902, 61

22 Amalgamated Woodworkers, ASCJ Records; TTLC, Minutes, 12 Sept. 1901

23 For Hamilton, London, and Toronto, see Bricklayers, Masons and Plasterers International Union (Washington), 28th Annual Report; notes in PAC, MG28II03, V. 247, 4; *Labor Union* (Hamilton), 20 Jan. 1883; *Spectator*, 10, 16 Feb., 7, 8 July 1881; 25 Jan. 1882; 9 Jan. 1885; *Palladium of Labor*, 14 Feb., 11 April 1885; *Daily Advertiser* (London), 2–3, 6, 10 May 1887; *Labour Gazette*, II, 575, 646, 721, 762; *American Federationist*, June 1899, 90.

24 For Brantford, see Local 9, Minutes, 1899–1902; *Daily Expositor*, 19 May, 13 Aug., 3 Nov. 1886; 7 Jan. 1888; 3 April 1890; 18 Aug. 1894; 3, 5 Sept. 1896; 2 Sept. 1899, 16 Feb. 1901; 24 June 1904; 31 Aug. 1907; 18 April 1908. The local started with 29 members; by August 1907 it had 70.

25 For Ottawa, see notes in PAC, MG28II03, V. 247, 4; *Citizen*, 2 May 1890; 8, 10, 12 June 1893; 9 May, 28 July 1899; 4, 5, 9, 14 June 1900; 4 May 1901.

26 For Halifax, see Halifax TLC, *Labor Journal: History of the Labor Movement in Halifax* (Halifax, 1935), 15; *Labour Gazette*, I, 459, 531.

27 For Vancouver and New Westminster, see notes in PAC, MG28II03, V. 247, 4; BMPIU (Washington, DC), 28th Annual Report; *Labour Gazette*, II, 186; *Province*, 18, 30 March, 8, 10, 12, 14 April, 9 Dec. 1899; 30 March, 2, 5, 7, 11, 27 April, 21 Aug. 1900. The eight-hour policy of the international had been communicated to the TLC on 17 March 1899.

28 *Carpenter* (Indianapolis), January, February, April 1882; *Spectator*, 23 Dec. 1881

29 *Carpenter*, May, June, July 1882

30 UBCJ, *Proceedings*, 1884, Report of the general secretary; notes in PAC, MG28I1O3, V. 247, 2; Victoria TLC, *Labor Annual* (1948), 43; *Palladium of Labor*, 2 May, 22 Aug. 1885; *Colonist* (Victoria), 4 March 1884

31 UBCJ, *Proceedings*, 5th Annual Report, 14–15, 18, 21; 6th Annual; 7th Annual, 22–3; 8th Annual; 9th Annual, 15, 28, 30, 33; 10th Annual, 33, 35–6; 11th Annual, 51, 53

32 UBCJ, Local 617 (Vancouver), Minutes; Vancouver TLC, Minutes, 21 Nov. 1889, 14 Feb. 1890

33 The following account is drawn from the minutes of Local 617, ibid., and from the *Province*, 26 April 1899; 30 March, 2, 26 April, 4 May 1900.

34 *Labour Gazette*, I, 397; II, 7–8, 62, 64, 75, 124, 126; *Citizen*, I, 6, 11, 12, 27, 29 June, 5, 9 July 1901

35 *Labour Gazette*, II, 2, 64

36 Ibid., 166, 731; III, 512; *Evening Record* (Windsor), 14 May, 2, 13 Aug. 1901; 19, 27 May 1902. By the end of 1902, the local had 115 members.

37 *Voice* (Winnipeg), 15 July, 5 Aug. 1898; 5, 12 May 1899; 4 Oct. 1901; *Labour Gazette*, II, 167, 205, 211; III, 54

38 *Labour Gazette*, II, 736–7, 762

39 UBCJ, *Proceedings*, 7th Annual Report, 23; 8th Annual; notes in PAC, MG28I1O3, V. 247, 2; *Labour Gazette*, III, 109; Lorne Thompson, 'The Rise of Labor Unionism in Alberta' (typewritten ms), PAC, Forsey Collection

40 The union was FLU 9583 (Carpenters), formed 23 Jan. 1902 (AFL records). On the strike, see *Labour Gazette*, III, 419, 478–9

41 Hamilton TLC, 12 Nov. 1888; 30 Aug., 27 Sept. 1895; Ontario, Bureau of Labor, *Report*, 1905, 33; TLCC, *Proceedings*, 1892, 5; notes in PAC, MG28I1O3, V. 248, 15

42 TTLC, Minutes, 4 May 1888; 6 Dec. 1891; Ontario, Bureau of Industries, *Report*, 1892, 39; *Citizen* (Ottawa), 6 Dec. 1892

43 *La Presse*, 21, 25 fév., 15 mars 1890

44 *Labour Gazette*, II, 572, 614, 643, 673–4, 719; *Citizen* (Ottawa), 12 May 1900; 26 May 1902

45 *Labour Gazette*, I, 399, 437; II, 78, 127, 401, 468, 575, 646, 674

46 Ibid., I, 549; *Province* (Vancouver), 20 Jan., 17 March, 2, 4 April, 16 June 1900; 20, 22 April 1901

47 TTLC, Minutes, 4 Jan. 1889; *Labour Gazette*, II, 246; *Morning Chronicle* (Halifax), 1 Aug. 1888

48 TTLC, Minutes, 3 Aug., 21 Sept. 1888; 18 Oct. 1889; for list of locals, see notes in PAC, MG28I1O3, V. 248, 16.

49 *Voice*, 20 May 1898; 5, 12 May 1899

50 *Labour Gazette*, II, 642, 717, 763; III, 52

51 Ibid., III, 17, 51, 53, 108

52 Ibid., 131, 187, 209, 270
53 *Province* (Vancouver), 5 May, 16 June 1900
54 TTLC, Minutes, 4 May, 20 July, 31 Aug. 1888; Ontario, Bureau of Labor, *Report*, 1905, 42, 76; *Procès-Verbal du Conseil Fédéré des Métiers et du Travail de Montréal*, 1902; *Citizen* (Ottawa), 5 Sept. 1892; 30 Aug. 1898; 5 Sept. 1899; 10 May, 14 June 1900; *Daily Advertiser* (London), 2, 8 Sept. 1896; 7 Sept. 1897; 6 Sept. 1898; 5 Sept. 1899; 4 Sept. 1900; *Daily Free Press*, 3 Sept. 1901
55 *Citizen*, 7, 8, 10, 12 June 1893; 10 May, 4, 5, 9, 11, 14, 16 June 1900
56 *Labour Gazette*, I, 468, 541; II, 646
57 See notes in PAC. MG28I103, v. 248, 13; *American Federationist*, July 1902, 399; *Procès-Verbal du Conseil Fédéré des Métiers et du Travail de Montréal*, 6 janv. 1898; *Labour Gazette*, II, 384; *La Patrie*, 24 août, 8 sept. 1896.
58 *Labour Gazette*, II, 7, 65, 441

CHAPTER 9

1 For the preceding, see TTU, Minutes.
2 For the preceding, see TTLC, Minutes.
3 Unless otherwise noted, the following is based on TTU, Minutes.
4 As well as ibid., see also TTLC, Minutes, 23 Nov. 1899; 25 Jan. 1900.
5 *Labour Gazette*, I, 145, 207, 288
6 Ibid., II, 647, 722; TTLC, Minutes, 27 Nov., 11 Dec. 1902
7 The following account of the Saint John local is based on the local's minutes. Only additional sources are noted.
8 Rice, 'Organized Labour in Saint John,' 132–41
9 In addition to Saint John TU, Minutes, see ibid., 141–3.
10 See also Rice, 'Organized Labour,' 145–54.
11 See also Saint John TLC, Minutes, and *Progress* (Saint John), 12 Nov. 1892.
12 See also TLCC, *Proceedings*, 1901, 40, and *Labour Gazette*, II, 496.
13 Saint John TU, Minutes, 13 Jan., 10 March 1883; Halifax TU, Minutes, 1 Dec. 1883; *Morning Chronicle* (Halifax), 11 July 1881; 9 Jan. 1882. The following account of the Halifax local is based on the local's minutes. Only additional sources are noted.
14 The *Herald* printed a statement of its position on 28 July; on 14 October it said the union had asked businessmen to withdraw their advertising or face publication of lists of *Herald* and *Mail* advertisers.
15 This and the following account are based on Kingston TU, Minutes.
16 The following account of the Vancouver local is based on George Bartley, *An Outline History of Typographical Union No. 226, Vancouver, B.C., 1887–1938* (Vancouver, 1938), 6–14, 16–21. Only additional sources are noted.

17 See also Vancouver TLC, Minutes, 21 Oct. 1892.

18 Ibid., 21 July 1893

19 See also *Province*, 6–7 Feb. 1899.

20 For example, see Vancouver TLC, Minutes, 21 Nov. 1889; 14 Feb. 1890.

21 Tracy, *History of ITU*, 353–4; see notes in PAC, MG281103, v. 248, 27.

22 Canada, Royal Commission on the Relations of Capital and Labor, 1889, Quebec Evidence, III, 321–4, 327, 331, 333, 355, 359, 365, 445–57

23 Hamelin, *Répertoire des grèves*, 105–6

24 *La Presse*, 6, 9, 22, 25 fév., 13 mars 1893

25 *Labour Gazette*, I, 265, 324, 395–6, 465; *Province* (Vancouver), 21 Oct. 1899

26 Tracy, *History of ITU*, 334; Saint John TU, Minutes, 10 Nov. 1883; TTU, Minutes, 20 April, 4 June 1892; *Citizen*, 6 April 1886

27 *Citizen*, 10 Sept. 1900

28 *Labour Gazette*, I, 397–8, 537

29 Ibid., II, 439, 500. This union is listed in Ontario, Bureau of Labor, *Report*, 1902, 71. See also *American Federationist*, April 1901, 117.

30 *Trades Union Advocate*, 11 May, 9, 16 Nov. 1882; TTU, Minutes, 4 Nov. 1882

31 Winnipeg TLC, *Souvenir Programme*, 23; *Labour Gazette*, II, 511–12

32 See notes in PAC, MG281103, v. 248, 27; *L'Evénement*, 4 sept. 1900 (35 is the number that marched in the Labour Day parade); *Labour Gazette*, I, 202, 264.

33 See notes in PAC, ibid.; *Voice*, 26 Aug., 30 Sept., 4 Nov. 1898.

34 Davis, 'History of Labour in London,' 70–1

35 *Iron Molders International Journal*, 30 Sept. 1880, 11; CMIU, Fifteenth Session, supplement to *Cigar Makers Journal*, 1883; Sixteenth Session, 21 Sept. 1885; Seventeenth Session, Oct. 1887; Eighteenth Session, Oct. 1889; Nineteenth Session, Sept. 1891. The Toronto local adopted the eight-hour day in November 1885, effective 1 May 1886: TTLC, Minutes, 27 Nov. 1885. One Toronto strike, in the spring of 1888, was for an icrease of $1 and $2 per thousand on mould and hand-work: *Journal of United Labor*, 19 May 1888, 2635.

36 *Palladium of Labor*, 14 Feb. 1885, 7; *Spectator*, 27 May, 11, 30 June 1881; 16 April, 4 Aug. 1883. The 1881 success may have prompted the manufacturers to form an association in the fall of 1882, which in turn may have helped produce the 1883 strike. The Hamilton association tried to get other cigar manufacturers to organize also: *Trades Union Advocate*, 7 Dec. 1882, 2.

37 *Palladium of Labor*, 22 May, 8; 3 July, 3; 17 July, 3; 14 Aug. 1886, 7; Ontario, Bureau of Industries, *Report*, 1886, cxxxiv

38 *Trades Union Advocate*, 21 Sept., 3; 28 Dec. 1882, 2; *Daily Advertiser*, 14 Feb., 20 Oct., 4 Dec. 1882

39 Canada, Royal Commission on Capital and Labor, *Report*, 1889, Ontario Evidence, 650–3, 656; *Daily Advertiser*, 27 Aug. 1886

40 Ontario, Bureau of Industries, *Report*, 1892, 10, 38; *Labour Gazette*, I, 49, 308, 334, 364, 474–5, 517, 590; II, 126, 144, 167, 374, 483, 525

41 Ontario, ibid., 1892, 38; *Daily Expositor*, 16 Aug. 1887; see also 3 Sept. 1894 for various features of this local.

42 For the Toronto local, see reports in TTLC, Minutes, 1, 15 June, 6, 20 July 1888; 17 Jan., 7, 27 Feb., 26 March, 9 April, 14 May, 22 July, 12, 26 Aug. 1896; 27 April, 11 May, 1899; *Voice*, 5 May 1899, 1.

43 Saint John TLC, Minutes, 7 June 1894

44 *Labour Gazette*, I, 381

45 Canada, Royal Commission on Capital and Labor, *Report*, 1889, Quebec Evidence, 24, 33, 36, 41–6, 56–9, 84, 101, 105, 124–9, 135–6, 143

46 Hamelin, *Répertoire des grèves*, 78, 121–2, 126–7, 130–1, 136–7, 143–5, 159–61; Saint John TLC, 17 Oct. 1894; TTLC, Minutes, 6 Sept. 1895; 23 March, 13 April 1899; *Procès-Verbal du Conseil Fédéré des Métiers et du Travail de Montréal*, 1898; TLCC, *Proceedings*, 1899, 21; *La Presse*, 31 janv. 1893; 6–7 juillet, 3 août, 20 sept., 5 déc. 1894; 18 juin, 4, 19, 24, 29 juillet, 1, 28 août, 20 sept., 4 nov. 1895; 7 mars 1899

47 *Labour Gazette*, I, 465, 513, 589–90; II, 64, 126, 166, 211, 298, 360, 413, 483, 498, 525, 570, 613–14, 674, 762; *American Federationist*, Jan. 1902, 44; *Voice*, 19 Sept. 1902; *Gazette* (Montreal), 20 April 1901

48 *Labour Gazette*, II, 66, 126; *Gazette*, 25 June 1901. These cigar makers had won a two-day strike, 27–29 March 1901, for increased wages: *Labour Gazette*, I, 437.

49 Ibid., II, 3–4, 66, 126, 166; *American Federationist*, Aug. 1901, 366; Jan. 1902 44

50 *Voice*, 11 Nov. 1898; 6 Jan., 20 Sept. 1899; 19 Sept. 1902; see also *Labour Gazette*, III, 513.

51 See notes in PAC, MG28I103, V. 248, 25. Division 30 was one of the few *bona fide* unions to register under the Trade Unions Act of 1872: PAC, RG68, Office of Registrar General, General Index, 1867–1908, f. 395, no 3.

52 *Motorman and Conductor* (Detroit), Nov. 1898, 526–7; *Industrial Banner* (London), Dec. 1898, 1–3; TTLC, Minutes, with insert, 10 Nov. 1898

53 *Motorman and Conductor*, Sept. 1899, 625–6; Oct., 636; *Industrial Banner*, April 1899, 1; Jan. 1900, 1; Davis, 'History of Labour in London,' 62–4

54 TLCC, *Proceedings*, 1899, 26; 1900, 19; *Province* (Vancouver), 23 Dec. 1899; 20 Jan. 1900; *Citizen* (Ottawa), 19 May 1900

55 *Motorman and Conductor*, Nov. 1899, 648; *Industrial Banner*, Jan. 1900, 4; 29 June 1900, 1; Aug. 1901, 4; Aug. 1902, 1; TLCC, *Proceedings*, 1900, 25; Davis, 'History of Labour in London,' 63–4

56 *Motorman and Conductor*, Nov. 1899, 648

57 *Labour Gazette*, I, 4–5, 47

58 Ibid., II, 8–9; *Motorman and Conductor*, Oct. 1900, 777

59 *Labour Gazette*, III, 35–9
60 Ibid., 737; *Citizen*, 8 Oct. 1902
61 *Motorman and Conductor*, Oct. 1899, 635–6; April, 711–12; Nov. 1900, 796–7
62 See mimeographed notes of the proceedings of the eighth convention, supplied by the international office of the Amalgamated Transit Union, in PAC, MG28I103, V. 248, 25.

CHAPTER 10

1 AEW (England), ASE, Records
2 Creighton, *Dominion of the North* (Toronto, 1957), 353–4
3 *Iron Molders Journal*, monthly reports of locals, 1881–95
4 Ibid., 1881: 31 May, 20–1; 31 Aug., 19; 1882: 28 Feb., 9; 31 March, 13; 30 April, 11–12; 31 May, 12; 1883: 31 Jan., 1, 6; 28 Feb., 14–15; 31 March, 13; 31 Oct., 19; 30 Nov., 19; see also report of the Molders' international convention in ibid., 1882, 10–12; and *Daily Advertiser* (London), 27, 31 March, 14 April 1882.
5 *Iron Molders Journal*, 1884: 31 Jan., 22; 28 Feb., 14, 22; 31 March, 13; 30 April, 4; 31 May, 22; 30 June, 14; 30 Nov., 21
6 Ibid., 1885: 31 Aug., 20; 30 Sept., 30; 1886: 31 March, 12; 31 May, 15; 31 July, 14; 1887: 30 June, 13; 31 July, 13, 20; 31 Aug., 20; IMIU, Convention Report, 1888 (printed in ibid.), 27, 41, 44; Ontario, Bureau of Industries, *Report*, 1892, 38
7 *Iron Molders Journal*, 1889: 28 Feb., 13; 30 Sept., 21; 31 Oct., 21; IMIU, Convention Report, 1890, 19, and list of locals. See also Ontario, Bureau of Industries, *Report*, 1892, 40–1, for the Ayr strike.
8 IMIU, Convention Report, 1890, 20
9 Ibid., 23, 26; *Iron Molders Journal*, 1890: 31 March, 19; 30 April, 17
10 IMIU, Convention Report, 1890, 26–27, 36
11 Ibid., 29–30, 36; 1895, 44, 46; *Iron Molders Journal*, 1890: 28 Feb., 9, 15; 31 March, 9, 14; 30 April, 12; 31 May, 7, 13; 31 Aug., 7, 10; 30 Sept., 11; 31 Oct., 11; 30 Nov., 13; 31 Dec., 14; 1891: 31 Jan., 3; 31 March, 13; 30 April, 11; Ontario, Bureau of Industries, *Report*, 1892, 39
12 *Iron Molders Journal*, 1890: 30 Nov., 13; 31 Dec., 14; 1891: 31 Jan., 13; Ontario, Bureau of Industries, *Report*, 1892, 39
13 *Iron Molders Journal*, 1890: 30 Nov., 20; 31 Dec., 21; 1891: 31 May, 19; 30 June, 19; 31 Oct., 19; IMIU, Convention Report, 1895, 32
14 *Iron Molders Journal*, 1892: 31 Jan., 20; 28 Feb., 24; Ontario, Bureau of Industries, *Report*, 1892, 38
15 *Iron Molders Journal*, 1892: 31 Jan., 13; 28 Feb., 12; 31 March, 11; 30 April, 10; 31 May, 9; 30 June, 2; 31 Aug., 10; 30 Sept., 10; 31 Oct., 10; 1893: 31 Jan., 12; 31 March, 9; IMIU, Convention Report, 1895, 11, 32, 46; Ontario, Bureau of Industries, *Report*, 1892, 44

16 *Iron Molders Journal*, 1892: 31 March, 24; 30 April, 24; 31 May, 23; 30 June, 24; 31 July, 24; IMIU, Convention Report, 1895, 47
17 Ibid., 47; *Iron Molders Journal*, 1892: 30 April, 25–6; 31 May, 25; 30 June, 10
18 Ibid., 1893: 31 March, 25; 31 July, 25
19 Hamelin, *Répertoire des grèves*, 148–9; *La Presse*, 6, 9, 10, 18, 22, 25–27, 29–31 mai, 1–3, 5, 8–9, 19, 21 juin 1899
20 *Daily Expositor*, 6, 14 April, 28 June, 10, 13 July 1900; 16 Feb. 1901
21 *Labour Gazette*, I, 46, 87, 208
22 Ibid., I, 46, 87, 405, 437, 460, 472, 516–17, 542; II, 3, 13, 64, 71, 126, 133, 166, 211, 298, 390
23 Ibid., II, 435, 483, 496, 525, 614, 647, 649, 652, 732, 762–3; III, 11, 52, 72, 133, 187, 214, 216–17, 269–71, 303, 379–80, 406, 478, 566
24 *Iron Molders Journal*, 1881: 30 June, 5; 1883: 31 Aug., 2
25 Ibid., 1884: 31 Jan., 3–4; 28 Feb., 4–5
26 Ibid., 1886: 31 July, 3–4, 10; *Journal of United Labor*, 10 Jan. 1885, 883
27 *Iron Molders Journal*, 1886: 30 Sept., 4
28 Ibid., 1887: 31 Jan., 8–9; 1888: 31 Jan., 4; 28 Feb., 4–5; 31 March, 1–2, 6–7
29 Ibid., 1883: 31 July, 11; 1893: 31 May, 4; IMIU, Convention Reports, 1882, 1886, 1888, 1890, 1895
30 The following account is drawn from IMIU, Local 191 (Peterborough), Minutes, and from the *Examiner*, 8 Aug., 4 Sept. 1888.
31 TLCC, *Proceedings*, 1890, 4; 1891, 4; TTLC, Minutes, 15 Jan., 19 Aug., 1892; J.D. Thwaites, 'The International Association of Machinists in Canada to 1919' (unpub. MA thesis, Carleton University, 1966), esp. 48, 52–6; notes in PAC, MG28II03, V. 248, 8
32 *Labour Gazette*, I, 71–5; *Province*, 7, 13–14, 17 Oct. 1899; 16 July, 4, 7–9, 16–18, 23, 27, 30 Aug., 1 Sept. 1900. The arbitrators gave the union what it had asked for gang bosses; generally, one cent less than it had asked for fitters and machinists; some increases for the apprentices.
33 *Labour Gazette*, I, 118, 147, 165, 209, 250, 273, 287
34 Ibid., I, 551, 589; II, 20; *Province*, 21, 23, 25, 30 May, 1, 4 June 1901; PAC, MG28II03, V. 248, 8
35 *Labour Gazette*, I, 537, 590; II, 7, 64, 75, 126, 166, 197, 211
36 Ibid., II, 645, 675, 719–20, 762; III, 16, 53, 108, 132, 186; Thwaites, 'The IAM in Canada,' 77–80; TTLC, Minutes, 14 Aug. 1902; TLCC, *Proceedings*, 1902, p. 76
37 *Labour Gazette*, III, 225–6
38 TTLC, Minutes, 21 Aug., 16 Oct. 1891; 3 Aug. 1894; 28 Sept. 1899; *Industrial Banner* (London), Nov. 1895; 24 May 1897; Peterson, *Handbook of Labor Unions*, 241; *Labour Gazette*, II, 252; *Daily Advertiser*, 5 Sept. 1893; 3 Sept. 1895; *Province*, 5 Aug. 1899; Fink, *Labor Unions*, 221

39 J.B. Casey, 'A Short History of the International Brotherhood of Boilermakers, Iron Ship Builders and Helpers of America,' photostat of an article that appeared in the *Boiler Makers and Iron Ship Builders Journal*, in PAC, MG28II03, v. 247, 8. Boilermakers who marched in the Hamilton demonstration of 4 August 1884 (*Spectator*) were evidently a local union on the verge of becoming international; the union which appeared in the Central Labor Union in Feb. 1886 (*Spectator*, 26 Feb.) was pretty certainly Local 21.

40 TTLC, Minutes, 18 Aug. 1893; 12 Jan. 1894; 15 Feb. 1895; *Labour Gazette*, II, 252; *La Presse*, 1 sept. 1894; 31 août 1895; *La Patrie*, 7 sept. 1897

41 *American Federationist*, 1900: Oct., 323; Nov., 355; 1902: March, 147; June, 176; *Labour Gazette*, II, 343, 360; III, 50, 53; Hamelin, *Répertoire des grèves*, 167

42 TTLC, Minutes, 8 Dec. 1898; 9, 23 Nov., 1899; 23 Jan. 1900; Winnipeg TLC, *Souvenir Programme*, 27; *American Federationist*, 1900: Oct., 329; Dec., 390; 1901: April, 117; 1901: May, 179; *Labour Gazette*, I, 401, 469; II, 254; III, 148–9; Ontario, Bureau of Labor, *Report*, 1902, 63; Babcock, 'The AFL in Canada,' chap. IV, 9; notes in PAC, MG28II03, v. 247, 6; *Province*, 9, 17, 30 Aug. 1900

43 *American Federationist*, 1900: Nov., 368; 1902: Jan., 32; April, 187–8; TTLC, Minutes, 23 Jan., 13 Feb., 27 March, 10 April, 8, 22 May, 12 June, 11, 25 Sept., 9 Oct., 13 Nov., 11 Dec. 1902; *Labour Gazette*, I, 103; II, 252, 482–3, 524–5, 576, 613–14, 650, 674, 692; *La Presse*, 2 sept. 1899; *Daily Expositor* (Brantford), 2 Sept. 1899

44 *American Federationist*, 1901: Feb., 54; 1902: Aug., 460; *Labour Gazette*, II, 248; IV, 680

45 *Labour Gazette*, I, 467; II, 252, 692; V, 882; Ontario, Bureau of Labor, *Report*, 1902, 63, 68, 71, 75; *Daily Expositor*, 2 Sept. 1899

46 Hamilton TLC, Minutes, 20 March 1889; 31 Jan. 1896; *Labour Gazette*, I, 92, 402; II, 370; III, 136, 187, 418, 477–8, 505, 566–7. A Hatters Union marched in the Labour Day parades of 1897 and 1900: *Spectator*, 7 Sept. 1897; *Evening Times*, 4 Sept. 1900. In March 1901 the Hamilton union was said to be the only one in Canada, and 'declining.'

47 *Tailor*, Dec. 1889; April 1890; July–Dec. 1891

48 Ibid., May 1890; Jan. 1891; Aug.–Oct. 1893; July 1895

49 Ibid., March–April, June 1892; Oct. 1893; Sept.–Oct. 1894; Jan. 1895; Feb., April–May 1896; May 1897; March, Oct.–Dec. 1899; Jan.–April, Oct. 1900; TTLC, Minutes, 21 Sept. 1894; 1 Nov. 1895; 3, 17 Jan., 7, 27 Feb., 12, 26 March 1894

50 *Tailor*, Jan.–Feb., April–June 1891; Dec. 1892; Dec. 1895; Feb. 1898; June 1899

51 Ibid., Oct. 1890; July 1891; April, June 1892; Aug.–Oct. 1893

52 Ibid., Oct. 1890; June–July 1891; Nov.–Dec. 1892; Jan.–April 1893

53 Ibid., Dec. 1890; Feb., April–May, Aug. 1891

54 Ibid., May 1891, April, Nov. 1892; Sept. 1893

55 Ibid., Aug. 1891; Aug.–Sept. 1893; Feb.–March 1898; March–July 1899; Vancouver TLC, Minutes, 15 Sept. 1893; *Province*, 18 March, 8, 10, 12, 14–15, 17–18, 22, 24, 29 April, 2–6, 9, 13, 23 May 1899

56 *Tailor*, June 1892; March–April, June 1893; July–Oct. 1900; *Labour Gazette*, I, 50

57 *Tailor*, May 1893; Sept. 1894; Nov. 1896; Oct. 1897

58 Ibid., Sept. 1894; May, Dec. 1897; Jan.–April, Aug. 1898

59 Ibid., Sept. 1896; May–Oct. 1897

60 Ibid., Dec. 1897

61 *Labour Gazette*, I, 471, 516–17; II, 298, 572, 612, 614–15, 674; III, 217

62 For Vancouver and Victoria, see ibid., I, 339–41; III, 318; for Kingston and St Thomas, see ibid., II, 8; I, 336.

63 *Tailor*, May 1896; Oct. 1897 (Belleville and Prescott); Nov. 1902, 24; information on Nova Scotia and Prince Edward Island from Prof. R.H. Babcock

64 Hamilton TLC, 21 April 1890; 20 May 1892; TTLC, Minutes, 2 April, 7 July 1890; 6 March, 2 Oct. 1891; 19 Feb. 1892; 21 July, 18 Aug. 1893; 17 Oct. 1896; 14, 28 April, 12, 26 May, 9 June 1898; TLCC, *Proceedings*, 1890, 4; 1892, 5; 1893, 4; 1902, 5; *American Federationist*, 1901: Jan., 22; 1902: Dec., 954; *Labour Gazette*, II, 694; III, 274, 447; Ontario, Bureau of Labor, *Report*, 1902, 66; Peterson, *Handbook of Labor Unions*, 57; *Labor Unions*, ed. Fink, 38; Kealey, 'Artisans Respond to Industrialism,' 150

65 *American Federationist*, 1901: March, 82–3; June, 218; Oct., 522; TLCC, *Proceedings*, 1902, 6; *Labour Gazette*, I, 265, 394; II, 370

66 TTLC, Minutes, 2 Feb., 2 March 1894; 14, 28 April, 12 May, 9 June 1898; 24 Jan. 1901; TTU, Minutes, 7 May, 2 July 1898; TLCC, *Proceedings*, 1900, 25; *Labour Gazette*, I, 207, 269

67 TTLC, Minutes, 26 Sept. 1901

68 *Garment Worker*, 1899: Aug., 8

69 TTLC, Minutes, 28 Sept. 1899

70 *Voice*, 10, 13, 17, 24 Feb., 5, 10, 17 March, 28 April 1899; 22 Nov. 1901

CHAPTER 11

1 See notes in PAC, MG28I103, v. 248, 26; *Voice*, 28 Jan. 1896; TTLC, Minutes, 10 Dec. 1896.

2 See notes in PAC, ibid.; *Voice*, 23 Dec. 1898; *Herald* (Halifax), 22–24 Dec. 1898.

3 *Labour Gazette*, II, 396–7, 722

4 *Tailor*, 1889: Dec., 5; *Morning Chronicle* (Halifax), 1 Aug. 1888

5 Halifax TU, Minutes, 7 Feb., 6 March 1891; *Morning Chronicle*, 10, 12 May 1890; *Daily Telegraph*, 20 May 1890

6 *Voice*, 2, 9, 23 May, 27 June, 4, 11, 18, 25 July, 1, 8, 15, 22 Aug., 28 Nov. 1902;
  Labour Gazette, II, 732–3; III, 26, 52–3, 90, 108, 110

7 *Labour Gazette*, II, 724, 763; III, 19, 53, 136

8 Ibid., III, 320

9 TTLC, 8 May, 12 June, 24 July, 27 Nov. 1902; *Labour Gazette*, II, 320, 575

10 See notes in PAC, MG28I103, v. 248, 18; Peterson, *Handbook of Labor Unions*, 313. The
   Toronto lodge appears in TTLC, Minutes, 3 Feb., 15 Sept. 1893; 17 Aug., 21 Sept.
   1894. It disappeared at some date (unknown to the international union) between then
   and 14 Feb. 1901, where the TTLC records a request from the Winnipeg lodge asking
   it to organize a new lodge in Toronto.

11 *Labour Gazette*, II, 342; III, 517–18

12 TTLC, Minutes, 16 Dec. 1892; 16 Oct. 1893; *American Federationist*, 1896: Oct., 169;
   Labour Gazette, II, 254; *Citizen* (Ottawa), 3 Sept. 1895

13 *Labour Gazette*, I, 5

14 Ibid., III, 478–9

15 TTLC, Minutes, 17 March 1893; 15 March 1895; *Labour Gazette*, II, 318; Ontario,
   Bureau of Labor, *Report*, 1901, 56; *La Presse*, 6 avril, 1 sept. 1893; 6 juin, 1 sept.
   1894; *La Patrie*, 7 sept. 1897

16 *Labour Gazette*, I, 537; II, 8, 62, 75, 122–4, 126; *Citizen* (Ottawa), 1, 3, 11–12, 19,
   27, 29 June, 2, 5–6 July 1901

17 *Labour Gazette*, II, 333, 387, 407–8, 413

18 Ibid., II, 610

19 Charlie Buhler, *In Appreciation* (Toronto, 1963), 2, citing the *Telegram*, 16 June
   1893; *Labour Gazette*, III, 303, 416

20 TLCC, *Proceedings*, 1897, 4; *American Federationist*, 1899: Aug., 137; 1900: Sept., 287;
   Labor Unions, ed. Fink, 346

21 TTLC, Minutes, 2 Feb. 1894; 11 March 1897; 28 April, 12 May, 28 July, 11 Aug.
   1898; 26 Jan., 9 Feb. 1899; CFMTM, *Procès-Verbal*, 1902; *Labour Gazette*, II, 309, 318

22 TTLC, *Minutes*, 6 Feb. 1891; *Labour Gazette*, II, 428, 696; *La Presse*, 1 sept. 1894

23 See notes in PAC, MG20I108, v. 247, 7; *Voice*, 19 June 1897; 7 Jan., 2 Sept. 1898;
   American Federationist, 1901: Feb., 61; *Labour Gazette*, I, 474, 542–3; II, 8, 275,
   398, 446, 576; Ontario, Bureau of Labor, *Report*, 1902, 40, 47, 69, 73–5.

24 See notes in PAC, MG28I103, v. 248, 21; *American Federationist*, 1899: Aug., 137;
   1902: July, 398; 1902: Oct., 729; *Voice*, 22 Nov. 1901; *Labour Gazette*, II, 9, 254,
   692; Ontario, Bureau of Labor, *Report*, 1902, 66, 69–70.

25 *Labour Gazette*, I, 398; II, 7–8, 64; *Citizen*, 3, 11–13 June 1901

26 TTLC, Minutes, 14 Aug., 11 Sept., 27 Nov. 1902; TLCC, *Proceedings*, 1902, 71; *Labour
   Gazette*, III, 18, 134, 415; Margaret Mackintosh, *Trade Union Law in Canada*
   (Ottawa, 1935), 35–6

27 *Labour Gazette*, II, 498, 716, 763

28 Ibid., I, 322; *American Federationist*, 1900: Nov., 358

29 NATSE, *Proceedings*, 1895, 16, 18, 23; 1897, 39–40; 1898, 51–2, 54, 59, 61, 67; 1899, 70, 82, 84; TTLC, Minutes, 15 Feb. 1895; 8, 22 Sept. 1898; *Voice*, 17 Feb. 1899; *Daily Mail and Empire* (Toronto), 6 Sept. 1898

30 NATSE, *Proceedings*, 1901, 114, 119–20; 1902, 131, 133, 139; 1903, 145–6, 160

31 TTLC, Minutes, 24 Oct. 1898; 27 March, 10 April 1902; *American Federationist*, 1899: May, 62; 1900: March, 70; 1901: Feb., 57; *Labour Gazette*, II, 723, 764; VI, 885; VIII, 984; *Province*, 21 Oct. 1899

32 TTLC, Minutes, 26 Jan. 1899; see notes in PAC, MG28II03, v. 248, 3.

33 *Voice*, 31 Jan. 1902

34 *Retail Clerks National Advocate* (Denver), Aug.–Nov. 1899; May 1900; July–Aug., Sept. 1901; Feb.–April, June, Nov.–Dec. 1902; Jan., Aug. 1903; *American Federationist*, 1899: Aug., 134; 1900: April, 114; 1902: May, 258; Nov., 831; 1903: Jan., 13; TLCC, *Proceedings*, 1902, 5; *Labour Gazette*, I, 334, 543; II, 210, 486, 554, 556, 566, 576, 624, 647, 738; III, 21, 55, 306, 378; IV, 681; V, 884; VII, 891; Ontario, Bureau of Labor, *Report*, 1902, 66–7, 71, 77

35 TTLC, Minutes, 26 Sept. 1901; *American Federationist*, 1902: Nov., 831; *Labour Gazette*, II, 45, 211, 298, 318, 360, 412–13, 692, 722, 761, 763; III, 52, 439, 441, 443–4; V, 882; VI, 884; XI, 866; Ontario, Bureau of Labor, *Report*, 1902, 46, 65–6, 70, 72, 76, 79

36 TTLC, Minutes, 8 May, 23 Oct. 1902; *American Federationist*, 1899: Aug., 137; 1901: April, 134; 1902: Aug., 460; *Labour Gazette*, I, 413, 415, 467; II, 210, 430, 566, 647, 698, 709; III, 154–5, 416; X, 1004; *Report on Labour Organization in Canada*, 1914, 228; Ontario, Bureau of Labor, *Report*, 1902, 50–1, 65, 73, 79

37 *Labour Gazette*, II, 330, 360; III, 297, 381

38 Ibid., II, 636, 667–71, 675; III, 304

39 See notes in PAC, MG28II03, v. 248, 22; TTLC, Minutes, 23 Oct. 1902; *American Federationist*, 1899: Oct., 200; *Motorman and Conductor*, 1899: Oct., 635.

40 Notes in PAC, ibid.; *American Federationist*, 1902: June, 329; *Labour Gazette*, II, 635, 674; VI, 885

41 See notes in PAC, MG28II03, v. 248, 12; *Labour Gazette*, I, 334, 474; II, 576.

42 *Labour Gazette*, II, 318, 692

43 Ibid., I, 48, 93, 118; II, 374; TLCC, Minutes, 14 Aug. 1902; *American Federationist*, 1899: Aug., 137; Ontario, Bureau of Labor, *Report*, 1902, 66

44 TTLC, Minutes, 14, 28 Aug., 11, 25 Sept. 1902; TLCC, *Proceedings*, 1902, 76; *Labour Gazette*, III, 80, 109–10, 134–5, 211, 270. The Guelph local got a 15 per cent increase without a strike: *American Federationist*, 1902: Oct., 729.

45 IBEW, *Proceedings*, 1970, 233–6, 239–40, 242–3. See also TTLC, Minutes, 9 March 1899; *American Federationist*, 1899: May, 3; June, 90; 1900: Feb., 40; *Labour Gazette*, I, 330; II, 250, 692; Ontario, Bureau of Labor, *Report*, 1902, 74

46 TTLC, Minutes, 12 June 1902; *American Federationist* 1902: July, 399; *Labour Gazette*, II, 576, 672, 675; III, 18, 50, 53, 80, 82, 108, 135, 185, 187, 214, 260–1, 270, 272; *Citizen*, 19, 21, 23, 26 June 1900

47 *Labour Gazette*, III, 477, 479, 517, 565–7. Victoria had a strike 2 July, when 5 linemen went out for a 4½ per cent increase (to 31 cents an hour), and lost: ibid., II, 89.

48 TTLC, Minutes, 25 Jan. 1900

49 Ibid., 12 March 1900

50 Ibid., 3 Nov. 1893; *American Federationist*, 1902: Jan., 44; *Voice*, 5 Sept. 1902; *Labour Gazette*, I, 398–9; II, 554; IX, 698

51 *Labour Gazette*, II, 248, 576, 646, 721–2, 763; III, 18, 51–2; *American Federationist*, 1900: Aug., 250; 1901: July, 258; Dec., 592; TTLC, Minutes, 23 Oct. 1902; *Daily Mail and Empire*, 3 Sept. 1901

52 *Labour Gazette*, II, 443, 554, 576; III, 148; *American Federationist*, 1901: June, 209

53 *Lather*, 1901: March, Nov., lists of locals; TTLC, Minutes, 27 Sept. 1900; *American Federationist*, 1900: Oct., 358; *Voice*, 10 Oct. 1902; *Labour Gazette*, II, 199

54 TTLC, Minutes, 22 May 1902; *Labour Gazette*, I, 203; II, 374; XI, 966

55 TTLC, Minutes, 7, 21 Nov. 1884; 13 Sept. 1900; *American Federationist*, 1900: Dec., 393; *Labour Gazette*, II, 488

56 Hamilton TLC, Minutes, 6 Feb. 1891; Canada, Royal Commission on the Relations of Capital and Labor, *Report*, 1889, Ontario Evidence, 790; *Labour Gazette*, I, 206; II, 167; Ontario, Bureau of Labor, *Report*, 1902, 67; *Spectator*, 10 June 1882; 4 Aug. 1884; *Citizen*, 8 Sept. 1891; *La Presse*, 31 août 1891; 3 sept. 1892; 2 sept. 1893

57 See notes in PAC, MG28I103, v. 248, 10; *Labour Gazette*, I, 549; II, 10, 385, 554; IV, 681; Davis, 'History of Labour in London,' 72; *La Presse*, 2 sept. 1898; 2 sept. 1899; *Province*, 18 April 1901.

58 TTLC, Minutes, 24 Jan. 1901; *American Federationist*, 1901: March, 84; *Labour Gazette*, I, 308, 329, 364

59 See notes in PAC, MG28I103, v. 247, 6; TTLC, Minutes, 23 May, 14 Nov. 1901; 13 Nov. 1902; *American Federationist*, 1902: Aug., 444; *Labour Gazette*, I, 540; II, 78, 254, 724.

60 *Toiler*, 14 April 1902; *Labour Gazette*, II, 502, 575, 646, 672–3, 675, 722, 762; III, 51–2

61 TTLC, Minutes, 13 Nov. 1902; *American Federationist*, 1901: June, 209; 1902: Nov., 831; *La Presse*, 1 sept. 1900

62 Peterson, *Handbook of Labor Unions*, 93; *American Federationist*, 1901: Oct., 443; 1903: Feb., 117; *Labour Gazette*, V, 882

63 *American Federationist*, 1901: Dec., 552; *Labour Gazette*, III, 298, 408, 412, 482, 498, 552

64 See notes in PAC, MG28I103, v. 247, 5; TTLC, Minutes, 28 Aug., 23 Oct. 1902; *American Federationist*, 1903: Jan., 117; *Labour Gazette*, II, 650; III, 80, 118, 136, 174, 378, 482, 510.

65 *Labour Gazette*, II, 443

66 Ibid., II, 322, 694; IV, 680; Peterson, *Handbook of Labor Unions*, 278, 357; TTLC, Minutes, 27 Sept. 1900; *American Federationist*, 1899: Nov., 225

67 TTLC, Minutes, 27 March, 10 April, 12 June 1902; *American Federationist*, 1902: Aug., 444; *Labour Gazette*, II, 576, 647; III, 50, 53

68 *Labour Gazette*, II, 696; III, 891; X, 1004

69 Ibid., II, 645, 681; TLCC, *Proceedings*, 1902, 5; *American Federationist*, 1902: Oct., 729; Ontario, Bureau of Labor, *Report*, 1902, 79; TTLC, Minutes, 24 April 1902

70 AFL-CIO Archives, Nation Union Files, Reel 11, Herbert Scott, 14 Sept. 1902; *American Federationist*, 1902: Nov., 832; *Labour Gazette*, III, 137, 217, 274; Ontario, Bureau of Labor, *Report*, 1902, 77

71 TTLC, Minutes, 23 Oct. 1902; *Labour Gazette*, II, 723, 754

72 *Labour Gazette*, III, 12

73 TTLC, Minutes, 28 Aug. 1902; Ontario, Bureau of Labor, *Report*, 1902, 76

74 Vancouver, TLC Minutes, 16 Oct. 1902; *Labour Gazette*, VI, 884

75 TTLC, Minutes, 13 Nov. 1902

76 *American Federationist*, 1902: Aug., 460; Oct., 729; *Labour Gazette*, III, 416; IX, 967

77 TLCC, *Proceedings*, 1896, 15–16, 29; 1897, 10; 1898, 17, 30; 1899, 4; *American Federationist*, 1897: May, 61; Babcock, 'The AFL in Canada,' chap. II, 9–11

78 Babcock, ibid., chap. IV, 5; the figures came from comparisons (Prof. Babcock's and mine) between AFL organizers' reports and *Labour Gazette* records of unions organized. In general, see *American Federationist*, 1899: May, 62; June, 90; Aug., 134–5, 137, 143; Oct., 208; Nov., 225; Dec., 252, 258; 1900: Jan., 40; March, 77; April, 114; June, 175; 1901: Aug., 319; Oct., 443; Nov., 462; Dec., 552; 1902: Jan., 43; April, 204; Sept., 650; Oct., 729; 1903: Jan., 35.

79 Information supplied by Prof. Babcock from AFL charter books, supplemented by the *Labour Gazette*, notably the lists in v. II.

80 *American Federationist*, 1901: Aug., 319; *Labour Gazette*, I, 101–3; H.S. Ferns and Bernard Ostry, *The Age of Mackenzie King: The Rise of the Leader* (London and Toronto, 1955), 55–6

81 *American Federationist*, 1901: July, 258; 1902: Jan., 44; June, 140; July, 398; Aug., 460; 1903: Jan., 37

82 Ibid., 1901: July, 258; *Labour Gazette*, I, 538

83 *American Federationist*, 1900: Dec., 393; 1902: Aug., 460; *Labour Gazette*, I, 476, 545

CHAPTER 12

1 Canada, Royal Commission on the Relations of Capital and Labor, *Report*, 1889, Nova Scotia Evidence, 107–8; *Morning Chronicle*, 18 July 1893; 3 Sept. 1901; 1 Sept. 1902; *Labour Gazette*, II, 252

2 *Acadian Recorder*, 6, 25 June 1881; 9 March, 16 April 1882

3 *Trades Union Advocate*, 28 Sept. 1882; *Wage-Worker*, 15 March 1883; *Morning Chronicle*, 6, 24 March 1883; 29 May 1884

4 See notes in PAC, MG28II03, v. 247, 2; *Labour Gazette*, II, 188.

5 *Morning Chronicle*, 11 July 1881; 9 Jan. 1882

6 Halifax TU, Minutes, 4 May, 5 Oct., 2 Nov. 1895; *Labour Gazette*, II, 320; *Morning Chronicle*, 23–24 July 1890 (the Coopers made 'their first appearances as a union in yesterday's demonstration'); 20, 23 July 1891; 19, 21 July 1892; 17, 20 July 1893; 4 Sept. 1895; 5 Sept. 1899

7 See notes in PAC, MG28II03, v. 247, 2.

8 *Acadian Recorder*, 8 April 1882; 10 Jan. 1883; *Citizen and Evening Chronicle*, 28 July, 11, 14 Aug. 1883; *Morning Chronicle*, 15 April 1884

9 Canada, Royal Commission on the Relations of Capital and Labor, *Report*, 1889, Nova Scotia Evidence, 102–3

10 *Acadian Recorder*, 18–19 Aug. 1885

11 Halifax TU, Minutes, 5, 19 Sept., 3 Oct., 7 Nov., 5 Dec. 1891; 5 March 1892

12 See notes in PAC, MG28II03, v. 248, 15; *Morning Chronicle*, 1, 3 Aug. 1888; 22 July 1889; 23–24 July 1890; 20, 23 July 1891; 19, 21 July 1892; 17, 20 July 1893; 4 Sept. 1895; 5 Sept. 1899.

13 *Acadian Recorder*, 8, 14 April 1882; *Morning Chronicle*, 3 Aug. 1888

14 *Acadian Recorder*, 9 June, 13 July, 11, 21 Aug. 1882; *Citizen and Evening Chronicle*, 22 Aug., 1 Nov., 6 Dec. 1882

15 *Acadian Recorder*, 7, 9 April 1883. The Labourers had a picnic to McNab's Island in 1883. St Patrick's Brass Band was to 'discourse a choice selection of music on the boat and the grounds,' and Gilday's String Band to provide the dance music. 'With the exception of one or two rows conducted by some roughs, not members of the association ... the day passed off pleasantly': *Citizen and Evening Chronicle*, 18, 20–1 Aug. 1883.

16 *Acadian Recorder*, 6, 15–17 May 1884

17 *Morning Chronicle*, for dates cited in note 12

18 *Labour Gazette*, II, 70

19 *Acadian Recorder*, 24 April 1882; 18 Aug., 14 Nov. 1884

20 *Morning Chronicle*, 1, 3 Aug. 1888

21 *Morning Chronicle*, 10 May 1882

22 Halifax TLC, *Labor Journal*, 15; *Acadian Recorder*, 6 June 1882; *Morning Herald*, 4 May 1883

23 *Morning Herald*, 10–11, 14–15, 17–18 Aug. 1883; *Citizen and Evening Chronicle*, same dates, and 20 Aug.

24 See notes in PAC, MG28II03, v. 247, 4; Halifax TLU, *Labor Journal*, 15.

25 Halifax TU, Minutes, 8 Aug. 1896; 1 Nov. 1902; *Labour Gazette*, II, 246; *Morning Chronicle*, for dates given in footnote 12, and 3 Sept. 1901 and 1 Sept. 1902. In 1899, 1901, and 1902 the union is described as Granite and Freestone Cutters.

26 *Acadian Recorder*, 30 March 1883; *Citizen and Evening Chronicle*, 15 May, 2 Aug. 1883 (Weavers' strike for a wage increase, beginning of May, Nova Scotia Cotton plant; whether there was a union is not clear); *Morning Chronicle*, 1, 3 Aug. 1888; 22 July 1889; 23–24 July 1890; 19, 21 July 1892

27 *Labour Gazette*, I, 87; *Acadian Recorder*, 19 March 1884; *Morning Chronicle*, 23 July 1891; 21 July 1892; 4 Sept. 1895; 5 Sept. 1899; 3 Sept. 1901; 1 Sept. 1902

28 *Labour Gazette*, VII, 891

29 Ibid., II, 428

30 Ibid., II, 248, 370; *Morning Chronicle*, 23 July 1890; 5 Sept. 1899; 3 Sept. 1901

31 *Morning Chronicle*, 20 July 1891

32 Ibid., 23–24 July 1890; 20 July 1891

33 Ibid., 23–24 July 1890

34 *Morning Herald*, 20, 31 May 1890

35 *Morning Chronicle*, for dates cited in note 12

36 Ibid., 23 July 1891; 21 July 1892

37 Ibid., 20, 23 July 1891; 21 July 1892; 17, 20 July 1893

38 *Labour Gazette*, II, 244; *Morning Chronicle*, 5 Sept. 1899; 3 Sept. 1901; 1 Sept. 1902

39 *Morning Chronicle* for dates cited in note 12; *Morning Herald*, 5 Sept. 1899

40 Halifax TU, Minutes, 4 July 1896; 3 July 1897

41 PWA, Grand Council, Minutes, 1 April 1887; *Trades Journal*, 30 March, 27 April, 11 May 1887

42 PWA, Grand Council, Minutes, 29 Sept. 1897; *Trades Journal*, 23 Jan., 29 May, 5 June 1889

43 *TLC Proceedings*, 1901, 70; *Labour Gazette*, vol. III, 155

44 *Daily Telegraph*, 11 Aug., 3 Oct. 1883; *Globe* (Saint John), 10, 20 Aug., 20 Sept. 1883; *Daily Sun*, 20 Sept. 1883

45 Saint John TLC, *History*, 73

46 *Citizen and Evening Chronicle*, 30 Sept. 1882

47 Saint John TLC, *History*, 73; *Daily Telegraph*, 11, 21, 28–29 Aug., 1, 3, 4, 8, 11, 12, 15, 19, 20 Sept., 2, 8 Oct. 1883; *Globe*, 10 Aug., 20 Sept. 1883; *Daily Sun*, 8 Aug., 20, 22, 29 Sept. 1883. There is mention also of millmen and confectioners.

48 *Morning Chronicle*, 9 Aug. 1887

49 Canada, Royal Commission on the Relations of Capital and Labor, *Report*, 1889, New Brunswick Evidence, 89, 95, 141, 164, 225

50 *Globe*, 15–18, 23 July 1889; *Daily Sun*, 24 July 1889; Rice, 'Organized Labour in Saint John,' 59

51 Rice, ibid., 117–18

52 Ibid., 109

53 See notes in PAC, MG28I103, v. 247, 2; *Daily Telegraph*, 29 April 1890

54 *Daily Telegraph*, 3–4 Sept. 1894; 3 Sept. 1895

55 Saint John TLC, *History*, 39, 61, 73; Rice, 'Organized Labour in Saint John,' 109

56 *Globe*, 1 Feb. 1895

57 *Labour Gazette*, I, 46, 306

58 *American Federationist*, 1901: Nov., 462

59 *Globe*, 1 Sept. 1902. The Lumber Surveyors Society organized 22 Jan. 1901 (*Labour Gazette*, I, 263), if it was really a union, seems to have lapsed.

60 Canada, Royal Commission on the Relations of Capital and Labor, *Report*, 1889, New Brunswick Evidence, 164, 209–10, 232, 235; *Labour Gazette*, I, 45; Rice, 'Organized Labour in Saint John,' 103–9; *Daily Telegraph*, 25 Nov. 1882; *Globe*, 6 June 1882; *Daily Sun*, 18, 20 Jan. 1887; *Morning Chronicle*, 30 April 1883; *La Presse*, 7–8, 10, 13 avril 1896. The employers must have brought in strikebreakers, or tried to, for *La Patrie*, 17 avril 1896, says the strike was won thanks to a municipal by-law imposing a fine of $20 for every outsider hired. See also *Labour Gazette*, I, 45.

61 *Daily Telegraph*, 20 Feb. 1883

62 Canada, Royal Commission on the Relations of Capital and Labor, *Report*, New Brunswick Evidence, 95; Rice, 'Organized Labour in Saint John,' 116

63 Saint John TU, Minutes, 11 July 1891; Rice, ibid., 119; *Daily Telegraph*, 3 June 1890

64 *Loyalist Centennial Souvenir* (Saint John, 1883), 55; *Daily Telegraph*, 3 Nov. 1882; 11–12, 15 Sept., 3 Oct. 1883; 4 Sept. 1894; *Daily Evening News*, 2 Oct. 1883

65 Centennial souvenir of the Typos, in *Daily Telegraph*, 2 Oct. 1883; *Globe*, 25 Sept. 1883

66 *Globe*, 1 Sept. 1902

67 *Labour Gazette*, I, 532; *Morning Chronicle*, 19 May 1882

68 Ibid., II, 690 (union formed 15 March 1900); III, 11, 50, 53

69 Hattenhauer, 'History of Nfld Labour,' 93–6, 114–16, 118–19, 123–8, 130–1, 134–5, 139–45, 149; J.J. Fogarty, 'The Seal-Skinners' Union,' and J.J. Power, 'The Coopers' Union,' *Book of Newfoundland*, ed. Smallwood, I, 100; Halifax TU, Minutes, 2 Dec. 1893; 6 Jan. 1894; TTU, Minutes, 2 Nov. 1894

70 Bélanger, *Les Travailleurs québécois*, 204–8, 210–11, 213–15, 217; *La Justice* 18 juillet 1886; *Trades Union Advocate*, 11 May 1882; *Labour Gazette*, II, 430; III, 73, 118, 241; *L'Evénement*, 12 juin, 31 août 1891; 2 sept. 1893; 31 août, 3 sept. 1895; 3 sept. 1898; *La Presse*, 23 fév., 30 août, 16 sept. 1899; 1er et 4 sept. 1900; 3 sept. 1901

71 *L'Evénement*, 31 août 1891; *La Presse*, 29 août 1899; 4 sept. 1900

72 Cooper, 'The Quebec Ship Labourers' Benevolent Society,' *CHR*, XXX, 343

73 Hamelin, *Répertoire des grèves*, 95–6

74 Canada, House of Common, *Debates*, 1887, 862, 1075, 1152–5, 1229–31, 1532–3; 1888, 46–67. The Toronto Trades and Labor Council unanimously appointed a delegation to Ottawa to oppose the bill: Minutes, 14, 15, 17 June 1887.

75 Canada, Royal Commission on the Relations of Capital and Labor, *Report*, 1889, Quebec Evidence, II, 803–6, 873–6, 878, 881–4, 888–91, 899, 1074–5, 1079–85, 1132–3

76 Ibid., 880

77 *Labour Gazette*, I, 513–15, 533. The *American Federationist*, Jan. 1902, 44, reports the Ship Labourers in receivership; but they survived.

78 *L'Evénement*, 11–13, 15–16, 19 juin, 3 juillet, 13 oct. 1891

79 Hamelin, *Répertoire des grèves*, 152

80 *Labour Gazette*, II, 567–9, 638–40, 672, 712; III, 12, 53

81 Bélanger, *Les Travailleurs québécois*, 207; for Labour Day lists see notes following; for the Progressive Union, *La Presse*, various dates, 6 janv.–31 oct. 1893. The Stone Cutters may have gone into the international union in 1898, when they named their first delegate to the Federated Trades and Labor Council: *La Patrie*, 22 avril 1898.

82 *Labour Gazette*, II, 430; Bélanger, *Les Travailleurs*, 215; *La Patrie*, 16 août 1882; *La Presse*, 13 fév., 4 mars, 11 avril, 19 juin, 3 juillet, 1889; 3 avril, 24 juillet 1890; 30 août 1892; 16 mars 1895; 8 sept. 1896; 18 juin 1898; 30 mai 1899; 12, 22 juin 1901; 2 sept. 1902

83 See notes in PAC, MG281I03, v. 247, 4; Bélanger, *Les Travailleurs*, 204; *La Presse*, 3 sept. 1889; 2 sept. 1890; 31 août 1891; 2 sept. 1893; various dates, 5 janv.–5 oct. 1894; 31 août 1895.

84 *La Patrie*, 25 juin 1881; 27 juin 1882; Bélanger, *Les Travailleurs*, 207 (nailmakers), 213 (bakers), 214 (longshoremen), 217 (merchants' clerks). On the bakers, see also *La Patrie*, 17–19, 23 oct., 30 nov. 1882. On a Merchants' Clerks' strike, 1881, see Hamelin, *Répertoire des grèves*, 66–7.

85 Bélanger, *Les Travailleurs*, 207; Hamelin, *Répertoire*, 114–17; *La Presse*, 11 sept. 1893; 23 janv., 1er sept. 1894; 31 août 1895; 2 sept. 1899

86 *La Presse*, 20 août 1889; 28 août 1891; 3 mai, 1894; 17 août; 1er, 7, 8 sept.; 31 août 1895; *La Patrie*, 8 fév. 1896

87 *La Presse*, 30 oct., 3, 6, 13, 20, 27 nov., 4, 18 déc. 1894; 7 nov. 1895

88 TLCC, *Proceedings*, 1893, 4; Bélanger, *Les Travailleurs*, 213; *La Presse*, 20 juillet, 20 août 1889; 3 juillet, 6 sept. 1893; 18 juin 1898; 12 juin 1899; *La Patrie*, 9, 23 juin 1897; *Le Monde* (Montreal), 5 sept. 1896

89 TLCC, *Proceedings*, 1890, 4; 1893, 4; Bélanger, *Les Travailleurs*, 209; *La Presse*, 31 août 1891; 3 sept. 1892; 2 sept. 1893; 1er sept. 1894; 9, 23 juin 1897; 12 juin, 2 sept. 1899; *La Patrie*, 9, 23 juin 1897

90 *La Presse*, 6 sept. 1886; 3 sept. 1888; 3 sept. 1889; 28 août 1890; 31 août 1891; 3 sept. 1892; 2 sept. 1893; 1er sept. 1894; 31 août 1895; 26 mai (separated from the American Knights), 26 août 1896; *La Patrie*, 7 sept. 1886; Garlock, 'Structural Analysis'

91 *Labour Gazette*, II, 372, 694; Bélanger, *Les Travailleurs*, 213; Hamelin, *Répertoire des grèves*, 93–4; *La Presse*, 12 juillet, 3 sept. 1889; 28 août 1890; 31

août 1891; various dates, 1er mars–1er déc. 1893; various dates, 5 janv.–2 nov.
1894; various dates, 15 fév.–31 août 1895; *La Patrie*, 19, 23 oct., 30 nov. 1882

92 *La Presse*, 28 août 1890; 31 août 1891; 2 sept., 2 nov. 1893; 1er sept. 1894; 31
août 1895; 28 fév. 1896; 6 sept. 1898; 2 sept. 1899; 1er sept. 1900; 31 août 1901

93 TTLC, Minutes, 1 Dec. 1882; 2 Feb. 1883; *Trades Union Advocate*, 3 Aug., 21, 28
Dec. 1882; 4, 25 Jan. 1883; *La Patrie*, 22, 24, 27–30 nov., 1er, 5, 11, 14, 16, 18,
20, 23, 27 déc. 1882

94 Hamelin, *Répertoire des grèves*, 211; *La Presse*, 21 juin 1902

95 Hamelin, *Répertoire*, 210; *La Patrie*, 6 oct. 1882

96 Bélanger, *Les Travailleurs*, 211; *La Patrie*, 7 sept. 1886; 6 sept. 1898; *La
Presse*, 6 sept. 1886; 29 nov. 1893; 17 août 1894 (still an 'Assemblée'); 1er sept.
1894 ('Union'); 31 août 1895 ('Local 24,' probably Local 249 of the international
Boot and Shoe Workers); 3 sept. 1896; 2 sept. 1897; 2 sept. 1899; 31 août 1901

97 Bélanger, *Les Travailleurs*, 206; *La Presse*, 3 sept. 1888; 3 sept. 1889; 2 sept.
1890; 31 août 1891

98 TLCC, *Proceedings*, 1902, 7; Bélanger, *Les Travailleurs*, 217; *La Presse*, 2, 17 août,
6, 8, 19 oct., 24 nov. 1894; 19 janv., 9 fév., 2–30 mars, 20 avril, 3–18 mai, 1er,
15 juin, 13, 18 juillet, 1er–31 août, 6–28 sept., 5–26 oct., 2–23 nov. (Barbers' LA
187, all these) 1895; 25 mai, 11 juin, 22 oct. 13 nov. 1894; 7 janv., 20 mars, 11
avril, 3, 8 sept. 1896; 4 déc. 1899 (union, all these)

99 Bélanger, *Les Travailleurs*, 206; *La Presse*, 28 août 1890; 31 août 1891; 3 sept.
1892; 2 sept. 1893; 29 mars 1894; 5 mai 1896

100 Bélanger, *Les Travailleurs*, 211; *La Presse*, 31 août 1891; 3 sept. 1892; 2 sept.
1893; 8, 15 janv., 13, 19 fév. 1894; 21 juin 1895

101 Canada, Royal Commission on the Relations of Capital and Labor, *Report*, 1889,
Quebec Evidence, I, 156; Bélanger, *Les Travailleurs*, 214; Hamelin, *Répertoire des
grèves*, 67, 71–2; *La Patrie*, 16, 26 août, 4 nov. 1882

102 All three of these appear in the Labour Day lists of 1889–95, and LA also in 1899,
and in the *Labour Gazette*, II, 560. On the LAS, see Garlock, 'Structural Analysis,'
and *La Presse*, 2 sept. 1890; 26 août 1891; 3 sept. 1892; 1er sept. 1894; 31 août
1895.

103 TTLC, Minutes, 23 Oct. 1902; *Labour Gazette*, II, 196, 430; but V, 882, indicates it
continued.

104 Bélanger, *Les Travailleurs*, 217; Hamelin, *Répertoire des grèves*, 66–7; *La
Presse*, 24 juillet, 21 août, 2 sept. 1885; 22–23 juin 1889; 26 juillet, 11 nov. 1890;
various dates, 11 janv.–2 déc. 1893; 11 janv. 1895; 9, 14, 21 juin 1897; 18 juin
1898; 12 juin, 6 oct. 1899; *La Patrie*, 19, 28 fév., 18 mars, 20 avril 1896

105 *La Presse*, 26–27 janv. 1894; 11, 14 janv., 6, 28 fév., 14 mai 1895; *La Patrie*,
20 avril 1896; 18 juin 1898; 12 juin 1899; 22 juin 1901

106 TLCC, *Proceedings*, 1900, 5; 1901, 5; 1902, 5; Bélanger, *Les Travailleurs*,
209; Hamelin, *Répertoire des grèves*, 70–1; *La Presse*, 20 août 1889; 28 août

1890; 31 août 1891; 3 sept. 1892; 1er sept. 1893; 1er sept. 1894; 31 août 1895; 13 mars, 10 avril, 10, 12 juillet 1896; *La Patrie*, 2 sept. 1897; 6 sept. 1898; 2 sept. 1899

107 Bélanger, *Les Travailleurs*, 217

108 Ibid., 206; Hamelin, *Répertoire des grèves*, 77, 102–3, 157–8; *La Presse*, 7–8, 11, 17, 20 fév., 1er, 4 mars 1890

109 Bélanger, *Les Travailleurs*, 206, 217; *La Presse*, 3 sept. 1888; 20 août 1889; 28 août 1890; 31 août 1891; 3 sept. 1892; 2 sept. 1893; 1er sept. 1894; 12 juin 1897; 2 sept. 1899; *La Patrie*, 20 avril 1896

110 *La Presse*, 3 sept. 1889; 28 août 1890; 31 août 1891 ('Charretiers,' first two years 'Voituriers'); 3 sept. 1892; various dates, 16 janv.–29 déc. 1893; various dates, 4 janv.–25 oct. 1894; various dates, 30 janv.–20 déc. 1895; 8 avril–2 sept., 8 sept. 1896; 2 sept. 1897; 9 janv., 12 juin, 2 sept. 1899; 1er sept. 1900; *La Patrie*, 7 sept. 1897. *La Patrie*, 7 fév. 1896, notes an 'Assemblée indépendante des charretiers,' which may indicate that the KOL assembly was in process of becoming the independent union, and that *La Presse*'s 1896 references to the assembly may be to this transitional organization.

111 *Labour Gazette*, II, 694; Bélanger, *Les Travailleurs*, 212; *La Presse*, 3 sept. 1889; 28 août 1890; 31 août 1891; 27 juin, 30 août, 3 sept. 1892; 27 fév., 6, 8, 9 mars; 2 sept. 1893; 1er sept. 1894; 15 juin, 31 août 1895

112 Bélanger, *Les Travailleurs*, 205; CFMTM, *Etat de compte*, sept., nov. 1902; *La Presse*, 3 sept. 1889; 28 août 1890; 31 août 1891; 2 sept. 1893; 13 mars, 24 avril 1894; 19 avril 1895; *La Patrie*, 21 janv., 11, 18 fév., 3, 17 mars 1896

113 *Labour Gazette*, II, 488; Bélanger, *Les Travailleurs*, 216; *La Presse*, 3 sept. 1889; 2 sept. 1890; 31 août 1891; 3 sept. 1892

114 *La Presse*, 3 sept. 1889; 28 août, 2 sept. 1890. The 'Union' in one 1890 list and the 'Assembly' in the other may well be the same body.

115 *La Presse*, 28 août 1890; 31 août 1891; 3 sept. 1892; 9 mars 1893; 14 mai 1894; 15 oct. 1895

116 Bélanger, *Les Travailleurst*, 207; *La Presse*, 31 août 1891; 3 sept. 1892

117 Bélanger, *Les Travailleurs*, 216; *La Presse*, 30 août 1891; 3 sept. 1892; 2 sept. 1893

118 Bélanger, *Les Travailleurs*, 206; *La Presse*, 19 juin, 12 août, 2 sept., 7 nov., 5 déc. 1893; 21 avril, 11 mai, 27 nov. 1894; various dates, 6 avril–17 déc. 1895; 2 sept. 1897; 2 sept. 1899; 1er sept. 1900; *La Patrie*, various dates, 14 janv.–14 avril 1896

119 Bélanger, *Les Travailleurs*, 207

120 Ibid., 217; *La Presse*, 20 août 1889; 28, 30 avril, 4, 5, 7, 21, 26 mai, 7, 12, 21 juillet, 2 août, 20, 29 sept., 5 déc. 1894; 15 juin 1895

121 *La Presse*, 30 mars 1895

122 *Labour Gazette*, II, 490
123 CFMTM, *Procès-Verbal*, 1er sept. 1898; *La Presse*, for dates already noted.
124 Bélanger, *Les Travailleurs*, 209–10; *La Presse*, 2 sept. 1899; *Labour Gazette*, I, 265; II, 692; CFMTM, *Etat de compte*, 1902
125 *La Presse*, 23–24 janv., 28 mars, 19–20 avril 1899; 31 août 1901
126 *La Presse*, 12 juillet, 1er sept., 9 oct.–26 déc. 1899; 1er sept. 1900; 31 août 1901; 2 sept. 1901
127 Bélanger, *Les Travailleurs*, 208
128 CFMTM, *Etat de compte*, 1900–02
129 *Labour Gazette*, II, 6; information from M. Martin
130 *Labour Gazette*, II, 570; AASRE, *Proceedings*, 1903
131 Bélanger, *Les Travailleurs*, 207, 212; *Labour Gazette*, III, 482; *La Presse*, 2 sept. 1902
132 *Labour Gazette*, I, 395, 437; II, 195, 210, 558, 642
133 Hamelin, *Répertoire des grèves*, 149–50; *Labour Gazette*, I, 202; II, 372. A Tanners and Curriers Union went international in January 1901: *Labour Gazette*, I, 305.
134 Bélanger, *Les Travailleurs*, 217; *Labour Gazette*, II, 554; III, 499
135 *Labour Gazette*, II, 178; III, 242
136 Ibid., II, 558; III, 240. An 'Aylmer Union' marched in the 1899 Ottawa Labour Day parade, and 'Aylmer Mill Men' in 1900: *Citizen*, 5 Sept. 1899; 1 Sept. 1900.
137 *Labour Gazette*, III, 242
138 Ibid., III, 174
139 Bélanger, *Les Travailleurs*, 217

CHAPTER 13

1 Kingston TU, Minutes, 12 June, 10 July 1896; Ontario, Bureau of Labor, *Report*, 1902, 44, 68
2 TLCC, *Proceedings*, 1889, 7; 1890, 4; Ontario, Bureau of Labor, *Report*, 1902, 71; *Citizen*, 5 Jan., 1889; 21 Feb., 12 April 1890; 8, 24 Sept. 1891; 5 Sept. 1892; 4 Sept. 1893; 3 Sept. 1895; 8 Sept. 1896
3 TLCC, *Proceedings*, 1886, 9; *Labour Gazette*, II, 244; see notes in PAC, MG28I103, v. 248, 16; *Citizen*, 21 Feb. 1889. The 1901 report of the Ontario Bureau of Labor, 45, says the Plumbers Union was formed in 1888.
4 Ontario, Bureau of Industries, *Report*, 1887, pt IV, 44
5 See notes in PAC, MG28I103, v. 248, 15; *Citizen*, 21 Feb. 1889. The 1900 report of the Ontario Bureau of Labor, 24, says the Painters Union began in 1887.
6 *Citizen*, 21 Feb. 1889; 2 Sept. 1890; 8 Sept. 1891; 5 Sept. 1892; 26 Jan., 2 Sept. 1893; 14 Aug., 4 Sept. 1894; 3 Sept. 1895; 8 Sept. 1896; 7, 25 Sept. 1897; 3 May,

18, 30 Aug. 1898; 1 May, 5 Sept. 1899; 15 Aug., 1 Sept., 1 Dec. 1900; 2 Sept. 1901; 2 Sept. 1902; TLCC, *Proceedings*, 1890, 4; 1893, 4; 1894, 4; Ontario, Bureau of Labor, *Report*, 1902, 71; see also notes in PAC, MG28II03, v. 247, 2, 4. Note: the UBCJ has no record of the Carpenters and Joiners Local 28; neither the TLCC nor the AFL seems to have any record of the 'Federal' union of 1897.

7 *Citizen*, 6 May, 4, 8 July, 19, 30 Aug. 1898

8 *Labour Gazette*, III, 443; Ontario, Bureau of Labor, *Report*, 1902, 71; *Citizen*, 13 June 1901

9 *Citizen*, 29 Sept. 1902

10 *Trades Union Advocate*, 12 Oct. 1882; Ontario, Bureau of Industries, *Report*, 1887, pt IV, 45; *Examiner*, 4 Sept. 1888; 30 Aug. 1902

11 Ontario, Bureau of Labor, *Report*, 1902, 70

12 TTLC, Minutes, 23 July, 13 Aug., 3 Sept., 18 Nov. 1881; 20 Jan., 17 Feb., 16 June, 6 Oct. 1882

13 See notes in PAC, MG28II03, v. 247, 4.

14 *Journal of United Labor*, 1882: Oct., 323

15 TTLC, Minutes, 6, 20 Jan., 17 Feb., 17 March, 7, 21 April, 5, 19 May, 2 June, 2, 21 July, 15 Sept., 6 Oct., 3, 17 Nov., 1, 15 Dec. 1882; *Trades Union Advocate*, 4, 11 May, 22 June, 20, 27 July, 14, 21, 28 Sept., 4, 12, 26 Oct., 9 Nov. 1882. The Coopers had been organized in January 1883, and reorganized in April, when they got a wage increase to $2 a day. At their first anniversary supper, January 1883, John Hewitt (described as ex-president of the international union) replied to the toast to that body: *Trades Union Advocate*, 4 May, 8 June 1882; 11 Jan. 1883.

16 There seems to have been a House Painters Union organized in March 1882 (TTLC, Minutes, 17 March). Whether it was this union or the earlier one which became Local 3 is not clear. For Local 3's charter date, see notes in PAC, MG28II03, v. 248, 15.

17 See notes in PAC, ibid., v. 247, 4.

18 *Daily Mail*, 23 July 1883

19 TLCC, *Proceedings*, 1883, 7; 1886, 8; 1887, 11; 1888, 8; 1890, 4; 1891, 4; 1892, 4; 1893, 4; *Daily Mail*, 30 July 1885; 13 Sept. 1886; 15 Jan., 13 Sept. 1886; 12 Sept. 1892; 7 Sept. 1897

20 Statements in the following paragraphs regarding the years of appearance and activities of the various Toronto local unions are based on references made in the minutes of the TTLC in the years noted. Only additional sources are cited.

21 *Daily Mail*, 23 July 1883; 30 July 1885; 13 Sept. 1886; 3 Oct. 1887; 12 Sept. 1892; 5 Sept. 1899; 4 Sept. 1900; and Ontario, Bureau of Labor, *Report*, 1900, 27, 31; 1902, 76

22 *Daily Mail*, 12 Sept. 1892

23 *Trades Union Advocate*, 4 May, 29 June 1882; Canada, House of Commons, *Journals*, 22 Feb. 1884, 135

24 *Journal of United Labor*, 10 May 1886, 2068; TLCC, Accounts, 1893

25 *Labour Gazette*, III, 372

26 *Journal of United Labor*, 10 May 1885, 2069; Garlock, 'Structural Analysis'; *Daily Mail*, 23 July 1883; 30 July 1885. The *Labour Gazette*, III, 416, says that in November 1902 a Ship Labourers Union joined the international local union.

27 Although the *Labour Gazette*, II, 347, gives the date of formation of the Stone Masons Union as 1884, this date is plainly wrong. This is probably the date when the union went international. The TTLC minutes of 7 July 1882 record a request from the union 'for advice has [sic] to uniting with the Branches on the other side and the best method to adopt. Information was given how other societies done in cases of this kind and it was left in his hands to report and adopt if thought practible'; see also 4 May 1883, 15 Feb., 21 March 1884.

28 *Journal of United Labor*, 10 April 1885, 959

29 Ibid., 10 June 1884, 720; *Labour Gazette*, II, 318; *Daily Mail*, 23 July 1883

30 *Trades Union Advocate*, 11 Jan. 1883; Canada, House of Commons, *Journals*, 18 Feb. 1884, 117

31 AFL charter books; *Labour Gazette*, II, 320; *Daily Mail*, 20 July 1883. A Silver Gilders Union marched in the Labour Day parade in 1900, and a Gilders Union in 1901 and 1902; *Daily Mail*, 4 Sept. 1900; 3 Sept. 1901; *Globe*, 2 Sept. 1902.

32 *Daily Mail*, 23 July 1883; *Globe*, 2 Sept. 1902

33 *Journal of United Labor*, Sept. 1883, 560; Garlock, 'Structural Analysis'

34 *Journal of United Labor*, 10 May 1886, 2069; Garlock, 'Structural Analysis'

35 *Wage-Worker*, 5 April 1883

36 *Daily Mail*, 23 July 1883

37 *Daily Mail*, 3 Oct. 1887

38 Ibid., 6 Sept. 1898

39 TTU, Minutes, 3 March 1894; *Journal of United Labor*, 10 Dec. 1885, 1148; Garlock, 'Structural Analysis'

40 TTU, Minutes, 5 Jan. 1901; *Daily Mail*, 7 Sept. 1897

41 *Journal of United Labor*, 10 Feb. 1886, 1193; Garlock, 'Structural Analysis'; *Daily Mail*, 12 Sept. 1892. There had been a Pick and Shovel Union in 1885: TTLC, Minutes, 18 Sept. 1885.

42 TLCC, *Proceedings*, 1892, 4; *Daily Mail*, 3 Sept. 1895; *Mail and Empire*, 8 Sept. 1896; 7 Sept. 1897; 6 Sept. 1898; 5 Sept. 1899; 4 Sept. 1900

43 *Daily Mail*, 12 Sept. 1892. For LA 7210, see *Journal of United Labor*, 10 June 1886, 2093; TTLC, Minutes, 1 Oct. 1886.

44 TLCC, Proceedings, 1892, 4; *Daily Mail*, 12 Sept. 1892; *Mail and Empire*, 8 Sept. 1896. On 20 Nov. 1891 the TTLC had had a letter from the International Union of Slate and Tile Roofers, asking that an enclosed circular be forwarded to the Slate Roofers Union if there was one in Toronto, and that, if not, steps be taken to organize one. The council referred the letter to its organizing committee.

45 *Daily Mail*, 12 Sept. 1892

46 Ibid.

47 TTU, Minutes, 18 March 1893

48 Ontario, Bureau of Labor, *Report*, 1901, 56, says the union was formed 4 Oct. 1894.

49 Ibid., 27, says No 2 was formed 6 April 1894; but the report for 1902, 54, says 1895.

50 *Mail and Empire*, 8 Sept. 1896; 7 Sept. 1897; 6 Sept. 1898; 5 Sept. 1899; 4 Sept. 1900; 3 Sept. 1901; *Globe*, 2 Sept. 1902. The *Labour Gazette*, II, 488, says No 1 was formed in 1895, and No 2 on 6 April 1894.

51 *Labour Gazette*, II, 250

52 TLCC, *Proceedings*, 1902, 64; Ontario, Bureau of Labor, *Report*, 1901, 54; 1902, 75

53 *Mail and Empire*, 3 Sept. 1901; AFL, charter books

54 *Labour Gazette*, III, 447, 552

55 *Trades Union Advocate*, 4 May 1882, records an extraordinary expression of union solidarity in the various strikes of the spring of 1882. The Crispins gave $50 to the Female Shoe Fitters, the Bricklayers $250 to the Carpenters. The Stone Cutters, 'weak in numbers' but 'with large hearts,' gave all their funds to the strikes; the Seamen's Union 'emptied its treasury,' and its president, John D. Murphy, gave a month's wages.

56 *Trades Union Advocate*, 3 April, 4, 11, 25 May, 1 June, 6, 27 July, 10, 17, 24, 31 Aug., 7 Sept., 12, 19, Oct., 2, 9 Nov., 14 Dec. 1882; TTLC, Minutes, 18 April 1884; *Citizen and Evening Chronicle* (Halifax), 18 Dec. 1882

57 *Wage-Worker*, 15, 22, 29 March 1883

58 Ibid., 29 March, 5, 12 April 1883

59 Ibid., 29 March 1883

60 *Dominion Annual Register and Review* (Toronto), 1885, 373

61 *Trades Union Advocate*, 16 Nov. 1882

62 *Spectator*, 10, 16 Feb., 7–8 July 1881

63 *Journal of United Labor*, Oct. 1882, 322; HTLC, Minutes, 3 Dec. 1888; *Spectator*, 9 May 1881; 28 March 1882

64 TLCC, *Proceedings*, 1886, 9; 1887, 11; HTLC, Minutes, 12 Nov., 3 Dec. 1888; 14 Jan. 1889; *Palladium of Labor*, 19 July 1884; Ontario, Bureau of Industries, *Report*, 1889, pt IV, 24; *Spectator*, 3, 5 May, 8 July 1881

65 *Spectator*, 27 May 1881; 4 Aug. 1883

66 Ibid., 29 Aug. 1881; 23 Jan. 1882; 25 Feb. 1886. The *Trades Union Advocate*, 8 June 1882, 2, says the Bakers got a wage increase and were stamping their bread 'U.B.,' and that the other unions' members had decided to buy only bread so stamped.

67 *Trades Union Advocate*, 12 Oct. 1882; *Spectator*, 25 Oct. 1881; 8 April 1882

68 *Palladium of Labor*, 3 May 1884; 25 April 1885; 24 July 1886; *Spectator*, 18 Feb. 1882; 4 Aug. 1883; 4 Aug. 1884; 23 April 1885

69 *Spectator*, 10, 14, 18, 29 March, 4, 20, 29 April 1882; HTLC, Minutes, 3 Dec. 1888; 27 Jan. 1889

70 *Spectator*, 4 May, 18–19 July, 1883; on the Firemen, see 10 June 1880; 5 Nov. 1881.

71 Ibid., 4 Aug. 1883; *Daily Mail*, 3 Aug. 1883

72 TTLC, Minutes, 21 March 1884; *Spectator*, 4 Aug. 1884

73 *Spectator*, 4 Aug. 1883; 15 July 1884; 18, 22 July 1885; 29 Sept. 1887; *Journal of United Labor*, May 1883, 470; *American Federationist*, 1902: Feb., 61; TLCC, *Proceedings*, 1888, 4; Garlock, 'Structural Analysis'; HTLC, Minutes, 28 Feb. 1889

74 *Journal of United Labor*, 10 July 1886; 2 June 1888; *Times*, (Hamilton) 3 Sept. 1895

75 Ontario, Bureau of Industries, *Report*, 1883, 36; *Journal of United Labor*, Feb. 1884, 651; 10 March 1886; *Spectator*, 4 Aug. 1884; HTLC, Minutes, 26 May, 2, 16 June, 7 July 1890. On 20 June the TTLC minutes record an appeal from the Weavers for help.

76 TTLC, Minutes, 21 Aug. 1885; *Spectator*, 20 Jan. 1886

77 HTLC, Minutes, 12 Nov. 1888; 13 Sept. 1895; *American Federationist*, 1902: Feb., 61; *Spectator*, 25 Feb. 1886

78 HTLC, Minutes, 28 Feb. 1889; 15 April 1891; *American Federationist*, 1902, 61; Ontario, Bureau of Labor, *Report*, 1902, 68; *Spectator*, 7 Sept. 1897

79 *Spectator*, 6–10 Sept. 1892

80 Ibid., 7 Sept. 1897

81 See notes in PAC, MG28I103, v. 247, 7 (Barbers) and v. 248, 12 (Butchers); *Times*, 4 Sept. 1900; *Labour Gazette*, I, 146, 194; II, 430; Ontario, Bureau of Labor, *Report*, 1902, 67.

82 *Labour Gazette*, I, 146, 194; II, 430; Ontario, Bureau of Labor, *Report*, 1902, 67, 68. The TTLC minutes, 13 Dec. 1900, mention a Hamilton Cab and Express Union.

83 *Trades Union Advocate*, 31 Aug., 12 Oct. 1882; *Spectator*, 29 Aug. 1881; Davis, 'History of Labour in London,' 11–12 (which says the old local union was dissolved 6 Aug. 1878); *Daily Advertiser*, 7 Feb., 6 Oct. 1882.

84 *Daily Advertiser*, 16 June, 30 July 1885; Ontario, Bureau of Industries, *Report*, 1887, IV, 44; 1888, pt IV, 17; 1889, pt IV, 22, 24

85 See notes in PAC, MG28I103, v. 247, 7; *Labour Gazette*, II, 554; *Daily Advertiser*, 6 Sept. 1892; 5 Sept. 1893; 4 Sept. 1894; 3 Sept. 1895; 8 Sept. 1896; 5 Sept. 1899; 2 Sept. 1902; *Industrial Banner*, June, 1895; TLCC, Proceedings, 1895, 4; Davis, 'History of Labour in London,' 53.

86 *Industrial Banner*, Nov. 1895; financial report of the international union, 1898, 2

87 *Labour Gazette*, II, 246; *Daily Advertiser*, 8 Sept. 1896; 7 Sept. 1897; 6 Sept. 1898; 5 Sept. 1899; 4 Sept. 1900; 2 Sept. 1902; *Daily Free Press*, 2, 3 (calls it local 8) Sept. 1901

88 *Daily Advertiser*, 8 Sept. 1896; 7 Sept. 1897; 6 Sept. 1898; 5 Sept. 1899 (Western Coopers Union); 4 Sept. 1900; *Daily Free Press*, 2 Sept. 1901; *Labour Gazette*, II, 250; Ontario, Bureau of Labor, *Report*, 1902, 69; Davis, 'History of Labour in London,' 53

89 *Daily Advertiser*, 5 Sept. 1899; 4 Sept. 1900; *Industrial Banner*, April 1899; Ontario, Bureau of Labor, *Report*, 1902, 69–70; Davis, ibid., 53

90 *Industrial Banner*, April 1899

91 See notes in PAC, MG28I103, v. 247, 7; *Daily Expositor*, 25 Jan., 9 May, 22 July 1887; 16 Jan., 7 Feb., 24 April 1894.

92 *Daily Expositor*, 17, 22 June 1887; 26 April 1900

93 See notes in PAC, MG28I103, v. 247, 2; *Daily Expositor*, 7 May 1889.

94 *Tailor*, April 1890, 7; *Daily Expositor*, 7 May 1889

95 See notes in PAC, MG28I103, v. 247, 4 (Bricklayers), v. 248, 15 (Painters); *Daily Expositor*, 18, 19 Aug. 1894; 12 March 1897; 18 Sept. 1901 (supplementary issue); 16 Jan. 1904; *American Federationist*, 1899; Aug., 137; Ontario, Bureau of Labor, *Report*, 1902, 63. The Tinsmiths' international was chartered by the AFL 23 April 1889; charter recalled, 20 Oct. 1896: AFL-CIO Archives, list of active and inactive international unions.

96 *Labour Gazette*, II, 554; Ontario, Bureau of Labor, *Report*, 1902, 52, 74; *Daily Standard*, 10 Oct. 1894; 11 May 1897; 15, 23 Nov. 1898

97 Ontario, Bureau of Industries, *Report*, 1887, pt IV, 45; 1889, pt IV, 25

98 See notes in PAC, MG28I103, v. 248, 15 (Painters); *Daily Standard*, 29 April, 11 May 1897; *Labour Gazette*, II, 246.

99 *Daily Standard*, 8, 10, 13, 15 Oct. 1894

100 *Labour Gazette*, I, 471, 512

101 *Retail Clerks International Advocate* (Washington), Nov. 1902; *Labour Gazette*, III, 306, 378; *Daily Standard*, 29 April, 11 May 1897

102 *Labour Gazette*, III, 502

103 Files in Carpenters' international union office; *Tailor*, Nov. 1890, 5; *Labour Gazette*, III, 444

104 TTLC, Minutes, 14 April, 4 May 1888; *Labour Gazette*, III, 482; IV, 1065; Ontario, Bureau of Industries, *Report*, 1887, pt IV, 44; 1888, pt IV, 17; 1889, pt IV, 24; Guelph city directories, 1882 and 1887

105 Ontario, Bureau of Industries, *Report*, 1887, pt IV, 45; Bureau of Labor, *Report*, 1902, 63, 75; *Labour Gazette*, II, 250, 490, 560; *Daily Standard*, 6 March 1896; 4 March, 27 June, 18 July 1899

106 TTLC, Minutes, 8 Aug. 1901; *American Federationist*, 1902: May, 261; AFL-CIO Archives, AFL charter books; *Labour Gazette*, II, 578; Ontario, Bureau of Labor, *Report*, 1902, 71

107 *Citizen*, 20–22 June, 30 Aug., 3 Sept. 1898

108 Ontario, Bureau of Labor, *Report*, 1902, 70, 73

109 *Labour Gazette*, VII, 889; Ontario, Bureau of Industries, *Report*, 1889, pt IV, 22–3; a riot in Collingwood between union and non-union sailors over the non-unionists' taking lower than union wages suggests a Sailors' Union, local or international; *Tribune* (Welland), 14 Aug. 1891.

110 *Daily Tribune*, 5, 19 Feb., 26 March, 2, 16 April, 14 May, 11 June, 30 Aug., 4 Sept. 1894; 3 Sept. 1895 (supplement); *Manitoba Morning Free Press*, 8 Sept. 1896;

Voice, 22 May, 11 Sept. 1897; 7 Jan., 3 June, 2, 9 Sept. 1898; *Labour Gazette*, II, 372

111 *Voice*, throughout 1898, beginning 18 March; *Manitoba Morning Free Press*, 5 Sept. 1899; see also notes in PAC, MG28I103, v. 248, 29 (Lathers), and, for the Plumbers, the financial report of the international, 1898, 2.

112 *Daily Tribune*, 3 Sept. 1895 (supplement); *Manitoba Morning Free Press*, 8 Sept. 1896; 5 Sept. 1899; *Voice*, 8 May, 19 June 1897; 10 Feb. 1899; 28 June, 23 Aug., 27 Sept., 4, 11, 18, 25 Oct., 1, 8, 15, 22 Nov. 1901; 3 Jan., 7 March, 9 May, 8 Aug., 10 Oct., 7 Nov. 1902; Winnipeg TLC, *Souvenir Programme*, 10, 33

113 *Manitoba Morning Free Press*, 8 Sept. 1896; *Voice*, 12 June, 11 Sept. 1897; 24 June, 1 July 1898; 10, 17 Feb., 17 March 1899; 3, 17 Jan., 8 Aug., 7 Nov. 1902; Winnipeg TLC, *Souvenir Programme*, 10, 33; *Labour Gazette*, II, 430

114 *Voice*, 19 July, 23 Aug., 6, 27 Sept., 4, 11, 18, 25 Oct., 1, 8, 15, 22 Nov., 6 Dec. 1901; 3 Jan., 4 April, 11 July, 8 Aug., 10 Oct., 7, 21 Nov., 13 Dec. 1902; Winnipeg TLC, *Souvenir Programme*, 9–10, 19, 29, 33, 35; *Labour Gazette*, VI, 886

115 See notes in PAC, MG28I103, v. 248, 21 (Sheet Metal Workers); *Labour Gazette*, III, 895; VI, 883.

116 *Labour Gazette*, III, 55; V, 880; *American Federationist*, 1902: June, 329; *Retail Clerks International Advocate*, Aug. 1903

117 Vancouver TLC, Minutes, 2 July 1892; 8 May, 4 Dec. 1896; 17 April, 3 July, 16 Oct., 18 Dec. 1902; TLCC, *Proceedings*, 1903, 50; *British Columbia Federationist* (Vancouver), 5 April, 6 May 1912; UBC, Local 617 (Vancouver), Minutes, 1 Dec. 1892; *Labour Gazette*, I, 413; II, 428, 430; *Province*, 15, 29 April, 15 May 1899; 21–3, 27–8 Feb., 3, 6, 8 March, 10, 19 April, 13 July 1900

118 Vancouver TLC, Minutes, 21 Nov. 1889; 31 Jan., 14 Feb. 1890; 13 Feb. 1891; 17 June 1892; UBC, Local 617, Minutes, 18 May 1891; 21 July 1892

119 See notes in PAC, MG28I103, v. 247, 4; Vancouver TLC, Minutes, 10 Jan. 1890; 12 Nov. 1902.

120 Vancouver TLC, Minutes, 31 Jan., 14, 28 Feb., 25 Aug., 26 Sept. 1890; 17, 31 July 1891; 17 June 1892

121 See Vancouver TLC, Minutes, and UBC, Local 617, Minutes; see also TLCC, *Proceedings*, 1902, 64; *Province*, 30 Sept. 1899.

122 Vancouver TLC, Minutes, and UBC, Local 617, Minutes, 3 Sept. 1891; *Labour Gazette*, II, 246

123 Vancouver TLC, Minutes, 4 Aug. 1893

124 *Colonist*, 11, 18 April 1899; *Province*, 10 April 1899

125 *Labour Gazette*, I, 50–1; II, 252; III, 1019; *Province*, 12 Sept. 1900; 5 Jan., 2 March, 22 April, 20, 22 May 1901

126 *Labour Gazette*, I, 480, 512; III, 319, 378; VI, 883; *Province*, 18 April 1901

127 *Labour Gazette*, II, 252

128 See notes in PAC, MG28I103, v. 247, 4 (Bricklayers and Masons) and v. 248, 15
(Painters); *Labour Gazette*, II, 184; *Times*, 31 Jan. 1890; Victoria TLC, *Labor Annual*, 45.

129 *Colonist*, 4, 6 July 1890; 6 Jan. 1899; *Free Press* (Nanaimo), 13 Jan. 1891

130 The *Labour Gazette*, II, 428, says Feb. 1901; the TLCC, *Proceedings*, 1902, 38, say the Victoria Marine Firemen 'were quite six months organized without a charter' and ultimately went into the ILA.

131 Letter from the general secretary-treasurer of the Hotel and Restaurant Employees and Bartenders international union, 12 Oct. 1967; *Labour Gazette*, III, 227, 274, 1020; VIII, 984

132 *Free Press*, 29 Nov. 1889; 4 Jan., 14 Feb., 30 Sept. 1890; 11 July, 7 Dec. 1891

133 UBC, office files; *Free Press*, 13 Sept. 1890

134 *Free Press*, 29 Sept., 2 Oct. 1890; 7 Dec. 1891

135 *Labour Gazette*, II, 252, 430, 738; III, 1017

136 TLCC, *Proceedings*, 1900, 18; *Labour Gazette*, II, 374; III, 1017; *Colonist*, 28 Nov. 1899

137 *American Federationist*, 1900: July, 224; *Labour Gazette*, II, 188; III, 1018

138 *Labour Gazette*, II, 430, 554, 558, 698; III, 1016–18

139 *Labour Gazette*, II, 556; III, 55, 896. The *Toiler* (Toronto), 4 April 1902, mentions the Yukon Carpenters.

140 TLCC, *Proceedings*, 1901, 63–7

141 *Labour Gazette*, II, 558

CHAPTER 14

1 The following account of the PWA is based primarily on information drawn from the minutes of its grand council: the dates are those mentioned in the text. Only additional sources are cited.

2 *Trades Journal*, 9 Nov., 14 Dec. 1881

3 Ibid., 29 June, 13, 20 July, 10 Aug., 19 Oct. 1881; 10 Oct. 1883; 20 May 1885; 10 Aug. 1887; 5 Dec. 1888

4 Ibid., 28 Feb., 7 March, 30 May, 12 Sept. 1883; 11 June 1884

5 PWA, Grand Council, Minutes, Oct. 1884, 63. It is interesting to compare these figures with some earlier ones. In November 1879 the PWA had 850 members; by April 1880 it had 741; by March 1881, about 750 (250 in Pioneer Lodge, the rest in Pictou County, where only 80 mine workers were non-members). In July and August 1881, the new Cape Breton lodges enrolled 1051 members; by the end of October, they had 1202. By October 1882, total membership in the province was over 2000 (Fidelity Lodge alone close to 300). See *Trades Journal*, 14 April 1880; 13 April, 3, 31 Aug., 26 Oct. 1881; 18 Oct. 1882.

6 *Trades Journal*, 26 March 1884; 20 April 1887; 8, 22 Feb., 4 April, 20 June 1888; 21 Jan. 1891

7 Ibid., 27 Jan. 1891

8 *Labour Gazette*, II, 376

9 In 1890 the grand secretary had reported that the years 1888–89 had been perhaps 'the lowest in our history,' but that the PWA was now holding its own; PWA, Grand Council, Minutes, Oct. 1890, 212; Oct. 1891, 227.

10 *Trades Journal*, 6 March 1889

11 *Labour Gazette*, II, 376. This lodge appears in the Grand Council's minutes, Sept. 1900, 361; Sept. 1902, 380; Sept. 1903, 404

12 *Labour Gazette*, II, 238, 261–2; 376; XI, 964

13 Ibid., I, 321; II, 376, 380; XI, 964

14 PWA, Grand Council, Minutes, iv

15 *Trades Journal*, 18, 25 Feb., 21, 27 April, 18 May, 22, 29 June 1881; 29 March, 10, 24 May, 5 July 1882

16 Ibid., 29 March, 5 April, 10 May, 21 June, 19 July, 23 Aug., 13 Sept., 11, 18 Oct., 1 Nov., 6 Dec. 1882; 10, 17, 24, 31 Jan., 21, 28 Feb., 21 March, 2 May, 4 July 1883; *Citizen and Evening Chronicle*, 12 Oct. 1882; 21–22, 24, 26–30 March, 2, 12–14, 18–19 April, 9, 12 May, 23 June 1883

17 *Trades Journal*, 26 March, 2, 23 April, 21, 28 May 1884; 3, 17, 24 June 1885

18 Ibid., 2, 9 Feb., 30 March, 6, 20, 27 April, 4, 11, 18, 25 May 1887

19 Ibid., 23 May 1888

20 Ibid., 26 June, 17, 31 July 1889

21 Ibid., 22 April 1891

22 *Labour Gazette*, I, 306–7, 379, 507–8; II, 21–3

23 *Trades Journal*, 28 Jan. 1885; Forsey, 'Economic and Social Aspects of the Nova Scotia Industry' 81–3

24 Forsey, 'Economic and Social Aspects,' 84–7. The 1925 strike pretty well put an end to the stores.

25 *Trades Journal*, 21 June 1882; 10 Oct. 1883; 27 May, 8 July, 4, 11 Nov. 1885; 2 Feb. 1887; 8 Feb., 7 March, 12 Sept. 1888; 6 Feb., 4, 18 Sept., 6, 13 Nov. 1889. At least eight are mentioned.

26 Ibid., 7 June 1882; 4 Nov. 1885; 2 Feb. 1887; 30 Jan. 1889; 4 Dec. 1889; Cameron, *Political Pictonians, 1767–1967*, 171, 260

27 *Trades Journal*, 16 July 1884

28 Ibid., 23 Aug. 1882; various dates, spring of 1884, 6 Feb. 1889; *Journal and Pictou News* (Stellarton successor to the *Trades Journal*), 30 Sept. 1891; Forsey, 'Economic and Social Aspects of the Nova Scotia Coal Industry' 89

29 TLCC, *Proceedings*, 1898, 10; PWA, Grand Council, Minutes, 1901, 375; *American Federationist*, 1902: Jan., 43; R.H. Babcock, *Gompers in Canada: A Study in American Continentalism before the First World War* (Toronto and Buffalo, 1974), 121–2

30 *Free Press*, 8, 15, 18 Aug., 13 Oct., 14, 28 Nov., 29 Dec. 1883

31 *Journal of United Labor*, Feb. 1884, 651; 10 Oct. 1884; 10 May 1885 (LA 3429, Wellington, lapsed); *Journal of the Knights of Labor*, 10 April 1890; *Free Press*, 8 March 1884; I, 3–4, 14, 20 Feb., 19, 21, 23 May 1890

32 TLCC, *Proceedings*, 1890, 4, 7, 13, 20; 1896, 4; 1897, 4; 1898, 4; 1899, 4–8; 1903, 50; AFL charter books; *Labour Gazette*, I, 341 ('local unions' at all the Dunsmuir mines trying, Jan. 1901, to amalgamate into a 'general union'); II, 276 ('movement on foot for the affiliation of the different unions of all the collieries on the island,' Oct. 1901); 344 (movement not successful 'so far because of the opposition of the management of the Wellington Coal Co.,' but 'a mass meeting of the miners of the different collieries' to be held 7 Dec., 'when the matter will be fully discussed and probably settled'); IV, 680; *Province*, 19 Jan. 1901

33 TLCC, *Proceedings*, 1896, 12, 16, 19, 26; 1897, 5, 18–19, 23; 1898, 17, 32; 1899, 24; 1900, 6–8, 29; 1901, 5–9, 75

34 Vancouver TLC, Minutes, 25 Aug., 14 Nov. 1890; 13 Feb., 13 March 1891; Phillips, *No Power Greater*, 19–20; *Free Press*, 19 May 1890

35 Vancouver TLC, Minutes, 26 Sept., 6 Nov. 1890

36 Ibid., 13 Feb. 1891; 18 Nov. 1892

37 Phillips, *No Power Greater*, 22, 24, 30

38 *Province*, 13 March 1899

39 Ibid., 29 Aug., 11 Sept. 1900; *Labour Gazette*, I, 51, 97, 127

40 *Labour Gazette*, I, 97

41 TLCC, *Proceedings*, 1900, 14; *Labour Gazette*, I, 217, 250, 282, 341, 416; II, 20; *Province*, 24 Dec. 1900

42 For the following five paragraphs, see *Labour Gazette*, I, 416, 483, 552; II, 20, 344–5, 360, 659.

43 Vancouver TLC, Minutes, 15 May, 3 July, 17 July 1902

44 TLCC, *Proceedings*, 1903, 50; Phillips, *No Power Greater*, 38

45 Gladstone and Jamieson, 'Unionism in the Fishing Industry,' 153–4; Ralston, 'The 1900 Strike of Fraser Fishermen,' 49–59, 61, 71, 80; *Province*, 9 July 1900

46 Gladstone and Jamieson, 'Unionism,' 155; Ralston, 'The 1900 Strike,' 83, 85, 90, 93–4, 97–102, 105–8, 110–11, 113–15, 117–39, 141–9, 152–67; *American Federationist*, 1900: Sept., 292; *Labour Gazette*, II, 488, 698; *Province*, 29 Jan., 17 March, 5 May, 16 June, 2, 9–11, 16–21, 25–28 July, 4 Aug. 1900

47 TLCC, *Proceedings*, 1902, 60; 1903, 50; TLCC, Official Book (Toronto, 1902); *Labour Gazette*, I, 340, 380 (four locals in Feb. 1901); II, 486, 488, 551, 698; Ralston, 'The 1900 Strike,' 168–9, 175; *Province*, 27 Aug. 1900

48 *Labour Gazette*, II, 87–8, 125; III, 28; *Province*, 24, 27, 29 June 1901

49 Vancouver TLC, Minutes, 2, 16 Dec. 1892; 21 July 1893; 27 April 1894; 1 March, 21 June, 27 Sept. 1895; 3 April, 18 Sept. 1902; UBC, Local 617 (Vancouver), Minutes, 23 March, 26 Oct. 1893; TLCC, Proceedings, 1901, 70; *Labour Gazette*, II, 428; IV, 681

50 *Labour Gazette*, I, 483, 512; II, 398, 412, 428, 589; III, 1020; *Free Press*, 8, 15 Oct. 1892

51 *Labour Gazette*, I, 551; *Province*, 11 Jan. 1901

52 *Labour Gazette*, II, 554; III, 241; Canada, *Census*, 1891, I, 370; *L'Evénement*, 3 sept. 1895; *La Presse*, 4 déc. 1899

53 *Labour Gazette*, I, 265; II, 370, 372; *La Presse*, 3, 6 sept. 1898; 2 sept. 1899; *La Patrie*, 6 sept. 1898; *L'Evénement*, 1er sept. 1900. The St Hyacinthe local of the United Shoemakers appears in *La Presse*, 15 mai, 8 juin, 12 août 1899; the Lasters' Local, 15 mai, 12 août. There was a Leather Cutters Union, 17 mai; by 12 Aug. it may have been gone, as *La Presse* speaks of 'les deux associations de St-Hyacinthe.'

54 TLCC, *Proceedings*, 1902, 6; *Labour Gazette*, II, 384, 438

55 HTLC, Minutes, 1 Feb. 1895; TTLC, Minutes, 1 Feb. 1895

56 Hamelin, *Répertoire des grèves*, 142; *La Presse*, 1er sept. 1898; 1er mars 1899

57 Hamelin, *Répertoire*, 146, 150, 156; *La Presse*, 3, 19 janv., 8, 11, 14 mars, 13, 17 mai, 19 déc. 1899

58 *Labour Gazette*, I, 325, 364, 437, 516

59 Ibid., I, 394; Hamelin, *Répertoire*, 158; *La Presse*, 17 nov. 1899

60 *Labour Gazette*, I, 134–5, 153–9, 202, 229–30, 263, 294–7, 322, 394, 462–3; II, 4, 72, 259

61 TLCC, *Proceedings*, 1896, 4; *Gazette du Travail*, II, 250, 681 ('fusion des Ingénieurs-Mécaniciens [sic],' avril 1902), 692; *La Presse*, 4 fév., 19 avril, 28–29 oct., 2 déc. 1895; 20 janv.–31 août 1896 (various dates); 9 fév.–23 mai 1899 (various dates); 1er sept. 1900; 3 sept. 1901; 21 juin 1902; *L'Evénement*, 31 août, 3 sept. 1895; 1er sept. 1900. The new local union of 1902 may have been an amalgamation of the Cour St-Laurent and a Cour St-Jacques which appears in *La Presse*, 7 oct. 1895.

62 TLCC, *Proceedings*, 1895, 4; *Industrial Banner*, 1895 (fragment), 4; Nov. 1895; April, 1897, 3; *American Federationist*, 1900: Dec., 393; *Labour Gazette*, IV, 681; Davis, 'History of Labour in London,' 24, 26–8; *Daily Advertiser*, 5 Sept. 1893; 4 Sept. 1894; 3 Sept. 1895; 8 Sept. 1896; 7 Sept. 1897; 5 Sept. 1899; 4 Sept. 1900; *Daily Free Press*, 2 Sept. 1901

63 *Industrial Banner*, 1895 (fragment), 4; Nov., 1895, 2; June, 1897, 3; Davis, 'History of Labour,' 25, 27–8

64 TLCC, *Proceedings*, 1895, 4; 1897, 4; 1899, 4; 1900, 4; 1901, 4; 1902, 4; Davis, 'History of Labour,' 27, 29, 45

65 TLCC, *Proceedings*, 1895, 20–1, 26–7; 1900, 38; 1902, 68

66 *Daily Standard*, 7 June 1899

67 And Babcock, *Gompers in Canada*, 79, notes an attempt by members of the United Carpenters' Nelson local to form a national union.

68 *Daily Expositor*, 22 July 1887. A clipping from the *Labor Record*, 10 June 1887, in TLCC, Minutes, 14 June 1887, says the Builders' Labourers unions of Hamilton, St

Thomas, Brantford, St Catharines, and Toronto were to meet in Guelph to form a provincial union.

69 *Labour Gazette*, I, 78; III, 209, 299, 378; *Citizen*, 7 Sept., 23 Oct. 1897; 30 Aug. 1898; 1 Sept. 1900; 2 Sept. 1901

70 *La Presse*, 16 mai 1896

72 Ibid., 19 nov. 1895; *Citizen*, 8 Sept., 16 Oct. 1896; 7 Sept. 1897

72 *Voice*, 11 Oct., 8, 15 Nov. 1901; *Labour Gazette*, II, 331

73 See notes in PAC, MG281103, v. 24811; *Labour Gazette*, II, 488; IV, 681.

74 PAC, MG26, 1(a), v. 175, Sir John Thompson Papers, letter of 4 Feb. 1893, with enclosure

75 TLCC, *Proceedings*, 1892, 33; 1898, 17; 1901, 69; 1902, 65; 1903, 11, 13; Canada, *Statutes*, 1902, 2 Edw. VII, c. 28

76 TLCC, *Minutes*, 1, 15 March 1889; 13 March, 10 April, 8, 22 May 1902; Ontario, Bureau of Labor, *Report*, 1902, 57 (Toronto Council organized 1868, reorganized 11 Jan. 1900)

77 TLCC, *Proceedings*, 1903, 51; *Labour Gazette*, II, 250, 692; Coats, *Labour Movement*, 316 (NAME formed in 1900; took in Toronto and Saint John unions, which had existed for several years).

78 TTLC, Minutes, 5 Oct. 1894; *Labour Gazette*, II, 250; *Report on Labour Organization in Canada*, 1911, 19; *La Presse*, 28 août 1890; 12 sept. 1893; *Province*, 17 April 1900 (comments in the Vancouver TLC)

CHAPTER 15

1 TTLC, Minutes, 23 July 1881. It was to be 'non partisan or Political.'

2 TTLC, Minutes, 16 Dec. 1881; 6 Jan. 1882; 28 Dec. 1887; *Spectator*, 27 March, 29 April 1882; 23, 25 Feb. 1886; HTLC, *Official Programme and Souvenir of the Labor Day Demonstration, 1897* (Hamilton, 1897), 3

3 TTLC, Minutes, 2 Dec. 1888, 128; HTLC, Minutes, 12 Nov., 3, 16 Dec. 1888. The *American Federationist*, Aug. 1900, 250, says that 'Organizer Sam Landers ... reports that a Trades and Labor Council has also been formed in Hamilton representing the cigarmakers, machinists, carpenters, woodworkers, railwaymen and garment workers'; but the TLCC, *Proceedings*, 1899, 4, show the Hamilton Trades and Labor Council represented by John Flett; and the 1900 *Proceedings* show the council represented by Flett and Henry Obermeyer.

4 *Morning Chronicle*, 23 Aug. 1882; *Trades Union Advocate*, 31 Aug., 28 Sept. 1882. The Typographical Union must have been in the ATU from the beginning, as the executive was elected by 'a convention consisting of four members of each union,' and the corresponding secretary was James Faltz, a Typo. The ATU appears in the Typos' minutes, 20 July 1895; but those minutes show a Trades and Labor Council

from 5 Sept. 1891 to 5 March 1892. 'History of the Labor Movement in Halifax,' *Labour Journal* (1935), 5, says 'internal dissensions' caused 'disbandment' of the ATU in 1897.

5 Halifax TU, Minutes, 3 Sept., 5 Nov. 1898; 'History of the Labor Movement,' 7; *Labour Gazette*, II, 184. The *Labour Gazette* says the council was formed in August; the Halifax TLC, 'History of the Halifax Labor Movement,' says November; Halifax TU, Minutes, 3 Sept., suggest that at that date the council either had just been formed or was in process of formation. The *Herald*, 3 Nov. 1898, reports 'talk' of a new central labour organization, the Federated Workmen; on 21 Nov. it records a meeting of the United Labor Party. The TTLC, Minutes, 13 Oct. 1898, record a letter from Nova Scotia Provincial Trades and Labor Council.

6 TTLC, Minutes, 1 Dec. 1882; *Trades Union Advocate*, 7 Sept., 30 Nov. 1882; *Daily Advertiser*, 15 Aug., 29 Sept., 4 Nov., 2, 4, 11 Dec. 1882; 6, 27 Jan., 10 March 1883; Davis, 'History of Labour in London,' 1

7 TTLC, Minutes, 6 June 1884

8 TTLC, *Proceedings*, 1883, 29

9 TTLC, Minutes, 19 June, 29 Dec. 1885; 7 Feb. 1887; 16 March 1894; 13, 27 Feb., 13 Nov. 1902; Ontario, Bureau of Industries, *Report*, 1888, pt IV, 17; *Labour Gazette*, II, 184

10 *Le Monde*, 1er sept. 1894; *L'Evénement*, 3 sept. 1895. The Toronto Trades and Labor Council had an inquiry from Montreal about forming a council, early in 1883; Minutes, 2 Feb. See also 18 June 1886 (Oshawa); *Labour Gazette*, II, 184, and *Daily Expositor*, 8 June, 25 Aug. 1886 (Brantford); and TLCC, *Proceedings*, 1886, 8 (St Thomas).

11 *Labour Organization in Canada* (1914), 226

12 CFMTM, *Procès-Verbal*, 20 avril 1897; *La Patrie*, 2 sept. 1899. *La Presse*, 23 mars 1896, reports a movement to organize a new, AFL council over a year earlier; the AFL issued a new charter, 26 April 1913: copy furnished by AFL-CIO (Washington, DC).

13 TTLC, Minutes, 3, 17 Sept. 1886; 7 Feb. 1887; TLCC, *Proceedings*, 1887, 11; Ontario, Bureau of Industries, *Report*, 1889, pt IV, 25

14 *Labour Gazette*, II, 184–5; *Daily Expositor*, 25 Jan. 1887; 3 April 1890; 25 Oct., 8 Nov., 12 Dec. 1892; 19 Oct. 1963. The council got an AFL charter in 1902.

15 TLCC, *Proceedings*, 1886, 8, 41; TTLC, Minutes, 7 Feb. 1887; 13 Sept. 1900; 27 Feb., 10 April, 8, 22 May 1902; *Labour Gazette*, I, 214; Ontario, Bureau of Labor, *Report*, 1900, 19

16 TTLC, Minutes, 15 April 1887; 16 March 1894, 86; letter from Professor A.B. McCormack, University of Winnipeg, 8 Sept. 1971; *Daily Tribune*, 5 Feb. 1894; 14 Sept. 1907, says Building Trades Council formed in 1889, Trades and Labor Council 15 March 1890.

17 TLCC, *Proceedings*, 1889, 7; 1902, 4; *Tailor*, Sept. 1896, 5; *Labour Gazette*, II, 184

18 *Citizen*, 5 Jan., 21 Feb. 1889; 28 Aug. 1897 (giving the new name)

19 *Labour Gazette*, II, 184, says the assembly was formed in June 1889. The *Victoria Times*, 31 Jan. 1890, says 'recently.' The TLCC, *Proceedings*, 1890, 14–15, have a letter from the Assembly, dated 25 Aug. 1890.

20 *Examiner*, 20 March 1902; BMIU, Local 17 (Peterborough), Minutes, 25 March, 1, 15 April 1902. The Toronto Trades and Labor Council had word, 5 Jan. 1902, that the Peterborough unions were about to form a council.

21 Vancouver TLC, Minutes, 21 Nov. 1889

22 *L'Evénement*, 3 Sept. 1895; CNMTC, *Procès-Verbal*, 1903, 6. The first Quebec council may not have had an uninterrupted existence: *La Presse*, 20 janv. 1899, speaks of its 'reconstitution,' and, 20 fév., of its 'first meeting since its reconstitution.'

23 Vancouver TLC, *Minutes*, 28 Feb., 25 April, 5 Sept. 1890; TTLC, Minutes, 3 June 1892; HTLC, Minutes, 3 June 1892. The New Westminster council does not appear in the list in the *Labour Gazette*, II, 184.

24 Saint John TU, Minutes, 13 April, 8 June, 10 Aug. 1889; 12 April, 10, 17 May, 14 June, 13 Sept., 11 Oct. 1890; 11 July 1891; Saint John TLC, *50th. Anniversary Banquet Programme* (1903), 1; *Daily Telegraph*, 29 May 1890; TLCC, *Proceedings*, 1897, 4; 1908, 25; 1910, 27; *Labour Gazette*, II, 382; Rice, 'Organized Labour in Saint John,' 117–18, 121

25 TLCC, Minutes, 16 April 1890 (inquiry on forming a council); TLCC, *Proceedings*, 1890, 3, and insert pasted in before p. 1; *Evening Record*, 5 Feb., 2 April 1894; interviews with veteran unionists J. Howard and W. Laing.

26 TLCC, *Proceedings*, 1903, 49; Rose, 'A Brief History of the Windsor and District Labor Council,' 28; information gathered locally by Lloyd Atkinson; *Evening Record*, 31 Dec. 1901; 25 June 1902.

27 *Labour Gazette*, II, 184; Vancouver TLC, Minutes, 1 May, 17 July 1902; CMTC, *Procès-Verbaux*, 1904, 41; *Free Press*, 5, 7, 22 Dec. 1891; *Province*, 2 July, 4 Aug., 17 Nov. 1900. The *American Federationist*, April 1900, 114, reported the formation of a new council, but the *Labour Gazette*'s list indicates a continuous life from 1891.

28 Kingston TU, Minutes, 7 Sept. 1894; CMTC, *Procès-Verbaux*, 1904, 41; *Labour Gazette*, II, 184

29 Hattenhauer, 'History of Nfld Labour,' 225–7

30 TLCC, *Proceedings*, 1898, 4; 1899, 4; 1901, 4; TTLC, Minutes, 4 Oct. 1901; 2 Jan. 1902; *Official Book of the Trades and Labor Congress of Canada*, 1902; *Labour Gazette*, II, 184; *Province*, 10 June 1899

31 *American Federationist*, Dec. 1899, 258, 261; AFL charter books; copy of application and charter from AFL-CIO (Washington, DC); *Labour Gazette*, II, 184

32 *American Federationist*, July 1901, 258; *Labour Gazette*, I, 203; II, 184; VII, 889

33 TLCC, *Proceedings*, 1900, 20; 1901, 4; CMTC, *Procès-Verbaux*, 1904, 41; TTLC, Minutes, Jan. 1903 (probably about 22 Jan.; clipping pasted in); *Voice*, 25 July 1902; *American Federationist*, March 1900, 77; *Province*, 19 Feb. 1901

34 TLCC, *Proceedings*, 1901, 4; 1902, 4; CMTC, *Procès-Verbaux*, 1904, 41; TTLC, Minutes, 13
   March 1902 (letter from Berlin council about incorporation); *Labour Gazette*, II, 184
35 CMTC, *Procès-Verbaux*, ibid.; TTLC, Minutes, 27 March 1902; *Labour Gazette*, II, 184
36 *Labour Organization in Canada*, 1911, 121; Ontario, Bureau of Labor, *Report*, 1911,
   79
37 TLCC, *Proceedings*, 1901, 4; 1902, 4; 1903, 4; 1905, 52; 1906, 69; 1907, 58; 1908,
   57; 1910, 57; 1911, 68; CMTC, *Procès-Verbaux*, 1904, 41; copy of application and
   charter from AFL-CIO (Washington, DC); *Labour Organization in Canada*, 1913, 179
   (which says the council was dissolved in that year).
38 TLCC, *Proceedings*, 1901, 4; 1902, 56–8, 64–5, 74–5; CMTC, *Procès-Verbaux*, 1904, 41;
   Labour Gazette, II, 184
39 TLCC, *Proceedings*, 1902, 43; CMTC, *Procès-Verbaux*, ibid.; *Labour Gazette*, II, 567
   (which says 26 March)
40 Letter from G.S. Borgford, CLC general representative, Calgary, citing Calgary *Labor
   Day Annual*, 1942; TTLC, Minutes, 22 May, 28 Aug. 1902; CMTC, *Procès-Verbaux*, ibid.
41 TLCC, *Proceedings*, 1901, 48–9; 1902, 18–19; *Labour Gazette*, II, 551–2; III, 158–9; IX,
   968; Eugene Forsey, 'Some Notes on the Early History of Unions in PEI,' 347–9
42 TLCC, *Proceedings*, 1903, 20, 50
43 CMTC, *Procès-Verbaux*, 1904, 41; *Labour Gazette*, II, 551, 736, 754; III, 55
44 *Labour Gazette*, VI, 886
45 Copy of application and charter from AFL-CIO (Washington, DC); CMTC, *Procès-Verbaux*,
   1904, 41; *Labour Gazette*, VI, 886; *Labour Organization in Canada*, 1913, 179 (says
   the council was established in 1892, which seems unlikely; perhaps there was an
   earlier council). The *Labour Gazette*, I, 333, reported only one union, the Cigar
   Makers, in Galt in Feb. 1901.
46 Copy of Sarnia application and charter from AFL-CIO (Washington, DC); CMTC, *Procès-Verbaux*, 1904, 41; *American Federationist*, Oct. 1902, 729
47 *Trades Union Advocate*, 28 Sept., 19 Oct. 1882; 25 Jan. 1883; *Morning Chronicle*, 23
   Aug. 1882; 24, 30 March 1883; 21 Jan. 1884; *Acadian Recorder*, 28 Feb. 1884
48 The above account is based on entries in the minutes of the Halifax TU, and on the
   Morning Chronicle, 23 July 1890.
49 'History of the Labor Movement in Halifax,' *Labour Journal* (1935), 5
50 Ibid.; Halifax TU Minutes, 3 Sept., 5 Nov. 1898
51 Halifax TU, Minutes, 4 Feb., 1 April, 7 Oct. 1899; TLCC, *Proceedings*, 1901, 49–50;
   1902, 41–2; *American Federationist*, 1901: Oct., 443; Dec., 552
52 Rice, 'Organized Labour in Saint John,' 131; Saint John TLC, Minutes, 1894–95;
   Saint John TU, Minutes, 11 May, 13 July, 10 Aug. 1895; 12 Oct. 1901; TLCC, *Proceedings*, 1897, 4–5, 15, 23–4; 1901, 40; 1902, 43; 1903, 5, 22; CMTC, *Procès-Verbaux*,
   1904, 20. The 'success' was somewhat qualified.
53 *Bulletin du Travail* (Québec), 1er sept. 1900. These figures were compiled by
   Jacques Martin; he does not say that all the organizations were affiliated. My own
   investigations suggest that the total number of organizations was larger; so it seems

probable that M. Martin's figures refer rather to council affiliates. See also *L'Evé-nement*, 8 oct. 1894; 3 sept. 1895; 15 fév. 1896; *La Presse*, 17 janv. 1894.

54 TLCC, *Proceedings*, 1890–97, 1899–1902

55 *Le Monde*, 27 oct., 24 nov. 1892; 1er sept. 1894; *La Presse*, 18 août 1892; 31 août 1893; 4 sept. 1894

56 See, for example, *La Presse*, 18 oct. 1894; 17 janv. 1896.

57 *La Presse*, 6 sept. 1886, 3 sept. 1888; 3 sept. 1889; 2 sept., et 27 déc. 1890; 31 août 1891; 3 sept. 1892; 2 sept. 1893; 3, 17 août, 1er sept. 1894; 8 janv. 1895; 4 avril, 31 août, 8 sept. 1896; 6 sept. 1898; 2 sept. 1899; 31 août 1901; *Le Monde*, for dates cited in note 55.

58 TLCC, *Proceedings*, 1889–98, 1900–01

59 *La Presse*, 2, 6 sept. 1898; 2 sept. 1899; 1er sept. 1900; 3 sept. 1901

60 TLCC, *Proceedings*, 1889–1902

61 *La Presse*, 22, 25, 27 nov. 1902

62 The Central Council's 1899 Labour Day parade seems to have had five or six international locals (*La Presse*, 2 sept.); CCMTM, *Procès-Verbal*, 1899, 1900; CFMTM, *Procès-Verbal*, 1898, 1900; Conseil Fédéré, *Etat de Compte*, 1900. The figures are estimates by M. Martin on the basis of the two councils' minutes, and newspaper reports. On certain activities, see *La Presse*, 22, 25, 27 nov. 1902.

63 CFMTM, *Procès-Verbal*, 18 août 1897; 2 fév., 24 mars, 15 déc. 1898; 5 janv., 16 fév., 6 avril, 18 mai, 15 juin, 3 août, 17 nov. 1899; 2 mars, 15 mars, 21 juin, 6 déc. 1900; 8 mai, 18 juillet, 16 nov. 1901; 2 oct. 1902; Alfred Charpentier, 'Le mouvement politique ouvrier à Montréal, 1883–1929,' *Relations Industrielles* (Université Laval, Quebec), mars 1955, 76–7

64 TLCC, *Proceedings*, 1899–1902, 1905–08; CMTC, *Procès-Verbaux*, 1904, 45

65 *La Presse*, 22, 25, 27 nov. 1902

66 The following account of the Ottawa council is based on reports in the *Citizen*, 12, 22 April, 16 May 1890; 24 Feb., 3 Nov., 21 Dec. 1891; 26 May, 15 Dec. 1892; 20 Jan., 23 Feb., 9, 11, 23 March, 8 June, 27, 29 July, 26 Oct., 2, 16, 30 Dec. 1893; 25 May, 25 Oct., 15, 28 Nov. 1894; 28 Feb., 15 March, 6, 9 May, 11 July, 16, 28 Nov. 1895; 8 Sept., 16 Oct. 1896; 28 Aug., 7 Sept., 23 Oct., 13 Nov. 1897; 11 June, 10 Dec. 1898; 1 May, 28 July 1899; 29 Sept., 22, 29 Dec. 1900; 15 July, 7, 17, 28 Dec. 1901; 3, 7 Jan., 29 Sept., 31 Dec. 1902; and on TLCC, *Proceedings*, 1890, 3, 32; 1892, 4; 1893, 3, 15, 17, 25; 1894, 4, 12, 16, 19; 1895, 4, 6, 17, 19–21, 23; 1896, 3, 19–22, 24; 1897, 4, 16, 24; 1899, 4, 24; 1900, 4, 23–4, 29, 33; 1901, 4, 62–3, 67–8, 73, 75–6; 1902, 4, 11–13, 59, 65, 67

67 The following account of the TTLC is based entirely on entries in its minute books.

68 For the TTLC's congress activities, see TLCC, *Proceedings*, 1883, 1886–1901.

69 See TTLC, Minutes, for the years noted.

70 For the Oshawa Council, see ibid., 18 June, 3, 17, Sept. 1886; TLCC, *Proceedings*, 1886, 9, 11, 20, 22, 26, 30–1, 33–4, 37–9, 41.

71 *Palladium of Labor,* 25 April 1885; *Spectator,* 25 Feb. 1886

72 *Palladium of Labor,* 28 Feb., 28 March, 25 April, 26 Dec. 1885; 11 Dec. 1886; *Spectator,* 14, 26 Feb., 29 Oct. 1885; 11 Dec. 1886

73 TLCC, *Proceedings,* 1886, 9, 11–16, 18–19, 22, 25, 27–8, 30, 33, 35–6, 40–1; 1887, 11

74 The following account of the Hamilton council is based on entries in HTLC, Minutes.

75 TLCC, *Proceedings,* 1889, 1892, 1895–1902

76 Davis, 'History of Labour in London,' 2–3

77 *Daily Advertiser,* 24, 31 Sept. 1886

78 Ibid., 27 Aug. 1886; a new union was organized in 1895; ibid., 2 Sept. 1902. See also Davis, 'History of Labour in London,' 31.

79 Davis, 'History of Labour,' 30; *Industrial Banner* 1895, (fragment), 3; interviews by Lloyd Atkinson

80 Davis, 'History of Labour,' 33–9

81 Ibid., 29, 45, 53, 68–70; *Industrial Banner,* 1895 (fragment), 3

82 Davis, 'History of Labour,' 40–2, 44–5, 47–9, 52

83 TLCC, *Proceedings,* 1888, 1890, 1894–95, 1897, 1899–1902

84 Davis, 'History of Labour in London,' 53

85 *Daily Expositor,* 10, 25 Jan., 9 May 1887; 3 April 1890; TLCC, *Proceedings,* 1887, 11, 30

86 Brantford *Daily Expositor,* 25 Jan. 1887; 29 Dec. 1892; 9 Jan., 6 Feb. 1893; 27 April 1897; 14 Feb. 1901; 19 Oct. 1963; TLCC, *Proceedings,* 1900–02

87 For the St Thomas council, and the councils that follow, see TLCC, *Proceedings,* 1886, 1890, 1899–1902; see also *American Federationist,* April 1902, 202, for Berlin.

88 *Voice,* 11 Sept. 1897; 7 Jan., 22 April, 20 May, 4 Nov. 1898; 6 Jan., 10, 17 Feb. 1899

89 Ibid., 5 July, 23 Aug., 22 Nov. 1901; 17 Jan., 4 April, 8 Aug., 19 Dec. 1902

90 Ibid., 22 May, 5 Nov., 3 Dec. 1897; 4, 11, 18 Feb., 11 March, 3, 8 April, 6 May, 24 June, 8 July 1898; 10 Feb., 17 March, 21 April 1899; 12 July 1901; 9, 23 May, 27 June, 7 July, 1, 8 Aug., 7, 21, 28 Nov., 19 Dec. 1902; see also Robin, *Radical Politics,* 37–9. The *Voice* began in 1894. The Winnipeg council probably had a hand in organizing the Painters, Plumbers, Lathers, Photographers' Employees, Teamsters, Team Owners, Retail Clerks, and Delivery Men.

91 TLCC, *Proceedings,* 1895–1902

92 The following account of the Vancouver council is based on entries in Vancouver TLC, Minutes; only additional sources are cited.

93 *Province,* 1 April 1899

94 Ibid., 6 Feb. 1899

95 Ibid., 6 Feb., 17 April 1899; 3, 19 Feb., 18 Aug. 1900

96 Ibid., 9, 23 Dec. 1899

97 Ibid., 19 Feb., 14 March, 21 April, 5, 10, 17, 25, 28 May, 2, 16 June, 5 July, 22 Sept., 6, 20 Oct. 1900

98 Ibid., 11 Jan., 6, 7 Feb., 15 April, 10 June, 16, 20, 30 Sept., 14 Oct., 18 Nov. 1899; 27 Feb., 13, 17 March 1900; 19 Jan. 1901

99 TLCC, *Proceedings*, 1895–1902

100 *Province*, 9, 21 Dec. 1899

101 TLCC, *Proceedings*, 1890–93, 1895, 1898

102 Vancouver TLC, Minutes, 8 Aug. 1890, and 19 June 1902, give cases where the council's committee certainly did the organizing.

103 *Province*, 11 Nov., 9, 23 Dec. 1899

104 Ibid., 1, 15, 29 April, 13 May, 9 June, 8 Nov. 1899

105 Ibid., 9, 23 Dec. 1899; 3 Feb. 1900

106 Ibid., 23 Jan., 6 Feb., 1 April, 7 Nov. 1899; 7 April, 3 Nov. 1900

107 Bartley, *An Outline History of Typographical Union No. 226*, 19; *Province*, 6 Feb., 27 May, 10 June 1899; 3, 19 Feb. 1900

108 *Province*, 4 Aug. 1900

109 TLCC, *Proceedings*, 1890, 21, 25; 1891, 10–13; 1892, 20–3; 1893, 18–23; 1895, 11–13; see also 1898, 17, 27.

110 Vancouver TLC, Minutes, 25 Aug. 1890; 26 Feb. 1892; 16 July, 13, 27 Aug. 1897; 15 May 1902; *Province*, 11 April 1899

111 TLCC, *Proceedings*, 1890, 14–15; 1892, 19–20

112 Ibid., 1898, 4, 27–8; 1899, 20

113 Vancouver TLC, *Minutes*, 21 Oct., 18 Nov. 1892; 27 Oct. 1893; 1 May, 17 July 1902

114 TLCC, *Proceedings*, 1901, 4, 69, 75, 80

115 Ibid., 1898, 4, 16–17, 27–8, 32; 1899, 4, 23–5, 28; 1901, 4

CHAPTER 16

1 Unless otherwise noted, the information in this chapter is drawn from the appropriate proceedings of the TLCC: TLCC, *Proceedings*, 1883–1903.

2 TTLC, Minutes

3 J.T. Carey (St Catharines) and J.D. Murphy (Toronto) appear as delegates of the Seamen's Union, Thomas Hanlon (Toronto) of the Sailors Union.

4 Forsey, 'A Note on the Dominion Factory Bills of the Eighteen-Eighties,' 580–3

5 TTLC, Minutes, 2, 16 May, 19 Sept., 3 Oct. 1884

6 Ibid., 3 Sept. 1886

7 As late as 1901 there were 707,924 people gainfully employed in agriculture, as against 229,027 in manufacturing, 89,100 in construction, and 81,161 in transport and communication: Canada, *Census*, 1941, VII, 6.

8 The Toronto council had done an enormous amount of work on the union label; see, for example, TTLC, Minutes, 18 Nov. 1881; 4, 18 Sept., 6 Nov. 1885; 21 Oct. 1892;

5 Oct. 1894; 4 Jan., 1, 15 Feb., 21 June 1895; 21 March, 23 July 1896; 27 April, 24 June 1897; 13 April, 11 May, 9 Nov. 1899; 22 Feb., 10 May, 13 Sept., 13 Dec. 1900; 11 April, 22 Aug., 12 Sept. 1901.

CHAPTER 17

1 Unless otherwise noted, the information in this chapter is drawn from the appropriate proceedings of the TLCC: TLCC, *Proceedings*, 1883–1903.
2 Babcock, *Gompers in Canada*, 70
3 CMTC, *Procès-Verbaux*, 1904, 10
4 Babcock, *Gompers in Canada*, 16–17
5 TLCC, *Proceedings*, 1896, 15–16, 29; Babcock, *Gompers in Canada*, 16–17; see also Babcock, 'The AFL in Canada,' chap. II, 2–3.
6 Babcock, *Gompers in Canada*, 24–6, 28, 33–4, 36, 40–1; TLCC, *Proceedings*, 1897, 10; 1898, 33; 1900, 15–17
7 Babcock, *Gompers in Canada*, 58–9
8 Phillips, *No Power Greater*, 22, 32; Robin, *Radical Politics*, 64, 66
9 Babcock, *Gompers in Canada*, 66; *Labour Gazette*, I, 2, 44, 86
10 TLCC, *Official Book* (Toronto) 1901; 1902; Ontario, Bureau of Labor, *Report*, 1902, 31–2
11 Babcock, *Gompers in Canada*, 83–9
12 TTLC, Minutes, 28 Dec. 1903
13 TLCC, *Proceedings*, 1903, 46–7, 50–1; CMTC, *Procès-Verbaux*, 1904, 40
14 NTLCC, *Proceedings*, 1903, 7; *Labour Gazette*, IV, 333

Bibliography

MANUSCRIPT COLLECTIONS

Archives, Libraries, etc.
British Columbia Archives. Shipwrights and Caulkers Association, Constitution and By-laws; Victoria Typographical Union, Constitution and By-laws; Western Federation of Miners, Canadian District 6, Proceedings
Canada, Department of Labour, Library. Provincial Workingmen's Association, Grand Council, Minutes
New Brunswick Museum. Saint John Typographical Union, Minutes; Letter Book
Public Archives of Canada. Ward Chipman Papers; Canadian Labour Congress Collection; E.A. Forsey Collection; Sir John Thompson Papers; Toronto Musicians Association, Minutes; Toronto Trades Assembly, Minutes; Toronto Trades and Labor Council, Minutes; Toronto Typographical Union, Minutes
Trent University (Gainey Collection). Bricklayers and Masons International Union, Local 17 (Peterborough), Minutes; Iron Molders International Union, Local 191 (Peterborough), Minutes
Public Archives of Nova Scotia. Halifax Typographical Union, Minutes
University of British Columbia, Library (Special Collections). Vancouver Trades and Labor Council, Minutes

Union Archives
Amalgamated Engineering Workers (England). Amalgamated Society of Engineers, Records
Amalgamated Woodworkers (England). Amalgamated Society of Carpenters and Joiners, Records
American Federation of Labor – Congress of Industrial Organizations, Archives. American Federation of Labor, Charter Books; National Union Files

Bricklayers and Masons International Union, Local 9 of Ontario (Brantford), Minutes, 1899–1903 (in the possession of Mr Percy Fisher, Brantford)
Cigar Makers International Union (Washington), Convention Proceedings
Cigar Makers International Union, 100th. Anniversary Journal (Washington)
Hamilton Labour Council, Hamilton Trades and Labor Council, Minutes
International Typographical Union, Local 204 (Kingston), Minutes
Saint John Labour Council, Saint John Trades and Labor Council, Minutes
United Brotherhood of Carpenters and Joiners, Local 617 (Vancouver), Minutes

PRINTED PRIMARY SOURCES

Barnes New Brunswick Almanac (Saint John), 1867
Canadian Historical Association, *Papers* (Ottawa), 1973
Canadian Directory of Parliament, 1867–1967 (Ottawa, 1968)
Canadian Parliamentary Companion (Ottawa), 1885, 1887, 1891
Canadian Parliamentary Guide (Ottawa), 1968
Dominion Annual Register and Review (Toronto), 1885
Guelph City Directories, 1882, 1887
Halifax Trades and Labor Council, *Labor Journal: History of the Labor Movement in Halifax* (Halifax, 1935)
Hamilton Trades and Labor Council, *Official Programme and Souvenir of the Labor Day Demonstration, 1897* (Hamilton, 1897)
Hamilton and District Trades and Labor Council, *Diamond Jubilee Programme* (Hamilton, 1948)
Alfred Hawkins [?], *Remarks upon the Desertion of Seamen at the Port of Quebec*, 1852
Loyalist Centennial Souvenir (Saint John, 1883)
McAlpin's Saint John Directory, 1869–70
McAlpin's City Directory, 1872–73 (Saint John)
McMillan's New Brunswick Almanac (Saint John, 1866)
St Catharines General and Business Directory (St Catharines, 1874)
Saint John and Its Business (Saint John, 1875)
Saint John Caulkers' Association, *Act of Incorporation and By-laws* (Saint John, 1866)
Saint John Trades and Labor Council, *History of Saint John Labor Unions* (Saint John, 1929)
L'Union typographique Jacques-Cartier, *Programme-souvenir du cinquantième anniversaire* (Montréal, 1920)
Victoria Trades and Labor Council, *Labor Annual* (Victoria, 1948)
Windsor, Ontario and Kent County Trades and Labor Council, *Labor Review and Union Buyers' Guide, 50th. Golden Anniversary Edition* (Windsor, 1952)
Winnipeg Trades and Labor Council, *Labor Day Souvenir Programme* (Winnipeg, 1903)

GOVERNMENT REPORTS, ETC.

Canada, House of Commons, *Journals, Debates*
- *Census*, 1870–71, 1891, 1941
- *Gazette du Travail*
- *Labour Gazette*
- *Report on Labour Organization in Canada*, 1911, 1913, 1914, 1938, 1958
- Royal Commission on the Relations of Capital and Labor in Canada, *Report*, 1889
- Statutes, 1875
New Brunswick, Legislative Assembly, *Journals*
Ontario, Bureau of Industries, *Reports*
- Bureau of Labor, *Reports*
- Statutes, 1875

UNION PROCEEDINGS

Amalgamated Association of Street Railway Employees, *Convention Proceedings*
Bricklayers, Masons and Plasterers International Union, *Annual Reports*
Canadian Labor Union, *Proceedings of the Congresses, 1873–77* (Montreal, 1951)
Congrès des Métiers et du Travail du Canada, *Procès-Verbaux*
Congrès National des Métiers et du Travail du Canada, *Procès-Verbaux*
Conseil Central des Métiers et du Travail de Montréal, *Procès-Verbaux*
Conseil Fédéré des Métiers et du Travail de Montréal, *Etats de Compte*
Conseil Fédéré des Métiers et du Travail de Montréal, *Procès-Verbaux*
International Brotherhood of Electrical Workers, Convention *Proceedings*
Iron Molders International Union, *Convention Reports* (printed in *Iron Molders Journal*)
Knights of Labor, General Assembly, *Proceedings*; General Executive Board, *Reports*
Knights of St Crispin, International Grand Lodge, Annual Meetings, *Reports*
National Alliance of Theatrical Stage Employees, Convention *Proceedings*
National Union of Molders, Convention *Proceedings*; *Quarterly Reports*
Trades and Labor Congress of Canada, *Proceedings*, 1883–1902; *Official Book*, 1901, 1902
United Brotherhood of Carpenters and Joiners, Convention *Proceedings*

NEWSPAPERS AND JOURNALS

Acadian Recorder (Halifax)
American Federationist (Washington)
Boilermakers and Iron Shipbuilders Journal (Kansas City)
British Colonist (Halifax)

British Columbia Federationist (Vancouver)
British Whig (Kingston)
Bulletin du Travail (Québec)
Canadian Historical Review (Toronto)
Canadian Journal of Economics and Political Science (Toronto)
Canadian Monthly and National Review (Toronto)
Carpenter (Indianapolis)
Cigar Makers Journal (Washington)
Citizen (Ottawa)
Citizen and Evening Chronicle (Halifax)
Colonist (Victoria)
Commercial (Winnipeg)
Daily Advertiser (London)
Daily Citizen (Ottawa)
Daily Expositor (Brantford)
Daily Mail (Toronto)
Daily Mail and Empire (Toronto)
Daily News (Saint John)
Daily Standard (St Catharines)
Daily Sun (Saint John)
Daily Sun (Winnipeg)
Daily Telegraph (Saint John)
Daily Times (Winnipeg)
Daily Tribune (Winnipeg)
Daily Union (Ottawa)
L'Evénement (Québec)
Evening Express and Commercial Record (Halifax)
Evening Herald (St John's)
Evening Record (Windsor)
Evening Reporter (Halifax)
Evening Times (Hamilton)
Examiner (Peterborough)
Fincher's Trades Review (Philadelphia)
Free Press (London)
Free Press (Nanaimo)
Garment Worker (New York)
Gazette (Hamilton)
Gazette (Montreal)
Gazette (Victoria)
Globe (Saint John)

Globe (Toronto)

Herald (Halifax)

Industrial Banner (London)

Iron Molders Journal (Cincinnati)

Journal and Pictou News (Stellarton)

Journal (St Catharines)

Journal of Economic History (various places of publication)

Journal of the Knights of Labor (Philadelphia)

Journal of United Labor (Philadelphia)

Juridical Review (London, Eng.)

Labor Union (Hamilton)

La Justice (Québec)

La Patrie (Montréal)

La Presse (Montréal)

Lather (Cleveland)

Leader (Toronto)

Le Monde (Montréal)

Manitoba Morning Free Press (Winnipeg)

Miramichi Gleaner (Chatham)

Morning Chronicle (Halifax)

Morning Chronicle (Quebec)

Morning Freeman (Saint John)

Morning Free Press (Winnipeg)

Morning News and New Brunswick Railway Advocate (Saint John)

Morning News (Saint John)

Morning Post and Shipping Gazette (St John's)

Motorman and Conductor (Detroit)

New Brunswick Courier (Saint John)

North American (Toronto)

Observer (Lambton)

Ontario History (Toronto)

Ontario Workman (Toronto)

Palladium of Labor (Hamilton and Toronto)

Pilot (Montreal)

Post (Thorold)

Progress (Saint John)

Province (Vancouver)

Recorder (Brockville)

Relations Industrielles (Québec)

Retail Clerks International Advocate (Washington)

Social History (Ottawa)
Spectator (Hamilton)
Tailor (New York)
Times (Hamilton)
Times (Ottawa)
Toiler (Toronto)
Trades Journal (Stellarton)
Trades Union Advocate (Toronto)
Transactions of the Royal Society of Canada (Ottawa)
Tribune (Welland)
Union (Ottawa)
Voice (Winnipeg)
Wage-Worker (Toronto)
Watchman (Saint John)
Weekly Citizen (Halifax)
Weekly News (St Catharines)
Workingman's Advocate (Chicago)
Workingman's Journal (Hamilton)

SECONDARY SOURCES

Babcock, R.H. *Gompers in Canada: A Study in American Continentalism before the First World War* (Toronto and Buffalo, 1974)
Bartley, George *An Outline History of Typographical Union No. 226, Vancouver, B.C., 1887–1938* (Vancouver, 1938)
Bélanger, Noël *et al. Les Travailleurs québécois et le syndicalisme* (Montréal, n.d.)
Brooks, T.R. *Toil and Trouble: A History of American Labor* (New York, 1964)
Buhler, Charlie *In Appreciation* (Toronto, 1963)
Cameron, J.M. *Political Pictonians* (New Glasgow, 1966)
Careless, J.M.S. *Brown of the Globe* (2 vols, Toronto, 1963)
Coats, R.H. *The Labour Movement in Canada*, vol. IX of *Canada and Its Provinces* (Toronto, 1913–17)
Commons, J.R. *et al. History of Labor in the United States* (New York, 1917)
Creighton, D.G. *Dominion of the North* (Toronto, 1957)
Fergusson, C.B. *The Labour Movement in Nova Scotia before Confederation* (Halifax, 1964)
Ferns, H.S. and Ostry, Bernard *The Age of Mackenzie King: The Rise of the Leader* (London and Toronto, 1955)
Fink, G.N. (ed.) *Labor Unions* (Westport, Conn., and London, 1977)
Firth, E.G. (ed.) *The Town of York, 1815–1834* (Toronto, 1966)
Foner, P.S. *History of the Labor Movement in the United States from Colonial Times to the Founding of the American Federation of Labor* (New York, 1947)

Forsey, E.A. *Economic and Social Aspects of the Nova Scotia Coal Industry* (Toronto, 1926)

Griffin, Harold *The People's Story* (Vancouver, 1958)

Hamelin, Jean *et al. Répertoire des grèves dans la province de Québec au XIXe siècle* (Montréal, 1971)

Hann, R.G. *et al. Primary Sources in Canadian Working Class History, 1860–1930* (Kitchener, 1973)

Hertel, D.W. *History of the Brotherhood of Maintenance of Way Employees, Its Birth and Growth* (Washington, 1955)

ITU *A Study of the History of the International Union, 1852–1963* (Colorado Springs, 1964)

Kennedy, D.R. *The Knights of Labor in Canada* (London, Ont., 1956)

Lawson, J.M. *Reminiscences of Yarmouth County* (Yarmouth, NS, 1902)

Lescohier, D.D. *The Knights of St Crispin, 1867–1874* (Madison, 1910)

Lipton, Charles *The Trade Union Movement in Canada, 1827–1959* (Montreal, 1966)

Logan, H.A. *Trade Unions in Canada* (Toronto, 1948)

Mackintosh, Margaret *Trade Union Law in Canada* (Ottawa, 1935)

MacNutt, W.S. *New Brunswick: A History 1784–1867* (Tornonto, 1963)

Miller, Orlo *A Century of Western Ontario: The Story of London, the 'Free Press' and Western Ontario, 1849–1949* (Toronto, 1949)

Parkin, George *The Great Dominion* (London and New York, 1895)

Peterson, Florence *Handbook of Labor Unions* (Washington, 1944)

Phillips, A.P. *No Power Greater* (Vancouver, 1967)

Robin, Martin *Radical Politics and Canadian Labour, 1880–1930* (Kingston, 1968)

Robinson, C.B. *History of Toronto and County of York, Ontario* (Toronto, 1885)

Scott, B. *The Economic and Industrial History of London, Canada* (London, Ont., 1930)

Smallwood, J.R. (ed.) *The Book of Newfoundland* (6 vols, St John's, 1936–37)

Tracy, G.A. *History of the Typographical Union* (Indianapolis, 1913)

ARTICLES

Allen, George 'History of the Labor Movement in Halifax,' Halifax TLC, *Labor Journal* (Halifax, 1935)

Armstrong, F.H. 'Reformer as Capitalist: William Lyon Mackenzie and the Printers' Strike of 1836,' *Ontario History*, (Toronto), LIX, 191–95

Armstrong, John 'Sketch of the Early History of No 91,' ITU Convention *Proceedings*, 1905

Casey, J.R. 'A Short History of the International Brotherhood of Boilermakers, Iron Ship Builders and Helpers of America,' *Boilermakers and Iron Ship Builders Journal* (Kansas City), photostat

Conner, J.M. 'Trade Unions in Toronto,' in J.E. Middleton, *Municipality of Toronto: A History* (Toronto, 1923)

Cooper, J.I. 'The Quebec Ship Labourers' Benevolent Society,' *Canadian Historical Review*, XXX (1949), 336–43

Creighton, D.G. 'George Brown, Sir John Macdonald and the "Workingman,"' *Canadian Historical Review*, XXIV (1943), 362–76

Desrosiers Richard, and Denis Héroux 'Les Chevaliers du Travail,' *Recherches historiques*, XLIII

Forsey, Eugene 'A Note on the Dominion Factory Bills of the Eighteen-Eighties,' *Canadian Journal of Economics and Political Science*, XIII (1947), 580–3

– 'Some Notes on the Early History of Unions in PEI,' *Canadian Historical Review*, XLVI (1965), 346–51

– 'The Telegraphers' Strike of 1883,' Royal Society of Canada, *Transactions*, series 4, IX (1971), 245–59

Gladstone, Percy and Jamieson, Stuart 'Unionism in the Fishing Industry of British Columbia,' *Canadian Journal of Economics and Political Science*, XVI (1950), 1–11

Grob, G.N. 'The Knights of Labor and the Trade Unions,' *Journal of Economic History* (various places of publication), XVII

Kealey, G.S. 'Artisans Respond to Industrialism: Shoemakers, Shoe Factories and the Knights of St Crispin in Toronto,' Canadian Historical Association, *Papers*, 1973

MacEwan, P.W. 'The PWA,' *Cape Breton Highlander*, 8 December 1965

McKenna, Edward 'Unorganized Labour versus Management: The Strike at the Chaudière Lumber Mills, 1891,' *Social History*, V (1972), 186–211

Ostry, Bernard 'Conservatives, Liberals and Labour in the 1870's,' *Canadian Historical Review*, XLI (1960), 93–127

Pryke, K.G. 'Labour and Politics: Nova Scotia at Confederation,' *Social History* (1970)

Smith, Goldwin. 'The Labor Movement,' *Canadian Monthly and National Review* (Toronto)

THESES AND OTHER UNPUBLISHED MANUSCRIPTS

Appleton, P.C. 'The Sunshine and the Shade: Labour Activism in Central Canada, 1850–1860' (unpub. MA thesis, University of Calgary, 1974)

Ayer, S.A. 'The Locomotive Engineers' Strike on the Grand Trunk Railway in 1876–1877' (unpub. MA thesis, McGill University, 1961)

Babcock, R.H. 'The AFL in Canada, 1896–1908' (unpub. PHD thesis, Duke University, 1968)

Chan, V.O. 'The Canadian Knights of Labor with Special Reference to the 1880s' (unpub. MA thesis, McGill University, 1949)

Conner, J.M. 'The Labour and Socialist Movement in Canada' (typewritten ms, Toronto Reference Library)

Davis, W.L. 'History of the Early Labour Movement in London, Ontario' (unpub. undergrad. thesis, University of Western Ontario, 1930)

Forsey, E.A. 'Economic and Social Aspects of the Nova Scotia Coal Industry' (unpub. MA thesis, McGill University, 1926)

Garlock, Jonathan 'A Structural Analysis of the Knights of Labor' (unpub. PHD thesis, University of Rochester, 1974)

Hattenhauer, Rolf 'A Brief History of Newfoundland Labour' (unpub. ms, prepared for the Royal Commission on Labour Relations in Newfoundland and Labrador, 1970)

Kealey, G.S. 'The Working Class in Toronto in the Late Nineteenth Century' (draft PHD thesis, University of Rochester)

Ralston, H.K. 'The 1900 Strike of Fraser Sockeye Salmon Fishermen' (unpub. MA thesis, University of British Columbia, 1965)

Rice, Richard 'A History of Organized Labour in Saint John, New Brunswick' (unpub. MA thesis, University of New Brunswick, 1968)

Shields, E.J. 'A History of Trade Unionism in Nova Scotia' (unpub. MA thesis, Dalhousie University, 1945)

Spector, David 'The Knights of Labor in Winnipeg' (unpub. undergrad. thesis, University of Winnipeg, 1974)

Spector, David 'The 1883 Locomotive Engineers' Strike in the Canadian North West (unpub. ms., University of Winnipeg, 1976)

Thwaites, J.D. 'The International Association of Machinists in Canada to 1919' (unpub. MA thesis, Carleton University, 1966)

Thompson, Lorne 'The Rise of Labor Unionism in Alberta' (typewritten ms, PAC, Forsey Collection)

Index

Most of the entries will be found under several general headings: Employers, corporate; Employers' organizations; International union bodies; Knights of Labor; Labour and socialist papers; Labour and socialist parties; Local central organizations; Local unions; National central organizations; National unions; Persons, ecclesiastical; Persons, employers; Persons, labour; Persons, other; Persons, political; Places; Regional unions and organizations; Subjects discussed by unions; and Women's unions.

582 Index